Midrash Rabbah Genesis Volume I - Primary Source Edition

Maurice Simon

MIDRASH RABBAH

GENESIS I

MIDRASH RABBAH

TRANSLATED INTO ENGLISH
WITH NOTES, GLOSSARY AND INDICES
UNDER THE EDITORSHIP OF

RABBI DR. H. FREEDMAN, B.A., PH.D.
AND
MAURICE SIMON, M.A.

WITH A FOREWORD BY
RABBI DR. I. EPSTEIN, B.A., PH.D., D.LIT.

IN TEN VOLUMES

THE SONCINO PRESS
LONDON

First Edition 1939
Second Impression 1951
Third Impression 1961

PRINTED IN ENGLAND BY
STEPHEN AUSTIN AND SONS, LTD., HERTFORD

GENESIS

IN TWO VOLUMES

I

TRANSLATED BY

RABBI DR. H FREEDMAN, B.A., PH.D.

CONTENTS

Foreword by Rabbi Dr. I. Epstein	*page* ix
Editorial Preface	xxv
Introduction to Genesis Rabbah	xxvii
Bereshith	1
Noach	233
Lech Lecha	313
Vayera	406

FOREWORD

by

RABBI DR. I. EPSTEIN, B.A., PH.D., D.LIT.

In the earliest periods of the history of Israel and Judah, when yet the twelve tribes were warring with each other, when the ideas of king and priest were yet elementary and vague, we find leaders who proclaimed that God is and must remain the sole ruler of the tribes, and that through the government of the Lord who is One and Everlasting, the unity of the individual, the nation, and humanity must be found

This only God and Supreme King had spoken to their ancestors at Sinai through the Law, and continued to speak to them through priest and prophet. What He had said and commanded was gathered up in books, which became The Book, the Torah, by which their individual and national life was to be guided. Thus arose and developed the religion of Israel. Grounded in the Book and centred in God, it was not like the Roman religion, the creature of the State, nor was it ever to derive its inspiration from political feeling. For the Jews, religion itself was to be an independent and positive source of inspiration, and its acceptance the chief foundation upon which the Jewish State was to rear itself.

But surrounding nations surged against them. Conquering Empires rose and fell. Israel was taken captive and disappeared from history as a separate entity. Judah too fell a prey to Babylonia, but was restored after Babylon fell to the Medes. Then began within Judah a centuries-long, heroic struggle for the inviolability of the Book. Its laws and precepts and ordinances had to be interpreted both literally and spiritually. The changes in the people's circumstances could not be neglected. Besides the written

Law there had been from the first, from the divine communications to Moses, onwards, an unwritten Law handed down from generation to generation—an unwritten Law which lawgiver and prophet strove to engrave in the heart of the people The written and unwritten must co-operate in the guidance of the Jewish people struggling against the inrolling civilisations of Greece and Rome, the unwritten being the dynamic factor of change, the written the abiding fundamental factor.

THE BEGINNINGS OF THE MIDRASH

A decisive move in this struggle on behalf of the Book was made by Ezra. It was in the year 444 B.C.E.; twelve years after his return from Babylonia Fired by the zeal to make the reign of the Torah supreme in the newly re-created lives of the returned Exiles, he summoned a large gathering of the people and secured in their presence by means of a covenant signed by their leaders the acceptance of the Torah as the constitution of the new community in Judea. He inaugurated this memorable convocation, which proved to be the turning-point in the history of the Jewish people, by a public reading of the Law. Himself '*a ready* Sofer (lit. "Bookman", "Student")[1] *of the Law of Moses which the Lord had given*',[2] he took the lead in the reading, while others who stood by '*gave the sense*': '*And they read in the book, in the Torah of God, distinctly; and they gave the sense, and caused them to understand the reading.*'[3]

Thus began the Midrash—orally at first. The people evidently would not have understood a reading which was completely out of touch with the currents of thought of their time or in conflict with their collective aspirations and traditions. In their endeavour to cause the people to understand the reading, Ezra and his associates (the *Soferim*) had to build bridges between the past and the

[1] V. Strack, H. L., *Introduction to the Talmud and Midrash* (English Ed), p. 201.

[2] Ezra VII, 6.

[3] Neh. VIII, 8.

present. For these spiritual guides of Israel it was inconceivable that the sense of the Torah of God might be in conflict with the fundamental conditions of Jewish life. The letters of the Holy Writ were not meant to kill the spirit. They were intended as containers ever to be filled with the wine of good, new vintage. Has not after all 'Every word of the Scripture "seventy aspects"'? שבעים פנים לתורה.[1] These 'aspects' were latent; and as generation after generation found expression for some or other of these aspects, they revealed again and anew the Torah which Moses received on Sinai.

ITS EARLIEST INFLUENCE

The Midrash thus created and brought into shape by the *Soferim* for the purpose of expounding the Torah—and later also other parts of the Hebrew Scriptures—fulfilled a vital necessity. For centuries after Ezra, it represented the most important medium for the expression of Jewish thought and teaching. Midrash was in fact during the whole of the Soferic period (which came to an end about 270 B.C.E.) the Queen of Jewish spiritual life. With the emergence of Mishnah about the second century, Midrash was obliged to share in the realms of the *Halachah* its kingdom with its new rival[2]; but despite its disputed rule Midrash did not cease to exercise sway over the heart and mind of the people. There were as yet no reasons for the rift between *Halachah* and *Haggadah*

[1] אותיות דר׳ עקיבא.

[2] On the problem as to the priority of the Midrash-form of study over the Mishnah-form, v. Lauterbach, L. Z., *JQR.* (N.S.), v, pp. 503–527, and vi, pp. 23–95, 303–323, Herford, R. T., *Talmud and Apocrypha*, pp. 46 ff., and Tchernowitz, Ch., *Toledoth Ha-Halakah* (*History of the Halakah*), i, pp. 37–61. In this connection the illuminating statement of Moore (*Judaism*, i, p. 150) may be quoted as apposite: 'The question which is the older method of study, Midrash or Mishnah, is one of those simplified alternatives to which a simple answer cannot be given. There is a strong presumption that the biblical studies of the ancient *Soferim* and of the learned in the priesthood were primarily directed to the interpretation of the Scriptures, so far as they dealt with the laws and the more precise understanding and application of what the Scripture enjoined or forbade. In this sense the Midrash-form is older.'

that developed, as we shall see, in the course of the Talmudic period and which eventually led Midrash to become an independent branch of Rabbinic literature; and during the whole of the post-scriptural and pre-talmudic period the teaching both of *Halachah* and *Haggadah* was conducted in Midrash-form.

Midrash, as one of the literary forms in which the Jewish creative genius in the realms in *Haggadah* expressed itself, left its deep impress on the Bible itself. In one of its functions as a collection of contributions to the history of Israel, Midrashic elements were assimilated to the Hebrew Scriptures. We find in Chronicles passages which are Midrashic glosses, supplementing in many details the narratives in the Book of Kings.[1] There is also a Midrash to the Book of Kings mentioned in II Chronicles XXIV, 27, whilst reference to the Midrash of Iddo the Prophet is made in II Chronicles XIII, 22. We may thus suppose that we have in Chronicles the first elements of Haggadic Midrash handed down in writing in their original form. After the completion of the Hebrew Scriptures, Midrashic creation in *Haggadah* obtained a dominating position in the spiritual life of Jewry. For a long period it was the vehicle for Jewish ideas, thoughts, feelings, and knowledge. Among the oldest Haggadic Midrashim is undoubtedly The Haggadah recited on Passover evening, which according to one authority[2] was compiled between the second half of the third century and the first half of the second century B.C.E.

MIDRASH AND THE DEVELOPMENT OF HALACHAH

A specimen of an early Halachic Midrashic exposition of the Torah emanating according to competent authorities[3]

[1] On the Midrashic character of Chronicles v Elmslie, W. A. L., *Introduction to Chronicles*, Cambridge Bible.

[2] Finkelstein, L., *The Oldest Midrash*, *The Harvard Theological Review*, 1938, pp. 291 ff.

[3] V. Herford, R. T., *Talmud and Apocrypha*, p. 48.

from the Soferic school is preserved in the Mishnah Soṭah, VII, 2. It expounds Deut XX, 3. 'The priest anointed for battle . . . *shall say unto them . . . against your enemies,*' but not against your brethren, not Judah against Simeon nor Simeon against Benjamin, so that if you fall into their hand they shall have mercy upon you, as it is said, *And the men which have been expressed by name rose up, and took the captives, and with their spoil clothed all that were naked among them, and arrayed them, and shod them, and gave them to eat and to drink, and anointed them, and carried all the feeble of them upon asses, and brought them to Jericho, the city of palm-trees, unto their brethren; then they returned to Samaria* (II Chron. XXVIII, 15).

Here we have one of the earliest typical examples of a Midrashic exposition of the Torah. The interpretation seems to adapt the law of the Torah to a new situation which had not been provided for in the text. There is no distinction in the original text of the Torah between '*enemy*' and '*enemy*'. Strictly speaking, the word '*enemy*' denotes any foe with whom one goes to battle. In the exposition cited a distinction is made, owing to the fact that a sort of 'Red Cross service' for the sick and wounded seems to have been created, the scope of which, however, was restricted to wars among Jews themselves. This new situation involved a modification of the law at least in certain of its regulations[1] in respect of such civil wars. The Midrash gives apparently the whole process of reasoning which led to such a modification, and thereby holds open the way for further development, any fundamental change in the methods of warfare being bound to react on the laws concerned. Should 'frightfulness', for example, be given up by other peoples too, should they also exercise mercy on their prisoners and wounded enemies, then the Law would be generally modified and the introduction of a certain measure of 'conscript' service would be permissible.

[1] Particularly the prohibition of conscription implied in Deut. XX, 8: *What man is there that is fearful and fainthearted? let him go and return unto his house.*

MIDRASH AND MISHNAH

This Halachic Midrash exemplifies more clearly than any Haggadic Midrash could do the formal and material differences of Midrash and Mishnah. As to the form, the Mishnah teaches the *Halachah* without reference to any Scriptural text. Evidently the Mishnah represented a progress in the method of teaching While Midrash was tied to the texts of the respective Scriptures, the Tannaim were able through the Mishnah-form to put at will on the order of the day such subjects as they desired. The need for methodical regrouping could, however, have been satisfied without abandoning the Midrash-form and all its implications. The Scriptural text could still have remained the basis of the 'expositions' in a Midrash whose contents needed only to be regrouped according to subjects. This method, which would have been a kind of re-editing of Midrashic expositions, was not resorted to. We may assume that there were other reasons apart from pedagogical, for introducing Mishnah as a rival of Midrash. The final victory of the Mishnah-form with its logical sequence, the Halachic Gemara, bore witness to the determination of the learned of Israel to build up an unalterable system of directives. There was now no question any longer of a bridge between past and present. Mishnah and Gemara were meant to be a fortress able to offer resistance to any enemy possessing even the most dangerous weapons, from the Sadduceans down to the Karaites, their latter-day spiritual descendants.

HALACHAH AND HAGGADAH

We do not know when the words *Halachah* and *Haggadah* were first introduced.[1] But we would probably not be mistaken if we suppose that the time of their first divorce coincides with the introduction of the Mishnah-form.

The emergence of two distinct terms need not necessarily have meant a rift or rivalry between the respective

[1] V. Herford, *op cit.*, p. 50

disciplines these terms represented. The fact that Midrashic exposition in the Soferic and pre-Talmudic period found no difficulty in following the Scriptures verse by verse regardless of whether their character was Halachic or Haggadic proves that in all respects harmony and equality between Halachic and Haggadic exposition reigned. The teachers were the same, and the form of teaching was the same. When the same person was building up a system of which *Halachah* and *Haggadah* were the component parts, the full harmony of the system was obviously safeguarded. But even if different persons happened to expound separately verses of Halachic and Haggadic character, they had—if ever such a necessity arose—to co-ordinate their expositions, in view of the fact that they all started from the same point, from Scriptural texts, from the Law of Moses. Under these conditions *Halachah*, representing the religious rules of practical life, and *Haggadah*, embodying the philosophy of the generation, existed side by side in complete unity.

FREEDOM OF SPIRIT IN THE MIDRASH

The sharp distinction which we find later between the significance of the two terms *Halachah* and *Haggadah* was a result of Talmudic development. The personal unity came to an end. There were teachers of the *Haggadah* (*rabbanan di-Aggadeta*), who presumably restricted their activity to Midrashic exposition of exclusively Haggadic character; while Mishnah supplemented by Gemara took more and more the form of categorical pronouncements on the religious law, and the discussion and application of its details. The characteristic Mishnaic form was the formulation of a decision which closed a debate. In many cases the Gemara reopens the debate, but only in order to close it again as categorically as the Mishnah did, though often on a different plane, embodying adaptations which the process of time had rendered necessary. These adaptations were adopted only after prolonged arguments between conflicting schools representing in many cases the forces of cautious conservatism on the one hand, and impatient progress on the other. More often the decision lagged behind the times, change being barred by definitive Mishnaic law and precedent. The *Haggadah*, however, in so far as it did not serve only to justify an *a posteriori* Talmudic decision already fixed, and as such unalterable, retained, especially in the Midrashim, its old freedom and its full potentialities. It, too, was governed in its interpretation of the Bible by certain norms of exposition which served as a check against the riot of untrammelled imagination. But whereas the *Halachah* was restricted to seven rules which even when expanded by Rabbi Ishmael (*c.* 90–130 C.E.) became no more than thirteen, the *Haggadah* enjoyed the greater latitude allowed by the thirty-two rules for Haggadic interpretation formulated by his contemporary R. Jose ha-Gelili (the Galilean). As ever before, the Haggadic Midrash continued to express the ideas, aspirations, hopes, fears, and collective thoughts of the people of Israel in successive generations. Many of the thoughts in the Haggadic Midrash were due to poetic inspiration, and these were often ahead of their times. In this sense they were prophetic, and in respect of function they continued the prophetic tradition, though formally and chronologically they were the direct descendants of the Scriptures, children of their verses, souls of their soul.

PERIOD OF MIDRASHIC CREATIVE ACTIVITY

The abandonment by the *Halachah* of the Midrash-form gave rise to the production of Haggadic writings which henceforth became synonymous with Midrashim. Simeon b. Pazzi in the first half of the third century was known as an editor of *Haggadah* (*Mesadder Aggadeta*)[1]; and R. Joḥanan is more explicit still in regard to the existence of Haggadic compilations when he declares, 'A covenant has been effected : whoever learns *Haggadah* from a

[1] Ber. 10*a*. V., however, Strack, *op. cit.*, p. 14

book will not easily forget it.'[1] The opinions recorded against the writing down of Haggadic creation are only further proofs of the fact that there were others who did put these *Haggadoth*, i.e. Midrashim, into writing.

The most flourishing period of Haggadic activity was in Palestine in the third and fourth centuries, when the Academics were on the decline and spiritual life in Palestine found its only refuge in the Synagogue in which the Torah was taught and sermons delivered. The teacher and preacher often took the same floor and a probably unintentional competition developed between them which often worked out to the disadvantage of the teacher. The popularity of the exposition of the Holy Writ, with the help of legend, parable, story, saw, and maxim, was ever growing. The masses of the people were drawn to the sermons which were full of such expositions and usually delivered on Sabbath and holy days. Hieronymus, who lived in Palestine, reports as an eye witness (about 420) that Jews would call one to another, 'Let us go and listen to this or that preacher who possesses a wonderful talent.'[2]

LATER MIDRASHIC COMPILATIONS

Some of the Midrashic creations of the Talmudic epoch found their way into the Talmud. This happened mostly when Haggadic motives of one kind or another entered into the course of some Halachic discussion. This was often the case; and therefore the Mishnah, Tosefta, and both the Babylonian and Jerusalem Talmuds are rich in Haggadic material. With the close of the Talmudic period creative Haggadic (and therefore Midrashic) activity came to an end. In the post-Amoraic and Geonic period the Midrashic activity was restricted to the field of collecting and revising the transmitted Midrashic material. The Karaite insurrection in the

[1] J. Ber. v, 1

[2] V. Dubnow, S. M., *Weltgeschichte des jüdischen Volkes*, vol. III, p. 281.

eighth century was favourable neither to Halachic nor to Haggadic activity: yet as a medium of literary expression the Midrash did not fall into disuse even after the Talmud had long been completed, and Midrashim were compiled down to the eleventh century.

Midrashic creation and compilation extend, as we have seen, in an unbroken line from the days of Ezra to the eleventh century. In the later part of this period the only kind of Midrash produced was the Haggadic. The Midrashim compiled concurrently with or just after the process of the creation of the Talmud were Midrashim in every sense of the word, and as a spiritual factor—owing to their Haggadistic contents—became more and more separated from the *Halachah* which dwelt exclusively in the Talmud.

STYLE AND CHARACTERISTICS

In all the Midrashic compilations either of contemporary creation or as the result of purely 'editorial' work, no attempt was made to reproduce in full dress the contents of the sermons of the great masters of the *Haggadah*. They merely record the central ideas from which flowed the whole process of thought of the preachers and round which they wove their orations and picturesque homilies. This accounts for their style being laconic, pithy, and terse, at times to the point of obscurity. It is well to remember this before criticising the Midrash for its apparent unintelligibility in places, as is sometimes done. It should also be borne in mind that some Midrashic paragraphs owe their preservation to the very obscurity of their meaning. This meaning might have consisted in political allusions, and contemporaries certainly possessed the key to many of the passages which to us appear a confusing mass of words. And these same Midrashim, if 'decoded' by the research and investigation of savants, may be made to throw new light on the life, religion, and history of a past age. Thus more material may be added to the historical facts embedded in the traditional lore in the Midrash, which have already proved to be invaluable data for the knowledge of the history of Israel.

Another criticism levelled against the Midrash is the simplicity exhibited in its construction and modes of expression. In truth, simple forms are proofs of inner strength, based upon the harmony of ideas and facts. Complicated forms are on the contrary signs of decline, as they betray difficulties in the endeavour to reconcile ideas with facts, formal truths with organic truth, aspirations with possibilities of attainment.

POPULARITY OF THE MIDRASH

The purely Haggadic character of the Midrash has been the cause of its immense popularity—a popularity which the passage of years has only served to confirm and strengthen. As ever in the past the Midrash retains to-day for the religious Jew the significance attached to it in the classical sentence: 'If thou wishest to know Him at whose command the world came into existence, learn *Haggadah*, for thereby shalt thou know the Holy One, blessed be He, and cling to His ways.'[1] Its sweet and potent influences have, moreover, been all-pervasive. Not only has it ever served as an inexhaustible source of inspiration to teacher and preacher, but it has also enriched the literature and liturgy of the Jew and his very life. Charged with messages, infinite in variety, which age cannot wither nor custom stale, the Midrash has ever proved an unfailing spring with the power to refreshen and renew, sustain and strengthen the Jew athirst for the word of the Living God. Whether in joy or sorrow, storm or sunshine, it never failed to yield the right message of moral sustenance and help. And to the present day, the learned Jewish layman will turn to the Midrash for solace and comfort from the turmoil and strife of work-a-day life, and the assiduous student of the law finds in it a welcome and refreshing retreat from the rigorous discipline of the battlefield of the *Halachah*.

[1] Sifre to Deut. XI, 22

ITS UNIVERSAL INFLUENCE

The influence of Jewish Midrashic activity was not restricted to Jews. Its sway extended far and wide, and much of the religious, moral, and ethical thought and teaching alike of Christianity and Islam was fashioned by the ideas to which the Midrash gave birth and which they adopted either *in toto*, or after reshaping them for their own ends. Apart from the New Testament, which so abounds with Midrashic elements that it has been not unjustly termed 'a masterpiece of the *Haggadah*',[1] the Church Fathers fully understood the importance of the Midrashic method employed with telling effect by contemporary Jewish preachers in the service of the Jewish spirit, and resolved to resort to the same spiritual weapon in order to place the dogmatic system of the Church on a firm basis. Eusebius (d 350) already praises Midrashic preachers, the '*Deuterotai*' (as distinguished from the Halachic teachers, the '*Sophoi*'), as 'men armed with extraordinary reasoning powers able to penetrate into the deepest meaning of the Holy Writ'. Ephraem Syrus, Chrysostom the 'golden mouthed', Augustine introduced Midrash in their apologetic works. Hieronymus especially drew extensively upon Midrashic sources, and thanks to his association with Palestinian Amoraim has been able to hand down to us a number of most daring Midrashic expositions.[2]

The considerable indebtedness of Mahommed to the Midrash for the legendary and other material which he incorporated in the Koran has already been proved over a century ago by Abraham Geiger in his work, *Was hat Mohammed aus dem Judenthume aufgenommen?*[3] Midrash also played its part in leading the thought of the Middle Ages into new channels and preparing the way for what was of permanent value in the Renaissance. Guillaume D'Auvergne (first half of the thirteenth century), the

[1] Renan, E., *Histoire du Peuple d'Israel* (1893), v, p. 321.
[2] V Dubnow, S. M., *op. cit.*, p 286.
[3] Published first at Bonn 1833.

first representative of the new spirit in scholasticism, shows in his *De Universo* marked traces of Midrashic influence.[1] Nicholas de Lyra, the most learned Christian Hebraist of the fourteenth century, whose influence on Luther is expressed in the well-known tag: *Si Lyra non lyrasset Lutherus non saltasset*,[2] made much use of Midrashic material in his *Postillae Perpetuae*.[3] And during the post-Reformation period, while Pascal in France was pressing Midrashic ideas into the service of Jansenism in his theological writings,[4] Milton in Puritan England was constructing his great epic *Paradise Lost* and its sequel *Paradise Regained* out of material supplied to him from Midrashic sources.[5]

ITS UNBROKEN CONTINUITY

We have seen the evidence of the centuries-long Midrashic activity, and in the Midrash Rabbah we have before us a monumental collection of the written testimony to this activity. It exhibits an unbroken row of pearls all of the same high quality, the first of which was strung by the early *Soferim* and the last perhaps by an anonymous scribe 1,500 years later. If ever a work was created by the collective spirit of a people, such a work is the Midrash. If ever the spirit of a people could claim to possess the highest degree of consistency, then the spirit which created the Midrash would entitle the Jews to make that claim.

At the same time the Midrash, in virtue of the amazing consistency of its creation, is also a most valuable proof of the progressive spirit of the Jewish people. It is a fundamental characteristic of Midrash that it keeps its gates open. It never closes a debate—that would be

[1] V. Guttmann, J., *R.E.J.*, XVIII, pp. 245 ff.

[2] If Lyra had not played the lyre (the tune), Luther would not have danced.

[3] V. Neumann, J., *R.E.J.*, XXVI, pp. 177 ff.

[4] V. Seidmann, E., *Pascal und das Alte Testament*, pp. 19–20.

[5] V. Fletcher, H. F., *Milton's Semitic Studies*, and *Milton's Rabbinical Readings*.

inconsistent either with its form or spirit. It is neither categorical nor exclusive There was in the 1,500 years during which the Midrash was being built up no epoch in the history of Israel—a history, alas, so rich in fateful changes—in which Midrashic debate would have been closed, so that Israel's philosophical activity should be ready to agree to be muzzled. This people was spiritually on the move even at a time when politically an extreme conservative attitude was to be expected. The Temple was rebuilt, a hierarchy of royal priests was installed, and the social order was stabilised. All this militated against ideological changes. And yet during this epoch when the nation was settling down, the urge for 'Quest' (*Derash*), for the search into the depth of truth was going on with a force which we do not expect to meet in times of political tranquillity.

This urge to bring the formal truth into line with the organic truth, to fill the written law—where the necessity arose—with the contents of tradition and aspiration, out of which the Midrash came into being, was never tamed in the course of the next fifteen centuries of Midrashic history. The 'Quest' has gone on and on unabated in its spirit of freedom. The hammer which awakens the slumbering sparks in the rocks (Sanhedrin 34*b*) was never used in nailing down the lid on the coffin of spiritual freedom.

THE SONCINO TRANSLATION OF THE MIDRASH

To render more accessible this heritage from which humanity has drawn much that is best in its religion, social life, and ethics is the chief aim of this translation, which has been designed on a scale hitherto unattempted in any language. The Editors and Translators alike have executed their work judiciously and conscientiously, making every possible effort to present the work in a simple, lucid, literary style whilst conforming as much as possible to the original in matter and sequence, and providing footnotes wherever necessary to remove surface difficulties. The Publishers, too, have contributed much by presenting the work in a form which makes the reading pleasant and easy.

The appeal made is not only to the student but also to the general reader 'who cares for some of these things', and is unacquainted with Jewish and Rabbinic thought. The first will have a new guide to the original which will help him over many difficulties and enable him more easily to discover the greatness lying concealed in apparent littleness, and the unity of outlook underlying differences as well as agreement, Eastern imagery as well as Western fact. The latter (the general reader) will have thrown open to him a vast treasure-house into which have been gathered the faith, the ideals, the hopes and aspirations of the people of Israel which enabled them to overcome persecutions and temptations greater than any that have confronted other peoples.

The era over which the work of the Midrash extends seems far distant and the methods of expressing thoughts, registering fears, hopes, and aspirations have greatly changed, but this translation comes at a time when the achievements of that era can provide a great sustaining and stimulating force to this generation and the generations that are to come.

I. EPSTEIN.

JEWS' COLLEGE, LONDON.
Tebeth 8, 5699.
December 30, 1938.

EDITORIAL PREFACE

THIS first complete and unabridged English translation of the Midrash Rabbah, one of the monumental productions of Rabbinic literature, owes its origin to the enterprise and idealism of Mr. J. Davidson, the Governing Director of the Soncino Press. The magnitude of the undertaking may be judged from the fact that the Midrash Rabbah is a collection of ten separate works, and this is the first time that a complete rendering has been made of all of them into any foreign language.

It has been the aim of the Editors and Translators to produce a translation which shall on the one hand be absolutely faithful and accurate, and on the other hand as agreeable to read as the original itself. We hope that it will be found literary enough to satisfy the æsthetic taste, and at the same time literal enough to be of service to those who require help in unravelling the original.

Notes have been added chiefly for the purpose of explaining difficulties and allusions in the text. They have been kept as brief as possible, and all elaborate discussion of scholastic points has been avoided. Each component work of the Midrash Rabbah is prefaced with an Introduction giving its date and place of origin as far as these can be ascertained, and pointing out its distinguishing features and characteristics.

Full use has naturally been made of the standard commentaries on the Midrash—the *Matnoth Kehunah*, the works of Einhorn and Jaffe, the glosses of Luzzatto and Strashun, etc. Where these differ, one opinion has usually been selected, but alternative renderings are mentioned in the notes where they seem to offer points of special interest. The Talmudical dictionaries of Levy and Jastrow have of course been of great help, especially in the elucidation of the foreign—mostly Greek words, of which so many occur in the Midrash Rabbah.

In spite, however, of the labours of all these scholars, and in spite of the fact that the Midrashic exposition of the Rabbis, being meant for the general public, had by its very nature to be easily intelligible, there remain in the Midrash Rabbah a number of passages which for one reason or another have become involved in obscurity, and the meaning of which is more or less a matter of conjecture. This is especially the case with passages containing some loan word or words from a foreign language which a copyist, ignorant of that language, has transformed almost out of recognition. In such cases the Editors have usually given the translation which appeared to them most probable, without entering into lengthy explanations.

In conclusion we wish to express our warmest thanks to our colleagues who have co-operated so loyally with us, and to associate with them the name of Mr. A M. Rueff, of the Soncino Press, who has given most valuable and devoted help in checking references and assuring the accuracy of the work in many other ways.

H. FREEDMAN.
M. SIMON.

INTRODUCTION

Bereshith Rabbah, to give the present work its Hebrew title, was also known under the names of Bereshith derabbi Osha'yah (Hosha'yah), Bereshith Rabbah derabbi Oshaya (Hoshayiah), Bereshith derabbi Hosha'yah rabba, and Baraitha derabbi Oshaya. It is one of the oldest Midrashim, its redaction dating not much later than the close of the Jerusalem Talmud, as will be seen further on.

In form it differs from the other Rabbah Midrashim, in that it is a running commentary on Genesis, verse by verse, and often even word by word, whereas the others are homiletic Midrashim and do not comment on each verse separately. The author of Halachoth Gedoloth ranged it not with the other Rabbah literature but with the Tannaitic Midrashim, such as the Sifra, Sifre and Mekilta, on the other books of the Pentateuch. These latter Tannaitic Midrashim being concerned mainly with Halachah, it was natural that they omitted Genesis, which contains very little Halachic matter, and thus the present work might be considered as supplementary to them. Nevertheless it differs from the Tannaitic Midrashim which are fragmentary in character, chiefly in that the *parashiyyoth* (sections, chapters) of Genesis Rabbah begin with proems, such as always characterise the beginnings of homilies collected in the homiletic Midrashim. Each chapter of the work is headed by the verse which is to be explained, and prefaced by a number of comments on a different verse of the Bible, the last of which always leads back directly to the verse of Genesis under discussion. Most of these introductory passages are anonymous, and may be partly ascribed to the author of Genesis Rabbah. Thus it is a combination of the running commentary with the homily complete in itself.

The *parashiyyoth* are numbered in the MSS. and the printed edd. The total number varies from 97 to 101. Nearly all MSS. and all edd. count 96 chapters up to the exposition on Gen. XLVII, 28 (beginning of Vayechi). The principle of division was based on the 'closed' and 'open' *parashiyyoth* of the Biblical text itself, but not on the present division of the Pentateuch into pericopes or weekly portions, whereby the whole Pentateuch is divided so that its public reading may be completed in one year. Though in the present translation, as also in the edd., the work is divided according to the pericopes for the sake of convenience, the pericopes of the one-year cycle are not marked at all in the best MSS., nor in the *editio princeps*.

The material consists of homiletic and ethical interpretations of the text. The Rabbis were not concerned to elucidate the meaning of the Biblical text according to the strictly scientific canons of scholarship, but rather to find in it teachings and messages needed by the problems which they encountered in their own days. Thus the text was seen through the spectacles of contemporary thought. The Creation story, for example, was utilised as a means of combating heretical views on the dual nature of the God-head, while in particular the story of Jacob and Esau, with all its drama and moving episodes, became a reflex of the struggle between Judea and Rome, Esau symbolising the military might of the Roman Empire and its ruthless conquest of the peoples.

Ancient tradition ascribed the authorship of the work to R. Hoshaya, a Palestinian scholar belonging to the first generation of Amoraim who flourished in the third century of the current era This tradition may mean that he was responsible for the work in its original form, but undoubtedly much of the present work was added later and swelled its size, and it is possible indeed that it was then given the name 'Bereshith Rabbah' (the great Bereshith) to distinguish it from the original work, which was naturally of much smaller compass. It has been observed that the material on the first pericope, Bereshith, has been compiled on a far more lavish scale than that on the other eleven pericopes; indeed, its twenty-nine chapters constitute more than a quarter of the whole. This has led to the theory that it may have formed part of a larger Haggadic work on Genesis which was either lost or remained incomplete. This larger work may have been called Bereshith Rabbah to distinguish it from the present smaller work preserved in the other eleven pericopes, but subsequently the name was applied not only to the first pericope but to the whole. The first scholar mentioned in this work in the edd. is R. Hoshayah Rabbah, and this has given rise to yet another theory that the name Bereshith Rabbah is a contraction of Bereshith derabbi Hoshayah Rabbah (the Bereshith of Rabbi Hoshayah the Great). This theory, however, is negatived by the fact that in the best MSS., as in the present edition, he is simply called R. Hoshayah, not R. Hoshayah Rabbah. But whatever its origin, the designation 'Rabbah' which originally belonged to Genesis alone, was subsequently applied to the other Midrashic works on the books of the Pentateuch, as well as to the five '*Megilloth*' ('Scrolls,' viz., Song of Songs, Ecclesiastes, Esther, Ruth and Lamentations), and thus ten distinct works were eventually included under the single title Midrash Rabbah.

Genesis Rabbah is a Palestinian work, and as has been stated above, its editing took place some time after the redaction of the Jerusalem Talmud. Zunz holds that it was collected and edited in the sixth century C.E. But even then the text was still subject to accretions, and from Vayyishlach we find extensive passages bearing marks of the later Haggadah. In Vayyigash the commentary is no longer verse by verse, while much of Vayechi was probably drawn from the Tanḥuma homilies. Attention to such passages has been drawn in the notes.

The present translation is based on Theodor's critical edition, which in turn is based on the Codex Add. 27169 of the British Museum. Where this differs considerably from the edd., as it often does, attention has been drawn to the fact. In the cur. edd. many passages are also found which are absent from the critical edition; these have been added either in the notes or in the text, within brackets.

H. FREEDMAN.

GENESIS

Chapter I

BERESHITH

1. R. Oshaya commenced [his exposition thus]: *Then I was by Him, as a nursling* (amon); *and I was daily all delight* (Prov. VIII, 30). '*Amon*' means tutor, '*amon*' means covered; '*amon*' means hidden[1]; and some say, '*amon*' means great. '*Amon*' is a tutor, as you read, *As an* omen *(nursing-father) carrieth the sucking child* (Num. XI, 12). '*Amon*' means covered, as in the verse, Ha'emunim (*they that were clad*—i e. covered) *in scarlet* (Lam. IV, 5). '*Amon*' means hidden, as in the verse, *And he concealed* (omen)[2] *Hadassah* (Est. II, 7). '*Amon*' means great, as in the verse, *Art thou better than No-amon* (Nah. III, 8)? which is rendered, Art thou better than Alexandria the Great, that is situate among the rivers?[3] Another interpretation: '*amon*' is a workman (*uman*). The Torah declares: 'I was the working tool of the Holy One, blessed be He.' In human practice, when a mortal king builds a palace, he builds it not with his own skill but with the skill of an architect. The architect moreover does not build it out of his head, but employs plans and diagrams to know how to arrange the chambers and the wicket doors. Thus God consulted the Torah and created the world, while the Torah declares, IN THE BEGINNING GOD CREATED (I, 1), BEGINNING referring to the Torah, as in the verse, *The Lord made me as the beginning of His way* (Prov. VIII, 22).[4]

[1] The speaker is the Torah (Wisdom) personified, referring to the pre-Creation era. The Torah was with God as with a tutor, reared, as it were, by the Almighty (this is similar to E V.), it was also covered up and hidden. This may mean that the laws of the Torah were unknown until the Revelation at Sinai, while some of them remained 'hidden' even then, i.e. their reasons are not known. [2] E.V. '*brought up*'. The Midrash understands it to mean that Mordecai concealed her from the public gaze. [3] Translation of the second half of the verse.
[4] Here too the speaker is the Torah. Thus the verse is translated: By means of the 'beginning', sc. the Torah, God created, etc.

5.[1] R. Huna quoted in Bar Ḳappara's name: *Let the lying lips be dumb*—te'alamnah (Ps. XXXI, 19): this means, Let them be bound, made dumb, and silenced. 'Let them be bound,' as in the verse, *For, behold, we were binding sheaves*—me'allemim allumim (Gen. XXXVII, 7); 'Let them be made dumb,' as you read, *Or who made a man dumb*—illem (Ex. IV, 11); while 'Let them be silenced' is its literal meaning. *Which speak* 'athak (E.V. '*arrogantly*') *against the righteous* (Ps. *loc. cit.*), meaning, [which speak] against [the will of] the Righteous One, who is the Life of all worlds, on matters which He has withheld (*he'etik*) from His creatures.[2] *With pride* (*ib.*)! in order to boast and say, 'I discourse on the Creation narrative!' *And contempt* (*ib.*): to think that he contemns My Glory! For R. Jose b. R. Ḥanina said: Whoever elevates himself at the cost of his fellow man's degradation has no share in the World to Come. How much the more then [when it is done at the expense of] the glory of God! And what is written after it? *Oh how abundant is Thy goodness, which Thou hast laid up for them that fear Thee* (*ib.* 20). Said Rab: Let him[3] have nought of Thine abundant goodness.[4] In human practice, when an earthly monarch builds a palace on a site of sewers, dunghills, and garbage, if one says, 'This palace is built on a site of sewers, dunghills, and garbage,' does he not discredit it? Thus, whoever comes to say that this world was created out of *tohu* and *bohu*[5] and darkness, does he not indeed impair [God's glory]! R. Huna said in Bar Ḳappara's name: If the matter were not written, it would be impossible to say it, viz., GOD CREATED

[1] The Midrash here is in some disorder. The passages that follow are sections 5 and 6 in cur. edd., but are placed here in Th.'s ed.

[2] Sc. the mysteries of Creation, which were regarded as a subject of esoteric teaching fit for the very select few only.

[3] Who irreverently disseminates esoteric teaching, and so is not of '*them that fear Thee*'.

[4] Lit. 'nought in "*Oh how abundant is Thy goodness*".'

[5] E.V. (in Gen. I, 2) '*unformed and void*'. Here, however, they are regarded, together with darkness, as forms of matter which according to some who deny *creatio ex nihilo* was God's raw material in the creation of the world. The object of the Midrash here is to refute that view.

HEAVEN AND EARTH; out of what? Out of NOW THE EARTH WAS TOHU AND BOHU (I, 2).[1]

6. R. Judah b. Simon quoted: *And He revealeth the deep and secret things*—mesatratha (Dan. II, 22). '*The deep things*' are the Gehenna, as it is written, *But he knoweth not that the shades are there, that in the depths of the nether world are her guests* (Prov. IX, 18). '*And secret things*' refers to the garden of Eden, as it is written, *And for a refuge and for a covert* (le-mistor), etc. (Isa. IV, 6).[2] Another interpretation: '*And He revealeth the deep things*' refers to the deeds of the wicked, as it is written, *Woe unto them that seek deep to hide their counsel from the Lord* (*ib.* XXIX, 15). *He knoweth what is in the darkness* (Dan. *loc. cit.*): this too refers to the deeds of the wicked, as it is written, *And their works are in the darkness* (Isa. *loc. cit.*). *And the light dwelleth with Him* (Dan. *loc. cit.*) refers to the deeds of the righteous, as it is written, *Light is sown for the righteous* (Ps. XCVII, 11). R. Abba of Serungayya[3] said: '*And the light dwelleth with him*'[4] alludes to the royal Messiah. R. Judah b. R. Simon said: From the commencement of the world's creation '*He revealeth the deep things,*' etc.,[5] for it is written, IN THE BEGINNING GOD CREATED THE HEAVEN, but it is not explained how. Where then is it explained? Elsewhere: *That stretcheth out the heavens as a curtain* (Isa. XL, 22); AND THE EARTH, which is likewise not explained. Where is that explained? Elsewhere: *For He saith to the snow: Fall thou on the earth*, etc. (Job XXXVII, 6). AND GOD SAID: LET THERE BE LIGHT (I, 3), and the manner of this, too, is not explained. Where is it explained? Elsewhere: *Who coverest Thyself with light as with a garment* (Ps. CIV, 2).

[1] God first created *tohu* and *bohu*, and out of these He created the world. But this is not to be taught publicly (Y.T.).
[2] *Covert* is understood to mean the Garden of Eden.
[3] A place near Tiberias.
[4] With a small *h*, in view of his interpretation.
[5] He reveals to the prophets matters in connection with the Creation which were hidden and unknown heretofore; 'E.J. and Th.

7. R. Isaac commenced with, *The beginning of Thy word is truth, and all Thy righteous ordinance endureth for ever* (Ps. CXIX, 160). Said R. Isaac: From the very commencement of the world's creation, '*The beginning of Thy word is truth.*' Thus, IN THE BEGINNING GOD CREATED [corroborates the statement,] *But the Lord God is the true God* (Jer. X, 10).[1] Therefore '*And all Thy righteous ordinance endureth for ever* (Ps *loc. cit.*). For in regard to every single decree which Thou dost promulgate concerning Thy creatures, they affirm the righteousness of Thy judgment and accept it with faith. And no person can dispute and maintain that two powers gave the Torah or two powers created the world. For '*And* the Gods *spake*' is not written here, but, *And* God *spake all these words* (Ex. XX, 1)[2]; *In the beginning* the Gods *created* is not written here, but IN THE BEGINNING GOD CREATED.[3]

2.[4] R. Joshua of Siknin[5] quoted in R. Levi's name: *He hath declared to His people the power of His works, in giving them the heritage of the nations* (Ps. CXI, 6). Why did the Holy One, blessed be He, reveal to Israel what was created on the first day and on the second day, etc.? So that the nations of the world might not taunt Israel and say to them: 'Surely ye are a nation of robbers: think of that!' But Israel can retort: 'And do ye not hold yours as spoil, for surely *The Caphtorim, that came forth out of Caphtor, destroyed them, and dwelt in their stead* (Deut. II, 23)! The world and the fullness thereof belong to God. When He wished, He gave it to you; and when He wished, He took

[1] Rashi and 'E J : The opening statement of the Bible thus proclaims the truth that the Lord is God, and there is none beside Him, for it is He alone who created the world. Mah. *Elohim* (God) is His attribute as a God of justice, and the opening verse of the Bible, IN THE BEGINNING *ELOHIM* CREATED, is an assertion that He created the world on the basis of justice and truth

[2] This is the verse which introduces Revelation.

[3] The point is that though *Elohim* (God) is plural in form, the accompanying verb is always in the singular. This passage is directed against the Gnostics, v. Graetz, *History of the Jews* (Eng. trans.), vol. II, pp. 377 *seq.*

[4] Cf. p. 2, n 1. [5] North of Jotapata in Galilee.

it from you and gave it to us.' Hence it is written, '*In giving them the heritage of the nations, He hath declared to His people the power of His works*': He declared the beginning to them, viz., IN THE BEGINNING GOD CREATED, etc.

3. R. Tanḥuma commenced with: *For Thou art great, and doest wondrous things*, etc. (Ps. LXXXVI, 10). R. Tanḥum b. R. Ḥiyya said: If a gourd has a hole even as small as the eye of a needle, all its air escapes; yet though man is formed with many cavities and orifices, his breath does not escape through them. Who achieved this? *Thou God alone (ib.)*.

When were the angels created? R. Joḥanan said: They were created on the second day, as it is written, *Who layest the beams of Thine upper chambers in the waters* (Ps CIV, 3), followed by, *Who makest the spirits Thine angels* (ib. 4).[1] R. Hanina said: They were created on the fifth day, for it is written, *And let fowl fly above the earth* (Gen I, 20),[2] and it is written, *And with twain he did fly* (Isa. VI, 2).[3] R. Luliani b. Ṭabri[4] said in R. Isaac's name: Whether we accept the view of R. Ḥanina or that of R. Johanan, all agree that none were created on the first day, lest you should say, Michael stretched [the world] in the south and Gabriel in the north, while the Holy One, blessed be He, measured it in the middle; but *I am the Lord, that maketh all things; that stretched forth the heavens alone; that spread abroad the earth by Myself*— me-itti (*ib.* XLIV, 24): *mi itti* (who was with Me) is written: who was associated with Me in the creation of the world? Ordinarily, a mortal king is honoured in his realm and the great men of the realm are honoured with him. Wherefore? Because they bear the burden [of state] with him.

[1] The former verse is interpreted as a poetic description of the dividing of the upper from the nether waters, which took place on the second day (Gen I, 6-8), and on the same day He created the angels, as is shown by the latter verse. [2] This was on the fifth day

[3] Thus angels too fall within the category of beings that fly, and were created on the same day as all flying creatures.

[4] I.e. Julianus b. Tiberius

The Holy One, blessed be He, however, is not so, but He alone created His world, He alone is glorified in His universe. R. Tanḥuma quoted: '*For Thou art great and doest wondrous things.*' Wherefore?[1] Because '*Thou God art alone*': Thou alone didst create the world. Hence, IN THE BEGINNING GOD CREATED.

4. IN THE BEGINNING GOD CREATED. Six things preceded the creation of the world; some of them were actually created, while the creation of the others was already contemplated.[2] The Torah and the Throne of Glory were created. The Torah, for it is written, *The Lord made me as the beginning of His way, prior to His works of old* (Prov. VIII, 22).[3] The Throne of Glory, as it is written, *Thy throne is established of old*, etc. (Ps. XCIII, 2). The creation of the Patriarchs was contemplated, for it is written, *I saw your fathers as the first-ripe in the fig-tree at her first season* (Hos. IX, 10).[4] [The creation of] Israel was contemplated, as it is written, *Remember Thy congregation, which Thou hast gotten aforetime* (Ps. LXXIV, 2). [The creation of] the Temple was contemplated, for it is written, *Thou throne of glory, on high from the beginning, the place of our sanctuary* (Jer. XVII, 12). The name of Messiah was contemplated, for it is written, *His name existeth ere the sun* (Ps. LXXII, 17). R. Ahabah b. R. Ze'ira said: Repentance too, as it is written, *Before the mountains were brought forth*, etc. (*ib.* XC, 2), and from that very moment, *Thou turnest man to contrition, and sayest: Repent, ye children of men* (*ib.* 3). I still do not know which was first, whether the Torah preceded the Throne of Glory or the Throne of Glory preceded the Torah. Said R. Abba b. Kahana: The Torah preceded the Throne of Glory, for it says, '*The Lord made me as the beginning of His way, ere His works of old,*' which means, ere that whereof it is written, '*Thy throne is established of old.*'

[1] I.e wherein does His greatness lie?
[2] And, generally speaking, contemplation and decision are identical and simultaneous with God. [3] The speaker is the Torah personified, and '*works of old*' means the Creation.
[4] 'I saw' is probably interpreted 'I approve', i.e. I decided to create them

R. Huna, reporting R. Jeremiah in the name of R. Samuel b. R. Isaac, said: The intention to create Israel preceded everything else. This may be illustrated thus: A king was married to a certain lady, and had no son by her. On one occasion the king was found going through the market-place and giving orders: 'Take this ink, inkwell, and pen for my son,' at which people remarked: 'He has no son: what does he want with ink and pen? Strange indeed!' Subsequently they concluded: 'The king is an astrologer, and has actually foreseen that he is destined to beget a son!' Thus, had not the Holy One, blessed be He, foreseen that after twenty-six generations[1] Israel would receive the Torah, He would not have written therein, *Command the children of Israel!*[2]

R. Banayah said: The world and the fullness thereof were created only for the sake of the Torah: *The Lord for the sake of wisdom* [i.e. the Torah] *founded the earth* (Prov. III, 19). R. Berekiah said: For the sake of Moses: *And He saw the beginning* [i.e. the Creation][3] *for Himself, for there a portion of a ruler* [sc. Moses] *was reserved* (Deut. XXXIII, 21).[4]

R. Huna said in R. Mattenah's name: The world was created for the sake of three things: *ḥallah*, tithes, and first-fruits, as it is said, IN THE BEGINNING (BERESHITH) GOD CREATED. Now *reshith* alludes to *ḥallah*, for it is written, *Of the first* (reshith) *of your dough* (Num. XV, 20); again, *reshith* alludes to tithes, for it is written, *The first-fruits* (reshith) *of thy corn* (Deut. XVIII, 4); and finally, *reshith* alludes to first-fruits, for it is written, *The choicest* (reshith) *first-fruits of thy land*, etc. (Ex. XXIII, 19).[5]

8. R. Menaḥem and R. Joshua b. Levi said in the name of R. Levi[6]: A builder requires six things: water, earth,

[1] Viz., 10 from Adam to Noah, 10 from Noah to Abraham (Aboth V, 2), and then Isaac, Jacob, Levi, Kohath, Amram, and Moses, making twenty-six in all. [2] E.g. Num. XXVIII, 2. [3] E V. '*And he chose a first part.*' [4] I.e. God created the world for the sake of Moses who was to be born in it. [5] Hence the verse is translated: For the sake of (the preposition ב can have that meaning) *reshith* God created heaven and earth. [6] Bacher is inclined to read: R. Joshua of Siknin in the name of R. Levi.

timber, stones, canes, and iron. And even if you say, He is wealthy and does not need canes,[1] yet he surely requires a measuring rod, as it is written, *And a measuring reed in his hand* (Ezek. XL, 3). Thus the Torah preceded [the creation of the world] by these six things,[2] viz., *ḳedem* ('the first'), *me-'az* ('of old'), *me-'olam* ('from everlasting'), *me-rosh* ('from the beginning'), and *mi-leḳadmin* ('or ever'), which counts as two.[3]

9. A certain philosopher asked R. Gamaliel, saying to him: 'Your God was indeed a great artist, but surely He found good materials which assisted Him?'[4] 'What are they,' said he to him? '*Tohu, bohu,* darkness, water, wind (*ruaḥ*), and the deep,' replied he. 'Woe to that man,' he exclaimed. 'The term "creation" is used by Scripture in connection with all of them.' *Tohu* and *bohu*: *I make peace and create evil* (Isa. XLV, 7)[5]; darkness: *I form the light, and create darkness* (*ib.*); water: *Praise Him, ye heavens of heavens, and ye waters that are above the heavens* (Ps. CXLVIII, 4)—wherefore? *For He commanded, and they were created* (*ib.* 5); wind: *For, lo, He that formeth the mountains, and createth the wind* (Amos IV, 13); the depths: *When there were no depths, I was brought forth* (Prov. VIII, 24).[6]

[1] The word probably means bamboos or reeds which were only used in poor houses.

[2] The idea is that six expressions of precedence are employed in reference to the Torah (Y.T. and 'E J.).

[3] This is an allusion to Prov VIII, 22 f· *The Lord made me* (sc. the Torah) . . *the first* (kedem) *of His works of old* (me-'az). *I was set up from everlasting* (me-'olam), *from the beginning* (me-rosh), *or ever* (mi-kadme = mi-likadmin in Aramaic) *the earth was*. *Ḳadme* is plural in form

[4] He believed that God had created the world, but maintained (in the form of a question) that He had used primeval matter, which was eternal.

[5] By *tohu* and *bohu* the philosopher meant primeval matter, without form Thereupon R. Gamaliel quoted: I make *shalom* (that which is whole, i e. what contains both matter and form) and evil, i.e. that which is defective, consisting of matter only without form. Thus that too was created. V Husik, *A History of Mediaeval Jewish Philosophy*, pp. XXIX f. Perhaps too this is an allusion to the view that matter is a source of evil.

[6] Since at one time there were no depths, God must have created them.

10. IN THE BEGINNING (BE-RESHITH) GOD CREATED. R. Jonah said in R. Levi's name: Why was the world created with a *beth?*[1] Just as the *beth* is closed at the sides but open in front, so you are not permitted to investigate what is above and what is below, what is before and what is behind.[2] Bar Ḳappara quoted: *For ask now of the days past, which were before thee, since the day that God created man upon the earth* (Deut. IV, 32): you may speculate from the day that days were created, but you may not speculate on what was before that. *And from one end of heaven unto the other* (*ib*) you may investigate, but you may not investigate what was before this. R. Judah b. Pazzi lectured on the Creation story, in accordance with this interpretation of Bar Ḳappara.[3]

Why was it created with a *beth?* To teach you that there are two worlds.[4] Another interpretation: why with a *beth?* Because it connotes blessing (*berakah*).[5] And why not with an *alef?*[6] Because it connotes cursing.[7] Another interpretation: Why not with an *alef?* In order not to provide a justification for heretics to plead, 'How can the world endure, seeing that it was created with the language of cursing?'[8] Hence the Holy One, blessed be He, said, 'Lo, I will create it with the language of blessing, and would that it may stand!' Another interpretation: why with a *beth?* Just as a *beth* has two projecting points, one pointing upward and the other backward,[9] so when we ask it, 'Who

[1] ב is the first letter: בראשית.
[2] Tosaf. in Hag. 11*a* s v. יכול explains that this may refer either to space or to time, or to both space and time.
[3] I.e. since the beginning of the Creation. Thus one may actually study or lecture (v. Hag 11*b*) on the Creation itself.
[4] *Beth* (ב) has the numerical value of two.
[5] Beth is the first letter of the word *berakah* (ברכה)
[6] The first letter of the Hebrew alphabet.
[7] Alef (א) is the first letter of *arur* (ארור), cursed
[8] Cf Aboth V, 1, where it is stated that the wicked destroy the world. But they would have been able to plead that it could not endure in any case.
[9] This refers to the two *taggin* ('daggers') on the top of the *beth*, thus ב. one points upwards and the other backwards The edd. read: and one *below*, at the back; this would refer to the backward projection of the *beth*, whereby it differs from the *kaf*, thus: *beth* ב, *kaf* כ.

created thee?' it intimates with its upward point, 'He who is above created me.' And if we ask further, 'What is His name?' it intimates to us with its back point: 'The Lord is His name.'[1] R, Leazar[2] b. Abinah said in R. Aḥa's name: For twenty-six generations[3] the *alef* complained before the Holy One, blessed be He, pleading before Him: 'Sovereign of the Universe! I am the first of the letters, yet Thou didst not create Thy world with me!' God answered: 'The world and its fullness were created for the sake of the Torah alone. To-morrow, when I come to reveal My Torah at Sinai, I will commence with none but thee: *I* (anoki)[4] *am the Lord your God'* (Ex. XX, 2). Bar Huṭah said: Why is it called *alef?* Because it denotes the sum of a thousand, viz. *The word which He commanded for a thousand* (elef)[5] *generations* (Ps. CV, 8).[6]

11. R. Simon said in the name of R. Joshua b. Levi: *Manẓapak*[7] is a Mosaic *halachah* from Sinai.[8] R. Jeremiah said in the name of R. Ḥiyya b. Abba: They are what the *ẓofim* [i.e. Seers] instituted.[9] It once happened on a stormy day that the Sages did not attend the House of Assembly [i.e. the Academy]. Some children were there and they said, 'Come and let us study [the letters instituted by] the Seers. Why are there two forms for *mem, nun, ẓade, peh,* and *kaf?*[10] It teaches [that the Torah was transmitted]

[1] J. Ḥag. *ad loc.* reads: י״י is His name, *adon* (אדון) is His name. Thus the backward projection points back to the *alef*, standing for אדון. But Yalḳut reads: 'the Lord is One (אחד) is His name; i.e. it points back to א, which is numerically one.

[2] More familiarly known as 'Eleazar', but these Palestinian forms are retained in the translation Edd. R. Eleazar b. Ḥanina.

[3] V p. 7, n. 1 [4] אנכי. [5] Heb. אלף.

[6] Mah. interprets He (God) agreed (i.e. contemplated) to give the Torah for a thousand (*elef*) generations, v. *infra*, XXVIII, 4, and Ḥag 13*b* bottom *seq*. V. also S S. R., p. 243, n. 3.

[7] This is a mnemonic i e. the letters מנצפכ. These have different forms when they come at the end of a word, viz. םןץףך; v Shab. 104*a* and notes *ad loc.* in Sonc. ed.

[8] The double forms were then instituted.

[9] Hence the mnemonical form *manzapak*, connected with *ẓofim*, instead of *kamanpaz*, following the order of the Hebrew letters.

[10] Lit. 'why is it written *mem mem, nun nun*,' etc.?

from utterance to utterance, from Faithful to faithful, from Righteous to righteous, from mouth to mouth, and from hand to hand. (From utterance to utterance—from the utterance of the Holy One, blessed be He, to the utterance of Moses. From Faithful to faithful—from the Almighty, who is designated, "God, faithful King," to Moses, who is designated faithful, as it is written, *He* [sc. Moses] *is faithful* (E.V. *"trusted"*) *in all My house* (Num. XII, 7). From Righteous to righteous—from God, who is designated righteous, as it is written, *The Lord is righteous in all His ways* (Ps. CXLV, 17), to Moses who is designated righteous, as it is written, *He executed the righteousness of the Lord* (Deut. XXXIII, 21)[1] From mouth to mouth—from the mouth of the Holy One, blessed be He, to the mouth of Moses. From hand to hand:)[2] from the hand of the Holy One, blessed be He, to the hand of Moses.' The scholars noted them, and they grew to be great sages in Israel; some say that they were R. Eliezer, R. Joshua, and R. Akiba.[3] They applied to them the verse, *Even a child is known by his doings*, etc. (Prov. XX, 11).

12. IN THE BEGINNING GOD CREATED. R. Judah said in the name of Akilas[4]: Him it is fitting to designate God. In human practice an earthly king is honoured in his realm even before he has built them public baths or provided them with private baths.[5] (Simeon b. 'Azzai quoted: *And Thy condescension* [modesty] *hath made me great* (II Sam. XXII, 36). A human being states his name first and then his title, thus: So-and-so the Prefect, So-and-so of whatever title it may be.[6]) But the Holy One,

[1] The verse (v. first half, which mentions *the ruler*) is understood to refer to Moses. [2] The bracketed passage is added from various MSS.

[3] In the corresponding passage in J. Meg. I R. Akiba is omitted; apparently with reason, since he was a pupil of R. Eliezer and R. Joshua, and began his studies at an advanced age (v. Ned. 50*a*). Radal, however, justifies the inclusion of his name

[4] The famous proselyte who translated the Bible into Greek, and who was said to be a relation by marriage to Hadrian; v. *J.E.* s.v. Aquila.

[5] Or perhaps: or bestowed gifts upon them.

[6] Thus his name comes first and then his claim to greatness in the form of the title he bears, which testifies to his achievements.

blessed be He, is not so, for He recorded His name only after creating the requirements of His universe: IN THE BEGINNING CREATED, and then GOD.

13. R. Simeon b Yoḥai taught: How do we know that one must not declare '[I vow this] to the Lord as a burnt-offering,' 'to the Lord as a meal-offering,' 'to the Lord as a peace-offering'; but must declare: '[This be] a burnt-offering to the Lord,' 'a meal-offering to the Lord,' 'a peace-offering to the Lord'? Because it is stated: *When any man of you bringeth an offering unto the Lord* (Lev. I, 2).[1] Now you can surely argue from this: If when one is going to dedicate [a sacrifice] the Torah directs, Let him cause the Divine Name to be related to nought but the sacrifice[2], then they who revile, blaspheme, and engage in idolatry, will surely be blotted out from the world!

THE HEAVEN AND THE EARTH. The Rabbis said: Mortal man builds an edifice, and if he succeeds according to his intentions, he can widen it as the building rises;[3] but if not, he must broaden it below and narrow it at the top. The Holy One, blessed be He, is not so, however; He built *the* heaven, i.e. the heaven which he originally contemplated, and *the* earth, viz. the earth which He originally contemplated.[4] R. Huna said in the name of R. Eliezer, the son of R. Jose the Galilean: Even those whereof it is written, *For, behold, I create new heavens* (Isa. LXV, 17), have been created long ago, since the six days of Creation, as it is written, *For as the new heavens . . . remain before Me* (*ib.* LXVI, 22): not 'new' is written here, but '*the new*'.[5]

[1] For the actual reason v. Ned. 10*a*. [2] I.e God's name must be mentioned only *after* the sacrifice. [3] Only if it turns out as strong as he planned it can the upper portions be broader than the lower
[4] He had no need to modify His original designs. This explains the use of the definite art. 'the', for otherwise, since these were new creations, Scripture should have written, 'God created heaven and earth'
[5] The def. art. implies the specific new heavens, viz. those created aforetime 'E.J.' it intimates therefore that the new heavens are already created, but only potentially, i.e. in God's thought. Mah. explains it differently.

14. ETH THE HEAVENS AND ETH THE EARTH.[1] R. Ishmael asked R. Akiba: 'Since you have studied twenty-two years under Nahum of Gimzo,[2] [who formulated the principle that] *ak* (save that) and *rak* (except) are limitations, while *eth* and *gam* (also) are extensions,[3] [tell me], what of the *eth* written here?' Said he to him: 'If it stated, "In the beginning God created heaven and earth," we might have maintained that heaven and earth too are divine powers.'[4] Thereupon he cited to him, *For it is no empty thing from you* (Deut. XXXII, 47), and if it is empty, it is so on your account,[5] because you are unable to interpret it [rightly]. No: ETH THE HEAVENS is to include the sun and moon, the stars and planets; WE-ETH THE EARTH is to include trees, herbage, and the Garden of Eden.[6]

15. THE HEAVEN AND THE EARTH. Beth Shammai maintain: The heaven was first created; while Beth Hillel hold: The earth was first created. In the view of Beth Shammai this is parallel to the case of a king who first made his throne and then his footstool, for it is written, *The heaven is My Throne, and the earth is My footstool* (Isa. LXVI, 1). On the view of Beth Hillel this is to be compared to a king who builds a palace; after building the nether portion he builds the upper, for it is written, *In the day that the Lord God made earth and heaven* (Gen. II, 4). R. Judah b. R. Ilai said: This supports Beth Hillel, viz *Of old Thou didst lay the foundations of the earth*, which is followed by, *And the heavens are the work of Thy hands* (Ps. CII, 26). R. Ḥanin said: From the very text which [apparently] supports Beth Shammai,[7] Beth Hillel refute them, viz. *And the earth was* (Gen. I, 2), meaning

[1] *Eth* is the sign of the acc. [2] A town in Judea. By a play on words this name is frequently connected with *gam zu*, 'this too,' because whatever happened Nahum would say, 'This too shall be for good' (v. Ta'an. 21*a*). [3] Which extend and add to the verse.
[4] I.e. without the sign of the accusative they might be regarded as nominatives and additional subjects of 'created', or ('E.J.) as in apposition to 'God' [5] The מ of מכם may be causative: if you find it empty, it is through your own fault (Mah.). [6] V. Ḥag. 12*a* where this is repeated with some variations. [7] Viz. our text, in which heaven comes first.

that it had already existed [before heaven][1] R. Johanan, reporting the Sages, said: As regards creation, heaven was first; as regards completion, earth was first. Said R. Tanhuma: I will state the grounds [of this opinion]: as regards creation heaven was first, as it is written, IN THE BEGINNING GOD CREATED THE HEAVEN; whereas in respect of completion earth took precedence, for it is written, *In the day that the Lord God made earth and heaven*. R. Simeon observed: I am amazed that the fathers of the world[2] engage in controversy over this matter, for surely both were created [simultaneously] like a pot and its lid, [as it is written], *When I call unto them* [sc. heaven and earth], *they stand up together* (Isa. XLVIII, 13). R. Eleazar b. R. Simeon observed: If my father's view is right, why is the earth sometimes given precedence over the heaven, and sometimes heaven over earth? In fact it teaches that they are equal to each other.[3]

Everywhere Abraham is mentioned before Isaac, and Isaac before Jacob; yet in one place it says, *Then will I remember My covenant with Jacob, and also My covenant with Isaac, and also My covenant with Abraham* (Lev. XXVI, 42): this teaches that the three are on a par.

Everywhere Moses is mentioned before Aaron, yet in one place it says, *These are that Aaron and Moses* (Ex. VI, 26): this teaches that they are on a par.

Everywhere Joshua is mentioned before Caleb, yet in one place it says, *save Caleb the son of Jephunneh the Kenizzite, and Joshua the son of Nun* (Num. XXXII, 12): this teaches that they are on a par.

Everywhere a father's honour is mentioned before the mother's honour, but in one place it says, *Ye shall fear every man his mother, and his father* (Lev. XIX, 3): this teaches that both are on a par.

[1] Translating *hayyethah* as a pluperfect: had been.

[2] The Sages, so called because by virtue of their teachings they were as spiritual fathers to all.

[3] But has no bearing on precedence Others, however, regard this as a confirmation: if it is as my father states, it is right that they are not always mentioned in the same order, and the verse teaches that they are of equal importance precisely because neither took precedence of the other.

Chapter II (BERESHITH)

1. Now the earth was unformed and void, and darkness was upon the face of the deep; and the spirit of God hovered over the face of the waters (I, 2). R. Berekiah quoted: *Even a child is known by his doings, whether his work be pure, and whether it be right* (Prov. xx, 11). Said R. Berekiah: While she [the earth] was as yet immature [in her infancy], she produced thorns; and so the prophet was one day destined to prophesy of her, *I beheld the earth, and, lo, it was waste and void* (Jer. iv, 23).

2. Now the earth was tohu E.V. 'unformed', etc. R. Abbahu and R. Judah b. R. Simon [gave the following illustrations]. R. Abbahu said: This may be compared to the case of a king who bought two slaves on the same bill of sale and at the same price. One he ordered to be supported at the public expense, while the other he ordered to toil for his bread. The latter sat bewildered and astonished[1]: 'Both of us were bought at the same price,' exclaimed he, 'yet he is supported from the treasury whilst I have to gain my bread by my toil!' Thus the earth sat bewildered and astonished, saying, 'The celestial beings [sc. the angels] and the terrestial ones [sc. man] were created at the same time: yet the celestial beings are fed by the radiance of the *Shechinah*, whereas the terrestial beings, if they do not toil, do not eat. Strange it is indeed!' R. Judah b. R. Simon said: Compare this case to a king who bought two bondmaids, both on the same bill of sale and at the same price One he commanded not to stir out from the palace, while for the other he decreed banishment. The latter sat bewildered and astonished. 'Both of us were bought on the same bill of sale, and at the same price,' she exclaimed, 'yet she does not stir from the palace while against me he has decreed

[1] The words are connected with *tohu* and *bohu*,—his mind not being able to formulate a reason and void of all understanding for the grounds of his treatment.

banishment. How amazing!' Thus the earth sat bewildered and astonished, saying, 'The celestial and the terrestial beings were created at the same time: why do the former live [eternally], whereas the latter are mortal?' Therefore, AND THE EARTH WAS TOHU AND BOHU (BEWILDERED AND ASTONISHED).[1] R. Tanhuma said: This may be compared to a royal infant sleeping in his cot while his nurse sat by anxious and troubled. Why? Because she knew that she was fated to receive punishment at his hand.[2] Thus the earth foresaw that she was destined to meet her doom at the hand of man, as it is written, *Cursed is the ground for thy sake* (Gen. III, 17). Therefore THE EARTH WAS TOHU AND BOHU (DESOLATE AND ANXIOUS).

3. NOW THE EARTH WAS UNFORMED, etc. R. Judah b. R. Simon interpreted the text as referring to the generations. NOW THE EARTH WAS UNFORMED: this refers to Adam, who was reduced to complete nothingness [on account of his sin]. AND VOID refers to Cain, who desired to turn the world back to formlessness and emptiness.[3] AND DARKNESS symbolises the generation of Enosh: *And their works are in the dark* (Isa. XXIX, 15).[4] UPON THE FACE OF THE DEEP, the generations of the Flood: *On the same day were all the fountains of the great deep broken up* (Gen. VII, 11); further, AND THE SPIRIT (RUAḤ) OF GOD HOVERED OVER THE FACE OF THE WATERS corresponds to *And God made a wind* (ruaḥ) *to pass over the earth* (*ib* VIII, 1). Said the Holy One, blessed be He: 'How long shall the Universe go on in darkness[5]: Let the light come!' So, AND GOD SAID: LET THERE BE LIGHT: this alludes to Abraham, as it is written, *Who hath raised up one from the east, whom He calleth in righteousness to His foot* (Isa. XLI, 2)?[6] AND GOD CALLED THE LIGHT DAY (I, 5) symbolises Jacob;

[1] Cf. p. 15, n. 1. [2] On his account
[3] Chaos being the inevitable result of lawlessness. [4] V. *infra* Ch. XXIV, 1, which refers to this generation [5] Sc. moral and religious darkness.
[6] Cf. *infra*, XLIII, 3 (p. 354).

AND THE DARKNESS HE CALLED NIGHT, Esau; AND THERE WAS EVENING—Esau; AND THERE WAS MORNING,—Jacob ONE DAY [teaches] that the Holy One, blessed be He, gave him one [unique] day: and which is that? the Day of Atonement.[1]

4. R. Simeon b. Laḳish applied the passage to the [foreign] Powers. NOW THE EARTH WAS TOHU (E.V. 'UNFORMED') symbolises Babylonia. *I beheld the earth, and, lo, it was tohu*—E.V. *'waste'* (Jer. IV, 23)[2]; AND BOHU (E.V. 'VOID') symbolises Media: *They hastened* (wa-yabhillu) *to bring Haman* (Est. VI, 14).[3] AND DARKNESS symbolises Greece, which darkened the eyes of Israel with its decrees, ordering Israel, 'Write on the horn of an ox that ye have no portion in the God of Israel.'[4] UPON THE FACE OF THE DEEP—this wicked State[5]: just as the great deep cannot be plumbed, so one cannot plumb [the depths of iniquity of] this wicked State. AND THE SPIRIT OF GOD HOVERED: this alludes to the spirit of Messiah, as you read, *And the spirit of the Lord shall rest upon him* (Isa. XI, 2) In the merit of what will [this spirit] eventually come? [For the sake of that which] HOVERED OVER THE FACE OF THE WATERS, i.e. in the merit of repentance which is likened to water, as it is written, *Pour out thy heart like water* (Lam. II, 19). R. Haggai said in the name of R. Pedath: A covenant was made with water[6] that even in the hot season a breeze stirs over it.[7]

[1] I e. it is the one day over which Satan, symbolising the wickedness of Esau, has no power, cf *infra*, III, 8.

[2] Jeremiah refers to the desolation wrought by the conquering might of Babylonia. *Tohu* and *bohu* are applied to Babylonia and Media (Persia) respectively in the sense that they caused chaos and destruction.

[3] This happened in Media, and *wa-yabhillu* is linked up with *'bohu'*. Or possibly *wa-yabhillu* is read: *wayabo bohu lo*, and they brought desolation to him —Mah.

[4] The reference is to Antiochus who endeavoured to annihilate Judaism and implant Hellenism in its stead, 'write on the horn of an ox' probably implies a public disavowal of Judaism.

[5] Pesiḳ. R · to the wicked State of Edom—i.e Rome.

[6] I.e. it is the eternal nature of water.

[7] He translates *'ruaḥ'* literally, wind, and also stresses the present tense of *meraḥefeth*, lit. 'hovers'; thus the verse means that at all times a breeze, caused by God, stirs over the waters.

It once happened that Simeon b. Zoma was standing wrapped in speculation, when R. Joshua passed and greeted him once and a second time, without his answering him. At the third time he answered him in confusion. 'What means this, Ben Zoma!' exclaimed he: 'whence are the feet?'[1] 'From nowhere, Rabbi,' replied he.[2] 'I call heaven and earth to witness that I will not stir hence until you inform me whence are the feet,' he urged. 'I was contemplating the Creation [and have come to the conclusion] that between the upper and the nether waters there is but two or three fingerbreadths,' he answered. 'For it is not written here, AND THE SPIRIT OF GOD blew, but HOVERED, like a bird flying and flapping with its wings, its wings barely touching [the nest over which it hovers].' Thereupon R. Joshua turned to his disciples and remarked to them, 'The son of Zoma has gone.'[3] But a few days elapsed and the son of Zoma was in his [eternal] home.

5. R. Abbahu and R. Ḥiyya Rabbah[4] were engaged in discussion. R. Abbahu said: From the very beginning of the world's creation the Holy One, blessed be He, foresaw the deeds of the righteous and the deeds of the wicked. Thus, NOW THE EARTH WAS FORMLESS AND VOID alludes to the deeds of the wicked; AND GOD SAID: LET THERE BE LIGHT, to the actions of the righteous. I still might not know in which of these He delights, the former or the latter. But from what is written, AND

[1] The passage is difficult. The commentaries offer several explanations, which are all rejected by Theodor, who thinks that this was an esoteric or mystical question on the Creation.
[2] Or possibly ר׳ is an abbreviation for רגלים (feet)—Theodor. In either case his reply seems to have been a refusal to answer, as R. Joshua's rejoinder shows.
[3] Passed away—he has immersed himself too deeply in supra-mundane thought—the Creation—and is no longer for this world.
[4] Since he is coupled with R. Abbahu, R. Ḥiyya b. Abba, an Amora, must be meant here. In Pesiḳ. XXI, however, this passage is introduced by 'R. Ḥiyya Rabbah taught (*tani*)', in which case it refers to R. Ḥiyya the Elder, a Tanna, and designated Rabbah (the Great or Elder) to distinguish him from the Amora of the same name.

GOD SAW THE LIGHT, THAT IT WAS GOOD (I, 4), it follows that He desires the deeds of the righteous, and not the deeds of the wicked. R. Ḥiyya Rabbah said: From the very beginning of the world's creation the Holy One, blessed be He, foresaw the Temple built, destroyed, and rebuilt. IN THE BEGINNING GOD CREATED [symbolises the Temple] built, as you read, *That I may plant the heavens, and lay the foundations of the earth, and say unto Zion: Thou art My people* (Isa. LI, 16).[1] NOW THE EARTH WAS TOHU (E.V. 'UNFORMED') alludes to [the Temple] destroyed, as you read, *I beheld the earth, and, lo, it was* tohu—E.V. '*waste*' (Jer. IV, 23). AND GOD SAID: LET THERE BE LIGHT, i.e. rebuilt and firmly established in the Messianic era, as you read, *Arise, shine, for thy light is come, and the glory of the Lord is risen upon thee*, etc. (Isa. LX, 1).

[1] I.e. the foundations are laid when God will say '*Thou art*', etc., which will come to pass with the rebuilding of Zion and the Temple.—Mah.

CHAPTER III (BERESHITH)

1. AND GOD SAID: LET THERE BE LIGHT (I, 3). R. Isaac opened with: *The opening of Thy words giveth light; it giveth understanding unto the simple* (Ps. CXIX, 130). R. Judah and R. Nehemiah disagree. R. Judah maintains: The light was created first, this being comparable to a king who wished to build a palace, but the site was a dark one. What did he do? He lit lamps and lanterns, to know where to lay the foundations; in like manner was the light created first. R. Nehemiah said: The world was created first, this being similar to the king who built a palace and then adorned it with lights. Thus far did R. Judan interpret. But R. Phinehas and R. Judah b. R. Simon came, and R. Ḥanin in the name of R. Samuel b. R. Isaac, and preached: '*The opening of Thy words giveth light*': The opening of Thy mouth was light to us: AND GOD SAID: LET THERE BE LIGHT.

2. R. Berekiah commenced in the name of R. Judah b. R. Simon: *By the word of the Lord were the heavens made, and all the host of them by the breath of His mouth* (Ps. XXXIII, 6): not by labour or toil but only by a word; thus, AND GOD SAID: LET THERE BE LIGHT.

3. R. Simeon b. Yohai commenced: *A man hath joy in the answer of his mouth, and a word in season, how good it is* (Prov. XV, 23)! '*A* Man *hath joy*' alludes to the Holy One, blessed be He: *The Lord is a* Man *of war* (Ex. XV, 3); '*In the answer of his mouth,*' viz. AND GOD SAID: LET THERE BE LIGHT; '*And a word in season, how good it is*': thus it is written, AND GOD SAW THE LIGHT, THAT IT WAS GOOD.

4. AND GOD SAID: LET THERE BE LIGHT, etc. R. Simeon b. R. Jehoẓadak asked R. Samuel b. Naḥman: 'As I have heard that you are a master of *haggadah*, tell me whence the light was created?' He replied: 'The Holy One, blessed be He, wrapped Himself therein as in

a robe and irradiated with the lustre of His majesty the whole world from one end to the other.' Now he had answered him in a whisper, whereupon he observed, 'There is a verse which states it explicitly: *Who coverest Thyself with light as with a garment* (Ps. CIV, 2), yet you say it in a whisper!' 'Just as I heard it in a whisper, so have I told it to you in a whisper,' he rejoined. R. Berekiah remarked: Had not R. Isaac taught it,[1] could we have said it![2] Before this, what did they say [on the matter]? R. Berekiah said in R Isaac's name: The light was created from the place of the Temple, as it is said, *And, behold, the glory of the God of Israel came from the east; and His voice was like the sound of many waters; and the earth did shine with His glory* (Ezek. XLIII, 2). Now '*His glory*' is nought else but the Temple, as you read: *Thou throne of glory, on high from the beginning, Thou place of our sanctuary* (Jer. XVII, 12).

5. R. Simon said: 'Light' is written five times [in this paragraph], corresponding to the Books of His Torah. NOW GOD SAID: LET THERE BE LIGHT corresponds to Genesis, in which is recorded that the Holy One, blessed be He, engaged in the creation of His world; AND THERE WAS LIGHT, to Exodus,[3] in which it is told how the Israelites went forth from Egypt, out of darkness into light; AND GOD SAW THE LIGHT, etc., to Leviticus, which is filled with numerous laws; AND GOD DIVIDED THE LIGHT, to Numbers, which divides between those who departed from Egypt and those who entered the [holy] land; AND GOD CALLED THE LIGHT [DAY], to Deuteronomy, which is filled with numerous laws. But, they [his hearers] objected, 'Is not Leviticus filled with numerous laws?'[4] — This passage, too, has, a repetition, viz. AND GOD CALLED THE LIGHT DAY: now surely light and day are identical![5]

[1] Th : publicly; and so explicitly in edd
[2] Certainly not, as we would have regarded it as esoteric lore.
[3] Lit. 'now these are the names'—the first words of Exodus; similarly the names of the Books which follow
[4] Why have two similar allusions?
[5] Hence it is fitting that this verse should correspond to Deuteronomy, which also contains much repetition of the previous Books (M.K.).

6. It was taught: The light which was created in the six days of Creation[1] cannot illumine by day, because it would eclipse the light of the sun, nor by night, because it was created only to illumine by day. Then where is it? It is stored up for the righteous in the Messianic future, as it says, *Moreover the light of the moon shall be as the light of the sun, and the light of the sun shall be sevenfold, as the light of the seven days* (Isa. xxx, 26). Seven! surely there were but three, seeing that the luminaries were created on the fourth day![2] It is like a man who says, 'I am providing so much for the seven days of my [wedding] feast'[3] R. Nehemiah said: It refers to the seven days of mourning for Methuselah, when the Holy One, blessed be He, lavished light upon them.[4]

AND GOD SAW THE LIGHT. R. Ze'ira, the son of R. Abbahu, lectured in Cæsarea[5]: Whence do we know that you must not recite a blessing over a lamp unless you can enjoy its light? From this: AND HE SAW . . . AND HE PRONOUNCED A DIVISION.[6] R. Judah b. R. Simon said: He [God] set it apart for Himself.[7] Our Rabbis said: He set it apart for the righteous for the future, just like a king who had a goodly portion [served to him at table],

[1] I e. the light which came into existence at God's command, not that shed by the sun.

[2] *The light of the seven days* is the special light created by God's fiat '*Let there be light*'. But this served for three days only, not seven, since the sun was created on the fourth day, which rendered the first light superfluous.

[3] Though he does not intend it to suffice for the whole period. Similarly we speak of the light of the seven days, though it did not serve for so long

[4] V. *infra*, XXXII, 7, and Sanh. 108*b*.

[5] Several cities bore that name: (i) Cæsarea by the Sea, originally called 'Strato's Tower', and some 75 miles from Jerusalem; (ii) Cæsarea Philippi, identical with Paneas; and (iii) Cæsarea in Cappadocia, of which it was the capital.

[6] A ceremony, called *habdalah* (division), is performed at the termination of Sabbaths and festivals, in which the distinction between these and non-holy days is mentioned. Part of the ceremony consists of pronouncing a blessing over light (v. Pes. 54*a*), and R. Ze'ira states that one must actually benefit from the light before he may pronounce the blessing *Wayyabdel* (E V '*divided*') is thus connected with the ceremony of *habdalah*, and we learn that it can be done only when the light is *seen*, i.e. enjoyed.

[7] This first light which He created.

but set it aside for his son. R Berekiah said: Thus did two men of world renown, R. Joḥanan and R. Simeon b. Laḳish, expound it: *'And he divided'* (wayyabdel) connotes a literal division. Imagine a king who had two chiefs of the guards, one in command by day and the other in command at night, who used to quarrel with one another, each claiming, 'I must have command by day.' Thereupon the king summoned the first and said to him, 'So-and-so, the day shall be your province'; summoning the second he addressed him, 'So-and-so, night shall be your province.' Thus GOD CALLED THE LIGHT [for service by] DAY, saying to it, 'The day shall be thy province'; AND THE DARKNESS CALLED HE [for service at] NIGHT, saying to it, 'Night shall be thy province.' R. Joḥanan observed: That is what the Holy One, blessed be He, said to Job: *'Hast thou commanded the morning?* (Job. XXXVIII, 12)—strange 'twere indeed! *And caused the dayspring to know its place* (*ib.*)—'twere amazing! hast thou really made it known which is its place [i.e. time—to function in]!'[1] R. Tanḥuma said: I can cite the grounds [for this statement]: *I form the light, and create darkness, I make peace* (Isa. XLV, 7); having created them, He makes peace between them.

AND GOD CALLED THE LIGHT, DAY (I, 5). R. Eleazar said: The Holy One, blessed be He, does not link His name with evil, but only with good. Thus it is not written here, *And God called the light Day, and the darkness* God *called Night,* but AND THE DARKNESS CALLED HE NIGHT.

7. AND THERE WAS EVENING, etc. R. Judah b. R. Simon said: 'Let there be evening' is not written here, but AND THERE WAS EVENING: hence we know that a time-order existed before this.[2] R. Abbahu said: This proves that the Holy One, blessed be He, went on creating

[1] *Yada'ta* (*ḳal*) can hardly be treated as a causative, as here, Y.T. thinks it probable that it is understood as *ya'adeta;* hast thou appointed a place for day, i.e. when it should function.

[2] By rendering· And evening (already) was—ere now.

worlds and destroying them until He created this one and declared, 'This one pleases Me; those did not please Me.' R. Phinehas said: This is R. Abbahu's reason: *And God saw everything that He had made, and*, behold, *it was very good* (Gen. I, 31): this pleases Me, but those did not please Me.[1]

8. R. Jannai said: From the very beginning of the world's creation the Holy One, blessed be He, foresaw the deeds of the righteous and the deeds of the wicked. '*And the earth was desolate*' alludes to the deeds of the wicked: '*And God said: Let there be light*,' to those of the righteous; '*And God saw the light, that it was good*,' to the deeds of the righteous; '*And God made a division between the light and the darkness*': between the deeds of the righteous and those of the wicked; '*And God called the light day*' alludes to the deeds of the righteous, '*And the darkness called He night*,' to those of the wicked; AND THERE WAS EVENING, to the deeds of the wicked, AND THERE WAS MORNING, to those of the righteous; ONE DAY: the Holy One, blessed be He, gave them one day, and which is that? It is the Day of Judgment.[2] R. Tanḥum said: It was on the day on which unique things were created, viz. heaven, earth, and light.[3] R. Judan said: The day in which the Holy One, blessed be He, was One in His universe. This agrees with R. Joḥanan but not with R. Ḥanina. For R. Johanan said: The angels were created on the second day, as it is said, *Who layest the beams of Thine upper chambers in the waters*, and it is written, *Who makest the spirits Thine angels* (Ps. CIV, 3f). R. Ḥanina said: The angels were created on the fifth day,[4] as it is written, *And let fowl fly above the earth* (Gen. I, 20), and it is written, *And with twain he did fly* (Isa. VI, 2). R. Luliani b. Ṭabri

[1] The deduction is from *behold* (hinneh), which implies that only what He *now* saw was very good in His eyes.
[2] I.e. the Day of Atonement. Cf. *supra*, II, 3, 5.
[3] Of each of these there is only one; cf. *infra*, XI, 9. Others translate: the day when a new heaven, earth, and light were created, cf. *supra*, I, 13.
[4] Hence it was not on the first day only that God was unique and alone in the universe

said in R. Isaac's name: Whether we accept the view of R. Ḥanina or of R. Joḥanan, all agree that none were created on the first day, lest you should say, Michael stretched [the world] in the south of the firmament and Gabriel in the north, while the Holy One, blessed be He, measured it in the middle; but *I am the Lord that maketh all things; that stretched forth the heavens alone; that spread abroad the earth by Myself*—me-itti (*ib.* XLIV, 24): *mi itti* (who was with Me?) is written; who was associated with Me in the creation of the world?[1]

9. R. Samuel b. Ammi said: From the beginning of the world's creation the Holy One, blessed be He, longed to enter into partnership with the mortals. For what will you: if it is a matter of time reckoning, it should say either one, two, three, or first, second, third,[2] but surely not, one, second, third![3] When did the Holy One, blessed be He, repay them? At the erection of the Tabernacle, as it says, *And he that presented his offering* the *first day* (Num. VII, 12), meaning, the first of the world's creation, for God said, 'It is as though on that day I created My world.'[4] That day took ten crowns[5]: it was the first of the creation,[6] first in respect of kings,[7] the princes,[8] the priesthood,[9] and the

[1] V. *supra*, I, 3.

[2] The creation narrative should either state, one day, two days, three days, etc., or the first day, the second day, etc. Instead of which it states '*one day*', and continues with '*the second day*', '*the third day*', etc. Hence '*yom ehad*' (one day) really means: the day when He designed to be at one with man, His handiwork.—The world thus requires the harmonious co-operation of God and man, and its harmony and unity are broken when man sins.

[3] When did He restore the designation '*first* day' which is lacking from the Creation narrative (M.K.).

[4] This is deduced from the def. art. '*the*'.—Thus the world is not really created until man does God's will, here symbolised by the erection of the Temple, and thereby His original design to be at one with man is fulfilled.

[5] It was pre-eminent in ten respects.

[6] I.e. it was the first day of the week.

[7] Kings date their reigns from the first day of Nisan (v. R.H. 2*a*), and on that day the Tabernacle was erected (Ex. XL, 2).

[8] On that day they began bringing their dedication gifts.

[9] This was the first day that the priesthood functioned in the sacrificial services, for previously the firstborn had performed these duties.

Shechinah,[1] (as it says, *And let them make Me a sanctuary, that I may dwell among them* (Ex. XXV, 8)); it was first in respect of blessing, sacrificial service,[2] the prohibition of high places,[3] killing at the north [side of the Altar], and the descending of fire,[4] as it is said, *And there came forth fire from before the Lord* (Lev. IX, 24).[5]

[1] The *Shechinah* dwelt there for the first time.

[2] The priestly blessing (v. Num. VI, 22-27) was pronounced for the first time, and the *public* sacrificial services were then inaugurated.

[3] Before the erection of the Tabernacle private sacrifices could be offered at any high place.

[4] Fire descended on that day from heaven for the first time.

[5] V. Shab. 87*b*, where there are several variations.

CHAPTER IV (BERESHITH)

1. AND GOD SAID: LET THERE BE A FIRMAMENT IN THE MIDST OF THE WATERS (I, 6). It is written, *Who roofs Thine upper chambers with water* (Ps. CIV, 3).[1] In human affairs, an earthly monarch builds a palace and roofs it over with stones, timber, and earth, but the Holy One, blessed be He, roofed over His world with nought but water, as it is said, '*Who roofs Thine upper chambers with water*'; thus, AND GOD SAID: LET THERE BE A FIRMAMENT, etc.[2]

2. AND GOD SAID: LET THERE BE A FIRMAMENT, etc. Our Rabbis said the following in the name of R. Ḥanina, while R. Phinehas and R. Jacob b. R. Bun said it in the name of R. Samuel b. Naḥman: When the Holy One, blessed be He, ordered, LET THERE BE A FIRMAMENT IN THE MIDST OF THE WATERS, the middle layer of water solidified, and the nether heavens and the uppermost heavens were formed. Rab said: [God's] handiwork [the heavens] was in fluid form, and on the second day it congealed; thus LET THERE BE A FIRMAMENT means 'Let the firmament be made strong'. R. Judah b. R. Simon said: Let a lining be made for the firmament, as you read, *And they did beat*[3] *the gold into thin plates* (Ex. XXXIX, 3). R. Ḥanina said: The fire came forth from above and dried up the face of the firmament. When R. Joḥanan came to the verse, *By His breath* [sc. fire] *the heavens are smoothed*—E.V. '*serene*' (Job XXVI, 13), he would say, 'R. Ḥanina taught me well.' R. Judan b. R. Simon said: The fire came forth from above and burnished the face of the firmament. R. Berekiah and R. Jacob b. R. Abina in R. Abba b. Kahana's name said: The creation story was used [by the prophet] to throw light upon Revelation, but was itself explained thereby.

[1] E.V. '*Who layest the beams of Thine upper chambers in the waters.*'
[2] V. Ex. R. XV, 22. [3] *Wayyeraḳe'u*, here connected with *raḳi'a*.

Thus: *As when fire burneth through into parts* (Isa. LXIV, 1),[1] which intimates that they divided [between the upper and the nether waters] Now when did the fire divide between the upper and the nether. surely at the Revelation! So it was, too, at the creation of the world.[2]

3. R. Phinehas said in R. Oshaya's name: As there is a void between the earth and the firmament, so is there a void between the firmament and the upper waters, as it is written, LET THERE BE A FIRMAMENT IN THE MIDST OF THE WATERS, meaning, midway between them. R. Tanḥuma said: I will state the proof. If it said, *And God made the firmament, and He divided between the waters . . . which are* upon *the firmament*, I would say that the water lies directly upon the firmament itself. Since, however, it is stated, '*And between the waters which are* above *the firmament*,' it follows that the upper waters are suspended by the word [of God].[3] R. Aha said: It is like [the flame of] a lamp,[4] and their fruits are the rain.[5]

4. A Samaritan asked R. Meir: 'Is it possible that the upper water is suspended by [God's] word?' 'Yes,' he answered. 'Bring me a water-clock,'[6] he added. When he

[1] E.V. '*As when fire kindleth brushwood*'.

[2] The meaning is this: The previous verse states, *O that Thou wouldst rend the heavens*, etc., which is followed by '*As when fire burneth into parts*'. The Midrash applies the former verse to Revelation, and interprets the verses as meaning that when God rent the heavens to give the Torah, it was even as when fire burned through and divided the upper from the nether waters Similarly, the fire at Revelation divided the terrestial beings (men) from the upper (celestial spheres). But it is not actually stated elsewhere that fire did act thus at the Creation, and so this verse, whose primary purpose is to teach us about Revelation by likening it to the Creation, tells us something new about the Creation itself.

[3] He stresses the word 'above' (*me-'al*), which is not the same as 'upon' (*'al*).

[4] Which seems to be suspended in the air.

[5] The upper waters drip through the heat of the firmament, the dripping being the rain we enjoy.

[6] The meaning of the word is doubtful. It would appear to mean a *clepsydra*, a contrivance for measuring time by the flow of water. The bottom was perforated with such small holes that if the upper aperture was completely closed the water would not flow out from the bottom. Levi: a syringe or squirt.

brought it, he placed a gold plate upon it, but the water did not stand still; then a silver plate, but the water did not stand still. But as soon as he placed his finger [upon the aperture], the water stood still.[1] 'But you have put your finger there,' he objected.—'If my finger stays the water, though I am but flesh and blood, how much more so the finger of the Holy One, blessed be He! Hence the upper waters are suspended by [God's] word.'

Said he to him: 'Is it possible that He of whom it is written, *Do I not fill heaven and earth?* (Jer. XXIII, 24) spoke to Moses from between the two staves of the Ark?' 'Bring me a large mirror,' said he. When he brought it he said to him, 'Look at your reflection,' and he saw it, large. 'Bring me a small[2] mirror.' He brought it. 'See your reflection in it.' He saw it, small. 'If you, who are but flesh and blood,' said he, 'can change yourself at will, how much more so He at whose word the world came into existence! Thus when He so wishes, "*Do I not fill heaven and earth?*", while when He wishes, He speaks to Moses from between the staves of the Ark.' R. Ania b. Susay said: At times the world and its fullness cannot contain His glory, yet at times He speaks to man from between the hairs of his head, as it is written, *Then the Lord answered Job out of the* sa'arah—E.V. '*whirlwind*' (Job. XXXVIII, 1), which means, from between the hairs (*sa'aroth*) of his head. Said he to him: 'Is it possible that *The river of God is full of water* (Ps. LXV, 10) since the six days of Creation and has not been diminished at all: it is incredible!'[3] 'Go in and bathe, and weigh yourself before you enter and after you have gone in,' replied he. He went and weighed himself, and his weight had not diminished at all. Said he to him: 'Now all that perspiration, did it not ooze from you?' 'Yes,' answered he. 'Then if your fountain [of perspiration] did not in any way diminish, though you are but a mere mortal, how much the more is this true of the fountain

[1] Thus remaining suspended in spite of the holes beneath it.
[2] Mah. and 'E.J. translate 'magnifying' and 'diminishing', the reference being to a convex and a concave mirror respectively.
[3] Whence then comes the rain?

of the Holy One, blessed be He! Hence "*The river of God is full of water*" since the six days of Creation, and it has not diminished at all.' R. Johanan said: The Holy One, blessed be He, took all the primeval water and poured half in the firmament and half into the ocean; hence the word *peleg* (the river),[1] meaning *palga* (half).

5. The firmament is like a lake, and above the lake is a vault, and through the heat of the lake the vault exudes moisture; it exudes heavy drops of water, which descend into the salt water yet do not combine with it.[2] R. Jonah observed: Do not wonder thereat, for lo! the Jordan passes through the lake of Tiberias yet does not mingle with it. The thing is indeed miraculous! For when a man is sifting wheat or stubble in a sieve, before they have dropped a distance of two or three fingerbreadths they intermingle, yet these [raindrops] have been travelling so many years without intermingling.[3] R. Judah b. R. Simon said: The reason is that He causes them to descend in measure. [Thus it is written,] *For He draweth away* (yigra') *the drops of water* (Job XXXVI, 27), [where *yigra'* is used] in the sense of *And an abatement shall be made* (we-nigra') *from thy valuation* (Lev. XXVII, 18).[4]

The thickness of the firmament equals that of the earth: compare, *It is He that sitteth above the circle* (ḥug) *of the earth* (Isa. XL, 22) with, *And He walketh in the circuit* (ḥug) *of the heaven* (Job XXII, 14): the use of '*hug*' in both verses teaches that they are alike. R. Aḥa said in R. Ḥanina's name: [It is but as] thick as a metal plate. R. Joshua b. R. Nehemiah said: It is about two fingers in thickness. The son of Pazzi said: The upper waters exceed the lower ones by about thirty *xestes*,[5] [for it is written,] AND LET IT DIVIDE THE WATERS FROM THE

[1] In the verse just quoted. [2] V. *infra*, XIII, 10.

[3] The Rabbis held that the rain descended from heaven, which is a distance of many years' journey above the earth, and yet no drop has ever touched another.

[4] The second verse obviously means a *calculated* deduction, and he understands the first in a similar sense: He calculatingly *draweth away*, etc.

[5] A dry and liquid measure, equalling nearly a pint.

WATERS (LA-MAYIM): *lamed*[1] is thirty.[2] Our Rabbis said: They are half and half [i.e. equal].

6. AND GOD MADE THE FIRMAMENT (I, 7). This is one of the verses over which the son of Zoma raised a commotion: He *made*—how remarkable! surely it [came into existence] at [God's] *word*, [as it is written,] *By the* word *of the Lord were the heavens made, and all the host of them by the breath of His mouth* (Ps XXXIII, 6).[3]

Why is *'that it was good'* not written in connection with the second day? R. Joḥanan explained, and it was also thus taught in the name of R. Jose b. R. Ḥalafta: Because on it the Gehenna was created, [as it is written,] *For Tofteh is ordered from yesterday* (Isa. XXX, 33),[4] which signifies a day to which there was a yesterday but not a day before yesterday.[5] R. Ḥanina said: Because in it schism was created, [as it is written,] AND LET IT DIVIDE THE WATERS. R. Ṭabyomi said: If because of a division made for the greater stability and orderliness of the world, *'for it was good'* is not written in connection with that day, then how much the more should this apply to a division which leads to its confusion! R. Samuel b. Naḥman said: Because the making of the waters was not finished[6]: consequently *'for it was good'* is written twice in connection with the third day, once in respect of the making of the waters and a second time on account of the work done on that day.

A [Roman] lady asked R. Jose: 'Why is "*for it was good*" not written in connection with the second day?' 'Even so,' replied he, 'it [the text] subsequently included them all [in this description], for it is said, *And God saw* everything *that He had made, and, behold, it was very good*'

[1] In למים.
[2] Hebrew letters have numerical values —He interprets the verse thus: and let there be a difference between the upper and nether waters of thirty (measures of) water. [3] Whereas *'made'* implies work. The difficulty remains unanswered (Theodor).
[4] *Tofteh* being the Gehenna E V. *'For a hearth is ordered of old'*.
[5] There was a 'yesterday' to the second day, but not a day before yesterday. [6] Whereas *'for it was good'* is applicable only to a completed work.

(Gen. I, 31). Said she to him. 'Supposing six men came to you and you gave a *maneh* to all but one, and then you gave a second *maneh* to all of them [jointly]: would not each now have a *maneh* and a sixth, while the one would only have one sixth!'[1] Then he explained it a second time in the same way as R. Samuel b. Nahman, viz. because the making of the water was not finished. Hence *'for it was good'* is written twice in connection with the third day, once on account of the making of the waters and a second time on account of the work done on that day.

R. Levi said in the name of R. Tanḥum b. Ḥanilai: It is written, *Declaring the end from the beginning* (Isa. XLVI, 10): from the very beginning of the world's creation God foresaw [the existence of] Moses who was called, *'for it was good'*[2] and that he was destined to be punished through them[3]; therefore *'for it was good'* is not written in connection therewith.

R. Simon said in the name of R Joshua b. Levi: This is similar to the king who had a very stern legion, and said, 'Since this legion is so stern, let it not bear my name.' Thus the Holy One, blessed be He, said, 'Since the generation of Enosh, the generation of the Flood, and the generation of the separation of races[4] were punished through them [the waters],[5] let "*for it was good*" not be written in connection therewith.'

7. AND GOD CALLED THE FIRMAMENT HEAVEN—SHAMAYIM (I, 8). Rab said: [*Shamayim* is a compound of] *esh* (fire) and *mayim* (water). R. Abba b. Kahana said in Rab's name: The Holy One, blessed be He, took fire and water and beat them up together, and from them the heaven was made.

SHAMAYIM is written, for they [the heavens] weigh

[1] Hence the subsequent inclusion still leaves the second day worse off than the others.

[2] In Sot. 12*a* R. Meir explained the verse, *And when she saw that he was good* (Ex. II, 2 *q.v.*) as meaning that his name was '*Ṭob*' (good)

[3] Sc. the waters, i.e. through his sin at the waters of Meribah (Num. XX, 12 f). [4] V. Gen. XI, 1–9. [5] V. *infra*, XXIII, 7.

up (*shamim*) the deeds of men: if one is worthy, *The heavens declare his righteousness* (Ps xcvii, 6); but if not, *The heavens shall reveal his iniquity* (Job xx, 27).

SHAMAYIM: [It is so called] because men wonder (*mishtommemim*) at it, saying: 'Of what (*shelmah*) is it composed? Of fire? Of water? 'Tis a mystery!' R. Phinehas said in R. Levi's name: It [Scripture] comes and explains it: '*Who layest the beams of Thine upper chambers in the waters*' (Ps. civ, 3): this shows that it is of water.

[SHAMAYIM means like] *sammim* (chemicals): just as some chemicals are blue, others red, some black and others white, so is heaven: sometimes it is blue, sometimes red, sometimes black and sometimes white.

R. Isaac said: [SHAMAYIM means] *sa-mayim*, i.e. be laden with water. Compare this to milk in a bowl: before a drop of rennet falls into it, it quivers, but as soon as a drop of rennet falls into it, it immediately curdles and stands still. Similarly, *The pillars of heaven quiver* (Job xxvi, 11); then the solidifying substance was infused into them, whereupon, '*And there was evening and there was morning, a second day*' (Gen. i, 8).[1] That agrees with Rab's dictum: [God's] handiwork was liquid and on the second day it congealed.

[1] I.e their solidifying was the work of the second day.

Chapter V (BERESHITH)

1. AND GOD SAID: LET THE WATERS UNDER THE HEAVEN BE GATHERED TOGETHER UNTO ONE PLACE, AND LET THE DRY LAND APPEAR (Gen. I, 9). It is written, *At Thy rebuke they fled* (Ps. CIV, 7), which explains, AND GOD SAID: LET THE WATERS . . . BE GATHERED TOGETHER, etc.[1]

LET THE WATERS BE GATHERED TOGETHER (YIKKAWU) UNTO ONE PLACE, etc. R. Berekiah explained it in the name of R. Abba b. Yoma: Let there be a measure set for the water, as you read, *And a line* (ḳaw) *shall be stretched forth over Jerusalem* (Zech. I, 16).[2] R. Abba b. Kahana explained it in R. Levi's name thus: Let the waters be gathered together for My purpose, [so as to perform] what I will one day do by means of them. Compare this to a king who built a palace and tenanted it with dumb people who used to rise early and pay their respects to the king with gestures, with their fingers and with their handkerchiefs.[3] Said the king, 'If these, who are dumb, rise early and pay their respects with gestures, with their fingers and with their kerchiefs, how much more would they do so if they possessed all their faculties!' Thereupon the king tenanted it with men gifted with speech, who arose and seized the palace, asserting, 'This is not the king's palace: it is our palace!' 'Then let the palace return to its original state,' the king ordered. Similarly, at the very beginning of the world's creation, the praise of the Almighty ascended from nought but the water, as it is written, *From the voices of many waters* (Ps. XCIII, 4); and what did they proclaim? *The Lord on high is mighty* (*ib.*). Said the Holy One, blessed be He: 'If these which have neither mouth nor speech praise Me, how much more [will I be praised] when man is

[1] The waters then fled to their appointed place, instead of covering the whole world. [2] '*Yiḳḳawu*' is thus derived from *ḳaw*, a measuring line, and translated. let the waters be confined to a definite measure or quantity. [3] Or, spears.

created!' But the generation of Enosh arose and rebelled against Him[1]; the generation of the Flood arose and rebelled against Him; the generation of the Separation [of tongues] arose and rebelled against Him. Thereupon the Holy One, blessed be He, said: 'Let these be removed and the former arise and come [in their place].' Hence it is written, *And the rain was upon the earth forty days and forty nights* (Gen. VII, 12).[2]

2. R. Judan and R. Berekiah observed: The whole world was one mass of water, yet you actually say, INTO ONE PLACE! This may be compared to ten inflated wine-skins lying in a chamber. When the king needs their place, what does he do to them? He unties them, permits their air to escape, and removes them into a corner. Even so did the Holy One, blessed be He, tread down all the primeval waters[3] and remove them into the Ocean, as it is written, *Behold, He [consumeth] the waters, and they dry up, also He sendeth them out, and they overturn the earth* (Job XII, 15); it also says, *And He treadeth upon the waves of the sea* (*ib.* IX, 8).

3. R. Levi said: The waters said to each other, 'Let us go and obey the fiat of the Holy One, blessed be He'; thus it is written, *The floods have lifted up their voice*, etc. (Ps. XCIII, 3). 'But whither shall we go,' asked they? '*Let the floods take up* (dokyam),'[4] replied He. R. Levi said: ['*Dokyam*'] means, *derek yam* (to the way of the sea). R. Abba b. Kahana interpreted it: To such and such a place (*dok*), to such and such a corner. R. Huna explained: To this sea (*ha-dak yama*). R. Joshua b. Ḥananiah said: To the receptacle (*diksa*) of the sea.[5] R. Eliezer said: The sea absorbed them, as you read, *Hast thou entered into the springs of the sea* (Job XXXVIII, 16)? Which means, into the

[1] V. *infra*, XXIII, 7. [2] It was for this purpose that the waters were to be *gathered together* at the Creation.
[3] The waters having been hitherto inflated, as it were, and He deflated them. [4] E.V. '*their roaring*'.
[5] I.e. to the place specially prepared to receive the waters.

waters absorbed by the sea. Our Rabbis interpreted it: We are crushed (*dakkim*): receive us; we are broken: receive us. R. Joshua b. R. Nehemiah said: The waters ascended mountains and descended into the depths, until they came to the Ocean [Mediterranean], as it is written, *They ascended the mountains, they descended into valleys unto the place which Thou hast founded for them* (Ps. CIV, 8): which place hast Thou founded for them? The Ocean.

4. R. Levi said: Some interpreters, e.g. the son of 'Azzai and the son of Zoma, interpret: The voice of the Lord became a guide[1] to the waters, as it is written, *The voice of the Lord is over the waters* (Ps. XXIX, 3).

R. Berekiah said: The upper waters parted from the nether waters with weeping, as it is written, *He bindeth the streams from weeping* (Job XXVIII, 11)[2] R Tanhuma adduced it from the following: *He hath made the earth by His power . . . at the voice of His giving a multitude of waters in the heavens* (Jer. X, 12 f). Now '*voice*' refers to nought but weeping, as you read, *A voice is heard in Ramah, lamentation and bitter weeping* (*ib*. XXXI, 15).

5. R. Johanan said: The Holy One, blessed be He, made a stipulation with the sea that it should divide before Israel; thus it is written, *And the sea returned* (le-ethano) —E.V. '*to its strength*' (Ex. XIV, 27): i.e. in accordance with its agreement (*li-tenao*) R. Jeremiah b. Eleazar said: Not with the sea alone did God make a stipulation, but with everything which was created in the six days of creation, as it is written, *I, even My hands, have stretched out the heavens, and all their host have I commanded* (Isa. XLV, 12). I commanded the sea to divide, and the heavens to be silent before Moses, as it says, *Give ear, ye heavens, and I will speak* (Deut. XXXII, 1); I commanded the sun and the moon to stand still before Joshua; I commanded the ravens to feed Elijah; I commanded the fire

[1] V. Jast. s.v מיטטור; i.e. He assigned their courses, etc.
[2] E.V. '*that they trickle not*'.

to do no hurt to Hananiah, Mishael, and Azariah; I commanded the lions not to harm Daniel; the heavens to open before Ezekiel; the fish to vomit forth Jonah.

6. R. Eleazar said: From the very beginning of the world's creation the Holy One, blessed be He, issued a decree, saying, '*Let the waters under the heaven be gathered together unto one place.*' Wherefore then [is it written], *That calleth for the waters of the sea, and poureth them out upon the face of the earth*, twice?[1] Once was in the generation of Enosh, and a second time in the generation of the Separation [of races]. *And God hath so made it* (Eccl. III, 14): all that He has done is in order *That men should fear before Him* (*ib.*). Compare this to a country that rebelled against its king, whereupon the king sent a strong legion and marched them round it, so that the inhabitants might see it and fear him. Even so, why *Gathereth He the waters of the sea together as a heap, and layeth up the deeps in storehouses* (Ps. XXXIII, 7)? In order that *All the inhabitants of the world may stand in awe of Him* (*ib.* 8).

7. In human practice, a man empties a full vessel into an empty one; does he ever empty a full vessel into a full vessel? Now the world was full of water everywhere, yet you say, UNTO ONE PLACE! In truth, from this we learn that the little held the much. Similarly, *And Moses and Aaron gathered the assembly together before the rock* (Num. XX, 10). Now R. Hanina said: It was but the size of the opening of a small sieve, yet all Israel stood there! In truth, from this we learn that the little held the much. Similarly, *Take to you handfuls of the soot of the furnace* (Ex. IX, 8): said R. Ḥana, Could then one fistful of Moses contain eight handfuls![2] For a fistful is not the same as a handful, one fistful equalling two handfuls, yet

[1] In Amos V, 8, and IX, 6. Thus He reversed His previous decree that the waters should be confined to one place.

[2] *Ḥofen* is the hollow of the hand formed by bending the fingers so as to touch the wrist; *ḳomez* is the bending of the three middle fingers over the hollow of the hand (Jast. s.v. חפן and קומץ). A *ḥofen* is normally

it is written, *And let* Moses *throw it* (*ib.*),[1] so that one fistful of Moses actually contained eight handfuls! From this, however, we learn that the little held the much. Similarly R Jose b. Ḥalafta observed: *The length of the court shall be a hundred cubits*, etc. (Ex. XXVII, 18), yet all Israel stood there![2] In fact, from this we learn that the little held the much. Similarly, *And Joshua said unto the children of Israel: Come hither*, etc. (Josh. III, 9) R. Huna said: He made them stand between the staves of the Ark. R. Ḥama said: He crowded them[3] between the staves of the Ark; our Rabbis said: He squeezed them between the two staves of the Ark. Said Joshua to them: *Hereby ye shall know that the living God is among you* (*ib.* 10). And in Jerusalem, too, they stood pressed together, yet when they prostrated themselves they had ample room.[4] R. Samuel b. R. Jonah said: Each had four cubits, a cubit on each side, so that none should hear his neighbour's prayer. And in the future, too, it shall be thus, viz. *At that time they shall call Jerusalem 'The Throne of the Lord', and all the nations shall be gathered unto it* (Jer. III, 17). R Joḥanan went up to inquire after the wellbeing of R. Ḥanina, and he found him sitting and lecturing on this verse: '*At that time they shall call Jerusalem "The throne of the Lord", and all the nations shall be gathered unto it.*' Said he to him: Can it then hold [them all]! It is amazing! —The Holy One, blessed be He, will order it: 'Lengthen [thy boundaries], enlarge [thy space], and receive thy hosts,' as it is said, *Enlarge the place of thy tent* (Isa. LIV, 2).

8. AND GOD CALLED THE DRY LAND ERETZ—EARTH (I, 10). Why ERETZ? Because she conformed (*razethah*) to His will (*razon*). R. Nathan commented in R. Aḥa's name, and R. Berekiah in R. Isaac's name: *I am* El Shaddai —E.V. '*God Almighty*' (Gen. XVII, 1). It was I who said

two *ḳemaẓim* (pl. of *ḳomez*), and Moses and Aaron both took a *ḥofen* in each hand, = 8 *ḳemaẓim* in all, and then Moses took it in one handful; v. Ex. R XI, 5. [1] I.e. Moses alone. [2] Cf. Lev VIII, 8.
[3] Lit. 'he made them lean'—perhaps it means that he made them stand so that one had to press against his neighbour (Th.). [4] Aboth V, 5.

to the earth,[1] '*day*' (enough), and to the world[2] '*day*'. For had I not said '*day*' to the heaven and '*day*' to the earth, they would have continued to extend even until now.

AND THE GATHERING TOGETHER OF THE WATERS CALLED HE SEAS (*ib*). Yet surely there is but one sea? Why then is it stated AND THE GATHERING TOGETHER OF THE WATERS CALLED HE SEAS?[3] The reason is because the taste of a fish caught at Acco is dissimilar from that of one caught at Sidon and Aspamia.[4]

9. AND GOD SAID: LET THE EARTH PUT FORTH GRASS etc. (I, 11). It was taught in R. Nathan's name: *Three* entered for judgment, yet *four* came out guilty. Adam and Eve and the serpent entered for judgment, whereas the earth was punished with them, as it is written, *Cursed is the ground* (Gen. III, 17), which means that it would produce accursed things for him [Adam], such as gnats, insects, and fleas. Then let it produce [pests as large as] a camel?[5] Said R. Isaac of Magdala[6]: In that there would be benefit too.[7] Now why was [the earth] punished? R. Judah b. R. Shalom said: Because she disobeyed [God's] command For the Holy One, blessed be He, said thus: LET THE EARTH PUT FORTH GRASS, HERB YIELDING SEED, AND FRUIT-TREE BEARING FRUIT: just as the fruit is eaten, so should the tree be edible. She, however, did not do thus, but AND THE EARTH BROUGHT FORTH GRASS, HERB YIELDING SEED AFTER ITS KIND, AND TREE BEARING FRUIT (I, 12): the fruit could be eaten but not the tree R. Phinehas said: She exceeded His command, thinking to do the will

[1] Interpreting *Shaddai(y)* as *sha-dav*, 'who (said) enough'
[2] 'World' will now connote heaven and earth.
[3] The Rabbis held that all seas are connected and therefore one Or possibly they are thinking here simply of the 'Great Sea' (the Mediterranean).
[4] Acco and Sidon are on the Phœnician coast. Th. conjectures that Aspamia refers to Apamea in the north of Palestine; cf B B. 74*b*· the sea of Aspamia.
[5] The bracketed addition gives Theodor's explanation of this passage.
[6] A town near Tiberias; v. *J.E.* s v.
[7] Though a pest, it could be killed and put to use

of her Creator: thus AND TREE BEARING FRUIT implies that even non-fruit-bearing trees yielded fruit. Now no difficulty arises on R. Judah's view. But on R. Phinehas's view, why was she cursed? It is in fact as one might say: 'Cursed be the breast that suckled such a one as this.'

AND THERE WAS EVENING AND THERE WAS MORNING, A THIRD DAY—SHELISHI (*ib.* 13); i.e. the day in which strong ones were created,[1] as you read, *Captains* (shalishim) *and councillors, all of them riding upon horses* (Ezek. XXIII, 23).[2] But when iron was created, the trees began to tremble. Said He to them, 'Why do you tremble? Let none of your wood enter it, and not one of you shall be harmed.'[3]

[1] I.e. strong and lofty trees.

[2] Thus *shalishim* means men of strength, transf captains.

[3] Iron cannot harm the tree unless the tree first furnishes a handle for the axe.

CHAPTER VI (BERESHITH)

1. AND GOD SAID: LET THERE BE LIGHTS (I, 14). R. Johanan began thus: *Who appointest the moon for seasons* (Ps. CIV, 19). R. Johanan commented: The orb of the sun alone was created to give light. If so, why was the moon created? *'For seasons'*: in order to sanctify new moons and years thereby.[1] R Shila of Kefar Temarta[2] said in R. Johanan's name: Yet even so, *The sun knoweth its coming (ib)*: from the sun one knows its coming [sc. of the month], for we count the beginning of the month only from sunset. Justa Ḥabra[3] said in R. Berekiah's name: *And they journeyed from Rameses in the first month, on the fifteenth day of the first month*, etc. (Num. XXXIII, 3): but if you count by the moon, then so far there were only thirteen sunsets?[4] Hence it follows that we count not from the moon but from sunset.

R. 'Azariah said in R. Ḥanina's name: The orb of the sun alone was created to give light; yet if so, why was the moon created? Because the Holy One, blessed be He, foresaw that the peoples of the world would treat them as divinities. Said the Lord: 'If they are two, opposed to each other,[5] and yet the peoples of the world treat them

[1] The Jewish year is lunar, and the actual fixing of the months and the years depends on the moon, though a month is intercalated in leap years in order to harmonise the lunar with the solar years.

[2] The townlet of Temarta in Judea; Ḥul 62*a*.

[3] Justa is an abbreviation of Justus or Justinus, Habra (חבריא) may either be part of the name or mean a *ḥaber*, an associate, one of a body who were particularly scrupulous in their observance of the laws of tithes and purity.

[4] This is based on the tradition that the Nisan (the first month of the Jewish year) in which the Exodus took place fell on a Thursday, while the actual New Moon occurred after midday on the preceding Wednesday; it is further assumed that when this happens the moon is not visible until the second evening following, i.e. the evening of Friday. Hence if we counted time solely from when the New Moon is visible, then by the Thursday on which they left, a fortnight after, there would only have been thirteen sunsets Since, however, it is called the fifteenth of the month, we see that the month was calculated from the first sunset after the New Moon.

[5] The reference is possibly to the eclipse of the sun and the moon (commentaries).

as divinities, how much more would they do so if there were but one!' R. Berekiah said in R. Simon's name: Both were created in order to give light, as it says, AND LET THEM BE FOR LIGHTS, etc.

AND LET THEM BE FOR SIGNS: this refers to the Sabbaths[1]; AND FOR SEASONS: to the three pilgrimage festivals; AND FOR DAYS: to the beginnings of the months; AND YEARS means the sanctification of the years.[2]

2. AND GOD MADE THE TWO GREAT LIGHTS (I, 16). It is written, *Thine is the day, Thine also the night* (Ps. LXXIV, 16). to Thee the day gives praise, to Thee the night gives praise. Just as the day is under Thy control, so is the night under Thy control. When Thou performest miracles for us by day, '*Thine is the day*'; and when Thou performest miracles for us by night, '*Thine also is the night.*' When Thou performest miracles for us by day, we utter song to Thee by day, and when Thou performest miracles for us by night, we utter song to Thee by night. Thou didst perform miracles for us by day, and we uttered song to Thee by day, thus: *Then sang Deborah and Barak the son of Abinoam on that day* (Judg. V, 1). Thou didst perform miracles for us by night, and we uttered song to Thee by night: *Ye shall have a song as in the night when a feast is hallowed* (Isa. XXX, 29). To Thee it is becoming to utter song by day and by night; wherefore? because *Thou hast established luminary and sun* (Ps. *loc. cit.*), and Thou hast made THE TWO GREAT LIGHTS.

3. R. Tanhum and R. Phinehas in R. Simon's name said: After calling them GREAT, He actually casts a slur [on one by writing] THE GREAT LIGHT . . . AND THE SMALL LIGHT (I, 16)! The reason is because it penetrated into its neighbour's territory.[3] R. Phinehas said:

[1] Cf Ex. XXXI, 17, where the Sabbath is called a sign
[2] I.e. the proclamation of the New Year by the proper authorities.
[3] The moon is sometimes seen by day too, and thus encroaches, as it were, upon the domain of the sun.

In respect of all other sacrifices it is written, *And one he-goat for a sin-offering*,[1] whereas in respect of New Moon it is written, *And one he-goat for a sin-offering for the Lord* (Num. XXVIII, 15): The Holy One, blessed be He, said: 'It was I who caused it to enter its neighbour's domain.'[2] Then if that [sc. the moon] which entered with permission was thus disparaged by Holy Writ, think how much more one is deserving of this who enters without permission!

R. Levi said in the name of R. Jose b. Lai: It is but natural that the great should count by the great, and the small by the small. Esau[3] counts [time] by the sun, which is large, and Jacob by the moon, which is small. Said R. Naḥman: That is a happy augury. Esau counts by the sun, which is large: just as the sun rules by day but not by night, so does Esau enjoy this world, but has nought in the World to Come. Jacob counts by the moon, which is small: just as the moon rules by day and by night, so has Jacob a portion in this world and in the World to Come. R. Naḥman made another observation, thus: R. Naḥman said: As long as the light of the greater luminary functions, the light of the smaller one is not noticeable, but when the light of the greater one sets, the light of the smaller one becomes noticeable; even so, as long as the light of Esau prevails, the light of Jacob cannot be distinguished; but when the light of Esau sets, that of Jacob shall be distinguished, as it is written, *Arise, shine, . . . For, behold, darkness shall cover the earth, and gross darkness the peoples, but upon thee the Lord will arise, and His glory shall be seen upon thee* (Isa. LX, 1 f).

4. AND THE STARS (I, 16). R. Aha said: Imagine a king who had two governors, one ruling in the city and the other in a province. Said the king: 'Since the former has humbled himself to rule in the city only, I decree that whenever he goes out, the city council and the people shall go out with him, and whenever he enters, the city

[1] Num XXVIII, 22; XXIX, 5, 11, *passim*.
[2] Therefore I need a sin-offering; cf Ḥul. 60*b*
[3] I.e. Rome.

council and the people shall enter with him.' Thus did the Holy One, blessed be He, say: 'Since the moon humbled itself to rule by night, I decree that when she comes forth, the stars shall come forth with her, and when she goes in [disappears], the stars shall go in with her.' Similarly we read, *And his brother's name was Joktan*—lit. 'he shall be small' (Gen. x, 25). R. Aha said. Why was he called Joktan? Because he humbled himself. What did he earn thereby?[1] He was privileged to beget thirteen families.[2] Now if this is so with the younger,[3] then when a great man is content with a humble position, how much the more so. Similarly, *And Israel stretched out his right hand, and laid it upon Ephraim's head, who was the younger* (*ib.* XLVIII, 14). Said R. Ḥunia: Do we not know from the birth records that he was the younger! But younger (*za'ir*) means that he reduced (*meẓa'ir*) himself. What did he earn thereby? He attained the birthright. Then if a great man contents himself with a humble position, how much the more [is he rewarded].

5. AND GOD SET THEM IN THE FIRMAMENT OF THE HEAVEN (I, 17). R. Jonathan said: Three things were given as a gift to the world, viz., the Torah, the luminaries, and rain. Whence do we know it of the Torah? *And He gave unto Moses . . . the two tables of testimony* (Ex. XXXI, 18). The luminaries? AND GOD GAVE (E.V. 'SET') THEM, etc. Rain? *Then I will give you rains* (Lev. XXVI, 4). R. 'Azariah said in the name of R. Judah b. R. Simon: Peace, too, as it says, *And I will give peace* (*ib* 6). R. Joshua b. R. Nehemiah said: Salvation too: *Thou hast also given me the shield of Thy salvation* (II Sam. XXII, 36). R. Tanḥuma said: Eretz Israel too: *And He gave them the lands of the nations* (Ps. CV, 44). Some say, vengeance too, as it says, *And I will give My vengeance upon Edom*, etc. (Ezek. XXV, 14). Our Rabbis say: Compassion too: *He gave them also to be pitied* (Ps. CVI, 46). R. Isaac b. Marion said:

[1] *Zakah* denotes 'to attain a privilege through merit'.
[2] He had thirteen children, who each produced a family (*ib*, 26–9).
[3] Joktan was Peleg's younger brother.

The crossing of the Great Sea too: *Thus saith the Lord, who giveth a way in the sea* (Isa. XLIII, 16)—from Pentecost until the Festival [sc Tabernacles]; *And a path in the mighty waters*—from the Festival until Ḥanukkah.[1]

R. Cohen, the brother of R. Ḥiyya b. Abba, was setting out on a sea voyage 'Pray for me,' he asked his brother. 'Why should we pray for you,' replied he: 'where you bind up your palm branch, bind your foot.[2] If you enter the synagogue and hear [the congregation] praying for rain, do not rely upon my prayers.'[3] R. Joshua b. Tanḥum b. R. Ḥiyya of Ḳefar Hagin was in Asia Minor[4] and wished to make a sea journey. Said a [Roman] matron to him: 'I am astonished that one should set out at this time of the year.' His father appeared to him in a dream [and admonished him]: 'My son! [would you die] without burial, [thus fulfilling the verse] *And moreover he have no burial'* (Eccl. VI, 3)? But he paid no heed to the words of either, and that [fate] did befall him.

6. Where are the spheres of the sun and the moon set? In the second heaven (*raḳi'a*),[5] as it says, AND GOD SET THEM IN THE RAḲI'A OF THE HEAVEN. R. Phinehas said in R. Abbahu's name: This verse is explicit, and the men of the Great Assembly[6] further explained, *Thou art the Lord, even Thou alone; Thou hast made the heaven, the heaven of heavens, with all their host* (Neh. IX, 6): thus where are all their hosts set? In the second *'raḳi'a'*, which is above the heaven.[7] From the earth to the *'raḳi'a'*

[1] The Feast of Lights, v. Shab 22*b*, i.e. from about the middle of October to the end of December, when the seas show their 'might', being storm-swept That one is able to travel at all then by sea is a gift of God.

[2] I e. do not travel after Tabernacles, as the sea is dangerous then.

[3] I can pray for your safety, but my prayers are submerged by those of the whole congregation, as rain naturally increases the dangers of sea travel.

[4] Or perhaps, Essa, east of the lake of Tiberias.

[5] The Rabbis believed that there were seven heavens, the name of the second being *raḳi'a* (firmament); v Ḥag. 12*b*.

[6] An institution consisting of 80 or 120 men (the sources vary) said to have been founded by Ezra.

[7] This is the meaning attached to *The heaven of heavens, heaven* itself meaning the first one.

is a five hundred years' journey, and the thickness of the '*raki'a*' is a five hundred years' journey,[1] and from the first '*raki'a*' to the next '*raki'a*' is a five hundred years' journey: see then how high it is! Again, it was taught: On the first day of the cycle of Tammuz [i.e. summer] no creature has a shadow,[2] for it is written, *And there is nothing hid from His sun* (Ps. XIX, 7).[3] The globe of the sun has a sheath. What is the proof? *In them hath He set a tent* [protective covering] *for the sun* (*ib.* 5); and a lake of water stands before it,[4] and when it goes forth, the Holy One, blessed be He, tempers its strength in the water, lest it go forth and burn up the world. But in the future the Lord will bare it from its sheath and burn it up.[5] What is the proof? *And the day that cometh shall set them ablaze* (Mal. III, 19). R. Jannai and R. Simeon b. Lakish said: There is no other Gehenna [in the future] save a day[6] which will burn up the wicked. What is the proof? *For, behold, a day cometh, it burneth as a furnace* (*ib.*). Our Rabbis maintain: There will be a Gehenna, for it is said, *Whose fire is in Zion, and his furnace in Jerusalem* (Isa. XXXI, 9). R. Judah b. R. Ila'i said: There will be neither a day nor a Gehenna, but a fire shall come forth from the bodies of the wicked themselves and burn them up. What is the proof? *Ye conceive chaff, ye shall bring forth stubble, your breath is a fire that shall devour you* (*ib.* XXXIII, 11). R. Joshua b. R. Bun quoted: *The heavens declare His righteousness* (Ps. L, 6): in the future the heavens will declare the righteousness [kindness] which the Lord did for His world in not setting them in the first '*raki'a*', for had He set them in the first '*raki'a*', no creature could have endured, on account of the burning heat of the day.

7. R. Levi said: The voice of three things travels from one end of the world to the other, yet no creature hears it, viz., the day [i.e. the sun], the rain, and the soul when

[1] Pes. 94*b*; cf. *supra*, IV, 5. [2] The sun being directly overhead.
[3] E.V. '*from the heat thereof*'. [4] Cf. *supra*, IV, 5.
[5] Sc. the world—of the wicked. Cur. edd.: and burn the wicked with it.
[6] I.e. the sun (Mah., 'E.J.).

it departs [from the body].[1] Whence do we know it of the day? Said R. Judah b. R. La'i: You may think that it glides in heaven, but it is not so, being rather like a saw which saws through wood.[2] Whence do we know it of the rain? Said R. Levi: It is written, *Deep calleth unto deep at the voice of Thy cataracts* (Ps. XLII, 8). And whence do we know it of the soul? From the story of R. Samuel, the brother of R. Phinehas b. Ḥama. He [R. Samuel] was a poor man and died in Sepphoris.[3] Now his colleagues were sitting with him [R. Phinehas], when something [ludicrous] happened and they began to laugh. Said [R. Phinehas] to them: 'How unhappy is the soul of that man's brother![4] it breaks down cedars, it breaks down oaks,[5] yet you sit here and do not know!'

8. How do the orbs of the sun and the moon set? R. Judah b. R. La'i and the Rabbis disagree. R. Judah said: Behind the vault[6] and above it. The Rabbis maintained: Behind the vault and below it. R. Jonathan said: The view of R. Judah b. R. La'i that it is behind the vault and above it is preferable in respect of summer, when the whole world is hot while the wells are cold; and the opinion of the Rabbis that it is behind the vault and below appears correct in respect of winter, when the whole world is cold and the wells are tepid. R. Simeon b. Yoḥai said: We do not know whether they fly through the air,[7] glide in the heaven, or travel in their usual manner.[8] It is an exceedingly difficult matter, and no person can fathom it.

9. AND TO RULE OVER THE DAY AND THE NIGHT (I, 18). R. Ḥilpa said: If that is [written] in respect of the luminaries, it has surely already been stated, '*The*

[1] Cf Ex. R.V 9; Yoma 20*b*.
[2] It must *force* its way through heaven, and makes a sound as it does so
[3] In Upper Galilee
[4] By 'that man' he meant himself, this being a common form of speech.
[5] The cry of the departing soul is so strong that it overthrows strong trees.
[6] The vault or arch of heaven, conceived as solid.
[7] Without a sphere (Th.)
[8] With an effort (Th.)

greater luminary to rule by day,' etc. Then what is taught by AND TO RULE OVER THE DAY AND THE NIGHT? It refers to the righteous, who have power over what was created to give light by day and what was created to give light by night, as it is written, *And the sun stood still, and the moon stayed . . . Is not this written in the book of Jashar?* (Josh. x, 13). What is this allusion to the book of Jashar?[1] R. Ḥilpa referred it to this: AND TO RULE OVER THE DAY AND THE NIGHT. R. Ḥanin in the name of R. Samuel b Isaac referred it to the latter portion of the Book, viz. *Howbeit his younger brother* [Ephraim] *shall be greater than he* [Manasseh], *and his seed shall become the fulness of nations* (Gen. XLVIII, 19). Now is that actually possible? Hence this must refer to Joshua who would spring from him and stay the sun and the moon, which rule from one end of the world to the other.[2] R. Ḥanin in the name of R. Samuel referred it to the end of the Torah [i.e. Deuteronomy]: *His firstling bullock, majesty is his; and his horns are the horns of the wild ox, with them he shall gore the peoples all of them, even the ends of the earth* (Deut. XXXIII, 17). Is that actually possible? Hence it refers to Joshua who would spring from him [Joseph], and stay the sun and the moon, which rule from one end of the world to the other. R. Simeon b. Yoḥai said: The Book of Deuteronomy was an ensign for Joshua.[3] When the Holy One, blessed be He, revealed Himself to him, He found him sitting with the Book of Deuteronomy in his hand. Said He to him, 'Be strong, Joshua, be of good courage, Joshua, *This book of the law shall not depart out of thy mouth'* (Josh. I, 8). Thereupon he took it and showed it to the orb of the sun which he apostrophised thus: 'Even

[1] There are two views as to what is meant by the term: R. Ḥilpa and R. Ḥanin (in the first version) hold that it is the Book of Genesis, while R. Ḥanin (in the second version) holds that it means Deuteronomy; v. 'A Z. 25*a*.

[2] The descendants of one man could not possibly become *the fulness of nations* (lit. translation), and therefore the verse is interpreted as alluding to Joshua, who stayed the sun which 'rules' (i.e. serves) *the fulness of nations*—the whole world.

[3] He used it as a commander uses his ensign, to enforce obedience.

as I have not stood still from [studying] this, so do thou stand still before me!' Straightway, '*And the sun stood still,*' etc. R. Isaac said: [He exclaimed to it], 'Thou evil servant, wert thou not indeed the chattel of my ancestor; did not my ancestor see thee thus in a dream: *And, behold, the sun and the moon and eleven stars bowed down to me*' (Gen. XXXVII, 9)![1] Straightway, '*And the sun stood still,*' etc.

[1] This passage is extremely difficult. Y.M. explains it by reference to Tanḥuma: Joshua said to it: Cannot a young man command his aged slave, 'Be silent!' And did not Abraham acquire you (Abraham was of course 'young' in comparison with the sun), as it says, *Blessed be Abraham of God most High, who possesses* (lit. translation, and making *who* refer to Abraham) *heaven and earth* (Gen. XIV, 19). Moreover, you ratified this purchase by bowing down to Joseph, his descendant.

CHAPTER VII (BERESHITH)

1. AND GOD SAID: LET THE WATERS SWARM WITH SWARMS OF LIVING CREATURES (I, 20). It is written, *There is none like unto Thee among the gods, O Lord, and there are no works like Thine* (Ps. LXXXVI, 8). In human practice a mortal king draws a figure on dry land, but the Holy One, blessed be He, draws figures in water, as it is said, AND GOD SAID: LET THE WATERS SWARM.

2. LET THE WATERS SWARM, etc. Jacob of Ḳefar Nibburaya[1] gave a ruling in Tyre that fish must be ritually slaughtered.[2] When R. Haggai heard thereof he ordered, 'Come and be flagellated.'[3] 'What!' exclaimed he, 'when a man gives a Scriptural ruling he is to be flagellated!' 'How do you know that this is Scriptural?' inquired he. 'Because it is written, LET THE WATERS SWARM WITH SWARMS OF LIVING CREATURES, AND LET FOWL FLY, etc.,' replied he: 'just as a bird must be ritually killed, so must fish be ritually killed.' 'You have not ruled well,' said he to him. 'And whence can you prove this to me?' he asked. 'Lie down [to be lashed] and I will prove it to you.' Said he to him: 'It is written, *If flocks and herds be slain for them, will they suffice them? or if all the fish of the sea be gathered together for them, will they suffice them?* (Num. XI, 22); "shall be slain" is not written here but "*be gathered together*".' 'Lay on me,' exclaimed he,[4] 'for thine exposition is good.'

Jacob of Ḳefar Nibburaya ruled in Tyre: It is permitted to circumcise the infant son of a Gentile woman[5] on the Sabbath. When R. Haggai heard this he said to him, 'Come and be flagellated.' 'Shall he who states a Scriptural ruling be punished!' exclaimed he. 'And how is this Scriptural?' 'Because it is written, *And they declared their pedigrees after their families, by their fathers' houses*' (Num. I, 18),

[1] Prob. Nimrin, near Tiberias (Jast.). [2] Before they are fit for food. [3] For this ruling. [4] Jacob of Kefar Nibburaya. [5] Born from a Jew.

he answered.[1] 'You have not ruled well,' said he to him. 'And whence can you prove this to me?' 'Lie down and I will prove it to you,' he retorted. 'It is written, *Now therefore let us make a covenant with our God to put away all the wives, and such as are born of them'* (Ezra X, 3).[2] 'And will you actually punish me on the strength of tradition!'[3] he protested. *'And let it be done according to the* Torah' (*ib.*), quoted he.[4] Said he: 'Hammer away thy hammering[5] [i.e. strike me], for it is well taught.'

3. AND LET FOWL FLY ABOVE THE EARTH. In ordinary practice a mortal king builds a palace and tenants the upper and the lower stories, but can he tenant the space between? Surely not! But the Holy One, blessed be He, placed denizens in the space between, as it is said, AND LET FOWL FLY ABOVE THE EARTH.

4. AND GOD CREATED THE GREAT SEA-MONSTERS—TANINIM (I, 21). R. Phinehas said in R. Idi's name: *Taninam*[6] is written, referring to Behemoth and Leviathan,[7] which have no mates. Resh Lakish said: Behemoth has a mate, but it has no desire, for it is said, *The sinews of his thighs are knit together* (Job XL, 17).[8]

R. Huna said in the name of R. Mattenah: The Zabua[9] is formed from a white drop; it contains three hundred and sixty-five different colours, as the days of the sun.

R. Jeremiah said: (R.) Kahana asked R. Simeon b.

[1] Thus he argued that the child follows his *father*, and was therefore like any other Jewish child, who is circumcised on the Sabbath if it is the eighth day from birth.
[2] Thus the children of mixed marriages follow their mothers, not their fathers. [3] The Prophets and the Hagiographa are thus termed.
[4] I.e. this law is affirmed to be Pentateuchal. There may be a reference here to Deut. VII, 4, as interpreted in Kid. 68*b*, q.v. *For he will turn away thy son from following Me.*
[5] Or (Rashi) pave thy paving, i.e. lie down (spoken by R. Haggai).
[6] תנינם, i.e. *singular.*
[7] Legendary sea-animals reserved for the righteous in the Messianic future.
[8] Perhaps he translates: are torn out—he lacks the organs of generation.
[9] 'Coloured' (animal); the leopard, or perhaps the striped hyæna.

Laḳish: 'What if one crosses different sea species?'[1] 'In their case, too, AFTER THEIR KIND is written,'[2] he answered. With this the son of Laḳish spread his net over (R.) Kahana.[3] Kahana, however, refuted him. 'Yet in the case of fish, too, AFTER THEIR KIND is written.'[4] With this Kahana spread his net over the son of Laḳish. Now how is it to be explained?[5] Said R. Judah: I can apply it [sc. '*after their kind*'] to the prohibition of driving: he brings two fish, one white and the other black, ties them with a reed rope and pulls them, for we learned: You may not plough with, pull, or drive them.[6]

AND EVERY LIVING CREATURE THAT CREEPETH . . . AND EVERY WINGED FOWL: This is the peacock.[7]

5. AND GOD SAID: LET THE EARTH BRING FORTH THE LIVING CREATURE, etc. (I, 24). R. Leazar said: LIVING CREATURE means the soul of Adam.[8]

AND GOD MADE THE BEAST OF THE EARTH (I, 25). R. Hoshaya the Elder said: This means the serpent. R. Ḥama b. R. Hoshaya said: In speaking of souls it enumerates four, but in speaking of bodies only three![9] Rabbi said: This [extra soul] refers to the demons whose soul the Holy One, blessed be He, created, but when He came to create their bodies the sanctity of the Sabbath commenced and He could not create them.[10] This gives

[1] Mammals are meant, not fish. Does that come under the prohibition of Lev. XIX, 19 (q.v.)?

[2] Each must breed with its own kind only: hence he has transgressed.

[3] Showed him deficient in knowledge.

[4] Though it is impossible to make fish copulate, owing to their inaccessibility. Hence '*after their kind*' cannot bear this meaning at all.

[5] According to Resh Laḳish.

[6] Sc. two different kinds of fish together; Kil. VIII, 2.

[7] Which, being a multicoloured bird, contains the hues of *every* winged fowl, i.e. all birds.

[8] *Infra*, VIII, 1.

[9] I, 24, says: *Let the earth bring forth the* soul (sic) *of a* living creature *after its kind*, cattle, *and* creeping thing, *and the* beast of the earth: thus *living creature* (ḥayyah), *cattle, creeping thing*, and *beast of the earth* are enumerated—four in all. Whereas I, 25, referring to the actual animals ('bodies') states: *And God made the beast of the earth . . . and the cattle . . . and everything that creepeth*—only three being enumerated.

[10] Hence they remained souls (spirits) without bodies.

you a lesson in behaviour from Scripture, viz., that if a man is holding in his hand a costly article or a precious stone on the eve of the Sabbath about sunset, we say to him, 'Throw it away,' for He at whose behest the world came into existence[1] was engaged in the creation of the world and had [already] created their souls, but when He came to create their bodies the holiness of the Sabbath commenced and He did not create them.

[1] Lit. 'who ordained and the world', etc., a phrase which is now liturgical.

CHAPTER VIII (BERESHITH)

1. AND GOD SAID: LET US MAKE MAN, etc (I, 26). R. Joḥanan commenced [his discourse]: *Thou hast formed me*[1] *behind and before*, etc. (Ps CXXXIX, 5). Said R. Joḥanan: If a man is worthy enough, he enjoys both worlds, for it says, '*Thou hast formed me for a later* [world] *and an earlier* [world].' But if not, he will have to render a full account [of his misdeeds], as it is said, *And laid Thy hand upon me* (*ib.*). R. Jeremiah b Leazar said: When the Holy One, blessed be He, created Adam, He created him an hermaphrodite [bi-sexual],[2] for it is said, *Male and female created He them and called their name Adam* (Gen. V, 2).[3] R. Samuel b. Naḥman said: When the Lord created Adam He created him double-faced, then He split him and made him of two backs, one back on this side and one back on the other side. To this it is objected: But it is written, *And He took one of his ribs*, etc. (Gen. II, 21)?[4] [*Mi-ẓalothaw* means] one of his *sides*, replied he, as you read, *And for the second side* (zela') *of the tabernacle*, etc. (Ex. XXVI, 20). R. Tanhuma in the name of R. Banayah and R. Berekiah in the name of R. Leazar said: He created him as a lifeless mass extending from one end of the world to the other; thus it is written, *Thine eyes did see mine unformed substance* (Ps. CXXXIX, 16). R. Joshua b. R Nehemiah and R Judah b. R. Simon in R. Leazar's name said: He created him filling the whole world How do we know [that he stretched] from east to west? Because it is said, '*Thou hast formed me behind* (ahor) *and before* (ḳedem).'[5] From north to south? Because it says, *Since the day that God created man upon the earth, and from the one end of heaven unto*

[1] E V. '*hemmed me in*.' Here *zartani* is derived from *ẓurah*, a figure: 'Thou hast made me into a figure.'

[2] Normally *androgynos* means one whose genitals are male and female; but here it means two bodies, male and female, joined together.

[3] Thus Adam himself was originally male and female.

[4] This certainly implies that woman was a separate creation.

[5] Now *ḳedem* can mean east, as in Gen. III, 24 q v ; hence *ahor*, which is obviously the opposite, means west.

the other (Deut. IV, 32). And how do we know that he filled the empty spaces of the world?[1] From the verse, '*And laid Thy hand upon me*' (as you read, *Withdraw Thy hand from me* (Job XIII, 21)).[2] R. Leazar interpreted it: He was the latest (*aḥor*) in the work of the last day, and the earliest (*kedem*) in the work of the last day.[3] That is R. Leazar's view, for he said: *Let the earth bring forth a soul of a living creature* (Gen. I, 24) refers to the soul of Adam.[4] R. Simeon b. Laḳish maintained: He was the latest in the work of the last day and the earliest in the work of the first day. That is consistent with the view of R. Simeon b. Laḳish, for he said: *And the spirit of God hovered* (*ib.* I, 2) refers to the soul of Adam, as you read, *And the spirit of the Lord shall rest upon him* (Isa. XI, 2). R. Naḥman said: Last in creation and first in punishment.[5] R. Samuel b. R. Tanḥum said: His praise [of God], too, comes only at the last, as it is written, *Hallelujah. Praise ye the Lord from the heavens*, the passage continuing until, *He hath made a decree which shall not be transgressed.* This is followed by, *Praise ye the Lord from the earth*, etc., and only after all that, *Kings of the earth and all peoples* (Ps. CXLVIII, 1–11). R. Simlai said: Just as his praise comes after that of cattle, beasts, and fowls, so does his creation come after that of cattle, beasts, and fowl. First we have '*And God said: Let the waters swarm*', and after them all, LET US MAKE MAN.

2. R. Ḥama b. R. Ḥanina commenced. *Knowest thou this of old time, since man was placed upon earth* (Job XX, 4).

[1] From the ground to the sky.

[2] Th. brackets this quotation, as its relevance is doubtful and it is absent in some versions. The proof lies in the first verse alone, Adam being pictured as lying upon the ground while God lays His hand, which is in heaven, upon him. Another explanation is that *kappeka* (E.V. '*Thy hand*') is now derived from *kippah*, the arch of heaven

[3] His body was the latest, but he received his soul before anything else which was made on the sixth day.

[4] The verse refers to the sixth day, and this was the earliest work of that day, as it is followed by, *And God made the beast of the earth*, etc

[5] Either, the first to receive an injunction whose violation was punished. Or, as in Ber. 61*a*, the first who was destroyed in the Flood (before the beasts).

Said R. Ḥama b. R. Ḥanina: This may be compared to a country which received its supplies from ass-drivers, who used to ask each other, 'What was the market price to-day?' Thus those who supplied on the sixth day would ask of those who supplied on the fifth day; the fifth of the fourth, the fourth of the third, the third of the second, the second of the first; but of whom was the first day supplier to ask? Surely of the citizens who were engaged in the public affairs of the country! Thus the works of each day asked one another, 'Which creatures did the Holy One, blessed be He, create among you to-day?' The sixth asked of the fifth, the fifth of the fourth, the fourth of the third, the third of the second, and the second of the first. Of what was the first to ask? Surely of the Torah, which preceded the creation of the world by two thousand years, as it is written, *Then I* [sc. the Torah] *was by Him, as a nursling, and I was His delight day after day* (Prov. VIII, 30); now the day of the Lord is a thousand years, as it is said, *For a thousand years in Thy sight are but as yesterday when it is past* (Ps. XC, 4). That is the meaning of '*Knowest thou this of old time?*' The Torah knows what was before the creation of the world, but you have no business to inquire about aught save '*Since man was placed upon earth*'. R. Leazar said in Bar Sira's name: About what is too great for thee inquire not; what is too hard for thee investigate not; about what is too wonderful for thee know not; of what is hidden from thee ask not; study what was permitted thee: thou hast no business with hidden things.

3. AND GOD SAID: LET US MAKE MAN, etc. With whom did He take counsel?[1] R. Joshua b. Levi said: He took counsel with the works of heaven and earth, like a king who had two advisers without whose knowledge[2] he did nothing whatsoever. R. Samuel b. Naḥman said: He took counsel with the works of each day, like a king who had an associate without whose knowledge he did nothing.

[1] This question arises because of the phrase LET *US* MAKE.
[2] The Hebrew implies knowledge and consent.

R. Ammi said: He took counsel with His own heart. It may be compared to a king who had a palace built by an architect, but when he saw it it did not please him: with whom is he to be indignant? surely with the architect! Similarly, *And it grieved Him at His heart* (Gen. VI, 6). R. Jassi said: This may be compared to a king who did some business through an agent and suffered loss: with whom is he to be indignant? Surely with the agent! Similarly, *'And it grieved Him at His heart.'*

4. R. Berekiah said: When the Holy One, blessed be He, came to create Adam, He saw righteous and wicked arising from him. Said He: 'If I create him, wicked men will spring from him; if I do not create him, how are the righteous to spring from him?' What then did the Lord do? He removed the way of the wicked out of His sight[1] and associated the quality of mercy[2] with Himself and created him, as it is written, *For the Lord regardeth the way of the righteous, but the way of the wicked* tobed—E.V. *'shall perish'* (Ps. I, 6): what does '*tobed*' mean? He destroyed it (*ibbedah*) from before His sight and associated the quality of mercy with Himself and created him. R. Ḥanina did not say thus, but [he said that] when He came to create Adam He took counsel with the ministering angels, saying to them, 'LET US MAKE MAN.' 'What shall his character be?' asked they. 'Righteous men shall spring from him,' He answered, as it is written, *'For the Lord knoweth* (yodea') *the way of the righteous,'* which means that the Lord made known (*hodia'*) the way of the righteous to the ministering angels; *'But the way of the wicked shall perish'*: He destroyed [hid] it from them. He revealed to them that the righteous would arise from him, but He did not reveal to them that the wicked would spring from him, for had He revealed to them that the wicked would spring from him; the quality of Justice would not have permitted him to be created.

[1] He deliberately disregarded it. [2] This is often hypostatised.

5. R. Simon said: When the Holy One, blessed be He, came to create Adam, the ministering angels formed themselves into groups and parties, some of them saying, 'Let him be created,' whilst others urged, 'Let him not be created.' Thus it is written, *Love and Truth fought together, Righteousness and Peace combated each other* (Ps. LXXXV, 11)[1]. Love said, 'Let him be created, because he will dispense acts of love'; Truth said, 'Let him not be created, because he is compounded of falsehood'; Righteousness said, 'Let him be created, because he will perform righteous deeds'; Peace said, 'Let him not be created, because he is full of strife.' What did the Lord do? He took Truth and cast it to the ground. Said the ministering angels before the Holy One, blessed be He, 'Sovereign of the Universe! Why dost Thou despise Thy seal?[2] Let Truth arise from the earth!' Hence it is written, *Let truth spring up from the earth* (*ib.* 12).

All our Rabbis say the following in the name of R. Ḥanina, while R. Phinehas and R. Hilkiah say it in the name of R. Simon. *Me'od* (E.V. '*very*') is identical with Adam[3]; as it is written, *And God saw everything that He had made, and, behold, it was good*—me'od (Gen. I, 31), i.e. and behold Adam was good. R. Huna the Elder of Sepphoris, said: While the ministering angels were arguing with each other and disputing with each other, the Holy One, blessed be He, created him. Said He to them: 'What can ye avail? Man has already been made!'[4]

6. R. Huna said in R. Aibu's name: He created him with due deliberation: He first created his food requirements, and only then did He create him. Said the ministering angels to the Lord: 'Sovereign of the Universe! *What is man, that Thou art mindful of him, and the son of man,*

[1] E.V. '*Mercy and truth are met together; righteousness and peace have kissed each other.*' The Midrash interprets *met* in the sense of fought, and derives *nashaḳu* (kissed) from *nesheḳ*, arms, rendering: have taken arms against each other. [2] Truth is the seal of God
[3] In the Hebrew the letters are the same, though differently arranged: מאד, אדם. [4] On this interpretation *ne'esah* (is made) is read instead of *na'aseh* (we will make).

that Thou thinkest of him? (Ps. VIII, 5). This trouble, for what has it been created?' 'If so,' said He to them, '*Sheep and oxen, all of them* (*ib.* 8), why were they created; why were *The fowl of the air and the fish of the sea* (*ib* 9) created? A tower full of good things and no guests—what pleasure has its owner in having filled it?' Said they to Him: 'Sovereign of the Universe! *O Lord, our Lord, how glorious is Thy name in all the earth* (*ib.* 10). Do what pleaseth Thee!'

7. R. Joshua of Siknin said in R. Levi's name: He took counsel with the souls of the righteous, as it is written, *These were the makers* [E.V. '*potters*'], *and those that dwelt among plantations and hedges; there they dwelt with the king in his work* (I Chron. IV, 23). '*These were the makers*': they are so termed on account of the verse, *Then the Lord formed* [made] *man*, etc. (Gen. II, 7); '*And those that dwelt among plantations*' corresponds to *And the Lord God planted a garden eastward* (*ib.* 8); '*And hedges*' corresponds to *I have placed the sand for the bound of the sea* (Jer. V, 22); '*There they dwelt with the king in his work*': with the supreme King of kings, the Holy One, blessed be He, sat the souls of the righteous with whom He took counsel before creating the world.

8. R. Samuel b. Naḥman said in R. Jonathan's name: When Moses was engaged in writing the Torah, he had to write the work of each day. When he came to the verse, AND GOD SAID: LET US MAKE MAN, etc., he said: 'Sovereign of the Universe! Why dost Thou furnish an excuse to heretics?'[1] 'Write,' replied He; 'whoever wishes to err may err.' 'Moses,' said the Lord to him, 'this man that I have created—do I not cause men both great and small to spring from him? Now if a great man comes to obtain permission [for a proposed action] from one that is less than he, he may say, "Why should I ask permission from my inferior!" Then they will answer him, "Learn

[1] For maintaining a plurality of gods.

from thy Creator, who created all that is above and below, yet when He came to create man He took counsel with the ministering angels."'

R. Hila[1] said: There is no taking counsel here, but it may be compared to a king who was strolling at the door of his palace when he saw a clod lying about. Said he, 'What shall we do with it?' Some answered: '[Use it in building] public baths'; others answered: 'private baths.' 'I will make a statue of it,' declared the king. Who then can hinder him?

9. The heretics asked R Simlai: 'How many deities created the world?' 'I and you must inquire of the first day,' replied he, as it is written, *For ask now of the first days* (Deut. IV, 32). Not, 'Since the day gods created (*baru*) man' is written here, but *God created*—bara (*ib.*).[2] Then they asked him a second time: 'Why is it written, *In the beginning Elohim* [plural] *created?*' '*In the beginning* baru Elohim is not written here,' answered he, 'but Bara Elohim *the heaven and the earth.*'

R. Simlai said: Wherever you find a point [apparently] supporting the heretics, you find the refutation at its side. They asked him again: 'What is meant by, AND GOD SAID: LET US MAKE MAN?' 'Read what follows,' replied he: 'not, "And gods created (*wa-yibre'u*) man" is written here, but "*And God created*—wa-yibra"' (Gen. I, 27). When they went out his disciples said to him: 'Them you have dismissed with a mere makeshift, but how will you answer us?' Said he to them: 'In the past Adam was created from dust and Eve was created from Adam; but henceforth it shall be *In our image, after our likeness* (*ib.* 26); neither man without woman nor woman without man, and neither of them without the Divine Spirit.'[3]

[1] So Theodor.
[2] *Elohim* is plural in form, but *bara* is singular, *bare'u* being plural. Thus he answered that the verb is in the singular, so that the plural form of *Elohim* is merely the plural of majesty. Similarly in the whole passage.
[3] He interprets the verse: man has already been made (cf. *supra*, 5 *ad fin*), and his seed shall henceforth be *in our image*, etc., as explained in the text.

10. R. Hoshaya said: When the Holy One, blessed be He, created Adam, the ministering angels mistook him [for a divine being] and wished to exclaim 'Holy' before him. What does this resemble? A king and a governor who sat in a chariot, and his subjects wished to say to the king, '*Domine!* (Sovereign)!' but they did not know which it was. What did the king do? He pushed the governor out of the chariot, and so they knew who was the king. Similarly, when the Lord created Adam, the angels mistook him [for a divine being]. What did the Holy One, blessed be He, do? He caused sleep to fall upon him, and so all knew that he was [but mortal] man; thus it is written, *Cease ye from man, in whose nostrils is a breath, for how little is he to be accounted* (Isa. II, 22)!

11. MALE AND FEMALE (NEḲEBAH) CREATED HE THEM (I, 27). This is one of the things which they altered for King Ptolemy[1]: 'Male with his apertures (*neḳubaw*) created He them.'[2]

R. Joshua b. R. Nehemiah said in the name of R. Ḥanina b. R. Isaac, and the Rabbis in the name of R. Leazar said: He created him with four attributes of the higher beings [i.e. angels] and four attributes of the lower beings [i.e. beasts].[3] [The four attributes of] the higher beings are: he stands upright, like the ministering angels; he speaks, like the ministering angels; he understands, like the ministering angels; and he sees, like the ministering angels. Yet does not a dumb animal see! But this one [man] can see from the side.[4] He has four attributes of the lower beings: he eats and drinks, like an animal; procreates, like an animal; excretes, like an animal; and dies, like an animal. R. Tifdai[5] said in R. Aḥa's name: The celestial

[1] King Ptolemy II Philadelphus, at whose command the Septuagint is said to have been produced, is probably meant here.

[2] This change is to explain the plural 'them' (v. *supra*, I), or (since he was created in God's image), to avoid the implication that God is male and female.

[3] Lit. 'He created in him four creations from above and four from below.'

[4] He can direct his gaze at an object sideways, without turning his head, which an animal cannot do

[5] He is mentioned only here and *infra*, XIV, 3.

beings were created in the image and likeness [of God] and do not procreate,[1] while the terrestial creatures [dumb animals] procreate but were not created in [His] image and likeness. Said the Holy One, blessed be He· 'Behold, I will create him [man] in [My] image and likeness, [so that he will partake] of the [character of the] celestial beings, while he will procreate, [after the nature] of the terrestial beings.' R. Tifdai said in R. Aḥa's name: The Holy One, blessed be He, said: 'If I create him of the celestial elements he will live [for ever] and not die, and if I create him of the terrestial elements, he will die and not live [in a future life]. Therefore I will create him of the upper and of the lower elements[2]: if he sins he will die; while if he does not sin, he will live.'

12. AND HAVE DOMINION (REDU) OVER THE FISH OF THE SEA (I, 28). R. Ḥanina said: If he merits it, [God says,] '*uredu*' (have dominion); while if he does not merit, [God says,] '*yerdu*' (let them descend).[3] R. Jacob of Ḳefar Ḥanan said: Of him who is in our image and likeness [I say] '*uredu*' (and have dominion); but of him who is not in our image and likeness [I say] '*yerdu*' (let them descend).[4]

AND GOD BLESSED THEM (I, 28). We learned elsewhere: A virgin is married on the fourth day of the week, and a widow on the fifth day.[5] Why is that? Because a blessing is written in connection with these days. But surely a blessing is written only in connection with the fifth and the sixth days? Said Bar Ḳappara. The fourth day is the eve of the fifth, and the fifth is the eve of the sixth.[6]

R. Leazar said in the name of R. Jose b. Zimra: *We-kibshuhah* [plural: and do *ye* subdue it] is actually

[1] Like God Himself. [2] His body of the earth and his soul of heaven.
[3] Or, let others (the beasts) rule over him. I.e ירדו instead of ורדו; וירדו is the word in v. 26.
[4] Man is entitled to pre-eminence only as long as he cultivates his God-like qualities, when he voluntarily abandons them he is even lower than the brute creation. [5] Keth. 2*a*. [6] Hence the marriages of the fourth and the fifth are consummated on the fifth and the sixth respectively.

written *we-kibshah* [singular: and do *thou* subdue it]: man is commanded concerning procreation, but not woman[1] R. Johanan b. Berokah said: Concerning both man and woman it says, AND GOD BLESSED THEM, etc.[2]

'*We-kibshah*' (and subdue her) is written: the man must master his wife, that she go not out into the market place, for every woman who goes out into the market place will eventually come to grief. Whence do we know it? From Dinah, as it is written, *And Dinah . . . went out*, etc. (Gen. XXXIV, 1). R. Isaac said in R. Ḥanina's name: The law is as stated by R. Johanan b. Berokah.

13. R. Abbahu said: The Holy One, blessed be He, took a cup of blessing[3] and blessed them. R. Judah b. R Simon said: Michael and Gabriel were Adam's 'best men'. R. Simlai said: We find that the Holy One, blessed be He, blesses bridegrooms, adorns brides, visits the sick, buries the dead, and recites the blessing for mourners.[4] He blesses bridegrooms, as it is written, AND GOD BLESSED THEM; He adorns brides, as it is written, *And the Lord God built the rib . . . into a woman* (*ib.* II, 22)[5]; He visits the sick, as it is written, *And the Lord appeared unto him*, etc. (ib. XVIII, 1)[6]; He buries the dead, as it is written, *And He buried him in the valley*, etc. (Deut. XXXIV, 6)[7]: R. Samuel b. Naḥman said: He also visits mourners, as it is written, *And God appeared unto Jacob again, when he came from Paddan-aram, and blessed him* (Gen. XXXV, 9).[8] How did He bless him? With the blessing of mourners.

[1] Since the order to subdue the earth is to man alone, the command of the first half of the verse (*Be fruitful*, etc) is likewise to man alone

[2] Hence both are subject to that command.

[3] In normal usage a cup of wine over which a benediction is pronounced on certain occasions, e.g at a marriage.

[4] V. Keth. 8*b*

[5] V. *infra*, XVIII, 1

[6] When Abraham was indisposed through circumcision.

[7] The proof that He recites the blessing for mourners is missing here, but is found in מנורת המאור . he comforts mourners, as it is written, *And it came to pass after the death of Abraham, that God blessed* (i e recited the blessing for mourners) *Isaac his son* (Gen. XXV, 1).

[8] This immediately follows the death of Deborah, Rebekah's nurse (v 8), and it is understood that Jacob was in mourning for her when God appeared to him.

CHAPTER IX (BERESHITH)

1. AND GOD SAW EVERY THING THAT HE HAD MADE, AND, BEHOLD, IT WAS VERY GOOD (I, 31). R. Levi in the name of R. Ḥama b. Ḥanina commenced: *It is the glory of God to conceal a thing, but the glory of kings is to search out a matter* (Prov. xxv, 2). Said R. Levi in the name of R. Hama b. Ḥanina: From the beginning of the Book [of Genesis] up to this point, '*It is the glory of God to conceal a thing*'; but from this point onward, '*The glory of kings is to search out a matter*': it is the glory of the words of the Torah, which are likened to kings, as it is said, *By me kings reign* (*ib.* VIII, 15), '*to search out a matter*'; hence, AND GOD SAW EVERY THING THAT HE HAD MADE, AND, BEHOLD, IT WAS VERY GOOD.[1]

2. R. Tanḥuma commenced: *He hath made every thing beautiful in its time* (Eccl. III, 11). Said R. Tanḥuma: The world was created when it was due, and the world was not fit to be created earlier. R. Abbahu said: Hence we learn that the Holy One, blessed be He, went on creating worlds and destroying them until He created these [sc. heaven and earth], and then He said: 'These please Me; those did not please Me.[2]; R. Phinehas said: The proof of R. Abbahu's statement is: AND GOD SAW EVERY THING WHICH HE HAD MADE, etc.[3]

[1] The meaning of the passage is that everything until the creation of man must be left in mystic obscurity and one must study the Torah only from the creation of man (Y.T.). It is for this reason that Scripture writes AND, BEHOLD, IT WAS VERY GOOD at this point, to indicate that from here one may '*search out a matter*'.

[2] He probably deduces this from the phrase, *Beautiful in its time*, which intimates that He made other worlds when the time was not yet ripe, and these were not beautiful, so that he destroyed them.

[3] Rendering: AND GOD SAW ALL THAT HE HAD MADE—i.e. all the *worlds* He had made—BUT BEHOLD, i.e. only what had *now* been made ('*behold*' has that significance: see now!) WAS VERY GOOD.

3. AND GOD SAW EVERY THING THAT HE HAD MADE, AND, BEHOLD, IT WAS VERY GOOD. R. Joḥanan and R. Simeon b. Lakish each commented thereon. R. Joḥanan said: When a mortal king builds a palace, he can only take in the upper stories with one look and the lower stories with another, but the Holy One, blessed be He, casts but a single look at the upper and the lower portions simultaneously.[1] R. Simeon b. Laḳish said: BEHOLD, IT WAS VERY GOOD implies this world, AND BEHOLD implies the next world[2]: The Holy One, blessed be He, cast but one look at this world and at the future world [together].[3]

Resh Lakish said in Leazar's name: *Ah Lord God! behold, Thou hast made the heaven and the earth* (Jer. XXXII, 17): since that moment [when Thou didst create the world] *there is nothing too hard for Thee* (*ib.*). R. Haggai quoted in R. Isaac's name: *And thou, Solomon my son, know thou the God of thy father, and serve Him with a whole heart and with a willing mind; for the Lord searcheth all hearts, and understandeth all the imaginations* (yeẓer) *of the thoughts* (I Chron. XXVIII, 9): even before a thought is born (*noẓerah*) in a man's heart, it is already revealed to Thee. R. Judan said in R. Isaac s name: Before even a creature is created, his thought is already revealed to Thee. R. Judah said on his own behalf: *For there is not a word in my tongue, but, lo, O Lord, Thou knowest it altogether* (Ps. CXXXIX, 4): before even my tongue gives expression to speech, '*Thou, O Lord*, already *knowest it altogether.*'

4. R. Ḥama b. R. Ḥanina and R. Jonathan explained it as follows. R. Hama b. R. Ḥanina said: Compare this to a king who built a palace. He saw it and it pleased him. 'O palace, O palace,' exclaimed he, 'mayest thou find favour in my eyes at all times just as thou hast found favour in my eyes at this moment!' Similarly, the Holy One, blessed

[1] Interpreting: AND GOD SAW *EVERY* THING THAT HE HAD MADE —in a single look. [2] AND being interpreted as an extending particle. [3] The idea underlying these two teachings is that heaven and earth, this world and the next, are all interlinked and have one purpose (Y.T.).

be He, apostrophised His world: 'O My world, O My world! mayest thou find favour in My eyes at all times just as thou hast found favour before Me at this moment.' R. Jonathan said: Imagine a king who gave his daughter in marriage and arranged a bridal chamber and a home for her, which he plastered, panelled, and painted. He saw it and it pleased him. 'My daughter, my daughter!' he cried to her, 'may this bridal chamber find favour before me at all times just as it has found favour before me at this moment' Even so said the Holy One, blessed be He, to His world, 'O My world, O My world! mayest thou find favour before Me at all times just as thou hast found favour before Me at this moment.'

5. In the copy of R. Meir's Torah [Pentateuch] was found written: AND, BEHOLD, IT WAS VERY (ME'OD) GOOD: and behold, death (*maweth*) was good.[1] R. Samuel b. Naḥman said: I was seated on my grandfather's shoulder going up from my own town to Ḳefar Ḥana via Beth-Shean,[2] and I heard R. Simeon b. R. Eleazar as he sat and lectured say in R. Meir's name: AND, BEHOLD, IT WAS VERY GOOD: and, behold, death was good.[3]

R. Ḥama b. R. Ḥanina and R. Jonathan said the following. R. Hama b. R. Ḥanina said: Adam deserved to be spared the experience of death. Why then was the penalty of death decreed against him? Because the Holy One, blessed be He, foresaw that Nebuchadnezzar and Hiram would declare themselves gods; therefore was death decreed against him Thus it is written, *Thou wast in Eden the garden of God* (Ezek. XXVIII, 13): was then Hiram in Eden? Surely not! But He said thus to him: 'It is thou who causedst him who was in Eden [sc. Adam] to die.' R. Ḥiyya, the son of R. Berekiah's daughter, quoted in R. Berekiah's name: *Thou wast the far-covering cherub*—kerub (*ib.* 14): it was thou who didst cause that youth

[1] This may mean either that the MS. read מות instead of מאד, or that this was inserted as a marginal comment.
[2] Scythopolis, in Galilee, v. 'A Z. (Sonc. ed.), p. 64, n. 7.
[3] Because it is a potent force for repentance.

(*robeh*—sc. Adam) to die. Said R. Jonathan to him: If so, He should have decreed death for the wicked but not for the righteous! But the reason is lest the wicked perform a fraudulent repentance, saying: 'Surely the righteous live only because they treasure up religious acts and good deeds; so shall we too lay up a store of religious acts and good deeds,' and as a result their performance of such would be with ulterior motives.

R. Joḥanan and R. Simeon b. Laḳish discussed this. R. Johanan said: Why was death decreed against the wicked? Because as long as the wicked live they anger the Lord, as it is written, *Ye have wearied the Lord with your words* (Mal. II, 17); but when they die they cease to anger Him, as it is written, *There the wicked cease from raging* (Job III, 17), which means, there the wicked cease from enraging the Holy One, blessed be He. Why was death decreed against the righteous? Because as long as the righteous live they must fight against their evil desires, but when they die they enjoy rest; that is the meaning of *And there the weary are at rest* (*ib.*): [they say]: We have laboured sufficiently.[1] R. Simeon b. Lakish said: [Death was decreed] in order to reward the righteous in double measure and to punish the wicked in double measure. To reward the righteous, who had not deserved to experience death, yet did accept the experience of death: *Therefore in their land they shall possess double* (Isa. LXI, 7); and to punish the wicked, since the righteous had not deserved death yet accepted it on their account; therefore, *And destroy them with double destruction* (Jer. XVII, 18).

6. R. Simeon b. Eleazar said: AND, BEHOLD, IT WAS VERY GOOD means, and, behold, sleep was good. Is there any sleep which is very good! Did we not learn thus: Wine and sleep when enjoyed by the *wicked* are beneficial to them and beneficial to the world![2] But [R.

[1] M.K.: in our fight against evil, Y.T.. we have laboured to attain a sufficient reward.

[2] When asleep they do no harm

Simeon meant this:] a man sometimes sleeps a little and arises and toils much in the study of the Torah.[1]

7. Naḥman said in R. Samuel's name: BEHOLD, IT WAS VERY GOOD refers to the Good Desire; AND BEHOLD, IT WAS VERY GOOD, to the Evil Desire. Can then the Evil Desire be very good? That would be extraordinary! But for the Evil Desire, however, no man would build a house, take a wife and beget children; and thus said Solomon: *Again, I considered all labour and all excelling in work, that it is a man's rivalry with his neighbour* (Eccl. IV, 4).[2]

8. R. Huna said: BEHOLD, IT WAS VERY GOOD refers to the dispensation of happiness; AND BEHOLD, IT WAS VERY GOOD, to the dispensation of suffering. Can then suffering actually be very good? It is in fact so because through its instrumentality men attain to the life of the future world[3]; and so said Solomon: *And reproofs of chastisement* [E.V. '*instruction*'] *are the way of life* (Prov. VI, 23) Say now, go forth and see which road leads man to the life of the future world? Surely it is suffering.

9. R. Ze'ira said: BEHOLD, IT WAS VERY GOOD refers to Paradise; AND BEHOLD, IT WAS VERY GOOD, to Gehenna. Is then the Gehenna very good? How remarkable! This, however, may be compared to a king who had an orchard, into which he brought workers. He built a treasure house by its entrance and said: 'Whoever will labour conscientiously in the work of the orchard may enter the treasure house, but he who will not show himself worthy in the work of the orchard may not enter the treasure house.' Thus for him who treasures up religious acts and good deeds, behold there is Paradise; while for him who does not lay up religious acts and good deeds, behold there is Gehenna.

[1] Such sleep is very good.
[2] It is the Evil Desire which in the first place inspires this rivalry which leads to great efforts.—One may triumph over his human failings by turning even them to noble purposes [3] Suffering chastens and purifies.

10. R. Samuel b. R. Isaac said: BEHOLD, IT WAS VERY GOOD alludes to the angel of life; AND BEHOLD, IT WAS VERY GOOD, to the angel of death. Is then the angel of death very good? Imagine a king who made a feast, invited the guests, and set a dish filled with all good things before them: 'Whoever will eat and bless the king,' said he, 'let him eat and enjoy it; but he who would eat and not bless the king, let him be decapitated with a sword.' Similarly, for him who lays up precepts and good deeds, lo! there is the angel of life; while for him who does not lay up precepts and good deeds, lo! there is the angel of death.

11. R. Simeon b. Abba said: BEHOLD, IT WAS VERY GOOD alludes to the dispensation of good; AND BEHOLD, IT WAS VERY GOOD, to the dispensation of punishment. Is then the dispensation of punishment very good? It means that He considered well how to bring it.[1]

R. Simon said in R. Simeon b. Abba's name: All measures have ceased,[2] yet the rule of measure for measure[3] has not ceased. R. Huna said in R. Jose's name[4]: From the very beginning of the world's creation the Holy One, blessed be He, foresaw that man will receive measure for measure; therefore Scripture said, AND, BEHOLD, IT WAS VERY GOOD, meaning, behold, there is a fitting dispensation.

God took good care that the Temple should be destroyed and the Jews be deported to Babylon in summer and not in winter, for they would never have survived the rigours and hardships of that long journey in winter. Mah · He was anxious how to make the punishment fit the wrongs committed so that the victims, recognising this, would be led to repentance. Others He caused the Temple to be destroyed two years before its time (translating He hastened to bring the punishment), for had He waited longer, Israel's sins would have condemned them to complete destruction. V. Lam. R. on 1, 14 (§ 42), Sanh 38*a*.

[2] The phrase is somewhat obscure In Sot. 8*b* a very similar phrase is explained as referring to the four modes of execution

[3] I.e punishment befitting the crime; v Soṭ. *ad loc.*

[4] I.e. the teacher known in the Babylonian Talmud as R. Joseph (not R. Jose the Tanna).

12. All our Rabbis said the following in R. Ḥanina's name, while R. Phinehas and R. Ḥilkiah said it in R. Simon's name: *Me'od* is identical with *adam* (man),[1] for the letters of both are identical. Thus it is written, AND GOD SAW EVERY THING THAT HE HAD MADE, AND, BEHOLD, IT WAS VERY (ME'OD) GOOD, i.e., and behold, *adam* (man) was good.

13. R. Simeon b. Laḳish said: BEHOLD, IT WAS VERY GOOD alludes to the kingdom of heaven; AND BEHOLD, IT WAS VERY GOOD, to the earthly kingdom.[1] Is then the earthly kingdom very good? How strange! [It earns that title] because it exacts justice for men; [hence it is written,] *I, even I, have made the earth, and created man* (adam) *upon it.* (Isa. XLV, 12).[2]

14. AND THERE WAS EVENING, AND THERE WAS MORNING, THE SIXTH DAY—HA-SHISHI (I, 31). R. Judan said: This intimates the extra hour which we add from the profane to the sacred,[3] and in it the work of creating the world was finished. HA-SHISHI: R. Simon said: There came a weakening (*metash*)[4] of the Creation: hitherto world time was counted,[5] but henceforth we count it by a different reckoning.[6]

[1] V. *supra*, VIII, 5, p. 58, n. 3.

[2] Theodor instead of *Adam* he reads *Edom*, a synonym in Talmudic and Midrashic literature for Rome, to which 'the earthly kingdom' alludes, this being also the reading in the Vilna ed.

[3] He interprets the additional def art. *heh* (ה) of הששי (in the case of other days we have a second, third, day, etc., without this def. art.) as intimating that the Sabbath must be commenced before actual nightfall, thus adding to the sacred period

[4] Presumably HA-SHISHI is connected here with *tashash*, to weaken

[5] I e., the second day, third day, etc., of the world's creation.

[6] I.e., first, second, third day of the week (Y.T., M.K.).

Chapter X (BERESHITH)

1. AND THE HEAVEN AND THE EARTH WERE FINISHED—WAYYEKULLU (II, 1). *I have seen an end to every purpose* (tiklah), *but Thy commandment is exceeding broad* (Ps. CXIX, 96): everything has a measure, heaven and earth have a measure, except one thing which has no measure: and what is it? The Torah, [of which it is written,] *The measure thereof is longer than the earth*, etc. (Job XI, 9).[1] Another interpretation: '*I have seen an end to every purpose*' refers to the work of the heaven, as it is said, AND THE HEAVEN AND THE EARTH WERE FINISHED.[2]

2. R. Ḥama b. R. Ḥanina commenced: *Take away the dross from the silver*, etc. (Prov. XXV, 4). R. Eliezer said: This may be compared to a bath full of water, in which were two beautiful bas-reliefs; as long as it was full of water the work of the bas-relief could not be seen, but when the plug was removed and the water emptied, the bas-relief could be seen. Even so, as long as formlessness and void were in the world, the work of heaven and earth could not be seen; but as soon as formlessness and void were eradicated from the world, the work of heaven could be seen. *And there cometh forth a vessel* (keli) *for the refiner* (*ib.*), i.e. they [heaven and earth] became finished articles (*kelim*): hence, AND THE HEAVEN AND THE EARTH WERE MADE INTO COMPLETED UTENSILS.[3]

3. AND THE HEAVEN AND THE EARTH WERE FINISHED, etc. How did the Holy One, blessed be He, create His world? Said R. Johanan: The Lord took two balls, one of fire and the other of snow, and worked them

[1] Possibly *wayyekullu* and *tiklah* are both derived here from *kul*, to measure, cf. Isa. XL, 12 *And comprehended* (we-kol) *the dust of the earth in a measure*. The verses will then be translated and the heavens . . . were measured off, for every thing I have seen a measure.

[2] On this interpretation '*finished*' and '*end*' mean in point of time.

[3] Deriving *wayyekullu* from *keli*.

into each other, and from these the world was created. R. Ḥanina said: [He took] four [balls], for the four corners [of the universe]. R. Ḥama said: Six. four for the four corners and one for above and one for below.[1]

Hadrian—may his bones rot![2]—asked R. Joshua b R. Ḥanina: 'How did the Holy One, blessed be He, create the world?' He answered him in accordance with R. Ḥama. 'Is that actually possible!' exclaimed he.[3] Thereupon he led him into a small chamber and said to him: 'Stretch out your hand to east, west, north, and south. Even so was the work [of Creation] before the Lord,' he added.[4]

4 R. Hoshaya said: R. Efes preached in Antioch[5]: The word WAYYEKULLU connotes nought but blows and destruction (*kelayah*). This may be compared to a king who entered a province, and its inhabitants praised him, which pleased him; thereupon he entertained them with many races and charioteers.[6] Subsequently they angered him, whereupon he reduced the race meetings and the charioteers. Similarly, there is a planet which completes its circuit in twelve months, e.g. the sun[7]; another completes its circuit in twelve years, viz Jupiter; yet another completes its circuit in thirty days, viz. the moon; still another completes its circuit in thirty years, viz. Saturn;

[1] 'E J. R. Johanan holds that the world was created by spreading outward from this ball, which was its centre, to the limits assigned to it; while R Ḥanina holds that it spread inwards, from four balls which were set on its outer limits R Ḥama agrees with R Ḥanina, but adds another two, which marked its upper and lower boundaries

[2] The tragedy of the revolt against Hadrian which ended in defeat at Bethar in 135 C.E. with the massacre of countless Jews, led to a deep hatred of him, and his name is generally followed by this imprecation.

[3] Could God really place balls at such widely separated points!

[4] He can encompass the four corners of the earth just as easily as you can touch these walls.

[5] The capital of Syria founded by Seleucus Nicator, situated on the Orontes (Jast.).

[6] These were very popular in ancient Roman times Jast. translates he increased for them the speed of the mail-bearers and the number of mail stations

[7] This of course is based on the ancient geo-centric conception of the universe.

except Mercury, Venus, and Mars, which complete their circuit in 480 years.[1]

R. Phinehas said in the name of R. Ḥama of Sepphoris: We learned: White figs have their Sabbatical year in the second year, because they produce in three years.[2] But on that day[3] the fruits were produced in one day.[4] And in the Messianic future the Holy One, blessed be He, will heal that injury, for it is said, *And He will heal the stroke of their wound* (Isa. XXX, 26), i.e. He will heal the wound of the world.

5. R. Joshua b. Levi said: The heaven was completed with the sun, moon, and planets; the earth was completed with trees, herbs, and the garden of Eden.[5] R. Simon said in the name of R. Joshua b. Levi: The works [of creation, i.e. heaven and earth] were completed[6] and went on expanding.[7]

AND ALL THE HOST (ZEBA) OF THEM. R. Eleazar said: There are three fixed periods[8]: a fixed period for

[1] These periods are discussed at length by Theodor *ad loc*, who substitutes '480 days' for 480 years. The greater length of time taken by some planets is similarly regarded as a punishment (destruction) for Adam's sin.
[2] Sheb. v, 1. The fruits of the Sabbatical year (v. Lev. xxv, 2-8) are subject to special laws, e g. one must not trade in them, while their owner may retain only sufficient for his own wants, and must declare the rest free to all. By the fruits of the Sabbatical year are meant those which take shape (termed חנטה *hanaṭah*) in the seventh year, no matter when they actually ripen. Now these figs take three years to ripen from the time of *hanaṭah;* consequently the laws of the Sabbatical year apply only to those which ripen in the second year of the septennate (seven-year cycle). [3] When they were first created
[4] Thus the fruits were 'smitten' for the future, to require such a long time, that is the meaning of '*wayyekullu*'.
[5] He translates '*wayyekullu*' literally, they were finished (cf. *supra*, I, 14). Mah. renders: The heaven was crowned (adorned) with the sun, etc., thus deriving '*wayyekullu*' from *kelil*, a wreath or crown.
[6] Each on its own day, e.g. the heaven on the first day, dry land on the third, etc. M.K. translates: the works were created in a general shape, without a clear-cut formation. [7] Until the sixth day, when their boundaries were finally determined He too translates '*wayyekullu*' literally.
[8] The passage is rather difficult, and commentators differ in their explanations. The translation adopted is that of Theodor and Y.T. Thus: heaven and earth were created for a definitely fixed time; a definite period is set for disciples when they shall attain the rank of teachers, and there is a fixed time beyond which a man's trials cease.—The word '*ẓeba*' probably means here 'a period of service', such as a soldier's.

heaven and earth, a fixed period for disciples, and a fixed period for suffering. A fixed period for heaven and earth, as it is written, AND THE HEAVEN AND THE EARTH WERE FINISHED, AND ALL THEIR FIXED PERIODS. A fixed period for disciples, as it is written, *All the days of my appointed time* (ẓeba'i)[1] *would I wait, till my relief should come* (Job XIV, 14), which means, until my substitute arises.[2] And there is a fixed period for suffering, [as it is written,] *Is there not a fixed period* (zeba) *to man upon earth* (*ib.* VII, 1)? Yet the whole desire of man is to be upon the earth [i.e. alive],[3] though what pleasure has he, seeing that *His days are like the days of a hireling* (*ib.*)?[4] Naḥman, the son of Samuel b. Nahman, said: If a man merits it, a host [of divine powers] is for him; if not, a host [of hostile powers] is against him.[5] If he erects a building and his work is successful, the host is for him; if he falls from it and dies, there is a host against him; if he eats his bread and it benefits him, there is a host for him; if it lodges in his throat and chokes him, there is a host against him. Many hosts has the Holy One, blessed be He, appointed against man to exact His penalties, many bears, lions, snakes, fiery serpents, and scorpions; moreover, '*His days are like the days of a hireling*'![6]

6. The son of Sira said: God caused drugs to spring forth from the earth; with them the physician heals the wound and the apothecary compounds his preparations.[7]

R. Simon said: There is not a single herb but has a constellation in heaven which strikes it and says, 'Grow,'[8]

[1] E.V. '*service*'.
[2] I.e. until one's own disciple can take his place; v. B B 116*a*.
[3] Others: all man's desires are in respect of earthly matters.
[4] I.e. full of labour and trials.
[5] He translates *ẓaba* in the last verse quoted 'host'—a host for a man may either mean for his benefit or one fighting against him
[6] Who at the end of the day must render an account of his work. So man, too, must render an account in the next world for his actions in this.
[7] Cf. Eccl. XXXVIII, 4, 7, 8 This, too, is a comment on *ẓeba'am*, which he translates 'their desires', i.e everything in creation serves a purpose (Mah.). [8] On *mazzal* cf. Sanh (Sonc. ed.), p. 629, n. 10; it is here applied even to plant life.

as it is written, *Knowest thou the ordinances of the heavens? Canst thou establish the dominion thereof* (mishṭaro) *in the earth* (Job XXXVIII, 33)?[1] *Canst thou bind the chains of the Pleiades, or loose the bands of Orion* (*ib* 31)? R. Ḥanina b. Papa and R. Simon said: Pleiades binds the fruit and Orion draws it out between knot and knot,[2] as it is written, *Canst thou lead forth the constellations* (mazaroth) *in their season* (*ib.* 32)? R. Tanḥum b. R. Ḥiyya and R. Simon said: ['*Mazaroth*' connotes] the constellation which ripens (*me-mazzer*) the fruits.

7. Our Rabbis said: Even those things which you may regard as completely superfluous to the creation of the world, such as fleas, gnats, and flies, even they too are included in the creation of the world, and the Holy One, blessed be He, carries out His purpose through everything, even through a snake, a scorpion, a gnat, or a frog.

R. Aha related this story: A man was standing by the bank of a river when he saw a frog bearing a scorpion and carrying it across the river; as soon as it had carried out its commission,[3] it carried it back to its place.[4]

R. Phinehas related in R. Ḥanan's name: It once happened that a man was about to reap the harvest of a field when he saw a certain grass which he plucked and plaited into a wreath for his head. Then a snake came up, but he struck and killed it. A man then came along and stood and looked at the snake wondering, who killed that snake? 'I killed it,' said the man. He then saw the grass wreath on his head, and said to him, 'Have you of a truth really killed it? Can you remove that herb from your head?' he continued. 'Yes,' replied he. When he had removed it he said to him, 'Can you approach the snake with your

[1] He appears to derive *mishtaro* from *shoṭer*, the court officer who inflicts the corporal punishment ordered by the court, thus. canst thou place the one which strikes it, etc.
[2] Pleiades binds, i e. gives shape and substance to the fruit in winter, but it is still in a shrivelled-up form until summer, when Orion draws it out, giving it the necessary fulness.
[3] Which was to kill someone. [4] Cf. story in Ned. 41*a*.

staff?' 'Yes,' replied he. As soon as he approached it, his limbs fell to pieces.[1]

R. Jannai was sitting and lecturing at the gate of his town, when he saw a snake coming on in great haste, slithering to and fro from side to side.[2] 'This [snake] is going to carry out a mission,' observed he. Immediately a report spread in the town, 'So-and-so has been bitten by a snake and died.'

R. Eleazar was sitting to ease himself in a privy, when a Roman came and drove him away and sat down. 'This has a purpose,' remarked he [R. Eleazar]. Immediately a snake emerged and struck and killed him. At that he applied to himself the verse, *Therefore will I give a man for thee* (Isa. XLIII, 4).

R. Isaac b. R. Eleazar was strolling on the cliffs of the sea of Cæsarea,[3] when he saw a thigh-bone; he hid it,[4] but it rolled out; he hid it again, and again it rolled out. 'This is intended to perform His [God's] commission, he remarked. Then a runner passed by, stumbled over it, fell and died. Then they went and searched him and found that he was bearing evil decrees against the Jews of Cæsarea.

When the wicked Titus entered the Holy of Holies, he dragged down the veil, blasphemed and reviled [God]. On his return a mosquito entered his nose and began piercing his skull. And when he died they split open his brain and found that it was like a bird weighing two pounds.[5]

8. AND ON THE SEVENTH DAY GOD FINISHED, etc. (II, 2). R. Hanina said: R. Ishmael b. R. Jose introduced me to a certain innkeeper, saying to me: 'Here my father recited the Sabbath prayer on the eve of the Sabbath.' R. Jeremiah, R. Ammi, and R. Joḥanan raised a difficulty:

[1] The snake had been commissioned to kill him, but the wreath had saved him. Now that he removed it the strength of its poison—probably it had bitten him before it was killed—had its effect and killed him. Cf Lev. R. XXII, 4.
[2] In Lev. R *loc. cit.*: driven from one place, it went to another, and so on.
[3] V. *supra*, III, 6.
[4] So that none might fall over it
[5] According to other sources the mosquito had grown to that size

What! 'Here my father recited the Sabbath prayer on the eve of the Sabbath!'[1] Yet they need have had no difficulty, for some ass-drivers came from Arab[2] to Sepphoris and reported: R. Ḥanina b Dosa has already commenced the Sabbath [by reciting the Sabbath prayers] in his town.[3] But if you do wish to raise a difficulty, raise it on the following. For R. Ḥanina said: R. Ishmael b. R. Jose introduced me to a certain innkeeper and said: 'Here my father recited the post-Sabbath prayer on the Sabbath.' Said R. Assi: This too need have presented no difficulty to them, for Rabbi was sitting and lecturing, when he said to Abdan his interpreter,[4] 'Announce to the congregation that they should recite the week-day prayer while it is still day.'[5] Furthermore, R. Hiyya b. Ba was sitting and lecturing, when he said to his interpreter, 'Announce to the congregation that they should recite the week-day prayer while it is still day.'

9. Rabbi asked R. Ishmael b. R. Jose: 'Have you heard from your father the actual meaning of AND ON THE SEVENTH DAY GOD FINISHED, etc.?'[6] Said he to him: 'It is like a man striking the hammer on the anvil, raising it by day and bringing it down after nightfall.'[7] R. Simeon b. Yoḥai said: Mortal man, who does not know his minutes, his [exact] times or his hours, must add from the profane to the sacred; but the Holy One, blessed be He, who knows His moments, His times, and His hours, can enter it by a hair's breadth. Genibah and the Rabbis discussed this. Genibah said: This may be compared to a king who made

[1] How is that possible?

[2] Near Sepphoris in Upper Galilee; v Neub. *Géogr.*, p 204. According to a slightly different reading: came on the eve (of the Sabbath) to Sepphoris. [3] Though they had left it while it was yet day, R. Ishmael had meant the same thing.

[4] In lengthy popular discourses the lecturer whispered his statements to an interpreter, who then spoke them aloud to the people.

[5] Sc. the Sabbath, for by the time they finished it would be night.

[6] For surely God finished His work on the *sixth*, not on the seventh day.

[7] In the second between his raising it and his bringing it down night has commenced. Similarly, God finished His work right at the end of the sixth day, so that in that very moment the Sabbath commenced.

a bridal chamber, which he plastered, painted, and adorned; now what did the bridal chamber lack? A bride to enter it. Similarly, what did the world still lack? The Sabbath.[1] The Rabbis said: Imagine a king who made a ring: what did it lack? A signet. Similarly, what did the world lack? The Sabbath. And this is one of the texts they changed for king Ptolemy, [making it read:] 'And He finished on the sixth day[2] and rested on the seventh.'

King Ptolemy[3] asked the elders in Rome: 'In how many days did the Holy One, blessed be He, create the world?' 'In six days,' they replied. 'And since then Gehenna has been burning for the wicked,' exclaimed he; 'woe to the world for the judgments it must render!'[4]

HIS WORK! Did not R. Berekiah say thus in the name of R. Judah b. R. Simon: Neither with labour nor with toil did the Holy One, blessed be He, create the world, yet you say, [AND HE RESTED . . .] FROM ALL HIS WORK! But it is [so stated] in order to punish the wicked who destroy the world which was created with labour, and to give a goodly reward to the righteous who uphold the world which was created with toil.[5] And what was created therein?[6] Tranquillity, ease, peace, and quiet. R. Levi said in the name of R. Jose b. Nehorai: As long as the hands of their Master were working on them they went on expanding; but when the hands of their Master rested, rest was afforded to them, and thus *He gave rest* to His world *on the seventh day* (Ex. XX, 11).[7]

[1] Thus by means of the Sabbath itself God completed His work, and so He actually finished it on the seventh day Without the higher longings inspired by the sanctity of a day consecrated by God mankind is incomplete. [2] He could not be expected to understand these explanations of the 'seventh'
[3] This is probably a copyist's error (Radal and Theodor). Read A certain philosopher. [4] The text is corrupt, and the translation adopted, based on the edd., is an attempt to reconstruct it
[5] Cf Aboth v, 1, and note *ad loc.* in Sonc. ed.
[6] On the Sabbath, after He rested, for the verse, *Because that in it He rested from all His work which God created to make* (lit. translation) implies that this resting itself was in order to make (i.e. create) something.
[7] Y T.: he interprets *wa-yishboth* (E.V. '*and he rested*'), 'he created a resting.'

R. Abba said: When a mortal king takes his army into quarters, he does not distribute largesse,[1] whilst when he distributes largesse he does not order a halt; but the Holy One, blessed be He, ordered a halt and distributed largesse, [as it is written,] AND HE RESTED . . . AND HE BLESSED.[2]

[1] That he does only before the troops are to go into battle or start on a march.
[2] Not only did He afford man a day of rest, but also made him the gift of a sacred day.

Chapter XI (BERESHITH)

1. AND GOD BLESSED THE SEVENTH DAY (II, 3). *The blessing of the Lord, it maketh rich* (Prov. X, 22): this refers to the Sabbath, as it is written, AND GOD BLESSED, etc. *And grief addeth nothing thereto* (*ib.*): this refers to mourning,[1] as you read, *The king grieveth for his son* (II Sam. XIX, 3).

2. AND GOD BLESSED THE SEVENTH DAY, AND HALLOWED IT. R. Ishmael said: He blessed it with manna and hallowed it with manna. He blessed it with manna, for every day of the week there descended one '*omer* [per person], but on the eve of the Sabbath two '*omers*. And He hallowed it through manna, which did not descend on the Sabbath at all. R. Nathan said: He blessed it with manna and hallowed it with a blessing. R. Isaac said: He blessed it with manna and hallowed it through the man who gathered [sticks].[2]

He blessed it with [the distinction of] robing.[3] R. Huna said: A man must change [his garments on the Sabbath]. R. Ḥiyya said in R. Johanan's name: A man must mingle [his garments].[4] Abin b. Ḥasde said: He must let [his cloak] hang down.[5] R. Jeremiah and R. Ze'ira were walking together [on the Sabbath], R. Jeremiah's cloak being tucked up, whereupon R. Ze'ira pulled it down. This shows that one must let his cloak hang down.

R. Liezer said: He blessed it in the matter of a lamp, and this happened in my case. I once lit a lamp for the Sabbath night, and when I came at the termination of the Sabbath I found it still burning and not at all diminished.

He blessed it with the light of a man's face: the light of

[1] Which is absent on the Sabbath.
[2] V. Num. XV, 32 The sanctity of the Sabbath was thereby emphasised.
[3] A special cloak should be worn on the Sabbath.
[4] If he cannot afford a complete change, he must have something different to mingle with his week-day attire.
[5] Instead of tucking it up as on the week-days, when he works in the fields.

a man's face during the week is not the same as it is on the Sabbath.

He blessed it in respect of the luminaries. R. Simeon b. Judah said: Though the luminaries were spoilt[1] on the eve of the Sabbath, yet they were not smitten until the termination of the Sabbath. This agrees with the Rabbis but not with R. Assi,[2] who maintained: Adam's glory did not abide the night with him.[3] What is the proof? *But Adam passeth not the night in glory* (Ps. XLIX, 13).[4] The Rabbis maintain: His glory abode with him, but at the termination of the Sabbath He deprived him of his splendour[5] and expelled him from the Garden of Eden, as it is written, *Thou changest his countenance, and sendest him away* (Job XIV, 20). As soon as the sun set on the night of the Sabbath, the Holy One, blessed be He, wished to hide the light, but He showed honour to the Sabbath; hence it is written, AND GOD BLESSED THE SEVENTH DAY: wherewith did He bless it? With light. When the sun set on the night of the Sabbath, the light continued to function,[6] whereupon all began praising, as it is written, *Under the whole heaven they sing praises to Him* (*ib.* XXXVII, 3)[7]; wherefore? Because *His light* [reaches] *unto the ends of the earth* (*ib*).[8] R. Levi said in the name of the son of Nezirah: That light functioned thirty-six hours,[9] twelve on the eve of the Sabbath [i.e. Friday], twelve during the night of the Sabbath, and twelve on the Sabbath [day]. When the sun sank at the termination of the Sabbath, darkness began to set in. Adam was terrified, [thinking,] *Surely* indeed *the darkness shall* bruise [E.V. '*envelop*'] *me* (Ps. CXXXIX, 11): shall he of whom it was written, *He shall* bruise *thy head* (Gen. III, 15), now come to attack me![10]

[1] Through Adam's sin it was decreed that the primeval light should be hidden *Var lec.:* cursed. [2] More correctly: R. Jose
[3] I.e. the primeval light, which was smitten immediately he sinned, before the Sabbath. [4] E.V. '*But man abideth not in honour*'.
[5] By hiding the primeval light. Others He deprived Adam's countenance of its lustre. [6] At night—this primeval light is meant.
[7] This derives *yishrehu* from *shir,* to sing E.V. '*He sendeth it forth under, etc.*' [8] On this night. [9] I e. for Adam, who was created on the sixth day. [10] Under cover of darkness.

What did the Lord do for him? He made him find two flints which he struck against each other; light came forth and he uttered a blessing over it; hence it is written, *But the night was light about me*—ba'adeni (Ps. *loc. cit.*), i.e. the night was light in my Eden (*be'edni*).[1] This agrees with Samuel, for Samuel said: Why do we recite a blessing over a lamp [fire] at the termination of the Sabbath? Because it was then created for the first time.[2] R. Huna in Rab's name, and R. Abbahu in R. Johanan's name said: At the termination of the Day of Atonement, too, we recite a blessing over it, because the fire rested the whole day.[3]

3. He blessed it by providing for additional expenditure. R. Levi said in the name of R. Jose b. R. Hanina: A blessing is written in connection with every day in which there is a decrease, and so it suffers no loss at all. [E.g.] on the fifth day birds and fish were created; now people kill birds and eat them, and catch fish and eat them, yet since a blessing is written in connection with it, the stock does not in any way decrease. Then what can you say of the seventh day?[4] R. Levi said in the name of R. Ḥama b. R. Ḥanina: [It is written] on account of the [additional] expenditure.[5] R. Leazar said in R. Jose's name: [The blessing was given] on account of people with delicate digestions.[6]

4. He blessed it with tasty dishes. Our Teacher[7] made a meal for Antoninus[8] on the Sabbath. Cold dishes were set before him; he ate them and found them delicious. [On another occasion] he made a meal for him during the week, when hot dishes were set before him. Said he to him: 'Those others I enjoyed more.' 'These lack a certain con-

[1] The meaning of the original is not clear, and the translation is a conjecture.
[2] Sc. artificial light.
[3] I.e. no fire was lit on that day. V. Pes. 53*b*, 54*a*.
[4] When nothing was created.
[5] Incurred, without one's wealth being thereby diminished; cf. Bez. 16*a*.
[6] The blessing enables them to enjoy the additional fare provided.
[7] R. Judah the Nasi, called Rabbi (teacher) *par excellence*.
[8] On the identity of Antoninus v. Sanh. (Sonc. ed.), p. 610, n. 7.

diment,' he replied. 'Does then the royal pantry lack anything?' he exclaimed. 'They lack the Sabbath,' he retorted; 'do you indeed possess the Sabbath?'[1]

R. Ishmael b. R. Jose asked Rabbi: On account of what virtue do the Babylonians live [a life of wealth]? In virtue of the Torah [which they study]. And in Eretz Israel? In virtue of the tithes. And the people of the Diaspora? Because they honour the Sabbaths and festivals. R. Ḥiyya b. Abba said: I was once invited by a man in Laodicea[2]; they brought before us a table borne on sixteen staves, and on it was of everything created in the first six days; a child sat in the middle and recited, *The earth is the Lord's, and the fulness thereof* (Ps. XXIV, 1). Why? So that the owner should not grow conceited. Said I to him, 'My son, whence did you merit all this wealth?' 'I was a butcher,' replied he, 'and whenever I saw a well-favoured animal, I set it aside for the Sabbath.'[3]

R. Tanḥuma said: It once happened in Rome on the eve of the great fast [sc. the Day of Atonement] that a certain tailor went to buy a fish, and it fell out that he and the governor's servant began bargaining for it. Each overbid the other until it reached twelve *dinars*, at which price the tailor bought it. At dinner the governor demanded of the servant, 'Why have you not served fish?' 'I will tell you the truth, sir,' he replied. 'A certain Jew did thus to me: did you really want me to bring you a single fish for twelve *dinars!*' 'Who was it?' inquired he. 'So-and-so, the Jew,' he answered. He had him summoned and said to him, 'A Jewish tailor can eat a fish at twelve *dinars!*' 'Sir,' replied he, 'we have one day when all our sins of the year are forgiven, and we honour it greatly.' When he produced proof of his words, he dismissed him.[4]

5. The wicked Tinneus Rufus[5] asked R. Akiba: 'Why does this day [the Sabbath] differ from other days?' 'Why does one man differ from other men?' he retorted.

[1] Shab. 119*a*. [2] A town of Syria. [3] V. Shab. 119*a*
[4] Cf story in Shab., *loc. cit.*, of a certain Joseph, who honoured the Sabbath. [5] A Roman governor of Judea; v. Sanh 65*b*.

'What did I ask you and what did you answer me?' inquired he. 'You asked me,' he replied, 'why does the Sabbath differ from all other days,' and I answered you, 'Why does Rufus differ from other men.' 'Because the emperor desired to honour him,' said he. 'Then this day, too, the Holy One wished to honour.' 'How can you prove it to me?'[1] 'Let the river Sambatyon prove it, which carries stones the whole week[2] but allows them to rest on the Sabbath.' 'You are evading the question,'[3] he exclaimed. 'Then let him who brings up [the dead by] his male genital prove it,' he replied, 'for every day he [the dead] comes up but not on the Sabbath.'[4] He went and made a test with his own father: every day he came up, but on the Sabbath he did not come up. After the Sabbath he brought him up [again]. 'Father,' said he, 'have you become a Jew after death! Why did you ascend during the whole week but not on the Sabbath?' 'He who does not keep the Sabbath among you of his own free will must keep it here in spite of himself.' 'But what toil have you there?' he demanded. 'The whole week we undergo judgment, but on the Sabbath we rest.' Then he went back to R. Akiba and said to him: 'If it is as you say that the Holy One, blessed be He, honours the Sabbath, then He should not stir up winds or cause the rain to fall on that day.' 'Woe to that man!'[5] he exclaimed; 'it is like one who carries [objects] four cubits.'[6]

6. A philosopher asked R. Hoshaya. 'If circumcision is so precious, why was it not given to Adam?'[7] 'If so,'

[1] That this is indeed the seventh day.
[2] The strong force of its current carries along stones and rubble, rendering it unnavigable. It is a mythical river; v Theodor *ad loc.* and Neub *Géogr.*, p 33. [3] Lit. 'you are drawing me away'—to a distant place; you quote as proof a distant river I have never seen.
[4] This refers to a kind of necromancer (*ba'al-ob*) who brought up the dead by means of the membrum virile
[5] Lit. 'let fainting come upon that man'.
[6] The whole universe is God's private domain, as it were, and when He moves the winds and rain it is to Him like carrying in private ground, which is permitted even on the Sabbath.
[7] I.e. why was he not born circumcised?

he replied, 'why do you shave the corners of your head and leave your beard?' 'Because it grew with me in folly,'[1] was the answer. 'If so, you should blind your eye and cut off your hands!'[2] 'To such an argument have we come!' observed he.[3] 'I cannot send you away empty-handed,' said he; '[the real reason is this:] whatever was created in the first six days requires further preparation, e.g , mustard needs sweetening, vetches need sweetening, wheat needs grinding, and man too needs to be finished off.'[4]

7. R Johanan said in R. Jose's name: Abraham, who is not reported to have kept the Sabbath,[5] inherited the world in [limited] measure, as it is written, *Arise, walk through the land in the length of it and in the breadth of it* (Gen. XIII, 17). But Jacob, of whom the keeping of the Sabbath is mentioned, viz *And he rested* [E.V. '*encamped*'] *before the city* (*ib.* XXXIII, 18), which means that he entered at twilight and set boundaries before sunset,[6] inherited the world without measure, [as it is written], *And thou shalt spread abroad to the west, and to the east,* etc. (*ib.* XXVIII, 14).

8. Now why did He bless it? R. Berekiah said: Because it has no mate. The first day of the week has the second, the third has the fourth, the fifth has the sixth, but the Sabbath has no partner. R. Samuel b. Nahman said: Because it cannot be postponed · a festival can be postponed, the Day of Atonement can be postponed,[7] but the Sabbath cannot be postponed.

R. Simeon b. Yohai taught: The Sabbath pleaded to the Holy One, blessed be He: 'All have a partner, while I have no partner!' 'The Community of Israel is your partner,' God answered. And when they stood before the mountain of Sinai, He said to them, 'Remember what I said to the

[1] In childhood and youth, before I reached the years of discretion Hence it is of less value and I cut it. [2] These, too, you have from birth.
[3] Your arguments are mere sophistries [4] By circumcision.
[5] Mah. · it is not stated *specifically* that he kept the Sabbath, but only in general terms that he kept God's law; v. *infra*, LXIV, 4.
[6] V. *infra*, LXXIX, 6 *ad fin*
[7] These are dependent on the day which the Court declares to be New Moon; thus if New Moon is declared a day later these too fall later.

Sabbath, that the Community of Israel is your partner, [hence,] *Remember the Sabbath day, to keep it holy'* (Ex. xx, 8).

9. BECAUSE THAT IN IT HE RESTED FROM ALL HIS WORK WHICH GOD CREATED TO MAKE (II, 3).[1] R. Levi said in the name of R. Ḥama b. R. Ḥanina: The Holy One, blessed be He, created three objects on each day: on the first, heaven, earth, and light; on the second, the firmament, Gehenna, and the angels; on the third, trees, herbs, and the Garden of Eden; on the fourth, the sun, the moon, and the constellations; on the fifth, birds, fish, and the Leviathan; on the sixth, Adam, Eve, and moving creatures.[2] R. Phinehas said: In the sixth He created six things: Adam, Eve, creeping things, cattle, beasts, and demons. R. Banayah said: *Which God created* and made is not written here, but WHICH GOD CREATED TO MAKE: whatever the Holy One, blessed be He, was to have made on the seventh, He created beforehand on the sixth.[3]

10. R. Phinehas said in R. Oshaya's name: Although you read: BECAUSE THAT IN IT HE RESTED FROM ALL HIS WORK WHICH GOD CREATED TO MAKE, He rested from the work of [creating] His world, but not from the work of the wicked and the work of the righteous, for He works with the former and with the latter. He shows the former their essential character, and the latter their essential character. And how do we know that the punishment of the wicked is called work? Because it is said, *The Lord hath opened His armoury, and hath brought forth the weapons of His indignation, for it is a work that the Lord God hath to do* (Jer. L, 25). And how do we know that the bestowing of reward upon the righteous is called work? Because it is said, *Oh how abundant is Thy goodness, which Thou hast laid up for them that fear Thee, which Thou hast wrought for them that take refuge in Thee, in the sight of the sons of men* (Ps. XXXI, 20)!

[1] Lit. translation. E.V. . . . '*Which God in creating had made.*'
[2] *Remes*, which in his view includes animals and wild beasts
[3] Rendering: God created what He was to make (on the seventh day). —Hence he made six things instead of three on the sixth day.

CHAPTER XII (BERESHITH)

1. THESE ARE THE GENERATIONS OF THE HEAVEN AND OF THE EARTH WHEN THEY WERE CREATED (II, 4). *Lo, these are but parts of His ways; and what blemish of aught is heard of Him! But the thunder of His mighty deeds who can understand* (Job XXVI, 14)? R. Huna said: Whatever things you see are but parts of the ways of the Holy One, blessed be He, as it says, '*Lo, these are but parts of His ways; and what blemish of aught is heard of Him*': what defect is heard of Him? '*But the thunder of His mighty deeds who can understand*'? R. Huna said: When thunder goes forth in its full force, no creature can understand it. It is not written, none understands, but '*who can understand?*'[1] The intelligent know His hints and His thoughts.[2] Said R. Huna: If you cannot comprehend the essential nature of thunder, can you comprehend the essence of the world! If a man tells you, 'I can comprehend the essential character of the universe,' say to him, '*For what is the man that cometh after the king*' (Eccl. II, 12)? i.e. after the King of the Universe, the supreme King of kings, the Holy One, blessed be He! R. Nahman said[3]: This may be compared to a thicket of reeds which no man could enter, for whoever entered therein lost his way. What did a certain clever man do? He cut down [some reeds] and entered, then cut down more and penetrated further; thus he entered through the clearing and went out; then all began to enter through his clearing R. Nahman gave another illustration. Imagine a large palace with many doors, so that whoever entered therein lost his way. What did a certain wise man do? He took a ball of cord and tied it near the door. Then all commenced to enter and go out

[1] Which implies that some may understand.
[2] Y T.: they understand it as a hint to introspection and repentance
[3] Mah : this is a comment on the first half of the verse just quoted, viz. *And I turned myself to behold wisdom*—i.e I (sc. Solomon) endeavoured to find a method to understand the wisdom of the Torah Cf. S.S. R. I, I, § 8.

by means of the clue. R. Simeon b. Yoḥai said: This may be compared to a mortal king who built a palace. People entered it and criticised: 'If the columns were taller it would be beautiful; if the walls were higher it would be beautiful; if the ceiling were loftier it would be beautiful.' But will any man come and say, 'Oh that I had three eyes or three feet!' Surely not.[1] It is not stated, 'That which He hath already made him,' but '*That which* they *have already made him*': if it were possible to say so, the supreme King of kings, the Holy One, blessed be He, and His court took a vote on every limb of thine and set thee up in proper trim: thus it is written, *He hath made thee, and established thee* (Deut. XXXII, 6).[2]

R. Levi b. Ḥaytha[3] said: If a mortal king builds a palace and sets its waterspout at its entrance, it is unbecoming. Yet the supreme King of kings, the Holy One, blessed be He, created man and set his spout [sc. the nose] over his entrance [mouth], and that constitutes his beauty and his pride. R. Isaac b. Merion said: It is written, THESE ARE THE GENERATIONS OF THE HEAVEN, etc., when their Creator praises them,[4] who may disparage them; when their Creator lauds them, who may find fault with them? But they are comely and praiseworthy; hence it is written, THESE ARE THE GENERATIONS OF THE HEAVEN, etc.

2. *For all these things hath My hand made* (Isa. LXVI, 2). R. Berekiah objected in the name of R. Judah b. R. Simon: Not with labour or wearying toil did the Holy One, blessed be He, create His world, yet you actually say, '*For all these things hath My hand made*'![5] R. Judan said: [It means that God created the world] for the sake of the Torah [which is referred to as 'these' in the verse,] *These are the statutes*

[1] Human achievements may fall short of perfection, but not the work of God. [2] Cf. Hul. 56*b* on this verse. [3] Other MSS.: Ḥama; R. Nahman. [4] This is deduced from the phrase THESE ARE, God pointing to them with pride, like a worker who draws attention to the fine quality of his work. [5] This implies physical labour, whereas God's fiat was sufficient; cf. *supra*, III, 2; X, 9.

and ordinances and laws—toroth (Lev. XXVI, 46)[1] R. Joshua b. R. Nehemiah said: For the sake of the tribes, [as it is written,] *Now these are the names of the tribes* (Ezek. XLVIII, 1).[2] *And so all these things came to be, saith the Lord* (Isa. *loc. cit.*): hence, THESE ARE THE GENERATIONS OF THE HEAVEN.

3. THESE ARE THE GENERATIONS OF THE HEAVEN, etc. R. Abbahu said: Wherever 'these are' (*eleh*) is written, it disqualifies [rejects] the preceding; 'and these are' (*we-eleh*) adds to the preceding. Here, where THESE ARE is written, it disqualifies the preceding. What does it disqualify? Formlessness and void.[3]

4. R. Judah and R. Nehemiah discussed this passage. R. Judah said: *And the heaven and the earth were finished* in their own time, *and all their host* in their own time.[4] Said R. Nehemiah to him: But it is written, THESE ARE THE GENERATIONS OF THE HEAVEN AND OF THE EARTH BE-HIBBARAM (WHEN THEY WERE CREATED), which means: they are [now] as when they were [first] created, i.e. on the very day they were created they brought forth their generations.[5] R. Judah countered: Yet surely it is written, *And there was evening and there was morning, one day . . . a second day . . . a third day . . . a*

[1] Pl. of Torah He renders: And for the sake of all these things (sc. the Torah) hath My hand made, etc.

[2] Other sources quote *All these are the twelve tribes of Israel* (Gen. XLIX, 28), or, *Now these are the names of the sons of Israel* (Ex I, 1), instead of the verse from Ezekiel, and these seem preferable; cf. Ex. R. XLVIII, 2.

[3] Y.T. If a passage commences with 'these are', it implies that only the things that follow are worthy to be so counted, but not what went before. If a passage commences with '*and* these are', it indicates that these too are worthy, in addition to what went before. According to the Rabbis, God created other worlds before the present one, but destroyed them, reducing them to formlessness and void. This is intimated in the present verse, THESE ARE THE GENERATIONS OF THE HEAVEN, etc., implying that the earlier worlds could not be called 'these', since they reverted to their original chaos. V. Ex. R. XXX, 3.

[4] I e heaven and earth were first created, and then the hosts of heaven and earth (M.K.).

[5] I e the heaven and the earth were created simultaneously with their generations.

fourth day . . . a fifth day . . . a sixth day?[1] Said R. Nehemiah: They were like those who gather figs, when each appears in its own time.[2] R. Berekiah observed in confirmation of this view of R. Nehemiah: *And the earth brought forth*, etc. (Gen. I, 12), implies something which was already stored within it.

5. R Nehemiah of Siknin said[3]: *For in six days the Lord made heaven and earth, the sea, and all that in them is* (Ex. XX, 11): these three things constitute the fundamental elements of the creation; they each waited three days and then produced three things. The earth was created on the first day, according to Beth Hillel, waited three days, viz , the first, second, and third, and brought forth three generations: trees, herbs, and the Garden of Eden. The firmament [heaven] was created on the second day, waited three days, viz., the second, third, and fourth, and brought forth three generations: the sun, moon, and constellations. The seas were created on the third day, tarried three days, viz., the third, fourth, and fifth, and produced three generations: birds, fish, and the Leviathan. R. 'Azariah, however, maintained: It is not so, but IN THE DAY THAT THE LORD GOD MADE EARTH AND HEAVEN teaches that two things constitute the fundamental elements of creation, and they waited three days and their work was completed on the fourth day. Heaven was created on the first day, as maintained by the School of Shammai; then it waited three days, viz., the first, second, and third, and its work was completed on the fourth. And what was the completion of its work? The luminaries, which were what the world lacked, as it is said, *And God set them in the firmament of the heaven* (Gen. I, 17). The essential creation of the earth

[1] On each of these days a generation of heaven or earth was created, whereas heaven and earth were themselves created on the first day.

[2] In a crop of figs all take shape about the same time, but they do not all ripen at the same time Similarly the hosts (*'generations'*) were created together with heaven and earth, but only completed each on the day assigned to it.

[3] Near Sepphoris. But in Soṭ. 18*b* we find: Neḥunia, the digger of wells.

was on the third day, as it is said, *And the earth brought forth* (*ib.* 12); also, *And let the dry land appear* (*ib.* 9).[1] It waited three days, viz., the third, fourth, and fifth, and its work was completed on the sixth day. And what was the completion of its work? Man, as it is written, *I, even I, have made the earth, and created man upon it* (Isa XLV, 12).

6. GENERATIONS (TOLEDOTH). All *toledoth* found in Scripture are defective,[2] except two, viz. *These are the toledoth* (generations) *of Perez* (Ruth IV, 18), and the present instance. And why are they defective? R. Judan said in R. Abun's name: The six [which they lack][3] corresponds to the six things which were taken away from Adam, viz., his lustre, his immortality [lit. 'life'], his height, the fruit of the earth, the fruit of trees, and the luminaries.[4] Whence do we know this of his lustre?—*Thou changest his countenance, and sendest him away* (Job XIV, 20). His immortality?—*For dust thou art, and unto dust shalt thou return* (Gen. III, 19). His height?—For it says, *And the man and his wife hid themselves* (*ib.* 8).[5] R. Aibu said: His height was cut down and reduced to one hundred cubits. The fruit of the earth and the fruit of the tree?—*Cursed is the ground for thy sake*, etc. (*ib.* 17). Luminaries?—R. Simeon b. Judah said: Though the luminaries were cursed on the eve of the Sabbath, they were not smitten until the termination of the Sabbath. This agrees with the Rabbis but not with R. Assi, who maintained: Adam did not retain his glory for a night. What is the proof? *But Adam passeth not the night in glory* (Ps. XLIX, 13). The Rabbis maintain: He passed the night in his glory, but at the termination of the Sabbath He deprived him of his splendour and expelled him from the Garden of Eden, as it is written, '*Thou changest his countenance, and sendest him away*' (Job XIV, 20). As soon

[1] Both quotations relate to the third day.
[2] Lacking a *waw*, i.e. תלדות instead of תולדות.
[3] The *waw* as a numeral is six.
[4] These were reduced, the earth and trees having originally produced fruit in one day, and the light of the luminaries being much greater than now, as explained in the text. [5] He originally filled the whole world (v. *supra*, VIII, 1), and now he was small enough to hide among the trees!

as the sun set on the night of the Sabbath, the Holy One, blessed be He, wished to hide the light, but He showed honour to the Sabbath; hence it is written, *And God blessed the seventh day*, etc. (Gen. II, 3): wherewith did He bless it? with light. When the sun set on the night of the Sabbath, the light continued to function, whereupon all began praising, as it is written, *Under the whole heaven they sing praises to Him* (Job XXXVII, 3); wherefore? Because *His light* [reaches] *unto the ends of the earth* (*ib.*). R. Levi said in the name of the son of Nezirah: That light functioned thirty-six hours, twelve on the eve of the Sabbath [i.e. Friday], twelve during the night of the Sabbath, and twelve on the Sabbath [day]. When the sun sank at the termination of the Sabbath, darkness began to set in. Adam was terrified, [thinking,] *Surely* indeed *the darkness shall bruise* [E.V. '*envelop*'] *me* (Ps. CXXXIX, 11): shall he of whom it was written, *He shall bruise thy head* (Gen. III, 15) now come to attack me! What did the Lord do for him? He made him find two flints which he struck against each other; light came forth and he uttered a blessing over it; hence it is written, *But the night was light about me*—ba'adeni (Ps. *loc. cit.*), i.e. the night was light in my Eden (*be-'edni*). This agrees with Samuel, for Samuel said: Why do we recite a blessing over a lamp [fire] at the termination of the Sabbath? Because it was then created for the first time. R. Huna in Rab's name, and R. Abbahu in R. Joḥanan's name said: At the termination of the Day of Atonement, too, we recite a blessing over it, because the fire rested the whole day.[1] R. Berekiah said in the name of R. Samuel b. Naḥman: Though these things were created in their fulness,[2] yet when Adam sinned they were spoiled, and they will not again return to their perfection until the son of Perez [viz. Messiah] comes; [for in the verse] '*These are the toledoth* (generations) *of Perez*', *toledoth* is spelled fully, with a *waw*. These are they[3]: his lustre, his

[1] For notes on this whole passage v. *supra*, XI, 2

[2] The fact that TOLEDOTH is spelled here fully, with a *waw*, intimates that they were created with their full power.

[3] The six things whose restoration is symbolised by the inclusion of the *waw*.

immortality, his height, the fruit of the earth and the fruit of trees, and the luminaries. Whence do we know it of his lustre?—*But they that love him shall be as the sun when he goeth forth in his might* (Judg v, 31). His immortality?—*For as the days of a tree shall be the days of My people* (Isa. LXV, 22)[1] His height?—*And I will make you go upright*—komemiuth (Lev. XXVI, 13). R. Ḥiyya taught: That means, with an erect bearing, fearing no creature. R. Judan said: It indicates a height of one hundred cubits. R. Simeon said: Two hundred. R. Eleazar b. R. Simeon said: Three hundred. Whence do we know it? From the word '*ḳomemiuth*': *komah* implies one hundred cubits, while *miuth* implies [another] two hundred cubits.[2] R. Abbahu said: Nine hundred cubits. R. Berekiah stated R. Abbahu's reason in R. Dosa's name: A sycamore tree continues growing in the earth six hundred years, while an infant comes out from his mother's womb a cubit and a half [in length]: go and calculate, a cubit and a half per annum, which gives nine hundred cubits.[3] Whence do we know it of the fruit of the earth and the fruit of the tree?—*For as the seed of peace, the vine shall give her fruit*, etc. (Zech. VIII, 12).[4] The luminaries?—*Moreover, the light of the moon shall be as the light of the sun, and the light of the sun shall be sevenfold, as the light of the seven days* (Isa. XXX, 26).

7. All have offspring. Heaven and earth have offspring: '*These are the offspring of the heaven and of the earth.*' Rain

[1] M.S.P adds. R. Simeon b. Yoḥai said: '*Tree*' refers to nought but the Torah, as it is said, *She is a tree of life to them that lay hold upon her* (Prov. III, 18). Hence man will be immortal like the Torah itself.

[2] *Miuth* is read as *me'oth*, hundreds. V. Sanh. 100*a*, B.B 75*a*.

[3] The passage is difficult. 'A cubit and a half' is based on a different reading, the text having 'a lopped-off cubit', i e rather less than a cubit. Y.T explains: R Abbahu refers to the verse, '*For as the days of a tree,*' etc As no tree is specified, he assumes it to mean the longest-lived one, viz. the sycamore, and holds that the point of similarity is not only the length of life, but also the manner of growth, the verse teaching that the height of men shall be as much as if they were to grow uniformly for six hundred years at one and a half cubits per annum, which is the average size of a new-born babe.

[4] *The vine shall give her fruit* implies, in the same measure and speed as when it was first created

has offspring: *Hath the rain a father* (Job XXXVIII, 28)? Dew has offspring: *Who hath begotten the drops of dew* (*ib.*)? R. Simeon b. Lakish said: That refers to the pearls of dew.[1] It was taught: Whatever has offspring dies, decays, is created, but cannot create, but what has no offspring neither dies nor decays, creates but is not created. R. 'Azariah said in the name of Rabbi: This was said in reference to the One above

8. Now all that you see are the offspring of heaven and earth, as it is said, *In the beginning God created the heaven and the earth.*[2] On the second day, His creations were of the celestial world: *And God said: Let there be a firmament*, etc. (Gen. I, 6), on the third, they were of the terrestial: *And God said: Let the earth put forth grass* (*ib.* 11); on the fourth, of the celestial: *Let there be light* (*ib.* 14); the fifth, of the terrestial: *Let the waters swarm*, etc. (*ib.* 20). On the sixth day, He came to create man. Said He: 'If I create him belonging to the celestial world, this will outnumber the terrestial by one creation, and there will be no peace in the universe; while if he is of the terrestial world it will be likewise. But lo! I will create him as partaking of both the celestial and the terrestial worlds, for the sake of peace.' Hence it is written, *Then the Lord God formed man of the dust of the ground, and breathed into his nostrils the breath of life* (*ib.* II, 7), which is of the upper world. And so Resh Lakish cited: *Dominion and fear are with Him; He maketh peace in His high places* (Job XXV, 2).

9. WHEN THEY WERE CREATED—BEHIBBARAM. R. Joshua b Karhah said: BEHIBBARAM is identical in lettering with *beabraham*[3]: i.e. for the sake of Abraham,

[1] Drops of water lying in the dew which look like pearls.—The offsprings of heaven are the luminaries, those of the earth are plant life and human life, those of dew are the fruit of the earth The deduction in respect of dew is from the words *father* and *begotten*, which imply that dew is in the category of things that beget (Y.T).
[2] And everything that followed was derived from these.
[3] Lit. 'for Abraham'. In Heb. both words contain the same letters, though in different order: בהבראם, באברהם.

whom He was one day to raise up. R. 'Azariah quoted on this statement of R. Joshua b. Ḳarhah the verse: *Thou art the Lord, even Thou alone; Thou hast made heaven* (continuing the whole passage) (Neh. IX, 6); and what was all this toil for? Because, *Thou art the Lord God, who didst choose Abram,* etc. (*ib* 7). R. Judan said: It is not written 'On the high mountains are the wild goats,' but, *The high mountains are for the wild goats* (Ps. CIV, 18): thus for whose sake were the high mountains created? For the sake of the wild goats Now the hind is weak and afraid of wild beasts; when therefore she wishes to drink, the Holy One, blessed be He, throws her into a state of panic and she beats with her horns [on the rocks]; the wild beast hears it and flees. *The rocks are a refuge for the conies* (*ib.*)· the coney takes shelter under the crag from the flying bird, lest it devour it Then if the Holy One, blessed be He, created His world thus for the sake of unclean things, how much the more for the sake of Abraham!

10. WHEN THEY WERE CREATED—BEHIBBARAM. R. Abbahu said in R Joḥanan's name: He created them with the letter *heh.*[1] All letters demand an effort to pronounce them, whereas the *heh* demands no effort[2]; similarly, not with labour or wearying toil did the Holy One, blessed be He, create His world, but *By the* word *of the Lord* (Ps. XXXIII, 6), and *The heavens were* already *made* (*ib.*).[3]

R. Judah the Nasi[4] asked R. Samuel b. Naḥman: 'As I have heard that you are a master of *haggadah*, tell me the meaning of, *Extol Him that rideth upon the skies, be-Jah is His name* (Ps. LXVIII, 5)?' Said he to him: 'There is not a single place which has not someone appointed to rule over it[5]: thus a commissioner in a province is appointed

[1] Reading בהבראם as two words: בה׳ בראם.
[2] Being a mere aspirate.—Lit. 'all letters take hold of the tongue', etc.
[3] A mere word, and the work was finished. Jewish thought knows nothing of recalcitrant matter fighting against God and refusing to be shaped into a world.
[4] This, of course, would not be the famous R. Judah the Nasi, compiler of the Mishnah, but his grandson, R. Judah II.
[5] Theodor. Jast.: There is not a place which has not an officer appointed over its highways.

to its governorship; a magistrate in a province is appointed to its governorship. Similarly, who is appointed to the governorship of His world? The Holy One, blessed be He· "*Be-Jah is His name*" means *biyah* (governorship) is His name.'[1] 'Alas for those who are gone and will not return!'[2] he exclaimed. 'I asked R. Eleazar, and he did not explain it thus. But the verse, *Trust ye in the Lord for ever, for the Lord* be-Jah *is an everlasting Rock* (Isa. XXVI, 4) means: By these two letters did the Lord create His world.'[3] Now we do not know whether this world was created with a *hé* or the next world with a *yod*, but from what R. Abbahu said in R. Joḥanan's name, viz. 'BE-HIBBARAM means, with a *hé* created He them,' it follows that this world was created by means of a *hé*. Now the *hé* is closed on all sides and open underneath: that is an indication that all the dead descend into *she'ol;* its upper hook is an indication that they are destined to ascend thence; the opening at the side is a hint to penitents.[4] The next world was created with a *yod:* as the *yod* has a bent [curved] back, so are the wicked: their erectness shall be bent and their faces blackened [with shame] in the Messianic future, as it is written, *And the loftiness of man shall be bowed down* (*ib.* II, 17). What will he [the wicked] say? *And the idols shall utterly pass away* (*ib.* 18).

BE-HIBBARAM. R. Berekiah said in the name of R. Judah b. R. Simon: Not with labour or wearying toil did the Holy One, blessed be He, create His world, but '*By the word of the Lord*, and *the heavens were* already *made*'.

BE-HIBBARAM: with a *hé* created He them. It was like a king who rebuked his servant, so that he stood still in bewilderment; even so, *The pillars of heaven tremble and are astonished at His rebuke* (Job XXVI, 11).[5]

[1] Reading *biyah* instead of *be-J(Y)ah.*
[2] I.e., the dead.
[3] Translating: for the Lord, by means of יה (*yod hé*) is the Rock (i.e. Creator) of worlds, viz. this world and the future world.
[4] That the way is open for a return to God.
[5] The universe went on expanding until rebuked by God (v. *supra*, VIII, 8). This rebuke was wordless and consisted of a single sound, like the letter *hé*

11. R. Eliezer and R. Joshua differed. R. Eliezer said: All that is in heaven was created out of heaven, and all that is on earth was created out of the earth. He proves this from the following: *Praise ye the Lord* [ye that were created] *from the heavens; Praise ye Him, all His angels . . . hosts . . . sun . . . moon . . .* etc. (Ps. CXLVIII, 1); *Praise the Lord* [ye that were created] *from the earth, ye sea-monsters . . . fire and hail . . . mountains . . . hills . . . beasts . . . cattle* (*ib.* 7 f). R. Joshua maintained: All that is in heaven and on earth was created from nought but heaven. He proves it from the following: *For He saith to the snow: Be thou on the earth*, etc. (Job XXXVII, 6). Just as the snow is created out of heaven, though its existence is on the earth; so everything that is in heaven and on earth was created from nought but heaven. R. Huna said in R. Joseph's name: Whatever is in heaven and on earth was created from the earth alone, as it is written, *For as the rain cometh down and the snow from heaven* (Isa. LV, 10): just as the rain's creation is from the earth, though it falls from heaven, so all that is in heaven and on earth was created from the earth alone.[1] R. Judan proved it from the following: *All go unto one place; all are of the dust*, i.e. earth (Eccl. III, 20). R. Naḥman said: Even the sun's orb, as it is said, *Who commandeth the sun* (ḥeres), *and it riseth not* (Job IX, 7).[2]

12. R. Joḥanan and Resh Laḳish discussed this. R. Joḥanan said: When a mortal king builds a palace, after having built the lower stories he builds the upper ones; but the Holy One, blessed be He, created the upper stories and the lower stories in a single act.[3] R. Simeon b. Laḳish said: When a human being builds a ship, first he brings the beams, then the ropes; after this he procures the anchors, and then erects the masts. But the Holy One, blessed be He, created them [heaven and earth] and their

[1] The proof is not clear and Th. assumes that some emendation of the text is necessary both here and in Eccl R. III, 20.

[2] The proof follows from a play on words, חרס (sun) being identified with חרש, a potsherd which is made from clay. thus even the sun was born out of the earth! [3] Cf. *supra*, I, 15, and IX, 3.

crew,[1] as it is written, *Thus saith God the Lord, He that created the heavens and stretched them forth*—we-noṭehem (Isa. XLII, 5), this is written *we-nawtehem* (and their mariners).[2]

13. R. Isaac and R. Simeon b. Lakish—R. Isaac said: When a mortal sets up a tent, after a while it is bound to slacken slightly; but here in truth, *Canst thou with Him spread out the sky* (Job XXXVII, 18)? And should you say that they are slack, therefore it is stated, *Which is strong as a molten mirror* (*ib.*). Resh Laḳish said: When a mere mortal makes a casting,[3] in the course of time it is bound to acquire rust; but in truth here they are '*Strong as a molten mirror*': they [the heavens] look like a [glittering] breastplate. R. 'Azariah observed in regard to this statement of R. Simeon b. Laḳish: It is written, '*Because that in it He rested from all His work which God in creating had made. These are the offspring of the heaven!*'[4] But a day ends and a day commences, a week ends and another commences, a month ends and another commences, a year ends and another commences, and yet they remain as WHEN THEY WERE CREATED, IN THE DAY THAT THE LORD GOD MADE EARTH AND HEAVEN.[5]

14. Beth Shammai and Beth Hillel differ. Beth Shammai maintain: The intention [to create was conceived] at night, while fulfilment [came] by day; whereas Beth Hillel say: Both intention and fulfilment were by day. R. Simeon

[1] The people, who carry on the world.

[2] Y.T.: Resh Lakish holds that heaven and earth are equal units in the universe, and both were created to carry out the design of the Divine Architect. Therefore he compares it to a ship, all whose parts co-operate in the one purpose of making it go. R. Joḥanan, however, holds that heaven plays the major role in God's scheme, earth being subsidiary to it. He thus compares the universe to a building in which the lower stories serve as a support to the upper ones.

[3] Lit. 'casts a lump of material'—whether of metal (as is obviously meant here) or glass.

[4] How strange that these two verses follow each other: what is the connection between them?

[5] Thus this proves the statement of Resh Laḳish.

b. Yoḥai observed: I am astonished! How could the fathers of the world, Beth Shammai and Beth Hillel, differ over the creation of heaven and earth! In truth, intention [was conceived] both by day and by night, while the fulfilment was at the standstill of the sun.[1]

15. . . . THE LORD GOD [MADE EARTH AND HEAVEN]. This may be compared to a king who had some empty glasses. Said the king. 'If I pour hot water into them, they will burst; if cold, they will contract [and snap].' What then did the king do? He mixed hot and cold water and poured it into them, and so they remained [unbroken]. Even so, said the Holy One, blessed be He: 'If I create the world on the basis of mercy alone, its sins will be great; on the basis of judgment alone, the world cannot exist. Hence I will create it on the basis of judgment and of mercy, and may it then stand!' Hence the expression, THE LORD GOD.[2]

16. EARTH AND HEAVEN. This may be compared to a legion which was the first to proclaim the king.[3] Said the king: 'Since this legion was the first to proclaim me king, I will give it a preferment which shall never be taken from it.' Even so said the Holy One, blessed be He: 'Because the earth was the first to fulfil My desire,[4] I will confer an honour upon her of which she will never be deprived.' Hence it is written, *Who didst establish the earth upon its foundations, that it should not be moved for ever and ever* (Ps. CIV, 5).[5]

[1] Jast . the time in the morning and the evening when the sun appears to stand still or be silent—dawn and sunset, immediately after the intention

[2] The Rabbis hold that *Adonai* (the Tetragrammaton) refers to God under His Attribute of Mercy, while *Elohim* describes Him as a God of judgment. [3] Before the other legions. This frequently happened in Rome under the Emperors. [4] Cf. *supra*, VIII, 8, 9.

[5] This is to explain why earth is mentioned here before heaven

CHAPTER XIII (BERESHITH)

1. NO TREE [E.V. '*SHRUB*'] OF THE FIELD WAS YET IN THE EARTH (II, 5) Here you say, NO TREE OF THE FIELD, etc., yet further on you read, *And the Lord God had made to grow out of the ground*, etc (*ib.* 9)?[1] Said R. Ḥanina· The verse below refers to the Garden of Eden,[2] whereas this refers to the inhabited world.[3] R. Ḥiyya taught· In both places nothing grew until rain descended upon them.[4]

2. NO SIAḤ (TREE) OF THE FIELD, etc. All the trees, as it were, conversed (*masiḥim*) with each other; all the trees, as it were, conversed with mankind; all the trees were created for man's companionship.[5] A man once gathered in the fruits of his vineyard and spent the night in it; then the wind blew[6] and caused him hurt.[7] All the conversation of mankind concerns the earth: 'Has the earth produced, or has the earth not produced?'[8] And all mankind's prayers concern the earth: 'Lord!

[1] The first verse implies that there was no plant-life yet on the sixth day (this being regarded as a continuation of Ch. I), while the second states that God *had* already made to grow, etc. (the Midrash treats the verb as *pluperfect*, in accordance with I, 12, which implies that plant life had already appeared on the *third* day). Cf. Ḥul. 60*b*.
[2] As appears from the rest of this verse and the following one.
[3] As distinct from the Garden of Eden.
[4] He reconciles the verses thus· The earth was endowed with plant-life on the third day, but the trees and herbs only reached the surface of the ground, until rain descended (in answer to Adam's prayer) and made them grow
[5] Others. were created for man's hurt—i e. he must take steps to protect himself from them This reading is more in accordance with the story that follows —The passage is based on the use of *siah* for tree instead of the more usual *'eẓ;* hence the Midrash connects it with the verb *siaḥ* to speak, converse. The sighing of the wind in the trees is poetically conceived as their speech.
[6] Others: then a spirit came—the spirits that dwell in trees.
[7] Mah. and 'E.J.: the fruit on the trees protects man from the wind that blows through them; hence when this man had gathered the grapes, leaving the vines bare, they no longer afforded protection M.K. interprets: though the trees are primarily for man's benefit, yet they sometimes harm him, as in the story quoted.
[8] This passage was possible only in a community essentially agricultural, such as was Palestine Jewry.

may the earth yield [fruit]'; or 'Lord, may the earth be successful!' All the prayers of Israel, however, are for the Temple: 'Lord, may the Temple be rebuilt!' and 'When will the Temple be rebuilt?'[1]

3. FOR THE LORD GOD HAD NOT CAUSED IT TO RAIN UPON THE EARTH. The full Name [of God] is employed in connection with a full world; it is similarly employed in connection with the fall of rain.[2] R. Simeon b. Yoḥai said: Three things are equal in importance, viz., earth, man, and rain. R. Levi b. Ḥiyyatha said: And these three each consist of three letters,[3] to teach that without earth there would be no rain and without rain earth could not endure; while without either man could not exist.

4. R. Hoshaya said: Wonderful is the might of rain, for it is reckoned as equivalent to the whole of creation. What is the proof?—*Who doeth great things and unsearchable* (Job v, 9); wherewith? By *Giving rain upon the earth and sending waters upon the fields* (*ib.* 10).[4] R. Aḥa proved it from the following: *He that hath made the earth by His power*, etc. (Jer. x, 12). *At the* sound *of His giving a multitude of waters in the heavens* (*ib.* 13).[5] Now '*sound*' signifies nought but rain, as you read: *Deep calleth unto deep at the* sound *of Thy cataracts* (Ps. XLII, 8).

5. R. Isaac said: It [rain] is evidence of propitiation, even as are sacrifices, as it is written, *Lord, Thou hast been favourable unto Thy land* (Ps. LXXXV, 2).[6] R. Simon said:

[1] Here *siaḥ* is connected with prayer, cf. *And poureth out his petition* (siḥo) *before the Lord* (Ps. CII, 1), while field is made to refer to the Temple; cf. *infra*, XXII, 7.
[2] God's full name, 'Lord God,' appears the first time in II, 4, after the world has been completed, similarly it is mentioned here, because rainfall is as important as the whole of creation, which is dependent on it.
[3] In Hebrew: ארץ, אדם, גשם.
[4] Thus these constitute '*great things and unsearchable*', which term is also applied to the creation, v. Ta'an 2*a*. [5] Thus the two are equated.
[6] *Thou hast been favourable* means with rain. Rain is withheld until God has allowed Himself to be propitiated for Israel's sins and forgiven them, this being also the object of sacrifices (Th. on the basis of Ta'an. 7*b*). Others translate and explain differently.

It will gather in the dispersed exiles[1]: *Thou hast turned the captivity of Jacob* (*ib.*). R. Joḥanan said: It dissipates [God's] wrath: *Thou hast withdrawn all Thy wrath* (*ib* 4). R. Tanḥum b. Ḥanilai said: It makes atonement for sins,[2] for it is said, *Thou hast forgiven the iniquity of Thy people* (*ib.* 3).[3]

6. R. Ḥiyya b. Abba said: It is as important as resurrection. R. Abba, son of R. Ḥiyya, said: The Sages too inserted it [the prayer for rain] in the blessing of the resurrection of the dead,[4] for 'hand' and 'opening' are used in connection with both. 'Hand' in connection with the one [resurrection]: *The* hand *of the Lord was upon me* (Ezek. XXXVII, 1)[5]; and 'hand' in connection with the other [rain]: *Thou openest Thy* hand, *and satisfiest every living thing with favour* (Ps. CXLV, 16). 'Opening' in connection with the one [rain]: *The Lord will* open *unto thee His good treasure the heaven to give the rain of thy land* (Deut. XXVIII, 12); 'opening' in connection with the other [resurrection]: *Behold, I will* open *your graves* (Ezek. *ib.* 12). R. Judan said in R. Eleazar's name: 'Song' is mentioned in connection with both. 'Song' in connection with the one: *Let those who dwell in the rock* sing (Isa. XLII, 11)[6]; 'song' in connection with the other [rain]. *Thou hast remembered the earth, and watered her . . . The valleys also are covered over with corn; they shout for joy, yea, they* sing (Ps. LXV, 10, 14). R. Ḥiyya b. Ba said: It is greater than resurrection, for whereas resurrection is for man alone, this is for man and beast; again, resurrection is for Israel, whereas this is for Israel and the nations.[7]

[1] 'E.J.' it is as beneficial as the gathering of the exiles.

[2] Probably this is similar in meaning to R. Isaac's teaching.

[3] All these follow '*Thou hast been favourable*', and are therefore regarded as indicating the influence or value of rain.

[4] The second blessing of the 'Eighteen benedictions', known as the '*Amidah*, which form the principal part of the daily service.

[5] This commences the narrative which relates the resurrection of the dry bones.

[6] *Those who dwell in the rock* are the buried dead: they are to sing when they are resurrected.

[7] Y.T: These symbolise the righteous and the wicked respectively, in accordance with the actual text in Ta'an. 7*a*, for the righteous of the Gentiles, too, will share in resurrection.

A certain Gentile asked R. Joshua, observing to him: 'You have festivals and we have festivals; we do not rejoice when you do, and you do not rejoice when we do.[1] When then do we both rejoice together?' 'When the rain descends.' What is the proof? *The meadows are clothed with flocks* (*ib.*); what follows? *Shout unto God, all the earth* (Ps. LXVI, 1): not priests, Levites, or Israelites is written here but, '*All the earth*'

R. Joshua b. Levi said: When rain falls [i.e. in spring], cattle long to rut. What is the proof? *The rams clothe the flocks*, etc., i.e. the males go up on the ewes, this being a more refined expression.

7. AND THERE WAS NOT A MAN TO TILL (LA'ABOD) THE GROUND (II, 5): i.e. there is no man to make men serve (*le'abbed*) the Holy One, blessed be He, as Elijah did.[2] What, there is no man to inspire service to the Lord?[3] —Man was created for nought but toil: if he is deserving, he toils in the Torah; if not, he labours in the soil. Happy is the man whose toil is in the Torah![4]

8. THE LORD GOD CAUSED IT TO RAIN UPON THE EARTH, though THERE WAS NOT A MAN: a covenant has been made with the earth, as it says, *To cause it to rain on a land where no man is, on the wilderness, wherein is no man* (Job XXXVIII, 26).[5]

9. BUT THERE WENT UP A MIST FROM THE EARTH, etc. (II, 6). *All the rivers run into the sea, yet the sea is not*

[1] Since our festivals do not coincide.

[2] The verse implies that rain falls for the sake of man. Hence when there is a drought, we must assume that the reason is because no man inspires service to God; this follows from reading *le'abbed* (to cause to serve) instead of *la'abod*, to serve (E.V. '*till*').

[3] Surely that is not the meaning of the verse!

[4] The verse is rendered thus: And when there is no man to make (men) serve (God), then they serve the ground (Th.).

[5] Theodor: Scripture writes, *For the Lord God had not caused it to rain and there was not a man*, etc., yet continues (v. 6): *but there went up a mist from the earth, and watered the whole face of the ground*. Thus even before man's creation there was rain, because a covenant, etc., i.e. rain, is a part of the scheme of Nature as created by God and is independent of man.

full (Eccl. I, 7). R. Eliezer and R. Joshua were once travelling on the great sea,[1] when their ship entered a non-flowing stretch of water.[2] Said R. Eliezer to R. Joshua: 'We have come here simply for a test.'[3] Thereupon they filled a barrel of water from there. When they arrived in Rome, Hadrian asked them, 'What is the nature of the water of the Ocean [i.e. the Mediterranean]?' 'It is water that absorbs other water,' replied they.[4] 'Show [i.e. prove] it to me,' he demanded. [They filled] a flaskful of that and poured more [ordinary] water therein, and the former absorbed it. In the opinion of R. Eliezer, *thither they return* (*ib.*) [is the essential meaning of the verse]; in the opinion of R Joshua, it is, '*thither they return to go on*' (*ib.*).[5]

How did the earth drink?[6] R. Judah, R. Nehemiah, and the Rabbis gave different answers. R. Judah said: Like the Nile which repeatedly waters [the land of Egypt].[7] R. Nehemiah said: Like a flood, like the Ḳebaria that grows and inundates [8] The Rabbis said: Like an overflowing river (*tuway*); there is a river in Babylonia named Tuway.[9] Even so did the earth drink: at first, THERE WENT UP A MIST FROM THE EARTH, AND WATERED THE

[1] I.e. the Mediterranean.

[2] Lit translation; i e. the water was quite stationary, and the vessel could not make its normal progress.

[3] It is the work of Providence that we have come to this place, so that we can carry out a test with this water, to prove that it possesses peculiar properties which corroborate the Scriptural assertion.

[4] For that reason it never becomes full, though all the rivers flow into it.

[5] This is difficult. 'Rashi': R. Eliezer, who suggested this test, knew the property of this water, though he had never been there before. The reason was that he interpreted the phrase *thither they return* as meaning that all waters discharge into the Ocean and remain there; hence the Ocean does not overflow only because it absorbs what it receives. R. Joshua, however, did not suggest this trial because he interpreted the verse, '*thither they return* in order *to go on*,' i.e. they enter at one point and flow out at another, eventually continuing their course in other rivers; hence he was not bound to R Eliezer's assumption. A different text in cur. edd. gives rise to an entirely different explanation by commentaries.

[6] M.K.: before the advent of rain.

[7] By its annual overflow. Similarly, the mist went up and watered the ground. [8] The river Ḳebaria has not been identified.

[9] Theodor thinks that the text is corrupt and suggests that it should be emended: R. Nehemiah said: Like the Kebaria; the Rabbis say: Like an overflowing river.

WHOLE FACE OF THE GROUND; but the Holy One, blessed be He, reconsidered the matter and decided that it should drink from above only. R. Ḥanan of Sepphoris said in the name of R. Samuel b. Nahman: On account of four things did the Holy One, blessed be He, subsequently decide that the earth should drink only from above: first, because of lawless men[1]; secondly, in order to wash away obnoxious vapours; thirdly, that the highlands might drink equally with the lowlands; and fourthly, that all might lift their eyes heavenwards; thus it is written, *That the lowly may lift* [their eyes] *heavenwards* (Job v, 11).[2]

10. And whence does the earth drink? R. Eliezer and R. Joshua disagree. R. Eliezer said: From the waters of the Ocean, for it is written, BUT THERE WENT UP A MIST FROM THE EARTH AND WATERED, etc. Said R. Joshua to him: But surely the waters of the Ocean are salty! They are sweetened in the clouds, replied he, for it is written, *Which the skies distil* (*ib.* XXXVI, 28): where are they distilled [i.e. sweetened]? In the skies [clouds]. R. Joshua said: [The earth drinks] from the upper waters, for it is written, *And drinketh water as the rain of heaven cometh down* (Deut. XI, 11); the clouds, however, mount up to heaven and receive them [the waters] as from the mouth of a bottle, for it is written, *They gather up* (yazoḳḳu) *water into its cloud* (*ib.*).[3] They distil it as from a sieve, not one drop touches another, for it is written, *Distilling waters from the thick clouds* (II Sam. XXII, 12).[4] Why are they [the clouds] called *sheḥaḳim?* Resh Laḳish said: Because they break up (*shoḥakim*) the [mass of] water [into rain drops]. Said R. Abba b. Kahana: They do this like the entrails of an animal.[5]

11. R. Joḥanan and Resh Laḳish discussed this. R. Joḥanan said: Clouds come from above, as it is written,

[1] Who would steal other people's water if it were gathered on the ground.
[2] E.V. '*So that He setteth up on high those that are low.*'
[3] E.V. '*Which distil rain from his vapour.*' Here, however, *yazoḳḳu* is connected with *ziḳa*, a water gourd, and the verse is translated: they gather water like a gourd. [4] E.V. '*Gathering of waters, thick clouds.*'
[5] Which break up the food in the process of digestion.

And, behold, with the clouds of heaven (Dan. VII, 13). Resh Laḳish maintained: Clouds come from below, for it says, *Who causeth the vapours* [clouds] *to ascend from the ends of the earth* (Ps. CXXXV, 7). In the view of R. Joḥanan it is like a man who presented his neighbour with a cask of wine together with the vessel.[1] In the view of Resh Lakish it is like a man who asked his neighbour, 'Lend me a *se'ah* of wheat,' to which he replied, 'Bring your basket and come and measure it out.' Similarly, the Holy One, blessed be He, says to the earth: 'Bring your clouds and receive rain.'

12. It [the cloud] has five names: *'ab, ed, 'anan, nasi, ḥaziz. 'Ab* (thick): because it thickens [i.e. darkens] the face of the sky, as it is said, *The thick clouds* ('abe) *of the skies* (II Sam. XXII, 12). *Ed:* BUT THERE WENT UP A CLOUD (ED) FROM THE EARTH: [it is so called] because it discomfits the speculators.[2] *'Anan:* because it makes men meek (*'anawim*) towards each other.[3] And it is written, *'With the clouds of* ('anane) *heaven.'*[4] *Nasi: Who causeth the clouds* (nesi'im) *to ascend* (Ps. CXXXV, 7): [it is so called] because it makes men princes (*nesi'im*) towards each other.[5] *Ḥaziz: And a way for the cloud* (ḥaziz E.V. *'storm'*) *of thunders* (Job XXVIII, 26): so called because it achieves [awe-inspiring] sights[6] in the

[1] Similarly, God supplies both the clouds from above and their rain.

[2] *Ed* (אד) is identified with *ed* (איד), calamity, destruction, in Deut. XXXII, 35: *For the day of their destruction* (edam) *is at hand.* Rain, by increasing the crops, frustrates the speculators who wish to force up prices.

[3] The realisation that all are dependent on it naturally tends to reduce their arrogance. Or as Mah.: One man may have a successful barley crop, another a successful wheat harvest, so that each needs the other.

[4] The relevance of this verse is not apparent, perhaps he translates: With the meek ones (sc the angels) of the heaven. Possibly, however, it is misplaced, and should be quoted at the beginning; *'anan,* as it is written, *'With the clouds of* ('anane) *heaven.'* The edd omit it altogether

[5] Either in the sense of independent of each other, because produce is very cheap when the rain has caused an abundant harvest, or arrogant, when one man's crops are successful while the other man's are a failure, and so he must become a suppliant of the other.

[6] *Ḥezyonoth* fr. *ḥizzayon.*

sky[1] and causes the Holy Spirit to rest upon men, as you read, *The vision* (hazon) *of Isaiah* (Isa. I, 1).

R. Simeon b. Gamaliel said: It [the earth] has four names: *ereẓ, tebel, adamah, arḳa.* The name *ereẓ* corresponds to the vernal equinox which forces up (*me-'alzah*) the crops[2]; *tebel,* to the summer solstice which lends savour to (*me-tabbeleth*) the crops; *adamah,* to the autumn, when the ground consists of clods of earth (*adamah*)[3]; *arḳa* corresponds to the winter[4] which causes the crops to wither (*moreḳeth*).

13. How much rain must descend that it may suffice for fructification[5]? As much as would fill a vessel of three handbreadths.[6] This is R. Meir's opinion. R. Judah said: In hard [soil], one handbreadth; in average [soil], two; in humid [soil], three.[7] R. Simeon b. Eleazar said: Not one handbreadth [of rain] descends from above without the earth bringing up two handbreadths [of moisture] to meet it. What is the proof? *Deep calleth unto deep at the voice of Thy cataracts* (Ps. XLII, 8).[8] R. Levi said: The upper waters are male while the lower are female,[9] and they say one to the other: 'Receive us; you have been created by the Holy One, blessed be He, whilst we are His messengers.' Immediately they receive them; thus it is written, *Let the sky pour down righteousness; let the earth open* (Isa XLV, 8)—like a female who receives the male; *That they may bring*

[1] The clouds causing the sky to assume various colours (v. *supra,* IV, 7).
[2] This connects *erez* with *alez,* to force. [3] The summer heat breaks up the ground and then the autumn rain kneads it into moist clods.
[4] Lit. the solstice of Tebeth. Tebeth is the tenth month, generally falling from about the middle of December to the middle of January.
[5] J Ber IX states that one must recite a blessing for rain when it descends in sufficient measure for fructification (*reb'iah*).
[6] *Var lec.:* As would fill the ploughing implement of three handbreadths. The plough dug three handbreadths into the soil, and this means that the rain too must penetrate this distance.
[7] There must be enough rain to penetrate three handbreadths into humid (lit. 'sated'—with moisture) soil, two into average soil, and one into hard soil.
[8] *Deep calleth unto deep* implies two parts from below as against the one part implied in *at the voice of Thy cataracts,* which refers to the rain from above. [9] V. *supra,* II, 4; V, 4.

forth (we-yifru) *salvation* (*ib.*)—in that they are fruitful (*parim*) and multiply[1]; *And let her cause righteousness to spring up together; I the Lord have created it* (*ib.*): this refers to the fall of rain. '*I the Lord have created it*': I have created it for the benefit and stability of the world.

14. R. Berekiah said: When there ascended contrition from the earth, then straightway IT WATERED THE WHOLE FACE OF THE GROUND.[2] That is consistent with R. Berekiah's view, for R. Berekiah said: *My doctrine* (likḥi) *shall drop* (ya'arof) *as rain* (Deut. XXXII, 2) means: let men break their stubbornness, and the rain shall immediately descend.[3] R. Menaḥma said in Rabin's name: In the Diaspora they are called 'the broken-necked people', for they break their necks [i.e. repent] and straightway rain descends.

15. How much rain must fall for one to recite a blessing?[4] R. Jose said in Rab Judah's name, and R. Jonah and Rab Judah said in Samuel's name: At the beginning, as much as will fructify [the earth]; at the end, even just a little.[5] R. Hiyya said in R. Joḥanan's name: At the beginning, sufficient to fructify; at the end, enough to wash the surface of the roof tiles. R. Jannai b. Ishmael said in the name of Resh Laḳish: At the beginning, sufficient to

[1] *Yifru* is derived from *parah*, to be fruitful.

[2] R. Berekiah, too, connects *ed*, cloud, with *ed*, destruction, and he translates thus Let there ascend from the earth the breaking of one's evil desires (or, the breaking of one's stubbornness against repentance), and then it shall water, etc

[3] He derives *ya-'arof* from *'araf*, to break the neck (cf Deut. XXI, 7: we-'arpu, *and they shall break the heifer's neck*); while 'neck' is a synonym for stubbornness in sin, cf. Ex. XXXII, 9, referring to the making of the golden calf; *It is a stiffnecked* (ḳeshe 'oref) *people*. Thus he translates: When My doctrine (or, teaching) shall break down their stubbornness, there shall be rain. [4] V. p. 107, n. 5.

[5] Theodor: 'At the beginning' and 'at the end' mean when the rain commences, and when it has already fallen respectively. Mah.: In the latter case the rain is more necessary, and so a blessing must be said even for a small quantity. 'E.J.: Because at the end the earth is already sated (therefore even a small rainfall is effective). 'Rashi'. 'At the end' means at the second rainfall (*reb'iah*); v. Ta'an. 6*b*.

fructify; at the end, enough to dissolve the bung [stopper].[1] But no matter how much rain descends the bung is not dissolved![2] But it must look as though it were dissolved.

How must one say the blessing?[3] Even as we learned: For rain and for good tidings one recites the blessing, '[Blessed is He] who is good and doeth good.'[4] R. Berekiah in the name of R. Levi derived this from the following: *As cold water to a faint soul, so is good news from a far country* (Prov. XXV, 25): just as for good news [one says], 'Blessed is He who is good and doeth good,' so for cold water [i.e. rain] one recites the blessing, 'Blessed is He who is good and doeth good.'[5] Rab Judah said: Thus did my father Ezekiel give praise: 'Thy Name be blessed, exalted, and magnified, for every single drop which Thou bringest down to us and keepest apart one from the other.'[6] R. Judan b. R. Simeon said: [He can keep them apart] because He causes them to fall in measure, [as it is written], *For He draweth away* (yigra') *the drops of water* (Job XXXVI, 27) ['*yigra'*' being used] in the sense of *And an abatement shall be made* (we-nigra') *from thy valuation* (Lev. XXVII, 18).[7]

R. Jose b. Jacob went up to visit R. Judan of Magdala[8] [in sickness], when he heard his voice blessing [God]: 'We must give thanks to Thy name countless times[9] for every single drop which Thou causest to descend for us, wherewith Thou requitest good to the unworthy.' Said he to him: 'Thus did R. Simon recite the blessing.'

R. Ze'ira said: Elsewhere we learnt: When cheapness rules in the world or a river [overflows and] supplies a country [with water], one recites: 'Blessed is He who is good and doeth good.'

16. AND WATERED THE *WHOLE* [FACE OF THE GROUND]. R. Eleazar said in the name of R. Jose b.

[1] The clay bung of a cask. [2] It is much too strong and firm.
[3] What is the formula? [4] Ber. 54*a*; *infra*, LVII, 2.
[5] R. Berekiah quotes the verse to explain why good tidings and rain are generally coupled in the sources.
[6] V. B.B. 16*a*. [7] V. *supra*, IV, 5. [8] Near Tiberias.
[9] Lit. 'a thousand thousand and ten thousand ten thousand.'

Zimra: Everything is blessed [by rain]: Commerce is blessed and merchants[1] profit.[2] R. Joḥanan b. Levi said: The feeble too are relieved. R. Ḥiyya b. Abba said: The sick too are relieved, for their limbs become more supple. Abimi, a member of [a sick visiting] society, used to visit the sick. When rain fell R Hiyya b. Ba would ask him· 'How are they [the sick] faring?' to which he would answer: 'They feel relieved.' Rabbi said: Even a precious stone feels [the rain].[3] The Rabbis said: Fish too feel it. R. Phinehas related: It once happened at Acco that a fish was caught and judged to weigh three hundred *liṭras*, yet when they weighed it it was only two hundred. An old fisherman who was present said to them, 'That is because rain has not fallen.' After rain fell they caught a fish and estimated it at two hundred *liṭras*, yet on weighing it they found it to be three hundred *liṭras!*

17. FACE OF THE GROUND. R. Eleazar b. Simeon said: The earth drinks only as far as its upper layer.[4] If so, what are the roots of the sycamore tree and the roots of the carob tree to do?[5] [Moreover], R. Hanina b. Iḳah and R Berekiah in the name of R. Judah said: The roots of wheat strike down fifty cubits into the earth; the soft roots of the fig-tree break through the rock? Said R. Levi: Once in thirty days the deep ascends and waters it. What is the proof? *I the Lord do guard it, I water it at certain moments* (Isa. XXVII, 3).[6]

R. Joshua b. Levi said: When the rain descends it makes a face for the ground.[7]

[1] M K. and 'Rashi'. Theodor prefers a different reading, בוטגריטין: the feeble-footed, those suffering with gout (*podagra*)
[2] Or, according to Th : are relieved.
[3] Its lustre increases.
[4] This follows from the phrase FACE OF THE GROUND.
[5] They go deeper than the crust.
[6] Viz once in thirty days E V. '*every moment*'.
[7] By covering it with plant life, whereas formerly it was bare. This too is deduced from FACE.

CHAPTER XIV (BERESHITH)

1. THEN THE LORD GOD FORMED MAN, etc. (II, 7). *The king by justice establisheth the land, but a man of gifts* (terumoth) *overthroweth it* (Prov. XXIX, 4). '*The king*' refers to the supreme King of kings, the Holy One, blessed be He; '*By justice establisheth the land*' means that He created the world on the basis of justice, as it is written, *In the beginning Elohim* (E.V. '*God*') *created* (Gen. I, 1)[1]; '*But the man of gifts overthroweth it*' refers to Adam, who was the *ḥallah*, the completion of the world,[2] while *ḥallah* is designated *terumah*, as it is written, *Of the first of your dough ye shall set apart* ḥallah (E.V. '*a cake*') *for a gift*—terumah (Num. XV, 20). R. Jose b. Ḳeẓarta[3] said: Like a woman who mixes her dough with water and separates *ḥallah* from the very centre, even so, at first, *There went up a mist from the earth and watered the whole face of the ground*, and then THE LORD GOD FORMED MAN OF THE DUST OF THE GROUND.

2. WAYYIYẒER (HE FORMED). This connotes two formations, viz. that of Adam and that of Eve.[4] [Another interpretation]: There is a viable birth at nine [months] and a viable birth at seven [months]. R. Huna said: When the fœtus is so formed as to be born at seven months,[5] and it is born either at seven or at nine months, it is viable; if born at eight months, it cannot live. When it is formed so as to be born at nine but yet it is born at seven months, it cannot live, and all the more so if it is born at eight months.[6] R. Abbahu was asked: 'How do we know that when the fœtus is fully developed at seven months it is

[1] *Elohim* being His name as a God of justice; v. *supra*, XII, 15.

[2] J. Shab. II explains: When a woman has poured water on the flour she separates *ḥallah*. Similarly, when God poured water on to the dust of the ground He separated *ḥallah*, which was man; v. also *infra*, XVII, 8.—The underlying idea is that man is the most sacred part of creation.

[3] Possibly. R. Jose the son of a laundress.

[4] This section gives various explanations why Scripture writes וייצר with two *yods*, instead of ויצר with one *yod*, as it is written in v. 19, in reference to animals.

[5] I.e. it is decreed at its formation that it should require nine months for its full development.

[6] So Th., M.K., 'Rashi,' and Mah. Y.T. and Y.M. translate differently.

viable?' 'From your own [language] I will prove it to you, replied he: 'Live, seven; go, eight.'[1]

3. WAYYIYẒER. There were two formations, [one partaking of the nature] of the celestial beings, [the other] of earthly creatures. R. Joshua said in the name of R. Ḥananiah, and the Rabbis in the name of R. Eleazar: He created him with four attributes of the higher beings [i.e. the angels] and four of the lower creatures [i.e. beasts]. [His attributes of the lower creatures are]: he eats and drinks, like animals; procreates, like animals; excretes, like animals; and dies, like animals. [His celestial attributes are]: he stands upright, like the ministering angels; and speaks, understands, and sees, like the ministering angels. But does not a dumb animal see? This one [man] can see from the side. R. Tifdai said in R. Aḥa's name: The celestial beings were created in the image and likeness [of God] and do not procreate, while the terrestial creatures procreate but were not created in [His] image and likeness. Said the Holy One, blessed be He: 'Behold, I will create him [man] in [My] image and likeness; [thus he will partake] of the [character of the] celestial beings, while he will procreate [as is the nature] of the terrestial beings.' R. Tifdai [also] said in R. Aḥa's name: The Lord reasoned: 'If I create him of the celestial elements he will live [for ever] and not die; while if I create him of the terrestial elements, he will die and not live [in a future life]. Therefore I will create him of the upper and the lower elements; if he sins he will die, and if he dies he will live [in the future life].'[2]

4. WAYYIYẒER: two formations, the good and the evil.[3] For if an animal possessed two [such] formations, it

[1] ζῆτα, the Greek letter *Zeta*, whose numerical value is seven, is phonetically like ζῆτω, let it live! while ἦτα (the letter η), whose numerical value is eight, sounds like ἴτω, lĕt it go! (i.e. die).
[2] For the whole passage v. *supra*, VIII, 11.
[3] This generally means the good and the evil side of man's nature. Here, however, the context shows that it means. discernment of what is good and what is evil—in a physical and material sense.

would die of fright on seeing a man holding a knife to kill it. But surely a man does possess these two faculties![1] Said R. Ḥanina (Ḥinena) b. Idi: *He bound up*[2] *the spirit of man within him* (Zech. XII, 1); for if that were not so, whenever a trouble came upon him he would remove and cast it from him.[3]

5. WAYYIYẒER: two formations, one in this world and one in the future world.[4] The School of Shammai and the School of Hillel disagree. The School of Shammai maintain: His formation in the next world will not be like that of this world. In this world skin and flesh are formed first, the sinews and bones last; but in the future he will commence with sinews and bones and finish with the skin and flesh, for thus it says in connection with the dead of Ezekiel: *And I beheld, and, lo, there were sinews upon them, and flesh came up, and skin covered them above* (Ezek. XXXVII, 8). Said R. Jonathan: We cannot learn from the dead of Ezekiel, for what did they resemble? A man who enters a bath: what he takes off first he puts on last. The School of Hillel said: Just as he is formed in this world, so will he be formed in the next world. In this world the skin and flesh come first, the sinews and bones last; so in the future will he begin with the skin and flesh and end with the sinews and bones. For thus says Job: *Wilt Thou not pour me out as milk and curdle me like cheese? Thou wilt clothe me with skin and flesh, and knit me together with bones and sinews* (Job X, 10 f.).[5] He does not say, 'Thou didst pour me out . . . and didst curdle me,' but '*Thou wilt pour me out . . . and wilt curdle me*'. It is not written here, 'Thou hast clothed me with skin and flesh,' but '*Thou wilt clothe me*', etc.; it is not written, '*And with bones and sinews Thou* hast *knit me together*,' but '*Thou* wilt *knit me together*'. Imagine a bowl full of milk: before rennet is put into it

[1] Yet he does not die of fright under similar circumstances.
[2] E.V. '*formed*'; *yozer* is derived here from *zarar*, to tie up.
[3] Sc. the spirit or soul within him which sustains life.
[4] At the resurrection. [5] Lit. translation. E.V. has the past, but the Midrash here points out that the *future* tense is used, not the past.

the milk is loose [liquid], but when rennet is put into it, the milk curdles and sets. Thus Job said: '*Wilt Thou not pour me out as milk . . . skin and flesh*' . . . *Thou hast granted me life and favour* (*ib.* 12).[1]

6. [THEN THE LORD GOD FORMED] THE MAN: for the sake of Abraham.[2] R. Levi said: It is written, *The greatest man among the Anakim* (Josh. XIV, 15): '*man*' means Abraham, and why is he called the greatest man? Because he was worthy of being created before Adam,[3] but the Holy One, blessed be He, reasoned: 'He may sin and there will be none to set it right. Hence I will create Adam first, so that if he sins, Abraham may come and set things right.' R. Abba b. Kahana said: In general practice, when a man joints a pair of beams [so that they meet] at a slope,[4] where does he place them? Surely in the middle of the chamber, so that they may support the beams in front and behind. Even so, why did the Lord create Abraham in the middle of generations? In order that he might bear the generations before and after him. R. Levi said: You bring a virtuous woman into the house of a corrupt one,[5] but you do not bring a corrupt woman into the house of a virtuous one.

7. '*AFAR* (OF THE DUST). R. Judah b. R. Simon said: [Read this] '*ofer* (a young man): he was created as a young man in his fulness.[6] R. Eleazar b. R. Simeon said: Eve too was created fully developed. R. Johanan said. Adam and Eve were created as at the age of twenty. R. Huna said: '*AFAR* (DUST) is masculine, while *adamah* (ground) is feminine: a potter takes male dust [coarse

[1] Cf. *supra* IV, 8; Lev. R XIV, 9.
[2] He interprets the def art: *THE* MAN, i.e., the outstanding man, viz , Abraham, cf. *supra*, XII, 9, *infra*, XV, 4, Ex. R. XXVIII, 1 *et passim*.
[3] V. Eccl. R. on Ch III, 11.
[4] Thus giving them greater strength than if they were laid flat.
[5] For the latter to learn from her.
[6] '*AFAR* (DUST) is superfluous, as Scripture could have stated, Then the Lord God formed man of the ground. By a play on words it is therefore connected with '*ofer* (עופר), a youth, strong man. 'Created in his fulness' means, with all his vigour and strength.

earth] and female earth [soft clay] in order that his vessels may be sound.[1]

A son of one of the notables of Sepphoris happened to die. Some say that he [the father] was a heretic, while others say that a heretic lodged with him. R. Jose b. R. Ḥalafta went up to visit him. He [the heretic], seeing him sitting and laughing, inquired, 'Why are you laughing?' 'We trust in the God of heaven that you will see his [the dead son's] face in the future world,' he replied. 'Have I not enough trouble,' he exclaimed, 'that you have come to trouble me more![2] Can broken potsherds be joined together? For is it not thus written, *Thou shalt dash them in pieces like a potter's vessel'* (Ps. II, 9)? He answered: 'An earthen vessel is made from water[3] and finished off with heat, while a glass vessel is made from fire and finished with fire; the one [sc. glass] when broken can be repaired, whereas the other [man] when broken cannot be repaired!'[4] '[The glass vessel can be repaired] because it is made by blowing,' said the other. 'Let your ears hear what your mouth speaks!' he retorted. 'If what is made with the breath of a mere mortal can be repaired, how much the more what is made with the breath of the Holy One, blessed be He!' R. Isaac said: It is not written, '*Thou shalt dash them in pieces like* earthen *vessels*,' but, '*Like a potter's vessels*,' which means, those which have not yet been baked, so that they can be reformed [when broken].[5]

8. OF THE GROUND (*ADAMAH*). R. Berekiah and R. Ḥelbo in the name of Samuel the Elder said: He was created from the place of his atonement,[6] as you read, *An altar of earth* (adamah) *thou shalt make unto me* (Ex. XX,

[1] R. Huna interprets the combination of 'AFAR and *adamah* in this verse [2] Or: has he not, etc. [3] Clay and mortar.
[4] Would you really maintain that broken man (i.e the dead) cannot be repaired, when you admit that a glass vessel can be.—In respect of an earthen vessel he argued that it naturally could not be repaired when broken, because the first step and the last in its manufacture are through mutually opposed elements, but man is rather like a glass vessel, as he proceeds to show. [5] Thus from the very verse he quoted he could have proved the possibility of resurrection. [6] The future site of the Temple.

21). The Holy One, blessed be He, said: 'Behold, I will create him from the place of his atonement, and may he endure!'

AND HE BREATHED INTO HIS NOSTRILS. This teaches that He set him up as a lifeless mass reaching from earth to heaven and then infused a soul into him.[1]

Because in this world [he was endowed with life] by breathing [therefore he is mortal]; but in the time to come he shall receive it as a gift, as it is written, *And I will put My spirit into you, and ye shall live* (Ezek. XXXVII, 14).[2]

9. THE BREATH OF (*NISHMATH*) LIFE. It has five names[3]: *nefesh, neshamah, hayyah, ruah, yeḥidah. Nefesh* is the blood: *For the blood is the* nefesh—E.V. '*life*' (Deut. XII, 23). *Ruaḥ:* this is so called because it ascends and descends[4]: thus it is written, *Who knoweth the* ruaḥ (E.V. '*spirit*') *of man whether it goeth upwards, and the* ruaḥ *of the beast whether it goeth downward to the earth* (Eccl. III, 21)?[5] *Neshamah* is the breath; as people say, His breathing is good.[6] *Ḥayyah* (lit. 'living')[7]: because all the limbs are mortal, whereas this is immortal in the body.[8] *Yeḥidah* (unique)[9]: because all the limbs are duplicated,[10] whereas this is unique in the body.

[1] Cf. *supra*, VIII, 1. [2] Therefore he will be immortal.
[3] Deut. R. II, 37 The five names may denote the different characteristics of the soul as the Rabbis understood it, or possibly some of these are conceived of as different things, v. Th and Y.T. *ad loc.*
[4] Just as the wind (*ruaḥ*) which travels about ('E.J).
[5] Th.: *nefesh* and *ruaḥ* are thus applied to both man and beast. With respect to *ruah*, the passage probably means. *ruaḥ* is that which ascends in the case of man and descends in the case of beast, as it says, *Who knoweth*, etc [6] Th. 'E J.: *neshamah* denotes the character (disposition), as people say, 'His character is good.'
[7] In the present verse: *And man became* nefesh ḥayyah (E.V. '*a living soul*'), *hayyah* possibly being treated as a substantive, not an adjective as in E.V. [8] Others: Because all the limbs are lifeless in themselves and this endows them with life.
[9] In Ps. XXII, 21. *Deliver my soul from the sword*, yeḥidathi (= *yeḥidah* + possessive suffix; E.V. '*mine only one*') *from the power of the dog*. Cf. also Ps. XXXV, 17.
[10] E g., eyes, ears, hands, feet. 'E J · The function of every limb is matched (or complemented) by that of another, whereas the function of this is unique and wholly distinct from the rest.

Thus it is written,[1] *If He set His heart upon man, if He gather unto Himself* ruho (*his spirit*) *and* nishmatho (*his soul*), *all flesh shall perish together, and man shall return unto the dust* (Job XXXIV, 14 f). R. Joshua b. R. Nehemiah and the Rabbis discussed this. R. Joshua b. R. Nehemiah interpreted it: '*If* God *set His heart upon* any *man*,'[2] his spirit (*ruho*) is already in His hand[3]; '*And if He gather his soul* (nishmatho) *unto him*' [sc. man], which means, into his body, then all men had already perished[4], but when man is sleeping the soul (*neshamah*) warms the body so that it should not waste and die. The Rabbis interpret: '*If* God *set His heart upon him*,' i.e. upon any man, his spirit (*ruḥo*) is already in His hand, '*And if He gather his soul* (nishmatho) *unto Himself*' above,[5] then all men had already perished, but that when man sleeps the soul (*neshamah*) warms man that he should not grow cold and die. R. Bisni, R. Aḥa, and R. Johanan in R. Meir's name said: The *neshamah* (soul) fills the body, and when man sleeps it ascends and draws life for him from above. R. Levi said in R. Ḥanina's name: It repeatedly ascends.[6] For every breath which a man takes[7] he must give praise to the Holy One, blessed be He. What is the reason? *Let every* neshamah (*breath*)[8] *praise the Lord* (Ps. CL, 6), which means, for every breath [let one praise Him].

10. AND MAN BECAME A *NEFESH ḤAYYAH* (E.V. '*LIVING SOUL*'). Judah b. Rabbi said: This teaches[9]

[1] This is not connected with the preceding, but a separate comment on *nishmath hayyim* (E.V. '*the breath of life*'), to show that life is dependent on the *neshamah* (Y.T., 'E J.) [2] To judge him.

[3] From the evening: When man goes to sleep he delivers his spirit (*ruaḥ*) to God.

[4] I.e. if He concentrated man's soul in one part of his body instead of permitting it to pervade all his limbs

[5] They translate, unto Him—to God.

[6] Not once only, but repeatedly ascends and re-enters man as he sleeps. Others: It returns to him (at each breath)

[7] Or possibly: every time that man recaptures his *neshamah*, which he does at each breath; v. preceding note.

[8] E.V. '*Let everything that hath breath*'.

[9] Sc. the word ḤAYYAH, lit., 'beast,' 'animal.'

that He provided him with a tail, like an animal, but subsequently removed it from him for the sake of his dignity. R. Huna said: He made him like a slave set free for himself,[1] who if he does not toil does not eat.[2] That is R. Huna's opinion, for R. Huna interpreted *The Lord hath delivered me into their hands* (bi-yede), *against whom I am not able to stand* (Lam I, 14): when my hands are at my own disposal[3] I am not able to stand: they toil day and night, yet do not attain a sufficiency.

R. Samuel, the son-in-law of R. Hanina, the colleague of the Rabbis, said: Here the *neshamah* (soul) is identified with *nefesh*,[4] whereas in another text the *neshamah* is equated with *ruaḥ*.[5] How do we know that the statement of the one text is applicable to that of the other and vice versa? Because 'life' (*hayyim*) is written in both texts, proving that they are analogous.[6]

[1] Presumably: set free, so that he is now responsible for himself. *Var. lec.* (as interpreted by commentaries) as a being eternally enslaved to himself—man is a slave to his wants.

[2] He interprets the verse thus: And man became obliged to keep his *nefesh*, i.e. soul, alive, *hayyah* meaning living.

[3] Reading *bi-yaddai* I.e. when I must bear my own responsibilities.

[4] Gen II, 7 *He breathed into his nostrils* nishmath hayyim (the *neshamah*—soul—of life) *and man became* nefesh ḥayyah (*a living soul*), thus *nefesh* is parallel to and the equivalent of *neshamah*

[5] Gen. XVII, 22. *All in whose nostrils was the breath of the spirit* (nishmath ruah) *of life*

[6] Hence the *neshamah* (soul) is both *nefesh* and *ruaḥ*

CHAPTER XV (BERESHITH)

1. AND THE LORD GOD PLANTED A GARDEN EASTWARD, IN EDEN (II, 8). The School of Jannai said: Why is the full Name[1] mentioned in connection with this planting? Because from the very beginning of its creation it required careful selection: before a tree develops out of its seed[2] one must determine its extent.[3]

Thus it is written,[4] *The trees of the Lord have their fill, the cedars of Lebanon, which He hath planted* (Ps. CIV, 16). R. Ḥanina said: At first they were like locusts' horns [i.e. small and puny], and then the Holy One, blessed be He, uprooted and replanted them in the garden of Eden[5]; hence it is written, '*The trees of the Lord have their fill,*' etc. Said R. Ḥanina: They have their fill in life, they have their fill in water, they have their fill in planting.[6]

R. Joḥanan said: The world was not worthy to enjoy the use of cedars. Why then were cedars created? For the sake of the Temple, as it is written, '*The trees* of the Lord *have* their fill, the cedars *of Lebanon*': '*Lebanon*' bears the same connotation as in the verse, *That goodly hill-country, and Lebanon* (Deut. III, 25).[7]

R. Samuel b. Naḥman said in R. Jonathan's name: There are twenty-four kinds of cedar,[8] the best are seven, as it is written, *I will plant in the wilderness the cedar, the acacia-tree,*

[1] V. *supra*, XIII, 3.
[2] Lit. 'its mother's womb'—the seed out of which the tree grows.
[3] Great care must be taken before a tree is planted to determine the best soil and position for it, to allow for the spreading of its branches and roots. Hence it requires all man's forethought, and therefore God's full name is used here to imply that He too, as it were, bent all His thought to determine where to plant this garden.
[4] This has no connection with the preceding statement
[5] He holds that '*And God planted*' instead of 'And God created' implies that they were already in existence and growing elsewhere, and God *re*planted them in the garden of Eden The verse quoted from the Psalms is also referred by him to the trees of the garden of Eden, for which reason they are called *the trees of the Lord*.
[6] I.e. whatever was planted from them would be like themselves.
[7] He interprets 'Lebanon' as a synonym for the Temple; cf. Lev R. I, 2.
[8] 'Cedar' is used here generically for trees.

and the myrtle, and the oil-tree; I will set in the desert the cypress, the plane-tree, and the larch together (Isa. XLI, 19). Rabbi said: They are but three[1]: *berosh* is the *beratha* (cypress); *tidhar* is the *adara*-tree[2]; *te'ashur* is the box-tree. Why is it called *te'ashur?* The Rabbis say: Because it is the most valuable (*me'ushar*) of all. To these they added another three: *alonim, armonin, almugin. Alonim* are oak-trees; *armonin* are plane-trees, and *almugin* are aloe-trees.

2. A GARDEN IN EDEN. R. Judah said: The Garden is larger than Eden, for it is written, *So that all the trees of Eden, that is*[3] *in the garden of God, envied it* (Ezek. XXXI, 9); and it is also said, *Thou wast in the Eden of the garden of God* (*ib.* XXVIII, 13). R. Jose said: Eden is larger than the garden, for it says, THEN THE LORD GOD PLANTED A GARDEN IN EDEN, etc. But surely it is written, *And a river went out of Eden to water the garden* (Gen. II, 10)?[4] On R. Jose's view, the drippings from a *beth kor* will water a *tarḳab*[5]; while on R. Judah's view, it is like a spring in the garden which waters the whole garden.[6] But R. Judah has two verses [to support his contention], whereas R. Jose has but one verse? Said R. Ḥanan of Sepphoris: The Holy One, blessed be He, illumined R. Jose's eyes and he found a verse supporting his view, viz. *And He hath made her wilderness* (midbar) *like Eden, and her desert* ('arabah) *like the garden of the Lord* (Isa. LI, 3).[7]

3. MIḲḲEDEM (E.V. 'EASTWARD'). R. Samuel b. Naḥmani said: You may think that it means before (*kodem*) the creation of the world, but that is not so; rather

[1] Those enumerated in the second half of the verse

[2] Jast.: a species of cedar, probably Spanish juniper.

[3] E.V. '*that were*', referring to the trees. But R. Judah relates 'that' to Eden.

[4] Implying that the garden was outside Eden, which contradicts R. Jose.

[5] *Beth kor* is a field requiring a *kor* of seed; *tarkab,* one requiring three *ḳabs* of seed; the latter is one-sixtieth of the former. He translates: And a stream of water drained off from Eden sufficient to water the garden which was in it, hence the garden was only one-sixtieth of Eden.

[6] Thus from the *smaller* area of Eden there flowed enough water to water the whole garden.

[7] *Midbar* is larger than '*arabah.*

it is, before Adam, for Adam was created on the sixth day, whereas the garden of Eden was created on the third. Hence it is written, *Yet God is my King, working salvation beforehand in the midst of the earth* (Ps. LXXIV, 12); it was a gracious act on the part of the Holy One, blessed be He, that He prepared my reward for me before ever I arose to labour.[1]

4. AND THERE HE SET (WAYYASEM) THE MAN. R. Judah and R. Jeremiah each commented. R. Judah said: He exalted him, [WAYYASEM having the same meaning] as in the verse, *Thou shalt in any wise set him* (tasim) *king over thee* (Deut. XVII, 15). R. Nehemiah said: He persuaded him [to enter and eat thereof], like a king who prepared a banquet and then invited guests.

THE MAN. For the sake of Abraham,[2] as it is written, *Thou knowest my downsitting and mine uprising, Thou understandest my thought afar off* (Ps. CXXXIX, 2). *'My downsitting'* means in the garden of Eden; *'My uprising'*—my expulsion thence; *'Thou understandest my thought afar off'*: for whose sake didst Thou determine to create me?[3] For the sake of him who came from afar [viz. Abraham], as it is written, *Calling a bird of prey from the east, the man of My counsel from a far country* (Isa. XLVI, 11).[4]

5. AND THERE HE PUT THE MAN WHOM HE HAD FORMED; as you read, *And* there *they are unto this day* (II Chron. V, 9).[5] R. Levi b. Zachariah said: Providing he stayed in this state of creation [i.e. without sin].

R. Isaac b. Merion said: It is written, *These are the generations of heaven*, etc. (Gen. II, 4). When their Creator praises them, who may disparage them; when their Creator lauds them, who may find fault with them? But they are comely and praiseworthy; hence it is written, *'These are*

[1] The fruits of the garden are man's reward for his toil, and they were created even before him. [2] V. *supra*, XIV, 6. [3] Cf. *supra*, VIII, 3 f.
[4] *From the east* is referred to Abraham (cf. *supra*, II, 3), who is likened to a bird of prey in point of swiftness; v. Rashi on Isa. *ad loc*
[5] Thus *there* implies for all time. Hence man was created to be permanently in the Garden of Eden.

the generation of the heaven and of the earth when they were created.'[1]

6. AND OUT OF THE GROUND MADE THE LORD GOD TO GROW EVERY TREE THAT IS PLEASANT TO THE SIGHT, AND GOOD FOR FOOD; THE TREE OF LIFE ALSO IN THE MIDST OF THE GARDEN (II, 9). It was taught: It was a tree which spread over all living things.[2] R. Judah b. R. Ila'i said: The tree of life covered a five hundred years' journey, and all the primeval waters branched out in streams under it. R. Judan said in the name of R. Judah b. R. Ila'i: Not only its boughs but even its trunk[3] was a five hundred years' journey.

7. AND THE TREE OF THE KNOWLEDGE OF GOOD AND EVIL (*ib.*). What was the tree whereof Adam and Eve ate? R. Meir said: It was wheat, for when a person lacks knowledge people say, 'That man has never eaten bread of wheat.' R Samuel b. Isaac asked R. Ze'ira: 'Is it possible that it was wheat?' 'Yes,' replied he. 'But surely TREE is written?' he argued. 'It grew lofty like the cedars of the Lebanon,' replied he.

R. Jacob b. Aḥa said: R. Nehemiah and the Rabbis are in conflict. R. Nehemiah said: [The benediction for bread is: 'Blessed art Thou . . .] who bringest forth (*ha-moẓi*) bread from the earth,' because He brought it forth in the past. The Rabbis maintain: [The benediction is . . .] 'bringest forth (*moẓi*),'[4] because He will bring it forth in the future,[5] as it is written, *There shall be an handful of corn* (pisath bar) *in the land* (Ps. LXXII, 16).[6]

[1] V. *supra*, XII, 1. It is quoted here to show that in man, too, God took pride, the phrase WHOM HE HAD FORMED being understood as though God pointed with pride at man, His handiwork.
[2] I.e. over the whole world. [3] Radal. M.K. translates: Not only the main branches, but even the side (minor) branches. [4] Without the def art.
[5] They differ on the bringing forth of bread itself, not mere wheat which must be made into bread. R. Nehemiah holds that *ha-moẓi* refers to the past, as God brought forth bread itself before Adam's sin, while the Rabbis say that *moẓi* must be said, which refers to the future, for it is then that God will cause bread to grow; cf Shab 30*b*.
[6] Rashi on Shab 30*b*: this implies corn as wide as a handbreadth, i.e. loaves of that width.

Lefeth[1]*:* two scholars, R. Ḥanina b. Isaac and R. Samuel b. Ammi, differ as to its meaning. One maintains: *Lefeth* means, it was *lo path*[2]; while the other maintains: In the future it will be *lo path.*

R. Jeremiah recited the blessing [for bread] before R. Zera: 'Who bringest forth (*ha-moẓi*) bread from the earth,' whereupon he praised him. Do we then rule as R. Nehemiah? surely not![3] But the reason was so as not to run the letters together.[4] If so, [are we to say] *ha-min ha-areẓ* ('that is from the earth')?[5]

R. Judah b. R. Ila'i said: It was grapes, for it says, *Their grapes are grapes of gall, they have clusters of bitterness* (Deut. XXXII, 32): those clusters brought bitterness [i.e. sorrow] into the world. R. Abba of Acco said: It was the *ethrog* (citron), as it is written, *And when the woman saw that the tree was good for food* (Gen. III, 6). Consider: go forth and see, what tree is it whose wood[6] can be eaten just like its fruit? and you find none but the *ethrog*. R. Jose said: They were figs. He learns the obscure from the explicit, and [the meaning of] a statement from its context, thus: This may be compared to a royal prince who sinned with a slave girl, and the king on learning of it expelled him from court. He went from door to door of the slaves, but they would not receive him; but she who had sinned with him opened her door and received him. So when Adam ate of that tree, He expelled him and cast him out of the garden of Eden; and he appealed to all the trees but they

[1] Something which goes with bread, vegetables (Jast.). Here we have an Haggadic dispute as to what the name connotes.

[2] Not bread; it was not food for man before he sinned, as bread fully seasoned grew out of the ground then. (Jast.)

[3] Seeing that the Rabbis, who are in a majority, differ from him.

[4] *Ha-moẓi* is immediately preceded by *ha-'olam* (the universe), and if *ha* is not interposed, *ha-'olam* and *moẓi* will sound like one word, since one ends and the next begins with a *mem* (מ).

[5] I.e. 'Who bringeth forth bread (*leḥem*) that is (*ha-min*)', etc., for otherwise *lehem* and *min* will be similarly run together. Yet we do not recite it thus, and the same should apply here. The difficulty remains unanswered.

[6] Heb. *'ez*, the same word as '*tree*' in the verse quoted, which is understood therefore as meaning that the tree itself, i.e. the wood, was good for food.

would not receive him. What did they say to him? Said R. Berekiah: 'Behold, a deceiver who deceived his Creator, who deceived his Master!' as it is written, *Let not the foot of presumption come unto me* (Ps. XXXVI, 12), which means, the foot that presumed against its Creator; *And let not the hand of the wicked shake*[1] *me* (*ib.*): i.e. let it not take a leaf from me.[2] But because he had eaten of its fruit, the fig-tree opened its doors and received him, as it is written, *And they sewed fig-leaves together*, etc. (Gen. III, 7). Of what species was that fig-tree? R. Abin said: It was the *berath sheva'*,[3] so called because it brought seven (*shiv'a*) days of mourning into the world.[4] R. Joshua of Siknin said in R. Levi's name. It was the *berath ali*,[5] because it brought lamentation and weeping into the world.

R. 'Azariah and R. Judah b. R. Simon in the name of R. Joshua b. Levi said: Heaven forfend [that we should conjecture what the tree was]! The Holy One, blessed be He, did not and will not reveal to man what that tree was. For see what is written: *And if a woman approach unto any beast, and lie down thereto, thou shalt kill the woman, and the beast* (Lev. XX, 16). Now if man has sinned, how did the animal sin? But [it is killed] lest when it stands in the market place people should say, 'Through this animal So-and-so was stoned.' Then if the Holy One, blessed be He, was anxious to safeguard the honour of his [Adam's] descendants, how much more his own honour![6]

[1] Deriving *tenidem* from *nadned*, to shake. E.V. '*drive me away*'.
[2] A tree is shaken when something is taken from it.
[3] A species of white fig, lit. 'a daughter of seven'.
[4] Death was decreed on its account, and for the death of a close relation one goes into full mourning for seven days.
[5] A different species; *ali* is connected here with *eli*, lamentation.
[6] Similarly, God did not reveal the nature of the tree that it might not be said, 'Through this tree Adam brought death into the world.'

Chapter XVI (BERESHITH)

1. AND A RIVER WENT OUT OF EDEN. R. Simon commenced: *Thou makest him strong for ever* (Job XIV, 20)[1]: the strength with which the Holy One, blessed be He, endowed Adam was intended '*for ever*', for all time; *But he goeth:* because he ignored God's wishes and followed the counsel of the serpent, *Thou changest his countenance*[2] *and sendest him away* (*ib*). R. Simon quoted: *With Him is counsel and might* (*ib.* XII, 13): when he [Adam] was at harmony with his Creator, he opened up the four river-heads with one thrust of the spade, and these are the four river-heads: AND A RIVER WENT OUT OF EDEN, etc.

2. THE NAME OF THE FIRST WAS PISHON (II, 11): so called because it makes flax (*pishton*) grow, and it flows with tranquillity (*be-shufi*).[3]

THAT IS IT WHICH COMPASSETH THE WHOLE LAND OF HAVILAH. Havilah was not yet in existence, yet you say, THAT IS IT WHICH COMPASSETH THE WHOLE LAND OF HAVILAH! But, *He declareth the end from the beginning* (Isa. XLVI, 10).

WHERE THERE IS GOLD: gold in its literal sense.[4]

AND THE GOLD OF THAT LAND IS GOOD (II, 12). Said R. Isaac: Fortunate is he who possesses it at home, and fortunate is he who possesses it on a journey[5]: R. Abbahu said: The Holy One, blessed be He, conferred a great boon upon the world, for a man changes one gold piece and can utilise it for many purposes. R. Simeon b. Lakish said: The world did not deserve to have the use of gold. Why then was gold created? For the sake of the Temple, as it is written, AND THE GOLD OF THAT LAND IS GOOD, which bears the same connotation as in the verse, *That goodly hill-country: Lebanon* (Deut. III, 25).[6]

[1] E.V. '*Thou prevailest for ever against him*'. [2] I.e. reduced his strength.
[3] PISHON, by transposing its letters, can be connected with *Shufi*.
[4] Not, as is stated *infra*, symbolically employed here for the Torah.
[5] This is R. Isaac's comment on the word *ṭob* (good); it is good for a man to possess it.
[6] Understood as a synonym for the Temple; cf. *supra*, XV, 1.

THERE IS BEDOLAḤ (E.V. 'BDELLIUM') AND ONYX STONE. R Aibu said: You might think that the *bedolaḥ* used by perfume-makers is meant[1]; therefore it says, *Its fellow* [i.e. parallel passage][2] *telleth concerneth it* (Job XXXVI, 33): just as the latter is a precious stone, so is the former a precious stone.

3. AND THE NAME OF THE SECOND RIVER IS GIHON; THE SAME IS IT THAT COMPASSETH THE WHOLE LAND OF CUSH (II, 13). Cush was not yet in existence, yet you say, THE SAME IS IT THAT COMPASSETH THE WHOLE LAND OF CUSH! But, '*He declareth the end from the beginning*'

AND THE NAME OF THE THIRD RIVER IS HIDDEKEL—E.V. 'TIGRIS' (II, 14): so called because it is a roaring stream (*ḥad be-kolo*).[3]

THAT IS IT WHICH GOETH TOWARD THE EAST OF ASSHUR. Asshur was not yet in existence, yet you say, THAT IS IT WHICH GOETH TOWARD THE EAST OF ASSHUR! But, '*He declareth the end from the beginning*'

AND THE FOURTH RIVER IS THE EUPHRATES. Rab said: The Euphrates is the mightiest of all rivers.[4] R. Ḥanina b. Igud and R. Joshua of Siknin in the name of R. Levi said: The Ubal is the most mighty of all rivers. But it is written, *As I was by the side of the great river, which is Hiddekel*—Tigris (Dan. X, 4)? That is because Daniel had two dreams, one by Ubal and the other by the Tigris, and as the Tigris appeared larger than Ubal, he calls it the large one.[5] But at the creation of the world this [river Euphrates] is not designated great; why then is it designated great elsewhere?[6] Because it flows on its way and encompasses Eretz Israel, of which it is written, *For what great nation is there, that hath God so nigh unto them*

[1] The sap of some tree (Th.).

[2] This derives *re'o* from *rea'*, a friend, companion. E.V. '*noise*'.

[3] So Th. and M K Lit. 'sharp in sound' Others translate differently.

[4] The word אוטירגטין may also imply that it is the mother and source of all rivers

[5] The passage contains a number of difficulties, and the text is probably corrupt, on the identity of Ubal v. Th. *ad loc.*

[6] In Gen. XV, 18, Deut. I, 7; Josh. I, 4.

(Deut. IV, 7)? Hence the popular saying: 'The king's servant is a king; cleave to heat and it will warm you.'[1]

Rab said to his son Ḥiyya: 'The Lybians are in Eretz Israel.'[2] 'Where do they dwell?' inquired he. 'By the ford of the river Bani,'[3] he replied. But Samuel maintained: As far as the river [Euphrates] flows is Eretz Israel. And what point is that? It is Tirbaḳnah.[4]

R. Judan and R. Huna disputed. R. Judan said: Perath (the Euphrates) is identical with Chebar[5]: Perath denotes that it grows (*parah*) and increases until it has to be traversed in ships; Perath denotes that its waters grow (*parin*) and increase[6]; Perath is so called because it goes on branching off into channels (*mafrid*) until it ends under the spade.[7] It is called Chebar because its waters come to an end.[8] Chebar, because its fruit[9] is large and cannot fall through a *kebara* (sieve). R. Huna maintained: The Euphrates and the Chebar are separate rivers.

R. Joshua of Siknin said in R. Levi's name: [The rivers] said to the Euphrates: 'Why is thy sound not audible?'[10] 'My deeds make me known,' it replied[11]; 'when a man plants a plant by me it matures in thirty days; when he sows a vegetable by me, it is full-grown in three days.' Said [the rivers] to the Tigris: 'Why is thy sound audible?' 'May

[1] Or (with a somewhat different text). associate with the governor and people will bow down to you.—Similarly, the Euphrates is called great because it compasses Eretz Israel, the home of a great nation.

[2] Th . I.e. they are considered as part of the Jewish Diaspora (*golah*) in Babylonia, which had a higher status than the Diaspora elsewhere. V. Ḳid. IV. [3] Which is east of the Tigris.

[4] On the upper reaches of the Euphrates northward. Bani is probably identical with Vanay. For the general identification of these names v. Ḳid. 71*b* and notes *ad loc.* in Sonc. ed. The present views of Rab and Samuel respectively are transposed there. [5] V. Ezek. I, 1.

[6] Th. and M K.: its waters cause fertility, the crops growing in abundance. Rashi in Bek. 53*b*: its waters increase even when there is no rain

[7] Th.: comes to an end because of the channels dug with the spade along its course to divert its waters. 'Rashi' a single spadeful of earth suffices to close it up.

[8] In the fields and orchards whither they are diverted, and so people say, 'The river has already (*kebar*) ceased' (commentaries).

[9] The fruit or produce which grows on the land this river irrigates.

[10] It is a quietly flowing river. [11] I need not shout my merits.

my voice be heard that I may be seen,' answered he. Said they to the fruit-bearing trees: 'Why is your sound not audible?' 'We do not need it,' they reply, 'as our fruits testify for us.' Said they to the non-fruit-bearing trees: 'Why is your sound audible?' 'Would that we could make our voice heard so that we might be seen,' they answered. R. Huna said: This is not the true reason; but because the food trees are heavy with fruit, their voice is not audible; and because non-fruit-bearing trees are light in fruit, their voice is audible, as it is written, *And his heart was moved and the heart of his people, as the trees of the forest are moved with the wind* (Isa. VII, 2).[1]

4. R. Menahma (others state, R. Tanhuma in the name of R. Joshua b. Levi) said[2]: The Holy One, blessed be He, will make the peoples of the world drink a cup of bitterness from the place whence this [river] issues. What is the proof? AND A RIVER WENT OUT FROM EDEN TO WATER THE GARDEN: This alludes to the four kingdoms, corresponding to the four heads [into which it was divided]. THE NAME OF THE FIRST IS PISHON: this is Babylon, so called with reference to the verse, *And their horsemen spread* (pashu) *themselves* (Hab. I, 8); also on account of the midget dwarf, who was smaller than a *pushka* (handbreadth).[3] THAT IS IT WHICH COMPASSETH THE WHOLE LAND OF HAVILAH: [this alludes to Nebuchadnezzar] who came up and surrounded the whole of Eretz Israel, whereof [sc. Eretz Israel] it is written, *Hope thou* (hohili) *in God; for I shall yet praise Him* (Ps. XLII, 6).[4] WHERE THERE IS GOLD: by this is meant the words of the Torah, which are '*more to be desired than gold, yea, than much fine gold*'.[5] AND THE GOLD OF THAT LAND IS GOOD: this teaches that there is no

[1] These sayings allegorically teach that if a man has real solid virtue to his credit he need not advertise his greatness.
[2] Text as emended by Th. and as in Lev. R XIII, 5.
[3] Viz. Nebuchadnezzar, according to Jewish legend.
[4] HAVILAH is thus connected with *hohili*.
[5] This is quoted from Ps. XIX, 1.

Torah (learning) like the Torah of Eretz Israel, and no wisdom like the wisdom of Eretz Israel. THERE IS BDELLIUM AND THE ONYX STONE: viz. Scripture, *Mishnah*, *Talmud*, *Tosefta*, and *Haggadah*. AND THE NAME OF THE SECOND RIVER IS GIHON: this alludes to Media, whose eyes Haman inflamed [with hate] like a serpent,[1] [so called] in allusion to the verse, *Upon thy belly* (geḥoneka) *shalt thou go, and dust shalt thou eat all the days of thy life* (Gen. III, 14). THE SAME IS IT THAT COMPASSETH THE WHOLE LAND OF CUSH, with allusion to the verse, *Who reigned from India even unto Cush*—E.V. *'Ethiopia'* (Est. I, 1). AND THE NAME OF THE THIRD RIVER IS ḤIDDEKEL: this alludes to Greece, which was sharp (*had*) and swift (*ḳal*) in its evil decrees, for she ordered Israel: Write upon the horn of an ox that ye have no portion in the God of Israel.[2] THAT IS IT WHICH GOETH BEFORE[3] ASSHUR: R. Huna said: In three things Greece was in advance of this wicked State [sc. Rome][4]: viz., in navigation, in the arrangement of camp-vigils,[5] and in language. R. Huna said in R. Aḥa's name: All kingdoms [which] are designated after the name of Asshur [are so called] because they enrich themselves (*mith-'ashroth*) at the expense of Israel. R. Jose b. R. Judah said: All kingdoms [which] are designated by the name of Nineveh are so called because they adorn themselves (*mith-na'oth*)[6] at the expense of Israel. R. Jose b. R. Ḥalafta said: All the kingdoms designated by the name of Miẓrayim (Egypt) are so called because they persecute (*meẓiroth*) Israel. AND THE FOURTH RIVER IS PERATH (EUPHRATES): that is Edom,[7] PERATH denoting that it upset (*hefirah*) and harassed His world; PERATH denoting that it was fruitful (*parath*) and increased through the blessing of that

[1] Th.: i.e. Media itself was not so very wicked, but Haman stirred up its evil passions. [2] *Supra*, II, 4.
[3] Heb. *ḳidmath*, here connected with *ḳodem*, before. E V. '*to the east of*'.
[4] To which Asshur is understood as an allusion (Y.T.).
[5] Jast Th.: in temples and in buildings.
[6] Nineveh is derived here from *na'eh*, beautiful, whence *mith-na'oth*.
[7] Edom is generally a synonym for Rome.

old man [sc. Isaac][1]; PERATH also denoting that I [God] will ultimately consign it to oblivion (*hafer*); [finally, it is called] PERATH on account of its ultimate destiny, as it is written, *I have trodden the winepress* (purah) *alone* . . . (Isa. LXIII, 3).[2]

5. AND THE LORD GOD TOOK THE MAN (II, 15). R. Judah and R. Nehemiah differed in their interpretations. R. Judah said: He exalted him, as you read, *And the peoples shall take them, and bring them to their place* (Isa. XIV, 2).[3] R. Nehemiah said: He persuaded him [to enter], as you read, *Take with you words, and return unto the Lord* (Hos. XIV, 3).[4]

AND PUT HIM INTO THE GARDEN OF EDEN. R. Judan and R. Berekiah each interpreted this differently. R. Judan said: He did actually give him repose, protect and delight him with all the trees of the garden of Eden. R. Berekiah said: [He put him there] *in order* to give him repose, protect and delight him with all trees of the garden of Eden.[5] WAYYANIHEHU (AND HE PUT HIM) means that He gave him the precept of the Sabbath, as you read, *And rested* (wayyanah) *on the seventh day* (Ex. XX, 11). LE-'ABEDAH (TO TILL IT): as you read, *Six days shalt thou labour*—ta-'abod (*ib.* 9). ULE-SHAMERAH (AND TO KEEP IT): *Keep* (shamor) *the Sabbath day* (Deut. V, 12). Another interpretation: LE-'ABEDAH ULE-SHAMERAH (TO TILL IT AND TO KEEP IT) is an allusion to sacrifices: thus it is written, *Ye shall serve* (ta-'abdun) *God upon this mountain* (Ex. III, 12); and, *Ye shall observe* (tishmeru) *to offer unto Me* (Num. XXVIII, 2).

[1] V Gen. XXVII, 39 f. Esau was regarded as the progenitor of Rome.
[2] This refers to Edom (Rome), the passage commencing: *Who is this that cometh from Edom* (*ib* 1)? [3] The passage deals with the future exalting of Israel. [4] Cf *supra*, XV, 4.
[5] M.K.: both connect *wayyanihehu* (E.V 'he put him') with *hanahah* (repose), *be-gan* (E.V. 'in the garden') with *haggen* (to protect), and Eden with *'adden* (to delight). R Judan holds that Adam actually enjoyed these benefits, while R. Berekiah maintains that they were potential only, but he never enjoyed them because of his sin. Mah . the controversy is the same as that recorded *supra*, XI, 2, as to whether God's punishment was deferred until after the Sabbath or not.

6. AND THE LORD GOD COMMANDED THE MAN, SAYING: OF EVERY TREE OF THE GARDEN THOU MAYEST FREELY EAT (II, 16). R. Levi said: He gave him six precepts[1]: AND HE COMMANDED (WAY-YEẒAW) alludes to idolatry, as you read: *Because he willingly walked after* ẓaw—i.e. idols (Hos. V, 11). THE LORD alludes to blasphemy, as you read, *And he that blasphemeth the name of the Lord* (Lev. XXIV, 16). GOD alludes to the [authority of] judges, as you read, *Thou shalt not revile God*—i.e. the judges (Ex XXII, 27). THE MAN: this alludes to bloodshed, as you read, *Whoso sheddeth man's blood* (Gen. IX, 6). SAYING alludes to incest,[2] as you read: *Saying: If a man put away his wife,* etc. (Jer. III, 1) OF EVERY TREE OF THE GARDEN THOU SHALT FREELY EAT: here He commanded him against theft.[3] The Rabbis interpreted the whole passage thus: AND THE LORD GOD COMMANDED. He said to him: 'What am I? God, [and I command] that I be treated as a God and not cursed ' How do we know [that Adam was forbidden] incest? [From the passage], *And cleave unto his wife* (Gen. II, 24), which implies, but not to his neighbour's wife, nor to a male, nor to an animal. OF EVERY TREE OF THE GARDEN THOU MAYEST FREELY EAT. R. Jacob of Kefar Ḥanan said: When does [an animal] become food, and when is it fit to be eaten? When it is ritually slaughtered. Thus He intimated [the forbidden character of] a limb torn from a living animal.[4]

BUT OF THE TREE OF THE KNOWLEDGE OF GOOD AND EVIL, THOU SHALT NOT EAT OF IT, FOR IN THE DAY THAT THOU EATEST THEREOF THOU SHALT SURELY DIE (MOTH TAMOTH) (II, 17): [this intimated] death for Adam, death for Eve, and death for his descendants.[5]

[1] *Infra*, XXIV, 5; Sanh. 56*b passim*. Generally seven are enumerated as being binding upon man before Revelation, the seventh being an injunction against eating flesh torn from a living animal Since Adam, however, was not permitted animal flesh at all, this is omitted here

[2] Which in its Hebrew usage includes adultery, pederasty, and bestiality.

[3] For the whole passage cf Sanh 56*b* and notes *ad loc.* in Sonc. ed.

[4] He probably interprets the verse thus: *akol tokel*, when it is food (*okel*) thou mayest eat it, v. *infra*, XVIII, 5; Sanh 58*a*.

[5] This is deduced from the doubling of the verb, which as usual is understood as an extension.

Chapter XVII (BERESHITH)

1. AND THE LORD GOD SAID: IT IS NOT GOOD THAT THE MAN SHOULD BE ALONE (II, 8). We learnt: By ten commands was the world created,[1] and these are they: *In the beginning God created* (Gen. I, 1); *And the spirit* (ruah) *of God hovered* (*ib.* 2)[2]; *And God said. Let there be light* (*ib.* 3); *And God said: Let there be a firmament* (*ib.* 6); *And God said: Let the waters be gathered together* (*ib.* 9); *And God said: Let the earth put forth grass* (*ib.* 11); *And God said: Let there be lights* (*ib.* 14); *And God said: Let the waters swarm* (*ib.* 20); *And God said: Let the earth bring forth* (*ib.* 24); *And God said: Let us make man* (*ib.* 26). Menahem b. R. Jose excluded, '*And the spirit of God hovered over the face of the waters,*' and included, AND THE LORD GOD SAID: IT IS NOT GOOD THAT THE MAN SHOULD BE ALONE. R. Jacob b. R. Kirshai said: A separate command was devoted to the wind.[3]

2. IT IS NOT GOOD. It was taught: He who has no wife dwells without good, without help, without joy, without blessing, and without atonement. 'Without good': IT IS NOT GOOD THAT THE MAN SHOULD DWELL ALONE. 'Without help': *I will make him a help meet for him.* 'Without joy'. *And thou shalt rejoice, thou and thy household* (Deut. XIV, 26).[4] 'Without a blessing': *To cause a blessing to rest on thy house* (Ezek. XLIV, 30).[5] 'Without atonement': *And he shall make atonement for himself, and for his house* (Lev. XVI, 11). R. Simon said in the name of

[1] Ab. v, 1; R H. 32*a*.
[2] These are interpreted as though they read · In the beginning God said, 'Let there be heaven and earth'; and God said, 'Let there be *ruah*' (E.V. 'spirit', but apparently rendered here 'wind')
[3] '*Ruaḥ*,' E.V. 'spirit'. M.K. explains. see the greatness of the wind, that its creation required a separate order! Thus he agrees with the first Tanna.
[4] *Household* is understood to refer to a wife, and the verse is interpreted: *And thou shalt rejoice* only when there is a '*household*' to rejoice with thee.
[5] Probably translated: *to cause a blessing to rest on* thee for the sake of *thy house,* viz. wife.

R. Joshua b. Levi: Without peace too, for it is said: *And peace be to thy house* (I Sam. XXV, 6). R. Joshua of Siknin said in the name of R. Levi: Without life too, for it is said, *Enjoy life with the wife whom thou lovest* (Eccl. IX, 9). R. Ḥiyya b. Gomdi said: He is also incomplete, for it is written, *And He blessed them, and called their name Adam*—i.e. man (Gen. V, 2).[1] Some say: He even impairs the Divine likeness: thus it is written, *For in the image of God made He man* (*ib.* IX, 6), which is followed by, *And you, be ye fruitful, and multiply* (*ib.* 7).[2]

3. I WILL MAKE HIM A HELP ('EZER) AGAINST HIM (KE-NEGDO)[3]: if he is fortunate, she is a help; if not, she is against him. R. Joshua b. Nehemiah said: If a man is fortunate, she is like the wife of Ḥananiah b. Ḥakinai; if not, she is like the wife of R. Jose the Galilean. R. Jose the Galilean had a bad wife; she was his sister's daughter, and used to put him to shame. His disciples said to him: 'Master, divorce this woman, for she does not act as benefits your honour.' 'Her dowry is too great for me, and I cannot afford to divorce her,' was his reply.[4] Now it happened once that he and R. Eleazar b 'Azariah were sitting and studying, and when they finished, the latter asked him, 'Sir, will you kindly permit that we go to your home together?' 'Yes,' replied he. As they entered, she cast down her gaze [in anger] and was making her way out, when he looked at a pot standing on the pot-range and asked her, 'Is there anything in the pot?' 'There's a hash in it,' she answered. He went and uncovered it, and found in it some chickens. Now R. Eleazar b. 'Azariah knew what he had heard,[5] and as they sat together and were eating he observed, 'Sir, did she not say it was hash, yet we have found chickens?' 'A miracle has happened,' replied he. When they finished he said to him: 'Master,

[1] Thus only both together are they 'man'.
[2] God's majesty, as it were, is impaired when man refuses to fulfil these functions. For the passage v. Yeb 62*a*: *infra*, XXXIV, 14.
[3] Lit translation of '*ke-negdo*'
[4] The dowry had to be returned on divorce.
[5] He understood the state of affairs

abandon this woman, for she does not treat you with proper respect.' 'Sir,' he replied, 'her dowry is too great for me and I cannot divorce her.' 'We [your pupils],' said the other, 'will apportion her dowry among ourselves,[1] so you can divorce her.' And they did so for him; they apportioned her dowry and had her divorced from him, and made him marry another and better wife. As a punishment for her sins she [the first wife] became married to the town watchman. After some time he was visited with affliction,[2] and she went about leading him round the whole town, begging in every district, but on coming to where R. Jose the Galilean lived she used to turn back. But since that man [her husband] was well acquainted with the town, he said to her, 'Why do you not lead me to the house of R. Jose the Galilean, as I have heard that he is charitably disposed?' 'I am his divorced wife,' she confessed, 'and I cannot bring myself to face him.' On one occasion they came begging in the vicinity of R. Jose the Galilean, when he began to maltreat her, and their cries brought a crowd and the whole town was shocked at them. Looking out, R. Jose the Galilean saw how they were being jeered at in the streets, whereupon he took and settled them in a room in his own house[3] and supported them for the rest of their lives, in accordance with the verse, *And that thou hide not thyself from thine own flesh* (Isa. LVIII, 7).

Another version of this story: R. Jose the Galilean was married to his sister's daughter, who treated him shamefully. Said his disciples to him, 'Divorce her.' 'I cannot pay her dowry,' he answered. 'We will pay it,' they said. So they gave it to him and he divorced her. She then married the town watchman. Later he became afflicted [with blindness] and she used to lead him by his hand through the streets of the town. But when she came to the street of R. Jose the Galilean she would stop. When he perceived this one day and a second day, he began beating her. Their cries brought down R. Jose, who said to him,

[1] Each will give something toward it.
[2] He became blind. [3] Or possibly: in a house of his.

'Why do you beat her?' 'She deprives me of the profit of this street every day,' was the reply. On hearing this R. Jose the Galilean took and settled them somewhere and supported them at his own expense, in accordance with the verse, '*And that thou hide not thyself from thine own flesh.*'

4. AND OUT OF THE GROUND THE LORD GOD FORMED (WAYYIẒER) EVERY BEAST OF THE FIELD (II, 19). R. Joḥanan b. Zakkai was asked: Since it is already written, *Let the earth bring forth the living creature* (I, 24), what is taught by AND OUT OF THE GROUND THE LORD GOD FORMED? [He replied]: The earlier verse refers to creation, whereas this treats of gathering them together,[1] as you read, *When thou shalt mass* (taẓur) *against a city a long time, in making war against it to take it* (Deut. XX, 19).[2] R. Aha said: When the Holy One, blessed be He, came to create Adam, He took counsel with the ministering angels, saying to them, '*Let us make man*' (I, 26). 'What will be the nature of this man?' they inquired. 'His wisdom will exceed yours,' He answered. What did the Lord do? He brought the animals, beasts, and birds before them and asked them, 'What should be the name of this?' but they did not know; 'of this?' and they did not know. Then He paraded them before Adam,[3] and asked him, 'What is the name of this?' 'An ox.' 'And of this?' 'A camel' 'And of this?' 'An ass.' 'And of this?' 'A horse.' Thus it is written, AND THE MAN GAVE NAMES TO ALL CATTLE, etc. (II, 20) Said He to him, 'And what is thy name?' 'It is fitting that I be called Adam, because I was created from the ground (*adamah*),' he replied. 'And what is My name?' 'It is fitting for Thee to be called *Adonai* (Lord), since Thou art Lord over all Thy creatures,' was the answer. R. Hiyya said: Thus it is written, *I am the Lord, that is My name* (Isa. XLII, 8), which means, That is My name by which Adam called Me. Then he paraded them again before him

[1] In order to name them, as the verse continues.
[2] Thus he renders: And the Lord God *assembled* all the beasts of the field (which were created) from the ground.
[3] Of course, after his creation.

in pairs, [male and female]. Said he, 'Every one has a partner, yet I have none': thus, BUT FOR ADAM THERE WAS NOT FOUND A HELP MEET FOR HIM! And why did He not create her for him at the beginning? Because the Holy One, blessed be He, foresaw that he would bring charges against her, therefore He did not create her until he expressly demanded her. But as soon as he did so, forthwith THE LORD GOD CAUSED A DEEP SLEEP TO FALL UPON THE MAN, AND HE SLEPT (II, 21)

5. THEN THE LORD GOD CAUSED A DEEP SLEEP TO FALL UPON THE MAN. R. Joshua of Siknin said in R. Levi's name: The beginning of a man's downfall is sleep: being asleep, he does not engage in study and does no work.[1] Rab said: There are three kinds of torpor (*tardemah*): the torpor of sleep, the torpor of prophecy, and the torpor of unconsciousness.[2] 'The torpor of sleep': THEN THE LORD GOD CAUSED A DEEP SLEEP TO FALL UPON THE MAN. 'The torpor of prophecy': *And it came to pass, that, when the sun was going down, a deep sleep fell upon Abram* (Gen. XV, 12). 'The torpor of unconsciousness': *And no man saw it, nor knew it, neither did any awake; for they were all asleep; because a deep sleep from the Lord was fallen upon them* (I Sam. XXVI, 12.) The Rabbis said: Also the torpor of folly, as it is written, *Stupefy yourselves, and be stupid! . . . For the Lord hath poured out upon you the spirit of deep sleep* (Isa. XXIX, 9 f). R. Ḥanina [or, Ḥinena] b. Isaac said: There are three incomplete phenomena: the incomplete experience of death is sleep; an incomplete form of prophecy is the dream; the incomplete form of the next world is the Sabbath. R. Abin added another two: the incomplete form of the heavenly light[3] is the orb of the sun; the incomplete form of the heavenly wisdom is the Torah.

6. AND HE TOOK ONE OF HIS RIBS (ẒAL'OTHAW).[4] R. Samuel b. Naḥmani said: He took one of his sides, as

[1] His point is: One causes man to fall, through sleep—a play on the verse.
[2] Or, a trance or catalepsy. [3] Cf *supra*, III, 6. [4] From *zela'*

you read, *And for the second side* (ẓela') *of the tabernacle, on the north side* (Ex. XXVI, 20).[1] But Samuel maintained: He took one rib from between two ribs, for it is not written, [*And He closed with flesh*] in its place, but '*And He closed with flesh in their places*.'[2]

R. Ḥanina, son of R. Adda, said: From the beginning of the Book until here no *samech*[3] is written, but as soon as she [Eve] was created, Satan[4] was created with her. While should one quote, *That is it which compasseth*—sobeb (Gen. II, 11),[5] answer him: the text refers there to rivers.[6]

AND HE CLOSED UP THE PLACE WITH FLESH INSTEAD THEREOF (TAḤTENNAH). R. Ḥanina b. Isaac said: He provided him with a fitting outlet (*naweh*) for his nether functions, that his modesty might not be outraged, like an animal.[7] Rabin [said]: Jannai and R. Jannai differed thereon.[8] One says: He provided him with a lock and a saddle cloth pressed over it,[9] so that he should not suffer pain when he sits. The other said: He provided him with cushions.[10] R. Ila and R. Ammi disagreed. One said: He instituted burial for him; while the other said: He made shrouds for him.[11]

7. A [Roman] lady asked R. Jose: 'Why [was woman created] by a theft?'[12] 'Imagine,' replied he, 'a man depositing an ounce of silver with you in secret, and you return him a *litra* [= 12 ounces] of silver openly; is that theft!' 'Yet why in secret?' she pursued. 'At first He

[1] V *supra*, VIII, 1. [2] Lit. translation, assuming the suffix in *taḥtennah* to be plural, and referring to the places of the two ribs.
[3] A Hebrew letter. [4] Here spelt with a *samech*: סטן, though usually שטן.—Satan is a synonym for the evil passions. [5] Heb. סובב.
[6] But this is the first time that the *samech* is used in reference to man.
[7] He interprets '*taḥtennah*' as *tahath na'ah*, seemly nether organs, i.e. He arranged that man should excrete through his nether part, and not from the side like an animal. [8] The text is doubtful. The translation follows Th., who suspects it to be corrupt If correct, it perhaps refers to R. Jannai the Younger and R. Jannai b R Ishmael.
[9] These are figurative terms for the lock of the buttocks (anus) and bones which close it in. [10] I e. the flesh of the buttocks.
[11] They both translate: and He closed up the flesh, i.e. the body, in the ground under him, and relate it either to the actual institution of burial or to the shrouds in which God decreed that man should be buried.
[12] God, as it were, stealing the rib.

created her for him and he saw her full of discharge and blood; thereupon He removed her from him[1] and created her a second time.' 'I can corroborate your words,' she observed. 'It had been arranged that I should be married to my mother's brother, but because I was brought up with him in the same home I became plain in his eyes and he went and married another woman, who is not as beautiful as I.'[2]

It once happened that a pious man was married to a pious woman, and they did not produce children. Said they, 'We are of no use to the Holy One, blessed be He,' whereupon they arose and divorced each other. The former went and married a wicked woman, and she made him wicked, while the latter went and married a wicked man, and made him righteous. This proves that all depends on the woman.[3]

8. R. Joshua was asked: 'Why does a man come forth [at birth] with his face downward, while a woman comes forth with her face turned upwards?' 'The man looks towards the place of his creation [viz. the earth], while the woman looks towards the place of her creation [viz. the rib],' he replied. 'And why must a woman use perfume, while a man does not need perfume?' 'Man was created from earth,' he answered, 'and earth never putrefies, but Eve was created from a bone. For example: if you leave meat three days unsalted, it immediately goes putrid.' 'And why has a woman a penetrating [shrill] voice, but not a man?' 'I will give you an illustration,' replied he. 'If you fill a pot with meat it does not make any sound, but when you put a bone into it, the sound [of sizzling] spreads immediately.' 'And why is a man easily appeased, but not a woman?' 'Man was created from the earth,'[3] he answered, 'and when you pour a drop of water on it, it immediately absorbs it[4]; but Eve was created from a bone,

[1] Th · He destroyed this creation. [2] Thus, had Adam seen Eve in the process of creation he would have found her repulsive.

[3] This story presupposes and proves another rendering of the verse, viz. 'And He delivered'. (Cf. Deut. XXIII, 16. *Thou shalt not deliver*—tasgir, of the same root as *wayyisgor* in the present verse) mankind (lit. 'flesh') into her power.—Th. and Y T.

[4] Thus man readily accepts an apology.

which even if you soak many days in water does not become saturated.' 'And why does the man make demands upon the woman, whereas the woman does not make demands upon the man?' 'This may be compared to a man who loses something,' replied he; 'he seeks what he lost, but the lost article does not seek him.' 'And why does a man deposit sperm within a woman while a woman does not deposit sperm within a man?' [He replied]: 'It is like a man who has an article in his hand and seeks a trustworthy person with whom he may deposit it.'[1] 'Why does a man go out bareheaded while a woman goes out with her head covered?' 'She is like one who has done wrong and is ashamed of people; therefore she goes out with her head covered.' 'Why do they [the women] walk in front of the corpse [at a funeral]?'[2] 'Because they brought death into the world, they therefore walk in front of the corpse, [as it is written], *For he is borne to the grave . . . and all* men *draw* after *him, as there were innumerable* before *him*' (Job XXI, 32 f)[3] 'And why was the precept of menstruation given to her?' 'Because she shed the blood of Adam [by causing death], therefore was the precept of menstruation given to her.' 'And why was the precept of "dough"[4] given to her?' 'Because she corrupted Adam, who was the dough (*ḥallah*) of the world,[5] therefore was the precept of dough given to her.' 'And why was the precept of the Sabbath lights given to her?' 'Because she extinguished the soul of Adam,[6] therefore was the precept of the Sabbath lights given to her.'[7]

[1] With the assurance that the same will be returned. A woman can give that assurance, since she has one husband only, but not a man, since he may have many wives.
[2] Sanh. 20*a*. [3] *Innumerable* before *him* is understood to refer to women, and in a *local*, not *temporal*, sense.
[4] V. Num. XV, 19 ff. The separation is naturally done by the woman who bakes the bread [5] V. *supra*, XIV, 1. [6] I.e. made him mortal.
[7] The attitude of Judaism towards woman is shown in these replies. In accordance with Scripture, she is charged with having brought death into the world through her disobedience, yet her punishment is not to be accursed, but on the contrary, hers is the privilege to emphasise the inviolate character of woman, to sanctify the bread one eats and spread the cheer of the Sabbath as symbolised by light.

Chapter XVIII (BERESHITH)

1. AND THE LORD GOD BUILT (WAYYIBEN) THE RIB, etc. (II, 22). R. Eleazar said in the name of R. Jose b. Zimra: She was endowed with more understanding (*binah*) than a man[1] For we learned elsewhere: The vows of an eleven-year-old maiden are subject to examination[2]; those of a twelve-year-old maiden are valid,[3] and we examine her in the whole of the twelfth year. The vows of a twelve-year-old youth are subject to examination; those of a thirteen-year-old youth are valid, and we examine him in the whole of the thirteenth year.[4] R. Jeremiah said in the name of R. Samuel b. R. Isaac: Some reverse it, because a woman generally stays at home, whereas a man goes out into the streets and learns understanding from people. R. Aibu—others state the following in R. Bannayah's name, and it was also taught in the name of R. Simeon b. Yoḥai—said: He [God] adorned her like a bride and brought her to Him, for there are places where coiffure is called building.[5] R. Hama b. R. Hanina said: What think you, that He brought her to him from under a carob tree or a sycamore tree![6] Surely He first decked her out with twenty-four pieces of finery[7] and then brought her to him! Thus it is written, *Thou wast in Eden the garden of God; every precious stone was thy covering, the carnelian, the topaz, and the emerald, the beryl, the onyx, and the jasper, the sapphire, the carbuncle, and the smaragd, and gold; the workmanship of thy settings and of thy sockets was in thee, in the day that thou wast created they were prepared* (Ezek. XXVIII, 13). The Rabbis and R. Simeon

[1] This connects '*wayyiben*' with *binah*, rendering and the Lord God made the rib into an understanding (intelligent) woman.
[2] Nid. 45*b*. She is examined as to whether she understands their import, and if she does, her vows are valid.
[3] She has reached maturity, and is assumed to understand their import.
[4] Thus a woman's understanding develops sooner than a man's.
[5] 'Coiffure' stands here for adornment in general Thus he translates: and the Lord God made the rib into a woman adorned
[6] As though she were an uncared-for foundling.
[7] The twenty-four are those enumerated in Isa. III, 18–24 q.v.

b. Lakish differ. The Rabbis say: There were ten canopies[1]; while R. Simeon b. Lakish maintained: There were eleven; R. Ḥama b. R. Ḥanina said: There were thirteen. R. Ḥama b. R. Hanina and R. Simeon b. Lakish both hold: Where we find a general term and a detailed enumeration, you regard the general term as additional to the detailed enumeration, and all are included [in the total]. Now '*Every precious stone was thy covering*' is a general term, while '*The carnelian, the topaz,*' etc., is a detailed enumeration: hence all are included [in the total], viz. '*Every precious stone was thy covering.*'[2] R. Levi and R. Simon,—one says that there were nine, while the other says ten. The view that there were ten agrees with the Rabbis; while he who says nine argues: the '*gold*' mentioned in this verse certainly does not allude to a canopy.[3] R. Aḥa b. Ḥanina said: He made the walls of gold and the covering of precious stones and pearls.[4] R. Eleazar b. Karsana said in R. Aḥa's name: He even made him hooks of gold.

2. R. Joshua of Siknin said in R. Levi's name: WAYYIBEN is written, signifying that He considered well (*hithbonnen*) from what part to create her. Said He: 'I will not create her from [Adam's] head, lest she be swelled-headed[5]; nor from the eye, lest she be a coquette[6]; nor from the ear, lest she be an eavesdropper; nor from the mouth, lest she be a gossip; nor from the heart, lest she be prone to jealousy; nor from the hand, lest she be light-fingered[7]; nor from the foot, lest she be a gadabout; but from the modest part of man, for even when he stands naked, that part is covered.' And as He created each limb

[1] One of every precious stone enumerated in this verse.—Since God set up so many canopies, He must certainly have adorned her as a bride.
[2] Ten stones are enumerated, indicating ten canopies. R. Simeon b. Lakish holds that '*every precious*', etc., indicates one more, while R. Ḥama b. R. Hanina regards '*precious*', '*stone*', and '*covering*' as three different canopies. [3] Since it is the last enumerated, v. B.B. 75*a*.
[4] Mah.: this does not refer to the canopies but to a special seat.
[5] Others read: light-headed, i.e. frivolous.
[6] Lit. 'a looker'—ogling men.
[7] Lit. 'one who touches things'—i.e. thievish.

He ordered her, 'Be a modest woman.' Yet in spite of all this, *But ye have set at nought all My counsel, and would none of My reproof* (Prov. I, 25). I did not create her from the head, yet she is swelled-headed, as it is written, *They walk with stretched-forth necks* (Isa. III, 16); nor from the eye, yet she is a coquette: *And wanton eyes* (*ib.*); nor from the ear, yet she is an eavesdropper: *Now Sarah listened in the tent door* (Gen. XVIII, 10); nor from the heart, yet she is prone to jealousy: *Rachel envied her sister* (*ib.* XXX, 1); nor from the hand, yet she is light-fingered: *And Rachel stole the teraphim* (*ib.* XXXI, 19); nor from the foot, yet she is a gadabout: *And Dinah went out*, etc. (*ib.* XXXIV, 1).

3. R. Ḥisda said: He built more chambers in her than in man,[1] fashioning her broad below and narrow at the top, so that she could receive child.

AND HE BROUGHT HER UNTO THE MAN. R. Abin observed: Happy the citizen for whom the king is best man![2]

4. AND THE MAN SAID: THIS IS NOW (ZOTH HA-PA'AM), etc. (II, 23). R. Judah b. Rabbi said: At first He created her for him and he saw her full of discharge and blood; thereupon He removed her from him and recreated her a second time. Hence he said: THIS TIME SHE IS BONE OF MY BONE.[3]

This is she of the previous occasion; this is she who is destined to strike the bell and to speak [in strife] against me,[4] as you read, *A golden bell*—pa'amon (Ex. XXVIII, 34); it is she who troubled me (*me-fa'amtani*) all night. All these remarks showed his amazement.[5]

[1] The reference is to the womb

[2] Here, God was 'best man' for Adam's bride.

[3] And no longer a mass of discharge and blood.—The translation follows Th.; cur. edd. THIS TIME SHE IS BONE OF MY BONE, (meaning) it is she who was created the first time Th, however, regards this as a separate statement.

[4] 'To strike the bell' is used metaphorically to bring charges and accusations

[5] *Pa'am* is given a twofold significance: (i) a bell, connecting it with *pa'amon*, and (ii) trouble, connecting it with the verb *pa'am*, to trouble, disquiet.—The translation and interpretation follow Th.

Resh Laḳish was asked: Why do not all other dreams exhaust a man, yet this [sc. a dream that intimacy takes place] does exhaust a man? Because from the very beginning of her creation she was but [formed] in a dream,[1] replied he.

BONE OF MY BONES, AND FLESH OF MY FLESH. R. Tanḥuma said When a man takes one of his relations to wife, of him it is said, BONE OF MY BONES, AND FLESH OF MY FLESH.

SHE SHALL BE CALLED, WOMAN (ISHAH), BECAUSE SHE WAS TAKEN OUT OF MAN (ISH). From this you learn that the Torah was given in the Holy Tongue.[2] R. Phinehas and R. Ḥelkiah in R. Simon's name said: Just as it was given in the Holy Tongue, so was the world created with the Holy Tongue[3]. Have you ever heard one say, *gini, ginia; itha, ittha; antropi, antropia; gabra, gabretha?*[4] But *ish* and *ishah* [are used]: why? because one form corresponds to the other.[5]

5. THEREFORE SHALL A MAN LEAVE HIS FATHER AND HIS MOTHER (II, 24). It was taught: If a man became a [Jewish] proselyte, and he was [previously] married to his paternal sister or to his maternal sister, he must, in R. Meir's opinion, divorce her. But the Sages maintain: He must divorce his maternal sister, but may keep his paternal sister, because Gentiles do not recognise paternity.[6] They raised an objection against him: Surely it is written, *And moreover she is my sister, the daughter of my father* (Gen. XX, 12)? He [Abraham] answered them in accordance with their own ideas,[7] was his reply. R. Ḥanan said: This

[1] Whilst Adam was sleeping.

[2] Sc. Heb. *ishah* is grammatically the fem. of *ish*, and Adam's remark is unintelligible unless he spoke in Hebrew

[3] I.e. Hebrew was the first language to be used.

[4] Gini (γυνή) and *antropi* (an assumed form for ἄνθρωπος) are woman and man respectively in Greek, *ittha* and *gabra* are the same in Aramaic. It is pointed out that these words lack the corresponding feminine or masculine forms, such as are seen in *ish* and *ishah*.

[5] This is regarded as evidence of the great antiquity of the language.

[6] V. Sanh. 58*a* and notes *ad loc.* in Sonc. ed.

[7] Since the Egyptians permitted a paternal sister. But in truth she was his niece, not his sister at all.

view was proved to us by the verse, THEREFORE SHALL A MAN LEAVE HIS FATHER AND HIS MOTHER, which means she who is related to his father and she who is related to his mother.[1] R. Abbahu objected: surely it is written, *And Amram took him Jochebed his father's sister to wife* (Ex. VI, 20)?[2] R. Simeon, the son of R. Abin, said: If so, the Israelites before Revelation did not even observe [the interdicts] of the children of Noah![3] Said R. Ila: But it was explained to us: THEREFORE SHALL A MAN LEAVE HIS FATHER AND HIS MOTHER means, the woman who is related *to himself* through his father and the woman who is related *to himself* through his mother.[4]

AND SHALL CLEAVE UNTO HIS WIFE, etc. R. Abbahu said in R. Johanan's name: The Noachides are culpable for [adultery with] married women, but not for [adultery with] betrothed women.[5] R. Jonah said in Samuel's name: If a harlot was standing in the street and two men had intercourse with her, the first is not culpable while the second is, on account of the verse, *Behold, thou shalt die . . . for she has been possessed by a man* (Gen. XX, 3).[6] But did the first intend to *acquire* her through cohabitation?[7] Hence this proves that cohabitation in the

[1] He renders. '*Therefore shall a man leave,*' i.e. divorce, his wife if she is related to *his father*, etc.

[2] If R. Meir's reason is as stated by R. Ḥanan, surely a father's sister is forbidden?

[3] This continues and emphasises R. Abbahu's objection.—'The children of Noah' or 'Noachides' is the technical designation for non-Jews, also frequently for Abraham and his descendants before the Giving of the Law.

[4] I.e. only a paternal or maternal *sister* is forbidden, not an aunt, such as Jochebed was to Amram, who is primarily related to his father or mother

[5] In ancient times marriage consisted of two stages: (i) *erusin* (betrothal), and (ii) *nesu'in* (marriage or home-taking). *Erusin* effected marriage, and the betrothed woman could not be free without a divorce; but cohabitation was forbidden until *nesu'in*. 'Betrothed' and 'betrothal' are used in this sense in the text and not in accordance with their modern connotation.

[6] Lit. translation. This proves that punishment is due merely because she had already cohabited with another, and not because she was married.

[7] Surely not.

case of the Noachides acquires, though that is not in accordance with [Jewish] law.[1] And how do we know that they have no divorce? R. Judah b. R. Simon and R. Ḥanan in R. Joḥanan's name explained this as meaning either that they have no law of divorce at all,[2] or that both can divorce each other.[3] R. Joḥanan said: His wife can divorce him and she gives him a double dowry.[4] R. Ḥiyya taught: If a Gentile divorced his wife and she went and married another, and then they both went and became converted [to Judaism], I do not apply to him the verse, *Her former husband, who sent her away, may not take her again to be his wife* (Deut. XXIV, 4).—Said R. Aḥa in the name of R. Ḥanina b. Papa[5]: Throughout the Book of Malachi *The Lord of hosts* is used, whereas here [in reference to divorce] we have *The God of Israel*, as it says, *For I hate putting away* [i.e. divorce], *saith the Lord, the God of Israel* (Mal. II, 16). It is as though one might say, His name has no bearing on divorce save in the case of Israel alone. R. Ḥanan said: When Nehemiah came up from the land of Exile [to Eretz Israel, he found that] the women's faces had been blackened by the sun, so that [their husbands] had gone and married strange [i.e. heathen] wives, while these would go round the altar weeping. Thus Malachi says, *And this ye do a second time* (*ib.* 13), i.e. ye actually repeat [the sin committed] at Shiṭṭim![6] *Ye cover the altar of the Lord with tears, with weeping, and with sighing* (*ib.*). The Holy One, blessed be He, said: 'Who will accept weeping and sighing from them?[7] Having robbed her, oppressed her, and deprived her of her beauty, thou castest

[1] In Jewish law intercourse acquires only when it is done with that purpose. [2] The husband can never divorce his wife

[3] I.e. they have no divorce as it is practised by Jews, where only the husband can divorce his wife but not the reverse.

[4] 'Rashi' and M K. Others: a divorce document.

[5] He reverts to the question, How do we know that a Gentile has no divorce? [6] V. Num. XXV, 1.

[7] Perhaps: who will pay heed to *their* (the husbands') tears, when they petition Me, seeing that they cause their own wives thus to weep? Or this may refer to the second half of the verse: *Insomuch that He regardeth not the offering any more* (*ib.* 13): Who would accept offerings from them, when they are responsible for their own wives' tears?

her away!' And how do we know that they are forbidden incest, like an Israelite? Because it says, AND HE SHALL CLEAVE UNTO HIS WIFE, which implies, but not unto his neighbour's wife; [UNTO HIS *WIFE*], but not to a male, nor to a beast.[1] R. Samuel, R. Abbahu, and R. Leazar in the name of R. Ḥananiah said: If a Noachide cohabits unnaturally with his wife, he is liable to death. R. Issi said: Every prohibition which is written in reference to the children of Noah is [technically] neither a positive nor a negative command.[2] Now how do you arrive [at the present law]?[3] [From the verse], AND HE SHALL CLEAVE UNTO HIS WIFE, AND THEY SHALL BE ONE FLESH: [that means that he shall cleave] to the place where both form one flesh.[4]

6. AND THEY WERE BOTH NAKED, AND WERE NOT ASHAMED—YITHBOSHASHU (II, 25). R. Leazar said: Three there were who did not remain in their tranquillity six hours, viz., Adam, Israel, and Sisera. Adam, for it is written, AND THEY WERE NOT ASHAMED (LO YITHBOSHASHU), which means, *lo ba'u shesh sha'oth* (six hours had not come). Israel: *And the people saw that Moses delayed*—boshesh (Ex. XXXII, 1), i.e. the six hours had come.[5] Sisera: *Why is his chariot so long* (boshesh) *in coming* (Judg. V, 28)? Every day he is wont to return at three hours or at four hours of the day, while to-day six hours have arrived (*ba'u shesh sha'oth*) yet he is not come![6]

[1] 'Incest' connotes here all forms of forbidden intercourse, and thus includes adultery, pederasty, and bestiality.—The whole of the preceding passage, which is really irrelevant, leads up to this piece of exegesis.
[2] Scriptural laws relating to Israelites are technically divided into these two categories; the violation of the former is not punishable at all (by Scriptural law), while that of the latter involves flagellation In the case of a Noachide, however, his prohibition ranks as neither, but is punishable by death (in theory only). [3] About unnatural intercourse
[4] I.e. only natural intercourse is permitted him. V. Sanh. 57*a*, 58*a* and *b*.
[5] V. Ex. R. XLI, 7
[6] In the case of Adam this means that from the time of his intercourse with Eve until his expulsion less than six hours elapsed; v. Sanh. 38*b*. Obviously it cannot have the same meaning in the case of Israel and Sisera, but that at the sixth hour on the day of their downfall they were no longer enjoying their usual tranquillity.—Mah.

AND THEY WERE NOT ASHAMED. NOW THE SERPENT WAS MORE SUBTLE, etc. Now surely Scripture should have stated, *And the Lord God made for Adam and his wife garments of skin* (Gen. III, 21)[1] [immediately after the former verse]? Said R. Joshua b. Karḥah: It teaches you[2] through what sin that wicked creature inveigled them, viz. because he saw them engaged in their natural functions, he [the serpent] conceived a passion for her.[3] R. Jacob of Kefar Ḥanan said: It is thus written in order not to conclude with the passage on the serpent.[4]

[1] The questioner holds that God made these garments *before* Adam sinned, and as a natural covering for their nakedness But in that case it should *immediately* have followed this verse

[2] Viz. the interpolation about the serpent

[3] Hence he sought to encompass Adam's death through sin.

[4] And the curse he brought Therefore '*And the Lord God made . . . garments*' is reserved for the ending, so as to conclude on the brighter note of God's care.

Chapter XIX (BERESHITH)

1. Now the serpent was more subtle, etc. (III, 1). *For in much wisdom is much anger, and he that increaseth knowledge increaseth sorrow* (Eccl. I, 18): Because man increases his wisdom he increases anger against himself, and because he increases his knowledge he adds to his sorrow.[1] Solomon said: Because I have multiplied wisdom to myself I multiplied anger against myself, and because I increased my knowledge I increased my sorrows. Did you ever hear anybody say: 'This ass went out and caught the sun [i e. ague], or caught a fever'?[2] And where is suffering prevalent? With human beings. Rabbi said: A scholar does not require a warning.[3] R Johanan said: It is like the fine linen garments which come from Beth Shean[4]: if they are even slightly blackened they are ruined; but as for the [coarse] linen garments which come from Arbel,[5] what is their value altogether?[6] R. Ishmael taught: According to the camel so is its load.[7] It often happens that two people enter a tavern; one orders, 'Bring me roast meat, white bread, and good wine,' while the other orders, 'Bring me bread and beets': the former eats and suffers afterwards, while the latter eats and does not suffer. Thus human ills weigh heavily upon the one but not upon the other. It was taught in R. Meir's name: According to the greatness of the serpent so was his downfall: because he was More subtle than all, he was *More cursed than all* (Gen. III, 14).

Now the serpent was more subtle than any

[1] Eccl. R I, 18.
[2] Animals, though lacking intelligence, are generally free from these ills.
[3] Sanh. 8*b*. Flagellation for violating a negative precept (v p. 146, n 2) is imposed only if the offender was previously warned, but in the case of a scholar this is unnecessary, as he is assumed to know that the act is forbidden Thus through increasing his knowledge he increases his sorrow, being punished where another would be exempt.
[4] Scythopolis in Galilee
[5] In Galilee, near Sepphoris.
[6] Very little, and a flaw does not matter. Similarly, the greater one is the greater is his punishment, and the same applies to the serpent, '*the most subtle*' of all animals.
[7] Sot. 13*b*.

BEAST OF THE FIELD. R. Hoshaya the Elder said: He stood out distinguished [erect] like a reed, and he had feet.[1] R. Jeremiah b. Eleazar said: He was an unbeliever.[2] R. Simeon b. Eleazar said: He was like a camel. He deprived the world of much good, for had this not happened, one could have sent his merchandise through him, and he would have gone and returned.[3]

2. AND HE SAID UNTO THE WOMAN: YEA (AF), HATH GOD SAID: YE SHALL NOT EAT OF ANY TREE OF THE GARDEN? R. Ḥanina b. Sansan said: Four commenced [their sin] with *'af'* (yea) and were destroyed through *'af'*.[4] And these are they: The serpent, the chief baker, the congregation of Korah, and Haman. The serpent: AND HE SAID UNTO THE WOMAN: YEA (AF), HATH GOD SAID, etc. The chief baker: *I also* (af) *saw in my dream* (Gen. XL, 16). The congregation of Korah: *Moreover* (af) *thou hast not brought us unto a land*, etc. (Num. XVI, 14). Haman: *Yea* (af), *Esther the queen did let no man come in*, etc. (Est. V, 12)

3. AND THE WOMAN SAID UNTO THE SERPENT: OF THE FRUIT OF THE TREES OF THE GARDEN WE MAY EAT (III, 2). Now where was Adam during this conversation? Abba Ḥalfon b. Koriah said: He had engaged in his natural functions [sc. intercourse] and then fallen asleep. The Rabbis said: He [God] took him and led him all around the world, telling him: 'Here is a place fit for planting [trees], here is a place fit for sowing [cereals].' Thus it is written, *Through a land that no man passed through, and where no man* (adam) *dwelt* (Jer. II, 6)[5]: i.e. Adam had not dwelt there.

BUT OF THE FRUIT OF THE TREE WHICH IS IN THE MIDST OF THE GARDEN, GOD HATH SAID: YE

[1] Cf. *infra*, XX, 1 [2] V. *infra*, XX, 1. [3] And none would have dared to attack it, owing to its great strength. Cf. Sanh. 59*b*

[4] Here is a play on words. *'Af'* means yea, moreover, too; they commenced their sin with the word *'af'*. *'Af'* also means wrath: they were punished through God's wrath [5] V. Ber. 3*a*.

SHALL NOT EAT OF IT, NEITHER SHALL YE TOUCH IT, LEST YE DIE (III, 3). Thus it is written, *Add not unto His words, lest He reprove thee, and thou be found a liar* (Prov. xxx, 6). R. Ḥiyya taught: That means that you must not make the fence more than the principal thing,[1] lest it fall and destroy the plants. Thus, the Holy One, blessed be He, had said, *For in the day that thou eatest thereof thou shalt surely die* (Gen. II, 17); whereas she did not say thus, but, GOD HATH SAID: YE SHALL NOT EAT OF IT, NEITHER SHALL YE TOUCH IT; when he [the serpent] saw her thus lying, he took and thrust her against it. 'Have you then died?' he said to her; 'just as you were not stricken through touching it, so will you not die when you eat it, but *For God doth know that in the day ye eat thereof*,' etc. (*ib.* 5).[2]

4. R. Tanhuma said: I was asked this question in Antioch.[3] I answered: It is not written, For the gods know (*yod'eim*), but, '*For God knows* (yodea').'[4]

R. Joshua of Siknin said in R. Levi's name: He [the serpent] began speaking slander of his Creator, saying, 'Of this tree did He eat and then create the world; hence He orders you, ye shall not eat thereof, so that you may not create other worlds, for every person hates his fellow craftsmen.' R. Judah b. R. Simon said: He argued: 'Whatever was created after its companion dominates it. Thus: heaven was created on the first day and the firmament on the second[5]: does it not bear its weight? The firmament was created on the second and herbs on the third: do they not interrupt its waters?[6] Herbs were created

[1] Adam, in order to emphasise the prohibition, added a fence to it by telling her that she must not even touch it (A R N). [2] Cf. Sanh 29*a*

[3] The end of the verse reads. *Then ye shall be as God, knowing good and evil; 'knowing'* is in the plural (*yode'e;* sing. *yodea'*), which implies more than one God.

[4] Hence the plural form of '*knowing*' refers back to *ye shall be*, not to God. Cf *supra*, VIII, 9. [5] V. *supra*, IV, 2, VI, 6.

[6] The herbs interrupt the flow of rain from the firmament Others read, 'does it (the firmament) not supply them with water'—thus being subservient thereto.

on the third day and the luminaries on the fourth;[1] the luminaries on the fourth and the birds on the fifth.' R. Judah b. R. Simon said: The *ẓiẓ*[2] is a clean bird,[3] and when it flies it obscures the orb of the sun.[4] 'Now you were created after everything in order to rule over everything; make haste and eat before He creates other worlds which will rule over you.' Hence it is written, *And the woman saw that it was good*, etc. (*ib.* III, 6): she saw [how plausible were] the words of the serpent.

5. THAT THE TREE WAS GOOD FOR FOOD, etc. R. Eleazar said in the name of R. Jose b. Zimra: Three things were said of the tree: it was good to eat, it was beautiful to the eyes, and it added wisdom, and the three were said in the same verse: AND THE WOMAN SAW THAT THE TREE WAS GOOD FOR FOOD: hence we learn that it was good to eat; AND THAT IT WAS A DELIGHT TO THE EYES: hence that it was beautiful to the eyes; AND THAT THE TREE WAS TO BE DESIRED TO MAKE ONE WISE (LE-HASKIL): hence that it added wisdom, as you read, *Maskil* (a song of wisdom) *of Ethan the Ezrahite* (Ps. LXXXIX, 1).

SHE TOOK OF THE FRUIT THEREOF, AND DID EAT. R. Aibu said: She squeezed grapes and gave him.[5] R. Simlai said: She came upon him with her answers all ready, saying to him: 'What think you: that I will die and another Eve will be created for you?—*There is nothing new under the sun* (Eccl. I, 9). Or do you think that I will die while you remain alone?[6] *He created it not a waste, He formed it to be inhabited*' (Isa. XLV, 18). The Rabbis said: She began weeping and crying over him.

ALSO is an extension[7]; she gave the cattle, beasts, and birds to eat of it. All obeyed her and ate thereof, except a certain bird named *ḥol* (phœnix), as it is written, *Then I*

1 And through the heat of the sun plant life matures and ripens.
2 Name of a bird; cf Ps. L, 11. 3 I.e. it may be eaten.
4 Thus it dominates the sun, as it were. 5 Cf. *supra*, XV, 7.
6 Jast. in public places (with none to care for).
7 In the passage, *And she gave also unto her husband*; cf. *supra*, I, 14.

said: I shall die with my nest, and I shall multiply my days as the ḥol—E.V. 'phœnix' (Job XXIX, 18). The School of R. Jannai and R. Judan b. R. Simeon differ: The School of R. Jannai maintained: It lives a thousand years, at the end of which a fire issues from its nest and burns it up, yet as much as an egg is left, and it grows new limbs and lives again. R. Judan b. R. Simeon said: It lives a thousand years, at the end of which its body is consumed and its wings drop off, yet as much as an egg is left, whereupon it grows new limbs and lives again.

6. AND THE EYES OF THEM BOTH WERE OPENED (III, 7). Were they then blind? R. Judan in the name of R. Joḥanan b. Zakkai, and R. Berekiah in the name of R. Akiba explained it by comparing them to a villager who was passing a glass-worker's shop and just when a basket full of goblets and cut-glass ware was in front of him he swung his staff round and broke them. Whereupon he [their owner] arose and seized him, saying to him, 'I know that I cannot obtain redress from you, but come and I will show you how much valuable stuff you have destroyed.' Thus He showed them how many generations they had destroyed.

AND THEY KNEW THAT THEY WERE NAKED, etc. Even of the one precept which they had possessed they had stripped themselves.[1]

AND THEY SEWED THE LEAVES OF THE FIG (TE'ENAH) TOGETHER. R. Simeon b. Yoḥai said; That is the leaf which brought the occasion (*to'anah*)—for death—into the world.[2] R. Isaac said: Thou hast acted sinfully: then take thread and sew![3]

AND THEY MADE THEMSELVES GIRDLES (ḤAGOROTH). R. Abba b. Kahana said: Not *ḥagorah* (a girdle) but ḤAGOROTH [plural] is written: now ḤAGOROTH implies shirts [or, embroidered girdles], robes, and linen

[1] They were naked of obedience.
[2] M.K.: which brought grief into the world; cf *supra*, XV *ad fin.*
[3] I.e. because of your sin you must henceforth toil.—Thus the immediate consequence of their sin was that they had to begin sewing.

cloaks; and just as these are made for man, so for woman are made girdles, hats, and hair nets.[1]

7. AND THEY HEARD THE VOICE OF THE LORD GOD TRAVELLING IN THE GARDEN TOWARD THE COOL OF THE DAY (III, 7). R. Ḥalapay said: We know [from here] that a voice may travel,[2] but we do not yet know that 'travelling' can apply to fire; and whence do we know that? From a verse elsewhere: *And the fire travelled down upon the earth* (Ex. IX, 23).

R. Abba b. Kahana said: Not *mehallek* but *mith-hallek*[3] is written here,[4] which means that it [repeatedly] leaped and ascended. The real home of the *Shechinah* was in the nether sphere; when Adam sinned it departed to the first *raḳia'* [firmament]; when Cain sinned, it ascended to the second *raḳia'*; when the generation of Enosh sinned, it ascended to the third; when the generation of the Flood sinned, to the fourth; with the generation of the separation [of tongues], to the fifth; with the Sodomites, to the sixth, with the Egyptians in the days of Abraham, to the seventh. But as against these there arose seven righteous men: Abraham, Isaac, Jacob, Levi, Kohath, Amram, and Moses, and they brought it down again to earth. Abraham [brought it down] from the seventh to the sixth, Isaac from the sixth to the fifth, Jacob from the fifth to the fourth, Levi from the fourth to the third, Kohath from the third to the second, Amram from the second to the first, while Moses brought it right down below. R. Isaac said: It is written, *The righteous shall inherit the land and dwell* (wayyishkenu) *therein for ever* (Ps. XXXVII, 29): then what are the wicked to do—are they to range in the air! What it means is that the wicked did not permit the *Shechinah* to dwell on earth.[5]

[1] ḤAGOROTH is plural, and it is understood to mean various kinds of garments.
[2] He applies 'travelling' to the 'voice', not to God.
[3] For 'travelling'. E.V. '*walking*'.
[4] The former belongs to the *pi'el* conjugation of the verb; the latter to the *hith-pa'el*. He understands the longer form as a frequentative.
[5] By reading *wayyashkinu* (and they caused—the *Shechinah*—to dwell) instead of *wayyishkenu*, and they dwell.

8. R. Berekiah said: For *wayyishme'u* (and they heard) read *wayyashmi'u* (and they caused to hear)[1]: they heard the voice of the trees saying, 'Lo the deceiver who deceived his Creator!'[2] R. Ḥanina b. Papa said: For *wayyishme'u* read *wayyashmi'u*: they heard the voice of the ministering angels saying, 'The Lord God is certainly going to those in the garden' [to punish them]. R. Levi and R. Isaac differed in their interpretation. R. Levi said: [The ministering angels were exclaiming], 'He of the garden is dead [and gone].'[3] R. Isaac said: [They exclaimed]: 'Does he still go about!'[4]

Said the Holy One, blessed be He, to them: ['He will die] LE-RUAḤ HA-YOM,'[5] i.e. *le-rewaḥ ha-yom* (after the day's respite): 'behold, I will give him the day's respite. For thus spoke I to him: "*For in the day that thou eatest thereof thou shalt surely die*" (Gen. II, 17) Now ye do not know whether that means one day of Mine or one day of yours. But behold! I will grant him one day of Mine, which is a thousand years,[6] and he will live nine hundred and thirty years and leave seventy for his children,' as it is written, *The days of our years are threescore years and ten* (Ps. XC, 10).

LE-RUAḤ HA-YOM. Rab said: He [God] judged him in the east side [of the universe]: LE-RUAḤ HA-YOM implies in the side (*ruaḥ*) which rises with the day [i.e. sun]. Zabdi b. Levi said: He judged him in the west side: LE-RUAḤ HA-YOM implies in the side which sinks with the day.[7] In Rab's view, He was severe toward him, just as the more the sun ascends the hotter it becomes. In Zabdi's view he was lenient toward him, just as the further the sun declines the cooler it grows.

[1] He relates this to the trees: the trees caused their voice to be heard.
[2] *Supra*, XV, 7. [3] He is doomed to die, reading *meth holek* (he goes as dead) instead of *mith-hallek*.
[4] When God has declared that disobedience would be followed by death. According to these interpretations the verse is rendered thus: And they heard the voice (of the angels declaring), etc. (either: 'O God, he'—man—'is dead and gone'; or, 'God is going to those in the garden'—to punish them; or, 'O God, does man still walk about!').
[5] E.V. '*in the cool of the day*' [6] V. Ps. XC, 4.
[7] As explained, east and west denote severity and mildness respectively.

AND THE MAN AND HIS WIFE HID THEMSELVES . . . AMONGST THE TREES OF THE GARDEN. R. Aibu said: His stature shrank to a hundred cubits.[1]

AMONGST THE TREES ('EẒ) OF THE GARDEN. R. Levi said: This was a sign for his descendants, that they would be placed within wooden (*'eẓ*) coffins.

9. AND THE LORD GOD CALLED UNTO THE MAN, AND SAID: WHERE ART THOU—AYEKKAH? (III, 9): 'How (*ek*) hast thou fallen![2] Yesterday [thou wast ruled] by My will, and now by the will of the serpent; yesterday [thou didst extend] from one end of the world to the other, whereas now [thou canst hide] AMONGST THE TREES OF THE GARDEN!'[3]

R. Abbahu said in the name of R. Jose b. R. Ḥanina: It is written, *But they are like a man* (Adam), *they have transgressed the covenant* (Hos. VI, 7). '*They are like a man* (Adam)' means like Adam: just as I led Adam into the garden of Eden and commanded him, and he transgressed My commandment, whereupon I punished him by dismissal and expulsion,[4] and bewailed him with *ekah* (how)! (I led him into the garden of Eden, as it is written, *And the Lord God took the man, and put him into the garden of Eden* (Gen. II, 15); and I commanded him: *And the Lord God commanded the man* (*ib.* 17); and he transgressed My commandment: *Hast thou eaten of the tree, whereof I commanded thee that thou shouldest not eat* (*ib.* III, 11)? and I punished him by dismissal: *Therefore the Lord God sent him forth from the garden of Eden* (*ib.* 23); and I punished him by expulsion: *So he drove out the man* (*ib.* 24); I bewailed him with *ekah* (how)! And said unto him: *ayyekah: ekah* is written [5]): so also did I bring his descendants into Eretz Israel and command them, and they transgressed My commandment, and I punished them

[1] V. *supra*, XII, 6, and notes *ad loc.*
[2] Lit. 'how is it with thee!' vocalising אַיֶּכָּה (*ayyekah*) as אֵיכָה (*ekah*, how! used in apostrophe). [3] Cf. *supra*, VIII, 1; XII, 6.
[4] Mah.: dismissal implies for a certain purpose, and hence, for a limited period,—here, until man should expiate his sin by hard work; whereas expulsion is more final, and does not imply a purpose or limit. [5] V. n. 2.

by sending them away and expelling them, and I bewailed them with *ekah!* I brought them into Eretz Israel, as it is written, *And I brought you into a land of fruitful fields* (Jer. II, 7); I commanded them: *And thou shalt command the children of Israel* (Ex. XXVII, 20), also, *Command the children of Israel* (Lev. XXIV, 2); they transgressed My command: *Yea, all Israel have transgressed Thy law* (Dan. IX, 11); I punished them by sending them away: *Send them away out of my sight, and let them go forth* (Jer. XV, 1); by expulsion: *I will drive them out of My house* (Hos. IX, 15); and I bewailed them with *ekah*: *Ekah* (how) *doth the city sit solitary* (Lam. I, 1).[1]

10. AND HE SAID: I HEARD THY VOICE . . . AND HE SAID: WHO TOLD THEE, etc. (III, 11 f)? R. Levi said: Imagine a woman borrowing vinegar,[2] who went in to the wife of a snake-charmer and asked her, 'How does your husband treat you?' 'He treats me with every kindness,' she replied, 'save that he does not permit me to approach this cask which is full of serpents and scorpions.' 'It contains all his finery,' said the other, 'he wishes to marry another woman and give it to her.' What did she do? She inserted her hand into it, and they began biting her. When her husband came he heard her crying out [with pain]. 'Have you touched that cask?' he demanded. Similarly, HAST THOU EATEN OF THE TREE, WHEREOF I COMMANDED THEE, etc.?

11. AND THE MAN SAID: THE WOMAN WHOM THOU GAVEST TO BE WITH ME, SHE GAVE ME OF THE TREE, AND I DID EAT (III, 12). Four there are upon whose flask the Holy One, blessed be He, knocked, only to find it a chamber-pot, viz.,[3] Adam, Cain, the wicked Balaam, and Hezekiah. Adam: AND THE MAN SAID, etc.; Cain: *And the Lord said unto Cain: Where is Abel thy brother* (Gen. IV, 9)? the wicked Balaam: *And God came*

[1] Lam. R. Proem V, 4.
[2] Poor women would go borrowing or begging vinegar, into which they dipped their bread (Radal). *Var. lec.*: a woman asking for leaven.
[3] A metaphor: God tested them by questions and found them wanting.

unto Balaam, and said: What men are these with thee (Num. XXII, 9)? Hezekiah: *Then came Isaiah the prophet unto king Hezekiah, and said unto him: What said these men?* etc. (II Kings XX, 14).[1] But Ezekiel was found superior to all of them: *Son of man, can these bones live? and I answered: O Lord God, Thou knowest* (Ezek. XXXVII, 3). R. Ḥanina b. Papa said: This may be compared to a bird in the hand of a hunter, who met a man and asked him: 'Is this dead or alive?' 'If you wish, it is alive; and if you wish, it is dead,' was the reply.[2] Thus: '*Can these bones live? And I answered: O Lord God, Thou knowest.*'

12. Thus it is written, *Then would I speak, and not fear Him; for I am not so with myself* (Job IX, 35). Job said: I am not like him [Adam]: he said, THE WOMAN WHOM THOU GAVEST TO BE WITH ME, etc.: thus he hearkened to his wife, but I did not hearken to my wife.[3]

R. Abba b. Kahana said: Job's wife was Dinah,[4] for he said to her: *Thou speakest as one of the vile women* (nebaloth) *speaketh* (*ib.* 10).[5] *What? shall we receive good at the hand of God, and shall we not receive evil* (Job *loc. cit.*)? Said R. Abba: It is not written 'shall I receive', but '*shall* we *receive*': shall we be upright in prosperity but not upright in times of evil![6] *For all this did not Job sin with his lips.* Said R. Abba: With his lips he did not sin, but with his heart he sinned.[7]

R. Abba said: Not *we-okalti* (and I did eat) but *wa-okel* is written: I did eat and I will eat.[8] R. Simeon b. Lakish

[1] V. Num. R. XX, 6 [2] Its life and death are in your hands.

[3] Translating: for I am not like (Adam, who said. '*The woman whom Thou gavest*') to be with me. When Job said that he would speak without fear of God, his friends pointed out that even Adam, though God's handiwork, could not stand before Him To which Job replied that he was not like Adam, who had obeyed his wife and sinned, whereas he had refused to obey her when she urged, *Blaspheme God, and die* (Job II, 9).

[4] Jacob's daughter.

[5] While of Dinah it is written. *Because he had wrought a vile deed* (nebelah) *in Israel in lying with Jacob's daughter* (Gen. XXXIV, 7).

[6] Th · the idea seems to be that Job's wife too was righteous, notwithstanding her counsel. [7] B.B. 16*a*.

[8] Different vocalisation of the same word changes its tense, thus: וָאֹכַל (*wa-okel*), and I did eat; וְאֹכַל (*we-okal*), and I will eat.

said: Adam was not banished from the garden of Eden until he reviled [God] and blasphemed, as it is written, *And he looked that it should bring forth grapes, and it brought forth wild grapes* (Isa. v, 2)[1]

AND THE WOMAN SAID: THE SERPENT BEGUILED ME (HISHI'ANI), AND I DID EAT. He incited me, he incriminated me, he beguiled me. 'He incited me,' as you read, *The enemy shall not incite* (yashi) *him* (Ps. LXXXIX, 23); 'he incriminated me,' as you read, *When thou dost lend* (tasheh) *thy neighbour* (Deut. XXIV, 10)[2]; 'he beguiled me,' as you read, *Now therefore let not Hezekiah beguile* (yashi) *you* (II Chron. XXXII, 15).

[1] Not only did it not produce the fine grapes of virtue and obedience, but it actually brought forth the wild grapes of blasphemy. V. also Num. R. XIII, 37.

[2] I.e. make him liable for repayment; here, he made me liable to punishment.

Chapter XX (BERESHITH)

1. AND THE LORD GOD SAID UNTO THE SERPENT: BECAUSE THOU HAST DONE THIS, CURSED ART THOU FROM AMONG ALL CATTLE, etc. (III, 14). *A slanderer shall not be established in the earth; the violent and wicked man shall be hunted with thrust upon thrust* (Ps. CXL, 12). R. Levi said: In the millennium the Holy One, blessed be He, will take the nations of the world and hurl them down into Gehenna, saying to them, 'Why did ye mulct My children?' and they will answer Him: 'Some of them were much addicted to slander.' Then the Lord will take both and hurl them into Gehenna. Another interpretation: '*A slanderer*' alludes to the serpent, who uttered slander against his Creator[1]; '*Shall not be established in the earth,*' as it is written, *Upon thy belly shalt thou go*;[2] '*The violent and wicked man shall be hunted*': not 'With a thrust' is written, but '*With thrust upon thrust*': Adam was cursed, Eve was cursed, and the serpent was cursed, as it is written, AND THE LORD GOD SAID UNTO THE SERPENT, etc.

2. *A froward man soweth strife, and a whisperer separateth familiar friends* (Prov. XVI, 28). '*A froward man*' refers to the serpent, who spake perversely of the Creator; '*And a whisperer*': [he is so called] because he whispered words against the Creator, viz. *Ye shall not surely die* (Gen. III, 4); '*Separateth familiar friends*': he separated the Prince of the world,[3] and because he separated the Prince of the world he was cursed: AND THE LORD GOD SAID UNTO THE SERPENT, etc.

AND THE LORD GOD SAID UNTO THE SERPENT, etc. With Adam He [first] discussed the matter, with Eve He [first] discussed the matter, but with the serpent He entered into no discussion.[4] The reason is that the Holy

[1] Cf *supra*, XIX, 4. [2] I.e. '*Shall not . . . earth*' means that the serpent will not walk upright, as hitherto; cf. *supra*, XIX, 1.
[3] He caused the *Shechinah* to depart. Cf. *supra*, XIX, 8.
[4] But cursed him forthwith.

One, blessed be He, said: 'This serpent is ready wi answers: if I discuss it with him, he will answer M "Thou badest them and I bade them: why did they igno Thy bidding and follow mine?"' Therefore He pr nounced his sentence summarily: hence, AND TH LORD GOD SAID UNTO THE SERPENT, etc.[1]

3. R. Ḥiyya taught: When conferring honour, v commence with the greatest; when subjecting to degrad tion, we commence with the smallest. When conferrir honour we commence with the greatest: *And Moses sa unto Aaron, and unto Eleazar and unto Ithamar, his so* (Lev. x, 6). But in subjecting to disgrace we commen with the smallest: AND THE LORD GOD SAID UNT THE SERPENT: BECAUSE THOU HAST DONE THI CURSED ART THOU . . . *Unto the woman He sai I will greatly multiply thy pain, etc. . . . And unto Adam I said: Because thou hast hearkened, etc.:* this teaches th [first] the serpent was cursed, then Eve, and finally Ada was cursed.[2]

All copulate face to back, save three who copulate fa to face, because the *Shechinah* spake with them, viz., Ma the serpent, and the fish. Whence do we know it of mar '*And unto Adam* (man) *He said: Because thou hast hearken unto the voice of thy wife.* Of the serpent? AND TH LORD GOD SAID UNTO THE SERPENT. Of the fish *And the Lord spoke unto the fish* (Jonah II, 11).

4. R. Hoshaya said: [The Almighty said to the serpent 'All that thou didst do was on account of this woma was not all thy labour for her sake?'[3] R. Judah b. R. Simo said in R. Hoshaya's name: From the beginning of tl Book [of Genesis] up to this point the Divine Name occu seventy-one times: this intimates that he [the serpen was judged by a full court.[4]

[1] Cf. Sanh. 29a. [2] Ber. 61a; Ta'an 15b.
[3] So that Adam might die and you could possess her, cf. *supra*, XVIII, *infra*, 5. [4] Sanhedrin—the great Court consisted of 71 member v. Num R. XIV, 12; Sanh 2a.

CURSED ART THOU, etc. R. Joshua of Siknin said in R. Levi's name· He cursed him with leprosy: for those scales [on the serpent] are leprosy.[1]

R. Eleazar said: Have you ever seen a man first beat his neighbour with a staff and then whip him again with a lash?[2] Thus, [when God declared,] CURSED ART THOU FROM AMONG ALL CATTLE, surely he is all the more cursed FROM AMONG ALL THE BEASTS OF THE FIELD![3] It was taught: Large clean cattle bear at nine months; large unclean cattle at twelve months; small clean cattle at five months; a dog at fifty days, a cat at fifty-two days, a swine at sixty days, a marten at seventy days, a deer and a fox at six months, and all other reptiles at six months; a lion, bear, leopard, elephant, ape, and the long-tailed ape[4] at three years, a serpent at seven years, and an adder at seventy years.[5]

A certain philosopher wished to know after what period of time a serpent bears. When he saw them copulating he took them and placed them in a barrel and fed them until they bore. When the Sages visited Rome he asked them how long it takes a serpent to bear. R. Gamaliel turned pale [with shame] and could not answer him. R. Joshua, meeting him and seeing his face wan, asked him, 'Why is your face wan?' 'I was asked a question,' replied he, 'and I could not answer it.' 'And what is it?' 'After how long does a serpent bear?' 'After seven years,' he told him. 'How do you know that?' he inquired? 'Because the dog, which is a wild beast,[6] bears at fifty days, while it is written, MORE CURSED ART THOU THAN ALL CATTLE, AND THAN ALL BEASTS OF THE FIELD: hence just as the cattle are seven times

[1] Ex. R. III, 13. [2] Which is lighter —Surely not!
[3] For cattle stand lower than beasts, since beasts are free, while cattle are under man's dominion (Th.). *Behemah* ('cattle') generally refers to domestic animals; *hayyah* ('beasts') to wild animals, beasts of the chase.
[4] *Var. lec* : hedgehog.
[5] Bek. 8*a*.—In this respect the serpent was more cursed than all living creatures. [6] In the ancient east dogs were semi-wild, not domesticated; v. *J E.* art. Dog.

more accursed than the beast,[1] so is the serpent seven times more accursed than the cattle.' At eventide he [R. Gamaliel] went and told it to him [the philosopher], who began to beat his head against the wall [in grief], crying out, 'All that for which I toiled seven years, this man has come and offered to me on the end of a cane!'[2]

5. UPON THY BELLY SHALT THOU GO. When the Holy One, blessed be He, said to him, UPON THY BELLY SHALT THOU GO, ministering angels descended and cut off his hands and feet,[3] and his cries resounded from one end of the world to the other. Thus the serpent comes to throw light upon the downfall of Babylonia and is itself illumined thereby, viz. *The cry thereof shall go like the serpent's* (Jer. XLVI, 22).[4]

R. Judan and R. Huna discussed this. One taught: [God said to the serpent]: 'Through thee My creatures go bent with grief (*geḥonim*) over their dead[5]; so thou too, UPON THY BELLY (GEḤONEKA) SHALT THOU GO.'[6]

R. Eleazar said: Even God's curse contains a blessing. For had not the Almighty decreed, UPON THY BELLY SHALT THOU GO, how could he flee to the wall and escape, or enter into a hole and escape?

AND EARTH [E.V. 'DUST'] SHALT THOU EAT. R Ḥilpi said: It does not mean every kind of earth; rather does it [the serpent] burrow down until it reaches a rock or virginsoil, and then it draws out fibres of earth and eats them.

[1] The unclean large cattle bearing at 12 months. He interprets the verse thus: more cursed art thou than all cattle, to the same extent that cattle are more cursed than beasts.

[2] An idiom for doing something with absolute ease.—Bek. 8*b*.

[3] Cf. *infra*, where it says that the serpent originally went upright like a man.

[4] The serpent's cry is employed as a simile to indicate the bitterness of Babylonia's downfall; but since the repercussions of the latter were world-wide, it follows in turn that the serpent's cry too filled the world. The verse quoted refers to *Egypt*, not Babylonia (V, 20), and elsewhere the reading is Egypt.

[5] Since but for the serpent there would have been no death.

[6] There is a lacuna in the text. Codex M. reads and the other said: Through thee My creatures go with (yearning) bowels over their dead, therefore thou too, UPON THY BELLY SHALT THOU GO.

R. Levi said: In the Messianic age all will be healed[1] save the serpent and the Gibeonite; the serpent, as it is written, *And earth shall be the serpent's food* (Isa. LXV, 25)[2]; the Gibeonite: *And they that serve the city, out of all the tribes of Israel, shall till it* (Ezek. XLVIII, 19), which means, all the tribes of Israel shall make them serve.[3]

R. Issi and R. Hoshaya in the name of R. Ḥiyya the Elder said four things: The Holy One, blessed be He, said to him [the serpent]: 'I made thee that thou shouldest be king over all cattle and beasts, but thou wouldst not have it; therefore, MORE CURSED ART THOU, etc.; I made thee that thou shouldest go upright like man, but thou wouldst not; hence, UPON THY BELLY SHALT THOU GO; I made thee that thou shouldst eat the food of man, but thou wouldst not; hence, AND EARTH SHALT THOU EAT; thou didst desire to kill the man [Adam] and take his wife: therefore, AND I WILL PUT AN ENMITY BETWEEN THEE AND THE WOMAN.' Thus what he desired was not given him, and what he possessed was taken from him. And we find the same in the case of Cain, Korah, Balaam, Doeg, Gehazi, Absalom, Adonijah, Uzziah, and Haman: what they desired was not given to them, and what they possessed was taken from them.[4]

6. UNTO THE WOMAN HE SAID: I WILL GREATLY MULTIPLY THY PAIN AND THY TRAVAIL, etc. (III, 16). R. Judah b. R. Simon and R. Joḥanan in the name of R. Eleazar b. R. Simon said: The Holy One, blessed be He, never spoke directly with a woman save with that righteous woman [viz. Sarah], and that too was due to a particular cause.[5] R. Abba b. Kahana said in R. Biryi's name: And what a roundabout way He went in order to speak with

[1] I.e. freed of their disabilities.
[2] This refers to the Messianic age; thus even then this curse shall lie upon it. [3] Who served hitherto—viz. the Gibeonites. Cf *infra*, XCV, 1.
[4] V. Soṭ 9*b*.
[5] Because she denied that she had laughed There is a lacuna in the text J. Soṭ. 21*b* reads: But it is written, UNTO THE WOMAN HE SAID: I WILL GREATLY MULTIPLY, etc.? Said R. Jacob of Kefar Ḥanin: (He spoke that) through an intermediary.

her! As it is written, *And He said: Nay; but thou didst laugh* (Gen. XVIII, 15). But it is written, *And she* [Hagar] *called the name of the Lord that spoke unto her*, etc. (*ib.* XVI, 13)? R. Joshua b. Nehemiah answered in R. Idi's name: That was through an angel. But it is written, *And the Lord said unto her*—Rebekah (*ib.* XXV, 23)? R. Levi said in the name of R. Ḥama b. R. Ḥanina: That was through an angel. R. Eleazar said in the name of R. Jose b. Zimra: That was through the medium of Shem [the son of Noah].[1]

I WILL GREATLY MULTIPLY (HARBEH ARBEH) THY PAIN AND THY TRAVAIL. R. Abba b. Zuṭra said in Samuel's name: Every [fœtus] that has [developed to the numerical value of] *harbeh*, I will multiply: i.e. a fœtus that has developed for two hundred and twelve days is viable.[2] R. Huna said: When the fœtus is so formed as to be born at seven months, and it is born either at seven months or at nine months, it is viable; if born at the eighth month, it cannot live. When it is formed so as to be born at nine, but is actually born at seven months, it cannot live, and all the more so if it is born at eight months. R. Abbahu was asked: How do we know that when the fœtus is fully developed at seven months it is viable? 'From your own language I will prove it to you,' replied he: 'Live, seven; Go, eight.'[3]

R. Berekiah and R. Biba in Samuel's name said: A woman can give birth only at two hundred and seventy-one, two hundred and seventy-two, or two hundred and seventy-three days, which is at nine months plus the days of conception.[4] Ḥiyya b. Adda was sitting before Rab, who was explaining a subject to him, but he could not grasp it. 'Why can you not grasp it?' he asked. 'Because my ass is about to foal, and I am afraid that it may catch cold and die.' 'Why does it worry you now?' he rejoined; 'sometimes it foals after a shorter period, sometimes after

[1] *Infra*, XLV, 10, *et passim*.
[2] The numerical value of הרבה is 212 (ה = 5, ר = 200, ב = 2, ה = 5 = 212). [3] V. *supra*, XIV, 2.
[4] A woman can conceive any time within three days of intercourse.

a longer period, but even when it foals after a shorter period, it gives birth not earlier than a lunar year [after conception], while if after a longer period, it gives birth not later than a solar year [after conception].'[1] Said he to him, 'But it is written, *Knowest thou the time when the wild goats of the rock bring forth? . . . Or canst thou mark the months that they fulfil'* (Job XXXIX, 1 f)?[2] 'That refers to the case of small cattle[3]; I am speaking of the case of large cattle,' he answered. 'But,' he rejoined, 'when Antoninus' herd were lying, and Rabbi's herd was made to copulate with them, some of them calved at the right time while others calved later?' 'There it was a case of clean [cattle],' he answered,[4] 'while here [we are discussing] an unclean animal.'

THY PAIN refers to the pain of conception; THY TRAVAIL, to the discomfort of pregnancy; IN PAIN, to the sufferings of miscarriages; SHALT THOU BRING FORTH, to the agony of childbirth; CHILDREN, to the suffering involved in the upbringing of children. R. Eleazar b. R. Simeon said: It is easier for a man to grow myriads of olives in Galilee than to rear one child in Eretz Israel.[5]

7. AND THY DESIRE SHALL BE TO THY HUSBAND. There are four desires: the desire of a woman is for none but her husband: AND THY DESIRE SHALL BE TO THY HUSBAND. The desire of the Tempter[6] is for none but Cain and his associates: *Sin coucheth at the door, and unto thee is its desire* (Gen. IV, 7). The desire of rain is for nought but the earth: *Thou hast remembered the earth, and them* [sc. the rains] *that desire her* (Ps. LXV, 10).[7] And the desire of the Holy One, blessed be He, is for none but Israel: *And His desire* (teshukatho) *is toward me* (S.S. VII, 11):

[1] But here it was well before even a lunar year; why then worry beforehand?
[2] I.e. even the months are not invariable, and it may bear before the usual twelve months.
[3] Their period cannot be known
[4] Their period is irregular.
[5] 'Er. 100*b*.
[6] Sin personified.
[7] E.V. '*and watered her*'.

We are weak (*tashim*), yet though weak [i.e. deficient in good deeds], we still hope (*meḳawim*) for the salvation of the Holy One, blessed be He,[1] and declare the unity of the Lord's Name twice daily, when we recite, *Hear, O Israel: The Lord our God, the Lord is One* (Deut. VI, 4).[2]

Another interpretation of AND THY DESIRE SHALL BE TO THY HUSBAND: When a woman sits on the birthstool, she declares, 'I will henceforth never fulfil my marital duties,' whereupon the Holy One, blessed be He, says to her: 'Thou wilt return to thy desire, thou wilt return to the desire for thy husband.' R. Berekiah and R. Simon in the name of R. Simeon b. Yohai said: Because she fluttered in her heart,[3] she must bring a fluttering sacrifice [i.e. a bird]: *She shall take two turtle-doves, or two young pigeons* (Lev. XII, 8).[4]

AND HE SHALL RULE OVER THEE. R. Jose the Galilean said: You might think that his dominion holds good under all conditions: therefore it is stated, *No man shall take the mill or the upper millstone to pledge* (Deut. XXIV, 6).[5] It is related that a certain woman of the house of Tabrinus[6] was married to a mean beggar.[7] When he came to the Sages he produced a golden candelabrum with an earthen lamp standing upon it, in fulfilment of the verse, AND THY DESIRE SHALL BE TO THY HUSBAND.[8]

8. AND UNTO ADAM HE SAID: BECAUSE THOU HAST HEARKENED UNTO THE VOICE OF THY WIFE (III, 17). R. Simlai said: She came upon him with her answers all ready, saying to him, 'What do you think? That I will die and another Eve will be created for you? *There is nothing new under the sun* (Eccl. I, 9). Or do you

[1] This is a play on תשוקתו, reading it as two words. תש (weak) and תקוה (hope). [2] S S. R. VII, 11.
[3] I.e. wavered in her faith; or ('Rashi') made a half-hearted vow of abnegation from her marital functions. [4] Nid. 31*b*.
[5] This refers to a woman debtor; one may not seize a pledge from a woman, *For he taketh a man's life to pledge* (*ib.*), i.e. the life that is destined to spring from her, while *ḥobel* (taketh to pledge) is perhaps translated: injureth. [6] A wealthy family of noble birth. [7] Text as emended (Th.).
[8] He, though lower in birth than his wife, yet ruled over her.

think that I will die while you remain idle? *He created it not a waste, He formed it to be inhabited'* (Isa. XLV, 18). The Rabbis said: She began weeping aloud (*be-ḳolah*) over him; hence it is written, AND UNTO ADAM HE SAID: BECAUSE THOU HAST HEARKENED UNTO THE VOICE (BE-ḲOL) OF THY WIFE: it is not written, 'To the *words* of thy wife,' but TO THE *VOICE* OF THY WIFE.[1]

AND HAST EATEN OF THE TREE: this supports the view of R. Abba of Acco that it was an *ethrog* (citron).[2]

OF WHICH I COMMANDED THEE TO SAY[3]: I commanded thee to forbid it to the cattle, beasts and birds[4]; yet not only didst thou not forbid them, but thou even gavest them and they ate thereof.

CURSED IS THE GROUND FOR THY SAKE, so that it will produce accursed things for you, such as gnats, midges, and fleas. Then let it produce [pests as large as] a camel for you? Said R. Isaac of Magdala: In that there would be benefit too, for he could sell them and enjoy the proceeds.[5]

9. IN TOIL (BE-'IẒẒABON) SHALT THOU EAT OF IT. R. Issi said: The difficulties of earning a livelihood are twice as great as those of childbirth. In respect of birth it is written, '*In pain* (be-'eẓeb) *shalt thou bring forth children*,' whereas in respect of a livelihood it is written, IN GREAT PAIN (BE-'IẒẒABON) SHALT THOU EAT OF IT.[6] R. Eleazar and R. Samuel b. Naḥman—R. Eleazar said: Redemption is likened to the earning of a livelihood, and the reverse: just as redemption [requires the working of] wonders [by God], so does the earning of a livelihood require the same; and just as the latter must be earned every day, so does redemption occur every day.[7] R. Samuel b. Naḥman said: It is even greater than

[1] Her voice raised in weeping. *Supra*, XIX, 5. [2] V. *supra*, XV, 7.
[3] E.V. '*saying*', v. next note. [4] Rendering: I commanded thee to say (to the animals too that it is forbidden). [5] V. *supra* V, 9.
[6] '*Eẓeb* and '*iẓẓabon* both belong to the same root, and the longer form implies intensification.
[7] God daily frustrates and redeems us from the evil machinations of our enemies (M.K.).

·demption, for redemption comes through an angel, hereas sustenance comes through the Holy One, blessed ᵉ He. Redemption comes through an angel, [as Jacob ɩid]: *The angel who hath redeemed me from all evil*[1]; hereas sustenance comes through the Lord: *Thou openest 'hy hand; and satisfiest every living thing with favour* ’s. CXLV, 16). R. Joshua b. Levi said: [Sustenance requires] ɩore effort than the dividing of the Red Sea, for it is ritten, *To Him who divided the Red Sea in sunder* (*ib.* ᴄXXVI, 13), and, *Who giveth food to all flesh* (*ib.* 25).[2]

10. THORNS (KOZ) ALSO AND THISTLES (DARDAR) HALL IT BRING FORTH TO THEE. ḲOZ is artichokes, hile DARDAR is cardoon.[3] Some reverse it: ḲOẒ cardoon, while DARDAR is artichokes, so called ecause it consists of rows (*darim*) above rows.[4]

AND THOU SHALT EAT THE HERB [GRASS] OF HE FIELD. R. Judah and R. Nehemiah [differ in their ɔmments]. R. Judah commented: Hadst thou merited , it would have brought forth of all the trees of the Garden f Eden for thy benefit; now that thou hast not merited, ıen THORNS ALSO AND THISTLES SHALL IT BRING ORTH TO THEE. R. Nehemiah said: Hadst thou merited , thou wouldst have taken herbs from the Garden of den and tasted in them all the delights of the world; ow that thou hast not merited it, THOU SHALT EAT HE HERB [GRASS] OF THE FIELD. R. Isaac said: This 'as said with reference to the present-day generations, 'hen a man repeatedly plucks his field and eats it [the ftermath] while it is still herbage. When Adam heard this, is face broke out into a perspiration [of anguish] and he ᵋclaimed, 'What! shall I be tied to the feeding-trough like beast!' Said the Holy One, blessed be He, to him, 'Since

Gen. XLVIII, 16.
The dividing of the Red Sea was for Israel only, whereas sustenance ust be provided for *all flesh* [3] A species of edible thistles (Jast.).
Artichokes grow in an imbricated form, i.e. overlapping each other like les or shingles These translations are based on the expression HALL IT BRING FORTH TO THEE, which implies edible growths

thy face has sweated, THOU SHALT EAT BREAD' (*ib.* 19).[1] R. Issi said: It had been better for him to remain with the first curse.[2]

IN THE SWEAT OF THY FACE SHALT THOU EAT BREAD. R. Abbahu said: This is one of the five things which are a favourable omen for an invalid, viz.: sneezing, perspiring, sleep, a dream, and semen. Sneezing, as it is written, *His sneezings flash forth light* (Job XLI, 10); sweat: IN THE SWEAT OF THY FACE SHALT THOU EAT BREAD[3]; sleep: *I had slept: then it were well with me* (Job III, 13)[4]; a dream: *Wherefore make me dream* [E V. *'recover Thou me'*] *and make me live* (Isa. XXXVIII, 16); semen: *He shall see seed* [i.e semen], *and prolong his days* (*ib.* LIII, 10). Our Rabbis of Cæsarea said: Also the natural motion of the bowels. What is the proof? *When the waste matter*[5] *is speedily eliminated, he* [the sick person] *shall not die* (*ib.* LI, 14). R. Haggai said in R. Isaac's name: Providing that *His bread shall not fail* (*ib.*).[6]

TILL THOU RETURN UNTO THE GROUND; FOR OUT OF IT WAST THOU TAKEN. Said He to him: 'Is not the handful of dust whence thou wast created as unlawful spoil in thy possession?'[7]

FOR DUST THOU ART, AND UNTO DUST SHALT THOU RETURN. R. Simeon b. Yoḥai said: Here Scripture hints at resurrection, for it does not say, FOR DUST THOU ART, AND UNTO DUST SHALT THOU go, but SHALT THOU RETURN.[8]

11. AND THE MAN CALLED HIS WIFE'S NAME EVE—ḤAWWAH, i.e. life (III, 2). She was given to him for an adviser, but she played the eavesdropper like the

[1] Translating: *On account of* (E.V 'in') *the sweat of thy face*, etc.
[2] Then he would have had less trouble in finding his food.—Pes. 118*a*.
[3] I e. it is a sign of returning health.
[4] E V. *'Then had I been at rest.'*
[5] This is a play on words, צעה being read as צואה. E.V. *'He that is bent down shall speedily be loosed'*. [6] I e. that he has an appetite for food.
[7] Which thou must give back to the earth.
[8] Which he interprets: thou shalt go to the dust, yet shalt thou return—at the resurrection.

serpent.[1] [Another interpretation]: He showed her[2] how many generations she had destroyed. R. Aḥa interpreted it: The serpent was thy [Eve's] serpent [i.e. seducer], and thou art Adam's serpent.[3]

BECAUSE SHE WAS THE MOTHER (EM) OF ALL LIVING. R. Simeon b. Eleazar said: That means that she is associated with (*'im*) all living. It was taught: If [her husband] becomes wealthy, she rises with him; if he becomes poor, she does not descend with him.[4] R. Simon said: THE MOTHER OF ALL LIVING means, the mother of all life.[5] For R. Simon said: Throughout the entire one hundred and thirty years during which Adam held aloof from Eve the male demons were made ardent by her and she bore, while the female demons were inflamed by Adam and they bore, as it is written, *If he commit iniquity, I will chasten him with the rod of men, and with the afflictions of the children of man*—Adam (II Sam. VII, 14), which means, the children of the first man.[6] (The reason for the view that house spirits are benevolent is because they dwell with him [man],[7] while the opinion that they are harmful is based on the fact that they understand man's evil inclinations.[8] He who maintains that the spirits of the field are benevolent does so because they do not grow up

[1] This is a play on '*hawwah*', which is connected here with both *hawweh* (sc. *da'ath*, an opinion), to show forth, i e. state (an opinion), and *hiwya*, a serpent.—As the serpent had eavesdropped when God commanded Adam to refrain from the forbidden tree, so did she in turn listen to the serpent when he incited her to disobedience—and persuaded Adam accordingly. Cur. edd.: but she counselled him as the serpent (bade her).

[2] V. preceding note. [3] *Infra*, XXII, 2.

[4] A wife must perform certain duties, but if she brings some servants with her as a dowry, she is free from them. Now if her husband becomes wealthy and buys them himself, she is likewise free; thus she rises with him. If on the other hand he becomes poor and must sell the slaves she brought as her dowry, she can still refuse to work, as she does not descend with him. Thus she is associated with him in living, sc. wealth, but not in death, poverty being so regarded.—Cf. Keth. 48*a*, 61*a*.

[5] Even of demons. *Infra*, XXIV; v. 'Er. 18*b*.

[6] *Afflictions* is understood to mean demons, and is in apposition to *the children of man*.

[7] And benefit from him: therefore they return good for good.

[8] Hence they know his weakness and vulnerability to harm.—Our evil inclinations lay us open to attack and hurt.

with him, while as for the view that they are harmful, the reason is because they do not comprehend his evil inclinations.)[1]

12. AND THE LORD GOD MADE FOR ADAM AND HIS WIFE GARMENTS OF SKIN ('OR), AND CLOTHED THEM (III, 21). In R. Meir's Torah it was found written, '*Garments of light* (or)'[2]: this refers to Adam's garments, which were like a torch [shedding radiance], broad at the bottom and narrow at the top. Isaac the Elder said: They were as smooth as a finger-nail and as beautiful as a jewel. R. Joḥanan said: They were like the fine linen garments which come from Bethshean,[3] GARMENTS OF SKIN meaning those that are nearest to the skin. R. Eleazar said: They were of goats' skin. R. Joshua said: Of hares' skin. R. Jose b. R. Ḥanina said: It was a garment made of skin with its wool. Resh Laḳish said: It was of Circassian wool, and these were used [later] by first-born children.[4] R. Samuel b. Naḥman said: [They were made from] the wool of camels and the wool of hares, GARMENTS OF SKIN meaning those which are produced from the skin.[5]

R. Levi said: The Torah teaches you here a rule of worldly wisdom: spend according to your means on food; less than you can afford on clothing, but more than you can afford on a dwelling. Spend according to your means on food, as it is written, *Of every tree of the garden thou mayest freely eat* (Gen. II, 16). Less than you can afford on clothing: AND THE LORD GOD MADE . . . GARMENTS OF SKIN, AND CLOTHED THEM.[6] More than you can afford on a dwelling: for lo! they were but two, yet they dwelt in the whole world.[7]

[1] M K. transposes 'benevolent' and 'harmful', which certainly improves the sense.
[2] I.e. אור light, instead of עור skin. [3] V. *supra*, XIX, 1.
[4] When they used to perform the sacrificial service, before the priests were chosen for it; v. *infra*, LXIII, 13; Num. R. IV, 8.
[5] Viz. the wool that comes off it.
[6] I.e. only simple, not expensive garments.
[7] Cf. Pes. 114*a*, Ḥul. 84*b*.

Chapter XXI (BERESHITH)

1. AND THE LORD GOD SAID: BEHOLD, THE MAN IS BECOME AS ONE OF US (III, 22). It is written, *Then I heard a holy one speaking; and another holy one said unto that certain one who spoke*, etc. (Dan. VIII, 13). '*One*' refers to the Holy One, blessed be He, as it is written, *The Lord our God, the Lord is one* (Deut. VI, 4). '*Holy*'—because all proclaim before Him, 'Holy!' '*Speaking*': pronouncing severe decrees against His creatures, viz: *Thorns also and thistles shall it bring forth to thee* (Gen. III, 18). '*And another holy one said unto that certain one* (lapalmoni) *who spoke*': R. Huna said: It means, to So-and-so [a certain person].[1] Akilas translated it: He spoke to him who was within,[2] which refers to Adam, whose partition was within that of the ministering angels.[3] *How long shall be the vision concerning the continual burnt-offering* (Dan. *loc. cit.*)? Shall the decree which was decreed against Adam continue for ever? Surely not! *And the transgression that causeth desolation* (*ib.*): shall his transgression make him desolate in the grave?[4] *To give both the sanctuary and the host to be trampled underfoot* (*ib.*): shall he and his descendants be trampled down by the angel of death![5] *And he said unto me: Until evening—morning two thousand and three hundred*[6]*; then shall the sanctuary be victorious* (*ib.* 14). R. 'Azariah and R. Jonathan b. Haggai in R. Isaac's name observed: Surely when it is evening it is not morning and when it is morning it is not evening? But the meaning is

[1] Rashi explains: i.e. this statement (in v. 14) was made to the one who cried (v. 13). [2] Translating *lapalmoni* as *lipnimi*.

[3] He was privileged to come more closely within the precincts of God than were even the angels. The picture is that of a series of partitions or barriers before God, and the more privileged one was, the nearer was he permitted to approach Him.

[4] 'E.J.: shall he remain desolate in the grave for ever on account of his sin and never experience resurrection?—The translation is somewhat conjectural. Mah. explains differently.

[5] Treating *sanctuary* as a metaphor for Adam, or translating *ḳodesh* directly: the holy one, viz. Adam, and 'host' his descendants.

[6] Lit. translation, which must be retained here

this: when the morning of the nations of the world turns to evening, and the evening of Israel to morning,[1] at that time, *'Then shall the sanctuary be declared righteous,'* i.e. I will declare him clear[2] of that decree: then, THE LORD GOD SAITH: BEHOLD, LET THE MAN BECOME AS ONE OF US.[3]

2. *I went by the field of the slothful man* (ish), *and by the vineyard of the person* (Adam) *void of understanding* (Prov. XXIV, 30). R. Huna said: Behold, if one buys a field or a vineyard and is designated person (*ish*) or man, yet is dubbed lazy, what benefit has one [from the title of 'man']?[4] *'I went by the field of the slothful man,'* however, refers to Adam, while, *'And by the vineyard of the person* (Adam) *void of understanding'* refers to Eve.[5] R. Huna said: Where do we find that Eve is called *Adam?—According to the beauty of Adam, to dwell in the house* (Isa. XLIV, 13).[6] *And lo, it was all grown over with thistles* (Prov. XXIV, 31), as it is written, *'Thorns also and thistles shall it bring forth to thee'* (Gen. III, 18). *The face thereof was covered with nettles* (Prov. *loc. cit.*): *In the sweat of thy face*, etc. (Gen. III, 19). *And the stone wall thereof was broken down* (Prov. *loc. cit.*): *Therefore the Lord God sent him forth from the garden of Eden* (Gen. III, 23): having sent him forth He began to bewail him, saying, BEHOLD, THE MAN *WAS* AS ONE OF US.[7]

3 *Though his stature* [E V. *'excellency'*] *mount up to the heavens, and his head reach unto the clouds* (Job XX, 6),

[1] I.e when the former are degraded and the latter elevated.
[2] Lit 'righteous'—as a person who having paid the penalty of his sin now starts with a clean sheet.
[3] Immortal, translating it as an imperative, as though it read הֱיֵה, not הָיָה
[4] I.e. it should simply say *slothful* and *one void of understanding*, man and person being understood
[5] Tanḥuma completes it: . . . to Adam, who was slothful to repent . . . to Eve, who was void of understanding in hearkening to the serpent. *And, lo, it was all grown over with thistles* (*ib.* 31)—i.e they spread punishment in the world. [6] Since it is woman who normally stays at home, *Adam* there must refer to her. [7] Lit. translation,—but is so no longer: he was immortal, but is now mortal.

i.e. until [his stature] reaches the clouds.[1] R. Joshua b. Ḥanina[2] and R. Judah b. R. Simon in R. Eleazar's name said: He created him extending over the whole world. How do we know [that he extended] from east to west? Because it is said, *Thou hast formed me behind* (aḥor) *and before*—ḳedem (Ps. CXXXIX, 5). How do we know, from north to south? Because it says, *Since the day that God created man upon the earth, and from one end of heaven unto the other* (Deut. IV, 32). How do we know that he filled the hollow spaces of the world also?[3] From the verse, *And Thou didst lay Thy hand upon me* (Ps. *loc. cit.*).[4]

Yet he shall perish for ever like his own rolling—E.V. '*dung*' (Job XX, 7): because he rolled away [i.e. disobeyed] an easy command, he was banished from the garden of Eden. *They that have seen him shall say: Where is he?* (*ib.*): i.e. where is man (Adam). Having sent him forth, He began to bewail him, saying, WHERE[5] IS THE MAN WHO *WAS* AS ONE OF US?

4. *Thou makest him strong for ever* (Job XIV, 20): the strength with which the Holy One, blessed be He, endowed Adam was intended to be '*for ever*', for all time; *But he goeth:* since he ignored God's wishes and went after the counsel of the serpent, *Thou changest his countenance and sendest him away* (*ib.*). Having sent him away, He began bewailing him, saying: BEHOLD, THE MAN *WAS* AS ONE OF US.[6]

5. BEHOLD, THE MAN HAS BECOME, etc. R. Pappyas lectured: BEHOLD, THE MAN HAS BECOME LIKE ONE OF US (MIMMENNU) means like one of the ministering angels. Said R. Akiba to him: Let that suffice thee, Pappyas.[7] How then do you interpret MIMMENNU?

[1] This is probably an explanation of שיאו, and intimates that it is to be translated stature [2] Th. amends: b. R. Nehemiah.
[3] I.e all the space from earth to heaven. [4] V. *supra*, VIII, 1, for notes.
[5] Translating הן (E.V. '*behold*') as the Aramaic הן where.
[6] He enjoyed our strength, but does so no longer. *Supra*, XVI, 1.
[7] You go too far (it is incorrect).

It means that the Holy One, blessed be He, set two ways before him, life and death, and he chose the other path.[1] R. Judah b. R. Simon interpreted: Like the Unique One of the universe,[2] as it is written, *Hear, O Israel; the Lord our God, the Lord is one* (Deut. VI, 4). Our Rabbis said: Like Gabriel: *And one man in the midst of them clothed in linen* (Ezek. IX, 2): like a snail whose garment is part of its body.[3] Resh Lakish said: [He has become] like Jonah, [of whom is written], *But as one was felling a beam*, etc. (II Kings VI, 5)[4]: just as the latter fled [from God's command],[5] so the former fled[6]; just as that one's glory did not stay the night with him,[7] so this one's glory too did not stay a night with him.[8] R. Berekiah said in R. Ḥanina's name: Like Elijah: just as he did not experience the taste of death, so [Adam] too was not meant to experience death.[9] The view of R. Berekiah in R. Ḥanan's name is that as long as there was [only] Adam he was one, but when his rib was taken from him, it was *To know good and evil.*[10]

6. AND NOW LEST (PEN) HE PUT FORTH HIS HAND. R. Abba b. Kahana said: This teaches that the

[1] That which God did not wish him to choose, viz. death. Th.. R. Akiba treats '*mimmennu*' as 3rd sing. ('of *himself*'), not 1st pl. ('of *us*'), translating Behold, the man has become as one who knows good and evil of himself, of his own free will, and thereby has himself chosen the path of death. V. S.S. R. I, 9, § 2. [2] Godlike and immortal, translating. *the man* was *like the One* who is among us, sc. God.

[3] Just as 'one' refers there to Gabriel, so here, too The relevance of 'like a snail' is not clear. It is perhaps best to regard it with Y.M. as a parenthetic remark: since the verse in Ezek refers to Gabriel, how then could an angel be dressed in linen? To which the answer is given that his dress, though appearing as linen, was an integral part of himself.

[4] The Midrash evidently assumes that this was Jonah. Similarly, in Seder 'Olam, ch. XVIII, the verse, *And Elisha . . called one of the sons of the prophets* (*ib.* IX, 1), is also applied to Jonah (Th).

[5] To carry the tidings of Nineveh's overthrow; v. Jonah I, 3.

[6] He too disobeyed God's command.

[7] The gourd which God caused to spring up for him, in his honour, as it were, was smitten in a single night (*ib.* III, 10).

[8] V. *supra*, XI, I. [9] But for his sin.

[10] I.e. the immediate effect of Eve's creation was that Adam should sin. He translates Behold, the man was as one, i.e. wholehearted in his obedience to God, but now (that he has Eve) he has been enabled *To know good and evil.*

Holy One, blessed be He, provided him with an opportunity of repentance. AND NOW: this can only refer to repentance, as you read, *And now, Israel, what doth the Lord God require of thee, but to fear the Lord thy God*, etc. (Deut. x, 12)[1]: PEN (LEST) can only mean 'not'.[2] Then the Holy One, blessed be He, said: SHALL HE PUT FORTH HIS HAND, AND EAT ALSO OF THE TREE OF LIFE? while if he does eat, HE WILL LIVE FOR EVER Therefore THE LORD GOD SENT HIM FORTH FROM THE GARDEN OF EDEN. Having sent him forth, He began lamenting him: '*Behold, the Man*,' etc.

7. THEREFORE THE LORD GOD SENT HIM FORTH FROM THE GARDEN OF EDEN (III, 27) R. Judah and R. Nehemiah differ. R. Judah said: He was sent forth from the garden of Eden in this world and in the next R. Nehemiah maintained: He was sent forth from the garden of Eden in this world, but not in the next. In R. Judah's view He laid a severe punishment upon him, while in that of R. Nehemiah He was lenient toward him. R. Huna said: R. Adda b. Ahawah and R. Hamnuna disputed on this, one agreeing with R Judah, the other with R. Nehemiah. Now the following supports R. Nehemiah: *As for me, I shall behold Thy face in righteousness; I shall be satisfied, when I awake, with Thy likeness* (Ps XVII, 15). [David said]: When he who was created in Thy likeness [viz. Adam] awakes, I shall be satisfied, and in righteousness I shall behold Thy face, and then I shall regard him as free of that decree.[3] Concerning that time [it is written], '*And the Lord God saith: Behold, the man has* [now] *become as one of us*,' etc.[4]

R. Joshua b. Levi said: When He created him, He

[1] Cf. *infra*, XXXVIII, 9.
[2] Thus God invited Adam to repent, but Adam said, I will not.
[3] The verse is thus rearranged, and is interpreted As for me (said David), I shall behold Thy face when Adam (i e. man) has expiated his sin and is thus completely righteous; I shall be satisfied on the awakening (the inf is used in the Hebrew, which may bear this meaning) of him who was created in Thy likeness.
[4] Free from sin

created him by His Attributes of Justice and Mercy,[1] and when He banished him, He likewise banished him in accordance with His Attributes of Justice and Mercy[2]: thus it is written, '*Behold, the man,*' etc.: O man, thou couldst not remain loyal to thy charge even for a single hour![3] Judah b. Padiah lectured: O that one might uncover the dust from thine eyes, O Adam, who couldst not remain loyal to thy charge even for a single hour, yet thy children wait for *'orlah* three years, as it is written, *Three years shall it be as forbidden* [lit. 'uncircumcised'] *unto you, it shall not be eaten* (Lev. XIX, 23)! R. Huna observed: When Bar Ḳappara heard this, he exclaimed: Thou hast taught well, O Judah the son of my sister![4]

8. SO HE DROVE OUT THE MAN (III, 24). R. Joḥanan said: Like the daughter of a priest who has been divorced[5] and cannot return [to her husband]; R. Simeon b. Laḳish said: Like the daughter of an Israelite [i.e. a non-priest] who has been divorced and is able to return.[6] In R. Joḥanan's view He was severe towards him[7]; in the view of R. Simeon b. Laḳish, He was lenient toward him.

SO HE DROVE OUT (WAYYEGARESH) THE MAN. [Read] *wayyagres*, which intimates that He showed him the destruction of the Temple, [in connection with which it is written], *He hath also broken* (wayyagres) *my teeth with gravel stones* (Lam. III, 16).[8] R. Lulianus b. Ṭibri [Tiberius] said in R. Isaac's name: He banished him to the open outskirts (*migrash*) of the Garden of Eden, and

[1] These two together were to be the foundations of God's rule over mankind.
[2] His expulsion was an act of justice, yet it was tempered with mercy, since he did not die immediately.
[3] An impression of commiseration for his frailty. [4] Lev R. XXV, 2.
[5] In Heb the same word connotes expulsion and divorce.
[6] By 'daughter', 'wife' is meant, as they generally married into their own rank. A priest might not remarry his divorced wife.
[7] He can never return to the garden of Eden, even in the next world
[8] By a play on words ויגרש is read ויגרס, and so made to veil an allusion to the destruction of the Temple. The Rabbis probably meant to convey that even here we find a hint that that catastrophe was the result of sin.

appointed watchmen to watch over it, as it is written, *I will also command the clouds, that they rain no rain upon it* (Isa. v, 6).[1]

9. AT THE EAST (MI-KEDEM). Rab said: In every case the east affords an asylum. To Adam: *So He drove out the man, and caused him to dwell* [sic] *at the east of the Garden of Eden* To Cain: *And Cain went out from the presence of the Lord, and dwelt in the land of Nod, on the east of Eden* (Gen. IV, 16). To a homicide: *Then Moses separated three cities beyond the Jordan towards the sun-rising*—i.e. in the east (Deut. IV, 41).

Another interpretation: MI-ḲEDEM teaches that the angels were created before (*ḳodem*) the Garden of Eden,[2] as it is written, *This is the living creature that I saw under the God of Israel by the river Chebar; and I knew that they were cherubim* (Ezek. X, 20). AND THE FLAMING SWORD: [the angels are so called] in accordance with the verse, *His ministers are as flaming fire* (Ps. CIV, 4). WHICH TURNS EVERY WAY: they [the angels] change [turn about]: sometimes they appear as men, sometimes as women, sometimes as spirits, sometimes as angels.[3]

Another interpretation: MI-KEDEM: before (*ḳodem*) the Garden of Eden the Gehenna was created, the Gehenna having been created on the second day, and the Garden of Eden not till the third. AND THE FLAMING SWORD [refers to Gehenna, so designated] in accordance with, *And the day that cometh shall set them aflame* (Mal. III, 19). THAT TURNS EVERY WAY: because it [Gehenna] revolves about man and burns him up from head to foot. Said Adam: 'Who will deliver my children from this flaming fire?' R. Huna said in R Abba's name. SWORD refers to circumcision, as it is written, *Make thee knives*[4] *of flint, and circumcise again*, etc. (Josh. v, 2). Our

[1] It appears that the whole passage there (Isa. v, 1 *seqq*) is applied to Adam. In this interpretation '*wayyegaresh*' is connected with *migrash*.
[2] Translating: and He caused the cherubim, i.e. the angels, to exist before the Garden of Eden (was created).
[3] Ex. R. xxv, 2.—Thus the whole passage is referred to angels.
[4] Heb. *ḥarboth*, pl. con. of *ḥereb*, sword.

Rabbis said: SWORD refers to the Torah, as it is written, *And a two-edged sword in their hand* (Ps. CXLIX, 6).[1] When Adam saw that his descendants were fated to be consigned to Gehenna, he engaged less in[2] procreation But when he saw that after twenty-six generations Israel would accept the Torah,[3] he applied himself to producing descendants; hence, *And Adam knew Eve his wife* (Gen. IV, 1).

[1] The idea is that the merit of circumcision and the study of the Torah would deliver his descendants from Gehenna (Y.T.).
[2] Lit. translation. Possibly it means here· he refrained (entirely).
[3] V. *supra*, I, 10.

CHAPTER XXII (BERESHITH)

1. AND THE MAN KNEW EVE HIS WIFE (IV, 1): *Remember, O Lord, Thy compassions and Thy mercies, for they have been from of old* (Ps. xxv, 6). R. Joshua b. Nehemiah interpreted it: [Show Thy mercies] wherewith Thou didst treat Adam, for thus saidst Thou to him, *For in the day that thou eatest thereof thou shalt surely die* (Gen. II, 17), and hadst Thou not given him one day *of Thine*, which is a thousand years, how could he have applied himself to begetting posterity [descendants]? Hence, AND THE MAN KNEW, etc.[1]

2. AND THE MAN KNEW, etc. R. Huna and R. Jacob in R. Abba's name said: No creature ever copulated before Adam: it is not written, man knew, but AND THE MAN[2]; KNEW intimates that he made known sexual functions to all. [Another interpretation]: He knew how he had been robbed of his tranquillity; he knew what his serpent [i.e. Eve, his tempter] had done to him.[3] R. Aḥa observed: The serpent was thy serpent, and thou wast Adam's serpent.[4]

AND SHE CONCEIVED AND BORE CAIN R. Eleazar b. 'Azariah said: Three wonders were performed on that day: on that very day they were created, on that very day they cohabited, and on that very day they produced off-spring. R. Joshua b. Karḥah said: Only two entered the bed, and seven left it: Cain and his twin sister, Abel and his two twin sisters.[5]

AND SHE SAID: I HAVE GOTTEN A MAN, etc. R. Isaac said: When a woman sees that she has children she exclaims, 'Behold, my husband is now in my possession.'[6]

[1] Cf. *supra*, VIII, 2, Num. R. XXIII, 13.
[2] The def. art. implies that he was so far unique in this respect.
[3] Viz. she aroused sexual desire. Thus KNEW is referred to both the preceding verses (Adam's expulsion from the Garden of Eden) and the following ones (sexual gratification).
[4] *Supra*, XX, 11 [5] *Infra*, XXIV, 6; v Sanh. 38*b*, 58*b*.
[6] I.e a child binds husband to wife. He translates: I have now a man (sc. *Adam*) in my possession, through having given birth to Cain.

WITH THE HELP OF (ETH) THE LORD. R. Ishmael asked R. Akiba: 'Since you have served[1] Nahum of Gimzo for twenty-two years, [and he taught], Every *ak* and *rak* is a limitation, while every *eth* and *gam* is an extension, tell me what is the purpose of the *eth* written here?' 'If it said, "I have gotten a man the Lord,"' he replied, 'it would have been difficult [to interpret][2]; hence ETH [WITH THE HELP OF] THE LORD is required.' Thereupon he quoted to him: *For it is no empty thing from you* (Deut. XXXII, 47), and if it is empty, it is so on your account,[3] because you do not know how to interpret it. Rather, ETH THE LORD [teaches this]: In the past, Adam was created from the ground, and Eve from Adam; but henceforth it shall be, *In our image, after our likeness* (Gen. I, 26): neither man without woman nor woman without man, nor both of them without the *Shechinah*.[4]

3. AND AGAIN (WA-TOSEF) SHE BORE HIS BROTHER ABEL (IV, 2). This supports what R. Joshua b. Ḳarḥah said: They ascended the bed two and descended seven, for AND SHE AGAIN BORE implies an additional birth, but not an additional pregnancy.[5]

AND ABEL WAS A KEEPER OF SHEEP, BUT CAIN WAS A TILLER OF THE GROUND. Three had a passion for agriculture, and no good was found in them: Cain, Noah, and Uzziah. CAIN WAS A TILLER OF THE GROUND; *Noah the husbandman* (Gen. IX, 20); Uzziah: *For he loved husbandry* (II Chron. XXVI, 10).[6]

4. AND AT THE END OF DAYS IT CAME TO PASS (IV, 3). R. Eliezer and R. Joshua disagree. R. Eliezer said: The world was created in Tishri; R. Joshua said:

[1] I.e. studied under. The term 'served' is generally employed because disciples gave personal service to their teachers.
[2] It might imply that she had begotten the Lord.
[3] Cf. *supra*, I, 14. [4] *Supra*, VIII, 9. This agrees with the E.V.
[5] Abel having been conceived simultaneously with Cain. The additional birth therefore is that two twin sisters were born with Abel, but only one with Cain.
[6] Cain became a murderer, Noah a drunkard, and Uzziah a leper.

In Nisan. He who says in Tishri holds that Abel lived from the Festival[1] until Ḥanukkah.[2] He who says in Nisan holds that Abel lived from Passover until Pentecost. In either case, all agree that Abel was not in the world more than fifty days.[3]

5. . . . THAT CAIN BROUGHT OF THE FRUIT OF THE GROUND: of the inferior crops,[4] he being like a bad tenant who eats the first ripe figs but honours the king with the late figs.[5]

AND ABEL, HE ALSO BROUGHT OF THE FIRSTLINGS OF HIS FLOCK AND OF THE FAT THEREOF (IV, 4). R. Eleazar and R. Jose b. R. Ḥanina differ. R. Eleazar said: The children of Noah[6] brought even peace-offerings[7]; R. Jose b R. Ḥanina said: They brought burnt-offerings.[8] R. Eleazar sought to refute R. Jose b. R. Ḥanina: But it is written, AND OF THE FAT THEREOF, implying that of which the fat is offered.[9] How did R. Jose b. R. Ḥanina answer him?—It means, of the fat ones [i.e. the best] R. Eleazar sought to refute R. Jose b. R. Ḥanina: But it is written, *And he sent the*

[1] Tabernacles, which commences on the 15th of Tishri.
[2] The feast of lights, commencing on the 25th of Kislew.
[3] The passage is difficult Both assume that AT THE END OF DAYS means at the end of one of the seasons of the year; and that Abel was murdered on the very day of the sacrifice. R. Eliezer applies it to autumn, R. Joshua to spring, so that AT THE END OF DAYS will mean about mid-winter (about 21st December) or midsummer (about 21st June), after which the seasons begin to change, and Ḥanukkah and Pentecost fall about these dates respectively. But 'Passover' and 'Tabernacles' are employed here loosely, the *beginning* of Nisan or Tishri being actually meant, and similarly Pentecost and Hanukkah, a date about a fortnight before being meant—otherwise the period is above 60 days. If on the other hand these are exact, then 50 is only stated approximately.
[4] This is deduced from the fact that it does not say, of the first of the fruit.
[5] The former were esteemed a special delicacy; v. Isa. XXVIII, 4; Jer XXIV, 2.
[6] 'The children of Noah' is a general term for all mankind before Revelation.
[7] And certainly burnt-offerings.
[8] But not peace-offerings, the fat of which was burnt on the altar while the flesh was eaten. Th.· because before the Revelation people were unworthy of enjoying any part of an animal consecrated to God. Y.T. states a somewhat similar reason. *Infra*, XXXIV, 9; Lev. R. IX, 6; Zeb. 116*a*.
[9] But not the whole,—hence a peace-offering.

young men of the children of Israel, who offered burnt-offerings, and sacrificed peace-offerings (shelamim) *of oxen unto the Lord* (Ex. XXIV, 5)?[1] How does R. Jose b. R. Ḥanina explain this?—It means that they were whole (*shelemim*) in their hide, without having been flayed or cut up.[2] R. Eleazar objected to R. Jose b. R. Ḥanina: But it is written, *And Jethro, Moses' father-in-law, took a burnt-offering and sacrifices* (*ib.* XVIII, 12)? How does R. Jose b. R. Ḥanina explain this?—He agrees with the view that Jethro came after Revelation. R Huna said: R. Jannai and R. Ḥiyya the Elder differ in this. R. Jannai said: Jethro came before Revelation; R. Ḥiyya the Elder said: Jethro came after Revelation. R. Ḥanina observed: They do not really differ: he who says that Jethro came before Revelation holds that the children of Noah might offer peace-offerings; while he who says that Jethro came after Revelation holds that they might offer burnt-offerings [only].[3] Now the following supports R. Jose b. R. Ḥanina: *Awake, O north wind* (S.S. IV, 16): this alludes to the burnt-offering, which was killed at the north [side of the altar].[4] To what does '*Awake*' apply? To something which was asleep and now awakes.[5] *And come, thou south* (*ib.*) alludes to peace-offerings, which were killed [even] at the south [side of the altar].[6] To what does '*come*' apply? To a new

[1] This was before Revelation (v. p. 182, n. 6). [2] He translates: .. who offered peace-offerings, and sacrificed the oxen whole.

[3] In the passage, *Jethro . . . took a burnt-offering and sacrifices*, '*sacrifices*' must refer to peace-offerings, since a burnt-offering is stated separately. Now actually there is nothing to indicate when Jethro came, but R. Jannai holds that the children of Noah might offer peace-offerings; therefore this incident may have happened even before Revelation. But R Hiyya the Elder holds that they could only offer burnt-offerings. Hence when we find Jethro sacrificing peace-offerings, it must have been after Revelation, when he accepted the Law and thus ceased to belong to the 'children of Noah'.—The fact that the incident is narrated before Revelation does not matter, as it is a principle of Rabbinic exegesis that the Bible is not necessarily in chronological order.

[4] Lev. I, 11, S.S. R. I, 2, § 1 (*Let him kiss me with the kisses of his mouth*).

[5] I.e. it had been practised long before, ceased for a time, and is now to be practised again.

[6] The peace-offering could be slain at any side of the altar.

practice.[1] R. Joshua of Siknin said in R. Levi's name: The following verse, too, supports R. Jose b. R. Hanina: *This is the law of the burnt-offering: that is the burnt-offering* (Lev. VI, 2),[2] viz. which the Noachides used to offer. But when it treats of peace-offerings, viz. *And this is the law of the sacrifice of peace-offerings* (*ib.* VII, 11), it is not written, 'Which they offered,'[3] but *Which they will offer* (*ib.*)—in the future.

6. AND THE LORD HAD RESPECT UNTO ABEL AND TO HIS OFFERING. He accepted it.[4]

BUT UNTO CAIN AND HIS OFFERING HE HAD NOT RESPECT (IV, 5). He did not accept it.

AND CAIN WAS VERY WROTH (WAYYIḤAR) AND HIS COUNTENANCE FELL: [His face] became like a firebrand.[5]

AND THE LORD SAID UNTO CAIN: WHY ART THOU WROTH? AND WHY IS THY COUNTENANCE FALLEN? IF THOU DOEST WELL, WILT THOU NOT RECEIVE[6] (IV, 6 f)—a blessing; AND IF THOU DOEST NOT WELL, RECEIVE (*ib.*)—a curse.[7] Another interpretation: IF THOU DOEST WELL, I will forgive thee[8]; but if not, thy sin[9] overflows the brim.[10] R. Berekiah quoted in R. Simeon's name: *Happy is he who is uplifted over transgression,*[11] *whose sin is pardoned* (Ps XXXII, 1): this means, happy is he who is [master] over his transgressions,[12] but his transgressions are not [master] over him.

[1] Thus it was only now, after Revelation, that the practice of sacrificing peace-offerings was introduced. v. S.S. R. *loc. cit.*
[2] E.V. '*It is that which goeth up*'.
[3] Which would connote, in the past, before Revelation.
[4] Lit. 'He was satisfied (propitiated) therewith.'
[5] Blackened. '*Wayyihar*' is derived from *harah*, to burn, cf. Ezek. XXIV, 10; Ps. CII, 4, and the verse is translated: And Cain was burnt up, i e blackened. [6] E.V '*Shall it not be lifted up*'.
[7] *Se'eth* is read with the preceding and the following clauses.
[8] This interprets *se'eth* in the sense of *nasa,* to bear with, forgive.
[9] Lit. 'the sin of that man.'
[10] Here too *se'eth* is read both ways, but when read with the clause that follows it it is derived from *se'ah,* a measure—the sin overflows the measure. [11] E.V. '*Whose transgression is forgiven*'.
[12] Who can master his evil propensities.

SIN COUCHETH (ROBEẒ) AT THE DOOR. Not *robeẓeth* [fem.] but ROBEẒ [masc.] is written here: at first sin is weak, like a woman, but then it grows strong, like a man R. Akiba said: At first it is like a spider's web, but eventually it becomes like a ship's rope, as it is written, *Woe to them that draw iniquity with trifling cords* [E.V. '*cords of vanity*'], *and sin as it were with a cart rope* (Isa. v, 18). R. Isaac said: At first it is like a [passing] visitor, then like a guest [who stays longer], and finally like the master of the house. Thus it is written, *And there came a traveller unto the rich man* (II Sam. XII, 4): [this represents the Tempter] as a traveller who passes on; *And he spared to take of his own flock and of his own herd, to dress for the guest* [E.V. '*wayfaring man*'] *that was come unto him* (*ib.*): now he is a guest; *And he dressed it for the man*[1] *that was come to him* (*ib.*): he is now the master.

R. Tanḥum b. Marion said: There are dogs in Rome that know how to deceive men. One [a dog] goes and sits down before a baker's shop and pretends to be asleep, and when the shopkeeper dozes off he dislodges a loaf near the ground,[2] and while the onlookers are collecting [the scattered loaves] he succeeds in snatching a loaf and making off.[3]

R. Abba b. Judan said: It is like a decrepit brigand who sat at the crossroads and ordered every passer-by to surrender his possessions, until a shrewd person passed by and saw that he was feeble, whereupon he began to crush him. Similarly, the Tempter destroyed many generations—the generation of Enosh, the generation of the Flood, and the generation of the separation [of races]. But when Abraham arose and saw how really feeble he was, he began to crush him, as it is written, *And I will beat to pieces his adversaries before him* (Ps. LXXXIX, 24).[4]

[1] He is no longer spoken of as a traveller or guest, but simply 'man'—the master of the house [2] Thus scattering the whole pile.

[3] Thus sin pretends to sleep until it catches its victim off his guard This is a comment on SIN COUCHETH (i.e. pretends to sleep).

[4] Thus SIN COUCHETH AT THE DOOR—his strength being only simulated.

R. Ammi said: The Tempter does not walk at the side [of the street] but in the broad highway,[1] and when he sees a person rolling his eyes, smoothing his hair [in self-satisfaction], and lifting his heel [in pride], he exclaims, 'This man belongs to me!' What is the proof? *Seest thou a man wise in his own eyes? The fool* [sc. sin] *hath hope of him* (Prov. XXVI, 12). R. Abin said: If one indulges his evil bent in his youth, it will eventually rule over him in his old age What is the proof? *He that indulgeth* [E.V. '*delicately bringeth up*'] *his servant in youth shall have him become a master at the last* (*ib.* XXIX, 21).[2]

R. Ḥanina said: If your Tempter comes to incite you to levity, cast him down with the words of the Torah, as it is written, *The* [evil] *imagination, when near to thee, thou shalt combat*—tiẓẓor (Isa. XXVI, 3).[3] And if you do so, I attribute merit to you as though you had created peace, [as the verse continues], *Thou createst* (tiẓẓor) *peace* (*ib.*)[4]: not *tinẓor* (thou shalt keep) is written, but '*tiẓẓor*' (thou shalt create). And should you argue that he is not in your power, then *Surely it is safe in thee* (*ib.*),[5] and I have already written for you in the Torah, AND UNTO THEE IS ITS DESIRE, BUT THOU MAYEST RULE OVER IT. R. Simon said. If your Tempter comes to incite you to levity, gladden it with the words of the Torah,[6] for it says, '*The evil imagination is gladdened* (samuk).'[7] And if you do so, I attribute merit to you as though you had created two worlds, for *shalom* (peace) is written here not once but twice.[8]

[1] Where the people crowd.

[2] Suk. 52*b* Rashi *ad loc.* explains that the Tempter is designated man's servant, since he can master him if he wishes, as it is written, *But thou mayest rule over it* (Gen. IV, 7).

[3] E.V. '*The mind stayed on Thee Thou keepest* (*in perfect peace*)'.

[4] In the first passage *tiẓẓor* is derived from *ẓarar*, to fight against; now it is derived from *yaẓar*, to form, create.

[5] E.V. '*Because it trusteth in thee.*'

[6] Perhaps this means. even your evil inclinations may be turned to good purpose; cf. *supra*, p. 68, n. 2.

[7] He appears to connect *samuk* (סמוך) with *simmah* (שמח), to gladden.

[8] Intimating that he effects peace in this world and in the next.

7. AND CAIN SPOKE UNTO ABEL HIS BROTHER, etc. (IV, 8). About what did they quarrel?[1] 'Come,' said they, 'let us divide the world.' One took the land and the other the movables. The former said, 'The land you stand on is mine,' while the latter retorted, 'What you are wearing is mine.' One said: 'Strip'; the other retorted: 'Fly [off the ground].' Out of this quarrel, CAIN ROSE UP AGAINST HIS BROTHER ABEL, etc. R. Joshua of Siknin said in R. Levi's name: Both took land and both took movables, but about what did they quarrel? One said, 'The Temple must be built in my area,' while the other claimed, 'It must be built in mine.' For thus it is written, AND IT CAME TO PASS, WHEN THEY WERE IN THE FIELD: now FIELD refers to nought but the Temple, as you read, *Zion* [i.e. the Temple] *shall be plowed as a field* (Micah III, 12).[2] Out of this argument, CAIN ROSE UP AGAINST HIS BROTHER ABEL, etc. Judah b. Rabbi said: Their quarrel was about the first Eve.[3] Said R. Aibu: The first Eve had returned to dust. Then about what was their quarrel? Said R. Huna: An additional twin was born with Abel,[4] and each claimed her. The one claimed: 'I will have her, because I am the firstborn'; while the other maintained: 'I must have her, because she was born with me.'

8. AND CAIN ROSE UP AGAINST HIS BROTHER ABEL, etc. R. Joḥanan said: Abel was stronger than Cain, for the expression ROSE UP can only imply that he [Cain] lay beneath him.[5] He [Cain] said to him, 'We two only are in the world: what will you go and tell our father [if you kill me]?' At this he was filled with pity for him; straightway he rose against him and slew him. Out of that incident was born the proverb, 'Do not do good to an evil man, then evil will not befall you.'

[1] The Midrash assumes that SPOKE means that they had a legal argument. [2] Cf. Pes. 88*a*.
[3] V. *supra*, XVIII, 4. Th , however, thinks it unlikely that the reference is to the Eve mentioned there, but thinks that in the Midrashic view there was yet another. [4] V. *supra*, 2. [5] They had already quarrelled and Abel had thrown Cain down.

With what did he kill him? R. Simeon said: He killed him with a staff: *And a young man for my bruising* (Gen. IV, 23) implies a weapon which inflicts a bruise. The Rabbis said: He killed him with a stone: *For I have slain a man for wounding me* (*ib.*) indicates a weapon which inflicts wounds. R. 'Azariah and R. Jonathan in R. Isaac's name said: Cain had closely observed where his father slew the bullock [which he sacrificed, as it is written], *And it shall please the Lord better than a bullock* (Ps. LXIX, 32), and there he killed him: by the throat and its organs.[1]

9. R. Joshua said in R. Levi's name: It is written, *The wicked have drawn out their sword* (Ps. XXXVII, 14)—this refers to Cain; *To cast down the poor and needy* (*ib.*) refers to Abel; *Their sword shall enter into their own hearts* (*ib.* 15), as it is written, *A fugitive and a wanderer shalt thou be in the earth* (Gen. IV, 12).

AND THE LORD SAID UNTO CAIN: WHERE IS ABEL, etc. (IV, 9). This may be compared to a prefect who was walking in the middle of the road, and found a man slain and another standing over him. 'Who killed him?' he demanded. 'I will ask you [that question] instead of your asking me,' rejoined the other. 'You have answered nothing,' he retorted.[2] Again, it is like the case of a man who entered a garden, and gathered mulberries and ate them. The owner of the garden pursued him, demanding, 'What are you holding?' 'Nothing,' was the reply. 'But surely your hands are stained [with the juice]!' Similarly, [God said to Cain], THE VOICE OF THY BROTHER'S *BLOOD* CRIETH UNTO ME FROM THE GROUND. Again, it is as if a man entered a pasture ground, seized a goat, and slung it behind him The owner of the pasture pursued him, demanding, 'What have you in your hand?'—'Nothing.' 'But it is bleating at your back!' exclaimed he. Similarly, [God rebuked Cain]: THE

[1] I.e. the gullet and the windpipe; cf Sanh. 37*b*.
[2] Seeing that it is you who are standing over him

VOICE OF THY BROTHER'S BLOOD CRIETH UNTO ME FROM THE GROUND.[1]

R. Judan, R. Huna, and the Rabbis each commented. R. Judan said: It is not written, 'Thy brother's blood' (*dam*—singular), but '*Thy brother's bloods*' (*deme*—plural): i.e. his blood and the blood of his descendants.[2] R. Huna observed: It is not written, 'Surely I have seen yesterday the blood (*dam*) of Naboth, and the blood (*dam*) of his sons,' but, '*Surely I have seen yesterday the bloods* (deme) *of Naboth, and the bloods* (deme) *of his sons*' (II Kings IX, 26), which means, his blood and the blood of his descendants. The Rabbis said: It is not written, 'His own servants conspired against him for the blood (*dam*) of the sons of Jehoiada,' but, . . . '*For the bloods of* (deme) *the sons of Johoiada*' (II Chron. XXIV, 25), namely, his blood and the blood of his descendants.

R. Simeon b. Yohai said: It is difficult to say this thing, and the mouth cannot utter it plainly.[3] Think of two athletes wrestling before the king; had the king wished, he could have separated them. But he did not so desire, and one overcame the other and killed him, he [the victim] crying out [before he died], 'Let my cause be pleaded before the king!'[4] Even so, THE VOICE OF THY BROTHER'S BLOOD CRIES OUT AGAINST *ME*.[5]

It [the blood] could not ascend above, because the soul had not yet ascended thither; nor could it go below, because no man had yet been buried there; hence the blood lay spattered on the trees and the stones.[6]

10. AND NOW CURSED ART THOU (IV, 11). R. Simeon b. Gamaliel said: In three places Scripture was

[1] Mah.: these three similes each illustrate something different. The first illustrates the futility of Cain's countering God's question with another; the second, Cain's bloody state, the third, the cry of blood.
[2] Not only he, but all his potential descendants cry out before Me.
[3] I.e. the verse condemns God Himself!
[4] I blame him for not sparing me.
[5] Reading '*alay* (עלי) for *elay* (אלי) '*From the ground*'.
[6] Hence, FROM THE GROUND. Cf. Sanh. IV, 5, where this is deduced from '*bloods*', which intimates that the blood was not in one place.

unduly sparing of its words: AND NOW CURSED ART THOU[1]; *But if the Lord make a new thing* (Num. XVI, 30)[2]; *For I have opened my mouth unto the Lord* (Judg. XI, 35).[3]

WHEN THOU TILLEST THE GROUND, IT SHALL NOT HENCEFORTH YIELD UNTO THEE HER STRENGTH (IV, 12). R. Eleazar said: To thee it shall not yield [her strength], but to another it shall yield it R. Jose b. R. Ḥanina maintained: Neither to thee nor to another. Similarly you read: *Thou shalt carry much seed out into the field, and shalt gather little in* (Deut. XXVIII, 38). R. Judah said: That means that a person will sow a *se'ah* and gather in a *se'ah*. Said R. Nehemiah: If so, how will he live? Rather, the field that ought to yield twenty measures will yield ten, and what ought to yield ten will yield five.

WHEN THOU TILLEST THE GROUND, IT SHALL NOT HENCEFORTH YIELD UNTO THEE HER STRENGTH. *Her* strength it shall not yield unto thee; thy strength, however, it shall yield unto thee.[4]

11. AND CAIN SAID UNTO THE LORD: MY SIN [E.V. 'PUNISHMENT'] IS TOO GREAT TO BEAR (IV, 14). Thou bearest the heavenly and the earthly, yet Thou canst not bear my transgression![5]

[Another interpretation]: My sin is greater than my father's. My father violated a light precept and was expelled from the Garden of Eden; this is a grave crime, to wit, murder; how much greater then is my sin!

BEHOLD, THOU HAST DRIVEN OUT, etc. Yesterday Thou DROVEST OUT my father AND NOW THOU DRIVEST ME OUT.[6] With monotony hast Thou fashioned the world[7]: how so?—BEHOLD, THOU HAST DRIVEN

[1] Without stating the manner or incidence of the curse.
[2] Without adding: by creating a mouth for the earth.
[3] The nature of the vow not being stated here.
[4] Man will still enjoy the fruit of his toil, though had he not sinned toil would have been unnecessary. [5] Interpreting the verse as a question and a protest. Cf. Sanh. 101*b*; Deut. R. VIII, 1.
[6] This interprets the *past* tense, hast driven out, which is made to refer to Adam. The verse is rendered: Behold, Thou *hast* driven out (my father, and Thou drivest out) me to-day ('me' follows 'driven out' in the Hebrew). [7] Text as emended; v. Th.

ME OUT THIS DAY—is it possible that FROM THY FACE I SHALL BE HID?[1]

12. AND THE LORD SAID UNTO HIM: THEREFORE (LAKEN) WHOSOEVER SLAYETH CAIN, etc. (IV, 15). R. Judah said: The cattle, beasts, and birds assembled to demand justice for Abel.[2] Said the Holy One, blessed be He, to him, 'I say to thee (*lak ani*), WHOSOEVER SLAYETH CAIN,' etc.[3] R. Nehemiah interpreted: Cain's judgment shall not be as the judgment of other murderers. Cain slew, but had none from whom to learn [the enormity of his crime], but henceforth, All who slay shall be slain.[4]

AND THE LORD SET A SIGN FOR CAIN. R. Judah said: He caused the orb of the sun to shine on his account. Said R. Nehemiah to him: For that wretch He would cause the orb of the sun to shine! Rather, He caused leprosy to break out on him, as you read, *And it shall come to pass, if they will not believe thee, neither hearken to the voice of the first sign*, etc. (Ex. IV, 8).[5] Rab said: He gave him a dog. Abba Jose said: He made a horn grow out of him. Rab said: He made him an example to murderers. R. Ḥanin said: He made him an example to penitents.[6] R. Levi said in the name of R. Simeon b. Lakish: He suspended his judgment until the Flood came and swept him away, as it is written, *And He blotted out every living substance*, etc. (Gen. VII, 23).[7]

13. AND CAIN WENT OUT, etc. Whence did he go out?[8] R. Aibu said: It means that he threw the words behind

[1] Surely not.—Thou hast but one, unvarying form of punishment, inflicting the same upon my father and myself.

[2] R. Judah explains that Cain's fear was due to the animals, seeing that there were no men on earth. [3] Reading '*laken*', *lak ani*, 'To thee I (say).' He thus assured him that he need have no fear of the animals

[4] He reads '*laken*' as *lo ken*, 'not so,' this being God's answer to the animals, not to Cain. [5] The reference is to leprosy, v. 6.

[6] Translating: And the Lord made Cain (direct object) a sign (to others)—according to Rab, of the fear that haunts a murderer, so that he needed a dog to protect him; according to R. Ḥanan, of the saving power of repentance, which Cain displayed, so that God did not put him to death immediately. [7] *Infra*, XXXII, 5; Eccl. R. VI, 3.

[8] For one cannot go out from the presence of God, who is everywhere.

him and went out, like one who would deceive the Almighty.[1] R. Berekiah said in R. Eleazar's name: He went forth like one who shows the cloven hoof,[2] like one who deceives his Creator. R. Ḥanina b. Isaac said: He went forth rejoicing, as you read, *He goeth forth to meet thee, and when he seeth thee, he will be glad in his heart* (Ex. IV, 14). Adam met him and asked him, 'How did your case go?' 'I repented and am reconciled,' replied he. Thereupon Adam began beating his face, crying, 'So great is the power of repentance, and I did not know!' Forthwith he arose and exclaimed, *A Psalm, a song for the Sabbath day: It is a good thing to make confession unto the Lord* (Ps. XCII, 1).[3]

[1] He rejected God's reproof, as though murder was a light matter.
[2] I.e. a hypocrite.—A swine shows his cloven hoof as though pretending to be clean
[3] E.V. '*to give thanks*'.

CHAPTER XXIII (BERESHITH)

1. AND CAIN KNEW HIS WIFE, etc. (IV, 17). It is written, *Their inward thought* (ḳirbam) *is, that their houses shall continue for ever*, etc. (Ps. XLIX, 12).[1] R. Judan and R. Phinehas discussed this. R. Judan explained it: What do the wicked think? *That within their houses* [they shall live] *for ever*,[2] *and their dwelling-places* [shall exist] *to all generations, and they will call their lands after their own names*, i.e. Tiberias after the name Tiberius, Alexandria after Alexander, Antioch after Antiochus? R. Phinehas interpreted it: '*Ḳirbam is their houses for ever*,' i.e. to-morrow their houses become their sepulchres (*ḳibram*)[3]; '*Their dwelling-places to all generations*,' i.e. they will neither live [i.e. be resurrected] nor be judged.[4] Moreover, '*They have called their lands after their own names*': thus it is written, AND HE BUILDED A CITY, AND CALLED THE NAME OF THE CITY AFTER THE NAME OF HIS SON ENOCH.[5]

2. AND UNTO ENOCH WAS BORN IRAD; AND IRAD BEGOT MEHUJAEL; AND MEHUJAEL BEGOT METHUSHAEL; AND METHUSHAEL BEGOT LAMECH (IV, 18). R. Joshua b. Levi said: All these names signify chastening. IRAD: I shall drive them (*'ordan*) out of the world [by the flood]; MEHUJAEL: I shall wipe them (*moḥan*) from the world; METHUSHAEL: I shall wear them out (*matishan*) from the world: what have I to do with Lamech and his descendants?[6]

AND LAMECH TOOK UNTO HIM TWO WIVES, etc.

[1] This verse and its interpretation are a comment on the *end* of the verse with which the section commences.
[2] That is his translation of the verse.
[3] He refers this to the generation of the Flood.—The flood will sweep them away in their houses, which will thus become their graves.
[4] They will remain in their grave-houses for all time, and not rise for judgment; v. *infra*, XXVI, 6; Sanh. XI, 3, 108*a*.
[5] These cities shall remain an everlasting memorial to their shame.
[6] Reading Lamech as *mah li*, what have I to do?

(IV, 19). R. 'Azariah said in R. Judah's name: The men of the generation of the Flood used to act thus: each took two wives, one for procreation and the other for sexual gratification. The former would stay like a widow throughout her life, while the latter was given to drink a potion of roots, so that she should not bear, and then she sat before him like a harlot, as it is written, *He devoureth the barren that beareth not, and doeth not good to the widow* (Job XXIV, 21). The proof of this is that the best of them, who was Lamech, took two wives, Adah, [so called] because he kept her away (*ya'ade*) from himself; and Zillah, to sit in his shadow (*ẓillo*).[1]

3. AND ADAH BORE JABAL; HE WAS THE FATHER OF SUCH AS DWELL IN TENTS AND HAVE CATTLE—U-MIKNEH (IV, 20). Formerly they used to provoke the Holy One, blessed be He, in secret, but subsequently they provoked Him openly, as it is written, *The image of jealousy, which provoketh to jealousy*—hamaḳneh (Ezek. VIII, 3).[2]

AND HIS BROTHER'S NAME WAS JUBAL; HE WAS THE FATHER OF ALL SUCH AS HANDLE THE HARP AND THE PIPE (IV, 21): i.e. organ players and flautists.

AND ZILLAH, SHE ALSO BORE TUBAL-CAIN, THE FORGER OF EVERY CUTTING INSTRUMENT OF BRASS AND IRON, etc. (IV, 22). R. Joshua said in R. Levi's name: This man perfected (*tibbel*) Cain's sin: Cain slew, yet lacked the weapons for slaying, whereas he was THE FORGER OF EVERY CUTTING INSTRUMENT, etc.[3]

AND THE SISTER OF TUBAL-CAIN WAS NAAMAH. R. Abba b. Kahana said: Naamah was Noah's wife; and why was she called Naamah? Because her deeds were pleasing (*ne'imim*). The Rabbis said: Naamah was a woman of a different stamp, for the name denotes that she sang (*man'emeth*) to the timbrel in honour of idolatry.

[1] I.e for sexual purposes only.

[2] *Ha-miḳneh* (E.V. 'cattle') is connected here with *ha-maḳneh*, that angereth, thus: . . . of such as provoke God in their tents, i.e. secretly. Cf. Lam. R. Proem XXII

[3] This interprets Tubal-Cain: he perfected (*tibbel*) Cain's work.

4. AND LAMECH SAID UNTO HIS WIVES, etc. (IV, 23 ff). R. Jose b. R. Hanina said: He summoned them to their marital duties. Said they to him: 'To-morrow a flood will come—are we to bear children for a curse?' He answered, 'FOR HAVE I SLAIN A MAN FOR MY WOUNDING—that wounds should come to me on his account! AND A YOUNG MAN CHILD FOR MY BRUISING—that bruises should come upon me![1] Cain slew, yet judgment was suspended for him for seven generations; for me, who did not slay, surely judgment will wait seventy-seven generations!'[2] (Rabbi said: This is a reasoning of darkness [i.e. fallacious]: for if so, whence is the Holy One, blessed be He, to exact His bond of debt? R. Jacob b. Idi asked R Johanan: If a man, why a child, if a child, why a man?[3] He was a man in deeds and a child in years.) Said he [Lamech] to them [his wives][4]: 'Come, let us go to Adam [and consult him].' So they went to him. He said to them: 'Do you do your duty, while the Holy One, blessed be He, will do His.'[5] 'Physician, physician, heal thine own limp!' retorted the other. 'Have you kept apart from Eve a hundred and thirty years for any reason but that you might not beget children by her!'[6] On hearing this, he [Adam] resumed his duty of begetting children, and forthwith, *And Adam knew his wife again* (Gen. IV, 25).

5. [AND ADAM KNEW HIS WIFE FURTHERMORE.] Desire was added to his desire.[7] Formerly he had experienced no desire when he did not see her, but now he desired her whether he saw her or not. R. Abba b. Judan said in R. Aha's name: This is a hint to seafarers to

[1] According to this he had not slain anyone. Other legends, however, relate that he *accidentally* killed Cain, and he argued that his punishment would be deferred for a greater time than that of Cain, who *intentionally* murdered Abel. [2] To their objection that a Flood was imminent he replied that it would certainly be postponed for many generations [3] Why does Lamech designate the same person both a man and a child? [4] This is a continuation of the discussion, which was parenthetically interrupted. [5] Your duty is to procreate, whatever God may do. [6] *Supra*, XX, 11. [7] This interprets '*od* (E.V. 'again') in the sense of more.

remember their homes [i.e. their wives] and repair thither immediately.[1]

AND SHE CALLED HIS NAME SETH: FOR GOD HATH APPOINTED ME ANOTHER SEED, etc. R. Tanḥuma said in the name of Samuel Kozith[2]: [She hinted at] that seed which would arise from another source,[3] viz. the king Messiah.

INSTEAD OF ABEL, FOR CAIN SLEW HIM. Through the sin against Abel, Cain was slain.[4] It was as if two trees were standing near each other, and a wind uprooted one of them, which fell upon the other and uprooted it too. Similarly, you read, INSTEAD OF ABEL, FOR HE SLEW CAIN.

6. AND TO SETH, TO HIM ALSO THERE WAS BORN A SON; AND HE CALLED HIS NAME ENOSH (IV, 26). Abba Cohen Bardela was asked: '[Why does Scripture enumerate] Adam, Seth, Enosh, and then become silent?'[5] 'Hitherto they were created in the likeness and image [of God],' he replied, 'but from then onward Centaurs were created.'[6]

Four things changed in the days of Enosh: The mountains became [barren] rocks, the dead began to feel [the worms],[7] men's faces became ape-like, and they became vulnerable to demons. Said R. Isaac: They were themselves responsible for becoming vulnerable (*ḥullin*) to demons, [for they argued]: What is the difference whether one

[1] When they return from the voyage. [2] The meaning of the word is doubtful; 'Ar. treats it as a surname, and it is so translated here.

[3] I.e. not from a Jewish stock, Messiah being descended from Ruth the Moabitess, v. *infra*, LI, 8

[4] Reading הרגנו as passive: for Cain was slain; or, for he slew Cain (active, as vocalised)—indirectly, since Cain eventually died on his account.

[5] Instead of continuing the genealogical record, the narrative is interrupted and recommences afresh with, *This is the book of the generations of man* (Gen. V, 1)

[6] Half man half beast—probably in a metaphorical sense, implying that the following generations were spiritually inferior, though an actual change of appearance, too, is meant.

[7] Their dead bodies putrefied (which had not been the case before) and so became the prey of worms.

prostrates himself before an image or prostrates himself before man? Hence, *Then man became degraded*[1] *to call upon the name of the Lord.*[2]

7. R. Simon said: In three places this term is used in the sense of rebellion [against God]: *Then they rebelled* (huhal) *to call upon the name of the Lord*[3]; *And it came to pass, when man rebelled* (hehel, E.V. *'began'*) *in multiplying on the face of the earth* (Gen. VI, 1); *He [Nimrod] rebelled* (hehel, E.V. *'began'*) *when he was a mighty one in the earth* (*ib.* X, 8). An objection was raised: but it is written, *And this is what they have rebelled* (hahilam, E.V. *'began'*) *to do* (*ib.* XI, 6)?[4] He replied: [God] smote Nimrod's head, exclaiming, 'It is he who has incited them to rebel!'[5]

R. Levi said: This may be compared to a woman who said to her husband, 'I saw you in a dream divorcing me.' Said he to her, 'Why only in a dream? here it is in actual fact.'[6] R. Aha said: Ye engaged in idolatry and gave yourselves [Divine] names[7]; therefore I too will summon the waters of the sea in My name and destroy those evil men from the world. R. Abbahu lectured: The Ocean [sc. the Mediterranean] is higher than the whole world. Said R. Eleazar b. Menahem to him: Is this not explicitly stated in a verse, *He calleth for the waters of the sea, and poureth them out upon the face of the earth* (Amos V, 8; IX, 6), which obviously means, like one who pours downward from above?

[1] *Huhal* being derived from *hullin*, profane matter, and as such, the victims of demons. E.V *'began'*. [2] They became degraded in their worship, adoring men and idols instead of the Lord —*Infra*, XXIV, 6.

[3] They called their idols 'Lord', thus rebelling against His sovereignty, The verse is apparently translated: then they rebelled by calling (their idols) by the name of the Lord; or, then they rebelled against calling upon the name of the Lord.

[4] Hence four should have been stated.

[5] Translating the last sentence, This man (v Nimrod) has incited them to revolt. Hence it is not an additional instance.—*Infra*, XXVI, 4.

[6] He derives *hahilam* from *halom*, a dream, and translates: And this against which they dream, viz. the possibility of being scattered, will become an actuality, and they will be scattered.

[7] Names indicating that you yourselves are gods. He translates: Then they rebelled by calling *themselves* by the name of the Lord (M.K. and Mah.).

'He calleth for the waters of the sea' is written twice, corresponding to the two times that the sea came up and inundated the world.[1] How far did it come up on the first occasion and how far on the second? R. Judan, R. Abbahu, and R. Eleazar in R. Ḥanina's name said: On the first it came up as far as Acco and Jaffa, while on the second it came up as far as the coasts of Barbary.[2] R. Huna and R. Aha in R Ḥanina's name said: On the first, as far as the coasts of Barbary; on the second, as far as Acco and Jaffa, as it is written, *And said: Thus far* ('ad poh) *shalt thou come, but no further*, etc. (Job XXXVIII, 11): *'Thus far* ('ad poh) *shalt thou come'* means as far as Acco: *And here shall thy proud waves be stayed* (u-foh yashith) intimates as far as Jaffa (*Yaffah*). R. Eleazar[3] said: At the first, as far as Calabria[4]; at the second, as far as the coasts of Barbary.

[1] V. *supra*, v, 6.
[2] This name is sometimes applied to Africa in general; sometimes to Azania (Barbary) in N. Africa
[3] *Var. lec.* R. Eleazar b. R. Jose
[4] The 'heel of Italy', lying in the S.E of that country.

CHAPTER XXIV (BERESHITH)

1. THIS IS THE BOOK OF THE GENERATIONS OF ADAM (V, 1): It is written, *Woe unto them that seek deep to hide their counsel from the Lord*, etc. (Isa. XXIX, 15). R. Levi said: This may be compared to a master builder who built a country with [secret] chambers, canals, and caves. Subsequently he became a tax-collector, and the inhabitants of the country hid from him in those chambers and caves. Said he to them, 'It is I who built all these chambers and caves; to what purpose then is your hiding?' Similarly, '*Woe unto them that seek deep!*' . . . *And their works are in the darkness*, etc. (*ib.*). *O your perversity! Shall the potter be esteemed as the clay* (*ib.* 16)? You liken the created object to its creator, the plant to its planter! *That the thing made should say of him that made it: He made me not*, etc. (*ib.*). *Is it not yet a very little while,*[1] *and Lebanon shall be turned into a fruitful field* (*ib.* 17)—i.e. into a royal palace; *And the fruitful field shall be esteemed as a forest*—i.e. as forests of men.[2] *And in that day shall the deaf hear the words of a book* (*ib.* 18), viz. the book of the generations of Adam; hence it is written, THIS IS THE BOOK OF THE GENERATIONS OF ADAM.[3]

2. *Thine eyes did see mine unformed substance, and in Thy book they were all written* (Ps. CXXXIX, 16). R. Joshua b. R. Nehemiah and R. Judah b. R. Simon in R. Eleazar's name said: When the Holy One, blessed be He, created Adam, He created him extending over the whole world. How do we know that he extended from east to west? Because it is said, *Thou hast formed me behind and before* (*ib.* 5). From north to south? Because it is said, *And from the one end of heaven unto the other* (Deut. IV, 32). And how do we know that he filled the hollow spaces of the world? From the verse, *And hast laid Thy hand upon me* (Ps. *loc. cit.*).[4] R. Tanḥuma in R. Banayah's name, and R. Berekiah

[1] If you repent. [2] So great shall be the multitude of men.
[3] Num. R. LXXXIX, 1; Deut. R. I, 3. [4] V. *supra*, VIII, 1.

in R. Eleazar's name said: He created him a shapeless mass, and he lay stretching from one end of the world to the other; as it is written, '*Thine eyes did see my shapeless mass.*' R. Judah b. R. Simon said: While Adam lay a shapeless mass before Him at whose decree the world came into existence, He showed him every generation and its Sages, every generation and its judges, scribes, interpreters, and leaders. Said He to him: 'Thine eyes did see unformed substance[1]: the unformed substance [viz. thy potential descendants] which thine eyes did see have already been written in the book of Adam': viz. THIS IS THE BOOK OF THE GENERATIONS OF ADAM.[2]

3. Bar Ḳappara commenced: *Let them be blotted out of the book of the living*, etc. (Ps. LXIX, 29): this means, from the book of the generations below [in this world]; *And not be written with the righteous* (*ib.*): from the book of the generations above [in the next world]. Bar Ḳappara taught: Wherever the word 'lived' occurs, it refers to a righteous person; e.g., *Shelah lived* (Gen. XI, 14), *Arpachshad lived* (*ib.* 12). Another interpretation of '*Let them be blotted out of the book of the living*,' etc.: '*Of the book of the living*' means of the book of the generations of Adam, as it is written, THIS IS THE BOOK OF THE GENERATIONS OF ADAM.

4. *For I will not contend for ever* (Isa. LVII, 16)—with Adam; *Neither will I be always wroth* (*ib.*)—with his descendants. *For the wind faileth before Me* (*ib.*): R. Huna said: When the wind goes out into the world, the Holy One, blessed be He, obstructs its passage by mountains and breaks its force on hills and commands it: Take heed to do no harm to [My] creatures. What is the proof? '*For the wind faileth* (ya'atof) *before Me.*' What is the meaning of '*ya'atof*'? He weakens it, as you read, *When my soul grew*

[1] In the sense of Adam's potential descendants. *Golmi* is now translated not *my* unformed substance, but simply 'unformed substance', the final '*i*' being regarded as poetical, while the speaker is God.
[2] Sanh. 38*b*, Ex. R. XL, 2, 3; Lev. R. XXVI, 7.

weak (behith'atef, fr. 'ataf) *within me, I remembered the Lord* (Jonah II, 8). R. Huna said: Through three winds the world would have been rendered desolate,[1] because they went forth with unmeasured force; these are they: one in the days of Jonah, another in the days of Job, and the third in the days of Elijah. R. Judan said: [The wind in the days] of Jonah was directed against that ship only, for it says, *But the Lord hurled a great wind into the sea . . .* so *that* the *ship was likely to be broken* (*ib.* I, 4).[2] That of Job was directed against his house only, for it says, *And, behold, there came a great wind from across the wilderness, and smote the four corners of the house* (Job I, 19). Hence of these [three] only that of Elijah was world-wide, for it says, *And, behold, the Lord passed by, and a great and strong wind rent the mountains, and broke in pieces the rocks* (I Kings XIX, 11).

R. Tanḥum—others state this in the name of the Rabbis—said: The royal Messiah will not come until all the souls which [God] contemplated creating have been created. What is the proof? *And the souls which I have made* (Isa. LVII, 16), i.e. for the sake of the souls which I have made.[3] And the souls are those referred to in the book of Adam, viz. THIS IS THE BOOK OF THE GENERATIONS OF ADAM.[4]

5. *Then did He see it, and declare it; He established it, yea, and searched it out* (Job XXVIII, 27). The Rabbis said: Every single statement which the Holy One, blessed be He, made to Moses, He said twice in His own mind and then once to Moses. What is the proof? '*Then did He see it, and declare it,*' denotes once; '*He established it, yea, and searched it out*' denotes once [again], and then '*And unto man He said*' (*ib.* 28), which refers to Moses. R. Aḥa said: [He said

[1] But for God. [2] *The* ship, but not other ships.

[3] The verse is now translated. For the spirit (i.e. Messiah, cf. *supra*, II, 4, where *ruaḥ*—spirit—is likewise referred to Messiah) shall be detained before Me until the souls which I made have been created.

[4] 'A.Z. 5*a*; Yeb. 62*a*. Th. assumes from these proems that an actual work, called the Book of Adam, is referred to; v. B.M. (Sonc. ed.), p. 493, n. 4.

it] four times [to Himself]: '*Then did He see it*' denotes once; '*And declare it,*' once; '*He established it,*' once; '*Yea, and searched it out,*' once; and after that, '*And unto man He said,*' by which Moses is meant.

R. Judah said: It was fitting that the Torah should have been given through Adam. Whence does this follow?—THIS IS THE BOOK OF THE GENERATIONS OF ADAM. The Holy One, blessed be He, said: 'He is the creation of My hands, and am I not to give it to him!' Subsequently, however, He said: 'I gave him six commandments,[1] and he did not remain loyal to them; how then shall I give him six hundred and thirteen precepts, viz. two hundred and forty-eight positive precepts and three hundred and sixty-five negative precepts?' Hence it is written, *And He said* la-adam—I will not give it to Adam.[2] But to whom will I give it? To his descendants: hence, THIS IS THE BOOK OF THE GENERATIONS OF ADAM.[3]

R. Jacob of Kefar Ḥanan said: It was fitting that the twelve tribes[4] should have sprung from Adam. What is the proof?—THIS (ZEH) IS THE BOOK OF THE GENERATIONS OF ADAM, implying the numerical value of *zeh*.[5] The Holy One, blessed be He, said: 'He is the creation of My hands, and am I not to give him [the privilege of begetting the twelve tribes]!' Subsequently He said: 'I gave him two sons, and one arose and slew the other; how then am I to give him twelve?' Hence, '*And He said* la-adam': not Adam: I will not give [them to him]. But to whom will I give them? To his sons: THIS (ZEH) IS THE BOOK OF THE GENERATIONS OF ADAM; i.e. the numerical value of *zeh*, the *zayin* being seven, and the *hé* being five, making twelve in all.[6]

[1] V. *supra*, XVI, 6 [2] Reading it *lo adam*, not Adam
[3] The deduction is from GENERATIONS, reading: This book (sc. the Torah) belongs to the *generations*, i.e. the descendants of Adam, but not to Adam himself.
[4] Which descended from Jacob.
[5] Which is twelve. He interprets: *Zeh*, i.e 12, should have been the generations (i e. the descendants) of Adam.
[6] Interpreting. *Zeh*, 12, shall be given to his generations, but not to him

6. THIS IS THE BOOK OF THE DESCENDANTS OF ADAM. These were descendants, while the earlier ones[1] were not descendants. What then were they? Divinities! [The answer is as] Abba Cohen Bardela was asked: [Why does Scripture enumerate] Adam, Seth, and Enosh, and then become silent? To which he answered: Hitherto they were created in the likeness and image [of God], but from then onwards Centaurs were created. Four things changed in the days of Enosh: The mountains became [barren] rocks, the dead began to feel [the worms], men's faces became ape-like, and they became vulnerable (*ḥullin*) to demons. Said R. Isaac: They were themselves responsible for becoming vulnerable to demons, [for they argued]: What is the difference whether one worships an image or worships man? Hence, *Then man became degraded to call upon the name of the Lord* (Gen. IV, 26).[2]

Another interpretation: These are descendants, but the earlier ones were not [human] descendants. What then were they? Demons. For R. Simon said: Throughout the entire one hundred and thirty years during which Adam held aloof from Eve the male demons were made ardent by her and she bore, while the female demons were inflamed by Adam and they bore, as it is written, *If he commit iniquity, I will chasten him with the rod of men, and with the afflictions of the children of man*—Adam (II Sam. VII, 14), which means, the children of the first [primeval] man. (The reason for the view that house spirits are benevolent is because they dwell with him [man], while the opinion that they are harmful is based on the fact that they understand man's evil inclinations. He who maintains that the spirits of the field are benevolent does so because they do not grow up with him; while as for the view that they are harmful, the reason is because they do not comprehend his evil inclinations.)[3]

These are the descendants of Adam, but the earlier ones were not descendants of Adam. Why? Because they were destroyed by the flood, for R. Joshua b. Levi said: All these

[1] Viz. Cain and Abel and Cain's descendants
[2] V. *supra*, XXIII, 6. [3] V. *supra*, XX, 11.

names signify chastening. *Irad:* I shall drive them (*'ordan*) out of the world; *Mehujael:* I shall wipe them (*moḥan*) from the world; *Methushael.* I shall wear them out (*matishan*) from the world; what have I to do with Lamech and his descendants?[1]

7. R. Tanḥuma in R. Eleazar's name and R. Menahamah in Rab's name said: Adam taught them all forms of craftsmanship. What is the proof? *And they are craftsmen from Adam* (Isa. XLIV, 11),[2] i.e from the first Adam. Rab said: Adam even taught the way of ruling parchment for the Scroll [sc. the Pentateuch]: THIS IS THE BOOK and its ruling.[3]

IN THE DAY THAT GOD CREATED MAN. This supports R. Leazar's teaching: Three miracles were performed on that day: on that very day they were created, they cohabited, and they produced offspring.[4]

Ben 'Azzai said: THIS IS THE BOOK OF THE DESCENDANTS OF ADAM is a great principle of the Torah. R. Akiba said. *But thou shalt love thy neighbour as thyself* (Lev. XIX, 18) is even a greater principle. Hence[5] you must not say, Since I have been put to shame, let my neighbour be put to shame. R. Tanhuma said: If you do so, know whom you put to shame, [for] *In the likeness of God made He him.*[6]

[1] V. *supra*, XXIII, 2.

[2] E.V. '*And the craftsmen skilled above men*' (me-adam, lit. 'from men'), the *mem* of *me-adam* being understood as a particle of comparison. Here it is interpreted to denote source, origin

[3] Translating: This is the Book which his descendants learned to write from Adam. A Scroll of the Torah must be ruled before it is written; THIS IS THE BOOK implies that it was drawn up according to regulations. [4] *Supra*, XXII, 2.

[5] This refers back to Ben 'Azzai, not to R. Akiba, v. next note.

[6] In the Sifra, Kedoshim IV, 12, the order is reversed. R. Akiba's view being stated first, viz, that *But thou shalt love . . .* is a great principle, and then Ben 'Azzai maintains that THIS IS THE BOOK, etc, is even a greater principle. For from R Akiba's verse it might be said that when a man is put to shame he may retaliate, since he is not bidden to love his neighbour *more* than himself. Whereas this verse stresses the sanctity of man even then, for he was created in God's likeness, and an insult to man is an insult to God.—Both these principles flow from the universal fatherhood of God, which implies the brotherhood and unity of man. V. Th. *ad loc.*

CHAPTER XXV (BERESHITH)

1. AND ENOCH WALKED WITH GOD, AND HE WAS NOT; FOR GOD TOOK HIM (V, 24). R. Ḥama b. R. Hoshaya said: [AND HE WAS NOT means] that he was not inscribed in the roll of the righteous but in the roll of the wicked. R Aibu said: Enoch was a hypocrite, acting sometimes as a righteous, sometimes as a wicked man. Therefore the Holy One, blessed be He, said: 'While he is righteous I will remove him.'[1] R. Aibu also said: He judged [i.e. condemned] him on New Year,[2] when he judges the whole world.

Some sectarians[3] asked R. Abbahu: 'We do not find that Enoch died?' 'How so?' inquired he. '"Taking" is employed here, and also in connection with Elijah,'[4] said they. 'If you stress the word "taking",' he answered, 'then "taking" is employed here, while in Ezekiel it is said, *Behold, I take away from thee the desire of thine eyes,*' etc. (Ezek. XXIV, 16).[5] R. Tanḥuma observed: He answered them well.

A matron asked R. Jose: 'We do not find death stated of Enoch?' Said he to her: 'If it said, AND ENOCH WALKED WITH GOD, and no more, I would agree with you. Since, however, it says, AND HE WAS NOT, FOR GOD TOOK HIM, it means that he was no more in the world, [having died,] FOR GOD TOOK HIM.'

2. AND HE CALLED HIS NAME NOAH, SAYING: THIS SAME SHALL COMFORT US (YENAḤAMENU fr. NAHEM) IN OUR WORK, etc. R. Joḥanan said: The name does not correspond to the interpretation [given to it], nor does the interpretation correspond to the name.

[1] Translating: While Enoch walked with God he was not, i.e. he died.
[2] The first of Tishri.
[3] Term generally used for Judeo-Christians, though by the time of R. Abbahu (third century C.E.) the break between Judaism and Christianity was complete, and therefore it would apply here to Christians or heretics in general
[4] II Kings II, 1. Hence just as there an assumption is meant, but not death, so here too.
[5] There it definitely refers to death.

The text should either have stated, 'This same shall give us rest (*yanihenu*),' or, 'And he called his name Naḥman, saying: This same *ye-nahamenu*'; but does Noah correspond to *ye-naḥamenu*?[1] The truth is that when the Holy One, blessed be He, created Adam, He gave him dominion over all things: the cow obeyed the ploughman, the furrow obeyed the ploughman.[2] But when he sinned, He made them rebel against him: the cow did not obey the ploughman, nor did the furrow obey the ploughman. But when Noah arose, they submitted: ease is mentioned here,[3] and ease is mentioned elsewhere, viz. *That thine ox and thine ass may be at ease* (Ex. XXIII, 12): just as the ease stated there means the ease of the ox, so the ease mentioned here implies the ease of the ox.[4]

Resh Lakish said: The name does not correspond to its interpretation nor does the interpretation correspond to the name. Scripture should have written either, '*The same* yaniḥenu [shall give us rest]' or . . . 'Naḥman . . . *the same* ye-naḥamenu [shall comfort us].' The fact is that before Noah arose, the waters used to ascend and inundate them [the dead] in their graves. For it is twice stated, *He calleth for the waters of the sea* (Amos V, 8; IX, 6),[5] corresponding to the two times [daily] that the waters came up and inundated them in their graves, once in the morning and once in the evening,[6] as it is written, *Like the slain that lie in the grave* (Ps. LXXXVIII, 6), i.e. even those who had died naturally[7] were like the slain.[8] But when Noah arose, they had rest; for 'resting' is mentioned here, and also elsewhere, viz. *He entereth into peace, they rest in their beds* (Isa. LVII, 2): just as there the rest of the grave is meant, so here too the rest of the grave is meant.

R. Leazar said: He was so named on account of his sacrifice, as it is written, *And the Lord smelled the sweet*

[1] Surely not. [2] Text as emended, also cur. edd.—I.e. nature, animate and inanimate, was readily responsive. [3] The name 'Noah' connotes that.
[4] I.e. it was easy to direct the ox in his work. [5] Cf *supra*, XXIII, 7.
[6] The general idea is that even in their graves the dead were not at rest.
[7] *Shokebe*, that lie, is understood to refer to such.
[8] Th.: like those who have died an unnatural death through drowning, and thus continue to be tossed about by the waves.

(niḥoaḥ) *savour* (Gen. VIII, 21).[1] R. Jose b. R. Ḥanina said: On account of the resting of the ark, as it is written, *And the ark rested*—wattanah (*ib.* 4).

R. Joḥanan said: The planets did not function the entire twelve months [of the Flood].[2] Said R. Jonathan to him: They did function, but their mark was imperceptible.[3] R. Liezer said: *They shall not cease* (*ib.* 22) implies that they never ceased.[4] R. Joshua deduced: '*They shall not cease*': hence it follows that they had ceased.

3. WHICH COMETH FROM THE GROUND WHICH THE LORD HATH CURSED (V, 29). Famine visited the world ten times. Once in the days of Adam: *Cursed is the ground for thy sake* (Gen. III, 17); once in the days of Lamech: WHICH COMETH FROM THE GROUND WHICH THE LORD HATH CURSED; once in the days of Abraham: *And there was a famine in the land* (*ib.* XII, 10); once in the days of Isaac: *And there was famine in the land, beside the first famine that was in the days of Abraham* (*ib.* XXVI, 1); once in the days of Jacob: *For these two years hath the famine been in the land* (*ib.* XLV, 6); once in the days when the judges judged: *And it came to pass in the days when the judges judged, that there was a famine in the land* (Ruth I, 1); once in the days of Elijah: *As the Lord, the God of Israel, liveth, before whom I stand, there shall not be dew nor rain these years* (I Kings XVII, 1); once in the days of Elisha: *And there was a great famine in Samaria* (II Kings VI, 25); one famine which travels about in the world; and once in the Messianic future: *Not a famine of bread, nor a thirst for water, but of hearing the words of the Lord* (Amos VIII, 11).[5] R. Huna and R. Jeremiah in the name of R. Samuel and R. Isaac said: Its occurrence ought properly to have been not in the days of David but in the

[1] *Noah* is thus connected with *miḥoah*. [2] Remaining stationary.
[3] The sun and moon did not provide the usual amount of illumination.
[4] M.K.: he translates the Heb. *'od . . . lo yishbothu,* they have never yet ceased.
[5] This actually gives eleven. Hence the ten must be assumed not to include the last. M K. emends and combines the last two· and one which will visit (lit. 'roll upon') the world in the future; cf. Ruth R. I, 4.

days of Saul, but because Saul was a shoot of a sycamore-tree,[1] the Holy One, blessed be He, postponed it and brought it in the days of David. Shila sins and Johanah is punished![2]—Said R. Ḥiyya: It is like the case of a glass-worker holding a basket full of goblets and cut glass, who when he wished to hang the basket up brought a nail, drove it [into the wall], suspended himself thereby,[3] and then hung up his basket. For that reason all these [famines] came not in the days of lowly [weak] men but in the days of mighty men, who could withstand it. R. Berekiah applied to them the verse, *He giveth power to the faint* (Isa. XL, 29). R. Berekiah said in R. Ḥelbo's name: There were two famines in the days of Abraham.[4] R. Huna said in R. Aḥa's name: There was one in the days of Lamech and one in the days of Abraham. The famine of Elijah's time was one of scarcity, one year yielding and one year not yielding. The famine in the days of Elisha was one of panic,[5] *Until an ass's head was sold for fourscore pieces of silver*, etc. (II Kings VI, 25). As for the famine during the days of the judges, R. Huna said in R. Dosa's name: From the price of two *se'ahs* [of wheat per *sela'*] it advanced to one *se'ah* [per *sela'*],[6] and it was taught[7]: A man must not emigrate abroad[8] unless two *se'ahs* cost a *sela'*.[9] R. Simeon observed. That is only when it is altogether unobtainable, but if it is obtainable, even at a *se'ah* per *sela'*, one must not go abroad.

[1] An idiom, denoting barren of thought or merit, or something that is easily broken, opp. of 'a shoot of an olive tree' (*infra*), which means rich in understanding or merit, not easily broken.—Thus Saul, lacking merit, would have been broken by a famine. [2] If Saul deserved punishment, was it to be postponed for David! [3] To test its weight.
[4] This was either a tradition or is deduced from the passage, *Beside the first famine that was in the days of Abraham*, whence it follows that there was also a second in his days, for if the contrast is merely with that in the time of Isaac, it should merely say, 'beside the famine,' etc. (Y.T.).
[5] There was food, but not enough to satisfy (Rashi, Th.). Jast. translates (on Ab. v, 8): a famine in consequence of (war) trouble.
[6] Text as emended (T., following זרע אברהם, reading מב' instead of מ"ב). The ordinary price was four *se'ahs* per *sela'* (Peah, VIII, 7).
[7] B.B. 91*a*. [8] From Palestine. [9] This indicating famine. But in the present case it was even twice as dear. On this interpretation this statement is cited as proof; but v. Ruth R. I, 4.

CHAPTER XXVI (BERESHITH)

1. AND NOAH WAS FIVE HUNDRED YEARS OLD; AND NOAH BEGOT SHEM, HAM, AND JAPHETH (V, 32). It is written, *Happy is the man that hath not walked,* etc. (Ps. I, 1): '*Happy is the man*' refers to Noah: '*That hath not walked in the counsel of the wicked,*'—R. Judah and R. Nehemiah differ on this. R. Judah said: It means through three generations, viz., of Enosh, the Flood, and the Separation [of tongues].[1] R. Nehemiah said: During the generation of Enosh he was but a child.[2] According to R. Judah's view, [the verse is to be interpreted thus:] '*In the counsel of the wicked*' refers to the generation of Enosh; *Nor stood in the way of sinners,* to that of the Flood; *Nor sat in the seat of the scornful,* to that of the Separation [of tongues]. *But his delight was in the law of the Lord* (*ib.* 2) alludes to the seven precepts which he was commanded.[3] *But in His law doth he meditate:* he inferred one thing from another, arguing, Why did the Holy One, blessed be He, order more clean animals [to be saved] than unclean ones? Surely because He desires that offerings should be made to Him of the former.[4] Forthwith, *He took of every clean beast,* etc. (Gen. VIII, 20). *And he shall be like a tree planted by streams of water* (*ib.* 3): the Lord planted him [i.e. saved] in the ark. *That bringeth forth its fruit in its season:* this alludes to Shem; *And whose leaf doth not wither:* to Ham; *And in whatsoever he doeth he shall prosper,* to Japheth: thus it is written, AND NOAH BEGOT SHEM, HAM, AND JAPHETH.

2. *Planted in the house of the Lord, they shall flourish in the courts of our God* (Ps. XCII, 14). '*Planted in the house of the Lord*' alludes to Noah, whom the Holy One, blessed be He, planted in the ark; '*They shall flourish in the courts*

[1] Noah lived through these, yet did not imitate the evil ways of his contemporaries. [2] Hence Scripture cannot refer to this.
[3] *Supra,* XVI, 6. He was given an additional precept, viz. the injunction not to eat a limb torn from a living animal. [4] *Infra,* XXXIV, 9.

of the God,' as it is written, AND NOAH BEGOT, etc.; *They shall still bring forth fruit in old age* (*ib.* 15) alludes to Noah.[1] *They shall be full of sap and richness* (*ib*), as it is written, AND NOAH BEGOT SHEM, HAM, AND JAPHETH.

AND NOAH WAS FIVE HUNDRED YEARS OLD, etc. (V, 32). R. Judan observed: All his contemporaries begot at a hundred or two hundred years, while he begot at five hundred years! The reason, however, is that the Holy One, blessed be He, said: 'If they [Noah's sons] are to be wicked, I do not desire them to perish in the flood[2]; while if they will be righteous, am I to put him to the trouble of building many arks?'[3] Therefore the Lord stopped his fountain and he begot at five hundred years. R. Nehemiah said in the name of R. Eliezer the son of R. Jose the Galilean: Even Japheth, who was the eldest,[4] was not at the time of the Flood a hundred years old so as to be liable to punishment.[5]

R. Ḥanina said: In the Messianic age there will be death among none save the children of Noah.[6] R. Joshua b. Levi said: Neither among Israel nor among the other nations, for it is written, *And the Lord God will wipe away tears from off* all *faces* (Isa. XXV, 8). How does R. Ḥanina explain this?—From off all faces of Israel. Yet surely it is written, *For the youngest shall die a hundred years old* (*ib.* LXV, 20), which supports R. Ḥanina; how then does R. Joshua explain it?—That means that he will then be liable to punishment.[7] But it is written, *Like sheep they are appointed for the nether-world; death shall be their shepherd* (Ps. XLIX, 15), which supports R. Ḥanina: how then does R. Joshua explain it?—Thus: whereas in this world Pharaoh [was

[1] Who begot children when 500 years old; Gen v, 32.
[2] For their father's sake. [3] Had he begotten children at the normal age, there would have been too many by the time of the Flood for one ark.
[4] Though he always comes last; cf. *infra*, XXXVII, 7.
[5] It was a tradition that before the Revelation the Heavenly Court did not punish for sins committed before that age.
[6] A general term for non-Israelites.
[7] V. n. 5 Mah.: 'death' is thus used to indicate punishment, which indeed redeems from death; it is not meant literally.

punished] in his time and Sisera in his time[1]; in the Messianic era He will appoint the angel of death their [sc. Pharaoh and Sisera's] officer,[2] as it is written, *And the upright shall have dominion over them in the morning, and their form shall be for the wearing away of the nether-world on account of His habitation* (*ib.*)[3]: this teaches that Sheol [the nether-world] will be destroyed, yet their bodies will not be destroyed.[4] And why such severity? '*On account of His habitation*,' i.e. because they stretched out their hands against His habitation [sc. the Temple], as it is written, *I have surely built Thee a house of habitation* (I Kings VIII, 13).[5]

3. SHEM, HAM, AND JAPHETH. Surely Japheth was the eldest? [Shem, however, is written] first because he was [more] righteous [than the others]; also, because he was born circumcised, the Holy One, blessed be He, set His name particularly upon him; [other reasons for his priority are that] Abraham was to arise from him, he was minister in the High Priesthood, and because the Temple would be built in his territory.[6] The son of Ḥuṭa said: [Shem is written first] because the Holy One, blessed be He, suspended [punishment] for the generations from the Flood until the Separation according to the numerical value of his name, viz. three hundred and forty years.[7]

4. AND IT CAME TO PASS WHEN MAN REBELLED—E.V. 'BEGAN' (Gen. VI, 1). R. Simon said: In three places this term is used in the sense of rebellion [against God]: *Then they rebelled* (huḥal) *to call upon the name of the Lord* (*ib.* IV, 26); AND IT CAME TO PASS, WHEN MAN

[1] Their punishment was but temporal, death ending it.
[2] So that their punishment will be eternal (continual).
[3] E.V. . . '*For the nether-world to wear away, that there be no habitation for it.*' [4] But they will be resurrected and their bodies continue to exist, so as to receive punishment.
[5] Cf. R.H. 17*a*. [6] V. Sanh. 69*b* for another explanation.
[7] ש = 300; מ = 40. Cf. Gen. XI, where it is said that the Separation occurred 338 years after Arpachshad's birth, which took place two years after the Flood.

REBELLED; *He* [Nimrod] *rebelled when he was a mighty one in the earth* (*ib.* x, 8). An objection was raised: But it is written, *And this is what they have rebelled to do* (*ib.* xi, 6)? He replied: [God] smote Nimrod's head, exclaiming, 'It is he who has incited them to rebel against Me!'[1]

TO MULTIPLY ON THE FACE OF THE EARTH. This teaches that they spilled their semen upon the trees and stones, and because they were steeped in lust the Holy One, blessed be He, gave them many women, as it is written, AND IT CAME TO PASS, WHEN MAN BEGAN TO MULTIPLY . . . AND DAUGHTERS WERE BORN UNTO THEM.

The wife of R. Simeon b. Rabbi gave birth to a daughter. When R. Ḥiyya the Elder met him he said to him: 'The Holy One, blessed be He, has begun to bless you.' 'What is the proof?'[2] inquired he. 'Because it is written, AND IT CAME TO PASS, WHEN MAN BEGAN TO MULTIPLY . . . AND DAUGHTERS WERE BORN UNTO THEM,'[3] he replied. When he [R. Simeon] went to his father he asked him, 'Did the Babylonian[4] congratulate you?' 'Yes,' he answered, 'and he said thus to me.' 'Nevertheless,' he [Rabbi] observed, 'both wine and vinegar, are needed, yet wine is more needed than vinegar; both wheat and barley are needed, yet wheat is more needed than barley. When a man gives his daughter in marriage and incurs expense he says to her, "May you never return hither."'[5]

R. Gamaliel gave his daughter in marriage. 'Father,' she requested, 'pray for me.' 'May you never return hither,' said he to her. When she gave birth to a son she again begged him, 'Father, give me your blessing.' 'May "woe" never leave your mouth,' replied he. 'Father,' she exclaimed, 'on both occasions of my rejoicing you have cursed me!' 'Both were blessings,' he replied. 'Living at

[1] V. *supra*, xxiii, 7, for notes. [2] That a daughter is a sign of a blessing.
[3] Thus daughters are a sign of increase. [4] R. Ḥiyya; v. Suk 20*a*; Ker. 8*a*.
[5] But live happily with your husband. Thus a daughter is eventually lost to her family.—This shows that the preference for sons was not based in any way on a lower opinion of women.—B.B. 16*b*.

peace in your home, you will not return here, and as long as your son lives, "woe" will not leave your mouth; "woe that my son has not eaten," "woe that he has not drunk," "woe that he has not gone to school."'

5. THAT THE SONS OF GOD (BENE ELOHIM) SAW THE DAUGHTERS OF MEN, etc. (VI, 2). R. Simeon b. Yohai called them the sons of nobles; [furthermore], R. Simeon b Yohai cursed all who called them the sons of God.[1] R. Simeon b. Yohai said: If demoralisation does not proceed from the leaders, it is not real demoralisation.[2] R. 'Azariah said in R. Levi's name: When the priests steal their gods, by what can one swear or to what can one sacrifice?[3]

Now why are they called the sons of God? R. Hanina and Resh Lakish said: Because they lived a long time without trouble or suffering.[4] R. Huna said in R. Jose's name: It was in order that men might understand [astronomical] cycles and calculations.[5] The Rabbis said: It was in order that they might receive their own punishment and that of the generations that followed them.[6]

THAT THEY WERE FAIR (ṬOBOTH). R. Judan said: Actually *ṭobath*[7] is written: when a bride was made beautiful for her husband, the chief [of these nobles] entered and enjoyed her first.[8] Hence it is written, *For they were fair*, which refers to virgins; *And they took them wives*, refers to married women.[9] *Whomsoever they chose:* that means males and beasts.

R. Huna said in R. Joseph's name: The generation of the Flood were not blotted out from the world until they

[1] Lit. translation. v. Hertz, *Pentateuch and Haftorahs* (Sonc. Ed), p. 18

[2] Since the leaders are in a position to stop it.

[3] The idea is the same: what hope is there when the leaders and guardians of religion themselves transgress? [4] As though they were divine.

[5] A long life was required for making the necessary observations.

[6] Through their long life of ease they were now fully liable for all the punishment their sins merited.

[7] Singular (טובת) instead of *ṭoboth* (טובות), plural, though it is read as plural. The idea is that one woman was taken by many men.

[8] An allusion to the *ius primae noctis*.

[9] They took women married to others.

composed nuptial songs[1] in honour of pederasty and bestiality. R. Simlai said: Wherever you find lust, an epidemic visits the world which slays both good and bad. R. 'Azariah and R. Judah b. R Simon in R. Joshua's name said: The Holy One, blessed be He, is long-suffering for everything save immorality. What is the proof? THE SONS OF MEN SAW, etc., which is followed by, *And the Lord said: I will blot out man* (Gen. VI, 7). R. Joshua b. Levi said in Bar Padiah's name: The whole of that night Lot prayed for mercy for the Sodomites. They [the angels] would have heeded him, but as soon as they [the Sodomites] demanded, *Bring them out unto us, that we may know them* (*ib.* XIX, 5)—for intercourse—they [the angels] said, '*Hast thou here any besides* (*ib.* 12)? Hitherto you may have pleaded in their defence, but you are no more permitted to do so.'

6. AND THE LORD SAID: MY SPIRIT SHALL NOT ABIDE (YADON) IN MAN FOREVER—LE-'OLAM (VI, 3). R. Ishmael interpreted this: I will not put My spirit in them when I give the righteous their reward.[2] R. Jannai and Resh Laḳish said: There is no other Gehenna [in the future] save a day which will burn up the wicked. What is the proof?—*And the day that cometh shall set them ablaze* (Mal. III, 19). The Rabbis maintain: There will be a Gehenna, for it says, *Whose fire is in Zion, and his furnace in Jerusalem* (Isa. XXXI, 9). R. Judah b. R. Ilai said: There will be neither a day nor a Gehenna, but fire shall come forth from the body of the wicked himself and burn him up. What is the proof? *Ye conceive chaff, ye shall bring forth stubble, your breath is a fire that shall devour you* (*ib.* XXXIII, 11).[3] R. Huna interpreted in R. Aḥa's name: When I restore the spirit to its sheath (*nadan*), I will not restore

[1] Or perhaps: until they wrote marriage deeds for males and beasts—i.e. they fully legalised such practices.
[2] I.e. they will not arise at the resurrection. The whole passage refers to the generation of the Flood; v. Sanh. X, 3; 108*a*. Th. conjectures that R. Ishmael derives *yadon* from *nadan*, a dowry, translating: I will not dower man (sc. the wicked) with My spirit *le-'olam* (in the world—to come; E.V. '*forever*'). [3] *Supra*, VI, 6.

their spirit to their sheath.[1] R. Ḥiyya b. Abba interpreted: I will not fill them with My spirit when I fill all other men with My spirit, because in this world it [My spirit] spreads[2] only through one of [the main] limbs, but in the future it will spread throughout the body, as it is written, *And I will put My spirit within you* (Ezek. XXXVI, 27). R. Judan b. Bathyra interpreted it: Never (*le-'olam*) again will I judge (*dan*) man with this judgment.[3] R. Huna commented in R. Joseph's name: *I will not again curse . . . I will not again smite* (Gen. VIII, 21): [the repetition implies], let this suffice. The Rabbis said: '*I will not again curse*' refers to the children of Noah; '*I will not again smite*,' to future generations.[4]

I intended that My spirit should judge [i.e. rule and guide] them, but they refused; behold, therefore, I will bend them[5] (*meshaggeman*) through suffering. I intended that My spirit should judge them, but they refused; behold, therefore, I will bend them [break their power] through each other, for R. Eleazar said: None becomes answerable for [injury done to] man save another man like himself.[6] R. Nathan said: Even a dog or a wolf is answerable. R. Huna b. Gorion said: Even a staff or a thong is answerable, as it is written, *For the yoke of his burden . . . Thou hast broken as in the day of Midian* (Isa. IX, 3).[7] R. Aḥa said: Even barren trees[8] will have to render an account. The Rabbis proved it from the following: *For the tree of the field is man* (Deut. XX, 19)[9]; just as man must render an account, so must trees render an account.

[1] Deriving *yadon* from *nadan*, a sheath, the casing of the spirit, viz. the body. [2] Th. Jast.: flashes in (i.e. seizes).

[3] Sc. a Flood. He derives *yadon* from *din*, judgment. Thus in his view, even before the Flood God stated that it would never be repeated.

[4] *Infra*, XXXIV, 10.

[5] Jast Th translates differently On all views this is a play on the word *beshagam*, E.V. 'for that also'. Here too *yadon* is derived from *dan*, to judge, in the sense of guide.

[6] But an animal is not answerable when it injures man. He translates: My spirit will not judge, i.e. punish, for injury done to man, save when he too—who inflicts the injury—is man.

[7] The yoke itself was punished, as it were.

[8] I.e non fruit-bearing. [9] E.V. '*Is the tree of the field man?*'

R. Joshua b. Nehemiah interpreted: Their spirit does not reason with itself that they are but flesh and blood[1]; therefore I will reduce their years, as I have determined[2] for them in this world, and then I will bend them through suffering. R. Aibu interpreted: What was the cause that they rebelled against Me? Was it not because I did not bend them through suffering? What keeps a door in position? Its hinges.[3]

R. Eleazar said: Wherever there is no judgment [below] there is judgment [above].[4] R. Bibi, the son of R. Ammi, interpreted, following R. Leazar: If they have not judged, then My spirit [will judge man]. R. Meir said: If they did not perform judgment below, am I too not to perform judgment above! Thus it is written, *Is not their tent-cord plucked up within them? They die, and that without wisdom* (Job IV, 21): i.e. through lacking the wisdom of the Torah. *Betwixt morning and evening they are shattered; they perish for ever without any regarding* (mesim) *it* (*ib.* 20). Now '*mesim*' can only refer to judgment, as you read, *Now these are the ordinances* [judgments] *which thou shalt set* (tasim) *before them* (Ex. XXI, 1) [5]

R. Jose the Galilean interpreted: No more shall My Attribute of Justice be suppressed [lit. 'judged'] before My Attribute of Mercy.[6] Rabbi interpreted: And the generation of the Flood said, 'The Lord will not judge my spirit.'[7] R. Akiba cited: *Wherefore doth the wicked condemn*

[1] And so they should not sin.

[2] This is the reading in several MSS. and is the most preferable Mah.: the long life they have hitherto enjoyed has blinded them to their mortality; hence I will shorten it. Th.'s ed. reads: I will grant them but few years, because I have been wroth with them; this involves the change of one letter only.

[3] Similarly man needs suffering to place him on a firm foundation. Suffering brings out the best in man.

[4] If a man's sins are unpunished in this world, they will be punished in the next.

[5] *Infra*, XXXI, 5; Deut. R. V, 5 Thus interpreting: They die, etc., because they did not execute justice on earth.

[6] M.K. and Mah.: *Ruḥi* (My spirit) connotes His mercy; *yadon*, His justice. Hitherto the former had prevailed; now the latter would come into its own.

[7] Instead of translating 'And the Lord said, My Spirit', etc., he treats 'the Lord' as the subject of *yadon* (judge), the subject of 'said' being the people, unexpressed, and so renders: And the people said, The Lord will not judge my (sc the people's) spirit—of rebellion.

God, and say in his heart, Thou wilt not require? (Ps. x, 13) meaning that there is no judgment or judge: [in truth] there is judgment and there is a Judge.

R. Ḥanina b. Papa said: Even Noah who was left of them was left not because he merited it, but because the Holy One, blessed be He, foresaw that Moses was destined to descend from him, *beshagam* and *Moshe* (Moses) both having the same numerical value.[1] The Rabbis adduced it from the following: *And his days shall be a hundred and twenty years.*[2]

7. THE NEPHILIM WERE IN THE EARTH . . . THE SAME WERE THE GIBBORIM (E.V. 'MIGHTY MEN') THAT WERE OF OLD (VI, 4). They were called by seven names: *Nephilim, Emim, Refaim, Gibborim, Zamzumim, Anakim,* and *Awim.*[3] *Emim* signifies that their dread (*emah*) fell upon all; *Refaim*, that all who saw them melted (*nirpeh*) like wax. *Gibborim:* R. Abba said in R. Joḥanan's name: The marrow of each one's thigh bone was eighteen cubits long.[4] *Zamzumim:* R. Jose b. R. Ḥanina said: They were the greatest of all masters of the arts of war.[5] *Anakim:* The Rabbis explained it as signifying that they were loaded with chains (*'anakim*) upon chains.[6] R. Aḥa said: Their necks reached (*'onkim*) the globe of the sun[7] and they demanded: 'Send us down rain.' *Awim* denotes that they cast the world into ruins, were themselves driven from the world in ruin, and caused the world to be ruined, as you

[1] Viz. 345: בשגם: ב (2)+ש (300)+ג (3)+ם (40); משה: מ (40)+ש (300) +ה (5)=345. He renders: My spirit will abide in man (sc. Noah) only for the sake of Moses (*beshagam*).

[2] I.e. for the sake of him who is to live 120 years (Moses). Cf. *infra*, XXVIII, 9. [3] V. Deut. II, 10 f, 20 f, 23.

[4] *Gibborim* denotes mighty, great.

[5] Th. holds that this does not actually explain the meaning of the word *zamzumim*, but is a comment on their might. Th. also conjectures that R. Jose connects *zamzumim* with *zamam*, to devise, intend, and it implies that owing to their superior military power they could always carry out their schemes.

[6] As ornaments. Jast (reading מרבים): they increased the chains (*'anaḳim*) around the necks (*'anakim*)—they subjugated many people.

[7] Th Jast.: they seized (fr. *anaḳ* 'to press', 'force,' 'rule') the globe of the sun.

read, *A ruin, a ruin, a ruin* ('awwah 'awwah 'awwah) *will I make it* (Ezek. XXI, 32). R. Leazar b. R. Simeon said: It signifies that they were as expert in the knowledge of different kinds of earth as a serpent, for in Galilee a serpent is called *'awwiah. Nefilim* denotes that they hurled (*hippilu*) the world down, themselves fell (*naflu*) from the world, and filled the world with abortions (*nefilim*) through their immorality.[1]

AND ALSO AFTER THAT. Judah b. Rabbi commented: The later generations would not learn from the earlier ones, i.e. the generation of the Flood from that of Enosh, and the generation of the Separation from that of the Flood.[2]

AND ALSO AFTER THAT, WHEN THE SONS OF GOD CAME IN UNTO THE DAUGHTERS OF MEN. R. Berekiah said: A woman would go out into the market place, see a young man, and conceive a passion for him, whereupon she would go, cohabit, and give birth to a young man like him.

THE MEN OF RENOWN (HASHEM). R. Aḥa quoted: *They are the children of churls, yea, children of ignoble men*—beli shem (Job XXX, 8), yet you say that they were MEN OF RENOWN![3] But it means that they laid the world desolate (*heshimu*), were driven in desolation from the world, and caused the world to be made desolate. R. Levi explained in the name of R. Samuel b. Naḥman: It means the men whose names are specified above,[4] for R. Joshua b. Levi said: All these names signify chastening: Irad: I shall drive them (*'ordan*) out of the world; Mehujael: I shall wipe them (*moḥan*) out of the world; Methushael: I shall wear them out (*matishan*) from the world: What have I to do with Lamech and his descendants?[5] R. Joḥanan interpreted: THE SAME WERE THE MIGHTY MEN THAT WERE OF OLD, THE MEN OF NAME: and

[1] Num. R. XVI, 11; Deut. R. I, 24; Yoma 10*a*, Shab 85*a*.
[2] *Infra*, XXXVIII, 4.
[3] The verse of Job is understood to refer to this generation of the Flood.
[4] In the preceding chapter, but does not necessarily imply renown.
[5] *Supra*, XXIII, 2.

who enumerates their deeds? THE MEN ENUMERATED BY NAME,[1] viz., Eliphaz the Temanite, Bildad the Shuhite, and Zophar the Naamathite.[2] For Rabbi said: Had Job come for no other purpose but to enumerate for us the deeds of the generation of the Flood, it would have sufficed him.[3] R. Ḥanan said: Had Elihu[4] come for no other purpose but to describe to us the action of the rainfall,[5] it would have sufficed him. For R. Johanan said: Every time *orah* (light) is stated in connection with Elihu,[6] it refers to the descent of rain. R. Hoshaya the Elder said: It refers to nought else but Revelation.[7] R. Aḥa said: Dissension is as great an evil as the generation of the Flood: It says here, MEN OF RENOWN, whilst elsewhere it says, *They were princes of the congregation, the elect men of the assembly, men of renown* (Num. XVI, 2).[8]

[1] This is R. Joḥanan's rendering of the phrase.
[2] Many verses in Job describing the deeds of the wicked were held to refer to the generation of the Flood, as stated in the text.
[3] The meaning seems to be, that alone justifies the whole work.
[4] Mentioned several times in Job, e.g., XXXII, 4; XXXV, 1.
[5] How God caused the Flood; e g , Job XXXVI, 27 *seq.*; XXXVII, 3 *seq.*
[6] E.g., Job XXXVI, 30, 32; XXXVII, 3, 11.
[7] Since the Torah is called light, v. Prov. XV, 23.
[8] The reference is to Korah and his rebellion.

Chapter XXVII (BERESHITH)

1. AND THE LORD SAW THAT THE WICKEDNESS OF THE MAN WAS GREAT IN THE EARTH, AND THAT EVERY IMAGINATION OF THE THOUGHTS OF HIS HEART WAS ONLY EVIL ALL DAY (VI, 5). It is written, *For there is a man whose labour is with wisdom*, etc. (Eccl. II, 21). R. Judan said: Great is the power of the prophets, who compare that which is created to its Creator, as it is written, *And I heard the voice of a man between the banks of the Ulai*, etc. (Dan. VIII, 16).[1] R. Judan b. R. Simon[2] said: We have other verses which display this more clearly than this one: *And upon the likeness of the throne was a likeness as the appearance of a man upon it above* (Ezek. I, 26).[3] '*With wisdom*,' as it is written, *The Lord by wisdom founded the earth* (Prov. III, 19); '*And with knowledge*' (Eccl. *loc. cit.*), as it is written, *By His knowledge the depths were broken up* (Prov. III, 20). '*And with skill*' (Eccl. *loc. cit.*): R. Berekiah said in the name of R. Judah b. R. Simon: Not with labour or toil did the Holy One, blessed be He, create the world, but '*By the word of the Lord*' (Ps. XXXIII, 6), and straightway, *The heavens have been made* (*ib.*).[4] *Yet to a man that hath not laboured therein shall he leave it for his portion* (Eccl. II, 21): that refers to the generation of the Flood.[5] *This also is vanity and a great evil* (*ib.*): thus it is written, AND THE LORD SAW THAT THE WICKEDNESS OF THE MAN WAS GREAT.

2. *For all his days are pains*, etc. (*ib.* 23): it means that they grieved the Holy One, blessed be He, with their evil deeds; *And his occupation vexation* (*ib.*): they vexed the Holy One, blessed be He, with their evil deeds. *Yea, even in the night his heart taketh no rest* (*ib.*)—from sin.

[1] God was speaking, as is clear from the second half of the verse, yet He is referred to as a man's voice.
[2] Th. . this is not the R Judan generally mentioned.
[3] *Man* in this verse certainly refers to God. Hence in Eccl. II, 21, it likewise refers to God. [4] V. *supra*, XII, 10.
[5] These were permitted to enjoy the results of God's work.

And how do we know that by day too [they did not cease from evil]? . . . WAS ONLY EVIL ALL DAY.

3. AND THE LORD SAW THAT THE WICKEDNESS OF MAN WAS GREAT. R. Hanina interpreted: It waxed ever greater. R. Berekiah said in R. Joḥanan's name: We know that the generation of the Flood was punished by water and the Sodomites by fire: whence do we know to apply what is stated here to the case below [sc. the Sodomites], and the reverse? Because 'great' is mentioned in both places, affording an analogy.[1]

WAS ONLY EVIL ALL DAY. From the rising until the setting of the sun there was no hope [of good] in them, as it is written, *The murderer riseth with the light* (Job XXIV, 14). But it is written, *In the dark they dig through houses* (*ib.* 16)?[2]—Why so? *Because they make a sign for themselves* [E.V. '*shut themselves up*'] *in the daytime* (*ib.*). What did they do? They brought balsam, smeared it over a stone, and would come at night and dig through it.[3] On the very night after R. Ḥanina taught this in Sepphoris, three hundred house-breakings took place.[4]

4. AND IT REPENTED (WAYYINNAḤEM) THE LORD THAT HE HAD MADE MAN ON THE EARTH (VI, 6). R. Judah said: [God declared:] 'It was a regrettable error on My part to have created him out of earthly elements,[5] for had I created him out of heavenly elements, he would not have rebelled against Me.' R. Nehemiah interpreted it:

[1] Heb. *gezerah shawah*. In reference to the Sodomites: *Verily, the cry of Sodom and Gomorrah is great* (Gen XVIII, 20). The analogy teaches that the punishment stated in the one case was also inflicted in the other.

[2] Then why say *Riseth with the light?*

[3] I.e. they marked in the daytime the spot most favourable for breaking in, and so as not to forget it they sprayed perfume there. Thus they made preparations by day and carried out their designs at night. V. Sanh 109*a* for a different version.

[4] The thieves took the hint.—Here follows in the original, 'What did the citizens of Sepphoris do there'? which is obviously only a fragment of a longer passage, and some MSS. omit it entirely.

[5] Or simply, below, on earth. Both stress, ON THE EARTH, this being the cause of God's regret.

I am comforted (*menuḥam*) that I created him below, for had I created him above, he would have incited the celestial creatures to revolt, just as he has incited the terrestrial beings to revolt. R. Aibu interpreted: It was a regrettable error on My part to have created an evil urge (*yeẓer ha-ra'*) within him, for had I not created an evil urge within him, he would not have rebelled against Me.[1] R. Levi interpreted: I am comforted that I made him from the earth.[2]

AND IT GRIEVED HIM AT HIS HEART. R. Berekiah said: If a king has a palace built by an architect and when he sees it, it displeases him, against whom is he to complain? Surely against the architect! Similarly, IT GRIEVED HIM AT HIS HEART.[3]

A certain Gentile asked R. Joshua b. Ḳarḥah: 'Do you not maintain that the Holy One, blessed be He, foresees the future?' 'Yes,' replied he. 'But it is written, AND IT GRIEVED HIM AT HIS HEART?'[4] 'Has a son ever been born to you?' inquired he. 'Yes,' was the answer. 'And what did you do?'—'I rejoiced and made all others rejoice,' he answered. 'Yet did you not know that he would eventually die?' 'Gladness at the time of gladness, and mourning at the time of mourning,' replied he. 'Even so was it with the Holy One, blessed be He,' was his rejoinder, 'for R. Joshua b. Levi said: Seven days the Holy One, blessed be He, mourned for His world before bringing the Flood, for it is said here, AND IT GRIEVED HIM, while elsewhere it says, *The king grieveth for his son'* (II Sam. XIX, 3).[5]

[1] Th.: possibly R. Aibu translates the end of the verse thus: and it grieved Him for his (man's) heart, i.e the desire to evil which the heart harbours.

[2] The commentaries (with a slightly different reading) explain: that I made him so as to remain in the earth, i e mortal and subject to burial —Sanh. 108*a*.

[3] Since God was His own Architect. Cf. *supra*, VIII, 3

[4] Why then was He originally pleased with the creation?

[5] Seven days is the period of deep mourning for a near relation. *Infra* XXXII, 7.

Chapter XXVIII (BERESHITH)

1. AND THE LORD SAID: I WILL BLOT OUT MAN WHOM I HAVE CREATED (VI, 7). It is written, *Therefore He taketh knowledge of their works, and He turneth [day] to night,*[1] *so that they are crushed* (Job XXXIV, 25). R. Ḥanina asked R. Jonathan. What does '*Therefore He taketh knowledge of their works*', etc. mean?—He answered: After the Holy One, blessed be He, has turned day into night[2] and put them at their ease, to be ready for punishment,[3] He then punishes them. Similarly, at first, *The Lord saw that the wickedness of man was great;* then, *It repented the Lord,* etc.; and finally, AND THE LORD SAID: I WILL BLOT OUT MAN.

2. AND THE LORD SAID: I WILL BLOT OUT MAN. R Berekiah said in the name of R. Abba b. Yema: It is written, *Let the waters be gathered together* (yiḳḳawu) *unto one place* (Gen. I, 9): that means, Let there be a measure set for the water, as you read, *And a line* (ḳaw) *shall be stretched forth over Jerusalem* (Zech. I, 16). R. Abba b. Kahana explained it in R. Levi's name thus: Let the waters be gathered together for My purpose, [so as to perform what I will one day do with them]. It is as if a king built a palace and tenanted it with dumb people, who used to rise early and pay their respects to the king with gestures, with their fingers and with their handkerchiefs. Said the king: 'If these, who are dumb, rise early and pay their respects with gestures, how much more zealous would they be if they possessed all their faculties!' Thereupon the king tenanted it with men gifted with speech, who arose and seized the palace, asserting, 'This palace is ours.' 'Then let

[1] E.V. '*Overturneth them in the night*'.
[2] By restraining the planets from functioning, so that it is perpetually dark; cf. *supra,* XXV, 2: R. Joḥanan said: The planets did not function for twelve months.
[3] I.e. that it shall come upon them unawares. *Var. lec.:* and has prepared them for punishment.

the palace return to its original state,' the king ordered. Similarly, at the beginning the praise of the Almighty ascended from nought but the water, as it is written, *From the voices of many waters, the mighty breakers of the sea* (Ps. XCIII, 4); and what did they proclaim? *The Lord on high is mighty* (*ib.*). Said the Holy One, blessed be He: 'If these, which have neither mouth nor speech, do thus, how much more will I be praised when I create man!' But the generation of Enosh arose and rebelled against Him; the generation of the Flood and that of the Separation [of tongues] arose and rebelled against Him. Thereupon the Holy One, blessed be He, said: 'Let these be removed and the former come [in their place].' Hence it is written, AND THE LORD SAID: I WILL BLOT OUT MAN.[1] 'What do they think? That I need armies [to combat them]? Did I not create the world with a word?[2] I will utter a word and destroy them!' R. Berekiah said: Surely I created them from the earth; what dissolves earth? Water. Then let the water come and dissolve the earth.

3. R. Levi said in R. Joḥanan's name: Even the nether stone of a millstone was dissolved.[3] R. Judah b. R. Simon said: Even the dust of Adam[4] was dissolved. R. Judah lectured thus, but the congregation would not accept it. R. Joḥanan said in the name of R. Simeon b. Jehozadak: Even the nut of the spinal column, from which the Holy One, blessed be He, will cause man to blossom forth in the future,[5] was dissolved.[6]

Hadrian—may his bones rot![7]—asked R. Joshua b. Ḥanania: 'From what part will the Holy One, blessed be He, cause man to blossom forth in the future?' 'From the nut of the spinal column,' he replied. 'How do you know that?' he asked. 'Bring me one and I will prove it to you,' he replied. He threw it into the fire, yet it was not burnt; he put it in water, but it did not dissolve; he ground it

[1] V. *supra*, V, 1. [2] Cf. *supra*, XXVII, 1.
[3] 'Blot out' and 'dissolve' are the same word in Hebrew.
[4] In his grave. [5] At the resurrection. [6] *Infra*, XXX, 8; Lev. R. XXXI, 10.
[7] V. p. 72, n. 2.

between millstones, but it was not crushed; he placed it on an anvil and smote it with a hammer; the anvil was cleft and the hammer split, yet it remained intact.[1]

4. I WILL BLOT OUT (EMḤEH) MAN WHOM I HAVE CREATED. I can impose an interdict (*me-maheh*) upon My creatures, but My creatures cannot impose an interdict upon Me.[2] R. Eleazar said: This may be compared to a king who possessed mixed stores,[3] and his subjects criticised him, saying, 'The king is miserly.'[4] What did the king do? He opened up for them the best, and they filled the country with stench, so that they had to sweep it out and cast it into the fire.[5] Similarly, these were the best of them, yet only *One man* [sc. Noah] *among a thousand* (elef) *have I found* (Eccl. VII, 28), [*elef* being used in the same sense] as when we learned, Best quality (*alfa*) wine,[6] and they have acted thus; therefore I WILL BLOT OUT MAN, THE BEST (ASHER) THAT I HAVE CREATED.[7] [God] contemplated creating a thousand generations, and how many of them were blotted out?[8] R. Huna said in the name of R. Eliezer, the son of R Jose the Galilean: Nine hundred and seventy-four. What is the proof?—*The word which he commanded after* [E.V. '*to*'] *a thousand generations*

[1] Hence it will remain as the nucleus of the resurrected man. Lev. R. XVIII, 1; Eccl. R. XII, 5.
[2] They may not criticise My actions, since there is much that is not revealed to them.—He derives '*emḥeh*' from *maḥa*, to forbid.
[3] Stores of commodities, good and bad mixed together. But even the best was poor.
[4] He is keeping all for himself.
[5] The worst would have been even more offensive and unbearable.
[6] Men. IX, 6. *Alfa* (alpha) is the first letter of Hebrew and Greek alphabets, and therefore denotes best quality. He translates: one man only (sc. Noah) out of the best (generations) have I found. As stated *infra*, the generations until the Flood, twenty-six in all, were the best of the thousand generations which God had contemplated creating, yet even so, *All flesh had corrupted their way*
[7] Connecting ASHER (E.V. '*whom*') with *ashar*, to be strong, happy, whence by transference, to be the best; hence translating: *I will blot out man* (though he is of) *the best that I have created*, for the other generations which I had intended to create would have been worse.
[8] I.e. remained uncreated.

(Ps. CV, 8), which refers to the Torah.[1] R. Levi said in the name of R. Samuel b. Naḥman: Nine hundred and eighty. What is the proof?—'*The word which he commanded after a thousand generations*' refers to circumcision.[2]

5. FROM THE FACE OF THE EARTH. R. Abba b. Kahana said: The ten tribes[3] did what was not done even by the generation of the Flood. With reference to the generation of the Flood, it is written, *And every imagination of the thoughts of his heart was only evil all day* (Gen. VI, 5), whereas with reference to the ten tribes it is written, *Woe to them that devise iniquity and work evil upon their beds* (Micah II, 1), implying, at night. And how do we know that they did so by day too? Because it is stated, *When the morning is light, they execute it* (ib.). Yet of those [the generation of the Flood] not a remnant was left, while of these a remnant was left. It was left only for the sake of the righteous men and women that were destined to arise from them, as it is written, *And, behold, there shall be left a remnant therein that shall be brought forth, both sons and daughters* (Ezek. XIV, 22): meaning, for the sake of the righteous men and women that were to arise from them.[4]

R. Berekiah said: The tribes of Judah and Benjamin did what was not done even in Sodom. With reference to Sodom it is written, *And, verily, their sin is exceeding grievous* (Gen. XVIII, 20), whereas of the tribes of Judah and Benjamin it says, *The iniquity of the house of Israel and Judah is most exceeding great* (Ezek. IX, 9)[5]; yet of the latter not a remnant was left, while of the former a remnant was left. But the reason is: the latter, *That was overthrown as in a moment* (Lam. IV, 6), never stretched forth their hands to

[1] Interpreting. The Torah was to have been commanded, i.e. revealed, after a thousand generations. Actually, however, it was revealed after 26 generations (from Adam to Noah, 10; from Noah to Abraham, 10; from Abraham to Moses, 6; total, 26), hence the other 974 were blotted out. [2] Which was enjoined upon Abraham, after only twenty generations—Eccl. R. I, 15; Ḥag. 13*b*.

[3] Comprising the Kingdom of Northern Israel. They were exiled to Assyria after the overthrow of their kingdom

[4] Cf. S.S. R. I, 4, § 3. [5] *Me'od* (exceeding) being repeated.

good deeds, as it is written, *Hands therein accepted no duties* (*ib.*),[1] which R. Tanḥuma interpreted: Hand did not join hand.[2] But the former stretched forth their hands to good deeds, as it is written, *The hands of women full of compassion have sodden their own children and provided the mourner's meal.*[3]

R. Huna said: What was perpetrated by the coastal cities[4] was not perpetrated even by the generation of the Flood,[5] for it is written, *Woe unto the inhabitants of the sea-coast, the nation of the Cherethites* (Zeph. II, 5), which means that they deserved to be annihilated (*kareth*). Yet for whose sake do they stand? For the sake of one nation[6] and one God-fearing person whom the Holy One, blessed be He, receives from their hands.[7]

'The nation of the Cherethites': [Others] interpret it in a laudatory sense, as you read, That maketh (*koreth*) the covenant.[8]

6. BOTH MAN, AND BEAST, AND CREEPING THING, AND FOWL OF THE AIR. R. Judan said: This may be illustrated by the case of a king who entrusted his son to a teacher who led him into evil ways, whereat the king became angry with his son and slew him. Said the king: 'Did any lead my son into evil ways save this man: my son has perished and this man lives!'[9] Therefore [God destroyed] BOTH MAN AND BEAST.[10] R. Phinehas said: A king

[1] E.V. '*No hands fell upon her*'
[2] To give assistance.—The rich never helped the poor.
[3] *Ib.* 10. The first meal eaten by a mourner after the funeral must not be his own but must be provided by his neighbours; this is called *se'udath habra'ah* (the meal of comfort), from which he derives *le-baroth*; v. Lam. R IV, 10 (13); Sanh. 104*b*. Having nothing else, they even cooked their own children for the purpose! 'E.J. softens this by explaining: they gave their last morsel, and so it was as though they had sodden their own children, since nothing was left for them and they had to die of hunger. V. Lam. R. on III, 10 (§ 13).
[4] Antioch, Gaza, Ashkelon, etc. [5] Yet the former are still in existence.
[6] *Var. lec.*: proselyte. [7] V. Schürer, *Geschichte*, III, 123, on the pious men (proselytes) who arose from the Gentiles.
[8] Th. conjectures that the reference is to Ps. L, 5: *Those that have made* (korethe) *a covenant with Me by sacrifice*, v. S.S R. I, 4, § 3.
[9] Surely not. [10] The fat animals and birds which they ate led them into evil.

gave his son in marriage and prepared a nuptial chamber for him, plastering, painting, and decorating it. Subsequently the king was angry with his son and slew him, whereupon he entered the nuptial chamber and broke the [supporting] rods, tore down the partitions, and rent the curtains, exclaiming: 'My son has perished: shall these remain!' Therefore [God destroyed] BOTH MAN AND BEAST,[1] as it is written, *I will consume man and beast*, etc. (Zeph. I, 3). [The verse continues], *And the stumblingblocks with the wicked* (*ib.*): It was they [the animals, etc.] which caused the wicked to stumble, for one would catch a bird and say to it, 'Go, fatten thyself, and then return,' whereupon it would go, fatten itself, and then return.[2]

7. R. Eleazar quoted: *Surely their substance is cut off* (Job XXII, 20). First the Holy One, blessed be He, destroyed their wealth, lest they should say, 'He needs our wealth.' *And their abundance the fire hath consumed* (*ib.*): they saw their chains of gold melted in the fire. R. Akiba said: All [the prophets] complained of the gold and silver which went forth with them from Egypt: e.g., *Thy silver is become dross* (Isa. I, 22); *And multiplied unto her silver and gold, which they used for Baal* (Hos. II, 10); *Of their silver and their gold have they made them idols*, etc. (*ib.* VIII, 4). R. Huna and R. Jeremiah in the name of R. Samuel b. Isaac said: It is not written, 'That they may be cut off,' but *That it may be cut off* (*ib.*),[3] as a man says: 'I will blot out the name of So-and-so who led my son into evil paths.'[4]

8. R. 'Azariah said in R. Judah's name: All acted corruptly in the generation of the Flood: the dog [copulated] with the wolf, the fowl with the peacock; hence it is written,

[1] Since the animals were created for the sake of man.
[2] I.e there was abundant prosperity, which led to evil. V. Sanh. 108*a*.
[3] Lit. translation, the text being in the singular.
[4] Similarly, that *it*, sc. their silver, may be cut off, since that led them into sin.

For all flesh *had corrupted their way*, etc. (Gen. VI, 12).[1] R. Julian [Lulianus] b. Tiberius said in R. Isaac's name: Even the earth acted lewdly; wheat was sown and it produced pseudo-wheat,[2] for the pseudo-wheat we now find came from the age of the deluge.

R. Joḥanan said: We learnt[3]: The judgment of the generation of the Flood lasted twelve months: having received their punishment, are they to enjoy a portion in the World to Come?[4]—Said R. Joḥanan: The Holy One, blessed be He, will boil up in Gehenna every single drop which He poured out on them, produce it and pour it down upon them. Thus it is written, *What time they wax hot, they vanish* (Job VI, 17), which means, they will be destroyed absolutely by scalding water. *As well their love* (Eccl. IX, 6)—i.e. they loved idolatry; *As their hatred* (*ib.*): they hated the Holy One, blessed be He, and provoked His jealousy; *Is long ago perished, neither have they any more a portion in the world* [to come] *on account of everything that was done* [by them] *under the sun* (*ib.*).[5]

FOR IT REPENTETH ME, etc. R. Abba b. Kahana observed: FOR IT REPENTETH ME THAT I HAVE MADE THEM AND NOAH—surely not![6] Even Noah, however, was left not because he deserved it, but because he found grace: hence, BUT NOAH FOUND GRACE IN THE EYES OF THE LORD.[7]

[1] Not only human beings.—Hence the Flood destroyed all. Cf. Sanh.—108*a* [2] Jast. (darnel or rye-grass). [3] 'Ed. II, 10.
[4] But it is stated in Sanh. X, 3 that they have no portion in the World to come.
[5] *Infra*, XXXIII, 7; Lev. R. VII, 6; Eccl. R. IX, 4.
[6] By disregarding the punctuation it appears that even Noah was included.
[7] Cf. *supra*, XXVI, 6; Sanh. 108*a*.

CHAPTER XXIX (BERESHITH)

1. BUT NOAH FOUND GRACE IN THE EYES OF THE LORD (VI, 8). *He delivereth him that is innocent* (i naki), *yea, thou shalt be delivered through the cleanness of thy hands* (Job XXII, 30). R. Hanina[1] said: Noah possessed less than an ounce (*unkia*)[2] [of merit]. If so, why was he delivered? Only '*Through the cleanness of Thy hands*'.[3] This agrees with what R. Abba b. Kahana said: *For it repenteth Me that I have made them and Noah.* But Noah was left only because he found grace; hence, BUT NOAH FOUND GRACE IN THE EYES OF THE LORD [4]

2. R. Simon quoted: *Thus saith the Lord: As, when wine is found in the cluster, one saith · Destroy it not, for a blessing is in it* (Isa. LXV, 8). It is related that a certain pious man went out to his vineyard and seeing a single [ripe] bunch pronounced a blessing over it, saying, 'This single bunch merits a blessing.' Even so, '*Thus saith the Lord: As, when wine is found in the cluster,*' etc.[5]

3. BUT NOAH FOUND GRACE IN THE EYES OF THE LORD. R. Simon said: The Holy One, blessed be He, found three treasures[6]: *And Thou foundest his* [Abraham's] *heart faithful before Thee* (Neh. IX, 8); *I have found David My servant* (Ps. LXXXIX, 21); *I found Israel like grapes in the wilderness* (Hos. IX, 10). His colleagues objected: Surely it is written, BUT NOAH FOUND GRACE IN THE EYES OF THE LORD?—*He* found, replied he, but the Holy One, blessed be He, did not find.[7] R. Simon interpreted:

[1] *Var. lec.:* R. Hanina of Anatoth said.
[2] This is a play on *i naki*, as though it read *unkia:* He delivereth him that hath an ounce of merit. [3] Referring it to God—i.e. as a special act of grace. [4] *Supra*, XXVIII *ad fin.* [5] He refers the verse to Noah.
[6] Lit. 'finds'—with whom He was pleased. Mah : He found these three when the moment was opportune: Abraham, to introduce the worship of the true God; Israel, to receive the Torah; and David, to wield sovereignty over Israel
[7] God did not find grace in him, because he was not actually righteous save by contrast with his contemporaries.

The people that were left of the sword have found grace in the wilderness (Jer. XXXI, 2): that means, for the sake of the generation of the wilderness.[1]

4. R. Ḥunia and R. Phinehas, R. Ḥanan and R. Hoshaia do not explain [what grace Noah found]; R. Berekiah in R. Joḥanan's name, R. Simeon b. Laḳish, and the Rabbis do explain. R. Johanan said: Imagine a man walking on a road, when he saw someone whom he attached to himself. To what extent? Until he was knit to him in love. Similarly, 'grace' is said here, while in another passage we read, *And Joseph found favour* [grace] *in his sight* (Gen. XXXIX, 3).[2] R. Simeon b. Laḳish said: Imagine a man walking on a road, when he saw someone whom he attached to himself. To what extent? So much that he conferred dominion upon him. Similarly, *'grace'* is said here, while elsewhere it says, *And Esther obtained favour in the sight of all them that looked upon her* (Est. II, 15).[3] The Rabbis said: It may be compared to one who was walking on a road, when he saw a man whom he attached to himself so strongly that he gave him his daughter in marriage. Similarly, *'grace'* is said here, while elsewhere it is said, *And I will pour upon the house of David and upon the inhabitants of Jerusalem the spirit of grace* (Zech. XII, 10).[4] How far [did God's favour to Noah extend]?—Until he knew which animal was to be fed at two hours of the day and which beast was to be fed at three hours of the night.[5]

5. R. Abbahu said: We find that the Holy One, blessed be He, shows mercy to the descendants for the sake of their

[1] Th.. this is mentioned in passing, because R. Simon has just spoken about 'finding'.
[2] *'Favour'* and 'grace' are the same in Hebrew (*hen*).—Thus Noah found as much favour in God's sight as Joseph in his master's.
[3] The result being that Ahasuerus made her queen so that she enjoyed honour and power
[4] Which will unite them as though in wedlock with the Almighty Each successive comparison connotes a higher degree of favour and intimacy. [5] V. Sanh. 108*b*.

forbears.[1] But how do we know that the Lord shows mercy to the forbears for the sake of their descendants? Because it says, BUT NOAH FOUND GRACE, which was for the sake of his offspring, as it is written, *These are the generations of Noah.*[2]

[1] Lit. 'later ones . . . earlier ones' [2] Interpreting. But Noah found grace because of these generations that followed him.

Chapter XXX
NOACH

1. These are the generations of Noah (vi, 9). *When the whirlwind passeth, the wicked is no more; but the righteous is an everlasting foundation* (Prov. x, 25). '*When the whirlwind passeth, the wicked is no more*'—this refers to the generation of the Flood; '*But the righteous is an everlasting foundation*'—this refers to Noah, as it is written, These are the generations of Noah: Noah was a righteous man.

The wicked are overthrown, and are not (*ib.* xii, 7): this refers to the generation of the Flood; *But the house of the righteous shall stand* (*ib.*)—this refers to Noah: These are the generations of Noah.

The house of the wicked shall be overthrown (*ib.* xiv, 11): this refers to the generation of the Flood; *But the tent of the upright shall flourish* (*ib.*)—this refers to Noah: These are the generations of Noah.[1]

2. *He is swift* (ḳal) *upon the face of the waters* (Job xxiv, 18): A decree was pronounced against them that they should perish by water[2]; *Their portion is cursed in the earth* (*ib.*), [as people curse], He who punished the generation of the Flood [punish them].[3] And why all this?—Because, *He turneth not by the way of the vineyards* (*ib.*): their intention was not to plant vineyards.[4] But Noah's only intention was to be fruitful and multiply in the world: hence, These are the generations of Noah.[5]

3. These: R. Abbahu said: Wherever 'these' (*eleh*) is written, it cancels the preceding; 'and these' (*we-eleh*) adds to the preceding. Here that 'these' is written, it

[1] I.e. Noah alone was blessed with generations which continued after him and formed the origins of the new world.
[2] *Ḳal* is connected with *ḳol*, a voice: there is a voice, i.e. a decree; cf. Dan. iv, 28. [3] Cf. B.M. 44*a*. I.e. they shall remain in the earth only as a means of cursing. [4] They indulged in sexual enjoyment without the intention to procreate. [5] Cf Sanh. 108*a*.

cancels the preceding. What does it cancel? The generation of the Flood.[1]

4. THESE ARE THE OFFSPRING OF NOAH: NOAH [WAS A RIGHTEOUS MAN]. R. Abba b. Kahana said: Whoever has his name thus repeated has a portion in this world and in the World to Come. They raised an objection to him: But it is written, *Now these are the generations of Terah. Terah begot Abram*, etc. (Gen. XI, 27): has he a portion in this world and in the future world? Even this does not contradict me, he replied, for R. Judan said in R. Abba's name: *But thou* [Abraham] *shalt go to thy fathers in peace* (*ib.* XV, 15): He [God] informed him that his father had a portion in the World to Come; *Thou shalt be buried in a good old age* (*ib.*): He informed him that Ishmael would repent.[2]

5. THESE ARE THE OFFSPRING OF NOAH: NOAH, etc. Surely Scripture should have written, 'These are the offspring of Noah: Shem,' etc.? It teaches, however, that he was a comfort to himself and a comfort to the world, a comfort to his fathers and a comfort to his children, a comfort to celestial beings and to mortals; [a comfort] in this world and in the World to Come.[3]

6. THESE ARE THE OFFSPRINGS OF NOAH: NOAH. Thus it is written, *The fruit of the righteous is a tree of life, and he that is wise taketh souls* (Prov. XI, 30): what is the fruit of the righteous? Life, religious actions, and good deeds.[4] *And he that is wise taketh souls:* for he fed and provided for [its inhabitants] the whole twelve months in the Ark. After all this praise, *Behold, shall the righteous be requited in the earth* (*ib.* 31)?[5] When he was about to leave it, was he requited? Surely R. Huna said in R. Liezer's

[1] Cf. *supra*, XII, 3 I.e. the generation of the Flood perished completely, so that its offspring are not to be counted. [2] *Infra*, XXXVIII, 12.
[3] Connecting *noaḥ* with *nahem*, to comfort, as in V, 29.
[4] Interpreting: The offspring of Noah were his righteousness and good deeds. [5] The Midrash understands this as a question

name: When Noah was leaving the Ark a lion set on him and maimed him, so that he was not fit to sacrifice,[1] and his son Shem sacrificed in his stead. Infer from this: *How much more the wicked and the sinner* (*ib.*), which refers to the generation of the Flood.[2]

7. [NOAH WAS IN HIS GENERATIONS] A MAN [RIGHTEOUS AND WHOLE-HEARTED]. Wherever '*a man*' occurs, it indicates a righteous man who warned [his generation]. For a whole one hundred and twenty years[3] Noah planted cedars and cut them down. On being asked, 'Why are you doing this?' he replied: 'The Lord of the universe has informed me that He will bring a Flood in the world.' Said they [his contemporaries] to him: 'If a Flood does come, it will come only upon your father's house!' Thus it is written, *A contemptible brand* (lappid buz) *in the thought of him that is at ease, a thing ready for them whose foot slippeth* (Job XII, 5). R. Abba interpreted: The Holy One, blessed be He, said: 'One herald arose for me in the generation of the Flood, viz. Noah.' For elsewhere[4] people say, 'Arouse him, stir him up!'[5] '*Buz*' (contempt) intimates that they despised him and called him, 'Contemptible old man!' *In the thought of* (le-'ashtoth) *him that is at ease:* this teaches that they were as hard as metal (*'ashtoth*).[6] *A thing ready for them whose foot slippeth:* two disasters were ready for them: a disaster from above and a disaster from below.[7]

[1] A maimed person may not engage in sacrificial service.

[2] In spite of his comparative righteousness, Noah was thus punished for his sins (v. *supra* · God did not find grace in Noah); how much more then are the really wicked to be punished!

[3] V. Gen. VI, 3, which according to the Rabbis meant that God gave 120 years' warning before bringing the Flood.

[4] Probably referring to Babylon, Genesis Rabbah being a Palestinian work.

[5] Aramaic *lepod*, to stir up. This is quoted to show that *lappid* (E.V. 'brand') means, 'arouse,' 'stir up.'

[6] Translating: to the metal-hearted who are at ease.

[7] Cf. Gen. VII, 11: . . . *Were all the fountains of the great deep broken up, and the windows of heaven were opened*. Thus their disaster came from below and above.

8. WHOLE-HEARTED. Bar Ḥuṭah said: Every man whom the Scripture designates '*Whole-hearted*' completed his years according to the measure of the Septennate.[1]

WAS. R. Joḥanan said: Every man of whom it is said that he 'was' (*hayah*) remained unchanged from beginning to end.[2] An objection was raised: But it is written, *Abraham was one, and he inherited the land* (Ezek. XXXIII, 24): was he then unchanged from beginning to end! That too does not refute me, he replied: R. Joḥanan and R. Ḥanina both said: Abraham was forty-eight years old when he recognised his Creator. Then how is 'was' to be understood in his case?[3] He was destined to lead the whole world to repentance.[4] [Similarly], *Behold, the man was* (Gen. III, 22)[5] means: destined to die. *The serpent was* (*ib.* I): destined to punishment. *Cain was* (*ib.* IV, 2): predestined to exile; *Job was* (Job I, I): destined to suffering; NOAH WAS: destined for a miracle[6]; *Moses was* (Ex. III, I): destined to be a redeemer; *Mordecai was* (Est. II, 5): destined for redemption.[7]

R. Levi said: Everyone of whom it is said that he 'was' (*hayah*) saw a new world. Said R. Samuel b. Naḥman: And they are five. Noah: yesterday [it was a case of] *The waters wear the stones* (Job XIV, 19), for R. Levi said in R. Joḥanan's name: Even the nether millstone was dissolved by the water;[8] whereas now you read, *And the sons of Noah that went forth*, etc. (Gen. IX, 18)! Thus he saw a new world. Joseph: yesterday, *His feet they hurt with fetters* (Ps. CV, 18), while now, *And Joseph was the governor over the land* (Gen. XLII, 6)! Thus he saw a new world. Moses: yesterday he was fleeing from Pharaoh, and now he plunges him into

[1] I.e. he lived a multiple of seven years after this epithet was applied to him. Thus Noah lived 350 years after the Flood Again, Abraham was told to be whole-hearted when he was commanded to circumcise himself at the age of 99, and lived to the age of 175, which is 77 years more, including the 99th year. Similarly, David lived 70 years. On the significance of 7 v. *J.E.* art. *Numbers and Numeral.*

[2] Lit. 'that was his beginning, that was his end'.

[3] Since there was a change in his life.

[4] From birth. Thus in that respect he remained unchanged.

[5] Lit. translation of *hayah*. E.V. 'is become'.

[6] Or possibly: destined to be a sign to his contemporaries.

[7] Ex R. II, 4; Est. R VI, 3. [8] *Supra*, XXVIII, 3.

the sea! Thus he saw a new world Job: yesterday, *He poureth out my gall upon the ground* (Job XVI, 13). While now, *And the Lord gave Job twice as much as he had before* (*ib* XLII, 10)! Thus he saw a new world. Mordecai: yesterday he was ready for the gallows, and now he executes his executioner! Thus he saw a new world. The Rabbis said: Every man of whom it is said that he 'was' (*hayah*) fed and sustained others. Noah fed and sustained [the inmates of the Ark] twelve months, as it says, *And take thou unto thee of all food that is eaten* (Gen. VI, 21). Joseph fed and sustained: *And Joseph sustained*, etc (*ib.* XLVII, 12). Moses fed and sustained [the Israelites] the whole forty years in the wilderness Job fed and sustained: *Or have I eaten my morsel myself alone*, etc. (Job XXXI, 17)?—did not the fatherless eat thereof! But did Mordecai actually feed and sustain?[1] Said R. Judan: On one occasion he went round to all the wet nurses but could not find one for Esther, whereupon he himself suckled her R. Berekiah and R. Abbahu in R. Eleazar's name said: Milk came to him and he suckled her.[2] When R. Abbahu taught this publicly, the congregation laughed. Said he to them: Yet is it not a Mishnah?[3] R. Simeon b. Eleazar said: The milk of a male is clean.[4]

9. IN HIS GENERATIONS. R. Judah and R. Nehemiah differed. R. Judah said: Only in his generations was he a righteous man [by comparison]; had he flourished in the generation of Moses or Samuel, he would not have been called righteous: in the street of the totally blind, the one-eyed man is called clear-sighted, and the infant is called a scholar. It is as if a man who had a wine vault opened one barrel and found it vinegar; another and found it vinegar; the third, however, he found turning sour. 'It is turning,' people said to him. 'Is there any better here?' he retorted. Similarly, IN HIS GENERATIONS he was a righteous man. R. Nehemiah said. If he was righteous even in *his* generation,[5] how much more so [had

[1] Surely there is no record of that!
[2] Always, and he never sought a wet-nurse. [3] Makshirin VI, 7.
[4] Est. R. *ib.*; cf. Shab. 53*b*. [5] In spite of his corrupt environment.

he lived] in the age of Moses. He might be compared to a tightly closed phial of perfume lying in a graveyard, which nevertheless gave forth a fragrant odour; how much more then if it were outside the graveyard ![1]

10. NOAH WALKED WITH GOD. R. Judah said: This may be compared to a king who had two sons, one grown up and the other a child. To the child he said, 'Walk *with* me,' but to the adult, 'Walk before me.' Similarly, to Abraham, whose [moral] strength was great, [He said,] '*Walk thou* before *Me*' (Gen. XVII, 1); of Noah, whose strength was feeble [it says], NOAH WALKED WITH GOD. R. Nehemiah said: He might be compared to a king's friend who was plunging about in dark alleys, and when the king looked out and saw him sinking [in the mud], he said to him, 'Instead of plunging about in dark alleys, come and walk with me.' But Abraham's case is rather to be compared to that of a king who was sinking in dark alleys, and when his friend saw him he shone a light for him through the window. Said he to him, 'Instead of lighting me through the window, come and show a light before me.' Even so did the Holy One, blessed be He, say to Abraham: 'Instead of showing a light for Me from Mesopotamia and its environs, come and show one before Me in Eretz Israel.'

Similarly, it is written, *And he blessed Joseph, and said: The God before whom my fathers Abraham and Isaac did walk*, etc. (Gen. XLVIII, 15). R. Berekiah in R. Joḥanan's name and Resh Laḳish gave two illustrations of this. R. Joḥanan said: It was as if a shepherd stood and watched his flocks.[2] Resh Laḳish said: It was as if a prince walked along while the elders preceded him.[3] On R. Joḥanan's view: We need His proximity.[4] On the view of Resh Laḳish: He needs us to glorify Him.[5]

[1] Sanh. 108*a*.
[2] Similarly, Abraham and Isaac walked before God and in His protection.
[3] As an escort, to make known his coming. Similarly, Abraham and Isaac walked before God, spreading His knowledge.
[4] Lit. 'place'. We must be near to God, as it were, so as to enjoy His protection.
[5] By propagating the knowledge of His greatness.

CHAPTER XXXI (NOACH)

1. AND GOD SAID UNTO NOAH: THE END OF ALL FLESH IS COME BEFORE ME; FOR THE EARTH IS FILLED WITH VIOLENCE THROUGH THEM (VI, 13). It is written, *Violence is risen up as a rod of wickedness; nought cometh from them, nor from their tumult* (hamonam), *nor from their turmoil* (hemehem); *neither is there eminency* (nohah) *among them* (Ezek. VII, 11). '*Violence is risen up*'—heaven forfend! It has not risen up. Yet if it has, it is as '*A rod of wickedness*'—to punish the wicked. '*Nought cometh from them, nor from their tumult* (hamonam).' '*Nor from their turmoil* (hemehem)': i.e. neither from them nor from their wealth[1] nor from their dazzling magnificence. Why so? Because '*Neither is there* nohah [E.V. "*eminency*"] *among them*'. No creature ever enjoyed satisfaction,[2] nor did the Holy One, blessed be He, receive satisfaction from them.[3] '*Neither is there* nohah *among them*': There was none to say to them: 'Let there be lamenting!'[4] Again: '*Neither was there* nohah *among them*' [is to be explained] as R. Abba b. Kahana commented: *For it repenteth Me that I have made them and Noah* (Gen. VI, 7 f.). But even Noah, who was left, was not worthy, save that he found grace as it is written, *But Noah found grace* (*ib*).[5] And because they were steeped in robbery, they were blotted out from the world, as it says, AND GOD SAID UNTO NOAH: THE END OF ALL FLESH IS COME BEFORE ME, FOR THE EARTH IS FILLED WITH VIOLENCE THROUGH THEM.[6]

2. *They made oil within their rows*, etc. (Job XXIV, 11): that means that they set up small oil-presses[7]; *They tread*

[1] *Hamon* is sometimes used in that sense; cf. Eccl. v, 9

[2] *Naḥath ruah*, lit. 'pleasing' or 'calming of the spirit'.

[3] Reading *nohah* (נה) as *noah* (נח); possibly too the latter was their actual reading. [4] Heb. *nehi*, i.e penitence. [5] Translating: Not even Noah among them was worthy; v. *supra*, XXVIII, 8.

[6] The idea of this ending here and the following passages is probably that notwithstanding all the other wrongs they perpetrated, the Flood actually came on account of robbery; cf. Sanh. 108*a*.

[7] Actually between the rows of olives, so as to press them immediately.

their wine-presses, and suffer thirst (*ib.*): even when they tread their wine-presses, they suffer thirst. R. Aibu said: Why do '*They tread their wine-presses, and suffer thirst*'? Because a curse rested upon the toil of the wicked. And because they were steeped in robbery, they were blotted out from the world: hence, AND GOD SAID UNTO NOAH, etc.

3. *They hate him that reproveth in the gate, and they abhor him that speaketh uprightly* (Amos v, 10). He [Noah] reproved them: 'Ye good-for-nothings! Ye forsake Him whose voice breaks cedars and worship a dry log!' And because they were steeped in robbery, they were blotted out from the world: hence, AND GOD SAID TO NOAH, etc

4. *By reason of the multitude of* (merob) *oppressions they cry out; they cry for help by reason of the arm of the mighty* (Job xxxv, 9): '*By reason of the multitude of oppressions they cry out*' refers to the oppressed; '*They cry for help by reason of the arm of the mighty*' to the oppressors: the latter contended with the former, and the former with the latter,[1] until the decree of their judgment was sealed. And because they were steeped in robbery they were blotted out from the world: hence, AND GOD SAID UNTO NOAH, etc.

5. THE END (ḲEẒ) OF ALL FLESH (BASAR) IS COME BEFORE ME: The time has come for them to be cut down (*hikkaẓeẓ*); the time has come for them to be treated as unripe grapes (*boser*)[2]; the term of their indictments has come. Why all this? BECAUSE THE EARTH IS FILLED WITH VIOLENCE (ḤAMAS) THROUGH THEM. What is '*ḥamas*' (violence) and what is *gezel* (robbery)? Said R. Ḥanina: '*Ḥamas*' (violence) refers to what is worth a *peruṭah*; *gezel* (robbery), to what is of less value than a

[1] Th. conjectures that *merob* (E.V. *multitude of*) is connected with *rib* and *meribah*, strife. [2] By a play on words, *ḳeẓ* (קץ) and *basar* (בשר) are connected with *hikkaẓeẓ* (הקצץ) and *boser* (בוסר) respectively.

perutah.[1] And this is what the people of the age of the Flood used to do: When a man brought out a basket full of lupines [for sale], one would come and seize less than a *perutah's* worth and then everyone would come and seize less than a *perutah's* worth, so that he had no redress at law. Whereupon the Holy One, blessed be He, said: 'Ye have acted improperly, so will I too deal with you improperly.'[2] Hence it is written, *Is not their tent-cord plucked up within them? They die, and that without wisdom* (Job IV, 21): i.e. without the wisdom of the Torah. *Betwixt morning and evening they are shattered; they perish for ever without any regarding* (mesim) *it* (*ib.* 20). Now '*mesim*' can only refer to judgment,[3] as you read, *Now these are the ordinances* [judgments] *which thou shalt set* (tasim) *before them* (Ex. XXI, 1).[4]

6. Another interpretation: FOR THE EARTH IS FILLED WITH ḤAMAS (VIOLENCE), etc. R. Levi said: '*Ḥamas*' connotes idolatry, incest,[5] and murder. Idolatry, as it is written, FOR THF EARTH IS FILLED WITH ḤAMAS.[6] Incest: *The violence done to me* (ḥamasi fr. ḥamas) *and to my flesh* (she'eri) *be upon Babylon* (Jer. LI, 35).[7] Murder: *For the* ḥamas [E.V. '*violence*'] *against the children of Judah because they have shed innocent blood* (Joel LV, 19). In addition, *ḥamas* (violence) bears its literal meaning also.[8]

7. BEHOLD, I WILL DESTROY THEM WITH THE EARTH. R. Huna and R. Jeremiah in R. Kahana's name

[1] A *perutah* being the smallest coin, in the latter case there was no redress. The commentaries reverse these definitions, and the text too demands it.
[2] I.e. in a way that you will not relish.
[3] Here in the sense of civil law—i.e. because they evaded its provisions.
[4] V. *supra*, XXVI, 6. [5] The term in Hebrew includes adultery.
[6] This is not altogether clear. It is explained in the לקח טוב thus: the verse implies that they rejected Him whose glory fills the earth, hence they engaged in idolatry. Others, however, read: *In that they fill the earth with* ḥamas (*violence*)—Ezek. VIII, 17, which refers to idolatry, of which the whole chapter treats; v. also Sanh. 57*a*.
[7] MSS. add: and *she'er* must refer to incest, cf. Lev. XVIII, 6: *None of you shall approach to* she'er besaro (E.V. '*any that is near of kin to him*'; besaro, lit. 'his flesh'). [8] Viz. robbery.

said: Even the three handbreadths of the earth's surface which the plough turns was washed away.[1] It is as if a royal prince had a tutor, and whenever he did wrong, his tutor was punished; or as if a royal prince had a nurse, and whenever he did wrong, his nurse was punished. Similarly, the Holy One, blessed be He, said, 'BEHOLD, I WILL DESTROY THEM WITH THE EARTH: behold, I will destroy them and the earth with them'[2]

8. MAKE THEE AN ARK, etc. (VI, 14). R. Issi said: In four places this phrase '*Make thee*' is employed; in three places it is explained,[3] while in one it is not explained. Thus: MAKE THEE AN ARK OF GOPHER WOOD, etc R. Nathan said: That means with beams of cedar.[4] *Make thee knives of flint* (Josh. V, 2) means flint knives. *Make thee two trumpets of silver* (Num. X, 2) is likewise clear in meaning. But the meaning of *Make thee a fiery serpent* (*ib.* XXI, 8) is not clear.[5] R. Judan said in R. Assi's name: *The wise man may hear, and increase in learning* (Prov. I, 6) applies to Moses, who reasoned thus: If I make it of gold (*zahab*) or of silver (*kesef*), these words do not correspond to the other.[6] Hence I will make it of *neḥosheth* (brass), since this word corresponds to the other, viz. *neḥash neḥosheth*—a serpent of brass (*ib.* 9): this proves that the Torah was given in Hebrew.[7] R. Phinehas and R. Hezekiah in R. Simon's name said: Just as the Torah was given in Hebrew, so was the world created with Hebrew: have you ever heard one say, *gini, ginia; itha, ittha; antropi, antropia; gabra, gabretha?* But [we do say] *ish* and *isha*: why? because one form corresponds to the other.[8]

9. WITH ḲINNIM [E.V. 'ROOMS'] SHALT THOU MAKE THE ARK: i.e. cells and chambers. R. Isaac said:

[1] Thus translating the verse literally.
[2] The earth too being regarded as man's nurse, as it were. Cf. *supra*, XXVIII, 6. [3] What was to be made. [4] A kind of cedar is meant.
[5] The material is left in doubt. [6] Viz. *naḥash* (serpent).
[7] For only in Hebrew do these words correspond. [8] V. *supra*, XVIII, 4.

Just as a *ken* (pair of birds) cleanses a leper,[1] so shall thy ark cleanse thee.[2]

AND THOU SHALT PITCH IT WITHIN AND WITHOUT WITH PITCH. Yet elsewhere it says, *And she daubed it* with slime *and with pitch* (Ex. II, 3)? There, since the water [of the Nile] was gentle, '*She daubed it with slime*' on account of the water, '*And with pitch*' on account of the odour.[3]

10. AND THIS IS HOW THOU SHALT MAKE IT (VI, 15). R. Judan said: AND THIS [is written where], THIS [would have sufficed]: [God intimated]: Another[4] is destined to measure with thy cubit, as it is written, *The length of the building after the ancient* [lit. 'first'] *measure was twenty cubits, and the breadth twenty cubits* (II Chron. III, 3).[5] And why is it [the cubit] called *tibikon?*[6] R. Huna said: Because it comes from Thebes.[7] The Rabbis said: On account of Noah's *tebah* (ark).[8]

THE LENGTH OF THE ARK THREE HUNDRED CUBITS, etc. Bar Ḥuṭa quoted: *I will meditate in Thy precepts . . . I will delight myself in Thy statutes* (Ps. CXIX, 15 f.): the Torah teaches you practical knowledge, that if

[1] V. Lev. XIV, 4 *seq.*

[2] This is a play on words, connecting *kinnim* with *ken*. v. *supra*, XXVIII, 9; even Noah was not worthy—hence he needed cleansing.

[3] Soṭ. 12*a*; Ex. R. I, 21. M.K and Y.T. reverse it: with slime on account of the smell and with pitch on account of the water—i e. pitch on the outside to make it watertight, slime on the inside but not pitch, which has an unpleasant odour. On the present reading the idea is somewhat similar: with slime on the inside as an additional means of making it watertight, and with pitch on the outside only, but not on the inside, on account of the smell.

[4] Sc. Solomon, '*And*' is regarded as an extension, God thereby intimating that one day another edifice of a different nature would be measured, viz. the Temple.

[5] The quotation is incorrect, and should read: *The length by cubits . . . was threescore cubits;* v. Ezek. XLI, 15, which may be the source of the error. The ancient (first) measure is taken to refer to Noah's measuring of the ark.

[6] Thebaic cubit, supposed to be the royal cubit of the Egyptians (Jast.).

[7] An ancient city of Egypt. Cur. edd.: because with it they fitted (the timber, etc.), i.e. they used this measure for building.

[8] *Tebah* and *tibikon* corresponding.

a man builds a ship which is to stand upright in harbour, he must make its breadth a sixth [of its length] and its height a tenth.[1]

11. A LIGHT (ẒOHAR) SHALT THOU MAKE TO THE ARK (VI, 16). R. Ḥunia and R. Phinehas, R. Ḥanan and R. Hoshaia could not explain [the meaning of ẒOHAR]; R. Abba b. Kahana and R. Levi did explain it. R. Abba b. Kahana said: It means a skylight; R. Levi said: A precious stone.[2]

R. Phinehas said in R. Levi's name: During the whole twelve months that Noah was in the Ark he did not require the light of the sun by day or the light of the moon by night, but he had a polished gem which he hung up: when it was dim he knew that it was day, and when it shone he knew that it was night.[3]

R. Huna said: Once we were taking refuge from [Roman] troops in the caves of Tiberias. We had lamps with us: when they were dim we knew that it was day, and when they shone brightly we knew that it was night.

AND TO A CUBIT SHALT THOU FINISH IT UPWARD. R. Judah and R. Nehemiah disagree. R. Judah said: It contained three hundred and thirty compartments, each compartment being ten cubits square, and two corridors each four cubits wide; the compartments ran along each side [of the corridor], and there were two cubits at the [outer] sides [of the compartments].[4] R. Nehemiah said: It contained nine hundred compartments, each being six cubits square, and three corridors of four cubits breadth, compartments running along each side and leaving two cubits at the [outer] sides.[5] On the view of R. Judah there

[1] These were the proportions of Noah's ark.
[2] Which provided light from itself. [3] Cf. Sanh. 108*b*.
[4] I.e. a gangway one cubit in breadth ran right round the outer side of the ark, thus accounting for two cubits.
[5] V. Figures in Mah. R. Judah holds that there were four rows of thirty compartments on each of the first and second stories, but only three rows on the third, owing to its greater narrowness. But R. Nehemiah maintains that there were six rows of fifty compartments on each of the three stories.

is no difficulty[1]; but on R. Nehemiah's view there is a difficulty?[2] As was its cubit below so was its cubit above: AND TO A CUBIT SHALT THOU FINISH IT UPWARD.[3] R. Nehemiah said: It was like a vaulted carriage, and he built it sloping inwards so that it tapered to a cubit.[4]

AND THE DOOR OF THE ARK SHALT THOU SET IN THE SIDE THEREOF. R. Isaac said: The Torah teaches you practical knowledge, that when you make a chamber ten cubits square, you should set its door at the side.

WITH LOWER, SECOND, AND THIRD STORIES SHALT THOU MAKE IT: the bottom storey for garbage, the second for himself and family and the clean animals, and the third for the unclean [ones]. Others reverse it: The bottom storey for the unclean animals, the second for himself and family and the clean animals, and the top for the garbage. How then did he manage?[5] He arranged a kind of trapdoor through which he shovelled it sideways.[6]

SHALT THOU MAKE IT. It helped [to build] itself.[7]

12. AND I, BEHOLD (VI, 17): I agree with the angels who urged, *What is man, that Thou art mindful of him* (Ps. VIII, 5)?[8]

BEHOLD, I DO BRING THE FLOOD OF WATERS. They were first waters, and as soon as they descended on the earth they became a flood.[9]

[EVERYTHING THAT IS IN THE EARTH] YIGWA' [E.V. 'SHALL PERISH']: i.e. shall shrivel up.[10]

[1] It tapered, hence the top storey contained only three rows.
[2] How could the top storey contain as many rows as the bottom ones?
[3] This passage is very obscure. M.K.: R. Judah holds that the same cubit that was used in measuring the bottom of the ark was used in measuring the top (cubits varied), and this is the meaning of the verse, viz and by the (same) cubit thou shalt finish it above.
[4] I.e. the three stories were of *equal* breadth, and they were topped by an inward sloping roof, the thirty cubits height being exclusive of this roof.
[5] To get the garbage (excrements) to the bottom, this question being based on the first view.
[6] Sanh. 108*b*. [7] This follows by reading תֵּעָשֶׂה, it shall make itself.
[8] Cf *supra*, VIII, 6; Sanh. 38*b*
[9] M.K.: a destroying and devastating deluge.
[10] Th.: and sink down into the depths like a stone.

BUT I WILL ESTABLISH MY COVENANT WITH THEE, etc. (VI, 18). Thou needest a covenant for the sake of the produce, that it should not decay or rot. Thou needest a covenant: the giants set their feet on the [opening of the] deep and closed it up, then each attempted to enter the Ark, whereupon his feet became entangled [in the water], as it is written, *The giants* [E.V. '*shades*'] *tremble beneath the waters and the inhabitants thereof*—shokenehem (Job XXVI, 5). [Read] *Shekenehem* (their neighbours)[1]: a lion would come to the Ark and his teeth would loosen, as it is written, *The lion roareth, and the fierce lion howleth and the teeth of the young lions are broken* (*ib.* IV, 10). R. Ḥiyya b. Abba explained: Thou wast indeed the builder, yet but for My convenant which stood thee in stead, couldst thou have entered the Ark?[2] Thus it is written, BUT I WILL ESTABLISH MY COVENANT WITH THEE: when [will that be proved]? When thou art brought into the Ark.[3]

THOU, AND THY SONS, etc. R. Judah b. R. Simon and R. Ḥanan in the name of R. Samuel b. R. Isaac said: As soon as Noah entered the Ark, cohabitation was interdicted to him; hence it is written, AND THOU SHALT COME INTO THE ARK, THOU, AND THY SONS—apart; AND THY WIFE, AND THY SONS' WIVES—apart. When he went out, He permitted it to him, as it is written, *Go forth from the ark, thou and thy wife*, etc. (Gen. VIII, 16).[4] R. Abin quoted: *They are lonely in want and famine* (Job XXX, 3): when want and famine visit the world, regard your wife as though she were lonely [i.e. menstruous]. R. Muna said: It is written, *And unto Joseph were born two sons* (Gen. XLI, 50): when? Before *the year of famine came* (*ib.*).[5]

[1] The wild beasts, of which the lion is quoted as an example.
[2] You would have been prevented from entering.
[3] On all views the 'covenant' here does not refer to the rainbow, but to God's assistance, without which Noah could never have made the Ark, or, having made it, would not have been able to keep out the great giants and wild animals.
[4] He and his wife being mentioned together.
[5] Cf. *infra*, XXXIV, 7; Sanh. 108*b*.

13. AND OF EVERY LIVING THING, OF ALL FLESH, etc. (VI, 19). R. Hoshaya said: Even spirits entered the ark with Noah; hence it is written, AND OF EVERY LIVING THING, OF ALL FLESH: i.e. of those for whom souls [spirits] were created but not bodies.[1]

R. Judah said: The *re'em*[2] did not enter the Ark,[3] but his whelps did. R. Nehemiah said: Neither he nor his whelps, but Noah tied him to the Ark, and he ploughed furrows [in the water] as great as from Tiberias to Susitha,[4] as it is written, *Canst thou bind the wild-ox with his hand in the furrow, or will he harrow the valleys after thee* (Job XXXIX, 10)? In the days of R. Ḥiyya b. Abba a [*re'em's*] whelp invaded Eretz Israel and did not leave a single tree which it did not uproot. A fast was proclaimed and R. Ḥiyya prayed, whereupon its mother bellowed from the desert and it [the whelp] went down [to the desert] at her voice.

THEY SHALL BE MALE AND FEMALE. [God instructed Noah]: 'If thou seest a male pursuing a female, accept him; a female pursuing a male, do not accept him.'

14. AND TAKE THOU UNTO THEE OF ALL FOOD THAT IS EATEN. R. Abba b. Kahana said: He took in pressed figs with him.[5] It was taught in R. Nehemiah's name: The greater part of his provisions consisted of pressed figs. R. Abba b. Kahana said: He took in branches for the elephants, *ḥazubah*[6] for the deer, and glass for the ostriches. R. Levi said: Vine-shoots for vine plantings, fig-shoots for fig trees, and olive-shoots for olive trees. In the view of R. Abba b. Kahana: *And it shall be for thee, and for them* implies something that is for thee and for them. In the view of R. Levi *And it shall be for thee, and*

[1] This follows by contrast: since OF ALL FLESH is mentioned separately, LIVING THING must refer to those that have life without flesh; cf. *supra*, VII, 5.
[2] Wild ox. A fabulous animal of enormous height.
[3] Being too high.
[4] Which lies on the opposite side of the Lake of Tiberias.
[5] These are eaten by all.
[6] A shrubby plant, prob. *cistus* (Jast. s.v. חצובה I).

for them implies, Thou art the principal and they are of secondary importance; *And gather it to thee:* a man does not gather [store] anything unless he needs it [for later].[1]

THUS DID NOAH; ACCORDING TO ALL THAT GOD COMMANDED HIM, SO DID HE (VI, 22). This text refers to the construction of the Ark.[2]

[1] He understands gather (ואספת) to mean store, hence it means for *future* use, viz for replanting Rashash *Infra*, XXXVI, 3.
[2] Noah made the Ark as God commanded him.

Chapter XXXII (NOACH)

1. And the Lord said unto Noah: Come thou and all thy house into the ark, etc. (VII, 1). It is written, *Thou destroyest them that speak falsehood,* etc. (Ps. V, 7): this refers to Doeg and Ahitophel; '*Them that speak falsehood*': them and their speech. R. Phinehas said: Them and their company.[1] *The man of blood and deceit* (*ib.*): the one permitted incest and bloodshed, and the other permitted incest and bloodshed. The one [Ahitophel] permitted incest and bloodshed, [when he counselled Absalom], *Go in unto thy father's concubines* (II Sam. XVI, 21). The other [Doeg] permitted incest: [Where do we find this]? Said R. Nahman b. Samuel b. Naḥman: He annulled his [David's] citizen rights and declared him an outlaw and as one dead, so that his blood was permitted and his wife was permitted. *The Lord abhorreth* (Ps. *loc. cit.*): this means that they will neither be resurrected nor judged. *But as for me* (*ib.* 8): as they have acted so have I acted[2]; yet what is the difference between me and them? Only that Thou hast shown me love and saidst to me, *The Lord also hath put away thy sin: thou shalt not die* (II Sam. XII, 13).

[Another interpretation]: It refers to the generation of the Flood: '*Thou destroyest them that speak falsehood*': them and their speech. '*The man of blood,*' as it is written, *The murderer riseth with the light,* etc. (Job XXIV, 14); '*And deceit,*' as it is written, *For the earth is filled with violence* (Gen. VI, 13). '*The Lord abhorreth*': they [the generation of the Flood] will neither be resurrected nor judged. '*But as for me*' [Noah]: as they have acted so have I acted,[3] yet what is the difference between me and them? Only that Thou showedst love to me and saidst to me: Come thou and all thy house into the ark.

[1] Deriving *dovere* (E.V. '*speak*') from *davar,* to lead: those who follow their lead. [2] In taking Bathsheba, Uriah's wife.
[3] Cf. the statement *supra,* XXVIII, 9, that Noah too was unworthy.

2. *For the Lord is righteous, He loveth righteousness; the upright shall behold His face* (Ps. XI, 7). R. Tanḥuma in R. Judah's name and R. Menaḥem in R. Eleazar's name said: No man loves his fellow-craftsman. A Sage, however, loves his compeer, e.g. R. Ḥiyya loves his colleagues and R. Hoshaya his.[1] The Holy One, blessed be He, also loves His fellow-craftsman[2]: hence, '*For the Lord is righteous, He loveth righteousness; The upright shall behold His face*' applies to Noah, as it is written, AND THE LORD SAID UNTO NOAH: COME THOU . . . FOR THEE HAVE I SEEN RIGHTEOUS BEFORE ME.[3]

3. *The Lord trieth the righteous; but the wicked and him that loveth violence His soul hateth* (Ps. XI, 5). R. Jonathan said: A potter does not test defective vessels, because he cannot give them a single blow without breaking them. Similarly the Holy One, blessed be He, does not test the wicked but only the righteous: thus, '*The Lord trieth the righteous.*' R. Jose b. R. Ḥanina said: When a flax worker knows that his flax is of good quality, the more he beats it the more it improves and the more it glistens; but if it is of inferior quality, he cannot give it one knock without its splitting. Similarly, the Lord does not test the wicked but only the righteous, as it says, '*The Lord trieth the righteous.*' R. Eleazar said: When a man possesses two cows, one strong and the other feeble, upon which does he put the yoke? Surely upon the strong one. Similarly, the Lord tests none but the righteous: hence, '*The Lord trieth the righteous.*' Another interpretation: '*The Lord trieth the righteous*' applies to Noah: hence, AND THE LORD SAID UNTO NOAH: COME THOU AND ALL THY HOUSE INTO THE ARK; FOR THEE HAVE I SEEN RIGHTEOUS, etc.[4]

FOR THEE HAVE I SEEN RIGHTEOUS, etc. R.

[1] Lit. 'R. Ḥiyya (those) of R. Ḥiyya', etc. Some suggest: E.g. R. Ḥiyya loved R. Hoshaya, etc. [2] He is righteous and loves those who are righteous, who are in that respect His fellow-craftsmen.

[3] Y.T.: the verse is quoted to show that God actually loves to see the righteous: hence, FOR THEE HAVE I SEEN, etc.

[4] *Infra*, XXXIV, 2, S S R. II, 16, § 2.

Eleazar b. 'Azariah said: We find that a portion of a man's merits may be declared in his presence, but all of them only in his absence. For thus it says in reference to Noah, FOR THEE HAVE I SEEN RIGHTEOUS,[1] whereas in his absence it says, *A man righteous and whole-hearted* (Gen. VI, 9). R. Eliezer b. R. Jose the Galilean said: We find that we utter but a portion of the praise of Him at whose word the world came into being, for it is said, *Say unto God: How tremendous is Thy work!* (Ps. LXVI, 3), and it says, *O give thanks unto the Lord, for He is good* (*ib* CXVIII, 1).[2]

4. OF EVERY CLEAN BEAST THOU SHALT TAKE TO THEE . . . AND OF THE BEASTS THAT ARE NOT CLEAN, etc. (VII, 2). R. Judan in R. Johanan's name, R. Berekiah in R. Leazar's name, and R. Jacob in R. Joshua's name said: We find that the Holy One, blessed be He, employed a circumlocution of three words in order to avoid uttering an unclean [indelicate] expression: It is not written, 'And of the unclean beasts,' but . . . THAT ARE NOT CLEAN.[3] R. Judan said: Even when [Scripture] comes to enumerate the signs of unclean animals, it commences first with the signs of cleanness [which they possess] it is not written, 'The camel, because he parteth not the hoof,' but, *Because he cheweth the cud but parteth not the hoof* (Lev. XI, 4); *The rock-badger, because he cheweth the cud but parteth not the hoof* (*ib.* 5); *The hare, because she cheweth the cud but parteth not the hoof* (*ib.* 6); *The swine, because he parteth the hoof, and is cloven-footed, but cheweth not the cud* (*ib.* 7).[4]

OF THE FOWL ALSO OF THE AIR, SEVEN EACH—E.V. 'SEVEN AND SEVEN' (VII, 3). If you say that it means seven of each kind,[5] one of them would lack a

[1] That was in speaking to him.
[2] 'Er. 18*b*. Whether this means in God's presence (i.e. when we are actually addressing Him, as in the first verse quoted) only or on all occasions is not quite clear, and the readings vary, v. Th. *ad loc.*
[3] In Heb. too four words are thus employed instead of one.
[4] Lev. R. XXVI, 1, Pes. 3*a*.
[5] While '*male and female*' might mean that the seven must include male and female—three of one and four of the other (Y.T. and Th.).

mate; hence it means seven males and seven females; 'not that I need them' [said God], 'but TO KEEP SEED ALIVE UPON THE FACE OF ALL THE EARTH.'

5. FOR YET SEVEN DAYS, etc. (VII, 4). R. Simeon b. Yohai said: They have transgressed the Torah which was given after forty days,[1] therefore I WILL CAUSE IT TO RAIN . . . FORTY DAYS AND FORTY NIGHTS. R. Johanan said: They corrupted the features which take shape after forty days,[2] therefore I WILL CAUSE IT TO RAIN . . . FORTY DAYS AND FORTY NIGHTS.

AND EVERY LIVING SUBSTANCE (YEKUM) THAT I HAVE MADE WILL I BLOT OUT. R. Berekiah said: That means, whatever exists (*kayomaya*) upon it.[3] R. Abin said: The one who arose against him [his brother].[4] R. Levi said in the name of Resh Lakish: He [God] kept him [Cain] in suspense[5] until the Flood came and swept him away: hence it is written, *And He blotted out every one that had arisen* (Gen. VII, 23).[6]

AND NOAH DID ACCORDING UNTO ALL, etc. (VII, 5). The present verse refers to the taking in of the animals, beasts, and birds.

6. AND NOAH WAS SIX HUNDRED YEARS OLD, etc. (VII, 6). R. Judah said: The year of the Flood is not counted in the number [of Noah's years].[7] Said R. Nehemiah to him: It is counted in the chronological reckoning.[8]

AND NOAH WENT IN, AND HIS SONS, etc. . . . BECAUSE OF THE WATERS OF THE FLOOD (VII, 7).

[1] Of Moses' stay in the mountain

[2] The features of a human embryo take shape after forty days. The idea of the expression is that sin is an essential degradation of the human dignity

[3] This translation of *yekum* corresponds to E.V.

[4] Viz. Cain, who arose against his brother, deriving *yekum* from *kam*, to arise. He was not punished at the time, but would now be punished.

[5] E.J.: i.e. He kept his judgment in suspense.

[6] Sc. Cain, cf. *supra*, XXII, 12. E.V '*Every living substance*'.

[7] For he was 600 years old when the Flood commenced, the Flood lasted a year in all, and he lived 350 years after the Flood (Gen. IX, 28), yet his total is given at 950 (*ib*. 29), not 951.

[8] When we count the number of years from the world's creation.

R. Joḥanan said: He lacked faith: had not the water reached his ankles he would not have entered the Ark.

7. AND IT CAME TO PASS AFTER THE SEVEN DAYS (VII, 10). This teaches that the Holy One, blessed be He, gave them a respite during the seven days' mourning for the righteous Methusaleh,[1] so that they might repent, yet they did not. Another interpretation. AND IT CAME TO PASS AFTER THE SEVEN DAYS: R. Joshua b. Levi said: Seven days the Holy One, blessed be He, mourned for His world before bringing the Flood, the proof being the text, *And it grieved Him* (Gen. VI, 6), while elsewhere we read, *The king grieveth for his son* (II Sam. XIX, 3).[2]

ON THE SAME DAY WERE ALL THE FOUNTAINS OF THE GREAT DEEP BROKEN UP, etc. (VII, 11). R. Jose b. Durmaskith said: They sinned through the eyeball,[3] which is like water, therefore the Holy One, blessed be He, punished them by water. R. Levi said: They abused their fountains,[4] therefore the Lord reversed the natural order: the natural order is for rain to descend and the deep to come up, but here, *Deep calleth unto deep* (Ps. XLII, 8).[5]

8. IN THE SELFSAME DAY ENTERED NOAH (VII, 13). R. Joḥanan said: Had Noah entered the Ark at night his whole generation would have said, 'We did not know what he was doing, but had we known we would not have permitted him to enter.' Hence he entered IN THE SELFSAME DAY [with the challenge], 'Let him who objects speak out!'[6]

[1] Cf. *supra*, III, 6.
[2] *Supra*, XXVII, 4. Sanh. 108*b*. The period of deep mourning for a near relation is seven days. [3] Through passion and lust.
[4] Cf. *supra*, XXVI, 4: 'they poured out their semen upon trees and stones.'
[5] Sanh. 108*a*. Th. prefers here the reading of cur. edd.: the natural order is for the rain to descend (first) and the deep to ascend (afterwards), as it is written, *Deep calleth unto deep at the voice of Thy cataracts* ('E.J.: the rain which descends causes the deep to ascend); whereas in the present instance, (first) '*All the fountains of the deep were broken up*'—i.e. the deep ascended—and after that '*The windows of heaven were opened*'—the rain descended [6] Cf. *infra*, XLVII, 9.

THEY, AND EVERY BEAST AFTER ITS KIND, etc. (VII, 14). They were the principals and all others were secondary.

EVERY BIRD OF EVERY WING.[1] R. Eleazar said: R. Jose interpreted this to his colleagues[2]: This excludes those which were moulting or maimed as unfit for the sacrifices of the Noachides.[3]

AND THEY THAT WENT IN, WENT IN MALE AND FEMALE OF ALL FLESH (VII, 16). Said he to Him: 'Am I a hunter!'[4] 'Does that matter to you,' He retorted; it is not written, 'And they that were brought,' but, AND THEY THAT WENT IN—of their own accord. R. Joḥanan quoted: *Seek ye out of the book of the Lord, and read* (Isa. XXXIV, 16): if they came of their own accord in order to be shut up twelve months in the Ark, how much the more [will they come] to gorge on the flesh of tyrants! Hence it is written, *And thou, son of man, thus saith the Lord God: Speak unto the birds of every sort, and to every beast of the field: Assemble yourselves, and come; gather yourselves on every side to My feast that I do prepare for you, even a great feast, upon the mountains of Israel, that ye may eat flesh and drink blood. The flesh of the mighty shall ye eat, and the blood of the princes of the earth shall ye drink*, etc. (Ezek. XXXIX, 17 f.).[5]

AND THE LORD SHUT HIM IN. R. Levi said. This may be compared to a king who decreed a general execution in a country, but took his friend, immured him in prison, and set his seal upon him.[6] Even so, AND THE LORD SHUT HIM IN.

9. AND THE WATERS INCREASED, AND BORE UP THE ARK, etc. (VII, 17). R. Phinehas said in R. Levi's name: Noah's ark thus sank in the water like a ship standing in harbour.

[1] Lit. translation. E.V. '*Of every sort*'. [2] Or possibly, to the scholars. [3] Hence: OF EVERY WING—i.e. were not maimed or lacking in feathers. As stated *supra* (XXVI, 1), some of these were required for sacrifices. Zeb. 116*a*. [4] How am I to know their sex? [5] Zeb., *loc cit.* [6] So that he might be spared.

AND THE WATERS PREVAILED . . . AND THE ARK WENT UPON THE FACE OF THE WATERS (VII, 18). R. Phinehas said in R. Levi's name: The ark thus floated upon the water as upon two planks[1] [covering a distance] as from Tiberias to Susitha.[2]

10. AND THE WATERS PREVAILED . . . AND ALL THE HIGH MOUNTAINS WERE COVERED (VII, 19). R. Jonathan was going up to worship in Jerusalem, when he passed the Palatinus[3] and was seen by a Samaritan, who asked him, 'Whither are you going?' 'To worship in Jerusalem,' replied he. 'Would it not be better to pray at this holy mountain than at that dunghill?' he jeered. 'Wherein is it blessed?' inquired he. 'Because it was not submerged by the Flood.' Now R. Jonathan momentarily forgot the teaching [on the subject], but his ass-driver said to him, 'Rabbi, with your permission I will answer him.' 'Do,' said he. 'If it is of the high mountains,' he answered, 'then it is written, AND ALL THE HIGH MOUNTAINS WERE COVERED. While if it is of the low ones, Scripture ignored it.' R. Jonathan immediately descended from his ass and made him [the driver] ride three miles and applied three verses to him: (i) *There shall not be male or female barren among you, or among your cattle* (Deut. VII, 14)—i.e. even among your cattle drivers[4]; (ii) Rakkathek [E.V. '*thy temples*'] *is like a pomegranate split open* (S.S. IV, 3): even the emptiest (*rekanim*) among you are as full of answers as a pomegranate [is of seeds]; and thus it is written, (iii) *No weapon that is formed against thee shall prosper; and every tongue that shall rise against thee in judgment thou shalt condemn* (Isa. LIV, 17).[5]

[1] I.e. it made very slow progress.
[2] V. *supra*, XXXI, 13, p. 247, n. 4—i.e. it covered but a short distance. Mah. and E. J. reverse the interpretation This and the preceding statement mean that at first, before the waters had risen to a considerable height, the ark remained as though grounded; but when they '*prevailed*' it was lifted up and floated (E.J.). [3] Lit. 'the Palatine Hill', a name given by the Samaritans to Mount Gerizim, which they held sacred.
[4] *Barren* in a metaphorical sense—of learning. [5] Cf. *infra*, LXXXI, 3.

11. FIFTEEN CUBITS UPWARD DID THE WATERS PREVAIL (VII, 20). R. Judah said: Fifteen cubits over the mountains and fifteen cubits over the plains.[1] R. Nehemiah said: Fifteen cubits over the mountains, but over the plains, any height.[2]

AND ALL THE FLESH PERISHED . . . ALL IN WHOSE NOSTRILS WAS THE BREATH OF (NISHMATH) THE SPIRIT OF (RUAḤ) LIFE, etc. (VII, 21 f.). R. Samuel the son-in-law of R. Ḥanina the colleague of the Rabbis said: Here the *neshamah* is made identical with *ruaḥ*, whereas in an earlier passage the *neshamah* is identified with *nefesh*. How do we know that we should apply the teaching of each passage to the other? Because 'life' is written in both places, proving that they are analogous.[3]

WHATSOEVER WAS IN THE DRY LAND, DIED. This excludes fish. But some maintain that they too were included among those who were to be gathered into [the ark], but they fled to the Ocean [the Mediterranean].[4]

AND HE BLOTTED OUT EVERY LIVING SUBSTANCE . . . AND NOAH ONLY (AK) WAS LEFT (VII, 23): AK is a diminishing particle: he too coughed blood on account of the cold.[5]

[1] The water thus reaching different levels—a miracle.
[2] The water had one level, consequently one cannot gauge how high it was above the plains—Yoma 76*a*.
[3] V. *supra*, XIV, *ad fin.*
[4] Sanh. 108*a*.
[5] I.e. even he was not left sound; cf *supra*, XXX, 6.

Chapter XXXIII (NOACH)

1. AND GOD REMEMBERED NOAH, AND EVERY LIVING THING, AND ALL THE CATTLE, etc (VIII, 1). *Thy righteousness is like the mountains of God; Thy judgments are like the great deep; man and beast Thou preservest, O Lord* (Ps. XXXVI, 7). R. Ishmael interpreted: To the righteous who accepted the Torah which was revealed on the mountains of God Thou shewest righteousness [i.e. love] reaching unto the mountains of God; but as for the wicked, who did not accept the Torah which was revealed on the mountains of God, Thou dealest strictly with them, even to the great deep. R. Akiba said: He deals strictly with both, even to the great deep. He deals strictly with the righteous, calling them to account for the few wrongs which they commit in this world, in order to lavish bliss upon and give them a goodly reward in the world to come; He grants ease to the wicked and rewards them for the few good deeds which they have performed in this world in order to punish them in the future world.[1]

R. Levi said: It [Scripture] gives a simile for the righteous in their dwelling, and for the wicked in their dwelling. The righteous in their dwelling: *I will feed them in a good pasture, and upon the high mountains of Israel shall their fold be* (Ezek. XXXIV, 14). The wicked in their dwelling: *In the day when he went down to the netherworld I caused the deep to mourn and cover itself for him* (*ib.* XXXI, 15). R. Judah said: *Hobalti* (I brought) is written[2]: a lid for a vat is made not of gold or silver but of earthenware, which is the selfsame material. Thus the wicked are darkness, Gehenna is darkness, and the deep is darkness: hence I brought the wicked to Gehenna and covered them with the deep: let darkness cover darkness.

R. Jonathan in R. Josiah's name transposed the verse: Thy righteousness [i.e. mercy] is above Thy judgments, just as the mountains of God are above the great deep: as

[1] Lev. R. XXVII, 1. [2] I.e. *he'ebalti* (I caused to mourn) with a different punctuation reads *hobalti*.

the mountains are endless, so are the righteous endless [1]; and as the mountains press back the deep so that it should not ascend and inundate the world, so do the righteous press back punishment, lest it go forth and burn up the world; and as the mountains are sown and yield fruit, so do the deeds of the righteous yield fruit; and as the deep is unfathomable, so is the punishment of the wicked unfathomable [i.e. immeasurable]. And as the deep cannot be sown to yield fruit, so the deeds of the wicked do not produce fruit, for if they produced fruit they would destroy the world.

When R. Joshua b. Levi visited Rome he saw there pillars covered with tapestry, in winter so that they should not contract, and in summer that they should not split. As he was walking in the street, he espied a poor man wrapped in a mat—others say, in half an ass's pack-saddle. To those pillars he applied the verse, '*Thy righteousness is like the mighty mountains*'—where Thou givest, Thou givest in abundance; while to the poor man he applied the verse, '*Thy judgments are like the great deep*'—where Thou smitest, Thou smitest with force.[2]

Alexander of Macedon visited King Ḳaẓia beyond the dark mountains.[3] He came forth, offering him golden bread on a golden tray. 'Do I then need your gold?' he demanded. 'Had you then nothing to eat in your own country that you have come here?' he retorted. 'I came only because I wished to see how you dispense justice,' was the reply. As he sat with him a man came with a complaint against his neighbour. 'This man,' he stated, 'sold me a dunghill and I found a treasure in it.' The buyer argued, 'I bought a dunghill only,' while the vendor maintained, 'I sold the dunghill and all it contained.' Said he [the king] to one: 'Have you a son?' 'Yes,' replied he. 'And have you a daughter?' he asked the other, 'Yes,' was the answer. 'Then marry them and let the treasure

[1] I.e. their reward is endless; v. Lev. R. *loc cit.*
[2] 'Rashi'· Thou cuttest down.
[3] A legendary king, so called because he was thought to live at the end (*ḳeẓ*) of the world.—Apparently the African interior is meant.

belong to both.' He noticed him [Alexander] sitting astonished, and asked him, 'Have I then not judged well?' 'Yes,' he replied 'Had this happened among you, how would you have judged?' 'I would have slain both and kept the treasure for myself.' 'Does rain descend in your country?' he asked. 'Yes.' 'Does the sun shine?' 'Yes.' 'Have you small cattle [sheep and goats]?' 'Yes,' he replied. 'By heaven!'[1] he exclaimed, 'it is not for your sake but for the sake of the cattle, as it is written, *Man and beast Thou preservest, O Lord:* Man for the sake of beast Thou preservest, O Lord.'

R Judah b. R. Simon referred the verse to Noah. The Holy One, blessed be He, said: 'The righteousness [mercy] which I showed to Noah in the ark I showed him nowhere save on the mighty mountains': as it is written, *And the ark rested in the seventh month, on the seventeenth day of the month, upon the mountains of Ararat* (Gen. VIII, 8).[2] *'Thy judgments are like the great deep':* the chastisement which I brought on his generation, I brought from nowhere else than the great deep, as it is written, *on the same day were all the fountains of the great deep broken up* (*ib.* VII, 11). And when I remembered him, not him alone did I remember, but him and all that were with him in the Ark, as it is written, AND GOD REMEMBERED NOAH, AND EVERY LIVING THING, etc.

2. *There was a little city* (Eccl. IX, 14): this alludes to the world; *And few men within it* (*ib.*), to the generation of the Flood; *And there came a great king against it, and besieged it* (*ib.*)—to the Holy One, blessed be He; *And built great bulwarks against it* (*ib.*)—ambushes and snares.[3] *Now there was found in it a man poor and wise* (*ib.* 15), viz.

[1] Lit. 'curse the man!'

[2] The meaning is apparently that God's mercy was manifest when the ark rested on these mountains. Yalkut reads: Thy righteousness to Noah was like the mighty mountains (in extent) . . . as for the judgment which Thou didst mete out to his contemporaries, Thou didst deal severely with them even to the great deep.

[3] From which He could, as it were, attack the city Jast. translates Craft and Guile—allegorical names of towers.

Noah; *And he by his wisdom delivered the city* (*ib.*), as it is written, *And he took of every clean beast*, etc. (Gen VIII, 20).[1] *Yet no man remembered that same poor man* (Eccl. *loc. cit.*): said the Holy One, blessed be He: 'Since none of you remember him, *I* will remember him': hence, AND GOD REMEMBERED NOAH, etc.[2]

3. *The Lord is good to all, and His tender mercies are over all His works* (Ps. CXLV, 9). R. Joshua b. Levi translated: The Lord is good to all, and His tender mercies are over all, because they are His works. R. Samuel b. Naḥman interpreted: The Lord is good to all, and His tender mercies are over all, for it is His nature to be compassionate.[3] R. Joshua interpreted in R. Levi's name: The Lord is good to all, and He inspires mankind with His [spirit of] compassion. R. Abba said: Should a year of famine commence to-morrow and men show compassion to each other, then the Holy One, blessed be He, will also be filled with compassion for them.

In the days of R. Tanḥuma Israel had need of a fast,[4] so they went to him and requested: 'Master, proclaim a fast.' He proclaimed a fast, for one day, then a second day, and then a third, yet no rain fell. Thereupon he ascended [the pulpit] and preached to them, saying: 'My sons! Be filled with compassion for each other, and then the Holy One, blessed be He, will be filled with compassion for you.' Now while they were distributing relief to the poor they saw a man give money to his divorced wife, whereupon they went to him [R. Tanḥuma] and exclaimed, 'Why do we sit here while such misdeeds are perpetrated!' 'What then have you seen?' he inquired. 'We saw So-and-so give his divorced wife money.' He summoned them and asked him, 'Why did you give money to your divorced wife?' 'I saw her in great distress,' replied he, 'and was

[1] He saved the world by sacrificing to God (cf. *supra*, XXVI, 1). Tanḥuma, however, reads: *Come thou and all thy house into the ark* (Gen. VII, 1), which seems preferable. [2] Eccl. R. IX, 14, 15. §1.
[3] Interpreting *His works* as the manner in which He rules.
[4] On account of drought

filled with compassion for her.' Upon this R. Tanḥuma turned his face upward and exclaimed: 'Sovereign of the Universe! This man, upon whom this woman has no claim for sustenance, yet saw her in distress and was filled with pity for her. Seeing then that of Thee it is written, *The Lord is full of compassion and gracious* (Ps. CIII, 8), while we are Thy children, the children of Thy beloved ones, the children of Abraham, Isaac, and Jacob, how much the more shouldst Thou be filled with compassion for us!' Immediately the rain descended and the world enjoyed relief.[1]

Our Teacher[2] was sitting and studying the Torah in front of the Babylonian Synagogue in Sepphoris, when a calf passed before him on its way to the slaughter and began to cry out, as though pleading, 'Save me!' Said he to it, 'What can I do for you? for this you were fashioned.' [As a punishment for his heartlessness] our Teacher suffered toothache for thirteen years. During these thirteen years no woman miscarried in Eretz Israel, and none suffered pain in childbirth.[3] After this period a creeping thing ran past his daughter. She was about to kill it, when he said to her, 'My daughter, let it be, for it is written, *And His tender mercies are over all his works.*'[4]

Our Teacher was very modest, and he used to say, 'I am prepared to do whatever any person tells me, except what the Family of Bathyra did for my ancestor [Hillel], for they relinquished their high office and promoted him.[5] And if R. Huna, the *Resh Galutha*, were to come up here [Palestine], I would rise before him, for he is descended from Judah, whereas I am from Benjamin; he is descended on the male side, while I am descended [from Judah] on the female side.'[6] Said R. Ḥiyya the Elder to him, 'Behold, he has come!' At this Rabbi's face turned pale. 'His

[1] Lev. R. XXXIV, 14. [2] Viz. R. Judah ha-Nasi.
[3] Because the sufferings of the righteous protect their generation.
[4] Cf. B M. 85*a*.
[5] For the story of Hillel's rise to greatness, v. Pes. 66*a*.
[6] I am descended from Judah on the female side only. It is not mentioned elsewhere that he was not descended through the male side.

coffin has come,' he added. 'Go and see who wants you without,' he ordered. He went out and found no one, whereupon he treated himself as banned for thirty days.[1] R. Jose [Assi] remarked: During these thirty days of his excommunication he taught Rab, his sister's son, all the [exegetical] principles of the Torah, while he [Rab] taught him the laws[2] of the Babylonians.[3] At the end of the thirty days Elijah, of blessed memory, came before Rabbi disguised as R. Ḥiyya the Elder,[4] laid his hand upon his teeth, and cured him. When R. Ḥiyya subsequently visited Rabbi he asked him, 'How is your tooth?' 'Since you laid your hand upon it it is cured,' he answered. 'I know nothing about it,' said he. On hearing this Rabbi showed him honour and set him on the inner [bench].[5] Said R. Ishmael b. R. Jose to him, 'Even before me?' 'Heaven forfend,' replied he, 'let such a thing not be done in Israel!'[6]

Our Teacher was singing the praises of R. Ḥiyya the Elder to R. Ishmael b. R. Jose. Said he [R. Ishmael b. R. Jose] to him: 'One day I saw him [R. Ḥiyya the Elder] at the baths but he did not make an obeisance before me.' 'Why did you not bow before him?' inquired he [our Teacher]. 'I was meditating on an *Aggadah* of the Psalms,' he answered. On hearing this he gave him two disciples who used to go in with him to the vapour room, lest he should stay too long there and become enfeebled.[7]

Another interpretation: '*The Lord is good to all, and His tender mercies are over all His works.*' As it is written, AND GOD REMEMBERED NOAH, etc.

AND ELOHIM (GOD) REMEMBERED NOAH. R. Samuel b. Naḥman said: Woe to the wicked who turn the Attribute of Mercy into the Attribute of Judgment. Wherever the Tetragrammaton ['Lord'] is employed it

[1] He understood this to be Rabbi's meaning.
[2] Perhaps: guiding principles of exegesis. [3] Rab being a Babylonian.
[4] Elijah was thought to visit men quite frequently.
[5] Nearest to Rabbi—this was a special mark of honour.
[6] I do not promote him at your expense.
[7] Meditating on sacred subjects in the baths is forbidden. Hence he assumed that he was given to absent-mindedness, in the course of which he might stay too long in the vapour room. Cf. Ḳid. 33*a*.

connotes the Attribute of Mercy, as in the verse, *The Lord, the Lord God, merciful and gracious* (Ex. XXXIV, 6), yet it is written, *And the* Lord *saw that the wickedness of man was great* (Gen. VI, 5), *And it repented the* Lord *that he had made man* (*ib.* 6), *And the* Lord *said: I will blot out man* (*ib.* 7). Happy are the righteous who turn the Attribute of Judgment into the Attribute of Mercy. Wherever *Elohim* (God) is employed it connotes the Attribute of Judgment: Thus: *Thou shalt not revile Elohim*—God (Ex. XXII, 27); *the cause of both parties shall come before Elohim*—God (*ib.* 8); yet it is written, *And* Elohim *heard their groaning, and* Elohim *remembered His covenant* (*ib.* II, 24); *And* Elohim *remembered Rachel* (Gen. XXX, 22); AND ELOHIM REMEMBERED NOAH.[1]

What did He remember in his favour?[2] That he provided for [the animals] the whole twelve months in the Ark, hence AND GOD REMEMBERED NOAH, and the spirit of justice approves it,[3] for the sake of the clean animals that were with him in the Ark. R. Leazar said: He was called [Noah] on account of his sacrifice, as it is written, *And the Lord smelled the sweet* (nihoaḥ) *savour* (Gen. VIII, 21). R. Jose b. R. Ḥanina said: On account of the resting of the Ark, as it is written, *And the ark rested*—wattanaḥ (*ib.* 4). R. Joḥanan said: The planets did not function the whole twelve months. Said R. Jonathan to him, They did function, but their mark was imperceptible. R. Liezer said: *They shall not cease* (*ib.* 22) implies that they never ceased. R. Joshua deduced: '*They shall not cease*': hence it follows that they had ceased.[4]

4. THE FOUNTAINS ALSO OF THE DEEP AND THE WINDOWS OF HEAVEN WERE STOPPED (VIII, 2). R. Leazar said: In connection with punishment it is written,

[1] Thus in the former case the wicked made *the Lord* decree punishment, while in the latter *Elohim* showed mercy. Cf. *supra*, XII, 15.
[2] Since there is no forgetfulness before Him, the Midrash assumes that the verse implies that He bore in mind something in his (Noah's) favour.
[3] I.e. Elohim, which connotes justice, approved Noah's actions.
[4] V. *supra*, XXV, 2, for notes.

On the same day were all *the fountains of the great deep broken up* (*ib.* VII, 11); but in connection with good it is written, THE FOUNTAINS ALSO OF THE DEEP . . . WERE STOPPED, but not *all* the fountains, the exceptions being the great well [of Biram], the gulf [of Gaddor], and the cavern spring of Paneas.[1]

AND THE ARK RESTED IN THE SEVENTH MONTH . . . UPON THE MOUNTAINS OF ARARAT (VIII, 4): i.e. upon the mountain range Cordyene.[2]

5. AND IT CAME TO PASS AT THE END OF FORTY DAYS, THAT NOAH OPENED THE ḤALON [E.V. 'WINDOW'] OF THE ARK (VIII, 6). This supports the view that it was a window [trapdoor].[3]

AND HE SENT FORTH A RAVEN (VIII, 7): thus it is written, *He sent darkness, and it was dark* (Ps. CV, 28).[4]

AND IT WENT FORTH TO AND FRO (YAẒO WA-SHOB). R. Judan said in the name of R. Judah b. R. Simon: It began arguing with him[5]: 'Of all the birds that thou hast here thou sendest none but me!' 'What need then has the world of thee?' he retorted; 'for food? for a sacrifice?'[6] R. Berekiah said in R. Abba's name: The Holy One, blessed be He, said to him [Noah]: 'Take it back, because the world will need it in the future.' 'When?' he asked. '*When the waters dry off from off the earth*' (*ib.*). He replied: 'A righteous man will arise and dry up the world,[7] and I will cause him to have need of them [the

[1] V. Sanh. 108*a* (Sonc. ed.), p. 740, n 8; the bracketed additions are in accordance with the reading there, Th. *ad loc.* identifying the first two mentioned here with the two quoted from there The hot springs of Tiberias are omitted, as only the strongest springs are mentioned, the cavern spring of Paneas being substituted. The last named is a city in the north of Palestine (Jast.: Cæsarea Philippi, modern Baneas) whence the Jordan issues.

[2] A district E. of the Tigris and S. of Armenia.

[3] V. *supra*, XXXI, 11.

[4] Translating: He (Noah) sent darkness, viz. the raven, which is dark-hued, and the raven found it dark—i e. without light or hope, and so returned.

[5] Lit. 'giving him answers, refutations'. '*Wa-shob*' (returning) is connected by a play on words with *hasheb*, the *hif'il* form, 'to answer.'

[6] You are fit for neither. Cf. Sanh 108*b*.

[7] Viz. Elijah, who threatened drought, and the threat was fulfilled.

ravens],' as it is written, *And the ravens* ('orbim) *brought him bread and flesh*, etc. (I Kings XVII, 6). R. Judah said: It refers to a town within the borders of Bashan called Arbo.[1] R. Nehemiah said: Ravens literally are meant, and whence did they bring him [food]? From Jehoshaphat's table.[2]

R. Akiba preached in Ginzak[3] on the theme of the Flood, and the audience did not weep, but when he mentioned the story of the raven they wept.[4] He then quoted this verse: *The womb* (reḥem) *forgetteth him; the worm feedeth sweetly on him, he shall be no more remembered; and unrighteousness is broken as a tree* (Job XXIV, 20). '*Reḥem* forgetteth': They [the generation of the Flood] forgot to be merciful to their fellow men,[5] therefore the Holy One, blessed be He, made His mercy forget them. '*The worm feedeth sweetly on him*': the worm became sweet through [feeding on] them.[6] '*He shall be no more remembered, and unrighteousness is broken as a tree*': R. Aibu said: It is not written, 'is uprooted,' but '*is broken*': i.e. like something which is broken, yet produces another stock in exchange; and to what does that allude? To the generation of the Separation [of races].[7]

6. AND HE SENT FORTH A DOVE . . . BUT THE DOVE FOUND NO REST, etc. (VIII, 8 f.): R. Judah b. Naḥman said in the name of Resh Laḳish: Had it found a place of rest, it would not have returned. Similarly, *She dwelleth among the nations, she findeth no rest* (Lam. I, 3): but had she [the nation] found rest, they would not have returned [to God]. Again, *And among these nations shalt thou have no repose, and there shall be no rest for the sole*

[1] Th. conjectures that it is El Arbain in Transjordania. R. Judah maintains that the citizens of this town were called Orbim, and it was they who supplied Elijah with food. [2] Lev R XIX, 1; Sanh. 113*a*, Ḥul. 5*a*.
[3] A city in the North of Media Atropatene; v. Neub. *Géogr.*, p. 375.
[4] Probably what is related at the beginning of this section, viz. that the raven would be required one day. They wept at God's marvellous foresight. The reading 'Job' of cur. edd. is obviously out of place.
[5] *Reḥem* is translated mercy, from *raḥem*, to be merciful: he forgetteth to be merciful. [6] This corresponds to E.V.
[7] Which succeeded the generation of the Flood in wickedness.

of thy foot (Deut xxviii, 65): but had they found it, they would not have returned.[1]

AND HE STAYED YET ANOTHER SEVEN DAYS (viii, 10 ff.). R. Jose b. R. Hanina said: There were three periods of seven days in all.[2]

AND AGAIN HE SENT FORTH THE DOVE . . . AND THE DOVE CAME IN TO HIM . . . AND LO IN HER MOUTH AN OLIVE-LEAF FRESHLY PLUCKED (ṬARAF). What does ṬARAF mean? Killed [slain], as you read, *Joseph is without doubt torn in pieces*—ṭarof ṭoraf (Gen. xxxvii, 33). He said to her: 'Had you left it, it would have grown into a great tree.'[3]

Whence did she bring it? R. Abba said: She brought it from the young shoots of Eretz Israel. R. Levi said: She brought it from the Mount of Olives, for Eretz Israel was not submerged by the Flood. Thus the Holy One, blessed be He, said to Ezekiel: *Son of man, say unto her: Thou art a land that is not cleansed, nor rained upon in the day of indignation* (Ezek. xxii, 24). R. Birai[4] said: The gates of the Garden of Eden were opened for her, and from there she brought it. Said R. Abbahu: Had she brought it from the Garden of Eden, should she have not brought something better, e.g. cinnamon or the balsam leaf? But in fact she gave him a hint, saying to him [in effect]: 'Noah, better is bitterness from this source [God], than sweetness from your hand.'[5]

AND HE STAYED YET OTHER SEVEN DAYS, etc. (viii, 12 ff.). This supports what R. Jose b. R. Ḥanina said: [He waited] three seven-day periods in all.

7. AND HE SENT FORTH THE DOVE, AND SHE RETURNED NOT AGAIN TO HIM ANY MORE, AND IT CAME TO PASS IN THE SIX HUNDRED AND FIRST

[1] Lam. R. I, 3, § 29.
[2] Two as stated in vv. 10 and 12, while YET OTHER SEVEN DAYS implies that he had already waited this period before, between the return of the raven and the sending forth of the dove.
[3] Thus she 'killed' its potentialities. Lev. R. xxxi end, Zeb. 113*a*.
[4] In Lev. R. *ad loc.* the reading is: R. Berekiah.
[5] Sanh. 108*b*.

YEAR, IN THE FIRST MONTH, THE FIRST DAY OF THE MONTH. We learned: The judgment of the generation of the Flood lasted twelve months.[1] How is this deduced? (i) *In the six hundredth year of Noah's life, in the second month, on the seventeenth day of the month . . . the windows of heaven were opened* (Gen. VII, 11); and it is written, (ii) *And the rain was upon the earth forty days and forty nights* (*ib.* 12). this embraces the rest of Marḥeshwan and Kislew; (iii) *And the waters prevailed upon the earth a hundred and fifty days* (*ib.* 24): this covers Tebeth, Shebat, Adar, Nisan, and Iyar; (iv) *And the ark rested in the seventh month, on the seventeenth day, upon the mountains of Ararat* (*ib.* VIII, 4): that means Siwan, the seventh month from the descent of the rain. For sixteen days the water diminished at the rate of a cubit per four days, which is one and a half handbreadths per day. You may thus infer that the Ark was eleven cubits in the water, and it all drained off in sixty days. Thus you read, *And the waters decreased continually until the tenth month* (*ib.* 5): that is Ab, the tenth from the descent of the rain.[2] Another interpretation[3]: (v) *And it came to pass in the six hundred and first year, in the first month* [i.e. Tishri], *on the first day of the month, the waters were dried up from off the earth* (*ib.* VIII, 13)[4]:

[1] *Supra*, XXVIII, 9

[2] From the descent of the rain means from the *beginning* of the Flood. Thus from 17th Marheshwan to 17th Iyar is seven months, while from Marheshwan to Ab inclusive is ten months. According to a different reading, however (which Rashi has adopted in his commentary on the Bible), the seventh month means from the *end* of the Flood, while the tenth is from the beginning. The calculation is the same, only we reckon from Kislew to Siwan inclusive.

[3] *Var. lec*: and it is written. This is perhaps preferable, since the verse that follows completes the calculation (v. next note).

[4] The verses are explained according to R. Eliezer's view (*supra*, XXII, 4) that the world was created in Tishri, the seventh month, so that the *second* month mentioned is Marḥeshwan. Commencing then on the 17th of Marḥeshwan, the forty days ended on the 27th of Kislew, the next 150 days thus included the rest of Kislew and the whole of Tebeth—Iyar (thus. 3 days in Kislew, and Tebeth (29) and Shebat—Iyar (118)—150). Then on the 1st of Siwan, the water began to abate, and the 15 cubits by which it had covered the mountains (Gen. VII, 20) was completely gone by the beginning of Ab, i.e. in 60 days; thus it abated at the rate of one cubit in four days. By the seventeenth of the month Siwan there-

it became like a marsh.[1] (vi) *And in the second month, on the seven and twentieth day of the month, was the earth dry* (*ib.* VIII, 14): it became like parched soil, which they sowed, but nothing would grow. Why was that? Because it [the Flood] had come as a curse, and a curse cannot turn into a blessing[2], so they waited until the next rainfall and then they sowed.

Now should not Scripture have said, 'On the *sixteenth* day of the month was the earth dry'[3]: why then is it stated, '*And in the second month, on the* seven and twentieth *day of the month, was the earth dry*'? Because of the eleven days by which the solar year exceeds the lunar year.[4] R. Simeon b. Gamaliel said: If you wish to prove for yourself that the solar year exceeds the lunar year by eleven days, make a mark on a wall on the day of the summer solstice; the following year at that season the sun will not reach it until eleven days later, and from this you may know that the solar year exceeds the lunar year by eleven days.

fore it had abated four cubits, and then the Ark rested on the mountain, so that it was sunk 11 cubits in the water. Now from the 1st of Ab until the 1st of Tishri, by which time the earth was dry (*ib.* VIII, 13), is a period of 60 days. Noah had waited 40 days after the tops of the mountains appeared (*ib.* 6) before sending out the dove hence three seven-day periods were spent in sending out the birds, and this supports R Jose b. R. Hanina.

[1] Lit. 'like oozing soil'—exuding enough water to moisten other objects.

[2] Therefore the water of the Flood disappeared completely, leaving the soil absolutely arid.

[3] Since the punishment of the generation of the Flood lasted twelve months, and the Flood commenced on the seventeenth day of the month in the previous year.

[4] The twelve months of punishment mean a *solar* year of 365 days, whereas the Jewish year is lunar, and consists of 354 days (to make up the deficiency extra months are intercalated at intervals).

Chapter XXXIV (NOACH)

1. AND GOD SPOKE UNTO NOAH, SAYING: GO FORTH FROM THE ARK, etc. (VIII, 15 f.). It is written, *Bring my soul out of prison, that I may give thanks unto Thy name; the righteous shall crown themselves because of me; for Thou wilt deal bountifully with me* (Ps. CXLII, 8). '*Bring my soul out of prison*' alludes to Noah, who was imprisoned twelve months in the Ark; '*That I may give thanks unto Thy name*': to give thanks to Thine [awe-inspiring] name; '*The righteous shall crown themselves because of me*': the righteous shall glory in me.[1] '*For Thou wilt deal bountifully with me*': Thou didst deal bountifully with me and say unto me: GO FORTH FROM THE ARK.

2. *The Lord trieth the righteous*, etc. (Ps. XI, 5). R. Jonathan said: A potter does not test defective vessels, because he cannot give them a single blow without breaking them. Similarly, the Holy One, blessed be He, does not test the wicked but only the righteous: thus, '*The Lord trieth the righteous.*' R. Jose b. R. Ḥanina said: When a flax worker knows that his flax is of good quality, the more he beats it the more it improves and the more it glistens; but if it is of inferior quality, he cannot give it one knock but it splits. Similarly, the Lord does not test the wicked but only the righteous, as it says: '*The Lord trieth the righteous.*' R. Eleazar said: When a man possesses two cows, one strong and the other feeble, upon which does he put the yoke? Surely upon the strong one. Similarly, the Lord tests none but the righteous; hence, '*The Lord trieth the righteous.*' Another interpretation: '*The Lord trieth the righteous*' applies to Noah [who stayed in the Ark until God said to him]: GO FORTH FROM THE ARK.[2]

[1] These last two interpretations or translations seem to be a quotation from some Targum (Th.). The E.V. actually covers them.
[2] Mah.. He remained in the Ark even after the earth became dry until he received God's command to leave it. *Supra*, XXXII, 3.

3. R. Judan commenced in Aibu's name: *In the transgression of the lips is a snare to the evil man* (Prov. XII, 13): through the rebellion of the generation of the Flood against the Holy One, blessed be He, they were brought to grief. *But the righteous cometh out of trouble* (*ib.*): this applies to Noah: hence, GO FORTH FROM THE ARK.[1]

4. *If the spirit of the ruler rise up against thee, leave not thy place* (Eccl. X, 4). This refers to Noah. Noah argued: Just as I entered the Ark only when I was permitted, so may I not go out save with permission. R. Judah b. R. Ilai said: Had I been there I would have broken it and gone out! Noah, however, said: I entered with permission and I will leave with permission. Thus: *Come thou into the ark—And Noah went in; Go forth from the Ark—And Noah went forth.*

5. *Wisdom is a stronghold to the wise man more than ten rulers* (Eccl. VII, 19): this alludes to Noah [to whom God said]: 'Of the ten generations from Adam to Noah I spoke with none but thee': hence, AND GOD SPOKE UNTO NOAH, SAYING.

6. *To everything there is a season, and a time to every purpose* (Eccl. III, 1): there was a time for Noah to enter the ark, as it is written, *Come thou and all thy house into the ark* (Gen. VII, 1), and a time for him to leave it: GO FORTH FROM THE ARK.

GO FORTH FROM THE ARK. He may be compared to an administrator who departed for a certain spot, putting someone in his place. On his return he said to the other, 'Leave your position.'[2] But he [Noah] was reluctant to go out, saying, 'Am I to go out and beget children for a curse?'[3] Until the Holy One, blessed be He, swore to him

[1] Cf. *infra*, LXVII, *ad fin.*
[2] Similarly, for twelve months Noah was in charge of the only creatures that were destined to live, and thus acted, as it were, as God's regent. Now he was to leave this exalted position.
[3] Sexual intercourse had been forbidden in the Ark but was now permitted, as stated *infra* and also *supra*, XXXI, 12.

that He would not bring another Flood upon the world, as it says, *For this is the waters of Noah unto Me; for as I have sworn that the waters of Noah should no more go over the earth*, etc (Isa. LIV, 9): thou wilt indeed be fruitful and multiply.

7. THOU, AND THY WIFE, etc. R. Judah b. R. Simon and R. Ḥanan in the name of R. Samuel b. R. Isaac said: As soon as Noah entered the Ark, cohabitation was forbidden to him, hence it is written, *And thou shalt come into the ark, thou, and thy sons* (Gen VI, 18)—apart; *And thy wife, and thy sons' wives*—apart. When he went out, He permitted it to him, as it is written, GO FORTH FROM THE ARK, THOU AND THY WIFE. R. Abin quoted: *They are lonely in want and famine* (Job XXX, 3): when want and famine visit the world, regard your wife as though she were lonely [i.e. menstruous]. R. Huna said: It is written. *And unto Joseph were born two sons* (Gen. XLI, 50): when? Before *the year of famine came* (*ib.*).[1]

8. BRING FORTH (HAYYEẒE) WITH THEE EVERY LIVING THING THAT IS WITH THEE . . . THAT THEY MAY SWARM IN THE EARTH (VIII, 18). R. Judan said: *Hozze* is written, but it is read HAYYEẒE[2]; THAT THEY MAY SWARM IN THE EARTH—but not in the Ark; AND BE FRUITFUL AND MULTIPLY UPON THE EARTH—but not in the Ark.

EVERY BEAST, EVERY CREEPING THING, AND EVERY FOWL, WHATSOEVER MOVETH (KOL ROMES) UPON THE EARTH (VIII, 19). R. Aibu said: KOL ROMES is written fully.[3] AFTER THEIR FAMILIES: this forbade heterogeneous breeding and emasculation.

[1] V. *supra*, XXXI, 12; Sanh. 108*b*.
[2] Th. and Mah: possibly no particular significance attaches to this, R. Judan merely recording the fact. Rashi on the Pentateuch comments: *Hayyeẓe* implies: order them out; if they refuse to go, then *hoẓẓe*: put them out—forcibly.
[3] Viz. רומש not רמש. Here too there may be no particular significance in this. Possibly, however, it is from this full form that the prohibition of castration is presently deduced, the full form implying that the animal must be complete.

The children of Noah were enjoined concerning seven things: Idolatry, incest, murder, cursing the Divine Name [blasphemy], civil law,[1] and a limb torn from a living animal.[2] R. Ḥanina said: Also concerning blood from a living animal. R. Leazar said: Also against cross-breeding. R. Simeon said: Also against witchcraft. R. Joḥanan said: Also against emasculation. R. Issi [Assi] said: The children of Noah were enjoined concerning everything stated in the following passage: *There shall not be found among you any one that maketh his son or his daughter to pass through the fire*, etc. (Deut. XVIII, 10).[3]

9. AND NOAH BUILDED (WAYYIBEN) AN ALTAR UNTO THE LORD (VIII, 20). *Wayyaben* (he understood) is written[4]: he considered the matter, reasoning: For what reason did the Holy One, blessed be He, order more clean animals [to be preserved] than unclean? Surely because He desired that sacrifices should be offered to Him of them. Straightway, AND TOOK OF EVERY CLEAN BEAST, etc.[5]

AND HE OFFERED BURNT-OFFERINGS ON THE ALTAR. R. Eliezer b. Jacob said: That means on the great altar in Jerusalem, where Adam sacrificed, as it is written, *And it shall please the Lord better than a bullock that hath horns and hoofs* (Ps. LXIX, 32).[6]

AND THE LORD SMELLED THE SWEET SAVOUR. R. Eleazar and R. Jose b. R. Ḥanina differ. R. Eleazar said: The children of Noah brought [even] peace-offerings; R. Jose b. R. Ḥanina said: They offered burnt-offerings [only]. R. Eleazar sought to refute R. Jose b. R. Ḥanina: But it is written, *And Abel, he also brought of the firstlings of his flock and of the fat thereof* (Gen. IV, 4), implying that of which the fat is offered. How did R. Jose b. R. Ḥanina answer him? It means, of the fat ones [i.e. the best]. R. Eleazar sought to refute R. Jose b. R. Ḥanina: But it is written, *And he sent the young men of the children of Israel*,

[1] Or possibly: obedience to the civil authorities. [2] Forbidding it.
[3] V. *supra*, XVI, 6. [4] I.e. the word can be so read.
[5] V *supra*, XXVI, 1. [6] V. 'A.Z. 8*a*, where this is referred to Adam. This interpretation is based on the def. art. THE ALTAR.

who offered burnt-offerings, and sacrificed peace-offerings (shelamim) *unto the Lord* (Ex. XXIV, 5)? How does R. Jose b. R. Ḥanina explain this? It means that they were whole (*shelemim*) in their hide, not having been flayed or cut up. R. Eleazar objected to R. Jose b. R. Ḥanina: But it is written, *And Jethro, Moses' father-in-law, took a burnt-offering and sacrifices* (*ib.* XVIII, 12)? How does R. Jose b. R. Ḥanina explain this? In accordance with the view that Jethro came after Revelation. R. Huna said: R. Jannai and R. Ḥiyya the Elder differ in this: R. Jannai said: Jethro came before Revelation; R. Ḥiyya the Elder said: Jethro came after Revelation. R. Ḥanina observed: Yet they do not differ [in an independent controversy]: He who says that Jethro came before Revelation holds that the children of Noah might offer peace-offerings; while he who says that Jethro came after Revelation holds that they might offer burnt-offerings [only]. The following supports R. Jose b. R. Ḥanina: *Awake, O north wind* (S.S. IV, 16): this alludes to the burnt-offering, which was killed at the north [side of the altar]. To what does '*awake*' apply? To something which was asleep and now awakes. *And come, thou south* (*ib.*) alludes to peace-offerings, which were killed [even] at the south [side of the altar]. To what does '*come*' apply? To a new practice. R. Joshua of Siknin said in R. Levi's name: This verse too supports R. Jose b. R. Ḥanina: *This is the law of the burnt-offering: that is the burnt-offering* (Lev. VI, 2)—viz. which the Noachides used to offer. But when it treats of peace-offerings, viz. *And this is the law of the sacrifice of peace-offerings* (*ib.* VII, 11), it is not written, 'which they *offered*,' but, *which they* will *offer* (*ib.*)—in the future.[1]

AND THE LORD SMELLED THE SWEET SAVOUR. He smelled the savour of the Patriarch Abraham ascending from the fiery furnace[2]; He smelled the savour of Hananiah, Mishael and Azariah ascending from the fiery furnace. This may be compared to a king's friend, who, to pay his respects, sent the king a fine gift, viz. some excellent

[1] V. the whole passage *supra*, XXII, 5. [2] V. *infra*, XXXVIII, 13.

brisket on a beautiful plate.[1] Then his son came and did not show him honour. Then his grandson came and showed him honour; whereupon he [the king] said to him, 'Your gift is like your grandfather's.'[2] He smelled the savour of the generation of destruction.[3] R. Shilum said in the name of R. Menaḥama b. R. Ze'ira: Imagine a king who wished to build a palace by the sea, but did not know where to build it. Finding a phial of foliatum, he followed its scent and built it there.[4] Thus it is written, *For He hath founded it upon the seas* (Ps. xxiv, 2): for whose sake? For the sake of [those of whom it is written], *Such is the generation of them that seek after Him, that seek Thy face, even Jacob, Selah* (*ib.* 6).[5]

10. AND THE LORD SAID TO HIS HEART. The wicked stand in subjection to their heart [i.e. passions. Thus it says], *The fool hath said* in *his heart* (Ps. xiv, 1); *And Esau said* in *his heart* (Gen. xxvii, 41); *And Jeroboam said* in *his heart* (1 Kings xii, 25); *Now Haman said* in *his heart* (Est. vi, 6). But the righteous have their hearts under their control; hence it is written, *Now Hannah, she spoke* at *her heart* (1 Sam. 1, 13); *And David said* to *his heart* (*ib.* xxvii, 1); *But Daniel purposed* to *his heart* (Dan. 1, 8); AND THE LORD SAID *TO* HIS HEART.[6]

I WILL NOT AGAIN CURSE THE GROUND, etc.: Let that indeed suffice. The Rabbis interpreted: I WILL NOT AGAIN CURSE—the children of Noah; NEITHER WILL I AGAIN SMITE, etc.—future generations.[7]

FOR THE IMAGINATION OF MAN'S HEART IS EVIL. R. Ḥiyya the Elder said: How wretched must be

[1] Or possibly: the gift being a beautiful salver. v. Th.
[2] Similarly Hananiah, Mishael, and Azariah made the same sacrifice as Abraham in order to sanctify God's name.
[3] The generation of the abortive and disastrous revolt of Bar Cochba, which after being crushed was followed by tremendous slaughter.
[4] The phial was in the ground; the king traced it to its exact spot and made that the site for his palace ('Rashi'). [5] Cf. Ex. R. xv, 7.
[6] The prepositions in these verses are translated literally, and thus imply that the wicked speak *in* (subjection to) their hearts, while the righteous speak *to* their hearts, giving them orders, as it were. *Infra*, lxvii, 8.
[7] V. *supra*, xxvi. 6.

the dough when the baker himself testifies it to be poor! [Thus man's Creator says] FOR THE IMAGINATION OF MAN'S HEART IS EVIL. Abba Jose the potter said: How poor must be the leaven when he who kneaded it testifies that it is bad! Thus: *For he knoweth our* [evil] *passions* [E V. *'frame'*], *He remembereth that we are dust* (Ps. CIII, 14).[1] The Rabbis said: How inferior must be the plant when he that planted it testifies that it is bad; thus, *For the Lord of hosts, that planted thee, hath spoken evil of thee* (Jer. XI, 17).[2]

Antoninus asked our Teacher[3]: 'When is the evil urge placed in man?' 'As soon as he is formed [in embryo],' he replied. 'If so,' he objected, 'he would dig through the womb and emerge; rather is it when he emerges [from the womb].' Rabbi agreed with him, because his view corresponds with that of Scripture, viz. FOR THE IMAGINATION OF MAN'S HEART IS EVIL FROM HIS YOUTH (MINE'URAW). R Judan said: This is written *mine'araw* (from his awakening), which means, from when he awakes to the world. He asked him further: 'When is the soul planted in man?' 'When he leaves his mother's womb,' replied he. 'Leave meat without salt for three days,' said he, 'will it not putrefy?[4] Rather, when his destiny is determined.'[5] Our Teacher agreed with him, for Scripture too supports him: *All the while my soul* [E.V. *'breath'*] *is in me, and the spirit of God is in my nostrils* (Job XXVII, 3), while it is written, *And Thy Providence hath preserved My spirit* (*ib.* X, 12): hence, when didst Thou place the soul in me? When Thou didst determine my fate.[6]

11. WHILE THE EARTH REMAINETH, SEEDTIME AND HARVEST, AND COLD AND HEAT, AND SUMMER AND WINTER, AND DAY AND NIGHT SHALL NOT CEASE (VIII, 22). R. Judan said in R. Aḥa's name: What did

[1] Leaven is a common simile for the evil passions (cf. Ber. 17*a*).
[2] Num. R. XIII, 4; cf. Ḳid. 30*b*.
[3] Viz. R. Judah ha-Nasi. For the identity of Antoninus v. *infra*, LXVII, 6, p. 611, n. 2. [4] Similarly the fœtus would putrefy without a soul.
[5] When, in accordance with Rabbinic lore, the destiny (to be rich or poor, wise or foolish) of the fœtus is determined. [6] Sanh. 91*b*.

the children of Noah think: that the covenant made with them would endure to all eternity?[1] That is not so, but only as long as the heaven and earth endure will their covenant endure.[2] But when that day cometh, of which it is written, *For the heavens shall vanish away like smoke, and the earth shall be worn out like a garment* (Isa. LI, 6), then [shall the verse be fulfilled], *And it* [sc. the covenant] *will be broken in that day* (Zech. XI, 11).

R. Aḥa commented: What was responsible for their rebelling against Me? Was it not because they sowed but did not cut down, i.e. they gave birth but did not bury?[3] Therefore henceforth there shall be SOWING AND CUTTING DOWN[4]: they shall bear and bury. COLD AND HEAT: [they shall suffer] fever and ague. SUMMER (ḲAYYIẒ) AND WINTER (ḤOREF): I will cause the birds to summer upon them,[5] as you read, *And the ravenous birds shall summer upon them, and all the beasts of the earth shall winter upon them* (Isa. XVIII, 6). It once happened that one of the great men of his time—some say that it was R. Samuel b. Naḥman—was suffering with headache, and he lamented: This is what the generation of the Flood did for us![6]

Another interpretation of WHILE THE EARTH REMAINETH, etc.: R. Huna said in R. Aḥa's name: What do the children of Noah think: that the covenant made with them will endure to all eternity? [No, for] thus said I to them: WHILE THE EARTH *REMAINETH*. But as long as day and night endure, their covenant will endure. Yet when that day cometh of which it is written, *And there shall be one day which shall be known as the Lord's, not day, and not night* (Zech. XIV, 7), at that time [shall be fulfilled the verse], '*And it will be broken in that day.*'

R. Isaac commented: What was responsible for their

[1] The covenant of the previous verse: *Neither will I again smite any more every living thing.* [2] Reading the two verses together: *Neither will I again smite . . . while the earth remaineth.* [3] I.e none ever died young [4] Lit. translation of the verse. [5] From the context this appears to mean that they would be exposed to the depredations of birds.
[6] He too understood HEAT to mean a high temperature.

rebelling against Me? Was it not because they sowed without having to reap?[1] For R. Isaac said: They used to sow once in forty years, and they travelled from one end of the world to the other in a brief period, cutting down the cedars of Lebanon in their course, making no more of the lions and leopards than of the vermin in their skin.[2]

How is this to be understood?[3] They enjoyed the climate [now usual] between Passover and Pentecost [right through the year].[4]

R. Simeon b. Gamaliel said in R. Meir's name, and R. Dosa too said thus: [The latter] half of Tishri, Marḥeshwan and the first half of Kislew is seedtime; the second half of Kislew, Tebeth and half of Shebat are the winter months; the second half of Shebat, Adar and the first half of Nisan are the cold season; the second half of Nisan, Iyar and the first half of Siwan is harvest time; the second half of Siwan, Tammuz and the first half of Ab is summer; the second half of Ab, Elul and the first half of Tishri are the hot season. R. Judah counted from Marḥeshwan. R. Simeon commenced with [the beginning of] Tishri.[5]

R. Joḥanan said: The planets did not function the whole twelve months [of the Flood]. Said R. Jonathan to him: They did function, but their mark was imperceptible. R. Eliezer said: THEY SHALL NOT CEASE implies that they never ceased. R. Joshua deduced: THEY SHALL NOT CEASE: hence it follows that they had ceased.[6]

12. AND GOD BLESSED NOAH AND HIS SONS, AND SAID UNTO THEM: BE FRUITFUL AND MULTIPLY (IX, 1). This [blessing conferred] here was a reward for their sacrifice.[7]

[1] Every year, a single harvest providing food for many years.
[2] This is a picture, exaggerated of course, of the extreme ease of their lives, which led to over-confidence in themselves and rebellion against God.
[3] This is a new passage. Since Scripture implies that *henceforth* there would be alternating seasons of cold and heat, how was the climate hitherto? [4] I.e. the weather of a mild spring or early summer.
[5] B.M. 106*b*. [6] V. *supra*, XXV, 2.
[7] For the blessing itself had already been uttered (Gen. VIII, 17).

AND THE FEAR OF YOU AND THE DREAD OF YOU (ḤITKEM) SHALL BE UPON EVERY BEAST OF THE EARTH (IX, 2): fear and dread returned, but dominion did not return.[1] When did it return? In the days of Solomon, as it is written, *For he had* dominion *over all the region* (I Kings V, 4).

It was taught, R. Simeon b. Eleazar said: For a live infant one day old the Sabbath is desecrated; for David king of Israel, dead, the Sabbath may not be desecrated. And thus too did R. Simeon b. Eleazar say: An infant one day old, alive, need not be guarded from mice or serpents to prevent them picking out his eyes: a lion sees him and flees, a serpent sees him and flees. Yet Og, King of Bashan, dead, must be guarded! For as long as a man is alive his fear lies upon the [lower] creatures; when he dies, his fear is removed from the lower creatures. Thus it is written, AND THE FEAR OF YOU AND THE LIFE OF YOU, etc.[2]

13. EVERY MOVING THING THAT LIVETH SHALL BE FOR FOOD FOR YOU . . . ONLY FLESH WITH THE LIFE THEREOF, WHICH IS THE BLOOD THEREOF, SHALL YE NOT EAT (IX, 3 f). R. Jose b. R. Abin said in R. Joḥanan's name: Adam, to whom flesh to satisfy his appetite was not permitted,[3] was not admonished against eating a limb torn from the living animal.[4] But the children of Noah, to whom flesh to satisfy their appetite was permitted, were admonished against eating a limb torn from the living animal.[5]

AND SURELY (WE-AK) YOUR BLOOD OF YOUR LIVES WILL I REQUIRE (IX, 5). This includes one who strangles himself.[6] You might think that even one in the

[1] God's blessing to *Adam* conferred upon him 'dominion over all creatures (Gen. I, 28 f) in addition to '*fear*' and '*dread*'; these prerogatives were lost at the Flood, and 'dominion' is not enumerated in this verse which restores them.
[2] Reading ḤITKEM as *ḥayyathkem* (only a change of punctuation is required for this), your life—thus, your fear will only be co-eval with your life. Eccl. R.V., 10, § 2; Shab. 151*b*.
[3] V. Gen. I, 29 f., where only plant life is permitted.
[4] Since all flesh was forbidden. [5] Sanh. 59*a*, *b*.
[6] A suicide is punished.

plight of Saul is meant[1]: therefore we have AK.[2] You might think, even one like Hananiah, Mishael and Azariah[3]: therefore we have AK.

AT THE HAND OF EVERY BEAST WILL I REQUIRE IT: this refers to the four kingdoms.[4] AT THE HAND OF MAN (HA-ADAM): R. Levi said: That means, from the hand of Edom.[5] EVEN AT THE HAND OF EVERY MAN'S BROTHER, as it is written, *Deliver me, I pray Thee, from the hand of my brother, from the hand of Esau* (Gen. XXXII, 12).[6] WILL I REQUIRE THE LIFE OF MAN: this refers to Israel, as it is written, *And ye My sheep, the sheep of My pasture, are men* (Ezek. XXXIV, 31).[7]

14. WHOSO SHEDDETH MAN'S BLOOD, etc. (IX, 6). R. Ḥanina said: All these are specifically Noachian laws, [viz. that a man is condemned] on the testimony of one witness, on the ruling of one judge, without a formal warning, [for murder committed] through an agent, and for [the murder of] an embryo. On the testimony of one witness and on the ruling of one judge, for it says, WHOSO SHEDDETH MAN'S BLOOD, BY ONE MAN SHALL HIS BLOOD BE SHED.[8] Without a formal warning, as it says, WHOSO SHEDDETH MAN'S BLOOD, BY MAN SHALL HIS BLOOD BE SHED.[9] [He who commits murder] through an agent, because it says, WHOSO SHEDDETH MAN'S BLOOD BY MAN, SHALL HIS BLOOD BE SHED: [i.e. if he slays] by means of another

[1] Who committed suicide to save himself from the Philistines, v. I Sam. XXXI, 4. [2] It is a principle of exegesis that *ak* and *raḳ* (excepting, save that) are limiting particles. [3] Who risked their lives, which is akin to suicide, in order to sanctify God's name.

[4] Viz. Babylonia, Persia, Greece, and Rome, with whom the 'four beasts' mentioned in Dan. VII, 3, 17, were identified.

[5] Reading this instead of *Adam*. Edom and Esau stand for Rome.

[6] I.e. this too refers to Esau (Rome).

[7] B.Ḳ. 91*b*. The verse is made to foretell the punishment of the kingdoms that have enslaved Israel, particularly Rome (Edom).

[8] 'One' is a deduction from the employment of the singular; i.e. one man alone, either as witness or as judge, may cause conviction.

[9] Th.: presumably he understands WHOSO SHEDDETH MAN'S BLOOD to imply extension—even one who was not warned previously.

person,[1] HIS BLOOD SHALL BE SHED. For [the murder of] an embryo, for it says, WHOSO SHEDDETH THE BLOOD OF MAN WITHIN [ANOTHER] MAN, SHALL HIS BLOOD BE SHED.[2] R. Judah b. R. Simon said: Also he who murders by strangling, and on his own testimony, as it says, WHOSO SHEDDETH MAN'S BLOOD [while retaining it] WITHIN MAN, SHALL HIS BLOOD BE SHED.[3] R. Levi said: Behold, if a man slew yet was not slain,[4] when will he be slain? When man comes [for final judgment[5]; thus it is written], WHOSO SHEDDETH MAN'S BLOOD, WHEN MAN COMES[6] SHALL HIS BLOOD BE SHED.[7]

R. Akiba lectured: He who sheds blood is regarded as though he had impaired [God's] likeness. What is the proof? WHOSO SHEDDETH MAN'S BLOOD, etc. What is the reason? FOR IN THE IMAGE OF GOD MADE HE MAN.[8] R. Eleazar b. 'Azariah lectured: He who refrains from procreation is as though he impaired [God's] image. What is the proof? FOR IN THE IMAGE OF GOD MADE HE MAN, which is followed by, AND YOU, BE YE FRUITFUL, AND MULTIPLY.[9] Ben 'Azzai lectured: He who refrains from procreation is as though he shed blood and impaired [God's] likeness. What is the proof? WHOSO SHEDDETH MAN'S BLOOD, etc.; why? FOR IN THE IMAGE OF GOD MADE HE MAN, which is followed by, AND YOU, BE YE FRUITFUL, AND MULTIPLY.[10] Said R. Eleazar to him: Teachings are becoming when they are uttered by those who practise

[1] Referring '*by man*' to '*sheddeth*', and ignoring the punctuation—*v.* Kid. 43*a*. [2] A man within another man is an embryo. For the whole passage cf. Sanh. 57*b* (pp. 390, 391, in Sonc. ed.).
[3] One can shed blood and yet retain it within the victim only by strangulation; further, the verse may be translated WHOSO . . . BLOOD, BY THAT SAME MAN—i.e. on his own confession—shall . . . shed.
[4] Having died peacefully in his bed. [5] Or it may mean: When Adam comes, *v. supra*, XXI, 7. Radal: when Messiah comes.
[6] This is a play on words, *ba'adam* (in man) being read *ba adam*, when man comes. [7] Deut. R. II, 25.
[8] Thus murder is punished by death because it impairs God's image, as it were.
[9] I.e. because man was made in God's image, therefore be ye fruitful.
[10] Thus, if the last is violated, the former two are transgressed

them, but you, son of 'Azzai, preach well, but do not fulfil your teaching![1] That is because I desire to study Torah,[2] he pleaded, while the world can be preserved through others.[3]

15. AND YOU, BE YE FRUITFUL, AND MULTIPLY; SWARM IN THE EARTH, AND MULTIPLY THEREIN (IX, 7). Resh Lakish said: A covenant has been made in favour of climates.[4] Resh Lakish was sitting and studying Torah in a small forest of Tiberias, when two women came out from there, one saying to the other, 'Praised be He who has led us out from that bad climate.' 'Whence do you come?' he called out to them. 'From Mazga,' they replied. 'I know about Mazga,' he observed, 'and it contains no more than two dwelling houses![5] Blessed is He who inspireth the inhabitants of a town with love for it!'

A disciple of R. Issi was sitting before him and could not comprehend what he was explaining to him. 'Why cannot you grasp it?' he asked, 'Because I am an exile from home,' he replied. 'Whence are you?' inquired he. 'From Gabath Shammai,' he replied. 'What is its climate?' he asked. 'When a child is born there we have to crush spices and smear his head with it, lest insects should eat him,' he replied. 'Blessed is He who inspireth the inhabitants of a place with love for it!' he exclaimed. In the future too it will be thus: *And I will take away the stony heart out of your flesh, and I will give you a heart of flesh*—leb basar (Ezek. XXXVI, 26), i.e., a heart which has no desire of (*boser*) his neighbour's portion.[6]

[1] Ben 'Azzai was unmarried, this being the reason that he is not designated by his own name (Simeon).
[2] Lit. 'My soul delights in the Torah'.
[3] Yeb. 63*b*.
[4] God has implanted in man a love of his native soil even in bad climates (M.K.).
[5] It is an insignificant place—quite unworthy of praise, and yet these women preferred it to Tiberias. *Var. lec.*: it contains no more than two stands (for scholars)—with similar meaning, Resh Lakish judging it from the point of view nearest to his heart.
[6] I.e. is satisfied with his own. Cf. *infra*, XXXVIII, 11; Sot. 47*a*.

CHAPTER XXXV (NOACH)

1. AND GOD SPOKE UNTO NOAH, AND TO HIS SONS WITH HIM, SAYING: AS FOR ME, BEHOLD, I ESTABLISH MY COVENANT WITH YOU, etc. (IX, 8, 9). R. Judah said: Because he transgressed [God's] command he was put to shame.[1] R. Nehemiah said: He went beyond [God's] command and acted with self-restraint.[2] Therefore he and his sons were favoured with [God's] allocution, as it is written, AND GOD SPOKE UNTO NOAH AND TO HIS SONS, etc.

2. AND GOD SAID: THIS IS THE TOKEN OF THE COVENANT . . . FOR PERPETUAL GENERATIONS—LEDOROTH (IX, 12). R. Judan said: This is written *le-dorath*,[3] which thus excludes two generations, the generation of Hezekiah and that of the Great Synagogue.[4] R. Hezekiah omitted the generation of the Men of the Great Synagogue and substituted that of R. Simeon b. Yoḥai.

Elijah of blessed memory and R. Joshua b. Levi were sitting and studying together,[5] when they came to a ruling of R. Simeon b. Yoḥai. Said one: 'Here is the author of the ruling: let us go and question him about it.'[6] So Elijah of blessed memory went to him, 'Who is with you?' he asked. 'The greatest of his generation, R. Joshua b. Levi,' he answered. 'Has the rainbow appeared in his days?'

[1] He was told to resume marital relations immediately on leaving the Ark, whereas he engaged first in planting a vineyard (v. 20), therefore he was put to shame by Ham (vv. 22 *seq*, *infra*, XXXVI, 4).

[2] This was not a transgression but on the contrary a more scrupulous observance of God's command. For whereas God had forbidden marital relations in the Ark only, he subdued his desires even after leaving the Ark

[3] Though read *le-doroth*. *Dorath* (lit. 'the generation of') is *singular*, and therefore implies limitation. Th.; he interprets the omissions of the two *waws* (לדרת instead of לדורות) as intimating the omission of two generations

[4] A body founded by Ezra to act as the official guardians of the Law. These generations did not need the sign of the rainbow, because they were completely righteous

[5] Elijah was believed to visit people quite frequently.

[6] R. Simeon b. Yoḥai of course was dead, having belonged to a much earlier generation (2nd century) than R. Joshua b. Levi (3rd century). But Elijah could still consult him.

he inquired; 'if it has, he is not worthy of being received by me.'[1]

R. Hezekiah related in R. Jeremiah's name: R Simeon b. Yoḥai had but to say, 'O field, O field, be filled with gold *dinars*,' and it was filled.[2]

R. Hezekiah related in R. Jeremiah's name: Thus did R. Simeon b. Yoḥai say If Abraham is willing, he can effectively intercede for [all generations] from his days until mine, while I can intercede for [all generations] from my time until the advent of Messiah. While if he is not willing, let Ahijah the Shilonite unite with me, and we can intercede for all from the days of Abraham until those of Messiah.[3]

R. Hezekiah said in R. Jeremiah's name: Thus did R. Simeon b. Yoḥai say: The world possesses not less than thirty men as righteous as Abraham. If there are thirty, my son and I are two of them; if ten, my son and I are two of them; if five, my son and I are two of them; if two, they are my son and I; if there is but one, it is I.[4]

3. I HAVE SET MY BOW (ḲASHTI) IN THE CLOUD (IX, 13): that means, My likeness (*ḳishuthi*), something that is comparable to Me.[5] Is that really possible? In truth, [the bow resembles God] as the straw resembles the grain.[6]

AND IT SHALL COME TO PASS, WHEN I BRING CLOUDS UPON THE EARTH (IX, 14). R. Judan said in name of R. Judah b. R. Simon: This may be compared to a man who was holding in his hand some hot flour,[7] and was going to give it to his son, but gave it to his servant instead.[8]

AND THE BOW SHALL BE IN THE CLOUD, etc. (IX, 16). It once happened that R. Isaac, R. Jonathan and R. Judan b. Giyori went to hear an exposition of the Torah—some say of the chapter on libations—from R. Simeon b.

[1] For in a truly righteous generation it would be unnecessary Keth. 77*b*.
[2] Ex. R. LII, 3. [3] Sanh. 97*b*. [4] V. *infra*, XLIX, 3; Ḥul. 92*a*.
[5] V. Ezek. I, 28. [6] It is but a faint reflection of God's glory.
[7] *Var. lec.*: a hot axe.
[8] To save his son the discomfort. (*Var. lec.* is perhaps preferable: he wished to pour it out on his son—in his anger—but poured it, etc.) Thus here too God promises that in His anger He will bring the clouds on the *earth*, not on man.

Yoḥai. Then they took their adieus from him,[1] but stayed on another day. Said they: We must bid him farewell a second time. One of them then expounded [a Scriptural passage],[2] saying to them: Since it is already written, *So Joshua blessed them, and sent them away; and they went unto their tents* (Josh. XXII, 6), why is it further stated, *Moreover when Joshua sent them away unto their tents, he blessed them* (*ib.* 7)? The reason is because when the Israelites were engaged in conquering and dividing the land, the tribes of Reuben and Gad were with them and likewise spent fourteen years there in conquering and dividing the country. After the fourteen years they received permission from Joshua to return home, but they stayed there another few days, and then asked permission a second time. Therefore it says, '*Moreover, when Joshua sent them away,*' etc. R. Judan said: The tribes of Reuben and Gad formed Joshua's personal retinue, and he accompanied them to the Jordan [on their return home]. When they saw that his retinue was thus diminished, they turned back and escorted him to his home His last blessing was greater than the first, as it is written, *And he spoke unto them, saying: Return with much wealth to your tents*, etc. (*ib.* 8).[3]

Another expounded thus: Since it is written, *On the eighth day he sent the people away, and they blessed the king* (I Kings VIII, 66), why is it stated, *And on the three and twentieth day of the seventh month he sent the people away, and they blessed the king* (I Chron. VII, 10)?[4] The reason, however, is that they obtained permission [to go on the twenty-second day], waited a couple of days,[5] and then received permission a second time; therefore it is said, *And on the three and twentieth day of the seventh month,*

[1] Lit. 'they received permission from him'—to go home.
[2] To prove that though permission had already been granted, it was necessary to receive it again since they had stayed on after it. [3] M.K 9*a*.
[4] Our edd. read: . . . *The people away unto their tents; And they blessed the king* is absent. Y.T.: the difficulty is not that the latter verse is superfluous, but that it contradicts the former, for the eighth day of the feast of Tabernacles, to which the former verse refers, is the twenty-second of the month, not the twenty-third.
[5] Viz the twenty-second and twenty-third. Others omit 'a couple of days', or read 'one day', which is preferable

etc. R. Levi said: It is written, *For they kept the dedication of the altar seven days and the feast* [sc. Tabernacles] *seven days* (*ib.* 9). Now the seven days before the Festival must include the Sabbath and the Day of Atonement,[1] yet during [all] these seven days the Israelites ate, drank, rejoiced and lit lamps. Subsequently, however, they were smitten with remorse, saying, 'Perhaps we have done wrong by desecrating the Sabbath and eating on the Day of Atonement?' In order to tranquillise them and assure them that the Holy One, blessed be He, had approved their actions, there came forth a heavenly voice and declared to them, 'Ye are all worthy of the Hereafter.' The last blessing was greater than the first; hence it says, *And they went unto their tents joyful and glad of heart* (I Kings, *loc. cit.*). R. Isaac observed: '*Joyful*,' because they found their wives clean, and '*glad of heart*' because they conceived male children. R. Levi said: There went forth a heavenly voice and proclaimed, 'Ye are all worthy of the Hereafter.'

The third expounded: It is already written, *So she went from him* (II Kings IV, 5)[2]; why then is it stated further, *Then she came and told the man of God* (*ib.* 7)?[3] The reason, however, is because it says *And the oil stayed* (*ib.* 6), which means that the market price advanced,[4] and she came to ask him whether to sell now or not.[5] His second blessing was greater than the first, viz. *And live thou and thy sons of the rest* (*ib.* 7)[6]: which means, until the resurrection of the dead.[7]

When he [R. Simeon b. Yoḥai] saw that they were men of such culture, he sent a couple of scholars with them, to hear what they would teach on the road. One of them expounded thus: It was already written, *And the angel of God, who went before the camp of Israel, removed and went behind them* (Ex. XIV, 19); why then is it further stated,

[1] The Feast of Tabernacles commences on the fifteenth of Tishri, while the Day of Atonement is on the tenth of that month.
[2] This refers to the woman whom Elisha saved from slavery by the miracle of the increasing oil. [3] That the miracle had been duly performed.
[4] Probably translating: *And the oil stood up*—i.e. advanced in price.
[5] But wait for a further increase.
[6] Whereas Elisha's first blessing had merely been that the oil would suffice to pay her debts. [7] Th.: not that they would live until then, but that the oil would sustain them even if they lived so long.

And the pillar of cloud removed from before them, and stood behind them (*ib.*)? It means that that very Attribute of Judgment,[1] which threateningly confronted Israel, was turned round by the Holy One, blessed be He, and directed against the Egyptians.

A second expounded: AND THE BOW SHALL BE IN THE CLOUD; AND I WILL LOOK UPON IT, THAT I MAY REMEMBER THE EVERLASTING COVENANT BETWEEN ELOHIM (GOD): this refers to the Attribute of Heavenly Judgment above; AND EVERY LIVING CREATURE OF ALL FLESH THAT IS UPON THE EARTH: this refers to judgment below: the judgment above is rigid while the judgment below is pliable.[2]

A third expounded: One verse says, [*For wisdom is better than rubies,*] *and all things desirable are not to be compared unto her* (Prov. VIII, 11); whereas another verse says, *And all* thy *desirable things are not to be compared unto her* (*ib.* III, 15)? '*Things desirable*' connotes religious acts and good deeds; '*Thy desirable things,*' gems and precious stones. R. Aḥa explained it in the name of R. Tanḥuma b. R. Ḥiyya: My desirable things and thy desirable things are not to be compared unto her,[3] for, *But let him that glorieth glory in this, that he understandeth, and knoweth Me* (Jer. IX, 23).[4]

[1] Judgment and mercy are often hypostasized as living personalities.

[2] The passage is somewhat obscure. Perhaps it means: heavenly judgment is exacting only when earthly judgment is lax, cf. *supra*, XXVI, 6. The whole story about these three scholars is quoted here for the sake of this verse.

[3] Sc. wisdom, in the sense of the knowledge and the fear of God, stands higher than material wealth and even than religious observances ('E.J.)—presumably because such wisdom is the foundation of all noble deeds.

[4] Several MSS. including cur edd. add the following: Arteban (the last Parthian king) sent our Teacher (R. Judah ha-Nasi) a priceless gem, with the request, 'Let me have in return an article as valuable as this.' So he sent him a *mezuzah*. He sent back word: 'I gave you a priceless object, whereas you returned me something worth but a *folar*' (a small debased coin). 'My desirable things and thy desirable things are not to be compared unto her,' he retorted (the *mezuzah* symbolising the knowledge of God). 'Moreover, you sent me something which I must guard, whereas I sent you something which guards you while you sleep at ease, as it says, *When thou walkest, it shall lead thee* (Prov. VI, 22)—in this world; *when thou liest down, it shall watch over thee* (*ib.*)—in the hour of death; *And when thou wakest, it shall talk with thee* (*ib.*)—in the Hereafter.'

CHAPTER XXXVI (NOACH)

1. AND THE SONS OF NOAH, THAT WENT FORTH FROM THE ARK, WERE SHEM, AND HAM, AND JAPHET (IX, 18). It is written, *When He giveth quietness, who then can condemn*, etc. (Job XXXIV, 29)? R. Meir interpreted it: He quieteneth Himself from His world, *And He hideth His face* (*ib.*) from His world, like a judge before whom a curtain is spread, so that he does not know what is happening without.[1] Let that suffice thee, Meir, said they to him.[2] Then what is meant by, '*When He giveth quietness, who can condemn?*' he demanded. Was not ease given to the generation of the Flood; who then can condemn them? they replied.[3] And what ease was given to them? *Their seed is established* (nakon) *in their sight with them, and their offspring before their eyes* (*ib.* XXI, 8); *They send forth their little ones like a flock*, etc. (*ib.* 11). R. Levi said: Their wives were pregnant but three days and then bore: for '*nakon*' is stated here, whilst elsewhere it is said, *Be ready* (nekonim, pl. of nakon) *against the third day* (Ex. XIX, 15): just as '*nakon*' there means for three days, so '*nakon*' here means for three days. The Rabbis said: Even after one day, for '*nakon*' occurs here, while elsewhere it is said, *And be ready* (nakon) *by the morning* (*ib.* XXXIV, 2): just as '*nakon*' there means in one day, so here too it means one day. '*And their offspring before their eyes*' means that they saw their children's children. '*They send forth their little ones* ('awilehem) *like a flock*': R. Levi

[1] He is unconcerned by what is done in this world and is not incensed by the deeds of the wicked—a remarkable teaching of God's transcendence Cur edd alter the meaning by adding: so said the generation of the Flood (according to this R. Meir merely puts these words into the mouth of the wicked), *Thick clouds are a covering to Him, that He seeth not* (Job XXII, 14). But in that case it is difficult to see why his colleagues so sharply rejected this interpretation. Cf. Lev. R. V, 1.

[2] You have said more than enough—heaven forfend that this teaching should be true!

[3] I.e when God is patient and long-suffering with the wicked, who can demand that He should have punished them sooner? Or perhaps: did He not give them tranquillity, and what did they lack? Their prosperity was complete.

said: In Arabia a child is called *'awila.*[1] *And their children dance (ib.)*—like demons, as you read, *And satyrs shall dance there* (Isa. XIII, 21).[2] When one of them gave birth by day she would say to her son, 'Go and bring me a flint to cut your navel cord.' If at night, she would say to her son, 'Go and light a lamp to cut [burn] through your navel cord.' It once happened that a woman who gave birth at night said to her son, 'Go and light me a candle to cut through your navel cord.' He went out, and the demon Shimadon [lit. 'Destruction'] met him and said to him, 'Go and inform your mother that the cock has crowed,[3] but if the cock had not crowed yet, I would have smitten and killed you.' 'Go and inform your mother that my mother had not yet cut my navel cord,' he retorted,[4] 'but had my mother cut my navel cord, I would have smitten and killed you.' Thus it is written, *Their houses are safe, without fear* (Job XXI, 9)—of demons: *Neither is the rod of God upon them (ib.)*—they are spared sufferings. Yet when He hid His face from them,[5] who said to Him, 'Thou hast not done well'?[6] And why did He hide his face from them? [Because as it is written], *Whether it be done unto a nation or unto a man, alike*—yaḥad (Job XXXIV, 29): '*Unto a nation*' refers to the generation of the Flood; '*And unto a man*,' to Noah; '*alike*': for from him [Noah] was the world established, and He can set up His world from a nation, and He can establish His word from a single person, as it is written, AND THE SONS OF NOAH, etc.[7]

2. *Mighty men do evil that is unfathomable* (Job XXXIV, 24)[8]: the men of the generation of the Flood did evil

[1] He translates *'awilehem*, which is a rare word in this sense, as E.V.
[2] The same word for dance is used in both places.
[3] It is daylight, when I am powerless; cf. Yoma 11*a*.
[4] So that I lack my full strength.
[5] Decreeing that they should all drown.
[6] This concludes the exegesis on Job XXXIV, 29, with which this section began: *And when He hideth his face, who then can behold Him* (ye-shurennu)? By a play on words *ye-shurennu* is connected with *ke-shurah*, right or just. [7] Since He can as easily establish the world from an individual, He destroyed the whole generation, as they were wicked
[8] E.V. '*He breaketh in pieces mighty men without inquisition.*'

with their wicked deeds; '*That is unfathomable*': their wicked deeds were unfathomable [endless] *And He setteth others in their stead* (*ib.*): viz., the children of Noah; hence AND THE SONS OF NOAH, etc

Yea, since the day was I am He, and there is none that can deliver out of My hand (Isa. XLIII, 13): none can deliver any of the world nations out of My hand. *I will work, and who can reverse it* (*ib.*)? In all the works and designs which I executed upon the people of the generation of the Flood, who could say to Me, 'Thou hast not done rightly'? But Noah entered [the Ark] in peace and left it in peace: thus, AND THE SONS OF NOAH, etc.

AND HAM IS THE FATHER OF CANAAN: He was the source of degradation.[1]

THESE THREE WERE THE SONS OF NOAH, AND OF THESE WAS THE WHOLE EARTH OVERSPREAD (IX, 19), as by a huge fish that spawned its eggs and filled the earth.

3. AND NOAH THE HUSBANDMAN BEGAN—WAYYAHEL (IX, 20). He was degraded (*nithḥallel*) and debased (*ḥullin*).[2] Why? Because HE PLANTED A VINEYARD (*ib.*). Should he have not planted something of use, such as a young fig-shoot or a young [olive-] shoot? Instead of which HE PLANTED A VINEYARD. And whence did he procure it? Said R. Abba b. Kahana: He took into the Ark with him vine shoots for planting, and young shoots for fig trees and olive trees, as it is written, *And thou shalt gather to thee* (Gen. VI, 21): a man gathers in only what he will need [in the future].[3]

THE HUSBANDMAN. Three had a passion for agriculture, and no good was found in them: Cain, Noah, and Uzziah. *Cain was a tiller of the ground* (*ib.* IV, 2); Noah: AND NOAH, THE HUSBANDMAN, BEGAN; Uzziah: *And he had husbandmen and vinedressers in the mountains and in the fruitful fields, for he loved husbandry* (II Chron. XXVI, 10).[4]

[1] To his father. 'Canaan' is treated as a substantive deriving from *kana'*, to subdue, subject; hence 'subjection', transf. lowliness, degradation.
[2] *Wayyaḥel* is thus connected with *ḥullin*, profane
[3] V. *supra*, XXXI, 14 [4] V. *supra*, XXII, 3.

A HUSBANDMAN [lit. 'A MAN OF THE GROUND': he was so termed] because he saved the face of the ground, since for his sake the ground was preserved; and because he filled the face of the ground. A MAN OF THE GROUND: just as a castle-guard is called by the name of the castle.[1]

R. Berekiah said: Moses was more beloved than Noah. Noah, after having been called *A righteous man* (Gen. VI, 9), is called A MAN OF THE GROUND[2]; but Moses, after having been called *An Egyptian man* (Ex. II, 19), was then called *The man of God* (Deut. XXXIII, 1). He was more beloved than Noah, who ended as a castrate.[3]

AND PLANTED A VINEYARD. As he was going to plant the vineyard the demon Shimadon met him and proposed, 'Come into partnership with me [in this vineyard], but take care not to enter into my portion, for if you do I will injure you.'

4. AND HE DRANK OF THE WINE, AND WAS DRUNKEN (IX, 21). He drank immoderately, became intoxicated, and was thus put to shame. R. Ḥiyya b. Ba said: He planted it, drank thereof, and was humiliated all on one and the same day.

AND HE WAS UNCOVERED (WAYYITHGAL) WITHIN HIS TENT. R. Judah b. R. Simon and R. Ḥanan in the name of R. Samuel b. R. Isaac said: Not WAYYGAL is written but WAYYITHGAL[4]: he was the cause of exile for himself and subsequent generations. The Ten Tribes were exiled only because of wine, as it is written, *Woe unto them that rise up early in the morning, that they may follow strong drink* (Isa. V, 11). The Tribes of Judah and Benjamin were exiled only on account of wine, as it is written, *But these also* [viz. Judah and Benjamin] *erred through wine* (*ib.* XXVIII, 7).

WITHIN HIS TENT (AHALOH): this is written *ahalah*

1 Jast. Th.: a land-worker is so called because he tills the land.
2 Now understood in a contemptuous sense.
3 V. *infra*, 7. The original is difficult and the translation is only a conjecture; cur. edd. omit it altogether.
4 This is a more intensive form; by a play on words it is derived from *galuth*, exile.

(her tent),[1] viz. his wife's tent. R. Huna said in R. Eliezer's name: When Noah was leaving the Ark a lion struck and mutilated him.[2] Now[3] he went to cohabit, but his semen was scattered and he was humiliated.

R. Joḥanan said: Beware of a passion for wine, because in this passage on wine *way* (woe) is written fourteen times, as it is written, *And Noah the husbandman began* (wayyahel), *and planted* (wayyiṭṭa) *a vineyard, And he drank* (wayyesht) *of the wine, and was drunken* (wayyishkar); *and he was uncovered* (wayyithgal). *And Ham saw* (wayyar) . . . *and told* (wayyagged) *his two brethren, and Shem and Japheth took* (wayyiḳḳah) *a garment, and laid it* (wayyasimu) *upon both their shoulders, and went* (wayyeleku) *backward, and covered* (wayyekassu) . . . *And Noah awoke* (wayyiḳḳez) . . . *and knew* (wayyeda') *what his youngest son had done unto him. And he said* (wayyomer): *Cursed be Canaan* (Gen. IX, 20–25).[4]

5. AND HAM, THE FATHER OF CANAAN, SAW . . . AND TOLD (WAYYAGGED) HIS TWO BRETHREN WITHOUT (IX, 22) He said to his brethren: Adam had but two sons, yet one arose and slew his brother; and this man [Noah] has three sons and yet he wants four! He spoke to them, and persuaded them.[5] R. Abba b. Zabdi said: Why does a slave go free for the loss of a tooth or an eye?[6] It follows from this: AND . . . HE SAW, AND TOLD.[7]

6. AND SHEM AND JAPHETH TOOK A GARMENT. R. Joḥanan said: Shem commenced the good deed, then

[1] Though punctuated *ahaloh*. [2] The reference is to his genital organs.
[3] Being drunk, he forgot that he was unfit for intercourse.
[4] In this passage *way* as part of the verb occurs fourteen times, and by a play on words it is translated 'woe'. Cf. Sanh. 70*a*.
[5] '*Wayyagged*' is derived now from *nagad*, to draw (with words), whence 'to persuade'. I.e. he tried to persuade them that their father had done wrong (v. 4). [6] V. Ex. XXI, 26 f.
[7] He saw with his eye and told with his mouth, his words being clipped, as it were, by his teeth. Thus on account of these organs he was condemned to slavery (Gen. IX, 25); consequently, when his master deprives him of one of them, he regains his freedom.

Japheth came and hearkened to him. Therefore Shem was granted a *ṭallith* and Japheth a *pallium*.[1]

AND LAID IT UPON BOTH THEIR SHOULDERS. Now since it is said, AND WENT BACKWARDS, do we not know that THEY SAW NOT THEIR FATHER'S NAKEDNESS? This, however, teaches that they hid their faces with their hands and walked backward,[2] giving him the respect due from a son to a father.[3] Said the Holy One, blessed be He, to Shem: 'Thou didst cover thy father's nakedness: By thy life! I will reward thee *When these men are bound in their cloaks* (be-sarbelehon),' etc. (Dan. III, 21).[4] (R. Judan and R Huna [differed as to the meaning of '*be-sarbelehon*']: R. Judan said: It means in their prayer cloaks; R. Huna said: It means in their robes of state.[5]) The Holy One, blessed be He, said to Japheth: 'Thou didst cover thy father's nakedness: By thy life, I will reward thee, for *It shall come to pass in that day, that I will give unto Gog a place fit for burial in Israel*' (Ezek. XXXIX, 11).[6] The Holy One, blessed be He, said to Ham: 'Thou didst bring thy father's nakedness into disgrace: By thy life, I will requite thee: *So shall the king of Assyria lead away the captives of Egypt, and the exiles of Ethiopia, young and old, naked and barefoot, and with buttocks uncovered to the shame of Egypt*' (Isa. XX, 4).

7. AND NOAH AWOKE FROM HIS WINE (IX, 24): he was sobered from his wine.

AND KNEW WHAT HIS YOUNGEST SON HAD DONE UNTO HIM. Here it means, his worthless son, as you read,

[1] A cloak fastened with clasps or buckles. *Ṭallith* here means a fringed garment, and R Joḥanan means that the reward of Shem (the ancestor of the Jews) was the precept of fringes (v. Num. XV, 38), while that of Japheth (i.e. the Greek) was the *pallium*—a cloak betokening his dignity.

[2] But actually facing Noah.

[3] It would have been disrespectful to turn their back on him.

[4] When Shadrach, Meshach, and Abed-nego, thy descendants, are cast into the fiery furnace, I will save them.

[5] Jast. Th.. in their breeches

[6] Burial in the land of Israel is regarded as a privilege—moreover, here it implies that they would enjoy the Messianic era. Gog is held to be a descendant of Japheth.

Because the brazen altar that was before the Lord was too little to receive the burnt-offering, etc. (I Kings VIII, 64).[1]

AND HE SAID. CURSED BE CANAAN (IX, 25): Ham sinned and Canaan is cursed! R. Judah and R. Nehemiah disagreed. R. Judah said: Since it is written, *And God blessed Noah and his sons* (Gen. IX, 1), while there cannot be a curse where a blessing has been given, consequently, HE SAID: CURSED BE CANAAN. R. Nehemiah explained: It was Canaan who saw it [in the first place] and informed them, therefore the curse is attached to him who did wrong.

R. Berekiah said: Noah grieved very much in the Ark that he had no young son to wait on him, and declared, 'When I go out I will beget a young son to do this for me.' But when Ham acted thus to him, he exclaimed, 'You have prevented me from begetting a young son to serve me,[2] therefore that man [your son] will be a servant to his brethren!' R. Huna said in R. Joseph's name: [Noah declared], 'You have prevented me from begetting a fourth son, therefore I curse your fourth son.'[3] R. Huna also said in R. Joseph's name: You have prevented me from doing something in the dark [sc. cohabitation], therefore your seed will be ugly and dark-skinned. R. Ḥiyya said: Ham and the dog copulated in the Ark, therefore Ham came forth black-skinned while the dog publicly exposes its copulation. R. Levi said: This may be compared to one who minted his own coinage[4] in the very palace of the king, whereupon the king ordered: I decree that his effigy be defaced and his coinage cancelled. Similarly, Ham and the dog copulated in the Ark and were punished.[5]

8. AND HE SAID: BLESSED BE THE LORD, THE GOD OF SHEM . . . GOD ENLARGE JAPHETH (IX,

[1] *Katon* is used in both verses, in the second in the sense that it was too small and consequently unfit; v. Zeb. 59*b*. Ham was actually not the youngest son, as appears from the order, Shem, Ham, and Japheth
[2] According to the Rabbis he castrated him.
[3] Sc. Canaan; v. X, 6.
[4] Coins bearing his own effigy.
[5] Copulating in the Ark is compared to minting one's coinage (producing offspring in one's own image) in the King's (i.e. God's) own house.

26 f.). This alludes to Cyrus who ordered the Temple to be rebuilt; yet even so, AND HE[1] SHALL DWELL IN THE TENTS OF SHEM: the *Shechinah* dwells only in the tents of Shem. Bar Kappara explained it: Let the words of the Torah be uttered in the language of Japheth [sc. Greek] in the tents of Shem.[2] R. Judan said: From this we learn that a translation [of the Bible is permitted].[3] Thus it is written, *And they read in the book, in the Law of God* (Neh. VIII, 8): this refers to Scripture; *distinctly* (*ib.*): to a translation; *And they gave the sense* (*ib.*)—i.e. the punctuation accents; *And caused them to understand the reading* (*ib.*)—this refers to the beginnings of the verses.[4] R. Hiyya b. Lulianus said: It refers to the grammatical sequence [of words].[5] The Rabbis of Cæsarea said: Here we have an allusion to the traditional text.[6]

R. Zera and R. Hananel said: Even if a man is as well-versed in the Torah as Ezra, he must not read it from memory and write it.[7] But it was taught[8]: It once happened that R. Meir visited Asia Minor,[9] and finding there no Scroll of Esther, he read it from memory and wrote it?[10] There [in Babylonia] they say: He wrote two Scrolls, suppressed the first and kept the second as valid [for use].[11]

[1] Sc God E V. '*And he*', i e. Japheth.
[2] V. Meg. 9*b* The reference is to the Septuagint.
[3] 'Targum' usually connotes the Aramaic translation of Onkelos, but it may also mean translation in general.
[4] Which are not marked in the original Scroll of the Bible.
[5] I.e. whether certain words are to be read with what follows or what precedes them; cf. *infra*, LXXX, 6. For the whole passage cf. Meg. 3*a*; Ned. 37*b*
[6] I.e. they taught the traditional vocalization, which does not always agree with the written text.
[7] I.e. he must not write a Scriptural Scroll from memory but copy from another.
[8] Meg. 18*b*
[9] Th.: Asia here means a tract of land including Lydia and some small portions of what is now Asia. It may also refer to a town, supposed to be Essa, east of the lake of Tiberias (v. Neub. *Géogr*, p. 38).
[10] R Meir was a skilled writer of Scrolls
[11] Because the first was written from memory, whereas the second was copied.

Chapter XXXVII (Noach)

1. The sons of Japheth: Gomer, and Magog, etc. (x, 2). R. Samuel b. Ammi said: These are Africa,[1] Germania,[2] Media, Macedonia and Mysia.[3] And Tiras: R. Simon said: That is the Euphrates region; the Rabbis said: It is Thrace.

And the sons of Gomer: Ashkenaz, and Riphath and Togarmah (x, 3): i.e. Asia,[4] Adiabene, and Germania R. Berekiah said: Germanicia.[5]

And the sons of Javan: Elishah, and Tarshish, Kithim, and Dodanim (x, 4): i.e. Hellas and Taras [Tarantum], Italia,[6] and Dardania.[7] One verse calls them Dodanim, while another verse calls them *Rodanim* (I Chron. I, 7)? R. Simon said: They are called Dodanim because they are the descendants of Israel's kinsmen (*dodim*); '*Rodanim*,' because they come and oppress (*rodim*) them. R. Ḥanan said: When Israel are elevated they say to them, 'We are the descendants of your kinsmen,' but when they are low they come and oppress them.

2. And the sons of Ham: Cush, and Mizraim, and Put, and Canaan (x, 6). Resh Laḳish said: We might have thought that the family of Put was absorbed,[8] had not Ezekiel came and explicitly enumerated him: *Ethiopia, and Put, and Lud, and all the mingled people . . . shall fall* (Ezek. xxx, 5).[9]

[1] Th.: this probably refers to ancient Phrygia in Asia Minor, not to Africa.
[2] The land of the Cimmerians, on the shores of the Caspian sea.
[3] A district of Asia Minor, Jast., with an emended text. Th., however, maintains with Graetz that the text is correct, *isamia* being another name for Javan (Macedonia); in that case several names are left unidentified.
[4] Th.: Asia proconsularis, ancient Phrygia.
[5] Town and district in the province of Commagene, near the borders of Cappadocia (Jast.).
[6] Especially the southern part of Italy, called Magna Graecia (Jast.).
[7] A district and city of Upper Mysia.
[8] In the other branches of the family, since Scripture does not enumerate the sons of Put, as it does the sons of the others.
[9] Thus the family of Put existed as a distinct entity in the days of Ezekiel.

AND CUSH BEGOT NIMROD (x, 8). This explains the text, *Shiggaion of David, which he sang unto the Lord, concerning Cush a Benjamite*—ish yemini (Ps. VII, 1). R. Joshua b R. Nehemiah said in the name of R. Ḥanina b. Isaac: He [David] composed this with reference to the seat of judgment of that wicked man[1] Was then Esau a Cushite?[2] [He is so called] because he acted like Nimrod. Hence it is written, LIKE NIMROD A MIGHTY HUNTER BEFORE THE LORD (x, 9): it is not written, Nimrod [was a mighty hunter], but LIKE NIMROD[3]: just as the one snared people by their words,[4] so did the other [Esau, i.e. Rome] snare people by their words, saying, '[True,] you have not stolen, [but tell us] who was your partner in the theft; you have not killed, but who was your accomplice in the murder.'

3. HE (HU) WAS A MIGHTY HUNTER, etc. Five times '*hu*' is found denoting a wicked character, and five times denoting a good one. It is employed five times to denote a wicked character: HE (HU) WAS A MIGHTY HUNTER; *This* (hu) *is Esau the father of the Edomites* (Gen. XXXVI, 43); *These are* (hu) *that Dathan and Abiram* (Num. XXVI, 9); *This same* (hu) *king Ahaz* (II Chron. XXVIII, 22); *This is* (hu) *Ahasuerus* (Est. I, 1). Five times '*hu*' denotes a good character: *Abram—the same is* (hu) *Abraham* (I Chron. I, 27); *These are* (hu) *that Moses and Aaron* (Ex. VI, 27); *These are* (hu) *that Aaron and Moses* (*ib.* 26); *This same* (hu) *Hezekiah* (II Chron. XXXII, 30); *This* (hu) *Ezra went up* (Ezra VII, 6). R. Berekiah said in the name of the Rabbis of the other country [i.e. Babylonia]: We have another that is better than all: *He is* (hu) *the Lord*

[1] Sc Esau, meaning Rome. I.e. the cunning of the Romans in verbally entangling those whom they accused until they inadvertently confessed to what they had never committed. It is not clear how he translates '*ben yemini*' (E.V. '*a Benjamite*') in that case. Rashash conjectures that it means a 'southerner', Edom, the land of Esau, lying to the south of Judea, whilst Benjamin's territory was in the south of Palestine.
[2] Surely not, being descended from Shem.
[3] Implying that there was another like him.
[4] Understanding hunter metaphorically.

our God (Ps. CV, 7), teaching that His mercy endures for ever.[1]

4 AND THE BEGINNING OF HIS KINGDOM WAS BABEL, AND ERECH, AND ACCAD, AND CALNEH (X, 10): i.e. Edessa,[2] Nisibis, and Ctesiphon.[3] IN THE LAND OF SHINAR: this is Babylonia. SHINAR connotes that it is emptied (*shemenu'ereth*) of precepts, lacking the precepts of *terumah*, tithes, and the Sabbatical year.[4] SHINAR connotes that its inhabitants die in anguish,[5] without a light and without a bath.[6] SHINAR connotes that its princes (*sarim*) die young (*ne'arim*). SHINAR finally connotes that its princes study the Torah in their youth.[7]

OUT OF THAT LAND WENT FORTH ASSHUR (X, 11 f.): from that scheme[8] Asshur dissociated himself.[9] When he saw them come to wage war against the Holy One, blessed be He, he quitted his country. Said God to Him. 'Thou hast departed from four places[10]; by thy life! I will give thee four'; hence, AND BUILDED NINEVEH, AND REHOBOTH-IR, AND CALAH, AND RESEN, [the last-named being] Talsar.[11] Yet he [Asshur] did not remain constant [in his righteousness], and when he came and joined them in destroying the Temple God said to him:

1 '*Hu*' is often understood to denote permanence, while 'Lord' describes God in His Attribute of Mercy (v. *supra*, XII, 15). 2 In Mesopotamia.
3 A city in the southern part of Assyria, on the eastern bank of the river Tigris (Jast.). 4 These, like all precepts bound up with the soil, were to be observed in Palestine only.
5 Lit. 'suffocation'. *Wa-yena'er* in Ex. XIV, 27 (E.V. '*overthrew*') is translated by the Targum 'suffocated'.
6 V Shab. 26*a* on the lack of oils for lighting in Babylonia, and Shab. 25*b* on the lack of baths
7 This last is absent in several MSS. Commentaries *ad loc.*, however, assume that in this clause 'princes' means scholars. But v. Proem XXIV to Lam. R., where מבעטים instead of מבינים is read: whose princes are youths and trample upon the Torah. In that case 'princes' must be understood literally. v. also Ber. 8*a*.
8 To build a city to heaven (Gen. XI, 1-9).
9 Lit 'went forth'. 10 Viz. Babel, Erech, Accad, and Calneh.
11 Th. conjectures that this may be identical with 'Telassar' mentioned in Isa. XXXVII, 12, which may have been the small kingdom of Bit-Adini on the Upper Euphrates.

'Yesterday a chicken and to-day an egg![1] Yesterday thou didst soar aloft with religious actions and noble deeds, whilst now thou art shut up like [a chicken in] an egg'[2]; therefore, *They have been an arm to the children of Lot* (Ps. LXXXIII, 9), which means, for a curse (*le-lewaṭ*).[3] THE SAME IS THE GREAT CITY. We do not know whether Resen is the great city or Nineveh; since, however, it is written, *Now Nineveh was an exceeding great city* (Jonah III, 3), it follows that Nineveh is the great city.

5. AND MIZRAIM [i.e. EGYPT] BEGOT, etc. (X, 13 f.). R. Abba b. Kahana said: The entire coinage of Egypt is thoroughly debased: thus Pathruthim implies degradation, Casluhim implies shame.[4] R. Abba b. Kahana said: The Pathruthim and Casluhim set up bazaars where they stole [interchanged] each other's wives. What came forth from them? THE PHILISTINES AND CAPHTORIM (X, 14): the Philistines were mighty men, while the Caphtorim were dwarfs.[5]

6. AND CANAAN BEGOT ZIDON HIS FIRSTBORN, etc. (X, 15–18). THE HIVITE: the inhabitants of Hildin[6]; THE ARKITE: i.e. Arkas of the Lebanon.[7] THE SINITE: Orthosia.[8] THE ARVADITE: Aradus[9] THE ZEMARITE: Ḥamats[10]; and why is it called Zemarite?

[1] You have retrogressed.

[2] I.e probably, you have stifled your good intentions.

[3] This is a play on words, לוט (Lot) being read לְוָט, a curse, it being loosely rendered: they have been delivered to a curse The first half of the verse reads: *Assyria also is joined with them.*

[4] The passage is extremely obscure, the translation being only a conjecture. He seems to mean that the name of Mizraim's children are all adjectival, descriptive of disgraceful types which originated in Egypt, but the meaning of the actual words in the text is very doubtful. Other MSS. have quite a different reading.

[5] *Kaftor* (כפתור) in Hebrew is a button, and he probably interprets 'Caphtorim' as meaning button-like—little and rotund people.

[6] If this is a place-name it has not been identified. Jast translates: the cave-dwellers.

[7] Also called Cæsarea Libani, a town at the north-western foot of Mount Lebanon.

[8] A Phœnician seaport, south of the river Eleutheros.

[9] On the Phœnician coast

[10] I.e. Emesa, a city of Syria on the eastern bank of the Orontes.

Because wool (*ẓemer*) is manufactured there. THE HAMATHITE: Epiphania.[1]

AND THE BORDER OF THE CANAANITE WAS . . . UNTO LASHA (X, 19): i.e. as far as Callirrhoe.[2]

7. AND UNTO SHEM, THE FATHER OF ALL THE CHILDREN OF EBER, THE ELDER BROTHER OF JAPHETH, TO HIM ALSO WERE CHILDREN BORN (X, 21). We do not know from this verse whether Shem or Japheth was the elder.[3] But since it is written, *Now these are the generations of Shem. Shem was a hundred years old, and begot Arpachshad two years after the flood* (Gen. XI, 10), it follows that Japheth was the elder.[4]

AND UNTO EBER WERE BORN TWO SONS; THE NAME OF THE ONE WAS PELEG [i.e. division], FOR IN HIS DAYS WAS THE EARTH DIVIDED (X, 25). R. Jose said: The ancients, since they knew their genealogy,[5] named themselves in reference to the events [of their days]. But we who do not know our genealogy name ourselves by our fathers. R. Simeon b. Gamaliel said: The ancients, because they could avail themselves of the Holy Spirit, named themselves in reference to [forthcoming] events[6]; but we who cannot avail ourselves of the Holy Spirit are named after our fathers. R. Jose b. R. Ḥalafta said: Eber must have been a great prophet, seeing that he named his child in reference to a [future] incident, as it is

[1] A city of Syria. [2] Warm springs on the eastern side of the Jordan, near the Dead Sea (Jast.). [3] The Hebrew may mean: the brother of the elder Japheth, and is therefore ambiguous.

[4] For Noah begot his first child at the age of 500, while the Flood occurred in his 600th year. Now his children are enumerated thus: Shem, Ham, and Japheth; consequently, if these were in the order of birth, Shem would have been 102 years old two years after the Flood, not 100. Hence we must assume that they are enumerated in order of wisdom, not of age, Shem being the youngest, Ham a year older, and Japheth the eldest (Sanh. 69*b*).

[5] And thus found it unnecessary to state who their fathers were. This is rather forced, and perhaps the reading in the Yalkuṭ, which reverses the statements (i.e. the ancients did *not* know), is more logical and preferable.

[6] Thus an infant's name corresponded to an event that might happen in his later life

written, AND UNTO EBER WERE BORN TWO SONS, etc.

And why was the other called 'Joktan'? Because he minimised (*maktin*) [the importance of] his affairs.[1] What did he thereby earn? He was privileged to found thirteen families. Now if a younger is thus rewarded because he minimises his affairs, how much more so when a great man minimises his importance! Similarly, *And Israel stretched out his right hand, and laid it upon Ephraim's head, who was the elder* (*ib.* XLVIII, 14). Said R. Huna: Do we not know from the birth records that he was the younger. But younger (*ẓa'ir*) means that he minimised (*maz'ir*) his importance. What did he thereby earn? He attained the birthright. Now if the younger is thus rewarded because he minimises his importance, how much the more so when an older minimises his importance!

8. AND JOKTAN BEGOT . . . AND HAZARMARETH (x, 26). R. Huna said: It refers to a place called Hazar Maweth,[2] where people eat leeks, wear garments of papyrus, and hope daily for death.[3] Samuel said: They did not even have garments of papyrus.

AND THEIR DWELLING WAS FROM MESHA (x, 30). R. Eleazar b. Pappos said: Mesene[4] is dead; Media is sick, and Elam is dying.[5] Ḥabil Yamma[6] is the glory of Babylon.[7] Ẓuẓira[8] is the glory of Ḥabil Yamma. R. Judah

[1] The reading *supra*, VI, 4, is 'because he made himself small'.

[2] I.e. this son founded that place. Ḥazar (*ḥaẓir*) is translated herbs, plants, while Maweth means death.

[3] It is a place of extreme poverty and misery. Th.: the reference is probably not to a place of that name in southern Arabia, which was rich and fertile

[4] The island formed by the Euphrates, the Tigris, and the Royal Canal.

[5] The Jews of Mesene are all unfit genealogically; in the other two they are mixed, but the majority of Media are pure, while the majority of Elam are not. (This is the explanation given in Ḳid. 71*b*.)

[6] Lit 'district of the sea'. that region of Babylon which is traversed by rivers and canals.

[7] Rashi in Ḳid. 72*a*: its inhabitants are of the purest birth in Babylon. It may also mean in general that it is the finest and most fertile district, as it actually was.

[8] In Ḳid. 72*a* it is called Zizura. A district not far from the Tigris, the waters of whose canal debouched into the Tigris between Baghdad and Madain; Obermeyer, *Landschaft*, p. 125.

said: Between the rivers[1] is as the Exile [sc. Babylon] in respect of genealogy.[2]

AS THOU GOEST TOWARD SEPHAR: i.e. Taphar[3]; UNTO THE MOUNTAIN OF THE EAST: i.e. the mountains of the East.[4]

[1] Jast.: between the Euphrates and the Tigris. Obermeyer, *loc. cit.*, pp. 100–1, rejects this and maintains that 'between the rivers' is the Talmudic designation for any region of island formation, and here applies to the Euphrates region from Hit (Ihi de Kira) to Anah.

[2] Its genealogy is pure. The genealogy of Babylon was regarded as even purer than that of Palestine; Ḳid 69*b*.

[3] A city in southern Arabia.

[4] The text is an Aramaic translation of the Hebrew

CHAPTER XXXVIII (NOACH)

1. AND THE WHOLE EARTH WAS OF ONE LANGUAGE, etc. (XI, 1). R. Leazar commenced his discourse in the name of R. Jose b. Zimra with the text: *Slay them not, lest my people forget, make them wander to and fro by Thy power, and bring them down, O Lord, our Shield* (Ps. LIX, 12). The Rabbis relate the verse to Doeg and Ahitophel: David said, '*Slay not* Doeg and Ahitophel, *lest my people forget,*' i.e. lest the generations that follow them forget.[1] '*Make them wander to and fro by Thy power,*' i.e. cast them about; '*And bring them down*' from their greatness; but for us, let '*The Lord be our Shield*'. *For the sin of their mouth, and the words of their lips* (*ib.* 13): this one permitted incest and bloodshed, and that one permitted incest and bloodshed. This one [Ahitophel] permitted them, [for he counselled], *Go in unto thy father's concubines* (II Sam. XVI, 21); [while he further said], *And I will come upon him while he is weary and weak-handed . . . and I will smite the king* (*ib.* XVII, 2). And the other [Doeg] permitted them: Naḥman b. Samuel said: He annulled his [David's] citizen rights and declared him an outlaw and as one dead, so that his blood was permitted [his life was forfeit] and his wife permitted.[2] R. Leazar in the name of R. Jose b. Zimra related the verse to the generation of the Separation [of races]. Israel said: '*Slay not* the generation of Separation, *lest my people forget*': lest the generations that follow them forget. '*Make them wander to and fro by Thy power*': cast them away, '*And bring them down*' from above to below.[3] But for us, may '*The Lord be our shield. For the sin of their mouth*': for the sin which they uttered with their mouth. They said: Once in one thousand six hundred and fifty-six years[4] the Firmament totters[5]; therefore let us go and make supports, one in the north, one in the south, one in the west, whilst

[1] Their sin and their punishment. [2] *Supra*, XXXII, 1.
[3] I.e. from the top of their tower.
[4] The period from the Creation to the Flood.
[5] But they refused to recognise the Flood as a Divine visitation for evil

at this spot [sc. Babylonia] will be its eastern support. '*And the word*[1] *of their lips*': thus it is written, AND THE WHOLE EARTH WAS OF ONE LANGUAGE, etc.

2. R. Abba b. Kahana began thus: *Though thou shouldest bray a fool in a mortar with a pestle among groats*, etc. (Prov. XXVII, 22). Said R. Abba b. Kahana: Like a man who pounds barley in a frame; so he [who chastises the fool] thinks to improve him,[2] yet even as it [the pestle] rises and falls,[3] *Yet will his foolishness not depart from him* (*ib.*). Thus the generation of the Flood was removed from the generation of Separation, but [two years, as it is written, *Shem begot Arpachshad*] *two years after the flood* (Gen. XI, 10),[4] yet, AND THE WHOLE EARTH WAS OF ONE LANGUAGE, etc.[5]

3. R. Joḥanan began thus: *Whoso rewardeth evil for good, evil shall not depart from his house* (*ib.* XVII, 13). Said R. Joḥanan: If your neighbour [first] entertained you with lentils and you [subsequently] entertained him with meat, you are still indebted to him; why? Because he showed hospitality to you first. R. Simeon b. Abba said: Not only '*Whoso rewardeth evil for good*', but even he who rewardeth evil for evil,[6] '*Evil shall not depart from his house.*' R. Alexandri commented on the verse '*Whoso rewardeth evil for good*': now the Torah said: *If thou see the ass of him that hateth thee lying under its burden, thou shalt forbear to pass by him; thou shalt surely release it with him* (Ex. XXIII, 5): of such Scripture saith, '*Whoso rewardeth evil for good, evil shall not depart,*' etc.[7] R. Berekiah related the

[1] The Hebrew has the singular. [2] This reading is preferable.
[3] Even while the fool is being chastised.
[4] With this the generation of the Separation was deemed to have begun, though actually the Separation took place 340 years after the Flood (*supra*, XXVI, 3). [5] The lesson was forgotten so soon—almost whilst the punishment was being inflicted.
[6] Translating, Whoso returneth evil instead of returning good.
[7] The point here is not quite clear. Mah. explains that R. Alexandri supports R. Simeon b. Abba, and quotes the verse, *If thou see*, etc., to prove that even if one has done evil to another, the latter must return good, for *him that hateth thee* implies that he had done him harm, yet he is bound to go to his assistance.

verse to these generations.[1] Now the generation of the Flood was removed from the generation of Separation but [two years, as it is written, *'Shem begot Arpachshad] two years after the flood'* (Gen. XI, 10), yet, AND THE WHOLE EARTH WAS OF ONE LANGUAGE, etc.

4. R. Judah b. Rabbi commenced: *They know not, neither do they understand; for their eyes are bedaubed, that they cannot see, and their hearts, that they cannot understand* (Isa. XLIV, 18). Thus it is written, *The Nephilim were in the earth in those days*, etc. (Gen. VI, 4). R. Judah b. Rabbi commented: The later generations would not learn from the earlier ones; viz. the generation of the Flood from that of Enosh, and the generation of the Separation from that of the Flood [from which it was but two years removed, as it is written, *'Shem begot Arpachshad] two years after the flood,'* yet, AND THE WHOLE EARTH WAS OF ONE LANGUAGE, etc.

5. R. 'Azariah commenced: *We would have healed Babylon, but she was not healed* (Jer. LI, 9): *'We would have healed Babylon'*—in the generation of Enosh; *'But she was not healed'*—in the generation of the Flood. *Forsake her, and let us go every one into his own country* (*ib.*)—as it is written, AND THE WHOLE EARTH WAS OF ONE LANGUAGE, etc.[2]

6. AND THE WHOLE EARTH WAS OF ONE LANGUAGE AND OF ONE SPEECH (AḤADIM). R. Leazar said: That means, of veiled deeds,[3] for the deeds of the generation of the Flood are explicitly stated, whereas those of the generation of Separation are not explicitly stated.

AND OF ONE SPEECH (AḤADIM): that means that they spoke against two who were unique [lit. 'one'],

[1] The generation of Separation. Though God had saved them from the Flood, they returned evil by rebelling against Him.

[2] As the narrative ends: *And from thence did the Lord scatter them abroad* (v. 9)—thus each went *'into his own country'*.

[3] This is his translation of *debarim aḥadim* (E.V. 'ONE SPEECH').

viz. against *Abraham* who *was one* (Ezek. XXXIII, 24) and against *The Lord our God, the Lord is One* (Deut. VI, 4). Said they: 'This Abraham is a barren mule[1] and cannot produce offspring.' Against '*The Lord our God, the Lord is One*' 'He has no right to choose the celestial spheres for Himself and assign us the terrestrial world! But come, let us build a tower at the top of which we will set an idol holding a sword in its hand, which will thus appear to wage war against Him.'

Another interpretation: AND ONE SPEECH (AḤADIM) means united in possessions,[2] what one possessed being at the other's disposal The Rabbis said: OF ONE LANGUAGE (SAFAH) may be illustrated by the case of a man who had a wine cellar. He opened one barrel and found it sour, another and found it sour, and a third and found it sour. 'This satisfies (*mashpo*) me that all the barrels are unfit,' he remarked.[3] R. Leazar said: Who is worse—the one who says to the king, 'Either you or I will dwell in the palace,' or the one who says, 'Neither you nor I will dwell in the palace'? Surely the one who says, 'Either you or I.'[4] Similarly, the generation of the Flood said, *What is the Almighty, that we should serve Him?* (Job XXI, 15), whereas the generation of Separation said: 'It does not rest with Him to choose the celestial spheres for Himself and assign the terrestrial world to us. Come, rather, and let us build a tower at the top of which we will set an idol holding a sword, that it may appear to wage war with Him.'[5] Yet of the former not a remnant was left, whereas of the latter a remnant was left! But because the generation of the Flood was steeped in robbery, as it is written, *They remove the landmarks, they violently take away flocks and feed them* (*ib.* XXIV, 2), therefore not a remnant of them was left. And since the latter, on the other hand, loved each other,

[1] The mule was held to be incapable of breeding.
[2] So Mah. Y.T . united in thought.
[3] This is a play on words, *safah* (language) being connected with *shafe*, to tranquillise, whence to satisfy, as in the text: they convinced God that they were uniformly evil. [4] For he means to usurp the king's throne, whereas the other wishes to drive him from it but not to usurp it.
[5] Thus they wished to supplant God—a more heinous offence.

as it is written, AND THE WHOLE EARTH WAS OF ONE LANGUAGE,[1] therefore a remnant of them was left.[2]

Rabbi said: Great is peace, for even if Israel practise idolatry but maintain peace amongst themselves, the Holy One, blessed be He, says, as it were, 'I have no dominion over them'; for it is said, *Ephraim is united in idol-worship*[3]*; let him alone* (Hos. IV, 17). But when their hearts are divided, what is written? *Their heart is divided; now shall they bear their guilt* (*ib.* X, 2).

Another interpretation: AND OF ONE SPEECH (AHADIM) means that they spoke sharp words (*hadim*), saying, 'Once in one thousand six hundred and fifty-six years the Firmament totters; therefore let us go and make supports for it, one in the north, one in the south, one in the west, while this spot will be its eastern support.' Thus it is written, AND ALL THE EARTH WAS ONE LANGUAGE OF SHARP WORDS.

7. AND IT CAME TO PASS, AS THEY JOURNEYED FROM THE EAST—MIKKEDEM (XI, 2).[4] They travelled from further east to nearer east.[5] R Leazar b. R. Simeon interpreted: They betook themselves away from the Ancient (*kadmon*) of the world, saying, 'We refuse to accept either Him or His Divinity.'

THAT THEY FOUND A PLAIN. R. Judah said: All the nations of the world assembled to discover which plain would hold them all, and eventually they found it. R. Nehemiah observed: THEY FOUND: thus it is written, *If it concerneth the scorners, He permits them to scorn* (Job III, 34).[6]

AND THEY DWELT THERE. R. Isaac said: Wherever

[1] I e. united. [2] A striking tribute to the value assigned to brotherly love and unity by the Rabbis. [3] E.V. '*Ephraim is joined to idols*'.
[4] Lit. translation.
[5] Th.· Since they came to Shinar (Babylon) which is itself in the east, the Rabbis maintain that they travelled from a still more easterly point
[6] E.V. '*He scorneth them*'. I.e. God gives all men the opportunity to follow their desires, whether good or bad—an assertion of free-will (cf Yoma 38*b*, Mah. 10*b*). Thus here, too, God permitted them to find a spot suitable for their purpose.

you find dwelling mentioned, Satan becomes active.[1] R. Ḥelbo said: Wherever you find contentment, Satan brings accusations.[2] R. Levi said: Wherever you find eating and drinking, the arch-robber [Satan] cuts his capers [is up to mischief].[3]

8. AND THEY SAID ONE TO ANOTHER (XI, 3). Who said to whom? Said R. Berekiah: Mizraim said to Cush.[4]

COME, LET US MAKE BRICKS, AND BURN THEM (WE-NISREFAH) THOROUGHLY: This is written *we-nissorfah*[5] (and we will be burnt): this people[6] is destined to be burnt out of the world.

AND THEY HAD BRICK FOR STONE, etc. R. Huna said: Their work prospered: a man came to lay one [stone] and he laid two; he came to plaster one [row] and plastered two.[7]

AND THEY SAID: COME, LET US BUILD US A CITY, AND A TOWER (XI, 4). R. Judan said: The tower they built, but they did not build the city. An objection is raised: But it is written, *And the Lord came down to see the city and the tower* (*ib.* 5)? Read what follows, he replied: *And they left off to build the city* (*ib.* 8), the tower, however, not being mentioned. R. Hiyya b. Abba said: A third of this tower which they built sank [into the earth], a third was burnt, while a third is still standing. And should you think that it [the remaining third] is small—R. Huna said in R. Idi's name: When one ascends to the top, he sees the palm trees below him like grasshoppers.

AND LET US MAKE A NAME (SHEM). The School of R. Ishmael taught: SHEM (A NAME) means nought else but an idol.[8]

LEST WE BE SCATTERED ABROAD UPON THE FACE

[1] By ישב the Rabbis understood to live in tranquillity, which rouses Satan's ire! [2] So as to disturb it.
[3] R. Levi translates: AND THEY SAT DOWN THERE—to eat and drink; v. *infra*, LXXXIV beginning; Ex. R. XLI, 7. [4] V. X, 6.
[5] I.e. the word may be read so with a different punctuation.
[6] I.e. they themselves. [7] The work seemed to grow of itself! He translates: And the brick turned *itself* for them into stone, etc.
[8] Cf. Sanh. 109*a*.

OF THE WHOLE EARTH. R. Simeon b. Ḥalputha [Ḥalafta] quoted: *A fool's mouth is his ruin* (Prov. XVIII, 7).[1]

9. AND THE LORD CAME DOWN TO SEE, etc. R. Simeon b. Yohai said: This is one of the ten descents mentioned in the Torah.[2]

WHICH THE CHILDREN OF MEN (ADAM) BUILDED. R. Berekiah said: Would we then have thought that asses or camels built it? It means, however, the children of the first man [Adam][3]: Just as Adam, after all the good which I bestowed upon him, said, *The woman whom Thou gavest to be with me*, etc. (Gen. III, 12),[4] so though the generation of the Flood [preceded that] of the Separation [by but two years, as it is said], '*Two years after the flood*' (*ib.* XI, 10),[5] yet, AND THE WHOLE EARTH WAS OF ONE LANGUAGE, etc.

AND THE LORD SAID: BEHOLD, THEY ARE ONE PEOPLE, etc. (XI, 6). R. Judah interpreted it: Since, BEHOLD, THEY ARE ONE PEOPLE AND THEY HAVE ALL ONE LANGUAGE,[6] if they repent I will accept them. R. Nehemiah explained it: What caused them to rebel against Me? Was it not because, BEHOLD, THEY ARE ONE PEOPLE AND OF ONE LANGUAGE?

AND NOW. R. Abba b. Kahana said: This teaches that the Holy One, blessed be He, gave them an opportunity to repent, for AND NOW indicates repentance, as it says, *And now, Israel, What doth the Lord thy God require of thee, but to fear the Lord thy God*, etc. (Deut. X, 12). But they said, 'No!'—THEN LET ALL WHICH THEY PURPOSE TO DO BE WITHHOLDEN FROM THEM (XI, 6),[7] decreed the Lord. When a vineyard does not yield fruit, what does its owner do to it? He uproots it!

[1] By saying this they unconsciously prophesied their fate and were themselves responsible for it. [2] One of the ten occasions when God came down. They are enumerated by Th.
[3] I.e. they showed themselves his spiritual heirs, both being ungrateful.
[4] He made God's very goodness the excuse for his sin.
[5] And the latter might easily have shared their fate.
[6] I.e. they live in unity; cf. *supra*, 6.
[7] R. Abba splits up the verse thus in three portions. E.V.: '*And now nothing will be withholden from them, which they purpose to do.*'

10. COME, LET US GO DOWN (XI, 7). This is one of the things which they[1] altered for King Ptolemy [changing it to] '*Come, I will go down, and there confound their language.*'[2] R. Abba interpreted it: Through their own lips will I destroy them.[3] Thus one said to his fellow-worker, 'Bring me water,' whereupon he would give him earth, at which he struck him and split his skull; 'Bring me an axe,' but he brought him a spade, at which he struck him and split his skull. Thus it is written, Through their own lips I will destroy them.[4]

SO THE LORD SCATTERED THEM ABROAD—WAYYAFEẒ (XI, 8). R. Judan said: The Tyrians went to Sidon and the Sidonites to Tyre, while Mizraim [Egypt] retains his land.[5] R. Nehemiah said: All the countries assembled within the angular points and each absorbed its own inhabitants.[6] The Rabbis said: WAYYAFEẒ (SCATTERED) is to be read *wayyaẓef* (swept away): the sea came up and swept away thirty families.[7] R. Phinehas said in R. Levi's name: No misfortune comes to a man which does not profit somebody. Whence were those thirty families replaced? From Abraham, sixteen from the sons of Keturah and twelve from Ishmael,[8] and as for the remaining two—*And the Lord said unto her: Two nations are in thy womb* (Gen. XXV, 23).

[1] The translators of the Septuagint.
[2] I.e. the singular instead of the plural—to obviate any idea of plurality in the Godhead. Cf. *supra*, VIII, 11.
[3] He reads *nablah* (E.V. '*confound*') as *nebalah* (meanness, obscenity, transf. destruction) and interprets *sefatham* (E.V. '*their language*') as referring to the words of their lips. [4] The verse is not written thus, and this is presumably his comment upon it.
[5] R. Judan and R. Nehemiah who follows both hold that the Separation took place *after* the nations had been apportioned their territories subsequently to the Flood, the Separation merely transposing them. 'While Mizraim (Egypt) retains his land' is obscure, and it is omitted in cur. edd. and in Yalḳuṭ.
[6] Th. The idea is as though points were taken on the inner borders (i.e. those nearest to the Tower of Babel) of all countries and joined by lines into a huge figure, and the nations entered within this and withdrew each those of its members who had gathered there to build the tower. Thus R. Nehemiah holds that the people remained in their own countries after the Separation, as they were before they gathered to build the Tower.
[7] The allusion is unknown. [8] V. Gen XXV, 2–4, 13–15.

11. THEREFORE WAS THE NAME OF IT CALLED BABEL (XI, 9). A disciple of R. Joḥanan was sitting before him and could not grasp his teaching. 'What is the cause of this?' he demanded. 'It is because I am exiled from my home,' replied he. 'Whence do you come?' inquired he. 'From Borsif,' he answered. 'Not that is its name,' he rejoined, 'but Balsif, in accordance with the text, BECAUSE THERE THE LORD DID CONFOUND (BALAL) THE LANGUAGE (SEFATH) OF ALL THE EARTH.'[1]

12. NOW THESE ARE THE GENERATIONS OF TERAH. TERAH BEGOT ABRAM, etc. (XI, 27). R. Abba b. Kahana said: Whoever has his name thus repeated has a portion in this world and in the World to Come. They raised an objection to him: But it is written, NOW THESE ARE THE GENERATIONS OF TERAH. TERAH BEGOT ABRAM, etc.? That too does not disprove it, replied he, for what is the meaning of, *But thou* [Abraham] *shalt go to thy fathers in peace* (*ib.* XV, 15)? He [God] informed him that his father had a portion in the World to Come; *Thou shalt be buried in a good old age* (*ib.*): He informed him that Ishmael would repent in his own days.

13. AND HARAN DIED IN THE PRESENCE OF HIS FATHER TERAH (XI, 28). R. Hiyya said: Terah was a manufacturer of idols. He once went away somewhere and left Abraham to sell them in his place. A man came and wished to buy one. 'How old are you?' Abraham asked him. 'Fifty years,' was the reply. 'Woe to such a man!' he exclaimed, 'you are fifty years old and would worship a day-old object!' At this he became ashamed and departed. On another occasion a woman came with a plateful of flour and requested him, 'Take this and offer it to them.' So he took a stick, broke them, and put the stick in the hand of the largest. When his father returned he

[1] Borsif was a city near the site of Babylon, and R. Johanan identified it with Babel, remarking at the same time that it should be called Balsif, this name being compounded of *balal* and *safah* and thus showing its origin.

demanded, 'What have you done to them?' 'I cannot conceal it from you,' he rejoined. 'A woman came with a plateful of fine meal and requested me to offer it to them. One claimed, "I must eat first," while another claimed, "I must eat first." Thereupon the largest arose, took the stick, and broke them.' 'Why do you make sport of me,' he cried out; 'have they then any knowledge!' 'Should not your ears listen to what your mouth is saying,' he retorted.[1] Thereupon he seized him and delivered him to Nimrod. 'Let us worship the fire!' he [Nimrod] proposed. 'Let us rather worship water, which extinguishes the fire,' replied he. 'Then let us worship water!' 'Let us rather worship the clouds which bear the water.' 'Then let us worship the clouds!' 'Let us rather worship the winds which disperse the clouds.' 'Then let us worship the wind!' 'Let us rather worship human beings, who withstand the wind.' 'You are just bandying words,' he exclaimed; 'we will worship nought but the fire. Behold, I will cast you into it, and let your God whom you adore come and save you from it.' Now Haran was standing there undecided. If Abram is victorious, [thought he], I will say that I am of Abram's belief, while if Nimrod is victorious I will say that I am on Nimrod's side. When Abram descended into the fiery furnace and was saved, he [Nimrod] asked him, 'Of whose belief are you?' 'Of Abram's,' he replied. Thereupon he seized and cast him into the fire; his inwards were scorched and he died in his father's presence. Hence it is written, AND HARAN DIED IN THE PRESENCE OF ('AL PENE) HIS FATHER TERAH.[2]

14. AND ABRAM AND NAHOR TOOK THEM WIVES, etc. (XI, 29 f.). Abram was a year older than Nahor and Nahor was a year older than Haran; [hence Abram was] two years older [than Haran]; [now deduct] the year of pregnancy with Milcah and the year of pregnancy with Iscah, and you find that Haran begot children at six years

[1] You deny their knowledge and yet you worship them!
[2] The Rabbis translate '*'al pene*' 'because of': he died because his father manufactured idols.

of age, yet you say that Abram could not beget a child! [The reason, however, was]: AND SARAI WAS BARREN; SHE HAD NO CHILD (*ib.* 30).[1]

R. Levi said: Wherever 'she had not' is found, it means that eventually she did have. Thus: AND SARAI WAS BARREN; SHE HAD NO CHILD: eventually she did have, as it is written, *And the Lord remembered Sarah* (Gen. XXI, 1). *And Peninah had children, but Hannah had no children* (I Sam. I, 2): eventually she did have, as it is written, *And she bore three sons*, etc. (*ib.* II, 21). Again, *She is Zion, there is none that careth for her* (Jer. XXX, 17). Yet eventually she will have [one to care for her, as it is written], *And a redeemer will come to Zion, and unto them that turn from transgression*, etc. (Isa. LIX, 20).

[1] According to the Rabbis, Iscah was Sarah. Now Abram was ten years older than Sarah (v. XVII, 17); since he was two years older then Haran, Sarah's father, Sarah was born when Haran was only eight years old. Again, she was his second daughter, and since the period of pregnancy and child-bearing is roughly a year for each child, Haran must have been six years old when he begot a child, i.e. when his wife conceived by him. The point of the difficulty, 'and yet you say that Abram could not beget child,' is not clear. משנת דרבי אליעזר says: If Haran, an unbeliever, could beget children at such an early age, surely it should have been granted to Abram to beget children! The Midrash answers that the fault was not in Abram but in Sarai, who was barren. ידי משה gives a rather more plausible explanation which, however, does not fit in so well with the text.

Chapter XXXIX

LECH LECHA

1. Now the Lord said unto Abram: Get thee out of thy country, etc. (xii, 1). R. Isaac commenced his discourse with, *Hearken, O daughter, and consider, and incline thine ear; forget also thine own people, and thy father's house* (Ps. xlv, 11). Said R. Isaac: This may be compared to a man who was travelling from place to place when he saw a building in flames.[1] Is it possible that the building lacks a person to look after it? he wondered. The owner of the building looked out and said, 'I am the owner of the building.' Similarly, because Abraham our father said, 'Is it conceivable that the world is without a guide?' the Holy One, blessed be He, looked out and said to him, 'I am the Guide, the Sovereign of the Universe.' *So shall the king desire thy beauty* (*ib.* 12): i.e. to make thee glorious in the world. *For he is thy Lord, and do homage unto him* (*ib.*): hence, The Lord said unto Abraham: Get thee, etc.

2. R. Berekiah commenced: *Thine ointments have a goodly fragrance* (S.S. i, 3). Said R. Berekiah: What did Abraham resemble? A phial of myrrh closed with a tight-fitting lid and lying in a corner, so that its fragrance was not disseminated; as soon as it was taken up, however, its fragrance was disseminated. Similarly, the Holy One, blessed be He, said to Abraham: 'Travel from place to place, and thy name will become great in the world': hence, Get thee, etc.

3. R. Berekiah commenced: *We have a little sister—aḥoth* (*ib.* viii, 8): this refers to Abraham, who united (*iḥah*) the whole world for us.[2] Bar Ḳappara observed:

[1] Similarly Abraham saw the world being destroyed by the flames of vice and wrongdoing.

[2] By proclaiming the unity and oneness of God, the corollary of which is the unity and brotherhood of man. This and the following are assumed to be said by God to the angels (Th.).

Like a person who sews a rent together. *'Little'*: even while young he stored up pious acts and good deeds. *And she hath no breasts* (*ib.*): no breasts suckled him[1] in piety or good deeds. *What shall we do for our sister in the day when she shall be spoken for* (*ib.*)? i.e. on the day when the wicked Nimrod ordered him to be cast into the fiery furnace. *If she be a wall, we will build upon her* (*ib.* 9): if he resists [Nimrod] like a wall, He [God][2] will build up [a defence] for him.[3] *And if she be a door* (deleth), *we will enclose* (nazur) *her with boards of cedar* (*ib.*): if he is poor (*dal*) in piety and noble deeds, '*We will enclose* (naẓur) *her with boards of cedar*': and just as a drawing (*ẓurah*) [on boards] is only temporary,[4] so will I protect him only for a time. Said he [Abraham] to Him: 'Sovereign of the Universe! *I am a wall* (*ib.* 10): I stand as firm as a wall; *And my breasts like the towers thereof* (*ib.*): my sons are Hananiah, Mishael, and Azariah.' *Then was I in his eyes as one that found peace* (*ib.*): he entered [the fiery furnace] in peace and left it unscathed: hence, NOW THE LORD SAID UNTO ABRAM: GET THEE.

4. *Wisdom maketh a wise man stronger than ten rulers* (Eccl. VII, 19)[5]: this refers to Abraham, [whom wisdom made stronger] than the ten generations from Noah to Abraham; out of all of them I spoke to thee alone, as it is written, NOW THE LORD SAID UNTO ABRAHAM.[6]

5. R. 'Azariah commenced: *We would have healed Babylon, but she was not healed* (Jer. LI, 9). '*We would have healed Babylon*'—in the generation of Enosh; '*But she was not healed*'—in the generation of the Flood; *Forsake her, and let us go every one into his country* (*ib.*), as it is written, NOW THE LORD SAID UNTO ABRAM: GET THEE.[7]

[1] He had none from whom to draw inspiration. [2] *Var. lec.*: we.
[3] Will save him—that is the probable meaning of the passage. Mah. translates: a world will be built upon him—he shall be the ancestor of a new order.
[4] It is easily rubbed off. He translates: We will treat her like a drawing.
[5] E.V. '*Wisdom is a stronghold to a wise man more than ten rulers that are in a city*'. [6] Cf. *supra*, XXXIV, 5. [7] *Supra*, XXXVIII, 5.

6. R. 'Azariah commenced in R. Aḥa's name thus: *Thou hast loved righteousness, and hated wickedness*, etc. (Ps. XLV, 8). R. 'Azariah in R. Aḥa's name referred the verse to our father Abraham. When Abraham our father stood to plead for mercy for the Sodomites, what is written there? *That be far from Thee to do after this manner* (Gen. XVIII, 25). R. Aḥa explained this: Thou hast sworn not to bring a deluge upon the world. Wouldst Thou evade Thine oath! Not a deluge of water wilt Thou bring but a deluge of fire? Then Thou hast not been true to Thine oath. R. Levi commented: *Shalt not the Judge of all the earth do justly* (*ib.*)? If thou desirest the world to endure, there can be no absolute justice,[1] while if Thou desirest absolute justice the world cannot endure, yet Thou wouldst hold the cord by both ends, desiring both the world and absolute justice. Unless Thou forgoest a little, the world cannot endure. Said the Holy One, blessed be He, to Abraham: '*Thou hast loved righteousness, and hated wickedness*[2]; *therefore God, thy God, hath anointed thee with the oil of gladness above thy fellows* (*ib.*). from Noah until thee were ten generations, and out of all of them I spoke with thee alone'; hence, NOW THE LORD SAID UNTO ABRAHAM.

7. Now what precedes this passage? *And Terah died in Haran* (*ib.* XI, 32), [which is followed by] NOW THE LORD SAID UNTO ABRAM: GET THEE (LEK LEKA). R. Isaac said: From the point of view of chronology a period of sixty-five years is still required.[3] But first you may learn that the wicked, even during their lifetime, are called dead.[4] For Abraham was afraid, saying, 'Shall I go

[1] I.e. justice untempered by mercy. [2] Translating. Thou hast loved to justify (thy fellowmen), and hated to condemn them as wicked.

[3] To bring the narrative to the death of Terah. For Terah was seventy years old at Abram's birth (Gen. XI, 26), whilst Abram departed from Haran at the age of seventy-five (*ib* XII, 4); hence Terah, whose age at death was two hundred and five (*ib.* XI, 32), died sixty-five years after this command, and yet it is narrated before

[4] Hence Terah is already in his lifetime called dead. (Though it is stated *supra*, XXXVIII, 12, that he repented, presumably this was much later.)

out and bring dishonour upon the Divine Name, as people will say, "He left his father in his old age and departed"?'[1] Therefore the Holy One, blessed be He, reassured him: 'I exempt thee (*leka*) from the duty of honouring thy parents, though I exempt no one else from this duty.[2] Moreover, I will record his death before thy departure.' Hence, '*And Terah died in Haran*' is stated first, and then, NOW THE LORD SAID UNTO ABRAM, etc.

8. GET THEE (LEK LEKA). R. Judah said: '*Lek leka*' (Go, go)[3] is written twice, one passage [referring to his departure] from Aram Naharaim, and the other [to his departure] from Aram Nahor. R. Nehemiah said: '*Lek leka*' is written twice, one passage [referring to his departure] from Aram Naharaim and Aram Nahor, and the other intimating that He made him fly from the Covenant between the pieces[4] and brought him to Haran.[5]

It is written: *Thy people* ('ammeka) *offer themselves willingly* (nedaboth) *in the day of thy warfare* (heleka), etc. (Ps. cx, 3). This means: I was with thee (*'immeka*) when thou didst willingly offer (*nadabta*) for My name's sake to enter the fiery furnace.[6] '*In the day of thy warfare*' [lit. 'retinue']; when thou didst bring Me all those bands.[7] *In the mountains*[8] *of holiness*: from the ancient mountain did

[1] This is one of the most important teachings of Judaism: a wrongful deed dishonours one's faith and one's God.

[2] This is deduced from the emphasis GET THEE (LEK LEKA), where *lek* ('go') alone would have sufficed.

[3] *Leka* (E.V. '*thee*') may mean 'go'; cf. Num. XXIII, 13: *Come* (leka), *I pray* thee. [4] V. Gen. xv.

[5] It is stated in Ex. XII, 41, that the Exodus took place at the end of 430 years, which can be proved, by comparing various figures mentioned in the Bible, to mean 430 years after the Covenant with Abraham; and this figure can be right only if Abraham was then 70 years old. Thus it *precedes* his departure from Haran, though it is recorded later. (The 400 years mentioned in the Covenant are calculated from Isaac's birth, 30 years later.) Therefore the Midrash states that God made him fly from the Covenant of the parts to Haran.

[6] The Hebrew may be made to mean this by a mere change of punctuation.

[7] Abraham's faith in the hour of trial won many converts

[8] בהררי. Our edd. of the Bible read בהדרי, in the adornments.

I sanctify thee.[1] *From the womb of the dawn*—mereḥem mishehar (*ib.*): from out of the womb of the world[2] have I sought thee (*shiḥartika*) for Me. *Thine is the dew of thy youth* (*ib.*): because Abraham was afraid and said to himself, 'Perhaps I bear guilt for having worshipped idols all these years,' God reassured him: '*Thine is the dew of thy youth*': even as dew evaporates, so have thy sins evaporated [disappeared]; as dew is a sign of blessing to the world, so art thou a sign of blessing to the world.

It is written: *And I said: Oh that I had wings like a dove! Then I would fly away, and be at rest* (Ps. LV, 7). Why like a dove? Said R. 'Azariah in the name of R. Judan b. R. Simon: Because all other birds, when tired, rest on a rock or a tree, but when a dove is tired she draws in one of her wings[3] and flies on with the other.[4] *Lo, then I would wander far off* (*ib.* 8): exile after exile, journey after journey. *I would lodge in the wilderness. Selah* (*ib.*): better is it to lodge in the deserts of Eretz Israel than in palaces abroad.[5] And should you object, if he [Abraham] had no qualms but rejoiced [to go to Eretz Israel],[6] why did he not emigrate [sooner]? Because he had not yet been permitted; but as soon as he was permitted, it is written, *So Abram went, as the Lord had spoken unto him, and Lot went with him* (Gen. XII, 4).

R. Levi said: When Abraham was travelling through Aram Naharaim and Aram Nahor, he saw its inhabitants eating and drinking and revelling. 'May my portion not be in this country!' he exclaimed. But when he reached the promontory of Tyre and saw them engaged in weeding and hoeing at the proper seasons, he exclaimed, 'Would that my portion might be in this country!' Said the Holy

[1] Th.: this may mean the mountain of Moriah out of which, according to tradition, the world was made to grow.
[2] This may mean either the Mount of Moriah (v. preceding note), or, from the very creation of the world.
[3] To her body and rests on it.
[4] Thus Israel, even when exhausted by persecution, still endeavour to progress.
[5] This is a comment on '*Get thee*', i.e. 'Go for thine own sake', Eretz Israel being so much superior.
[6] The translation is only a conjecture, but certainly gives the general meaning of the passage.

One, blessed be He, to him: *Unto thy seed have I given this land* (*ib.* XV, 18).

9. R. Levi said: '*Get thee*' is written twice,[1] and we do not know which was more precious [in the eyes of God], whether the first or the second.[2]

R. Joḥanan said: GET THEE OUT OF THY COUNTRY means, from thy province; AND FROM THY KINDRED—from the place where thou art settled; AND FROM THY FATHER'S HOUSE—literally, thy father's house. UNTO THE LAND THAT I WILL SHOW THEE: why did He not reveal it to him [there and then]? In order to make it more beloved in his eyes and to reward him for every step he took. This agrees with another teaching of R. Joḥanan, for R. Joḥanan said: *And he said: Take now thy son* (*ib.* XXII, 2)—'which one?' '*Thine only son.*' 'Each is the only one of his mother?' '*Whom thou lovest.*' 'I love them both: are there limits to one's emotions?' Said He to him: '*Even Isaac.*' And why did He not reveal it to him [without delay]? In order to make him even more beloved in his eyes and reward him for every word spoken, for R. Huna said in R. Eliezer's name: The Holy One, blessed be He, first places the righteous in doubt and suspense, and then He reveals to them the meaning of the matter. Thus it is written, TO THE LAND THAT I WILL SHEW THEE; *Upon one of the mountains which I will tell thee of* (*ib.*); *And make unto it the proclamation that I bid thee* (Jonah III, 2); *Arise, go forth into the plain, and I will there speak with thee* (Ezek. III, 22).

10. R. Berekiah b. R. Simon said in R. Nehemiah's name: This may be illustrated by a king who was passing from place to place, when a gem fell from his head. Whereupon the king halted and stationed his retinue there, gathered the sand in piles, and brought sieves. He sifted

[1] Once here, and again when he was commanded to go and sacrifice Isaac (Gen. XXII, 2). [2] This is apparently incomplete; v. *infra*, LV, 7.

the first pile but did not find it ; the second but did not find it; but in the third he found it Said they: 'The king has found his pearl.' Similarly, the Holy One, blessed be He, said to Abraham. 'What need had I to trace the descent of Shem, Arpachshad, Shelah, Eber, Peleg, Reu, Serug, Nahor, and Terah? Was it not on thy account?'[1] Thus it is written, *And* foundest *his heart* [Abraham's] *faithful before Thee* (Neh. IX, 8).[2] In like manner God said to David: 'What need had I to trace the descent of Perez, Hezron, Ram, Aminadab, Nachshon, Shalmon, Boaz, Obed, and Jesse? Was it not on thy account?' Hence it is written, *I have* found *David My servant; with My holy oil have I anointed him* (Ps. LXXXIX, 21).

11. AND I WILL MAKE OF THEE A GREAT NATION (XII, 2). Said he to Him: 'Yet hast Thou not caused the seventy nations to spring from Noah?'[3] He replied: 'That nation of which it is written, *For what* great *nation is there, that hath God so nigh unto them* (Deut. IV, 7), them will I raise up from thee.'

R. Berekiah said · It is not written, 'And I will give thee,' or 'And I will set thee,'[4] but, AND I WILL MAKE THEE: i.e. after I have created thee as a new creation[5] thou wilt be fruitful and multiply.

R. Levi b. Aḥyatha and R. Abba said Thrice is 'greatness' mentioned here, and 'blessings' four times[6]: He thus informed him that there would be three Patriarchs and four Matriarchs.

R. Berekiah said: Because travelling has three adverse

[1] All this led up to thee. [2] He was the pearl that God found.
[3] Seventy was thought to comprise all the possible nations—how then could another arise now? Or, wherein is my greatness? From Noah Thou hast raised seventy nations, but from me only one (Mah , Y.T.).
[4] אתנך and אשימך respectively: both these words could be used in the required sense.
[5] This may refer either to his circumcision or to his change of name to Abraham, through both of which he may have been regarded as a new creation.
[6] V. XII, 2 f. Actually 'greatness' is only mentioned twice. Some explain that '*I will make thee*' counts as one; others include Gen. XVIII, 18: *Seeing that Abraham shall surely become a great and mighty nation.*

effects, diminishing procreation, and reducing one's wealth and one's fame, [God gave him counter assurances]. Since it diminishes procreation [He said to him], AND I WILL MAKE OF THEE A GREAT NATION; it decreases one's wealth, hence, AND I WILL BLESS THEE; it diminishes one's name [fame], hence, AND MAKE THY NAME GREAT. And though the proverb says, 'When you travel from one house to another, you lose a shirt; from one country to another, you lose a life,'[1] yet in truth thou wilt lose neither life nor property.

R. Berekiah said in R. Helbo's name: It[2] means that his coinage was current in the world. There were four whose coinage became current in the world: (i) Abraham, as it is written, AND I WILL MAKE OF THEE, etc. And what effigy did his coinage bear? An old man and an old woman on one side, and a boy and a girl on the other.[3] (ii) Joshua, as it is written, *So the Lord was with Joshua, and his fame was in all the land* (Josh. VI, 27), which means that his coinage was current in the world. And what was its effigy? An ox on one side and a wild-ox on the other, corresponding to, *His firstling bullock, majesty is his, and his horns are the horns of a wild-ox* (Deut. XXXIII, 17).[4] (iii) David, as it is written, *And the fame of David went out into all the lands* (I Chron. XIV, 17), which means that his coinage was current. And what was its effigy? A staff and a wallet on one side,[5] and a tower on the other, corresponding to, *Thy neck is like the tower of David, builded with turrets* (S.S. IV, 4). (iv) Mordecai, as it is written, *For Mordecai was great in the king's house, and his fame went forth throughout all the provinces* (Est. IX, 4)—this too means that his coinage was current. And what was its effigy? Sackcloth and ashes on one side and a golden crown on the other.[6]

[1] Even a short distance causes some loss, while in a long journey a member of the household may easily die through the danger and fatigues of the road. [2] The promise of greatness.

[3] I.e. Abraham and Sarah, Isaac and Rebekah.

[4] This refers to Joseph, from whom Joshua was descended.

[5] Indicating that he was originally a shepherd.

[6] Cf. Est. IV, 1; VIII, 15.

R. Isaac said: [God promised Abraham]: 'I will set thee as a blessing in the Eighteen [Benedictions].[1] Yet thou dost not know whether Mine is first or thine is first.'[2] Said R. Aḥa in R. Ze'ira's name: Thine is before Mine; after having recited 'the shield of Abraham', we then recite 'who resurrectest the dead.'[3]

[AND I WILL MAKE THY NAME GREAT; this means, I will add the letter *he* to thy name.][4] R. Abbahu commented thereon: It is not written, 'Look now *hashamayim*' (at the heaven), but, *Look now* hashamaymah—E.V. '*toward heaven*' (Gen. XV, 5)[5]: with this *hé* I created the world[6]; behold, I will add it to thy name, and then thou wilt be fruitful and multiply. R. Judan said: The numerical value of the letters of thy name will equal those of WA-ABAREKEKA (AND I WILL BLESS THEE): just as WA-ABAREKEKA amounts to two hundred and forty-eight, so do the letters of thy name amount to two hundred and forty-eight.[7]

R. Levi said: No man ever priced a cow belonging to Abraham [in order to buy it] without becoming blessed, nor did a man ever price a cow [to sell] to him without his becoming blessed. Abraham used to pray for barren women, and they were remembered [i.e. they conceived]; and on behalf of the sick, and they were healed. R. Huna said: It was not necessary for Abraham to go to the sick person, for when the sick person merely saw him he was relieved. R. Ḥanina said: Even ships travelling the sea

[1] The principal part of the daily service. This is R. Isaac's comment on AND BE THOU A BLESSING.

[2] One of the eighteen is called '*aboth*', the patriarchs, the blessing referred to here, another is termed '*geburoth*' (strength), in which mention is made of God's strength in bringing rain and resurrecting the dead; this is referred to here as 'Mine'. The verse AND BE THOU A BLESSING does not indicate which of these two takes precedence.

[3] The concluding formulas of '*aboth*' and '*geburoth*' (v n. 2.) respectively. Presumably he translates. 'and be thou the first of the blessings.'

[4] The bracketed sentence has probably fallen out of the text. Radal and Th.

[5] I.e. השמימה with a ה (*hé*) at the end of the word instead of השמים.

[6] V. *supra*, XII, 10.

[7] ואברכך actually = 249. Th. assumes that he reads ואברככה with a *hé* (= 5) at the end, but omits the conjunctive *waw* at the beginning; this gives the required 248.

were saved for Abraham's sake. But did they not contain forbidden wine?[1] [There is a proverb]: 'Vinegar cheapens wine':[2] wherever Gentile wine is available, Jewish wine is cheap. R. Isaac said: To Job too He did thus, as it is written, *Thou hast blessed the work of his hands* (Job I, 10): no man who took a farthing from Job had to take a second one from him.

AND BE THOU A BLESSING (BERAKAH): this means, be thou a *berekah* (pool): just as a pool purifies the unclean, so do thou bring near [to Me] those who are afar.

R. Berekiah said: Seeing that it is already written, AND I WILL BLESS THEE, why is AND BE THOU A BLESSING added? He [God] said to him: 'Hitherto, *I* had to bless My world; henceforth the blessings are entrusted to thee: whom it pleases thee to bless, do thou bless.'

12. AND I WILL BLESS THEM THAT BLESS THEE (XII, 3). R. Jeremiah b. Eleazar said: The Holy One, blessed be He, was stricter in defence of the honour of the righteous than of His own honour. For in respect to His own honour it is written, *For them that honour Me I will honour, and they that despise Me shall be disgraced* (I Sam II, 30), which means through others; whereas concerning the honour of the righteous it is written, AND I WILL BLESS THEM THAT BLESS THEE, AND HIM THAT CURSETH THEE WILL I CURSE—I Myself.

It was taught[3]: At these benedictions one must bow: at the beginning and end of the first, and at the beginning and end of 'We give thanks'; and if a man bows at each benediction, he must be instructed to refrain. R. Isaac b. R. Naḥman said in the name of R. Joshua b. Levi: The High Priest bows at the beginning of each benediction, and a king must bow at the beginning and the end of each benediction. R. Simon said in the name of R. Joshua b. Levi: Once he [the king] had bent the knee, he did not

[1] I.e. these ships carried forbidden cargoes, what was the purpose then of saving them? [2] An abundance of vinegar, which may also be drunk, reduces the demand for wine and thus cheapens it. [3] Ber. 34*a*.

straighten himself until he finished his entire prayer, as it is written, *And it was so, that when Solomon had made an end of praying all this prayer and supplication unto the Lord, he arose from before the altar of the Lord, from kneeling on his knees*, etc. (I Kings VIII, 54). What is *keri'ah* and what is *berikah?*[1] R. Ḥiyya the elder showed Rabbi the action of *keri'ah*, and became lame, but was subsequently healed. Levi b. Susi showed Rabbi the action of *keri'ah*, he became lame and was not healed.

AND IN THEE SHALL BE BLESSED: rain and dew shall come for thy sake.

Now it is written, *And the thing became known to Mordecai, who told it unto Esther the queen*, etc. (Est. II, 22): he [Mordecai] was circumcised while the other [Ahasuerus] was uncircumcised, yet he had pity on him[2]! R. Judah quoted: *From my elders I receive understanding* (Ps. CXIX, 100): He [Mordecai] reasoned thus: Jacob blessed Pharaoh, as it is written, *And Jacob blessed Pharaoh* (Gen. XLVII, 7); moreover, did not Joseph reveal his dreams to him, and did not Daniel reveal his dreams to Nebuchadnezzar? So I too; hence, '*And he told it unto Esther the queen.*'[3] R. Nehemiah said: The Holy One, blessed be He, said to Abraham: AND IN THEE SHALL ALL THE FAMILIES OF THE EARTH BE BLESSED. Now if that is meant in respect of wealth, they are surely wealthier than we! But it was meant in respect of counsel: when they get into trouble they ask our advice, and we give it to them.

13. SO ABRAM WENT, AS THE LORD HAD SPOKEN UNTO HIM; AND LOT WENT WITH HIM (XII, 4): Lot was merely joined on with him.

AND ABRAM WAS SEVENTY AND FIVE YEARS OLD. Thus it is written, *And he brought up Hadassah* (Est. II, 7). Rab said: She was forty years old[4]; Samuel said: She was

[1] Both denote a form of bending the knee, but in different ways.
[2] This is a question: why did Mordecai care about the conspiracy of Bigthan and Teresh against Ahasuerus (v. v. 21 *ad loc.*)?
[3] The question is rhetorical, its purpose being to show the Jewish attitude of loyalty to his country of domicile.
[4] When chosen by Ahasuerus.

eighty years old; the Rabbis of that place [i.e. Babylonia] said: She was seventy-five years old. R. Berekiah observed in the name of the Rabbis: The Holy One, blessed be He, assured Abraham: 'Thou didst leave thy father's house when seventy-five years old; by thy life, the redeemer whom I will raise up from thee shall be seventy-five years old,' this being the numerical value of Hadassah.[1]

14. AND ABRAM TOOK SARAI HIS WIFE, AND LOT THEIR BROTHER'S SON, AND ALL THEIR SUBSTANCE WHICH THEY HAD GATHERED, AND THE SOULS THAT THEY HAD MADE[2] IN HARAN (XII, 5). R. Leazar observed in the name of R. Jose b. Zimra: If all the nations assembled to create one insect they could not endow it with life, yet you say, AND THE SOULS THAT THEY HAD MADE! It refers, however, to the proselytes [which they had made]. Then let it say, 'That they had converted'; why THAT THEY HAD MADE? That is to teach you that he who brings a Gentile near [to God] is as though he created him Now let it say, 'That *he* had made'; why THAT THEY HAD MADE? Said R. Ḥunia: Abraham converted the men and Sarah the women.[3]

15. AND ABRAM PASSED THROUGH THE LAND UNTO THE PLACE OF SHECHEM . . . AND THE CANAANITE WAS THEN IN THE LAND (XII, 6): so far they still had a right in the land.[4]

AND THE LORD APPEARED UNTO ABRAM, AND SAID: UNTO THY SEED WILL I GIVE THIS LAND; AND HE BUILDED THERE AN ALTAR (XII, 7): what is stated here is on account of the good tidings about Eretz Israel.[5]

AND HE REMOVED FROM THENCE UNTO THE

[1] הדסה: ה (5) + ד (4) + ס (60) + ה (5) = 74, to which the word as a whole is added, making 75.
[2] Lit. translation. E V. '*gotten*'. [3] Cf. *infra*, LXXXIV, 4.
[4] Their measure of sin was not yet full, that they should be expelled from the country; cf. Gen. XV, 16.
[5] It was on that account that he built the altar.

MOUNTAIN ON THE EAST OF (MI-KEDEM) BETH-EL (XII, 8): originally it was called Beth-el (house of God), but now it is called Beth-awen (house of iniquity).[1] R. Liezer said: He who does not merit being called *ben he-'amal* is called *ben he-'amad*.[2] R. Isaac b. Nahman said: There [in Palestine] a good worker is called *'amela* (industrious), while urine-soaked dung is called *'amidah.*

AND PITCHED HIS TENT (AHALO). R. Ḥanina said: *Ahalah* (her tent) is written[3]; after having pitched Sarah's tent he pitched his own.[4]

16. AND HE BUILDED THERE AN ALTAR UNTO THE LORD (XII, 16). R. Leazar said: He built three altars: one on account of the good tidings about Eretz Israel, another for his possession thereof,[5] and a third [as a prayer] that his descendants might not fall at Ai, as it is written, *And Joshua rent his clothes, and fell to the earth upon his face before the Ark of the Lord until the evening, he and the elders of Israel, and they put dust upon their heads* (Josh. VII, 6). R. Leazar b. Shamua' said: They began recalling the merit of our father Abraham, who said, *I am but dust and ashes* (Gen. XVIII, 27); did then Abraham build Thee an altar at Ai for aught but that his children should not fall there!

AND CALLED UPON THE NAME OF THE LORD: with prayer. Another interpretation of AND CALLED: he began to make converts.[6]

AND ABRAM JOURNEYED, GOING ON STILL TOWARD THE SOUTH (XII, 9): he drew a course and journeyed toward the [future] site of the Temple.

[1] '*Mi-ḳedem*' is translated: in former times; cf. Josh. VII, 2.
[2] '*Amal:* toil, '*amad* = heap of dung. he who does not earn for himself the epithet, a toiler in the Torah, earns for himself the other epithet
[3] Though vocalised *ahalo*, his tent.
[4] A deft touch, showing the honour paid in Judaism to women.
[5] V. XIII, 17. I.e. that he might possess Eretz Israel for the merit of having built this altar.
[6] Translating: and he summoned people to the name (i.e. glory) of the Lord.

Chapter XL (LECH LECHA)

1. AND THERE WAS A FAMINE IN THE LAND, etc. (XII, 10). It is written, *Behold, the eye of the Lord is toward them that fear him* (Ps. XXXIII, 18): this alludes to Abraham, of whom it is written, *For now I know that thou art a God-fearing man* (Gen. XXII, 12). *Toward them that wait for His mercy* (Ps. *loc. cit.*): thus it is written, *Thou wilt show faithfulness to Jacob, mercy to Abraham* (Micah VII, 20). *To deliver their soul from death* (Ps. XXXIII, 19): from the death decreed by Nimrod.[1] *And to keep them alive in famine* (*ib.*): thus it is written, AND THERE WAS A FAMINE IN THE LAND; AND ABRAM WENT DOWN INTO EGYPT TO SOJOURN THERE.

2. R. Phinehas commenced his discourse in the name of R. Ḥanan of Sepphoris: *Happy is the man whom Thou chastisest, O Lord* (Ps. XCIV, 12)· yet should he object,[2] then, '*And teachest out of Thy law*' (*ib.*): what is written of Abraham? *And I will bless thee, and make thy name great* (Gen. XII, 2). As soon as he set out, famine assailed him, yet he did not protest nor murmur against Him, but, AND ABRAM WENT DOWN INTO EGYPT, etc.

R. Joshua b. Levi commenced thus: *He hath given* ṭeref [E.V. '*food*'] *unto them that fear Him; He will be ever mindful of His covenant* (Ps. CXI, 5). Said R. Joshua b. Levi: In this world He hath given wanderings (*ṭiruf*) unto them that fear Him; but in the Messianic future, '*He will be ever mindful of His covenant.*' For what is written of Abram? '*And I will bless thee, and make thy name great*' (Gen. XII, 2). As soon as he set out, famine assailed him, yet he did not protest nor murmur against Him, but, AND THERE WAS A FAMINE IN THE LAND, etc.[3]

3. AND THERE WAS A FAMINE IN THE LAND, etc. Ten famines have come upon the earth. One in the days of

[1] V. *supra*, XXXVIII, 13. [2] Calling God's justice into question.
[3] I.e. he retained his faith and went on to Egypt.

Adam: *Cursed is the ground for thy sake* (*ib.* III, 17); one in the days of Lamech: *Which cometh from the ground which the Lord hath cursed* (*ib.* V, 29); one in the days of Abraham: AND THERE WAS A FAMINE IN THE LAND; one in the days of Isaac: *And there was famine in the land, beside the first famine that was in the days of Abraham* (*ib.* XXVI, 1); one in the days of Jacob: *For these two years hath the famine been in the land* (*ib* XLV, 6); one in the days when the judges judged: *And it came to pass in the days that the judges judged, that there was a famine in the land* (Ruth I, 1); one in the days of David: *And there was a famine in the days of David* (II Sam. XXI, 1); one in the days of Elijah: *As the Lord, the God of Israel, liveth, before whom I stand, there shall not be dew nor rain these years* (I Kings XVII, 6); one in the days of Elisha: *And there was a great famine in Samaria* (II Kings VI, 25); and there is one famine that travels about the world, and one will be in the Messianic future—*Not a famine of bread, nor a thirst for water, but of hearing the words of the Lord* (Amos VIII, 11). R. Huna and R. Jeremiah in the name of R. Samuel b. Isaac said: The proper time for its manifestation was in the days of David, and it ought really to have come in the days of Saul, but because Saul was the shoot of a sycamore tree, the Holy One, blessed be He, postponed it and brought it in the days of David. Shila sins and Joḥana is punished! Said R. Ḥiyya: Imagine a glass-worker holding a basket full of goblets and cut glass; when he wished to hang the basket up, he brought a nail and drove it [into the wall], and held on to it while he hung up his basket. For that reason all these [famines] came not in the days of lowly [weak] men but in the days of the mighty ones, who could withstand it. R. Berekiah applied to them the verse, *He giveth power to the faint* (Isa. XL, 29). R. Berekiah said in R. Ḥelbo's name: There were two famines in the days of Abraham. R. Huna said in R. Aḥa's name: There was one in the days of Lamech and one in the days of Abraham. The famine of Elijah's time was one of scarcity, one year being productive and the next year unproductive. The famine in the days of Elisha was one of panic, *Until an ass's head was sold for fourscore pieces of silver*, etc. (II Kings VI, 25). As for the famine during the days of the judges, R. Huna said in R. Dosa's name: From the price of two *se'ahs* [of wheat per *sela'*] it advanced to one *se'ah* [per *sela'*], whereas it was taught: A man must not emigrate abroad unless two *se'ahs* cost a *sela'*. R. Simeon observed: That is only when it is altogether unobtainable, but if it is obtainable, even at a *se'ah* per *sela'*, one must not go abroad.[1]

4. AND IT CAME TO PASS, WHEN HE WAS COME NEAR TO ENTER INTO EGYPT, etc. (XII, 11). She was with him all these years, yet *now* he says to her, BEHOLD, NOW I KNOW THAT THOU ART A FAIR WOMAN TO LOOK UPON! The reason, however, is because travelling takes toll of one's beauty.[2] R. 'Azariah said in the name of R. Judah b. R. Simon: [Abraham said to Sarah:] We have traversed Aram Naharaim and Aram Nahor and not found a woman as beautiful as you; now that we are entering a country whose inhabitants are swarthy and ugly, SAY, I PRAY THEE, THOU ART MY SISTER, THAT IT MAY BE WELL WITH ME FOR THY SAKE, etc. (*ib.* 13).

R. Phinehas said in the name of R. Reuben: Two people were principal actors and yet made themselves subordinate, viz. Abraham and Barak. Barak, as it is written, *And she sent and called Barak . . . And Barak said unto her: If thou wilt go with me, then I will go; but if thou wilt not go with me, I will not go* (Judg. IV, 6 ff.). R. Judah explained: If thou wilt go with me to Kadesh,[3] I will go with thee against Hazor[4]; whilst if thou wilt not go with me to Kadesh, I will not go with thee against Hazor. R. Nehemiah explained it: If thou wilt go with me in Song,[5] I will go with thee to battle; but if thou wilt not go with me in Song, I will not go with thee to battle. *And*

[1] For notes v. *supra*, XXV, 3. [2] Lit. 'through journeying a person becomes despised'—but Sarah retained her beauty.
[3] To summon the warriors of Zebulun and Naphtali; v. 9 f
[4] I.e. against Jabin who reigned in Hazor; v. 2. Y.T. suggests that Hazor is an error for Tabor.
[5] If you undertake to join me in singing praises to God; v. Judg. V.

she said: I will surely go with thee, notwithstanding (efes) *the journey that thou takest shall not be for thy honour* (*ib.* 9). R. Reuben said: [*Efes*] is a Greek word, as though to say *hafes* (let alone).[1] Said she to him: 'What thinkest thou? that the glory for the Song shall be given to thee alone!' He retired into the second place, as it is written, *Then sang Deborah and Barak the son of Abinoam*, etc. (*ib.* v, 1).[2] Abraham was the principal, as it is written, *And Abram took Sarai his wife* (Gen. XII, 5), but he made himself of secondary importance, saying, SAY, I PRAY THEE, THOU ART MY SISTER, whereupon he really became subordinate to her, as it is written, *And he dealt well with Abram for her sake* (*ib.* 16).

5. AND IT CAME TO PASS, THAT, WHEN ABRAM WAS COMING INTO EGYPT, etc. (XII, 14). And where was Sarah? He had put her in a box and locked her in it. When he came to the customs-house, he [the customs officer] demanded, 'Pay the custom dues.' 'I will pay,' he replied 'You carry garments in that box,' said he. 'I will pay the dues on garments.' 'You are carrying silks,' he asserted. 'I will pay on silks.' 'You are carrying precious stones.' 'I will pay on precious stones.' 'It is imperative that you open it and we see what it contains,' he insisted. As soon as he opened it the land of Egypt was irradiated with her lustre [beauty]. R. 'Azariah and R Jonathan in R. Isaac's name said: Eve's image was transmitted to the reigning beauties of each generation.[3] Elsewhere it is written, *And the damsel was very fair*—'ad me'od (I Kings I, 4), which means that she attained to Eve's beauty; but here in truth it is written, THE EGYPTIANS BEHELD THE WOMAN THAT SHE WAS VERY FAIR (ME'OD)—which means, even more beautiful than Eve's image.[4]

AND THE PRINCES OF PHARAOH SAW HER, AND PRAISED HER (XII, 15). R. Johanan said: They went on

[1] Gr. ἀφές. [2] Deborah first, as the principal [3] As a standard of beauty. [4] V. *supra*, VIII, 5, where '*me'od*' is treated as an allusion to Adam, and XXI, 2, where Eve is called Adam. The present comments are on the same lines (Th.). '*Ad* implies up to a certain point, but no further.

outbidding each other for her[1]: one said, 'I give a hundred *dinars* that I may enter [Pharaoh's palace] with her,' whereupon another bid, 'I give two hundred *dinars* to enter with her.'[2] I know this only of their advancement; whence do we know it of their degradation?[3] Because it says, *Then took they Jeremiah, and cast him into the pit* (Jer. XXXVIII, 6): they raised his price.[4] We know it only of this world: whence do we know it of the Messianic future? Because it is said, *And the peoples shall take them, and bring them to their place* (Isa. XIV, 2).

6. AND HE DEALT WELL WITH ABRAM, etc. (XII, 16). It is written, *And Pharaoh gave men charge concerning him*, etc. (*ib.* 20). R. Phinehas commented in R. Hoshaya's name: The Holy One, blessed be He, said to our father Abraham, 'Go forth and tread out a path for thy children.' For you find that everything written in connection with Abraham is written in connection with his children. In connection with Abraham it is written, *And there was a famine in the land* (*ib.* 10); while in connection with Israel it is written, *For these two years hath the famine been in the land* (*ib.* XLV, 6). Abraham: *And Abram went down into Egypt;* Israel: *And our fathers went down into Egypt* (Num. XX, 15). Abraham: *To sojourn there;* Israel: *To sojourn in the land are we come* (Gen. XLVII, 4). Abraham: *For the famine was sore in the land;* Israel: *And the famine was sore in the land* (*ib.* XLIII, 1). Abraham: *And it came to pass, when he was come near* (hiḳrib) *to enter into Egypt;* Israel: *And when Pharaoh drew nigh*—hiḳrib (Ex. XIV, 10).[5] Abraham: *And*

[1] Lit. 'she was progressively raised' (in price)
[2] This is a comment on the end of the verse: AND THE WOMAN WAS TAKEN INTO PHARAOH'S HOUSE
[3] Viz. that when the righteous are to be humbled and mishandled, people outbid each other for the privilege of doing so?
[4] As in last note
[5] This appears difficult, since the second phrase refers to Pharaoh, not Israel. Mah explains that in both verses *ḳarab*, the *kal* form, should have been used, not *hiḳrib*, the *hif'il*, which literally means, '*caused* to draw nigh' Hence the Midrash translates the fear of the Egyptians caused Abraham to bring himself near to God, and similarly Pharaoh, by casting his fear upon the Israelites, caused them to come near to God; cf. Ex. R XXI, 4.

they will kill me, but thee they will keep alive; Israel: *Every son that is born ye shall cast into the river, and every daughter ye shall save alive* (*ib.* I, 22). Abraham: *Say, I pray thee, that thou art my sister, that it may be well with me;* Israel: *And God dealt well with the midwives* (*ib.* 20). Abraham: *And it came to pass, that, when Abram was come into Egypt;* Israel: *Now these are the names of the sons of Israel, who came in Egypt* (*ib* I). Abraham: *And Abram was very rich in cattle, in silver, and in gold* (Gen. XIII, 2), Israel: *And He brought them forth with silver and gold* (Ps. CV, 37). Abraham. *And Pharaoh gave men charge concerning him, and they sent him away;* Israel: *And the Egyptians were urgent upon the people, to send them out* (Ex. XII, 33). Abraham: *And he went on his journeys* (Gen. XIII, 3); Israel: *These are the journeys of the children of Israel* (Num. XXXIII, I).

CHAPTER XLI[1] (LECH LECHA)

1. AND THE LORD PLAGUED PHARAOH AND HIS HOUSE WITH GREAT PLAGUES, etc (XII, 17). It is written, *The righteous shall flourish like the palm-tree; he shall grow like a cedar in Lebanon* (Ps. XCII, 13). As the palm and the cedar have neither crooked curves nor excrescences, so the righteous have neither crookedness nor excrescences[2]; as the shadow of the palm and the cedar is cast afar,[3] so is the reward of the righteous far away [in the future world]; as the heart of the palm and the cedar is directed upward, so are the hearts of the righteous directed toward the Holy One, blessed be He, as it is written, *Mine eyes are ever toward the Lord, for He will bring forth my feet out of the net* (*ib.* XXV, 15); as the palm and the cedar have desire,[4] so have the righteous desire. And what is their desire? The Holy One, blessed be He. R. Tanḥuma said: There was once a palm tree in Amatho[5] that did not yield fruit. A palm-gardener passed and saw it; said he: 'This ungrafted tree looks to [a male palm] from Jericho.' As soon as they grafted it, it yielded fruit. Or [will you argue]: as we cannot make utensils from a palm tree, so are the righteous! Therefore, it says '*like a cedar*'. R. Huna observed: There [in Babylonia] utensils are manufactured from it [the palm tree].[6] Then will you say: as the cedar does not produce fruit, so are the righteous? Therefore it is stated, '*The righteous shall flourish like the palm-tree*': as no part of the palm has any waste, the dates being eaten, the branches used for Hallel, the twigs for covering [booths],[7] the bast for ropes, the leaves for besoms, and the planed boards for ceiling rooms, so are there none worthless in Israel, some being versed in Scripture, others in Mishnah,

[1] In the British Museum MSS. Add 27169, which forms the basis of Theodor's critical edition, this is still Ch. XL. But in the cur. edd. and several other MSS. Ch. XLI commences here, and this has been adopted for the sake of convenience. From Ch XLIII the edd and MSS. are again alike. [2] In their character. [3] Their foliage being at the top. [4] To be grafted with the male palm standing at a distance (Th.).
[5] Th.: a place in Transjordania. *Var. lec.* Hamtham, also a place, one mile from Tiberias, v. Meg. 2*b*. [6] Cf. Pes 88*a*. [7] V. Lev. XXIII, 42.

some in Talmud,[1] others in *Haggadah.* And as whoever climbs to the top of the palm and the cedar and does not take care of himself falls and is killed, so whoever comes to attack Israel eventually receives his deserts on their account, the proof being that because Pharaoh took possession of Sarah for one night he and his household were smitten with plagues, as it is written, AND THE LORD PLAGUED PHARAOH, etc.

2. R. Simeon b. Laḳish said in Bar Ḳappara's name: Pharaoh was smitten with lupus. R. Simeon b. Gamaliel said: An old man suffering with boils met me in Sepphoris; said he to me: 'There are twenty-four varieties of boils, and out of all these the only one upon which a woman has an injurious effect is lupus'[2]; and therewith was the wicked Pharaoh smitten.

AND HIS HOUSE. R. Aḥa said: Even the beams of his house were smitten, and all exclaimed, 'It is BECAUSE OF SARAI ABRAM'S WIFE.' R. Berekiah said: Because he dared to approach the shoe of that lady. And the whole of that night Sarah lay prostrate on her face, crying, 'Sovereign of the Universe! Abraham went forth [from his land] on Thine assurance, and I went forth with faith; Abraham is without this prison while I am within!' Said the Holy One, blessed be He, to her: 'Whatever I do, I do for thy sake, and all will say, "It is BECAUSE OF SARAI ABRAM'S WIFE."' R. Berekiah said: Because he dared to approach the shoe of that lady.[3] R. Levi said: The whole of that night an angel stood with a whip in his hand; when she ordered, 'Strike,' he struck, and when she ordered, 'Desist,' he desisted.[4] And why such severity?

[1] The general discussions on the Mishnah.
[2] In both cases the translation is only a conjecture
[3] This repetition is absent in cur. edd. Its purpose is presumably to serve as an introduction to R. Levi's statement
[4] All these statements are deduced from the verse under discussion. *Al debar* (E.V. *'for the sake of'*) can also mean, 'by the word of'. Hence it is interpreted: By the word of all people, that this was on account of Sarai; again, by the word, i.e. prayer, of Sarah, and finally, by the word of Sarai to the angel. *'Abram's wife'* is superfluous, hence the comment: that he should have dared to approach Abram's wife!

Because she told him [Pharaoh], 'I am a married woman,' yet he would not leave her. R. Leazar said (the same was also taught in the name of R. Liezer b. Jacob): We know that Pharaoh was smitten with leprosy and Abimelech with the closing up [of the orifices]: how do we know that what is said here is to be applied there, and vice versa? Because *'for the sake of'* occurs in both places, that an analogy may be drawn.[1]

3. AND ABRAM WAS VERY RICH IN CATTLE, IN SILVER, AND IN GOLD (XIII, 2). Thus it is written, *And He brought them forth with silver and with gold; and there was none that stumbled among His tribes* (Ps. CV, 37)

AND HE WENT ON HIS JOURNEYS (XIII, 3): He returned by the same route by which he had come. R. Leazar said: He went to settle his debts.

AND LOT ALSO, WHO WENT WITH ABRAM, etc. (XIII, 5). Lot enjoyed four boons on account of Abraham: (i) *And Lot went with him* (Gen. XII, 4); (ii) AND LOT ALSO, etc, (iii) *And he also brought back his brother Lot, and his goods* (*ib.* XIV, 16); and (iv) *And it came to pass, when God destroyed the cities of the plain, that God remembered Abraham, and sent Lot out of the midst of the overthrow* (*ib.* XIX, 29). Now in return for these his descendants should have requited us with kindness, yet not alone did they not requite us with kindness, but they even did us evil. Thus it is written, *And he sent messengers unto Balaam . . . Come now therefore, I pray thee, curse me this people* (Num. XXII, 5 f.); again, *And he gathered unto him the children of Ammon and Amalek, and he went and smote Israel* (Judg. III, 13); also, *And it came to pass after this, that . . . the children of Ammon, and with them some of the Ammonites, came against Jehoshaphat to battle* (II Chron. XX, 1); also this verse, *The adversary hath spread out his hand upon all her treasures* (Lam. I, 10)[2] Their sin is

[1] V. Gen. XX, 18: *For the Lord had fast closed up all the wombs of the house of Abimelech, for the sake of Sarah Abraham's wife.*

[2] All these verses refer to the Ammonites or Moabites (v Lam. R. I, 10; Yeb. 16*b*), who were descended from Lot (v. Gen. XIX, 30–8).

recorded in four places: *An Ammonite or a Moabite shall not enter into the assembly of the Lord . . . because they met you not with bread and water in the way*, etc. (Deut. XXIII, 4 f.); *Because they met not the children of Israel with bread and water*, etc. (Neh. XIII, 2); *O My people, remember now what Balak king of Moab devised* (Micah VI, 5).[1] Four prophets arose and sealed their doom, viz. Isaiah, Jeremiah, Ezekiel, and Zephaniah. Isaiah said: *The burden of Moab*, etc. (Isa. XV, 1); Jeremiah: *Then I will cause an alarm of war to be heard against Rabbah of the children of Ammon*, etc. (Jer. XLIX, 2); Ezekiel: *I will open the flank of Moab . . . together with the children of Ammon, unto the children of the east . . . and I will execute judgments upon Moab*, etc. (Ezek. XXV, 9 ff.); Zephaniah: *Surely Moab shall be as Sodom, and the children of Ammon as Gomorrah*, etc. (Zeph. II, 9).

4. HAD FLOCKS, AND HERDS, AND TENTS. R. Ṭobiah b. R. Isaac said: He had two tents, viz. Ruth the Moabitess and Naamah the Ammonitess.[2] Similarly it is written, *Arise, take thy wife, and thy two daughters that are found* (Gen. XIX, 15)[3]: R. Ṭobiah said: That means two 'finds',[4] viz. Ruth and Naamah. R. Isaac commented: *I have found David My servant* (Ps. LXXXIX, 21): where did I find him? In Sodom.[5]

5. AND THERE WAS A STRIFE BETWEEN THE HERDMEN OF ABRAM'S CATTLE AND THE HERDMEN OF LOT'S CATTLE (XIII, 7). R. Berekiah said in R Judan's name: Abraham's cattle used to go out muzzled,[6] but Lot's did not go out muzzled. Said Abraham's herdmen to them: 'Has then robbery been permitted?' To which Lot's herdmen replied: 'Thus did the

[1] Only three are stated Th adds (v Lam R. I, 10): *Then Balak the son of Zippor, king of Moab, arose and fought against Israel: and he sent and called Balaam the son of Beor to curse you* (Josh. XXIV, 9).
[2] He understands tents figuratively, as meaning descendants.
[3] V. *infra*, L, 10 *ad fin.* [4] Two precious things
[5] He was descended from Lot who was saved from the destruction of Sodom. [6] So as not to graze in others' fields.

Holy One, blessed be He, say to Abraham: *Unto thy seed will I give this land* (Gen. XII, 7); now Abraham is a barren mule, who cannot beget children,[1] therefore Lot will be his heir; if they eat, they are eating their own.' Said the Holy One, blessed be He, to them: 'Thus did I say to him: *Unto thy seed have I given this land' (ib.* XV, 18): When? when the seven nations are uprooted from it.[2] Now, however, AND THE CANAANITE AND THE PERIZZITE DWELT THEN IN THE LAND, etc.: so far they still have a right in the land.[3]

6. AND ABRAM SAID UNTO LOT: LET THERE BE NO STRIFE, I PRAY THEE, BETWEEN ME AND THEE, etc. (XIII, 8). R. 'Azariah said in R. Judah's name: Just as there was strife between the herdmen of Abraham and the herdmen of Lot, so was there strife between Abraham and Lot, as it says, AND ABRAM SAID UNTO LOT: LET THERE BE NO STRIFE, etc.

FOR WE ARE BRETHREN. Was he then his brother? In fact he called him so because his features resembled his own.

IS NOT THE WHOLE LAND BEFORE THEE? SEPARATE THYSELF (HIPPARED) I PRAY THEE (XIII, 9). R. Ḥelbo said: Not *hibbadel*[4] is written, but HIPPARED: just as a *peredah* (mule) cannot develop semen, so is it impossible for this man [Lot] to mix with the seed of Abraham.

IF THOU WILT TAKE THE LEFT HAND, THEN I WILL GO TO THE RIGHT; OR IF THOU TAKE THE RIGHT HAND, THEN I WILL GO TO THE LEFT. He said to him: 'If thou goest to the left, I go to the south, while if I go to the south, thou goest to the left, so that in either case I go to the south.'[5] R. Johanan said: This may be compared to two men who had two stacks, one of wheat

[1] Cf. *supra*, XXXVIII, 5. [2] As follows from vv. 19 f.
[3] The Pesikta comments: a righteous man influences his household and servants to be likewise, while a wicked man makes his household wicked.
[4] Which has the same meaning. [5] Translating the second half of the verse: or if I take the right hand, then I will make thee go to the left.

and the other of barley. Said one to the other: 'If the wheat is mine, then the barley is yours, while if the barley is yours the wheat is mine, in either case then the wheat is mine.'[1] R. Ḥanina b. Isaac said: It is not written, *we-asme'elah* but *we-asme'ilah*[2]: in all events I will make that man [Lot] go to the left.

7. AND LOT LIFTED UP HIS EYES, etc. R. Naḥman b. Ḥanan said: Whoever is fired with immoral desire is eventually fed with his own flesh.[3] R. Jose b. R. Ḥanina said: The whole of this verse connotes immoral desire. Thus: AND LOT LIFTED UP HIS EYES, as you read, *And his master's wife lifted up her eyes to Joseph* (*ib.* XXXIX, 7). AND BEHELD ALL THE PLAIN (KIKKAR) OF THE JORDAN, as you read, *For on account of a harlot a man is brought to a loaf* (kikkar) *of bread* (Prov. VI, 26).[4] THAT IT WAS WELL WATERED (MASHKEH) EVERYWHERE, as you read, *And he shall make the woman drink*—wehishkah (Num. V, 24)[5]; BEFORE THE LORD DESTROYED (SHAḤETH) SODOM, as you read, *And it came to pass, when he went in unto his brother's wife, that he spilled*[6] *on the ground* (Gen. XXXVIII, 9).

LIKE THE GARDEN OF THE LORD, LIKE THE LAND OF EGYPT: LIKE THE GARDEN OF THE LORD in trees, and LIKE THE LAND OF EGYPT in cereals.

SO LOT CHOSE HIM ALL THE PLAIN OF THE JORDAN, etc. (XIII, 11). R. Jose b. Zimra said: He was like a man who covets his mother's dowry.[7]

AND LOT JOURNEYED EAST (MI-ḲEDEM): He betook himself from the Ancient (*ḳadmon*) of the world, saying, I want neither Abraham nor his God.[8]

[1] The probable meaning is: if you examine the wheat, you will see that it is mine; while if you examine the barley, you will see that it is yours.
[2] The first is intransitive, I will go left; the second is transitive, I will cause another to go left. [3] He commits incest.
[4] Translating: and beheld all the loaf—i.e. the immorality—of the Jordan. [5] The reference is to the water ordeal of a woman accused of adultery. [6] *We-shiheth*, lit. 'destroyed'.
[7] Lot was as eager for immoral pleasures as though they were his due heritage. [8] Cf *supra*, XXXVIII, 7.

AND THEY SEPARATED THEMSELVES THE ONE FROM THE OTHER. ABRAM DWELT IN THE LAND OF CANAAN, etc (*ib.* 11 f.). Rabbi said: There was no city more wicked than Sodom: when a man was evil he was called a Sodomite; and there was no nation more cruel than the Amorites; when a man was cruel he was called an Amorite. R. Issi said: There was no city [in the plain] better than Sodom, for Lot searched through all the cities of the plain and found none like Sodom. Thus these people were the best of all, yet, THE MEN OF SODOM WERE WICKED AND SINNERS (*ib.* 13)—they were WICKED to each other; SINNERS in adultery; AGAINST THE LORD in idolatry; while EXCEEDINGLY refers to bloodshed.

8. AND THE LORD SAID UNTO ABRAM, AFTER THAT LOT WAS SEPARATED FROM HIM (XIII, 14 f.). R. Judah said: There was anger [in heaven] against our father Abraham when his nephew Lot parted from him. 'He makes everyone cleave [to Me],' said the Holy One, blessed be He, 'yet he does not cause his brother's son to cleave [to Me]!' R. Nehemiah said: There was anger [in heaven] against the Patriarch Abraham when Lot his brother's son *went* with him. 'I promised him, *Unto thy seed have I given this land*' (Gen. XV, 18), said God, 'yet he attaches Lot to himself; if so, let him go and procure two common soldiers!' This explains the text: *Cast out the scorner* (Prov. XXII, 10), which alludes to Lot; *And contention will go out* (*ib.*), alluding to, *And there was a strife between the herdmen of Abraham's cattle*, etc. *Yea, strife and shame will cease* (*ib.*), as it says, *And Abram said to Lot: Let there be no strife. He that loveth pureness of heart, that hath grace in his lips, the king shall be his friend* (*ib.* 11): hence, AND THE LORD SAID UNTO ABRAM: . . . FOR ALL THE LAND WHICH THOU SEEST, TO THEE WILL I GIVE IT, etc.

9. AND I WILL MAKE THY SEED AS THE DUST OF THE EARTH (XIII, 16). Just as the dust of the earth is found from one end of the world to the other,

so shall thy children be found from one end of the earth to the other; and as the dust of the earth can be blessed only through water, so will thy children be blessed only for the sake of the Torah, which is likened to water[1]; and as the dust of the earth wears out even metal utensils yet itself endures for ever, so will Israel exist [for ever] while the nations of the world will cease to be; and as the dust of the earth is trodden upon, so will thy children be downtrodden under the heel of [foreign] powers, as it is written, *And I will put it into the hand of them that afflict thee* (Isa. LI, 23); which means, those who make thy wounds flow. Nevertheless, it is for thy benefit, for they purify thee of guilt,[2] as you read, *Thou makest her soft with showers*, etc. (Ps. LXV, 11).[3] *That have said to thy soul: Bow down, that we may go over* (Isa. *loc. cit.*). What did they do to them? They made them lie down in the streets and drew ploughs over them. R. 'Azariah said in R. Aha's name: That is a good augury: as the street outlives those who travel on it, yet itself remains for ever, so shall thy sons, [said God to Abraham], outlive the nations of the world while they will remain for ever.[4]

10. ARISE, WALK THROUGH THE LAND, etc. (XIII, 17). It was taught[5]: If he walks in the field, whether along its length or its breadth, he acquires it as far as he walks. This is the view of R. Liezer,[6] but the Sages maintain: He does not acquire it until he takes possession.[7] R. Jacob said: R. Eliezer's view is based on the verse, ARISE, WALK THROUGH THE LAND.[8]

[1] Cf. Isa. LV, 1. [2] Lit. 'they beat thee out of thy guilt'.
[3] Words of the same root are used for 'makest soft' and 'that afflict thee'. The Midrash understands the former in the sense of making the rain flow, and hence the latter too—to make the wounds flow.
[4] Nations that persecute the Jews are in the long run doomed to perish.
[5] B.B. 100*a*
[6] One of the legal methods of acquiring land is *hazakah*, taking possession, and R. Liezer holds that walking in the land to be acquired constitutes *hazakah*.
[7] E.g by fencing part of it. The translation follows the text as emended by Th , which agrees with the text in the Talmud.
[8] By this act of walking Abraham was to acquire the title to the land.

Chapter XLII (LECH LECHA)

1. AND IT CAME TO PASS IN THE DAYS OF AMRAPHEL, etc. (XIV, 1). R. Joshua commenced his discourse in the name of R. Levi: *The wicked have drawn out the sword*, etc. (Ps. XXXVII, 14). R. Liezer's brothers were once ploughing in the plain, while he was ploughing on the mountain, when his cow fell and was maimed. It proved fortunate for him that his cow was maimed, for he fled to R. Joḥanan b. Zakkai.[1] He ate there clods of earth[2] until his mouth emitted an offensive odour, and when they went and told R. Joḥanan b. Zakkai that the breath from R. Eliezer's mouth smelt foul, he said to him: 'As the smell of your mouth became unpleasant for the sake of the Torah, so will the fragrance of your learning be diffused from one end of the world to the other.' After some time his father came up to disinherit him, and found him sitting and lecturing with the greatest of the land sitting before him. Ben Ẓiẓẓith Hakeseth, Niḳodemon ben Gurion, and Ben Ḳalba Shabua. He was expounding this verse: '*The wicked have drawn out the sword, and have bent the bow*'; this alludes to Amraphel and his companions; *To cast down the poor and needy* (*ib.*)—to Lot; *To slay such as are upright in the way* (*ib.*)—to Abraham. *Their sword shall enter into their own heart* (*ib.* 15), as it is written, *And he fought against them by night, he and his servants, and smote them*, etc. (Gen. XIV, 15). Said his father to him, 'My son, I came up only to disinherit thee; now, however, all my property is given to thee as a gift.' 'Behold,' he replied, 'let it be *ḥerem* [accursed] to me[3]; I will take only an equal share with my brothers.' (Another interpretation: '*The wicked have drawn out the sword*' alludes to Amraphel and his allies, as it is written, AND IT CAME TO PASS IN THE DAYS OF AMRAPHEL).[4]

[1] To study in his academy. [2] Through poverty.
[3] He would not profit through his learning.
[4] The bracketed passage may be spurious, Th.

2. R. Samuel commenced his discourse: *And this also is a grievous evil, that in all points as he came, so shall he go* (Eccl. v, 15). Said R. Samuel: As he comes with slops, so he goes with slops.[1] R. Abin said: Just as he commenced with four kings, so will he conclude with four kings.[2] [He commences with four kings, viz.]: *With Chedorlaomer king of Elam, and Tidal king of Goiim, and Amraphel king of Shinar, and Arioch king of Ellasar* (Gen. xiv, 9); so he ends with four kingdoms: the kingdom of Babylon, the kingdom of Media, the kingdom of Greece, and the empire of Edom [i.e. Rome]. R. Phinehas quoted in R. Abin's name: *But they know not the thoughts of the Lord, neither understand they His counsel, for He hath gathered them as the sheaves to the threshing-floor* (Micah iv, 12). Thus, why *Came all these as allies* (Gen. xiv, 3)? In order that they might come and fall by the hands of Abraham; hence it is written, AND IT CAME TO PASS IN THE DAYS OF AMRAPHEL, etc.

3. AND IT CAME TO PASS (WAYYEHI) IN THE DAYS OF AMRAPHEL. R. Tanḥuma said in the name of R. Ḥiyya the Elder and R. Berekiah said in R. Eleazar's name: The following teaching came to us from the Exile[3]: wherever '*And it came to pass in the days of*' (wayyehi biyeme) occurs, it denotes trouble.[4] R. Samuel b Naḥman said: '*And it came to pass in the days of*' occurs five times: (i) AND IT CAME TO PASS IN THE DAYS OF AMRAPHEL: THAT THEY MADE WAR. This may be compared to a king's friend who dwelt in a province, and on his account the king used to visit the province and showed it favour. But when barbarians came to attack him [this friend] they lamented, 'Woe to us, for the king will no longer show favour to this province as was his wont, [if his friend is killed].' Thus it is written, *And they turned*

[1] At birth he can only eat slops, and in old age before death he is the same.
[2] R Abin relates the verse to the Jewish nation: just as his history commences with an engagement between Abraham and the four kings, so at an advanced stage of his history shall he be subject to four powers
[3] I.e. from Babylon
[4] By a play on words the phrase is read *way hayyah*, there was woe.

back and came to En-mishpat, etc. (*ib.* 7): R. Aḥa said: They came only in order to attack the eyeball of the world; the eye which executed judgment in the world[1] they desire to blind![2] *The same* (hi) *is Kadesh*: R. Aha said: This is written *hu* (he)[3]: it was he [Abraham] that sanctified (*kiddash*) the name of the Holy One, blessed be He, in the fiery furnace. Hence when barbarians came to attack him, all began lamenting 'woe!'; thus 'There was woe in the days of Amraphel.'[4]

(ii) *And it came to pass in the days of Ahaz* (Isa. VII, 1): [What]? *The Arameans on the east, and the Philistines on the west* (*ib.* IX, 11). This may be compared to the son of a king against whom his tutor plotted in order to kill him. Said he to himself: 'If I slay him now, my life will be forfeit to the king. Therefore I will rather withdraw his foster-mother from him, and he will die of himself.' Ahaz said likewise: If there are no kids there are no wethers; if there are no wethers there are no sheep; if there are no sheep there is no shepherd; if there is no shepherd there is no world. He reasoned thus to himself: No children, no adults; no adults, no disciples; no disciples, no sages; no sages, no elders; no elders, no prophets; and if there are no prophets the Holy One, blessed be He, will not cause His *Shechinah* to rest upon them. Thus it is written, *Bind up the testimony, shut up the instruction among My disciples* (*ib.* VIII, 16).[5] R. Ḥunia said in R. Leazar's name: Why was he called Ahaz? Because he seized (*aḥaz*) the synagogues and schools. R. Jacob said in R. Aḥa's name: Isaiah said: *And I will wait for the Lord, that hideth His face from the house of Jacob, and I will look for Him* (*ib.* 17): no hour is as grievous as that whereof it is written, *And I will surely hide my face*, etc (Deut. XXXI, 18), and since that hour I have hoped for Him, for He said to me, *For it shall not be forgotten out of the mouths of their seed* (*ib.* 21). And what did it avail him [sc. Ahaz]? *Behold, I and the*

[1] *En-mishpat* literally means 'the eye of judgment'.
[2] The reference is to Abraham
[3] Though read *hi*, feminine, its consonantal form is *hu*, masc., i.e. 'he'.
[4] V. p. 341, n. 4. [5] Understood in the sense of to shut it out from them

children whom the Lord hath given me shall be for signs and for wonders (Isa. VIII, 18). Were they then his children? Surely they were his disciples! This, however, teaches that they were dear to him, and so he called them his children.[1] But as soon as he seized the synagogues and schools, all began lamenting 'woe': thus there was woe in the days of Ahaz.

(iii) *It came to pass in the days of Jehoiakim* (Jer. I, 3)—*I beheld the earth, and lo, it was waste and void* (*ib.* IV, 23). This may be compared to a king who sent an ordinance to a province: what did its inhabitants do? They took it, tore it up, and burnt it in fire. [Similarly we read], *And it came to pass, when Jehudi had read three or four columns, that he cut it with the penknife, and cast it into the fire* (*ib.* XXXVI, 23). When they saw this all began crying 'woe': thus there was woe in the days of Jehoiakim.

(iv) *And it came to pass in the days when the judges judged* (Ruth I, 1)—*That there was a famine in the land* (*ib.*). This may be compared to a province that owed arrears to the king, and the king sent a treasury officer to collect them. What did the inhabitants do? They seized him, beat him and mulcted him. Then they cried, 'Woe to us when the king learns of this: what he wished to do to us we have done to him': similarly, woe to the generation that judged its judges![2] Thus, there was woe in the days when the judges were judged.

(v) *And it came to pass in the days of Ahasuerus* (Est. I, 1)—*Wherefore Haman sought to destroy all the Jews* (*ib.* III, 6). This may be compared to a king who had a vineyard, which three enemies attacked: the first plucked off single grapes, the second thinned the clusters, and the third uprooted the vines. Thus Pharaoh decreed, *Every son that is born ye shall cast into the river* (Ex. I, 22); Nebuchadnezzar deported *The craftsmen and the smiths a thousand* (II Kings XXIV, 16). (R. Berekiah said in R. Judah's name: That means, the craftsmen a thousand and the smiths a thousand. The Rabbis said: It means a thousand in all.) But Haman

[1] I.e. so far his attempt to kill Jewish education was a failure.

[2] This is the Rabbinical rendering of the present verse.

wished to pull up the very roots, as it is written, *To destroy, to slay, and to cause to perish all Jews* (*ib.* 13). When they saw this, all began lamenting 'woe': thus there was woe in the days of Ahasuerus.

R. Simeon [b. R. Abba] said in R. Joḥanan's name: Wherever *wayyehi* (and it came to pass) is employed it connotes either trouble or joy, if trouble, there was none like it; if joy, there was none like it. R. Samuel b. Naḥman came and drew a distinction: wherever *wayyehi* is stated, it denotes trouble, *we-hayah* denotes joy.[1] They objected: But it is written, *And God said: Let there be light and there was* (wayyehi) *light* (Gen. I, 3)? That still does not connote joy, he replied, since the world was not privileged to make use of that light.[2] (R. Judah said: By the light which was created on the first day man could have seen from one end of the world to the other; but when the Holy One, blessed be He, foresaw the wicked, He hid it away for the righteous, as it is written, *But the path of the righteous is as the light of dawn, that shineth more and more unto the perfect day* (Prov. IV, 18).) They objected: But it is written, *And there was* (wayyehi) *evening and there was* (wayyehi) *morning, one day* (Gen. I, 4)? That too was not an occasion of joy, replied he, for everything created on the first day is destined to wear out, as it is written, *For the heavens shall vanish away like smoke, and the earth shall wax old like a garment* (Isa. LI, 6).[3] They objected: But it is written, *And there was* (wayyehi) *evening and there was* (wayyehi) *morning, a second day* (Gen. I, 8) . . . *a third day* (*ib.* 13) . . . *a fourth day* (*ib.* 19), etc.? These still do not connote joy, he answered, for whatever was created in the first six days of Creation needs further preparation [before it is fit for use], e.g. mustard must be sweetened, wheat must be ground. They objected: But it is written, *And the Lord was* (wayyehi) *with Joseph* (*ib.* XXXIX, 2)? That too was not an occasion of joy,

[1] *Wayyehi* is the impf. of the verb to be with the *waw* conversive, generally translated, 'and it was,' 'and it came to pass', *we-hayah* is the perf with the *waw* conversive, generally rendered 'and it shall be', 'and it shall come to pass.' [2] V. *supra*, III, 6. [3] It should be noted that he understands 'joy' in the sense of a permanent joy.

because that she-bear [Potiphar's wife] assailed him. Another objection: But it is written, *And it came to pass* (wayyehi) *on the eighth day* (Lev. IX, 1)?[1] That does still not connote joy, he replied, because on that very day Nadab and Abihu died. But it is written, *And it came to pass* (wayyehi) *on the day that Moses had made an end of setting up the tabernacle* (Num. VII, 1)? That still does not connote joy, he answered, because it [the tabernacle] was hidden away at the building of the Temple.[2] But it is written, *So the Lord was* (wayyehi) *with Joshua, and his fame was in all the land* (Josh. VI, 27)? That still does not connote joy, he replied, since he eventually had to rend his garments.[3] But it is written, *And it came to pass* (wayyehi), *when the king dwelt in his house*, etc. (II Sam. VII, 1)?[4]—Nathan came and informed him, *Nevertheless, thou shalt not build the house* (I Kings VIII, 19). Said they to him: We have quoted our objections: do you quote your proofs. Thereupon he cited: *And it shall come to pass* (we-hayah) *in that day, that living waters shall go out from Jerusalem* (Zech. XIV, 8); *And it shall come to pass* (we-hayah) *in that day, that a great horn shall be blown*, etc. (Isa. XXVII, 13); *And it shall come to pass* (we-hayah) *in that day, that a man shall rear a young cow*, etc. (*ib.* VII, 21)[5]; *And it shall come to pass* (we-hayah) *in that day, that the Lord will set His hand again a second time to recover the remnant of His people* (*ib.* XI, 11); *And it shall come to pass* (we-hayah) *in that day, that the mountains shall drop down sweet wine* (Joel IV, 18). They objected: But it is written, *And he* (Jeremiah) *was there* (we-hayah) *when Jerusalem was taken* (Jer. XXXVIII, 28)? Even that connotes joy, was his reply, for on that very day Israel received full quittance for their sins, as R. Samuel b. Naḥman said: Israel received quittance in full measure for their sins on the day that the Temple was destroyed, as it is written, *The punishment of*

[1] The verse treats of the final consecration of Aaron to the priesthood.
[2] This implies that the Tabernacle was in existence (though probably not in its erected form) until the Temple was built.
[3] Over the defeat at Ai (*ib* VII, 6).
[4] The chapter treats of the building of the Temple.
[5] This refers to the Messianic era.

thine iniquity is complete, O daughter of Zion, etc. (Lam. IV, 22).

4. AND IT CAME TO PASS IN THE DAYS OF AMRAPHEL. He was called by three names: Cush, Nimrod, and Amraphel. Cush, because he was indeed a Cushite[1]; Nimrod, because he incited the world to revolt (*himrid*); Amraphel denotes: he made a declaration (*amar imrah*), 'I will cast down (*appilah*).'[2] [Another interpretation is] that he made sport of (*amar we-afle*) the world, also that he made sport of Abraham; again, that he ordered Abraham to be thrown (*amar we-hippil*) into the furnace.[3]

ARIOCH KING OF ELLASAR. R. Jose of Milhaya[4] said: Why are they [hazel-nuts] called *elsarin?* Because [they grow in the territory] of Ellasar.

CHEDORLAOMER KING OF ELAM, AND TIDAL KING OF GOIIM. R. Levi said: There is a place which is so called there [sc. in Babylon],[5] and [its inhabitants] took a certain man and made him king over them.[6] R. Johanan said: And his name was Tidal. Another interpretation: AND IT CAME TO PASS IN THE DAYS OF AMRAPHEL KING OF SHINAR: this alludes to Babylon; ARIOCH KING OF ELLASAR: that alludes to Greece; CHEDORLAOMER KING OF ELAM: that is Media; AND TIDAL THE KING OF GOIIM [lit. 'nations']: this alludes to the wicked Power [i.e. Rome] which levies troops from all the nations of the world. R. Eleazar b. R. Abina said: When you see the Powers fighting each other, look for the coming [lit. 'feet'] of the King Messiah. The proof is that in the days of Abraham, because these Powers fought against each other, greatness came to Abraham.

[1] That was his real name, as he was descended from Cush (Gen. x, 8)
[2] Th. Thus Amraphel is read as an abbreviation. Others translate differently. [3] The translation is conjectural. Neither the text nor its meaning is certain. [4] Probably in Galilee.
[5] The text reads: which is called there in Rome (or, in the Roman language, i e. Latin) This is hardly intelligible and is probably a gloss
[6] *Goiim* also means nations, peoples hence he interprets that he was king because the people had so appointed him.

5. THEY MADE WAR WITH BERA, etc. (XIV, 2). R. Meir used to interpret names: BERA signifies that he was an evil son (*ben ra'*); BIRSHA, that he was a wicked son (*ben rasha'*); SHINAB, that he amassed wealth (*sho'eb mammon*); SHEMEBER, that he flew[1] and procured riches; BELA, that its inhabitants were swallowed up (*nith-ball'u*).

ALL THESE CAME AS ALLIES UNTO THE VALE OF SIDDIM (XIV, 3). This was called by three names: The vale of Siddim, the vale of Shaveh, and the vale of Succoth.[2] Siddim signifies that oak trees (*saddanim*) grew there; again, that it was divided up into fields (*sadim*); and finally, that it suckled its children like breasts (*shadayim*). *The vale of Shaveh*: R. Berekiah and R. Ḥelbo in the name of R. Samuel b. Naḥman said: It was so called because there all the peoples of the world became unanimous (*hushewu*),[3] felled cedars, erected a large dais for him [Abraham] and set him on top, while uttering praises before him, saying: '*Hear us, my lord: thou art a prince of God among us; in the choice*', etc. (Gen. XXIII, 6). They said to him: 'Thou art king over us, thou art a god to us.'[4] But he replied: 'The world does not lack its king and the world does not lack its God.' 'Succoth,' implies that it was overshadowed (*me-sukak*) with trees. R. Tanḥuma said: These were the vine, fig, pomegranate, nut, almond, apple, and peach-trees.[5]

THE SAME IS THE SALT SEA. R. Aibu said: There was no sea there,[6] but the rocky banks of the river [Jordan ?] were broken through[7] and a sea [lake] was formed, as it is written, *He cutteth out channels among the rocks* (Job XXVIII, 10).

6. TWELVE YEARS, etc. (XIV, 4). R. Jose and R. Simeon b. Gamaliel disagreed. R. Jose said: Twelve years

[1] Reading the name *sam eber*, he made himself wings.
[2] V. v. 17, and Ps. LX, 8; the three are identified here.
[3] Identifying *shaveh* with *shaweh*, equal, alike—here, in thought and act.
[4] Reading 'prince' and 'God' as independent substantives
[5] The valley was probably pictured as terraced by rows upon rows of fruit trees. [6] At the time of this engagement.
[7] When Sodom was overthrown.

[service] and thirteen years [rebellion], thus amounting to twenty-five. R. Simeon said: It means thirteen in all. How then do I explain, AND THE FOURTEENTH YEAR?[1] It means their rebellion.

AND IN THE FOURTEENTH YEAR CAME CHEDORLAOMER. The owner of the beam has to bear the weight of it.[2]

AND THE KINGS THAT WERE WITH HIM, AND SMOTE THE REPHAIM IN ASHTEROTH—KARNAIM: i.e. in Ashtarta lying between the horns.[3]

AND THE ZUZIM IN HAM: that means the most illustrious of them (*ziwtane ba-hem*).[4] AND THE EMIM IN SHAVEH—KIRYATHAIM: They were twin cities both called Shaveh.[5]

AND THE HORITES (XIV, 6): Eleutheropolis [Freetown].[6] And why was it called Eleutheropolis? Because its inhabitants chose it and made themselves independent [free] in the generation of Separation.

UNTO EL-PARAN, WHICH IS BY THE WILDERNESS; i.e. by the plain of Paran.[7]

7. AND THEY TURNED BACK, AND CAME TO EN-MISHPAT—THE SAME IS KADESH (XIV, 7). R. Aḥa said: They came only in order to attack the eyeball of the world; the eye which executed judgment in the world they desire to blind! THE SAME (HI) IS KADESH: R. Aḥa said: This is written *hu* (he): it was he [Abraham] that

[1] On R. Jose's view

[2] This is a proverb. Since they had served Chedorlaomer, he had to be in the forefront now, his allies playing a subordinate part.

[3] Karnayim literally means two horns. I.e. between two mountains, v. Suk 2*a*.

[4] This connects ZUZIM with *ziw*, 'lustre' or 'brightness', and HAM with *bahem*, 'among them'

[5] Text as emended by Th., which is also similar to that of cur edd. 'Kiryathaim' is the dual form of *kiryah*, a city. On the present reading in Th's. ed., which is found in several MSS. ('they were two Ninevehs'), it is suggested there may be an actual reference to Nineveh, or to a town Navah in Bashan in the vicinity of Ashteroth—*karnayim*

[6] *Hori* is derived from *heruth*, freedom, and *ḥori*, free.

[7] Connecting El with *elone* in XIII, 18 *et passim*, which the Targum translates: the plain (of Mamre; E.V.: '*the terebinths of Mamre*').

sanctified (*kiddash*) the name of the Holy One, blessed be He, in the fiery furnace.[1]

AND THEY SMOTE ALL THE COUNTRY OF THE AMALEKITES. Amalek had not yet arisen, yet you say, AND THEY SMOTE ALL THE COUNTRY OF THE AMALEKITES! But, *He declareth the end from the beginning* (Isa. XLVI, 10).[2]

AND ALSO THE AMORITES, THAT DWELT IN HAZAZON—TAMAR: this means, in En-gedi of the palm-trees.[3]

AND THERE WENT OUT THE KING OF SODOM . . . FOUR KINGS AGAINST THE FIVE (XIV, 8 f). Four kings waged war with five and defeated them.

NOW THE VALE OF SIDDIM WAS FULL OF SLIME PITS—ḤEMOR (XIV, 10): full of pits producing asphalt (*ḥamor*).

AND THE KINGS OF SODOM AND GOMORRAH FLED, AND THEY FELL THERE, AND THEY THAT REMAINED FLED TO THE MOUNTAIN. R. Judah said: AND THEY FELL THERE refers to the troops, while AND THEY THAT REMAINED FLED TO THE MOUNTAIN refers to the kings. R. Nehemiah said: AND THEY FELL THERE refers to the kings, while AND THEY THAT REMAINED FLED TO THE MOUNTAIN refers to the troops Now on the view of R. Judah there is no difficulty.[4] But on the view of R. Nehemiah, R. 'Azariah and R. Jonathan in R. Isaac's name gave the following further explanation: When Abraham descended into the fiery furnace and was rescued, some of the nations believed [that it had happened], while others disbelieved But when the King of Sodom descended into the slime and was rescued, then all believed in Abraham retrospectively.

AND THEY TOOK ALL THE GOODS OF SODOM AND GOMORRAH, AND ALL THEIR VICTUALS (OKLAM),

[1] V. *supra*, 3 *ad init.*
[2] It is called THE COUNTRY OF THE AMALEKITES in anticipation.
[3] *Tamar* is a palm-tree v. II Chron. XX, 2
[4] The kings escaped, hence it states in v. 17: *And the king of Sodom went out to meet him.*

AND WENT THEIR WAY (XIV, 11). R. Judah said: Was it not a big thing to take ALL THEIR VICTUALS? Said R. Nehemiah: What is meant is dry dates.[1]

AND THEY TOOK LOT . . . AND HIS GOODS, etc They did this to Lot: they put him in a boat and took him with them. And why did he come to this? Because HE DWELT IN SODOM (*ib.*), thus fulfilling the verse, *He that walketh with wise men shall be wise, but the companion of fools shall smart for it* (Prov. XIII, 20).

8. AND THERE CAME ONE THAT HAD ESCAPED, AND TOLD ABRAM, etc. (XIV, 13). R. Simeon b. Laḳish said in the name of Bar Ḳappara: That was Og[2]; and why was he called Og? Because he came and found Abraham sitting and engaged in the precept of [unleavened] cakes (*'ugoth*) [3] He did not act from a pious motive, but he said to himself: 'This man Abraham is vindictive: I will apprise him that Lot is captured; then will he go out to battle and be slain, while I will take Sarah.' 'By thy life!' said the Holy One, blessed be He, to him, 'thou wilt receive reward for thy journey [footsteps] by living a long time in the world.[4] But because thou didst intend to slay that righteous man, thou wilt see myriads of his descendants and wilt ultimately fall into the hands of his sons,' as it is written, *And the Lord said unto Moses: Fear him not; for I have delivered him into thy hand*, etc. (Num. XXI, 34).[5]

AND TOLD ABRAM THE HEBREW (HA-'IBRI). R. Judah said: [HA-'IBRI signifies that] the whole world was on one side (*'eber*) while he was on the other side (*'eber*).[6] R. Nehemiah said: [It denotes] that he was descended from Eber. The Rabbis said: It means that he came from across the river[7]; further, that he spoke in the language of the dwellers across the river.

[1] These are easy to carry yet highly esteemed. [2] King of Bashan.
[3] It was Passover-time, and the Rabbis held that Abraham fulfilled all the precepts of the Torah even before they were promulgated. V. Deut. R. 1, 25, for a different version.
[4] Obviously, since he was alive in the time of Moses.
[5] The past tense *have delivered* implies before, viz. in the days of Abraham. [6] He alone of all mankind believed in the true God.
[7] V. Josh. XXIV, 3.

NOW HE DWELT BE-ELONE (E.V. 'BY THE TEREBINTHS OF') MAMRE, etc. R. Judah said: That means, in the plain of Mamra. R. Nehemiah said. In the palace of Mamre. On R. Judah's view a place called Mamre is meant; on R. Nehemiah's view, it refers to a person called Mamre. And why was he called Mamre? R. 'Azariah said in the name of R. Judah[1]. Because he rebuked (*himrah*)[2] Abraham When the Holy One, blessed be He, commanded Abraham to circumcise himself he went and took counsel with his three friends.[3] Aner said to him: 'You are already a hundred years old, yet you would inflict this pain upon yourself?' Eshcol said to him: 'Why should you go and make yourself distinguishable to your enemies?'[4] But Mamre said to him: 'When did He not stand by you—in the fiery furnace, in famine, and in your war with the kings? Will you not obey Him then in this matter!' Said the Holy One, blessed be He, to him: 'Thou gavest him good advice, to circumcise himself. by thy life! I will reveal Myself to him only in thy palace.' Hence it is written, *And the Lord appeared unto him in the palace of Mamre* (Gen. XVIII, 1).

[1] Probably R Judah b. R. Simon.
[2] Lit 'he showed a stern countenance'.
[3] V. v. 24. [4] By circumcision.

Chapter XLIII (LECH LECHA)

1. AND ABRAM HEARD THAT HIS BROTHER WAS TAKEN CAPTIVE (XIV, 14) It is written, *He shall not be afraid of evil things; his heart is steadfast, trusting in the Lord* (Ps CXII, 7); also, *And foundest his heart faithful before Thee* (Neh. IX, 8); also, *His heart is established, he shall not be afraid* (Ps. CXII, 8); also, *Fear not Abram* (Gen. XV, 1); also, *Until he gaze upon his adversaries* (Ps. *loc. cit.*). Consequently, *And he divided himself against them by night*, etc. (Gen. XV, 15).

2. AND ABRAM HEARD, etc. Thus it is written, *He stoppeth his ears from hearing of blood*, etc. (Isa. XXXIII, 15).[1]

HE LED FORTH (WAYYAREḲ) HIS TRAINED MEN, etc. R. Judah said: It was they who turned a wrathful countenance (*horiḳu panim*) upon Abraham, saying, 'Five kings could not defeat them, yet we are to defeat them!'[2] R. Nehemiah interpreted it: He turned a defiant countenance (*horik panim*) to them and exclaimed, 'I will go forth and fall in sanctifying the name of the Holy One, blessed be He.'[3] R. Abba b. Zabda said: He made them glitter (*horiḳan*) with weapons, as you read, *Burnish* (hareḳ—E.V. '*draw out*') *also the spear, and the battle axe, against them that pursue me; say unto my soul: I am thy salvation* (Ps XXXV, 3). R. Simeon b. Laḳish said: He made them glitter with precious stones and pearls, as you read, *With the shimmer of* (yeraḳraḳ) *gold* (*ib.* LXVIII, 14). R. Levi said: He thinned their numbers[4] by reading

[1] I e. Abraham would not hear of violence without seeking to remedy it.
[2] Lit. 'stand against them'. Both R. Judah and R. Nehemiah interpret *wayyareḳ*, he made pale (in anger) R Judah holds that he made his servants' faces pale, i e. they opposed him; while in R. Nehemiah's opinion he made himself pale by defying them.
[3] This is one of the cardinal teachings of Judaism: it is man's duty to act nobly and uprightly even at the cost of his life, for in so doing he sanctifies the Divine Name.
[4] Lit. 'he emptied them' (*heriḳan*).

the section of the heralds, as you read, *What man is there that is fearful* (yare) *and faint-hearted*—rak (Deut. xx, 8)?[1]

BORN IN HIS HOUSE. This means, those bearing his name, their name being Abram, like his own.[2]

THREE HUNDRED AND EIGHTEEN. R. Simeon b. Lakish said: It was Eliezer alone, the numerical value of Eliezer being three hundred and eighteen.[3]

AND PURSUED AS FAR AS DAN. Idolatry smites both before it comes and after it has departed. It smites in anticipation, as it is written, AND PURSUED AS FAR AS DAN. It smites retrospectively, as it is written, *The snorting of his horses is heard from Dan* (Jer. VIII, 16).[4]

3. AND THE NIGHT WAS DIVIDED AGAINST THEM (XIV, 15).[5] R Benjamin b. Jepheth said in R. Johanan's name: The night was divided of its own accord. The Rabbis say: Its Creator divided it.[6] The Holy One, blessed be He, said: 'Abraham has laboured with Me[7] at midnight; therefore I too will act for his sons at midnight' And when did that happen? In Egypt, as it says, *And it came to pass*

[1] He derives *wayyarek* from *rek*, empty: he 'emptied them', and was left with Eliezer only Cur edd.: he made them bright (encouraged them); i.e he inspired them with courage by pointing out that the faint-hearted need not go

[2] This connects *hanikaw* (E.V. '*his trained men*') with *hanikah*, a surname (v Jast. s.v. חניכה), hence rendered: the men bearing his name. 'E.J.: he understands BORN IN HIS HOUSE figuratively, i.e. *converted* by him, and as they were converted by Abraham they took his name

[3] א (1) + ל (30) + י (10) + ע (70) + ז (7) + ר (200) = 318. Cf. n. 1.

[4] The meaning is that the evil effects of idolatry are felt both before and after it is actually practised. Because Jeroboam was destined to set up a golden calf at Dan (1 Kings XII, 19), Abraham was weakened now when he came to that place and so could pursue them no further. Similarly, even after it was destroyed Jeremiah speaks of terror raging in Dan. Cf. Sanh. 96*a*.

[5] E.V. 'AND HE DIVIDED HIMSELF AGAINST THEM BY NIGHT'.

[6] Both explain the verse, AND THE NIGHT WAS DIVIDED AGAINST THEM to mean that exactly at midnight they suffered defeat and pursuit. But since a man cannot ascertain the exact moment of midnight (cf. Ex. R. XVIII, 1), R. Benjamin maintains that the night divided itself, showing Abraham the exact moment, while the Rabbis hold that God divided it for Abraham

[7] Abraham's rescue of the captives, being a noble action, is regarded as working with and assisting God.

at midnight (Ex. XII, 29). R. Tanhuma said: Some state this in a different form. The Holy One, blessed be He, said: 'Abraham went forth at midnight, therefore I too will go forth with his sons at midnight,' as it says, *Thus saith the Lord: About midnight will I go out*, etc (*ib.* XI, 4).

AND SMOTE THEM, AND PURSUED THEM. Does then a man pursue the slain?[1] Said R. Phinehas. Those who were pursued by Abraham were [already looked upon as] slain, as it says, *For they pursue him whom thou hast smitten* (Ps. LXIX, 27).

It is written, *Who hath raised up* (he'ir) *one from the east, Zedek* (Righteousness) *calling him to His feet* (Isa. XLI, 2)[2]: [this alludes to Zedek—the Righteous One] the Life of all worlds, who illumined (*me'ir*) his path wherever he went.[3] R. Berekiah said: The planet Zedek [Jupiter] illumined his path. R Reuben said: Righteousness[4] cried out and said: 'If Abraham will not perform me, none will perform me.'[5]

It is written, *He giveth nations before him, and maketh him rule over kings; his sword maketh them as the dust, his bow as the driven stubble* (*ib.*). R. Judah and R. Nehemiah differed. One maintained: This means that Abraham threw dust at them [the four kings] which turned to swords; stubble, and it turned to arrows. But the other argued: It is not written, 'He maketh dust,' but '*He maketh them* as *the dust*': they threw swords at Abraham which turned to dust; and arrows, which became stubble.

Again, it is written, *He pursueth them, and passeth on safely*—shalom (*ib.* 3). R. Levi and R. Eleazar in R. Jose's name said: Abraham's steps were three miles long.[6] R. Judah b. R. Simeon said: They were one mile long, for it says, *The way with his feet he treadeth not* (*ib.*).[7]

[1] AND HE SMOTE being understood in the sense of killed How then could he first smite and then pursue them?
[2] E.V. '*At whose step victory attendeth*'. [3] By a play on words העיר, to awaken, raise up, is connected with האיר, to illumine.
[4] The Attribute of Righteousness personified; cf *supra*, VIII, 5
[5] Rendering: Righteousness (personified) summoned him (Abraham) to his (righteousness') feet—i.e. to do it.
[6] *Shalom* (E.V. '*safely*') being read as an abbreviation of *shalosh milin*, three miles ('E.J.). [7] M.K.: a mile is the shortest distance which can be called *way*. Thus he passed over a whole mile without treading.

R. Neḥunia said in R. Bibi's[1] name: Their feet became no more dust-stained than those of one who goes from his home to the synagogue.[2]

4. AND HE BROUGHT BACK ALL THE GOODS . . . AND THE WOMEN ALSO, AND THE PEOPLE (XIV, 16) R. Judan said: They brought back the men and the women, but not the children.[3] Thereupon they arose and became proselytes and cut off the reproach of their fathers.[4] Thus it is written, *Wherefore I will bring the worst of the nations* (Ezek. VII, 24).[5] Who are '*The worst of the nations*'? Said R. Judah: The people of Sodom, as it says, *Now the men of Sodom were wicked and sinners* (Gen. XIII, 13).[6]

5. AND THE KING OF SODOM WENT OUT TO MEET HIM (XIV, 17). R. Abba b. Kahana said: He began putting on airs,[7] saying to him: 'Just as you descended into the fiery furnace and were saved, so did I descend into the slime and was saved.'

AT THE VALE OF SHAVEH—THE SAME IS THE KING'S VALE. R. Berekiah and R. Ḥelbo in the name of R. Samuel b. Naḥman said: It was so called because there all peoples of the world became unanimous, and said to Abraham: 'Be thou king over us.' But he replied: 'The world does not lack its king and its God.'[8]

6. AND MELCHIZEDEK KING OF SALEM BROUGHT FORTH BREAD AND WINE (XIV, 18). It is written, *And, O daughter of Ẓor* [E.V. '*Tyre*'], *the richest of the people*

[1] This is Th.'s conjectured emendation.
[2] I e. as though they had not trodden the way with their feet.
[3] 'E.J.: he renders *wayyasheb* ('he brought back') in the sense of restored to their place: Abraham restored the adults to their original place, but retained the children, to teach them righteousness. '*They* brought back' is thus meant generically Abraham's company. Cur. edd. '*he* brought back' is preferable. M.K. explains differently.
[4] I.e. they freed themselves from their fathers' evil ways. Y.T.: they underwent circumcision. [5] Sc. under the wings of the *Shechinah*.
[6] And it was the children of these that God brought back to Himself.
[7] Lit. 'he began wagging his tail against him', as a sign of familiarity. *Aliter* 'he began to fawn on him', in order to curry favour.
[8] V. *supra*, XLII, 5

shall entreat thy favour with a gift (Ps. XLV, 13). '*Daughter of Zor*' alludes to Abraham, who distressed (*hezar*)[1] kings and who was distressed by kings.[2] '*They shall entreat thy favour with a gift*,' as it is written, AND MELCHIZEDEK KING OF SALEM BROUGHT FORTH BREAD AND WINE.

AND MELCHI ZEDEK[3]: This place[4] made its inhabitants righteous.[5] [Another interpretation]: AND THE KING OF ZEDEK,[6] *The Lord of Zedek* (Josh. X, 1).[7] Jerusalem is called *Zedek* (righteousness), as it is written, *Zedek* (righteousness) *lodged in her* (Isa. I, 21).

KING OF SALEM (SHALEM). R. Isaac the Babylonian said: This implies that he was born circumcised.[8]

BROUGHT FORTH BREAD AND WINE. R. Samuel b. Naḥman said: He instructed him in the laws of the priesthood, BREAD alluding to the shewbread, and WINE to libations.[9] The Rabbis said: He revealed Torah to him, as it is written, *Come, eat of my bread, and drink of the wine which I have mingled* (Prov. IX, 5).[10]

AND HE WAS PRIEST OF THE GOD MOST HIGH. R. Abba b Kahana said: Wherever 'wine' is mentioned in the Torah it leaves its mark,[11] except in the present instance. R Levi said. Here too we have not escaped unscathed, for immediately after this it was revealed to him, *And they shall serve them; and they shall afflict them*, etc. (Gen. XV, 13).[12]

[1] Deriving *zor* from *zarar*, to vex, distress.
[2] This presumably refers to Abraham's pursuit of the four kings and his persecution by Nimrod (v *supra*, XXXVIII, 13) respectively, 'kings' in the second case being employed generically.
[3] Read as two words, as in the original.
[4] Sc Jerusalem (Salem in the English)
[5] This is the comment on the word '*Zedek*', which means righteousness.
[6] So translated now. [7] E.V. '*Adoni-zedek*'.
[8] Translating *Shalem* whole, complete, i e. the 'whole' king; cf Gen XVII, 1–10 [9] Both were in charge of the priests.
[10] The speaker is Wisdom personified (v. 1–3); hence '*bread*' and '*wine*' there refer to the Torah.
[11] Every mention of wine-drinking is followed by some record of trouble.
[12] In Ned. 32*b* this is stated to have been Abraham's punishment for complying with the request of the king of Sodom, *Give me the persons* (v. 21), instead of converting them to the true faith. R Levi perhaps holds that this complaisance was due to the convivial and friendly mood induced by the drinking of wine. Y T.

7. AND HE BLESSED HIM, AND SAID: BLESSED BE ABRAM OF THE GOD MOST HIGH, WHO HAS ACQUIRED (KONEH)[1] HEAVEN AND EARTH (XIV, 19). From whom then did He acquire them?—Said R. Abba: [ACQUIRED is attributive,] as one says, So-and-so has beautiful eyes and hair.[2] R. Isaac said: Abraham used to entertain wayfarers, and after they had eaten he would say to them, 'Say a blessing.' 'What shall we say?' they asked. 'Blessed be the God of the Universe of Whose bounty we have eaten,' replied he Then the Holy One, blessed be He, said to him: 'My Name was not known among My creatures, and thou hast made it known among them: I will regard thee as though thou wast associated with Me in the creation of the world.' Hence it is written, AND HE BLESSED HIM, AND SAID. BLESSED BE ABRAM OF THE GOD MOST HIGH, WHO [sc. ABRAHAM] HAS ACQUIRED HEAVEN AND EARTH.[3]

8. AND BLESSED BE GOD THE MOST HIGH, WHO HATH DELIVERED (MIGGEN) THINE ENEMIES INTO THY HAND (XIV, 8). R. Huna interpreted it: Who hath turned thy weapons[4] against thine enemies. R. Judan interpreted: By how many contrivances did I bring them[5] under thy hands! They were close friends and used to interchange gifts of dry dates[6] and other presents; yet I incited them to rebel against each other, so that they might fall into thy hands.

AND HE GAVE HIM A TENTH OF ALL. R. Judah said in R. Nehorai's name: In virtue of that blessing the three great pillars of the world, Abraham, Isaac, and Jacob, enjoyed prosperity. In the case of Abraham it is written, *And the Lord blessed Abraham in* all *things* (*ib.* XXIV, 1),

[1] E.V. '*Maker of*'. [2] I.e. *koneh* here means, in possession of.
[3] I.e. *koneh* does mean acquired, but it refers to *Abraham*, who acquired a partnership in the world. The purpose of the Creation was the making of man who should ever strive to come nearer to God. By diffusing the knowledge of God amongst men, Abraham thus became a partner in God's work. [4] *Magnun*, with which '*miggen*' by a play on words is connected; it may also mean, thy plans, schemes
[5] The kings [6] These were highly esteemed; cf. *supra*, XLII, 7.

as a reward for, AND HE GAVE HIM A TENTH OF ALL. Of Isaac it is written, *And I have eaten of all* (*ib.* XXVII, 33), as a reward for, AND HE GAVE HIM A TENTH OF ALL. Of Jacob it is written, *Because God hath dealt graciously with me, and because I have all* (*ib.* XXXIII, 11), as a reward for, AND HE GAVE HIM A TENTH OF ALL.

Whence were Israel privileged to receive the Priestly Blessing?[1] R. Judah said: From Abraham, [for in his case it is written,] *So* (koh) *shall thy seed be* (Gen. XV, 5), while there it is written, *So* (koh) *shall ye bless the children of Israel* (Num. VI, 23). R. Nehemiah said: From Isaac, for it is written, *And I and the lad will go yonder*—'ad koh (Gen. XXII, 5); therefore the Holy One, blessed be He, promised: '*So* (koh) *shall ye bless the children of Israel.*' The Rabbis taught: From Jacob, for it says, *So* (koh) *shalt thou say to the house of Jacob* (Ex. XIX, 3), to which corresponds, '*So shall ye bless the children of Israel*'

When will I magnify thy sons like the stars? R. Eleazar and R. Jose b. R. Ḥanina gave different replies. One maintained: When I reveal Myself to them with a message 'So', viz. '*So shalt thou say to the house of Jacob.*'[2] The other maintained: When I reveal Myself to their leaders with a message 'So', viz. *So* (koh) *saith the Lord: Israel is My son, My firstborn* (*ib.* IV, 22).[3]

9. AND THE KING OF SODOM SAID UNTO ABRAM . . . AND ABRAM SAID TO THE KING OF SODOM: I HAVE LIFTED UP (HARIMOTHI) MY HAND UNTO THE LORD (XIV, 21 f.). R. Judah said: He had separated *terumah* thereof,[4] as you read, *Then ye shall set apart* (waharemothem) *of it a gift* (terumah) *to the Lord* (Num. XVIII, 26). R. Nehemiah interpreted it: He had taken an oath in respect of it, as you read, *And he lifted up his right*

[1] V. Num. VI, 23–27

[2] This introduces the chapter of Revelation *So shall thy seed be* is preceded by, *Look now toward heaven, and count the stars.*

[3] The leaders are Moses and Aaron Cur edd : leader—sc. Moses.

[4] Of the spoil.

hand and his left hand unto heaven, and swore (Dan. XII, 7). The Rabbis said: He had uttered song [to God] on its account, as you read, *My father's God, and I will exalt Him*—aromemenhu (Ex. XV, 2). R. Berekiah said in R. Eleazar's name Moses said: 'With the very same language in which my ancestor uttered song, viz. *harimothi*, will I utter song, viz. "*My father's God, and I will exalt Him*—aromemenhu".'

THAT I WILL NOT TAKE A THREAD NOR A SHOE-LATCHET (XIV, 23). R. Abba b. Mammel said: The Holy One, blessed be He, assured him: 'Because thou saidest, I WILL NOT TAKE A THREAD, by thy life! I will give thy children the precept of fringes,' as you read, *And that they put with the fringe of each corner a thread of blue* (Num. XV, 38), which is rendered, a thread of blue wool.[1] NOR A SHOE-LATCHET: 'I swear to thee that I will give thy children the precept of *yebamah*, in connection with which you read, *Then shall she loose his shoe from off his foot*' (Deut XXV, 9).

Another interpretation. NOT A THREAD: this is an allusion to the Tabernacle, which was adorned with blue wool and purple wool; NOR A SHOE-LATCHET alludes to the badger skins.[2] Another interpretation: NOT A THREAD alludes to sacrifices, as we learned[3]: A thread of scarlet girdled it [the altar] about the middle.[4] NOR A SHOE-LATCHET: this alludes to the feet of the [festival] pilgrims, as it says, *How beautiful are thy steps in sandals* (S.S. VII, 2).

SAVE ONLY THAT WHICH THE YOUNG MEN HAVE EATEN AND THE PORTION OF THE YOUNG MEN WHICH WENT WITH ME; [also] LET ANER, ESCHOL, AND MAMRE TAKE THEIR PORTIONS (XIV, 24).[5] Thus

[1] The Aramaic translation of the Hebrew is given here.
[2] Shoes being made from animal hides. This too probably means that the Israelites obtained these in the merit of Abraham's self-denial.
[3] Mid. III, 1; Zeb. 53*a*. [4] Above or below which the blood of the different sacrifices was sprinkled, according to their nature
[5] Note the punctuation, which differs from E.V. According to this Aner, etc , had *not* accompanied Abraham, but kept guard in his absence, yet they were to receive their portion.

it is written, *Then answered all the wicked men and base fellows, of those that went with David, and said: Because they went not with us, we will not give them aught of the spoil . . . Then said David: Ye shall not do so, my brethren . . . For as is the share of him that goeth down to battle, so shall be the share of him that tarrieth by the baggage; they shall all share alike. And so it was from that day and above, that he made it a statute* (I Sam. XXX, 22–25). R. Judah said: It is not written, '[*From that day*] and onward,' but '[*From that day*] *and above*'[1]: from whom did he learn? From his ancestor Abraham, who said, SAVE ONLY THAT WHICH THE YOUNG MEN HAVE EATEN . . . [also] LET ANER, ESCHOL, AND MAMRE TAKE THEIR PORTION.

[1] Which means, and formerly. E.V. '*forward*'.

Chapter XLIV (LECH LECHA)

1. AFTER THESE THINGS THE WORD OF THE LORD CAME UNTO ABRAM IN A VISION, etc. (XV, 1). It is written, *As for God, His way is perfect; the word of the Lord is tried* (II Sam. XXII, 31) if His way is perfect, how much the more He Himself! Rab said: The precepts were given only in order that man might be refined[1] by them. For what does the Holy One, blessed be He, care whether a man kills an animal by the throat or by the nape of its neck? Hence its purpose is to refine [try] man.[2] Another interpretation: '*His way is perfect*' alludes to Abraham,[3] for it is written, *And thou foundest his* [sc. Abraham's] *way faithful before Thee*, etc. (Neh. IX, 8). '*The word of the Lord is tried*' intimates that the Holy One, blessed be He, tried him in a fiery furnace. *He is a shield unto all them that take refuge in Him* (II Sam. *loc. cit.*); hence, FEAR NOT, ABRAM, I AM THY SHIELD, etc.

2. *A wise man feareth, and departeth from evil* (Prov. XIV, 16): though thou art wise and departest from evil, yet thou fearest![4] [Therefore I say to thee] FEAR NOT, ABRAM.

Be not wise in thine own eyes; fear the Lord (*ib.* III, 7): Be not wise by what thou seest with thine own eyes[5]; canst thou say that I will cause thee to beget or that I will not cause thee to beget? '*Fear the Lord*'[6]: thus it is written, FEAR NOT, ABRAM, I AM THY SHIELD.

R. Abin commenced his discourse in R. Ḥanina's name: *The wicked doeth work of falsehood*[7]*; but he that soweth righteousness hath a sure reward* (*ib.* XI, 18). '*The wicked doeth work of falsehood*' alludes to Nimrod, whose works

[1] *Le-ẓaref*, of the same root as *ẓerufah* ('tried') in the verse just quoted.
[2] And this is the meaning of *The word of the Lord is tried.*
[3] The verse will then be translated: *O God! his (Abraham's) way*, etc.
[4] The verse is apparently rendered as a rhetorical question: a wise man, who departeth from evil, does he fear?
[5] According to the Rabbis (Shab. 156*a*) Abraham saw in his horoscope that he was not destined to beget children, and this was the cause of his fear. [6] But none else. [7] E.V. '*Earneth deceitful wages*'.

were of falsehood; '*But he that soweth righteousness*' alludes to Abraham, of whom it is written, *That they may keep the way of the Lord, to do righteousness and justice* (Gen. XVIII, 19); '*Hath a sure reward*', as it is written, FEAR NOT, ABRAM, I AM THY SHIELD, THY REWARD SHALL BE EXCEEDINGLY GREAT.

3. *But thou, Israel, My servant, Jacob whom I have chosen, the seed of Abraham My friend, thou whom I have taken hold of from the ends of the earth* (Isa. XLI, 8 f.)—i.e. from Mesopotamia and its country towns; *And called thee from its nobles* (*ib.*)[1]: I summoned thee from out of its distinguished men. *I have chosen thee and not cast thee away* (*ib.*): I chose thee when thou wast Abram, and did not cast thee away when thou wast Abraham.[2] *Fear not, for I am with thee, be not dismayed, for I am thy God* (*ib.* 10). R. Hoshaya said: When Isaac said to Jacob, *Come near, I pray thee, that I may feel thee* (Gen. XXVII, 21), perspiration poured over his legs, and his heart melted like wax; whereupon the Holy One, blessed be He, provided him with two angels, one at his right and one at his left, and these supported him by the elbows, that he might not fall. Hence He said to him, '*Be not dismayed* (tishta')'—i.e. be not wax-like (*teshawa'*), '*For I am thy God*'; *I strengthen thee, yea, I help thee; yea, I uphold thee with My victorious right hand. Behold, they shall all be ashamed and confounded that were incensed against thee* (*ib.* 10 f.)—this means, those who are hostile to thee; *They that strove with thee shall be as nothing, and shall perish* (*ib.*)—that means, those who engage in strife with thee; *Thou shalt seek them, and shalt not find them, even them that contended with thee* (*ib.* 12)—this refers to those who wage quarrels with thee. *For I the Lord thy God hold thy right hand, who say unto thee: Fear not* (*ib.* 13), as it is written, FEAR NOT, ABRAM, etc.

4. R. Levi explained this in two ways, the Rabbis in one. R. Levi said: Abraham was filled with misgiving,

[1] E.V. '*The uttermost parts thereof*'. [2] I.e. in old age (Mah. and Th.).

thinking to himself, Maybe there was a righteous or God-fearing man among those troops which I slew. This may be compared to a straw-merchant who was passing the king's orchards, and seeing some bundles of thorns, descended [from his wagon] and took them. [The king] caught sight of him, whereupon he tried to hide himself. 'Why do you hide?' he said to him, reassuringly, 'I needed labourers to gather them; now that you have gathered them, come and receive your reward.' Thus the Holy One, blessed be He, said to Abraham: 'Those troops that thou slewest were thorns already cut down'[1]; thus it is written, *And the peoples shall be as the burnings of lime; as thorns cut down, that are burned in the fire* (Isa. XXXIII, 12).

R. Levi made another comment: Abraham was fearful, saying, 'Perhaps the sons of the kings that I slew will collect troops and come and wage war against me.' Therefore the Holy One, blessed be He, said to him: 'FEAR NOT, ABRAM, I AM THY SHIELD: just as a shield receives all spears and withstands them, so will I stand by thee.'

The Rabbis explained it thus: Abraham was filled with misgivings, saying to himself, 'I descended into the fiery furnace and was delivered; I went through famine and war and was delivered: perhaps then I have already received my reward in this world and have nought for the future world?' Therefore the Holy One, blessed be He, reassured him: 'FEAR NOT, ABRAM, I AM THY SHIELD (MAGEN), meaning, a gift of grace (*maggan*) to thee, all that I have done for thee in this world I did for nought; but in the future that is to come, THY REWARD SHALL BE EXCEEDING GREAT', even as you read, *Oh how abundant is Thy goodness, which Thou hast laid up for them that fear Thee*, etc. (Ps. XXXI, 20).

5. AFTER (AḤAR) THESE THINGS. R. Judan and R. Huna both said in the name of R. Jose b. R. Judan. Wherever *aḥare* occurs it denotes 'in immediate connection with', whereas *aḥar* denotes that there is no

[1] I.e. doomed to death.

connection.[1] R. Huna said: Wherever *ahar* is stated it denotes 'in immediate connection with', whereas *ahare* implies that there is no connection.

AFTER THESE THINGS. Misgivings were entertained there.[2] Who entertained them? Abraham. He said to God: 'Sovereign of the Universe! Thou madest a covenant with Noah not to exterminate his children; then I arose and accumulated meritorious acts and pious deeds, whereupon my covenant superseded his. Perhaps another will arise and accumulate even a greater store of precepts and good deeds, and then a covenant with him will supersede Thy covenant with me?' Said the Holy One, blessed be He, to him: 'From Noah I did not set up shields of the righteous, but from thee I set up shields of the righteous.[3] Moreover, when thy children take to transgressions and evil deeds, I will see one righteous man amongst them who will be able to say to My Attribute of Justice, "Enough!" whereupon I will take him and make him atone for them.'

6. THE WORD OF THE LORD CAME UNTO ABRAM IN A VISION, etc. [Prophecy] is expressed by ten designations: prophecy, vision, preaching,[4] speech, saying, command, burden, parable, metaphor, and enigma. And which is the severest form? R. Leazar said: Vision, as it says, *A grievous vision is declared unto me* (Isa. XXI, 2). R Johanan said: Speech (*dibbur*), as it says, *The man, the lord of the land, spoke* (dibber) *roughly with us*, etc. (Gen. XLII, 30). The Rabbis said: Burden, as it says, *As a heavy burden* (Ps. XXXVIII, 5). Great then was the power of Abraham that [Divine] converse was held with him in vision and in speech.

[1] Both *aḥar* and *aḥare* (the second is the pl. const. form of the first) mean after. When a passage is introduced by *aḥare* it implies that its contents are closely connected with what precedes it; whereas *ahar* merely implies that one episode followed the other but was unconnected with it. Y. T.: this distinction holds good only in the phrase 'after these things'. [2] This is a play on words, *aḥar*, 'after,' being connected with *hirhur*, 'misgiving'.

[3] Th.: I did not say to Noah, 'I am thy shield,' as I said to thee Radal and Mah.: Noah's descendants could not shield their contemporaries, that I should forgive them for their sake. [4] Lit. 'flow of words'.

7. FEAR NOT, ABRAM. Whom did he fear? R. Berekiah said: He feared Shem,[1] as it is written, *The isles saw, and feared* (Isa. XLI, 5): just as islands stand out in the sea, so were Abraham and Shem outstanding in the world. '*And feared*': Each one feared the other. The former feared the latter, thinking, Perhaps he nurses resentment against me for slaying his sons. And the latter feared the former, thinking, Perhaps he nurses resentment against me for begetting wicked offspring. *The ends of the earth* (*ib.*): One dwelt at one end of the world and the other dwelt at another end of the world.[2] *They drew near, and came* (*ib.*): each approached the other. *They helped every one his neighbour* (*ib.* 6): each helped the other. One helped the other with blessings, as it says, *And he blessed him, and said: Blessed be Abram*, etc. (Gen. XIV, 19).[3] And the other helped the former with gifts, as it says, *And he gave him a tenth of all* (*ib.* 20). *So the carpenter encouraged* (Isa. XLI, 7): this alludes to Shem, who made the Ark[4]; *The refiner* (*ib.*): this is Abraham, whom the Holy One, blessed be He, refined [tried] in the fiery furnace. *And he that smootheth with the hammer him that smiteth the anvil*—pa'am (*ib.*): he smoothed with the hammer and beat all mankind into one path (*pa'am*).[5] *Saying of the join: It is good* (*ib.*): This refers to the nations of the world, who said: It is better to be joined to the God of Abraham than to the idol of Nimrod. *And he strengthened it with nails* (*ib.*): Abraham strengthened Shem in religious acts and pious deeds; *He shall not be moved* (*ib.*): viz. Abraham.

8. AND ABRAM SAID: O LORD GOD, WHAT WILT THOU GIVE ME (XV, 2)? R. Jonathan said: Three persons were bidden 'ask', viz.: Solomon, Ahaz, and the King Messiah. Solomon: *Ask what I shall give thee* (I Kings III, 5). Ahaz: *Ask thee a sign* (Isa. VII, 11).

[1] Whose descendants, viz. Chedorlaomer and his sons, Abraham had slain. [2] Th.: Abraham and Shem dwelt in Transjordania and Jerusalem respectively, which were regarded as ends of the world.
[3] Shem is identified with Melchizedek. [4] Together with Noah.
[5] He directed all to the fear of God.

The King Messiah: *Ask of Me*, etc. (Ps. II, 8). R. Berekiah and R. Aḥi in the name of R. Samuel b. Naḥman said: We can cite another two from the *Haggadah:* Abraham and Jacob. Abraham: WHAT WILT THOU GIVE ME? He could not say, WHAT WILT THOU GIVE ME, unless He [GOD] had previously said to him, 'Ask.' Jacob said, *And of all that Thou shalt give me* (Gen XXVIII, 22), and he would not say, '*And of all that Thou shalt give me*' unless He had previously said to him: 'Ask.'

9. R. Judan and R. Aibu in R. Johanan's name said: Two men said the same thing, Abraham and David. Abraham said: O LORD GOD: 'Sovereign of the Universe,' he cried out to Him, 'if I am destined to beget children who will anger Thee, 'twere better for me THAT I GO CHILDLESS.' David said: *Search me, O God, and know my heart, try me, and know my thoughts*—sar'appay (Ps. CXXXIX, 23)—know those who have sprung from me.[1] *And see if there be any way in me that is grievous, and lead me in the way everlasting* (*ib.* 24): 'Sovereign of the Universe!' he pleaded, 'if I am to beget children to provoke Thee, 'twere better for me that Thou didst lead me in the way everlasting.'[2]

AND HE THAT SHALL BE POSSESSOR (BEN MESHEḲ) OF MY HOUSE, etc. (XV, 2). R. Leazar said in the name of R. Jose b. Zimra: BEN MESHEḲ BETHI (MY HOUSE) alludes to Lot, whose soul, [said Abraham,] longs (*shoḳeketh*) to be my heir. IS DAMESEḲ ELIEZER [E.V. 'ELIEZER OF DAMASCUS']: this means, for whose sake I pursued the kings as far as Damascus and God helped me.[3] R Simeon b. Lakish said: BEN MESHEK BETHI means 'The son of my household'[4]; IS ELIEZER OF DAMASCUS—i.e. by his assistance I pursued the kings as far as Damascus, and his name was actually Eliezer, for it says, *He led forth his trained men, three*

[1] Th.: He appears to translate *sar'appay* 'my branches'—metaphorically, my sons; cf Ezek. XXXI, 5. [2] I.e. death.
[3] Reading *Eli 'ezer*: my God helped me.
[4] I e. the steward of my house (M.K.).

hundred and eighteen (Gen. XIV, 14), the numerical value of Eliezer being three hundred and eighteen.[1]

10. AND ABRAM SAID: BEHOLD, TO ME THOU HAST GIVEN NO SEED (XV, 3). R. Samuel b. Isaac commented: [Abraham said.] My planetary fate oppresses me and declares, 'Abram cannot beget a child.' Said the Holy One, blessed be He, to him: 'Let it be even as thy words: Abram and Sarai cannot beget but Abraham and Sarah can beget.'[2]

11. AND, BEHOLD, THE WORD OF THE LORD CAME UNTO HIM, etc. (XV, 4). R. Judan and R. Leazar in R. Jose's name said: [We have here,] THE LORD [SPOKE] TO HIM; THE WORD OF THE LORD CAME UNTO HIM; AND, BEHOLD, THE WORD OF THE LORD CAME UNTO HIM[3]: this signifies, angel after angel, angel after angel; speech after speech, speech after speech; implying, I and three of my angels reveal ourselves to thee and say to thee, 'Lot is accursed,[4] he shall not be Abraham's heir.' R. Huna and R. Leazar said in R. Jose's name: It is written, AND, BEHOLD, . . . THE LORD: thus *He* came and spoke with him.[5]

12. AND HE BROUGHT HIM FORTH WITHOUT—HA-ḤUẒAH (XV, 5). R. Joshua said in R. Levi's name. Did He then lead him forth without the world, that it says, AND HE BROUGHT HIM FORTH WITHOUT? It means, however, that He showed him the streets of heaven, as you read, *While as yet He had not made the earth, nor the outer spaces*—ḥuzoth (Prov. VIII, 26).[6] R. Judah b. R. Simon

[1] Cf. *supra*, XLIII, 2.
[2] By changing your names I will free you from your planetary fate.
[3] I.e. instead of the simple *And the Lord said*, which is usual, we have, The Lord (spoke) to him, as if that were not enough, THE WORD is added, and on top of that there is the further addition of AND, BEHOLD. Each addition implies an additional messenger of God's word. [4] This is a play on words, Lot is *liṭa*, accursed
[5] Not an angel The names cause some difficulty here. Th suggests that R. Huna stated that R. Eleazar said this in R. Jose's name, not as was previously stated.
[6] By contrast, *ḥuzoth* is understood to mean the heavens; E.V. '*the fields*' '*Ha-huẓah*' and *huzoth* are both derived from the same root

said in R. Joḥanan's name: He lifted him up above the vault of heaven; hence He says to him, LOOK (HABBEṬ) NOW TOWARD HEAVEN, HABBET signifying to look down from above.[1] The Rabbis said: [God said to him]: 'Thou art a prophet, not an astrologer,' as it says, *Now therefore restore the man's wife, for he is a prophet* (Gen. xx, 7).[2]

In the days of Jeremiah the Israelites wished to entertain this belief [in astrology], but the Holy One, blessed be He, would not permit them. Thus it is written, *Thus saith the Lord: Learn not the way of the nations, and be not dismayed at the signs of heaven*, etc. (Jer. x, 2): your ancestor Abraham wished to entertain this belief long ago, but I would not permit him.

R. Levi said: While the sandal is on your foot tread down the thorn; he who is placed below them fears them, but thou [Abraham] art placed above them,[3] so trample them down [ignore them].

R. Judan said in R. Leazar's name: Three things nullify a decree [of evil], viz. prayer, righteousness,[4] and repentance. And the three are enumerated in one verse: *If My people, upon whom My Name is called, shall humble themselves, and pray* (II Chron. VII, 14)—here you have prayer; *And seek My face* (*ib.*) alludes to righteousness, as you read, *I shall behold Thy face in righteousness* (Ps. XVII, 15); *And turn from their evil ways* (II Chron. *loc. cit.*) denotes repentance; after that, *Then will I forgive their sin* (*ib.*). R. Huna said in R. Joseph's name: Also change of name and good deeds. Change of name is learned from Abraham and Sarah.[5] Good deeds, from the people of Nineveh, for it says, *And God saw their works, that they turned from their evil ways* (Jonah III, 10). Some say, change of place, too, for it says, *Now the Lord said unto Abram:*

[1] Hence thou art now above thy fate, and canst ignore it
[2] Cf. Shab. 156*a* and Ned. 32*a* on this and the following passages.
[3] Either metaphorically: you are superior to the influence of planets; or actually, as stated above.
[4] Or, charity. The same word *zedakah* means both, charity being regarded as simple righteousness. [5] V. p. 367, n. 2.

Get thee out of thy country, etc (Gen. XII, 1).[1] R. Huna said: Also fasting, as it says, *The Lord answer thee in the day of trouble* (Ps. XX, 20).[2] Raba b. Meḥasia and R. Ḥama b. Guria said in Rab's name: Fasting is as effective for counteracting an evil dream as fire for consuming tow. R. Joseph said: Providing it is done on the same day, even on the Sabbath.

13. AND HE BELIEVED IN THE LORD . . . AND HE SAID UNTO HIM: I AM THE LORD THAT BROUGHT THEE OUT OF UR OF THE CHALDEES, etc. (XV, 6 f). R. Liezer b. Jacob said: Michael descended and rescued Abraham from the fiery furnace. The Rabbis said: The Holy One, blessed be He, rescued him; thus it is written, I AM THE LORD THAT BROUGHT THEE OUT OF UR OF THE CHALDEES.[3] And when did Michael descend? In the case of Hananiah, Mishael, and Azariah.

14. AND HE SAID: O LORD GOD, WHEREBY SHALL I KNOW THAT I SHALL INHERIT IT (XV, 8)? R. Ḥama b. Hanina said: [He spoke] not as one making a complaint, but he asked Him: 'Through what merit [will I inherit the land]?' God replied: 'Through the merit of the atoning sacrifices which I will institute for thy sons.'[4]

AND HE SAID UNTO HIM: TAKE ME A HEIFER OF THREE YEARS OLD (MESHULSHELETH), A SHE-GOAT OF THREE YEARS OLD (MESHULSHELETH), AND A RAM OF THREE YEARS OLD (MESHULASH), etc. (XV, 9 f.). He showed him three kinds of bullocks, three kinds of goats, and three kinds of rams.[5] Three kinds of bullocks: the bullock sacrificed on the Day of Atonement, the

[1] And only then *Will I make thee a great nation* (*ib.* 2), the change of place changing his destiny, which was to be childless.

[2] I e. in a day of fasting, which was proclaimed in dire trouble.

[3] This is the source of the famous legend that Abraham was thrown into a fiery furnace. The Hebrew for Ur is אור, which also means fire, and is so translated here. I brought thee forth from the *fire* of the Chaldees.

[4] As the next verse says. *Take me a heifer*, etc.

[5] The Midrash translates '*meshulsheleth*', three-fold, three kinds—i.e. for three different purposes, as explained in the text.

bullock brought on account of [the unwitting transgression of] any of the precepts,[1] and the heifer whose neck was broken.[2] Three kinds of goats: the goats sacrificed on festivals, the goats sacrificed on New Moon, and the goat brought by an individual.[3] Three kinds of rams. the guilt-offering of certain obligation,[4] the guilt-offering of doubt,[5] and the lamb [sin-offering] brought by an individual.[6] AND A TURTLE-DOVE (TOR) AND A YOUNG PIGEON (GOZAL): that is, a turtle-dove and a young pigeon.[7]

AND HE TOOK HIM ALL THESE, etc. R. Simeon b. Yoḥai said: The Holy One, blessed be He, showed Abraham all the atoning sacrifices save the tenth of an ephah [of fine meal].[8] The Rabbis said: He showed him the tenth of an ephah [of fine meal] also; for ALL THESE is stated here, while elsewhere it is said, *And thou shalt bring the meal-offering that is made of these things* (Lev II, 8).[9]

BUT THE BIRD DIVIDED HE NOT. He intimated to him that the fowl burnt-offering is divided, but the fowl sin-offering[10] is not divided.[11]

15. Another interpretation: TAKE ME A HEIFER THREEFOLD: this alludes to Babylonia, which produced three kings, Nebuchadnezzar, Evil-Merodach, and Balshazzar; AND A SHE-GOAT THREEFOLD: this alludes to Media, which produced three kings: Cyrus, Darius, and Ahasuerus[12]; AND A RAM THREEFOLD: this alludes to Greece. R. Leazar and R. Joḥanan explained how. R. Leazar said: She conquered all parts [of the world]

[1] V. Lev. IV, 13 f. [2] V. Deut. XXI, 1-9. [3] V. Lev. IV, 27 f.
[4] E.G., a leper when he became clean, a nazirite when he completed his naziriteship, and several other cases V Num. VI, 12; Lev XIV, 24; V, 15; XIX, 20. [5] To which one is liable when in doubt whether he committed a transgression which if certainly committed would have involved a sin-offering. [6] V. Lev. IV, 32.
[7] The Hebrew is translated into the more familiar Aramaic. All these are regarded as atoning sacrifices, as stated at the beginning of the section.
[8] V. Lev. V, 11. R. Simeon finds no allusion to this in the present verse.
[9] The use of *these* in both verses hints that the same thing is referred to in both cases [10] Which the dove and young pigeon symbolised.
[11] V Zeb. VI, 4, 5; Ḥul. 21*b*. [12] Only the kings who impinged upon Jewish history are taken into account.

save the east. Said R. Joḥanan to him: Even so it is written, *I saw the ram pushing westward, and northward, and southward; and no beasts could stand before him* (Dan. VIII, 4), and that is his [R. Eleazar's] reason too, since eastward is not stated.[1] AND A TURTLE-DOVE AND A YOUNG PIGEON (GOZAL). This refers to Edom [Rome]: it was a turtle-dove, but of a predatory nature.[2]

AND HE TOOK HIM ALL THESE. R. Judah said: He showed him the princes of the Gentile nations. R. Nehemiah said: He showed him the princes of Israel. On the view of R. Judah, [HE LAID EACH HALF OVER AGAINST THE OTHER symbolised] the throne of one [prince] opposing the throne of another.[3] According to R Nehemiah, it symbolised the place where the great Sanhedrin [Court] of Israel sat and determined the laws of Israel.[4]

BUT THE BIRD DIVIDED HE NOT. R. Abba b. Kahana said in R Levi's name: The Holy One, blessed be He, intimated to him that he who attempts to resist the wave is swept away by it, but he who bends before it is not swept away by it.[5]

16 AND THE BIRDS OF PREY CAME DOWN UPON THE CARCASES AND ABRAM DROVE THEM AWAY (XV, 11). R. Assi said: Abraham took a flail and beat them, but they were not smitten [killed], yet even so, ABRAM

[1] This verse of Daniel is understood to allude to Greece. Rashash, however, points out that in vv 20, 21, the ram is related to Media and Persia, while the he-goat symbolises Greece Consequently he reverses the reading here, too. Mah. does not reverse the text, but explains it differently.

[2] This interprets *gozal* not 'a young pigeon' but as an attribute (fr. *gazal*, to rob); a robber turtle-dove. This comment on Edom (Rome) was natural enough to the Rabbis.

[3] He showed him the hostility of the nations toward each other, in contrast with which the bird, symbolising Israel, was not to be divided but united ('E.J.).

[4] The Sanhedrin sat in crescent-shaped rows, so that the ends could see each other (Sanh. IV, 3), hence that too can be symbolised in this verse.

[5] Only by such a course could the bird—symbolical of Israel—be saved from being cut up and destroyed.

DROVE THEM AWAY (WAYYASHSHEB)—by repentance.[1] R. 'Azariah said: [God hinted to Abram]: When thy children become as carcases [corpses] without sinews or bones, thy merit will support them.[2]

17. AND IT CAME TO PASS, THAT, WHEN THE SUN WAS GOING DOWN, etc (XV, 12). R. Joshua of Siknin[3] said in R. Levi's name: The beginning of a man's downfall is sleep: being asleep, he does not engage in study and does no work. Rab said: There are three kinds of torpor (*tardemah*): the torpor of sleep, the torpor of prophecy, and the torpor of unconsciousness. The torpor of sleep: *Then the Lord God caused a deep sleep to fall upon the man, and he slept* (Gen. II, 21). The torpor of prophecy: AND IT CAME TO PASS, THAT, WHEN THE SUN WAS GOING DOWN, A DEEP SLEEP FELL UPON ABRAM. The torpor of unconsciousness: *And no man saw it, nor knew it, neither did any awake; for they were all asleep; because a deep sleep from the Lord was fallen upon them* (I Sam. XXVI, 12). The Rabbis said: Also the torpor of folly, as it is written, *Stupefy yourselves, and be stupid! . . . For the Lord hath poured out upon you the spirit of deep sleep* (Isa. XXIX, 9 f.). R. Ḥanina [or R. Ḥinena] b. Isaac said: There are three incomplete phenomena: the incomplete experience of death is sleep; an incomplete form of prophecy is the dream; the incomplete form of the next world is the Sabbath. R. Abin added another two: the incomplete form of the heavenly light is the orb of the sun; the incomplete form of the heavenly wisdom is the Torah.[4]

AND, LO, A DREAD, EVEN A GREAT DARKNESS, FELL UPON HIM (*ib.*). DREAD refers to Babylon, as it

[1] The birds of prey represent the nations swooping down on Israel. Abram—i.e. Israel—tried to beat them off by physical force but without success, and it is only when Israel turns to God in penitence that his enemies are driven off. '*Wayyashsheb*' is thus connected with *teshubah*, repentance

[2] He interprets the verse in the same way, but relates '*carcases*' to Israel defeated and despoiled; it is then that Abraham's merit will disperse the birds of prey

[3] North of Jotapata in Galilee

[4] The whole passage *supra*, XVII, 5

is written, *Then was Nebuchadnezzar filled with fury* (Dan. III, 19).[1] DARKNESS refers to Media, which darkened the eyes of Israel with fasting and tribulation; GREAT refers to Greece. R. Simon said: The Kingdom of Greece set up one hundred and twenty commanders, one hundred and twenty governors, and one hundred and twenty generals. The Rabbis said: Sixty of each, for it is written, *Serpents, fiery serpents, and scorpions* (Deut. VIII, 15)[2]: just as the scorpion lays sixty eggs at a time, so did the Greek state set up sixty of each. FELL UPON HIM alludes to Edom [Rome], as it is written, *The earth quaketh at the noise of their fall* (Jer. XLIX, 21).[3] Some reverse it. FELL UPON HIM (*ib.*) alludes to Babylon, as it is written, *Fallen, fallen is Babylon* (Isa. XXI, 9). GREAT alludes to Media, as it is written, *King Ashuerus did make great*, etc. (Est. III, 1). DARKNESS alludes to Greece that darkened the eyes of Israel with its decrees.[4] DREAD alludes to Edom, as it is written, *After this I saw . . . a fourth beast, dreadful and terrible* (Dan. VII, 7).[5]

18. AND HE SAID UNTO ABRAM: KNOW, YEA KNOW (XV, 13): Know that I shall disperse thy seed; know that I will gather them together, know that I will give them in pledge,[6] know that I will redeem them; know that I will allow them to be enslaved, know that I will free them.

THAT THY SEED SHALL BE A STRANGER IN A LAND THAT IS NOT THEIRS, AND SHALL SERVE THEM, AND THEY SHALL AFFLICT THEM FOUR HUNDRED YEARS: this means, until four hundred years after seed shall be granted to thee.[7] R. Judan said: The

[1] The word for 'fury' (חימה) is somewhat similar to that used for dread (אימה). [2] This is symbolically applied to Babylon, Media, and Greece respectively

[3] This refers to Edom, as is stated in the preceding verse *q.v.*

[4] Cf. *supra*, II, 4; XVI, 4. [5] The *fourth beast* was applied to Edom

[6] The exile is regarded as putting Israel in pledge to expiate their sins.

[7] I.e. FOUR HUNDRED YEARS does not apply to SERVE THEM, AND THEY SHALL AFFLICT THEM (in actual fact the oppression in Egypt lasted much less) but to THY SEED SHALL BE A STRANGER, and this period is counted from the birth of Isaac.

condition of being strangers, in servitude, and afflicted in a land not theirs was to last four hundred years, which was their decreed term.[1]

9. AND ALSO THAT NATION, WHOM THEY SHALL SERVE, etc. (XV, 14). R Ḥelbo said: Instead of, 'And that nation,' Scripture writes AND ALSO THAT NATION WHOM THEY SHALL SERVE: this indicates, also they [Abraham's descendants,] also Egypt and the four kingdoms[2] which will subjugate thee.[3]

WILL I JUDGE (DAN). R. Eleazar said in R. Jose's name: The Holy One, blessed be He, promised our forefather that He would redeem his children with these two letters[4]; but if they repented, He would redeem them with seventy-two letters. R. Judan said: In the passage, [*Or hath God assayed*] *to go and take Him a nation from the midst of another nation, by trials, by signs, and by wonders, and by war, and by a mighty hand, and by an outstretched arm, and by great terrors* (Deut. IV, 34), you will find seventy-two letters; and should you object that there are seventy-five, deduct the second '*nation*,' which is not to be counted.[5] R. Abin said: He redeemed them by His name, the Name of the Holy One, blessed be He, consisting of seventy-two letters.[6]

20. AND AFTERWARDS (AḤARE KEN) THEY SHALL COME OUT WITH GREAT SUBSTANCE. R. Aha said:

[1] The passage is rather obscure. It apparently means, like the preceding statement, that only the three things together would occupy four hundred years. Th. reduces the time still further by translating, would be spread over four hundred years, the time being counted from Isaac's birth, the condition of an alien being held to apply to Abraham when he had to dwell in the country of the Philistines, and to Isaac when in Gerar, and to Jacob in Haran.

[2] Sc. Babylon, Persia, Media, Rome. ALSO (Heb. *gam*) is generally treated as an extension; according to R. Ḥelbo's interpretation it means that not only should Abraham's seed serve strangers, but in the fulness of time Egypt and the other four kingdoms too would be subjugated

[3] Further, he appears to translate: And also the nation which will put thee to service. [4] Viz דן (I will judge)

[5] In the Hebrew that passage contains seventy-two letters.

[6] The longest form of God's name, of which there were several. V. *J.E* art. 'Names of God'.

Not *aḥar* is written here but AHARE[1]: this teaches, when I have visited ten plagues upon them, then THEY SHALL COME OUT WITH GREAT SUBSTANCE. Said he [Abraham] to Him: 'Shall I too be included in this servitude?' 'BUT THOU SHALT GO TO THY FATHERS IN PEACE; THOU SHALT BE BURIED IN A GOOD OLD AGE' (*ib.* 15), He assured him. R. Simeon b Laḳish said: Of three men was '*In a good old age*' said: Abraham deserved it, David deserved it, but Gideon did not deserve it. Why? Because, *And Gideon made an ephod thereof* (Judg. VIII, 27)—for idolatry.

21. AND IT CAME TO PASS, THAT, WHEN THE SUN WENT DOWN, AND THERE WAS THICK DARKNESS (XV, 17): there was intense darkness.[2]

BEHOLD A SMOKING FURNACE AND A FLAMING TORCH. Simeon b. Abba said in R. Johanan's name: He [God] showed him four things, viz. Gehenna, the [foreign] kingdoms,[3] Revelation, and the Temple, with the promise: As long as thy children occupy themselves with the latter two, they will be saved from the former two; if they neglect the latter two they will be punished by the former two. Wouldst thou rather that thy children descend into Gehenna or into the power of the [foreign] kingdoms? He asked him. R. Ḥinena b. Papa said: Abraham himself chose [subjection to foreign] powers. R. Judan, R. Idi, and R. Ḥama b. R. Ḥanina said: Abraham chose Gehenna, but the Holy One, blessed be He, chose [subjection to foreign] powers for him. Thus it is written, *How should one chase a thousand, and two put ten thousand to flight, except their rock had given them over* (Deut. XXXII, 30)—this alludes to Abraham; *And the Lord had delivered them up* (*ib.*)? this teaches that God approved his choice.[4] R. Huna said in R. Aḥa's name: Abraham sat wondering all

[1] אחרי Both mean after; here the longer form, containing an additional *yod* (= 10) is used.
[2] The Hebrew is translated by Aramaic.
[3] Which would conquer Israel, v. p. 374, n. 2.
[4] This agrees with R Ḥinena b. Papa.

day, thinking, 'Which should I choose?' Whereupon the Holy One, blessed be He, said to him, 'Make a decision without delay'; hence it is written, *In that day the Lord made*[1] *a covenant with Abram*, etc. (Gen. xv, 18). In this matter we come back to the controversy of R. Ḥinena b. Papa and R. Judan, R. Idi, and R. Hana b. R. Ḥanina. R. Ḥinena b. Papa said: Abraham himself chose [subjection to other] powers. R Judan, R. Idi, and R. Ḥama b. R. Ḥanina said on the authority of a certain sage in Rabbi's name: The Holy One, blessed be He, chose the [foreign] kingdoms for him. Thus it is written, *Thou hast caused men to ride over our heads* (Ps. LXVI, 12), meaning, Thou didst cause nations to ride over our heads, which is as though *We went through fire and through water* (*ib.*).[2] R. Joshua said: He also showed him the dividing of the Red Sea, for it is written, THAT PASSED BETWEEN THESE PIECES—GEZARIM (Gen. *loc. cit.*), GEZARIM having the same meaning] as in the verse, [*O give thanks* . . .] *to Him who divided the Red Sea in sunder*—gezarim (Ps. CXXXVI, 13).

22. IN THAT DAY THE LORD MADE A COVENANT WITH ABRAM (XV, 18) R. Judan said: R. Joḥanan b. Zakkai and R. Akiba disagree. One maintains: This world He revealed to him,[3] but not the next. The other maintains that He revealed to him both this world and the next. R. Berekiah said: R. Leazar and R. Jose b R. Ḥanina disagreed. One maintained: He revealed to him [the future] *until* that day; while the other said: He revealed to him the future *from* that day.[4]

UNTO THY SEED HAVE I GIVEN THIS LAND. R. Huna and R. Dostai said in the name of R. Samuel b.

[1] Lit. 'cut'—i.e. helped Abraham to make his decision.
[2] Sc. Gehenna—i.e. our servitude should now exempt us from Gehenna. V. Ex. R. LI, 7. [3] I.e. the future of Israel in this world.
[4] The discussion turns on the implication of IN THAT DAY. R. Berekiah apparently states that one held that God revealed Israel's future to Abraham only until that day, viz. when Israel would leave Egypt, while the other held that He revealed the future to him from the Exodus until Messiah's coming (M.K.).

Naḥman: The mere speech of the Holy One, blessed be He, is equivalent to action, for it says, UNTO THY SEED HAVE I GIVEN: not 'I will give', but HAVE I GIVEN.[1] R. Judan said in R. Abba's name: It is not written, *So let the redeemed of the Lord say whom* He redeemeth, but, *Whom He* hath *redeemed* (Ps. CVII, 2). R. Abin said: It is not written, *For the Lord* ransometh *Jacob*, but *For the Lord* hath *ransomed Jacob* (Jer. XXXI, 11). The Rabbis said: It is not written, *I will hiss for them, and gather them,* for I will redeem them, but '*For I* have *redeemed them*' (Zech. X, 8). R. Joshua said: It is not written, 'And the Lord will create (*we-yibra*),' but, *And the Lord has created* (u-bara)[2] . . . *a cloud and smoke by day*, etc. (Isa. IV, 5): it has long been created and ready.

23. THE KENITE, AND THE KENIZZITE, AND THE KADMONITE, AND THE HITTITE, AND THE PERIZZITE, AND THE REPHAIM, AND THE AMORITE, AND THE CANAANITE, AND THE GIRGASHITE, AND THE JEBUSITE (XV, 19 f.). R. Dostai said in the name of R. Samuel b. Naḥman: Because the Hivite is not mentioned here[3] the Rephaim are substituted in their stead. R. Ḥelbo said in R. Abba's name in R. Joḥanan's name: The Holy One, blessed be He, did at first contemplate giving Israel possession of ten peoples, but He gave them only seven, the other three being, THE KENITE, AND THE KENIZZITE, AND THE KADMONITE. Rabbi said: They are Arabia, the Shalamite, and the Nabatean. R. Simeon b. Yoḥai said: They are the Damascus region, Asia Minor,[4] and Apamea.[5] R. Liezer b. Jacob said: Asia Minor, Thrace, and Carthage.[6] The

[1] Thus His mere promise is as though it were already fulfilled

[2] E.V. '*will create*'. *U-bara* is perfect tense with the *waw* conversive, but R. Joshua translates it as a simple perfect: has created.

[3] V. Deut VII, 1

[4] Jast.. The Roman province embracing the west part of the peninsula of Asia Minor, bequeathed by King Attalus to the Roman Republic.

[5] Several towns, especially one in Bithynia, one in Mesopotamia, and one in Syria (Jast.)

[6] For a discussion of the various places mentioned in this passage, v. Th. *ad loc.*

Rabbis said: Edom, Moab, and the chief of the children of Ammon[1] are the three nations that were not given to them in this world, as it is said, *For I will not give you of their land*, etc. (Deut. II, 5). But in the days of the Messiah they shall once again belong to Israel,[2] in order to fulfil God's promise. Now, however, He has given them but seven, as it says, *Seven nations greater and mightier than thou* (*ib*. VII, 1). R. Isaac said: The swine grazes with ten of its young whereas the sheep does not graze even with one.[3] Thus, all these, viz THE KENITE, THE KENIZZITE, etc. [were promised to Abraham's seed], yet so far, *Sarai Abraham's wife bore him no children* (Gen XVI, 1)!

[1] The language is Biblical; v. Dan XI, 41.

[2] 'Once again'—as though through God's promise this had already been the case.

[3] This was proverbial. the unclean swine is always surrounded by a large litter of its offspring, whereas the clean sheep is alone.

CHAPTER XLV (LECH LECHA)

1. NOW SARAI ABRAM'S WIFE BORE HIM NO CHILDREN, etc. (XVI, 1). It is written, *A woman of valour who can find, for her price* (mikrah) *is far above rubies* (Prov. XXXI, 10). What does '*mikrah*' mean? R. Abba b. Kahana said: Her pregnancy,[1] as you read, *Thine origin* (mekuroth) *and thy nativity* (Ezek. XVI, 3).[2] Now Abram was a year older than Nahor, and Nahor was a year older than Haran; [hence Abram was] two years older [than Haran; deduct] the year of pregnancy with Milcah and the year of pregnancy with Iscah, and you find that Haran begot children at six years of age, yet you say that Abram could not beget? Hence, NOW SARAI ABRAM'S WIFE BORE HIM NO CHILDREN.[3]

DID NOT BEAR TO HIM. R. Judah said: TO HIM teaches that she did not bear to Abram, but had she been married to another she would have borne children. R. Nehemiah said: Neither to him nor to anyone else. How then does R. Nehemiah interpret DID NOT BEAR TO HIM? Interpret TO HIM and TO HER,[4] thus: She did not bear to herself—on Sarai's own account—nor TO HIM—on Abram's account.

AND SHE HAD A HANDMAID, AN EGYPTIAN. She was a handmaid of 'plucking'[5] whom he was bound to support but might not sell. R Simeon b. Lakish was asked: What is the meaning of what we learnt[6]: 'Servants of plucking'? 'What you pluck, you pluck,' he answered.[7]

[1] Y T.: Righteous women, as in the case of Sarah, find pregnancy more difficult of attainment than rubies.

[2] 'Origin,' by contrast with 'nativity', is understood to mean pregnancy, conception, and *mikrah* is now identified with *mekurah*, pl. *mekuroth*.

[3] V. *supra*, XXXVIII, 14, for notes.

[4] The verse continues: *And to her was a handmaid* (E.V. '*and she had a handmaid*'). R Nehemiah reads DID NOT BEAR together with TO HIM and (disregarding the punctuation) TO HER

[5] This is a technical term, describing the portion of a wife's dowry, the usufruct of which the husband enjoys without responsibility for loss or deterioration. From the term she *had* it is deduced that Abram's rights in her were limited.

[6] Yeb. VII, 1.

[7] I.e. you (sc. the husband) enjoy the usufruct without any further responsibility in the same.

R. Simeon b. Yohai said: Hagar was Pharaoh's daughter. When Pharaoh saw what was done on Sarah's behalf in his own house,[1] he took his daughter and gave her to Sarah, saying, Better let my daughter be a handmaid in this house than a mistress in another house'; thus it is written, AND SHE HAD A HANDMAID, AN EGYPTIAN, WHOSE NAME WAS HAGAR, he (Pharaoh) saying, 'Here is thy reward (*agar*).'[2] Abimelech, too, when he saw the miracles performed in his house on Sarah's behalf, gave his daughter to her, saying, 'Better let my daughter be a handmaid in this house than a mistress in another,' as it is written, *Kings' daughters are among thy favourites* (Ps. XLV, 10). viz. the daughters of [two] kings.[3] *At thy right hand doth stand the queen in gold of Ophir* (*ib.*)—this alludes to Sarai.

2. AND SARAI SAID UNTO ABRAM: BEHOLD NOW, THE LORD HATH RESTRAINED ME FROM BEARING, etc. (XVI, 2). Said she: I know the source of my affliction: it is not as people say [of a barren woman], 'she needs a talisman, she needs a charm,'[4] but BEHOLD NOW, *THE LORD* HATH RESTRAINED ME FROM BEARING.

IT MAY BE THAT I SHALL BE BUILDED UP THROUGH HER. It was taught: He who has no child is as though he were dead and demolished. As though dead: *And she said unto Jacob: Give me children, or else I am dead* (Gen. XXX, 1).[5] As though demolished: IT MAY BE THAT I SHALL BE BUILDED UP THROUGH HER, and only that which is demolished must be builded up.

AND ABRAM HEARKENED TO THE VOICE OF SARAI. R. Jose said: To the voice of the Holy Spirit,[6] as you read, *Now therefore hearken unto the voice of the words of the Lord* (1 Sam. XV, 1).

[1] V. Gen. XII, 17. [2] A play on the name Hagar.
[3] Viz. Pharaoh and Abimelech.
[4] Both the text and the meaning are doubtful, and the translation is only a conjecture.
[5] Lit translation. E.V. '*or else I die*'.
[6] Which he felt moved her to speak.

3. AND SARAI ABRAM'S WIFE TOOK HAGAR THE EGYPTIAN (XVI, 3). She persuaded [took] her with words: 'Happy art thou to be united to so holy a man,' she urged.

AFTER ABRAM HAD DWELT TEN YEARS IN THE LAND OF CANAAN. R. Ammi said in the name of Resh Laḳish: What is the source of what we learned[1]: If a man married a woman and spent ten years with her and she did not bear a child, he may not stay sterile?[2] This verse: AFTER ABRAM HAD DWELT TEN YEARS: this proves that the time he spent without the Land[3] was not included in the reckoning.

AND GAVE HER TO ABRAM HER HUSBAND TO BE A WIFE TO HIM, but not to another; TO BE A WIFE, but not a concubine.[4]

4. AND HE WENT IN UNTO HAGAR, AND SHE CONCEIVED (XVI, 4). R. Levi b. Ḥaytha said: She became pregnant through the first intimacy. R. Eleazar said: A woman never conceives by the first intimacy. An objection is raised: surely it is written, *Thus were both the daughters of Lot with child by their father* (Gen. XIX, 36)?[5] Said R. Tanḥuma: By an effort of will power[6] they brought forth their virginity, and thus conceived at the first act of intercourse. R. Ḥanina b. Pazzi observed: Thorns are neither weeded nor sown, yet of their own accord they grow and spring up, whereas how much pain and toil is required before wheat can be made to grow![7]

Why were the matriarchs barren? R. Levi said in R. Shila's name and R. Ḥelbo in R. Johanan's name: Because the Holy One, blessed be He, yearns for their prayers and supplications. Thus it is written, *O my dove, thou art as the clefts of the rock* (S.S. II, 14)[8]: Why did I make thee barren? In order that, *Let Me see thy countenance, let Me hear thy*

[1] Yeb. 64*a*. [2] But must remarry.
[3] Sc Palestine, the Land *par excellence*.
[4] Hagar was to enjoy all the rights of a wife.
[5] Though they were only once with him.
[6] Lit. 'they mastered themselves'.
[7] Thus Hagar conceived immediately, whereas Sarah had to wait a long time. [8] I e barren. E.V 'in *the clefts*,' etc

voice (*ib.*).[1] R. 'Azariah said in R. Ḥanina's name: So that they might lean on their husbands in [spite of] their beauty.[2] R. Huna and R. Jeremiah in the name of R. Ḥiyya b. Abba said: So that they might pass the greater part of their life untrammelled. R. Huna, R. Idi, and R. Abin in R. Meir's name said: So that their husbands might derive pleasure from them, for when a woman is with child she is disfigured and lacks grace. Thus the whole ninety years that Sarah did not bear she was like a bride in her canopy.

Ladies used to come to inquire how she was, and she would say to them, 'Go and ask about the welfare of this poor woman [Hagar].' Hagar would tell them: 'My mistress Sarai is not inwardly what she is outwardly: she appears to be a righteous woman, but she is not. For had she been a righteous woman, see how many years have passed without her conceiving, whereas I conceived in one night!' Said Sarah: 'Shall I pay heed to this woman and argue with her! No; I will argue the matter with her master!'[3]

5. AND SARAI SAID UNTO ABRAM: MY WRONG (ḤAMASI) BE UPON THEE (XVI, 5). R. Judan explained this in R. Judah's name: Thou wrongest me with words, since thou hearest me insulted yet art silent.[4] R. Berekiah explained it in R. Abba's name: I have a grievance against thee. For imagine two men incarcerated in prison, and as the king passes one of them cries out, 'Execute justice for me!' The king orders him to be released, whereupon his fellow-prisoner says to him, 'I have a grievance against you, for had you said, "Execute justice for *us*," he would have released me just as he has released you; but now that

[1] In prayer.

[2] The matriarchs, possessing both beauty and wealth, would have felt quite independent of their husbands had they also been blessed with children in their early years.

[3] This paragraph is a comment on the phrase, AND WHEN SHE SAW THAT SHE HAD CONCEIVED, HER MISTRESS WAS DESPISED IN HER EYES.

[4] '*Ḥamasi*' really means, 'what is stolen from me'. Sarah complained that Abraham robbed her of the words that he ought to speak on her behalf

you said, "Execute justice for *me*," he released you but not me.' Similarly, hadst thou said, '*We* go childless,' then as He gave thee a child so would He have given me; since, however, thou saidest, *And* I *go childless* (Gen. xv, 2), He gave thee a child but not me. This may [also] be compared to two people who went to borrow seed from the king. One of them asked, 'Lend me seed,' and he ordered, 'Give it to him.' Said his companion to him, 'I have a grievance against you. Had you asked, "Lend *us* seed," he would have given me just as he gave you; now however that you said, "Lend *me* seed," he has given you but not me.' Similarly, hadst thou said, 'Behold, to us Thou hast given no seed,' then as He gave thee so had He given me. Now however that thou didst say, '*Behold, to* me *Thou hast given no seed*' (*ib.* 3), He gave to thee but not to me.

R. Menahema [Nehemiah] said in R. Abin's name: She scratched his face.[1] The Rabbis said: Women are said to possess four traits: they are greedy, eavesdroppers, slothful, and envious. Greedy, as it says, *And she took of the fruit thereof, and did eat* (*ib.* III, 6); eavesdroppers: *And Sarah heard in the tent door* (*ib.* XVIII, 10); slothful: *Make ready* quickly *three measures of fine meal* (*ib.* 6); envious: *Rachel envied her sister* (*ib.* XXX, 1). R. Joshua b. Nehemiah said. She is also a scratcher and talkative. A scratcher: AND SARAI SAID UNTO ABRAM: MY SCRATCH BE UPON THEE. Talkative: *And Miriam spoke against Moses* (Num. XII, 1). R. Levi said: She is also prone to steal and a gadabout. Prone to steal: *And Rachel stole the teraphim* (Gen. XXXI, 19). A gadabout: *And Dinah went out* (*ib.* XXXIV, 1).[2]

THE LORD JUDGE BETWEEN ME AND THEE (U-BENEKA). R. Tanhuma said in the name of R. Ḥiyya the Elder, and R. Berekiah said in R. Eleazar's name: Whoever plunges eagerly into litigation does not escape from it unscathed. Sarah should have reached Abraham's years, but because she said, THE LORD JUDGE

[1] By a play on words *hamasi* (E.V '*my wrong*') is derived from *ḥimmes*, to scratch, and rendered: my scratch be upon thee

[2] Cf. *supra*, XVIII, 2.

BETWEEN ME AND THEE, her life was reduced by forty-eight years.

R. Hoshaya said: *Binka* (thy son) is written.[1] Seeing that it is already written, *And he went in unto Hagar, and she conceived*, why is it further stated, *Behold, thou* wilt *conceive* (*ib.* 11)?[2] This, however, teaches that an evil eye took possession of her and she miscarried.[3] R. Hanina observed: Had the prophet Elisha told her that by the Holy Spirit, it would have sufficed her.[4]

6. BUT ABRAM SAID UNTO SARAI: BEHOLD, THY MAID IS IN THY HAND (XVI, 6). Said he: 'I am constrained to do her neither good[5] nor harm.'[6] It is written, *Thou shalt not deal with her as a slave, because thou hast humbled her* (Deut. XXI, 14). after we have vexed her, can we now enslave her again? I am constrained to do her neither good nor harm It is written, *And Sarah dealt harshly with her, and she fled from her face* (Gen. *loc. cit.*), while it is written, *To sell her unto a foreign people he shall have no power, seeing he hath dealt deceitfully with her* (Ex. XXI, 8): after we have made her a mistress,[7] shall we make her a bondmaid again? I am constrained to do her neither good nor harm; hence it is written, AND SARAH DEALT HARSHLY WITH HER, AND SHE FLED FROM *HER* FACE.[8] R. Abba said: She restrained her from cohabitation. R. Berekiah said· She slapped her face with a slipper. R. Berekiah said in R. Abba's name. She bade her carry her water buckets and bath towels to the baths.[9]

[1] The word for AND THEE, Heb. וביניך is written ובנך, which may be read ובנך, and thy son, sc. the unborn Ishmael. Thus she called down God's wrath on him (In cur edd of the Bible וביניך is actually written, but according to tradition each *yod* (י) is dotted, which means that it is disregarded)

[2] Spoken by the angel to Hagar after her flight.

[3] Hence the angel told her that she would conceive again

[4] How much greater then was the honour conferred upon her in that an angel spoke to her!

[5] Because she has insulted you.

[6] Since she is now my wife

[7] I.e. given her the status of a wife.

[8] But not Abraham's.

[9] This was the work of a slave. Thus she did not actually ill-treat her but made her do work unsuited to her new status

7. AND THE ANGEL OF THE LORD FOUND HER . . . N THE WAY TO SHUR (XVI, 7): on the road of Ḥalizah.[1]

AND HE SAID: HAGAR, SARAI'S HANDMAID, etc. XVI, 8). So runs the proverb. 'If one man tells you that you have ass's ears, do not believe him; if two tell it to you, order a halter.' Thus, Abraham said: *Behold, thy maid is in thy hand* (*ib.* 6); the angel said: HAGAR, SARAI'S *HANDMAID*, etc. Hence, AND SHE SAID: I FLEE FROM THE FACE OF MY *MISTRESS* SARAI.[2]

AND AN ANGEL OF THE LORD SAID UNTO HER: RETURN TO THY MISTRESS, etc. . . . AND AN ANGEL OF THE LORD SAID UNTO HER: I WILL GREATLY MULTIPLY THY SEED, etc. (XVI, 9 f.). How many angels visited her?[3] R. Ḥama b. R. Ḥanina said: Five, for each time 'speech' is mentioned it refers to an angel. The Rabbis said: Four, this being the number of times 'angel' occurs. R. Ḥiyya observed: Come and see how great is the difference between the earlier generations and the later ones! What did Manoah say to his wife? *We shall surely die, because we have seen God* (Judg. XIII, 22)[4]; yet Hagar, a bondmaid, sees five angels and is not afraid of them! R. Aḥa said: The finger-nail of the fathers rather than the stomach of the sons! R. Isaac quoted: *She seeth the ways of her household* (Prov. XXXI, 27): Abraham's household were seers, so she [Hagar] was accustomed to them.

8. AND THE ANGEL OF THE LORD SAID UNTO HER: BEHOLD, THOU ART WITH CHILD, etc. (XVI, 11). R Isaac said: Three were called by their names before they were born, Isaac, Solomon, and Josiah. What is said in the

[1] The name in Aramaic. Shur was 'the wall' or fortification which protected Egypt on the east from the incursions of raiding Bedouins (Hertz on Genesis, *loc. cit.*).
[2] In spite of her higher status (v. *supra*, 3) she recognised Sarai as her mistress
[3] It is assumed that since AND AN ANGEL OF THE LORD SAID UNTO HER occurs more than once, though after the first time it is superfluous, different angels are referred to.
[4] Actually they had seen an angel; v. 13.

case of Isaac? *And God said: Nay, but Sarah thy wife shall bear thee a son; and thou shalt call his name Isaac* (Gen. XVII, 19). In the case of Solomon? *Behold, a son shall be born to thee, who shall be a man of rest; and I will give him rest from all his enemies round about; for his name shall be Solomon* (I Chron. XXII, 9). In the case of Josiah? *And he cried against the altar by the word of the Lord: O altar, altar, thus saith the Lord: Behold, a son shall be born unto the house of David, Josiah by name* (I Kings XIII, 2). Some add Ishmael among the nations [i.e. non-Jews]: BEHOLD, THOU ART WITH CHILD, AND SHALT BEAR A SON; AND THOU SHALT CALL HIS NAME ISHMAEL.

9. AND HE SHALL BE A PERE (E.V. 'A WILD ASS') OF A MAN (XVI, 12). R. Joḥanan and Resh Laḳish debated this. R. Joḥanan said: It means that while all people are bred in civilised surroundings, he would be reared in the wilderness. Resh Laḳish said: It means a savage among men in its literal sense, for whereas all others plunder wealth, he plunders lives.

HIS HAND SHALL BE AGAINST EVERY MAN, AND EVERY MAN'S HAND AGAINST HIM (KOL BO). His hand and his dog's (*kalbo*)[1] are alike. Just as his dog eats carrion, so does he eat carrion. R. Eleazar said: When SHALL HIS HAND BE AGAINST EVERY MAN AND EVERY MAN'S HAND AGAINST HIM? When he shall come of whom it is written, *And wheresoever the children of men, the beasts of the field, and the fowls of the heaven dwell, hath He given them into thy hand* (Dan. II, 38).[2] Hence it is written, *Of Kedar, and of the kingdoms of Hazor, which Nebuchadrezzar smote* (Jer. XLIX, 28): his name is written 'Nebuchadrezzar',[3] because he shut them up (*'aẓuran*)[4] in the wilderness and slew them.

AND HE SHALL DWELL IN THE FACE OF ALL HIS

[1] *'Kol bo'* being read *kalbo*, his dog.
[2] I.e. in the days of Nebuchadnezzar, whose ruthless policy of conquest aroused the whole world against him.
[3] Instead of the more usual Nebuchadnezzar.
[4] A play on the name, which, with the present spelling, ends in *aẓar* (אצר) and is read as though it were *'aẓar* (עצר), to shut up.

BRETHREN. Here you say, HE SHALL DWELL, while elsewhere you read, *He fell* (Gen. XXV, 17)? As long as Abraham lived, HE SHALL DWELL; as soon as he died, '*He fell.*' Before he stretched out his hand against the Temple, HE SHALL DWELL; as soon as he stretched out his hand against the Temple, '*He fell.*' In this world, HE SHALL DWELL; in the next world, '*He fell*' [shall be applicable to him].[1]

10. AND SHE CALLED THE NAME OF THE LORD THAT SPOKE UNTO HER (XVI, 13). R. Judah b. R. Simon and R. Joḥanan in the name of R. Eleazar b. R. Simeon said: The Holy One, blessed be He, never condescended to hold converse with a woman save with that righteous woman [viz. Sarah], and that too was through a particular cause. R. Abba b. Kahana said in R. Birya's name: And what a roundabout way He took in order to speak with her, as it is written, *And He said: Nay, but thou didst laugh* (*ib.* XVIII, 15)! But it is written, AND SHE [HAGAR] CALLED THE NAME OF THE LORD THAT SPOKE UNTO HER? R. Joshua b. R. Nehemiah answered in R. Idi's name: That was through an angel. But it is written: *And the Lord said unto her*—Rebekah (*ib.* XXV, 23)? R. Levi said in the name of R. Ḥama b. R. Ḥanina: That was through an angel. R. Leazar said in the name of R. Jose b. Zimra: That was through the medium of Shem.[2]

THOU ART A GOD OF SEEING (EL ROI). R. Aibu explained it: Thou seest the sufferings of the persecuted.

FOR SHE SAID: HAVE I EVEN HERE (HALOM) SEEN HIM THAT SEETH ME. She said: I have been granted not only speech [with the angel], but even with royalty too, as you read, *That Thou hast brought me thus far*—

[1] Bacher suggests that the statement that Ishmael (which is not to be identified with Rome) attacked the Temple alludes either to Aretes, King of Nabatea, who attacked Aristobulus and besieged Jerusalem (v. Josephus, *Ant.* XIV, 2, § 1), or to the Arabian Prince who joined Vespasian's army. V. Th. *ad loc.* on the bearing of this passage on the date of the composition of Gen. Rabbah.

[2] V. *supra*, XX, 6.

halom (II Sam. VII, 18).[1] I was favoured [to see the angel] not only when with my mistress, but even now that I am alone.[2] R. Samuel said: This may be compared to a noble lady whom the king ordered to walk before him. She did so leaning on her maid and pressing her face against her.[3] Thus her maid saw [the king], while she did not see him.

[1] Referring to David's royal rank. Thus here too '*halom*' expresses Hagar's gratitude that kings would spring from her. Cur. edd. have here: Not only was I favoured to see the angel together with my mistress, but even my mistress who was with me did not see him (while I did). This explains the comparison that ends the section.

[2] Rendering: I have seen (the angels in the wilderness) after having seen them (at home); v. *supra*, 7.

[3] Hiding her face in modesty.

CHAPTER XLVI (LECH LECHA)

1. AND ABRAM WAS NINETY YEARS OLD AND NINE, etc. (XVII, 1). It is written, *I found Israel like grapes in the wilderness, I saw your fathers as the first-ripe in the fig-tree at her first season* (Hos. IX, 10). R. Judan said: At first the fruit of a fig-tree is gathered one by one, then two by two, then three by three, until eventually they are gathered in baskets and with shovels.[1] Even so, at the beginning, *Abraham was one* (Ezek. XXXIII, 24); then there were Abraham and Isaac; then Abraham, Isaac, and Jacob. Until eventually, *And the children of Israel were fruitful, and increased abundantly, and multiplied*, etc. (Ex VII, 1). R. Judan said: Just as a fig contains nothing inedible save its stalk, and with its removal even this defect ceases, so did God say to Abraham: 'There is nought unworthy in thee save thy foreskin: remove it and the blemish ceases': hence, WALK BEFORE ME, AND BE THOU WHOLE.

2. AND WHEN ABRAM WAS NINETY YEARS OLD AND NINE, etc. It is written, *To everything there is a season, and a time to every purpose under the heaven* (Eccl. III, 1). There was a season when circumcision should be given to Abraham viz. *In the self same day was Abraham circumcised* (Gen. XVII, 26); there was a season when his descendants were to neglect it, viz. in the wilderness, as it is written, *For all the people that came out were circumcised; but all the people that were born in the wilderness by the way as they came forth out of Egypt, had not been circumcised* (Josh. V, 5).

Why should he not have circumcised himself at the age of forty-eight, when he recognised his Creator?[2] In order not to discourage proselytes.[3] Then why not be circumcised at the age of eighty-five, when [God] spoke with him between the pieces?[4] In order that Isaac might issue from

[1] At first single figs here and there ripen; then little clusters of twos and threes, but eventually the whole tree ripens. [2] Cf *supra*, XXX, 8.
[3] Who might otherwise think that it was too late in life for them to be circumcised. Lit. 'so as not to shut the door in the face of proselytes'.
[4] V. ch. XV There are several views as to Abraham's age at the time.

a holy source.[1] Then let him be circumcised at the age of eighty-six, when Ishmael was born?[2] Said R. Simeon b. Laḳish: [God said]: 'I will set up a cinnamon tree in the world· just as the cinnamon tree yields fruit as long as you manure and hoe around it, so [shall Abraham be] even when his blood runs sluggishly and his passions and desires have ceased.'[3]

3. [Abraham] asked: 'If circumcision is so precious, why was it not given to Adam?' Said the Holy One, blessed be He, to him: 'Let it suffice thee that I and thou are in the world.[4] If thou wilt not undergo circumcision, it is enough for My world to have existed until now, and it is enough for uncircumcision to have existed until now, and it is enough for circumcision to have been forlorn until now.'[5] Said he: 'Before I circumcised myself, men came and joined me [in my new faith]. Will they come and join me when I am circumcised?'[6] 'Abraham,' said God to him, 'let it suffice thee that I am thy God; let it suffice thee that I am thy Patron, and not only for thee alone, but it is sufficient for My world that I am its God and its Patron.'[7]

R. Nathan said in R. Aḥa's name, and R. Berekiah said in R. Isaac's name: I AM EL SHADDAI (GOD ALMIGHTY): It is I who said to My world, '*day*' (enough)! And had I not said '*day*!' to My world, the

[1] I.e. after Abraham's circumcision. [2] V xvi, 16.
[3] I.e. Abraham was to be like a cinnamon tree which no matter how old can be made to produce fruit, so was circumcision to renew his virility.
[4] I was not interested in the previous generations, because they did not acknowledge and recognise me. This and the following comments are based on the phrase, *I am* El Shaddai (God Almighty) By a play on words, *Shaddai* is derived from *day*, enough
[5] Since none practised it. I e the world must cease.
[6] I.e when a difficult operation is necessary.
[7] On this interpretation, which is similar to that of M.K., God assured Abraham that even if circumcision should deter would-be converts, it did not matter. This may therefore be directed against Paulinism, which abolished circumcision in order to facilitate the spread of Christianity. Th. Mah. and Y.T. translate differently: (Even) before I was circumcised, men fought against me; how much more when I am circumcised and so I emphasise the difference between us. Though God's reply, 'let it suffice thee that I am thy Patron,' lends colour to this interpretation, it does not on the whole seem very probable.

heaven would still have been spreading and the earth would have gone on expanding to this very day.

It was taught in the name of R. Eliezer b. Jacob : It is I whose Godhead outweighs the world and the fulness thereof.[1] Aḳilas[2] translated it: Sufficient and incomparable.

4. WALK BEFORE ME, AND BE THOU WHOLE. R. Levi said: This may be illustrated by a noble lady whom the king commanded, 'Walk before me.' She walked before him and her face went pale, for, thought she, who knows but that some defect may have been found in me? Said the king to her, 'Thou hast no defect, but that the nail of thy little finger is slightly too long; pare it and the defect will be gone.' Similarly, God said to Abraham, 'Thou hast no other defect but this foreskin: remove it and the defect will be gone.' Hence, WALK BEFORE ME, AND BE THOU WHOLE.

AND I WILL MAKE MY COVENANT, etc. (XVII, 2). R. Huna said in Bar Ḳappara's name: Abraham pondered[3] and drew an inference: *'orlah* (foreskin) is said here (v. 11), and *'orlah* occurs in reference to a tree (Lev. XIX, 23)[4]: just as *'orlah* in the case of trees refers to the place where it yields fruit, so *'orlah* employed in reference to man means the member which produces offspring [fruit]. Said R. Ḥanina to him. Had then reasoning by analogy already been given to Abraham? Surely not! But [he learned it from God's promise]: AND I WILL MAKE MY COVENANT BETWEEN ME AND THEE, AND WILL MULTIPLY THEE EXCEEDINGLY: hence, with [that member through which] I WILL MULTIPLY THEE EXCEEDINGLY, I WILL MAKE MY COVENANT BETWEEN ME AND THEE.

[1] The original is very difficult, and this is Th.'s conjecture '*Day*' (v.p 390, n 4) is accordingly understood in the sense of 'assessment'—the whole world cannot be assessed as having such greatness as Mine. The Targum that follows corresponds to these two meanings of '*day*', viz. 'sufficient' and 'assessed'.

[2] The author of a translation of the Bible into Greek in the second century. He was a proselyte. [3] Lit. 'sat'.

[4] Though translated differently, the Hebrew is the same in both cases.

5. R. Ishmael and R. Akiba [reasoned as follows]. R. Ishmael said: Abraham was a High Priest, as it says, *The Lord hath sworn, and will not repent: Thou art a priest for ever after the manner of Melchizedek* (Ps. CX, 4).[1] Again, it is said, *And ye shall be circumcised in the flesh of your* 'orlah (Gen. XVII, 11). If he circumcised himself at the ear, he would be unfit to offer sacrifices; if at the mouth, he would be unfit to offer; at the heart, he would be unfit to offer.[2] Hence, where could he perform circumcision and yet be fit to offer? Nowhere else than at the *'orlah* of the body [the foreskin]. R. Akiba said: There are four kinds of *'orlah*. Thus, *'orlah* is used in connection with the ear, viz. *Behold, their ear is* 'orlah—E.V. *'dull'* (Jer. VI, 10); the mouth, *Behold, I am* 'aral [E.V. *'uncircumcised'*][3] *of lips* (Ex. VI, 30); the heart: *For all the house of Israel are* 'arle [E.V. *'uncircumcised'*] *in the heart* (Jer. IX, 25). Now, he was ordered, WALK BEFORE ME, AND BE THOU WHOLE. If he circumcised himself at the ear, he would not be WHOLE; at the mouth, he would not be WHOLE; at the heart, he would not be WHOLE. Where could he circumcise himself and yet be WHOLE? Nowhere else than at the *'orlah* of the body.

Naḳdah said: It is written, *And he that is eight days old shall be circumcised among you, every male* (Gen. XVII, 12). Now if he is circumcised at the ear, he cannot hear; at the mouth, he cannot speak; at the heart, he cannot think.[4] Where then could he be circumcised and yet be able to think? Only at the *'orlah* of the body. R. Tanḥuma observed: This argument of Naḳdah is logical.

AND THE UNCIRCUMCISED MALE (XVII, 14). Is there then an uncircumcised female? The meaning, however, is that we must perform circumcision on the member which marks the distinction between male and female.

[1] V. Ned. 32*b* and Lev. R. XXV, 6, where the verse is applied to Abraham.
[2] In each case it would be a blemish, which disqualifies a priest. This is probably merely argumentation for its own sake, as appears from the reference to the heart.
[3] *'Aral* has the same root as *'orlah*.
[4] The heart was regarded as the seat of the emotions, and 'think' probably has that meaning here.

6. AND ABRAHAM FELL ON HIS FACE, etc. (XVII, 3). R. Phinehas said in R. Levi's name: Abraham fell on his face on two occasions.[1] In consequence, his children were deprived of circumcision once in the wilderness and once in Egypt[2]: In Egypt, Moses came and circumcised them; in the wilderness, Joshua came and circumcised them.[3]

7. AS FOR ME, BEHOLD, MY COVENANT IS WITH THEE, etc. (XVII, 4). It is related that R. Abba, R. Berekiah, R. Abba b. Kahana, and R. Samuel b. Ammi, when sitting and studying, once raised the question: How is *notarikon* [as a permissible method of exegesis] deduced from Scripture?[4] We know it from this: AND THOU SHALT BE AB HAMON (THE FATHER OF A MULTITUDE—OF NATIONS), the *resh* being lacking.[5]

8. NEITHER SHALL THY NAME ANY MORE BE CALLED ABRAM, BUT THY NAME SHALL BE ABRAHAM (XVII, 5). Bar Kappara said: Whoever calls Abraham 'Abram', violates a positive commandment. R. Levi said: A positive commandment and a negative commandment.

[1] Here, and when he was informed about the birth of Isaac; v. 17.

[2] His falling on his face is regarded as an indication of *unwilling* assent to God's command; but v. n. 3 for a different interpretation. According to the Rabbis the Israelites in Egypt were uncircumcised until just prior to their departure, when circumcision became essential for the eating of the passover-offering (v. Ex. XII, 48).

[3] V. Josh. v, 5. The above translation, though fitting in with the text, is not very probable, since it assumes Abraham's *unwillingness* (the second falling on the face can certainly not bear this connotation). E. J.: Abraham foresaw these two occasions when his descendants would not be circumcised, and he fell on his face *in prayer* that they might not lose it altogether. His prayer was answered through Moses and Joshua.

[4] *Notarikon* is a method of exegesis whereby words are broken up and each letter or syllable is treated as an abbreviation. In this treatment the *general* form of the word only is considered, while a particular letter or so may have to be ignored. Their question was: how do we know that even then *notarikon* is a permissible method of exegesis. Cf. Shab. 105*a*.

[5] His name was changed from אברם (Abram) to אברהם (Abraham), so that it might read *ab* (father of) *ham* (an abbreviation of *hamon*, 'multitude'). Hence the ר (*resh*) must be ignored in a case where Scripture itself provides the exegesis.

NEITHER SHALL THY NAME ANY MORE BE CALLED ABRAM—that is a negative command; BUT THY NAME SHALL BE ABRAHAM—that is a positive command. But surely the men of the Great Assembly[1] called him Abram, as it is written, *Thou . . . who didst choose Abram* (Neh. IX, 7). There it is different, as it means that He chose him while he was yet Abram. Then, by analogy, does one who calls Sarah 'Sarai' infringe a positive command?[2] No, for only he [Abraham] was enjoined respecting her.[3] Again, by analogy, if one calls Israel, 'Jacob,' does one infringe a positive command? [No, for] it was taught: It was not intended that the name Jacob should disappear, but that 'Israel' should be his principal name, while 'Jacob' should be a secondary one. R. Zebida interpreted in R. Aḥa's name: At all events, *Thy name is Jacob*, save that, *But Israel* [too] *shall be thy name* (Gen. XXXV, 10): 'Jacob' will be the principal name, while 'Israel' will be an additional one.

9. AND I WILL GIVE UNTO THEE, AND TO THY SEED AFTER THEE, THE LAND OF THY SOJOURNINGS, etc. (XVII, 8). R. Judan gave five interpretations of this. R. Judan said: God said: (i) 'If thy children accept My Divinity, I will be their God and Patron; if not, I will not be their God and Patron. (ii) If thy children enter the Promised Land, they accept My Divinity; if not, they do not accept My Divinity. (iii) If they accept circumcision, they accept My Divinity; if not, they do not accept My Divinity. (iv) If thy children accept circumcision, they will enter the Promised Land; if not, they will not enter the Promised Land.'[4] R. Berekiah and R. Ḥelbo in the name of R. Abin b. R. Jose said: It is written, *And this is the cause* (dabar) *why Joshua did circumcise* (Josh. V, 4): Joshua spoke a word (*dabar*) to them, and circumcised them.[5] 'What think you,' said he upbraiding them, 'that

[1] A body instituted by Ezra as the supreme ecclesiastical executive council The authorship of Nehemiah is here apparently ascribed to it. Y. B.B 15*a*.
[2] Surely not! [3] V. Gen. XVII, 15: Thou *shalt not call her name Sarai*.
[4] Only four are given here.
[5] Translating: And by this word did Joshua circumcise them.

you will enter the Land uncircumcised?' Thus did the Holy One, blessed be He, say to Abraham, 'AND I WILL GIVE UNTO THEE, AND TO THY SEED AFTER THEE, etc., providing that you fulfil the condition, AND AS FOR THEE, THOU SHALT KEEP MY COVENANT' (XVII, 9).

AND AS FOR THEE, THOU SHALT KEEP MY COVENANT. R. Huna in Rab's name and R. Joḥanan each commented. Rab said: AND AS FOR THEE means one like thee [must perform the actual circumcision]; hence it follows that only he who is himself circumcised may perform circumcision. R. Joḥanan said: *He must needs be circumcised*—himmol yimmol (*ib.* 13) teaches that the circumciser must himself be circumcised.[1] It was taught: An uncircumcised Israelite [Jew] may not circumcise, and how much more so an uncircumcised Gentile!

10. AND YE SHALL BE CIRCUMCISED (U-NEMALTEM) IN THE FLESH OF YOUR FORESKIN (XVII, 11). It [the prepuce] is like a sore (*numi*) hanging from the body[2]. Once Monabaz[3] and Izates,[4] the sons of King Ptolemy,[5] were sitting and reading the book of Genesis. When they came to the verse, AND YE SHALL BE CIRCUMCISED, one turned his face to the wall and commenced to weep, and the other turned his face to the wall and commenced to weep. Then each went and had himself circumcised.[6] Some time later they were sitting and reading the Book of Genesis; and when they came to the verse, AND YE SHALL BE CIRCUMCISED, one said to the other, 'Woe to thee, my brother!' to which he replied,

[1] This follows from the doubling of the verb.
[2] The grammatical form, *unemaltem*, is unusual, and so by a play on words it is read: *numi* (a sore) *maltem* (shall ye circumcise).
[3] The name of a king of Adiabene, also of one of his sons, who embraced Judaism; the second one is referred to here. V. Jos. *Ant.* xx, 2, § 1 *seq.*
[4] A prince of Adiabene, brother of the second Monabaz.
[5] The mention of King Ptolemy is surprising, since they were the sons of King Monabaz. He is possibly mentioned in error, for he too is counted elsewhere as one of the heathen kings who embraced Judaism.
[6] Without his brother's knowledge.

'Woe to thee, my brother, but not to me.' Thus they revealed the matter to each other. When their mother learned about it she went and told their father: 'A sore has broken out on our sons' flesh and the physician has ordered circumcision.' 'Then let them be circumcised,' said he. How did the Holy One, blessed be He, requite them? Said R. Phinehas: When he went out to battle a band of enemies attacked him, and an angel descended and rescued him.[1]

11. AND HE THAT IS EIGHT DAYS OLD SHALL BE CIRCUMCISED . . . HE THAT IS BORN IN THE HOUSE OR BOUGHT WITH MONEY (XVII, 12). It was taught: If a man buys the unborn child of a non-Jewish bondmaid belonging to a Gentile—R. Joḥanan said: He must be circumcised on the eighth day [after birth]. It was likewise taught, R. Hama b. R. Jose said: He must be circumcised on the eighth day, while Samuel taught the same.[2] Samuel's statement is based on the verse: *For a son, or for a daughter* (Lev. XII, 6); '*For a son*' means in all cases, and '*For a daughter*' means in all cases.[3]

12. HE SHALL SURELY BE CIRCUMCISED—HIMMOL YIMMOL (XVII, 13). This intimates circumcision, *per'i'ah,*[4] and removal of the shreds [of the corona].[5] HE SHALL SURELY BE CIRCUMCISED: this teaches that the circumciser must himself be circumcised. HE SHALL SURELY BE CIRCUMCISED: this signifies the inclusion of one who is born circumcised.

It was taught, R. Simeon b. Eleazar said: Beth Shammai

[1] V. Jos. *ad loc.* IV.
[2] V. Shab. 135*a* and *b*, with which this does not agree.
[3] I.e. whatever the circumstances in which the son is born, and whatever the status of his mother (the 'daughter'), circumcision must be on the eighth day. The verse actually treats of the mother's period of uncleanness, not of circumcision at all. Mah. suggests that it may have been regarded as superfluous, since its scope is covered by the preceding verses (*q.v.*), and therefore it was applied to circumcision. [4] The uncovering of the corona by splitting the membrane and pulling it down.
[5] This and the following statements are based on the emphasis and extension implied by the doubling of the verb, '*himmol yimmol.*'

and Beth Hillel agree that when one is born circumcised, the blood of the covenant must be made to flow from him,[1] because it is a suppressed foreskin. They disagree only about a man who became a proselyte when already circumcised. Beth Shammai maintain: The blood of the covenant must be made to flow from him, while Beth Hillel rule: It is unnecessary. R. Eleazar the son of R. Eleazar Haḳappar said: Beth Shammai and Beth Hillel agree that in both of these cases the blood of the covenant must be made to flow. They disagree about one who was born circumcised, and the eighth day after whose birth[2] fell on the Sabbath. Beth Shammai then maintain: The blood of the covenant must flow[3]; while Beth Hillel rule: It is unnecessary.[4] R. Isaac b. Naḥman said in R. Hoshaya's name: The *halachah* is as stated by the disciple.[5]

13. AND THE UNCIRCUMCISED MALE, etc. (XVII, 14). R. Haggai said in R. Isaac's name, and R. Berekiah said in R. Isaac's name: Is there then an uncircumcised female? The meaning, however, is that we must perform circumcision on the member which marks the distinction between male and female.[6]

HE HATH BROKEN MY COVENANT. This refers to one whose circumcision is disguised.[7] It was taught: He whose circumcision is disguised must re-circumcise. R. Judah said: He does not re-circumcise, because it is a suppressed foreskin.[8] Said they to R. Judah: Yet there

[1] I.e. a minor form of circumcision is necessary.
[2] When circumcision must be performed; v. Lev. XII, 3.
[3] On the eighth day, the Sabbath.
[4] Hence it must be postponed until after the Sabbath.
[5] Sc. R. Eleazar the son of R. Eleazar Hakappar. V. Yeb. 71*a*; Shab. *ad loc.* [6] Cf. *supra*, 5.
[7] Lit. 'drawn'—the skin over the prepuce. Under the Hellenising influence of the pre-Maccabean period, when Greek games were introduced into Judea, in which the competitors appeared naked, many underwent operations (epiplasm) to hide the fact that they were circumcised.
[8] In Yeb. 72*a* the reading is: because it endangers his life. On the present reading the meaning is that it is indeed circumcised, notwithstanding that it is hidden.

were many in the days of the son of Kosiba[1] who re-circumcised and yet gave birth to children after that.[2] Hence it is written, HE SHALL SURELY BE CIRCUMCISED—even four or five times: HE HATH BROKEN MY COVENANT—viz. he whose circumcision is disguised.

[1] The leader of the ill-starred revolt against Hadrian, which ended in the crushing defeat of Bithar in 135 C.E.

[2] They survived it. Th.'s text probably requires emendation. On the historical fact v. Graetz, *Geschichte* (fourth edition), IV, 73.

Chapter XLVII (LECH LECHA)

1. AND GOD SAID UNTO ABRAHAM: AS FOR SARAI THY WIFE, THOU SHALT NOT CALL HER NAME SARAI, BUT SARAH [i.e PRINCESS] SHALL HER NAME BE (XVII, 15). It is written, *A virtuous woman is a crown to her husband* (Prov. XII, 4). R. Aḥa said: Her husband was crowned through her, but she was not crowned through her husband.[1] The Rabbis said: She was her husband's ruler. Usually, the husband gives orders, whereas here we read, *In all that Sarah saith unto thee, hearken unto her voice* (Gen. XXI, 12).

THOU SHALT NOT CALL HER NAME SARAI, BUT SARAH SHALL HER NAME BE. R. Joshua b. Ḳarḥah said: The *yod* which the Lord took from Sarai soared aloft before God and protested: 'Sovereign of the Universe! Because I am the smallest of all letters,[2] Thou hast withdrawn me from the name of that righteous woman!' Said the Holy One, blessed be He, to it: 'Hitherto thou wast in a woman's name and the last of its letters; now I will set thee in a man's name and at the beginning of its letters,' as it says, *And Moses called Hoshea the son of Nun Joshua* (Num. XIII, 16).[3] R. Mana said: Formerly she was a

[1] He refers this verse to Sarah. Her original name was שרי; now the numerical value of י is 10, while that of ה is 5. Thus God took the י from her name and split it up into two ה s, one for her name, which became שרה (Sarah), and one to be added to Abraham's name, which was thus changed from אברם to אברהם. Hence Abraham was crowned (his name was changed to denote his greatness; v. XVII, 5) through Sarah, but Sarah was not crowned through him He deduces this from the words THY WIFE, which are apparently superfluous: hence he interprets: THY WIFE—who brings thee honour. The passage might also mean quite simply that Abraham derived honour and glory from her, as we find in connection with Pharaoh (v. XII, 16), but she did not derive honour from him Y.M. explains: was then her husband (Abraham) crowned through her while she was not crowned through him—surely each cast glory upon the other? To which the Rabbis answer that the meaning here is that she was to be a mistress (crown, sovereign) to him, etc. This seems the most plausible interpretation, but it would probably require a slight emendation of the text.

[2] In actual writing it is almost a mere dot (י).

[3] Changing הושע into יהושע

princess [Sarai] to her own people only, whereas now she is a princess [Sarah] to all mankind.[1]

2. AND I WILL BLESS HER, AND MOREOVER I WILL GIVE THEE A SON FROM HER; YEA, I WILL BLESS HER, etc. (XVII, 16). R. Judah said: This means, AND I WILL BLESS HER, that she should give thee a son; YEA, I WILL BLESS HER in respect of milk. Said R. Nehemiah to him: Had she then already been informed about her milk?[2] This teaches, however, that God restored to her her youth. R. Abbahu explained it thus in the name of R. Jose b. R. Ḥanina: I will inspire all peoples with awe of her, so that they should not call her, 'barren woman.' R. Judan said in the name of Resh Lakish: She lacked an ovary, but the Lord fashioned an ovary for her.

AND KINGS OF PEOPLES SHALL BE OF HER. R. Hama b. R. Ḥanina said: Abraham drew a deduction from this and took back Keturah.[3]

3. THEN ABRAHAM FELL UPON HIS FACE (XVII, 17). R. Phinehas said in R. Levi's name: On two occasions did Abraham fall on his face. In consequence, his children were deprived of circumcision, once in the wilderness and once in Egypt. In Egypt, Moses came and circumcised them; in the wilderness, Joshua came and circumcised them.[4]

[1] He holds that both *Sarai* and *Sarah* denote 'princess', but that the latter is more comprehensive.

[2] The passage is rather difficult. It apparently means that there was no need to inform her that she would be able to suckle her child, seeing that he was not even conceived yet. Another interpretation is this: R Judah said that God informed her that He would bless her with sufficient milk to suckle other children too (v. *infra*, LIII, 9), to which R. Nehemiah objected that she had so far not even been promised sufficient for her own child V. *infra*, LII, 5, from which the present passage might in error have come here

[3] V XXV, 1. According to the Rabbis (v. *infra*, LXI, 4) Keturah was Hagar. Abraham deduced that FROM *HER* he would have kings of peoples, which implied that he was also to beget children from another wife who would not be kings of peoples This implied prophecy could not refer to Ishmael, for he was already born Rash. explains it differently.

[4] V. *supra*, XLVI, 6.

AND SAID IN HIS HEART: SHALL A CHILD BE BORN UNTO HIM THAT IS A HUNDRED YEARS OLD, etc. R. Judan interpreted: SHALL A CHILD BE BORN UNTO HIM THAT IS A HUNDRED YEARS OLD? Why [this astonishment]? For, [said he], SHALL SARAH, THAT IS NINETY YEARS OLD, BEAR? A man does not grow aged, but a woman does.[1]

When is a woman to be regarded as aged? Said R. Simeon b. Lakish: When she is called 'Mother So-and-So' and does not mind.

4. AND ABRAHAM SAID UNTO GOD: OH THAT ISHMAEL MIGHT LIVE BEFORE THEE! (XVII, 18). R. Judah said in R. Judan's name: Imagine a king who wished to increase his friend's allowance. 'I intend to double your allowance,' the king informed him. 'Do not fill me with a false hope,' he rejoined; 'pray only that you do not withhold my present allowance!' Similarly Abraham said, OH THAT ISHMAEL MIGHT LIVE BEFORE THEE.[2]

5. AND GOD SAID: NAY, BUT SARAH THY WIFE SHALL BEAR THEE A SON . . . AND AS FOR ISHMAEL, I HAVE HEARD THEE, etc. (XVII, 19 f.). R. Joḥanan said in the name of R. Joshua b. Ḥananiah: Here the son of the bondmaid might learn [that he would be blessed] from the son of the mistress. For, BEHOLD, I HAVE BLESSED HIM refers to Isaac; AND WILL MAKE HIM FRUITFUL refers to Isaac; AND WILL MULTIPLY HIM refers to Isaac. AND AS FOR ISHMAEL, I have already informed thee[3] [about his blessing] through an angel.[4] R. Abba b. Kahana said in R. Biryai's name

[1] There was nothing improbable in his begetting children, and he was surprised only because of Sarah's age.

[2] And I shall not hope for another son.

[3] Reading *shim'atika* instead of *shem'atika* (E.V 'I HAVE HEARD THEE')

[4] Who spoke to Hagar, XVI, 10 Now that his name was coupled with Isaac's, Ishmael could be sure that his blessing too would be fulfilled; or (as 'E.J.) that even his blessing would be increased.

Here the son of the mistress might learn from the son of the bondmaid: BEHOLD, I HAVE BLESSED HIM refers to Ishmael; AND WILL MAKE HIM FRUITFUL refers to Ishmael; AND WILL MULTIPLY HIM refers to Ishmael. How much the more then WILL I ESTABLISH MY COVENANT WITH ISAAC. R. Isaac said: It is written, *All these are the twelve tribes* (shibte) *of Israel* (Gen. XLIX, 28)—these were the descendants of the mistress [Sarah]. Yet did not Ishmael too produce twelve [princes]?[1] In truth those were *nesi'im* (princes) in the same sense as you read, *As* nesi'im [E.V. *'vapours'*] *and wind*, etc. (Prov. XXV, 14) [2] But these were *maṭoth* (tribes) as you read, *Sworn are the* matoth [E.V. *'rods'*] *of the word. Selah* (Hab. III, 9).[3]

BUT MY COVENANT WILL I ESTABLISH WITH ISAAC, WHOM SARAH SHALL BEAR UNTO THEE AT THIS SET TIME (LA-MO'ED) IN THE NEXT YEAR (XVII, 21). R. Huna said in R. Idi's name: That year was intercalated.[4]

6. AND HE LEFT OFF TALKING WITH HIM. It was taught: He who departs from his neighbour, whether he is greater or smaller than he, must ask leave of him. From whom do we learn it? From Abraham. On one occasion Abraham was speaking to God, when the ministering angels came to speak to him. Said he to them, 'Let us take leave of the *Shechinah*, which is greater than you, and then I will speak with you.' When he had spoken with God all that he needed, he said to Him, 'Sovereign of the Universe!

[1] As the present verse continues TWELVE PRINCES (NESI'IM) SHALL HE BEGET. Wherein then lay Sarah's superiority?

[2] Their glory would be transient, and they would soon pass away.

[3] *Shebet* and *mateh* are synonyms, both meaning tribes and both meaning rods. Thus these tribes would endure like rods that are planted.

[4] He holds that these tidings were announced at the time of the Feast of Tabernacles (15th–22nd of Tishri), while *la-mo'ed* means at the Festival, sc. Passover, in Nisan. Since this gives an interval of only six months, we must assume that the year was prolonged by the intercalation of a month (Adar), which then gives seven months. The Jewish year is lunar, and consists of about 354 days To make up to the 365 days of the solar year a month was intercalated in certain years

I have need to speak [with the angels].' 'Then let Me take leave [of thee] in peace,' replied He. Thus it is written, AND GOD WENT UP FROM ABRAHAM.[1]

Resh Lakish said: The Patriarchs are [God's] Heavenly Chariot. Thus it is written, AND GOD WENT UP FROM UPON ABRAHAM; again, *And God went up from upon him* (Gen. XXXV, 13); further, *And, behold, the Lord stood upon him* (*ib* XXVIII, 13).[2]

7. AND ABRAHAM TOOK ISHMAEL HIS SON, AND ALL THAT WERE BORN IN HIS HOUSE (XVII, 23). R. Aibu said: When Abraham circumcised those that were born in his house, he set up a hillock of foreskins; the sun shone upon them and they putrefied, and their odour ascended to the Lord like sweet incense. God then said: 'When My children lapse into sinful ways, I will remember that odour in their favour and be filled with compassion for them.'

8. AND ABRAHAM WAS NINETY YEARS OLD AND NINE, WHEN HE WAS CIRCUMCISED IN THE FLESH OF HIS FORESKIN, AND ISHMAEL HIS SON WAS THIRTEEN YEARS OLD, WHEN HE WAS CIRCUMCISED IN (ETH) THE FLESH OF HIS FORESKIN (XVII, 24 f.). Here you say, BESAR 'ORLATHO, while in the second verse you say, ETH BESAR 'ORLATHO?[3] The reason is this: BESAR 'ORLATHO is written in the case of Abraham, because he had been made flabby through a woman; but since Ishmael had not been made flabby through a woman, ETH BESAR 'ORLATHO is written.[4]

[1] Understanding it as though God first asked leave The passage of course is a lesson in manners

[2] In these verses על is translated literally 'upon', as though, as it were, God rode upon them. The idea is that through the Patriarchs the knowledge of God was diffused among all peoples

[3] E.V. '*The flesh of his foreskin*'; but in the second verse referring to Ishmael it is preceded by *eth*, the sign of the accusative, and in Rabbinic exegesis denoting an extension.

[4] His flesh was firmer, and a severer operation was necessary, and that is indicated by the extending particle *eth*.

9. IN THE SELF SAME DAY WAS ABRAHAM CIRCUMCISED (XVII, 26). R. Berekiah said: It is written, *I have not spoken in secret* (Isa. XLV, 19). Thus the Holy One, blessed be He, said: 'Had Abraham been circumcised at night, all his contemporaries might have said: "We did not know of it, but had we known of it we would not have let him be circumcised." Hence he was circumcised IN THE SELF SAME DAY, [with the challenge], "Let him who objects speak out!"'[1]

WAS ABRAHAM CIRCUMCISED. R. Abba said: He felt the smart and suffered pain, so that the Lord might double his reward. R. Levi said: It does not say, 'Abraham circumcised himself,' but WAS ABRAHAM CIRCUMCISED: this intimates that he examined himself and found that he was [already] circumcised. R. Berekiah observed: It was at that time that R. Abba b. Kahana humiliated R. Levi, saying to him: 'It is a lie and a falsehood![2] He felt the smart and suffered pain,[3] so that the Lord might double his reward.'

10. AND ALL THE MEN OF HIS HOUSE, THOSE BORN IN THE HOUSE, AND THOSE BOUGHT WITH MONEY OF A FOREIGNER, WERE CIRCUMCISED WITH HIM (XVII, 27). It was taught[4]: You may attend a non-Jewish fair on the Intermediate Days of a Festival[5] to buy houses, fields, vineyards, and male and female slaves from them. R. Ammi said in the name of R. Simeon b. Laḳish: Not only circumcised, but even uncircumcised slaves, because you thereby bring them under the wings of the *Shechinah*. R. Joshua b. Levi asked Resh Laḳish: Is it permitted to buy uncircumcised [heathen] slaves from a Gentile? About when do you ask me, he replied, about a

[1] Cf. *supra*, XXXII, 8.
[2] To suggest that Abraham did not perform circumcision. Radal suggests: would you teach a lie and a falsehood?
[3] The passive indicating that he was made to feel his circumcision.
[4] 'A.Z 13*a*, *b*
[5] These possess a semi-sacred character, and only work which cannot be postponed is permitted on them. Some MSS. omit: on the Intermediate Days of a Festival.

festival? It was taught: This is permitted even on the Sabbath.[1] Hezekiah taught: [*Thou mayest build bulwarks against the city that maketh war with thee,*] *until it fall* (Deut. xx, 20): even on the Sabbath, for thus we find that Jericho was indeed reduced on the Sabbath.[2]

There were three annual fairs: the fair of Gaza, the fair of Acco, and the fair of Batnan [Batanea],[3] and none of them is so clearly [of an idolatrous character] as the fair of Batnan.[4]

Abraham said: 'Before I became circumcised, travellers used to visit me; now that I am circumcised, perhaps they will no longer visit me?' Said the Holy One, blessed be He, to him: 'Before thou wast circumcised, uncircumcised mortals visited thee; now I in My glory will appear to thee.' Hence it is written, *And the Lord appeared unto him* (Gen. xviii, 1).

[1] For the reason stated. He would not actually hand him the money then.
[2] Cf Num R. ii, 9
[3] Jast.: a town and district east of the Jordan.
[4] Y.T reverses the meaning. the fair of Batanea was the *least* idolatrous; but the parallel passage in Jer. 'A. Z *ad loc* proves the correctness of the translation adopted. Y.M.: only these three fairs may be visited on the Intermediate Days, as slaves are certain to be found there who may thus be initiated in Judaism. But slaves were not always procurable at other fairs, and therefore the Intermediate Days may not be desecrated.

CHAPTER XLVIII

VAYERA

1. AND THE LORD APPEARED UNTO HIM (XVIII, 1). It is written, *Thou hast also given me Thy shield of salvation, and Thy right hand hath holden me up, and Thy condescension hath made me great* (Ps. XVIII, 36). '*Thou hast also given me Thy shield of salvation*' alludes to Abraham[1]; '*And Thy right hand hath holden me up*'—in the fiery furnace, in famine, and in [my battle with] the kings; '*And Thy condescension hath made me great*': with what condescension did the Lord make Abraham great? In that he sat while the *Shechinah* stood; thus it is written, AND THE LORD APPEARED UNTO HIM . . . AS HE SAT.[2]

2. *And when after my skin this is destroyed* (nikkefu), *then through my flesh shall I see God* (Job XIX, 26). Abraham said: After I circumcised myself,[3] many proselytes came to attach themselves to this sign [of the covenant].[4] '*Then through my flesh shall I see God*': had I not done so, why should God have revealed Himself to me?[5] Therefore, AND THE LORD APPEARED UNTO HIM.

3. R. Issi commenced his discourse thus: *If I did despise the cause of my manservant, or of my maidservant, when they contended with me—what then shall I do when God riseth up? and when He remembereth, what shall I answer Him* (ib. XXXI, 13)? R. Issi's wife quarrelled with her maidservant, whereupon he gave her [his wife] the lie[6] in her presence. 'Why do you give me the lie before my own servant?' she complained. He replied: 'Did not Job say,

[1] Radal and Rash.: as it is written, *I am thy shield* (Gen. XV, 1).
[2] God did not permit him to rise on account of his age and the weakness caused by circumcision. [3] Translating: and after I removed my foreskin.
[4] Deriving *nikkefu* from *hikkif*, to surround, i.e. proselytes flocked, surrounding him, as it were.
[5] Hence through circumcision performed on my flesh shall I see God.
[6] He denied that his wife was in the right.

"If I did despise the cause of my manservant . . . what then shall I do when God riseth up? and when He remembereth, what shall I answer Him?"' Another interpretation: '*If I did despise the cause of my manservant*' alludes to Abraham, as it says, *And Abraham took Ishmael his son . . . and circumcised them* (Gen. XVII, 23).[1] Said he: 'Had I not done so, why should God have revealed Himself to me?'[2] Consequently, AND THE LORD APPEARED UNTO HIM, etc.

4. R. Isaac commenced thus: *An altar of earth thou shalt make unto Me* . . . [then] *I will come unto thee and bless thee* (Ex. XX, 21). Said R. Isaac: If I reveal myself to bless him who built an altar in My name, how much the more to Abraham who circumcised himself for My sake! Consequently, AND THE LORD APPEARED UNTO HIM, etc.

5. R. Levi commenced: *And* [take] *an ox and a ram for peace-offerings . . . for to-day the Lord appeareth unto you* (Lev. IX, 4). [God] said: 'If I reveal Myself to and bless him who sacrificed an ox and a ram for My sake, how much the more to Abraham, who circumcised himself for My sake!' Consequently, AND THE LORD APPEARED UNTO HIM, etc.

6. It is written, *The sinners in Zion are afraid* (Isa. XXXIII, 14). R Jeremiah b. Eleazar said: This may be illustrated by two children who ran away from school: when one is punished the other trembles.[3] R. Jonathan said: Whenever *hanufah* occurs in Scripture, it refers to heresy,[4] and the *locus classicus* for all cases is the verse, '*The sinners in Zion are afraid,*' *trembling hath seized the ungodly* (ha-ḥanefim). R. Judah b. R. Simon said: This may be illustrated by a robber chief who revolted against

[1] He did not despise the rights of his servants, but circumcised them too, this being a 'right' (privilege). [2] Translating: If I did despise, etc., what could I do that God should honour me by standing before me? [3] Similarly, when God punishes the heathens, the sinners in Zion are afraid. [4] *Hanufah* is generally translated hypocrisy, but it also means godlessness, faithlessness.

the king, and the king announced, 'I will give preferment to any man who captures him.' A man arose and caught him, and the king ordered them both to be guarded until morning. One was filled with anxiety, thinking what preferment the king would give him. The other was filled with anxiety, thinking what punishment the king would pronounce upon him. Thus, in the Messianic future Israel shall fear, viz. *And they shall come in fear unto the Lord and to His goodness* (Hos. III, 5); and the Gentiles will fear: '*The sinners in Zion are afraid.*' R. Judah b. R. Simon said: Why are they called *Everlasting burnings* (Isa. *loc. cit.*)? Because if they were given free passage they would burn up the whole world.

He that walketh righteously (*ib.* 15) alludes to Abraham, as it is written, *To the end that he* [sc. Abraham] *may command his children . . . that they may keep the way of the Lord to do righteousness and justice* (Gen. XVIII, 19). *And speaketh uprightly* (Isa. *loc. cit.*), as it is written, *The upright ones do love thee* (S.S. I, 4)[1] *He that despiseth the gain of oppressions* (*ib.*), as it says, *I will not take a thread or a shoe latchet* (Gen. XIV, 23). *That shaketh his hands from holding of bribes* (Isa. *loc. cit.*). *I have lifted up my hand unto the Lord, God Most High* (Gen. XIV, 22). *He shall dwell on high* (Isa. XXXIII, 16): R. Judah b. R. Simon and R. Ḥanin in R. Joḥanan's name said: He lifted him [sc. Abraham] up above the vault of heaven; hence He said to him, *Look now* (habbeṭ) *at heaven* (Gen. XV, 5): '*habbeṭ*' is applicable only when one looks downward from above.[2] *His place of defence shall be the munitions of rocks* (Isa. *loc. cit.*): this alludes to the clouds of Glory.[3] *His bread shall be given* (*ib.*)—*And I will fetch a morsel of bread* (Gen. XVIII, 4).—*His waters shall be sure* (Isa. *loc. cit.*).—*Let now a little water be fetched* (Gen. *loc. cit.*). *Thine eyes shall see the King in his beauty* (Isa. XXXIII, 17).—AND THE LORD APPEARED UNTO HIM.

[1] E.V. '*Sincerely do they love thee*'. In S.S.R. *ad loc.* this verse is applied to the Patriarchs. [2] Cf. *supra*, XLIV, 12
[3] Which frequented Abraham's home; cf. *infra*, LX, 16.

7. AS HE SAT (YOSHEB) IN THE TENT DOOR IN THE HEAT OF THE DAY. R. Berekiah said in R. Levi's name: This is written *yashab* (he sat)[1]: he wished to rise, but God said to him: 'Sit, and thou art a token to thy children: as thou sittest while the *Shechinah* is standing, so will thy children sit and the *Shechinah* stand,' as it says, *God standeth* (nizzab) *in the congregation of God* (Ps LXXXII, 1).[2] R. Haggai said in the name of R. Isaac: Not '*omed* (standing) is written here but '*nizzab*' (stationed at his post), which means ready, as you read, *And thou shalt be stationed* (nizzabta) *upon the rock* (Ex. XXXIII, 21).[3] R. Samuel b R. Ḥiyya and R. Judan in R. Ḥanina's name said: Every time that Israel praise the Holy One, blessed be He, He causes His *Shechinah* to rest upon them. What is the proof? *Yet Thou art holy, O Thou that art enthroned upon the praises of Israel* (Ps. XXII, 4).[4]

8. IN THE TENT DOOR. [God said to him]: 'Thou hast opened a good door for travellers; thou hast opened a good door to proselytes, for if not for thee I had not created heaven and earth,' as it says, *He spreadeth them out as a tent to dwell in* (Isa. XL, 22).[5] Again, but for thee I had not created the orb of the sun, as it says, *In them hath He set a tent for the sun* (Ps. XIX, 5) But for thee I had not created the moon, as it says, *Behold, even for the moon He doth not set a tent*—ya'ahil (Job XXV, 5).[6]

R. Levi said: In the Hereafter Abraham will sit at the entrance to Gehenna, and permit no circumcised Israelite to descend therein. What then will he do to those who have sinned very much? He will remove the foreskin from babes who died before circumcision and set it upon them

[1] I e it is written defectively ישב, instead of יושב, and accordingly it can be punctuated יָשַׁב.

[2] Cur. edd. add.: That is when Israel enter their synagogues and houses of study and recite the *shema'*, and thus they sit in My honour.

[3] Ready—to see God's glory E.V. '*And thou shalt stand*' God stands ready in the congregation of God—to answer Israel's prayers.

[4] Cf S.S R. I, 9, § 2, for the whole passage

[5] The statement is suggested by the use of the word *tent* in both verses.

[6] This derives *ya'ahil* from *ohel*, a tent E.V. '*Behold, even the moon hath no brightness*'. Mah. retains E.V.

[the sinners], and then let them descend into Gehenna; hence it is written, *He hath sent forth his hands to those that were whole*[1]; *he hath profaned his covenant.*[2] IN THE HEAT OF THE DAY: [this is an allusion to the time] when that day will come of which it is written, *For, behold, the day cometh, it burneth as a furnace* (Mal. III, 19).[3]

IN THE HEAT OF THE DAY. R. Ishmael taught: *And as the sun waxed hot, it melted* (Ex. XVI, 21) means at four hours.[4] You say, at four hours; yet perhaps that is not so, and it means at six hours? When it says, IN THE HEAT OF THE DAY, that must refer to six hours. Yet perhaps it is the reverse? At four hours it is cool in the shade and hot in the sun, whereas at six hours both the sun and the shade are equally hot.[5] R. Tanḥuma said: [IN THE HEAT OF THE DAY] means when people cannot find shade beneath it [the sun].[6]

R. Jannai said: The Holy One, blessed be He, made a hole in Gehenna, making the whole world intolerably hot to its inhabitants for a short while. 'Shall the righteous,' He said, 'be in pain while the whole world is at ease!' [That is the implication of] IN THE HEAT OF THE DAY.[7] From this it follows that heat is beneficial to a wound.

9. He [Abraham] complained: 'Before I was circumcised travellers used to visit me; now that I am circumcised, perhaps they will no longer visit me?' Said the Holy One, blessed be He, to him: 'Hitherto uncircumcised mortals visited thee; but now I and My retinue will appear to thee. Thus it is written, AND HE LIFTED UP HIS EYES AND LOOKED (XVIII, 2)—he saw the *Shechinah* and saw the angels.

[1] Sc the circumcised wicked. E.V. '*Against them that were at peace with him*'. [2] I.e. put an uncircumcised foreskin upon the wicked.
[3] This interpretation is presumably the basis of R. Levi's teaching here
[4] About 10 a.m.
[5] IN THE HEAT OF THE DAY implies that it was hot everywhere, that condition is fulfilled at noon. But *And as the sun waxed hot* indicates that it was hot only in the sun, but not in the shade.
[6] I.e. at midday or just after.
[7] Rashi in the Bible *ad loc* gives a different reason: so that travellers might pause to rest, and not be a burden on Abraham's hospitality.

R. Ḥanina said: The names of the months came up with us from Babylon. R. Simeon b. Laḳish said: Also the names of the angels, Michael, Rafael, and Gabriel R. Levi said: One appeared to him in the guise of a Saracen, the second in the guise of a Nabatean, and the third in the guise of an Arab.[1] Said he [Abraham]: 'If I see that the *Shechinah* waits for them, I will know that they are worthy; and if I see that they pay respect to each other, I will know that they are distinguished.' And when he did see them pay respect to each other, he knew that they were distinguished.

R. Abbahu said: The tent of the Patriarch Abraham opened at both sides R. Judan said: It was like a double-gated passage.[2] Said he: 'If I see them turn aside, I will know that they are coming to me.' When he saw them turn aside, immediately HE RAN TO MEET THEM.

10. AND SAID: MY LORD, IF NOW I HAVE FOUND FAVOUR IN THY SIGHT (XVIII, 3). R. Ḥiyya taught: He said this to the greatest of them, viz. Michael. LET NOW A LITTLE WATER BE FETCHED (XVIII, 4). God said to Abraham, 'Thou hast said, LET NOW A LITTLE WATER BE FETCHED. I swear that I will repay thy children (in the wilderness, in inhabited country [the Land—Eretz Israel], and in the Messianic future).'[3] Thus it is written, *Then sang Israel this song! Spring up, O well—sing ye unto it* (Num. XXI, 7)—that was in the wilderness. Where do we find it in the Land [sc. Eretz Israel]? *A land of brooks of water* (Deut. VIII, 7). And in the Messianic future? *And it shall come to pass in that day, that living waters shall go out from Jerusalem* (Zech. XIV, 8). 'Thou hast said: AND WASH YOUR FEET: I swear to thee that I will repay thy children.' *Then washed I thee in water* (Ezek. XVI, 9) refers to the wilderness. In the Land?[4] *Wash you, make you clean* (Isa. I, 16). In the Messianic

[1] Commentaries in cur. edd. translate: a baker, a master mariner, and an Arab (probably a Bedouin).
[2] The rendering is conjectural
[3] Bracketed passage added from cur. edd.
[4] Sc. Palestine; or perhaps here: in a civilised country.

future? *When the Lord shall have washed away the filth of the daughters of Zion* (*ib.* IV, 4). 'Thou hast said: AND RECLINE YOURSELVES UNDER THE TREE: by thy life, I will repay thy children.' *He spread a cloud for a screen* (Ps. CV, 39)—that was in the wilderness. In the Land? *Ye shall dwell in booths seven days* (Lev. XXIII, 42). In the Messianic future? *And there shall be a pavilion for a shadow in the day-time from the heat* (Isa. IV, 6). 'Thou didst say, AND I WILL FETCH A MORSEL OF BREAD (XVIII, 5): I swear that I will repay thy children.' Thus: *Behold, I will cause to rain bread from heaven for you* (Ex. XVI, 4)—that is in the wilderness. In the Land? *A land of wheat and barley*, etc. (Deut. VIII, 8). In the Messianic future? *He will be as a rich cornfield in the land* (Ps. LXXII, 16). 'Again, thou didst run after the herd: I swear that I will repay thy children.' Thus: *And there went forth a wind from the Lord, and brought across quails from the sea* (Num. XI, 27),[1] that is in the wilderness. In the Land? *Now the children of Reuben and the children of Gad had a very great multitude of cattle* (*ib.* XXXII, 1).[2] In the Messianic future? *And it shall come to pass in that day, that a man shall rear a young cow, and two sheep* (Isa. VII, 21). As a reward for AND HE STOOD BY THEM (XVIII, 8), *And the Lord went before them* (Ex. XIII, 21)—there you have the wilderness. In the Land? *God standeth in the congregation of God* (Ps LXXXII, 1). In the Messianic future? *The breaker is gone up, before them . . . and the Lord at the head of them* (Mic. II, 13).

11. AND I WILL FETCH A MORSEL OF BREAD, AND STAY YE YOUR HEART (XVIII, 5). R. Isaac said: In the Torah [i.e. the Pentateuch], the Prophets, and the Writings we find that bread strengthens the heart. In the Torah: AND I WILL FETCH A MORSEL OF BREAD, AND STAY YE YOUR HEART. In the Prophets: *Stay thy*

[1] This verse is not really appropriate, since it refers to *punishment*. It is merely quoted to prove that the quails came from God, while the verse treating of quails as a *reward* is in Ex XVI, 13: *And it came to pass in the evening, that the quails came up*. [2] In Transjordania, where they received their territory instead of on the west of the Jordan.

heart with a morsel of bread (Judg. XIX, 5). In the Writings: *And bread that stayeth man's heart* (Ps. CIV, 15).

R. Aha said: It is not written, 'And stay *le-babekem*,' but '*And stay* libkem' (*your heart*).[1] This proves that the Tempter has no power over angels.[2] That is R. Ḥiyya's view too, for R. Ḥiyya said: It is not written, 'Turn *lebabekem* (your hearts) to the dance,' but, *Turn* libekem (*your hearts*) *to the dance* (Ps. XLVIII, 17).[3] This proves that the Tempter will have no sway in the Messianic future.

SINCE FOR THIS PURPOSE YE ARE COME TO YOUR SERVANT. R. Joshua b. R. Nehemiah said: [Abraham urged:] Since the day when the Holy One, blessed be He, created you ye were destined to come to me. SINCE FOR THIS PURPOSE (KI 'AL KEN) YE ARE COME: [KEN has the same meaning here as in the verse] *So* (ken) *be the Lord with you* (Ex. X, 10).[4]

AND THEY SAID: SO DO THOU, AS THOU HAST SAID. 'As for us,' said they, 'we neither eat nor drink; but thou who dost eat and drink, SO DO THOU, AS THOU HAST SAID, and may this day be repeated in honour of the son [that will be born to thee].'[5]

12. AND ABRAHAM HASTENED INTO THE TENT UNTO SARAH, AND SAID: MAKE READY QUICKLY THREE MEASURES OF FINE MEAL (XVIII, 6). R. Abiathar said: She baked nine measures in all, three of cakes, three of *ḥabiẓ*,[6] and three of pastries.[7] KNEAD

[1] The shorter form לבכם is used, and he regards this as a limitation.

[2] Hence their hearts were all as one—to do good—and they did not have two hearts, as it were, one to do good and the other to do evil

[3] E.V. '*Mark ye well her ramparts*'—le-ḥelah. The Rabbis, however, read it *le-ḥolah*, which they derive from *meḥol*, a dance, and interpret it as referring to the life of happiness, as a dance, which the righteous will enjoy in the Messianic future.

[4] I.e. ye are come so—for this purpose.

[5] Then too you will have an opportunity of displaying hospitality to guests. Th Mah. and Rash.· this is deduced from the word תעשה, which is imperfect, lit. 'so *wilt* thou do—on a future occasion'.

[6] Jast.: a dish of flour, honey and oil beaten into a pulp

[7] The Heb is *ḳemah soleth* (E.V. '*fine meal*'). Actually *kemah* denotes a coarse flour, and so R Abiathar maintains that separate confections were made from *ḳemaḥ* and *soleth* respectively, while 'three measures' denotes yet other kinds of pastries.

IT, AND MAKE CAKES ('UGOTH).[1] It was the season of Passover.[2] R. Jonah and R. Levi in the name of R. Ḥama b. R. Ḥanina said: The wilderness of Sin and the wilderness of Alush[3] are one and the same. [The change of name to Alush teaches this]: On account of whose merit were Israel privileged to have the manna given to them? On account of [the merit of Abraham who said]: LUSHI (KNEAD IT), AND MAKE CAKES.[4]

13. AND ABRAHAM RAN UNTO THE HERD (XVIII, 7). R. Levi said: He ran to anticipate the people of whom it is written, *Ephraim is a heifer well broken, that loveth to thresh* (Hos. X, 11).[5]

AND FETCHED A CALF. You might think that it was full-grown[6]; therefore TENDER is stated.[7] If TENDER, you might think that it was lacking [in flavour][8]; therefore AND GOOD is stated. AND GAVE IT UNTO THE LAD: this was Ishmael, [Abraham's] purpose being to train him in good deeds.

14. AND HE TOOK BUTTER, AND MILK (XVIII, 8). R. Ḥanina said: Best [butter] is made from a hundredth part of the milk[9]; medium quality is from a fortieth part; while inferior [butter] is from a twentieth. Now where was the bread?[10] Ephraim Miḳsha'ah,[11] a disciple of R. Meir, said in R. Meir's name: Sarah became menstruous and the dough was defiled. The Rabbis said: He certainly brought

[1] '*Ugoth*' are thin wafers, in the form in which unleavened bread is baked, and the Rabbis understood it to mean unleavened cakes.
[2] Or, Passover eve, פרס meaning half—i.e. the second half of the day preceding Passover (Y.T.). [3] V. Num. XXXIII, 13.
[4] By a play on words Alush is derived from *lushi*. The manna was given to Israel in the wilderness of Sin (v. Ex XVI).
[5] 'Rashi': he ran to prepare atonement in anticipation for Ephraim.
[6] The Heb. בן בקר might mean a member of the herd, not necessarily a calf. [7] Heb. רך, which refers to the young
[8] So young that the flesh had not yet developed its proper taste.
[9] I.e from the creamiest part of its cream.
[10] It is not mentioned that he did actually give them bread.
[11] A nickname meaning one who was fond of raising difficulties. Others a cucumber merchant.

them bread too, for if he brought them what he had not offered,[1] how much more what he had offered![2]

AND HE STOOD OVER THEM. But earlier you read, *Three men stood over him* (Gen. XVIII, 2)? The explanation is this: before they had performed their mission, '*They stood over him*'[3]; but when they had performed their mission, HE STOOD OVER THEM: he inspired them with fear, and so he stood over them,[4] Michael trembled and Gabriel trembled. R. Tanhuma in R. Eleazar's name and R. Abun in R. Meir's name said: The proverb runs, 'When in Rome, do as Rome does.'[5] Above [in the celestial sphere] there is no eating and drinking; hence when Moses ascended on high he appeared like them [the angels], as it says, *Then I abode in the mount forty days and forty nights; I did neither eat bread nor drink water* (Deut. IX, 9). But below, where there is eating and drinking, we find, AND HE STOOD BY THEM UNDER THE TREE, AND THEY DID EAT. Did they then eat? They pretended to eat, removing each course in turn.

15. AND THEY SAID UNTO HIM (ELAW): WHERE IS SARAH THY WIFE (XVIII, 9)? The *alef*, *yod*, and *waw* are dotted, but the *lamed* is not dotted.[6] R. Simeon b. Eleazar said: Wherever you find the plain writing exceeding the dotted letters, you must interpret the plain writing; if the dotted letters exceed the plain writing, you must interpret the dotted letters. Here that the dotted letters exceed the undotted, you must interpret the dotted text. Thus, [the angels asked Sarah,] 'Where is he—Abraham?'[7] R. 'Azariah said: Just as they said to Abraham, 'WHERE IS SARAH,' so they said to Sarah, 'Where is Abraham?' AND HE SAID: BEHOLD, IN THE TENT. Thus it is

[1] Sc. milk and (butter) curd.
[2] Therefore the mention of it is omitted as superfluous.
[3] As though his superiors.
[4] Now that they had nothing more to do, he became their superior.
[5] Lit., 'when you enter a town, follow its customs'.
[6] The word אליו in this passage is traditionally written אֹלֹיֹו.
[7] The three dotted letters read איו, where is he. The question is probably meant in the sense of 'how is he?' and was asked as a matter of politeness, cf. B.M 87*a*.

written, *Blessed above women shall Jael be, the wife of Heber the Kenite, above women in the tent shall she be blessed* (Judg. v, 24) R. Eleazar said: It means, above the women of the generation of the wilderness. They gave birth to children, yet but for her [Jael] they [the children] would have been destroyed.[1] R. Samuel b. Nahman said: Above the Matriarchs. They gave birth to children, yet but for her they would have been destroyed.

16. AND HE SAID: I WILL CERTAINLY RETURN UNTO THEE WHEN THE SEASON COMETH ROUND . . . AND SARAH HEARD IN THE TENT DOOR, AND HE WAS BEHIND HIM (XVIII, 10). This refers to Ishmael: AND HE WAS BEHIND HIM, so that they [the angel and Sarah] should not be alone. Another interpretation[2]: AND HE WAS BEHIND HIM: she understood that the guest had come.[3]

NOW ABRAHAM AND SARAH WERE OLD (XVIII, 11). R. Joḥanan said: Since it is now written, NOW ABRAHAM AND SARAH WERE OLD, why is it again written, *Now Abraham was old* (Gen. XXIV, 1)?[4] The reason is because the Holy One, blessed be He, restored him to the days of his youth, therefore, '*And Abraham was old*' must then be written a second time. R. Ammi said: Here old age combined with virility is meant, while further on it means old age without virility.

IT HAD CEASED (ḤADAL) TO BE WITH SARAH AFTER THE MANNER OF WOMEN. [ḤADAL means], it had forborne, as in the verse, *But if thou shalt forbear* (te-ḥedal) *to vow* (Deut. XXIII, 23). Or, it had ceased; as in the verse, *And forbeareth* (we-ḥadal) *to keep the passover* (Num. IX, 13).[5]

[1] By Sisera. [2] This is the reading in M.K.
[3] Th : Presumably he reads *we-hi*, and *she* was behind him. She understood that Abraham had ordered the preparations for guests, and so she stood behind him to hear what they would say
[4] The second verse refers to a later period
[5] The translation follows Th We have here two renderings of '*ḥadal*': (i) it had forborne or refrained—i.e. her menses were now irregular; and (ii) they had altogether ceased.

17. AND SARAH LAUGHED WITHIN HERSELF (BE-ḲIRBAH), SAYING (XVIII, 12). This is one of the texts which they amended for King Ptolemy, reading it, AND SARAH LAUGHED before her relatives (*bi-ḳero-behah*), SAYING . . .[1] AFTER I AM WAXED OLD, I SHALL HAVE 'EDNAH [E.V. 'PLEASURE']. She said thus: 'As long as a woman is young she has finery, whereas AFTER I AM WAXED OLD, I SHALL HAVE 'EDNAH, that means finery, as in the verse, *I decked thee also with ornaments*—'edi (Ezek. XVI, 11). A woman, as long as she is young, has her regular periods, while AFTER I AM WAXED OLD, I SHALL HAVE 'EDNAH, i.e. menses.[2] The fact, however, is that MY LORD IS OLD.' Rab Judah said: He is virile, yet impotent. R. Judah b R Simon said: [The Holy One, blessed be He, said:] 'Ye declare yourselves young and your companions old,[3] yet I AM TOO OLD (XVIII, 13) to perform miracles!'[4]

18. AND THE LORD SAID UNTO ABRAHAM: WHEREFORE DID SARAH LAUGH, SAYING . . . SEEING THAT I AM OLD (XVIII, 13). Bar Ḳappara said: Great is peace, for even Scripture made a mis-statement in order to preserve peace between Abraham and Sarah. Thus, it is written, WHEREFORE DID SARAH LAUGH, SAYING: SHALL I OF A SURETY BEAR A CHILD? It does not say, '*Since* my lord *is old*,' but SEEING THAT *I* AM OLD.

19. IS ANYTHING TOO HARD FOR THE LORD (XVIII, 14). R. Judah said in the name of R. Judan b. R. Simon: This may be compared to a man who had in his hand

[1] V *supra*, p 61, n. 1. Rashi in Meg. 9*a*. they amended the text so that Ptolemy might understand that God was angry with Sarah because she had *publicly* laughed at the promise, whereas Abraham had laughed to himself (v. XVII, 17).
[2] According to this, she stated that she *would* become young.
[3] I.e even Sarah ridiculed the promise on account of *Abraham's* age, thus implying that she herself was young enough.
[4] This takes the AND I AM OLD in v. 13 to refer to God, spoken as a reproof.

two parts of a lock[1] and went to a smith and asked him: 'Can you repair these?' 'I can make them from the outset,' he replied, 'and you think that I cannot repair them!' So here, [God said], 'I can create man from the beginning, yet [you would say that] I cannot restore them to their youth!'

20. THEN SARAH DENIED, SAYING: I LAUGHED NOT, etc. R Judah b. R. Simon and R. Johanan in the name of R. Simeon b. Eleazar said: The Holy One, blessed be He, never condescended to converse with a woman save with that righteous woman [viz. Sarah], and that too was through a particular cause. R. Abba b. Kahana said in R. Biryi's name: And what a roundabout way He sought in order to speak with her, as it is written, AND HE SAID: NAY, BUT THOU DIDST LAUGH. But it is written, *And she* [Hagar] *called the name of the Lord that spoke unto her*, etc. (Gen XVI, 13)? Said R. Joshua in R. Nehemiah's name in R. Idi's name: That was through an angel. But it is written, *And the Lord said unto her*—Rebekah (*ib.* XXV, 23)? R. Levi said in the name of R. Ḥama b. R. Ḥanina: That was through an angel. R. Leazar said in the name of R Jose b. Zimra: That was through the medium of Shem.[2]

AND THE MEN ROSE UP FROM THENCE, AND LOOKED OUT TOWARD SODOM; AND ABRAHAM WENT WITH THEM TO BRING THEM ON THE WAY (XVIII, 16). So runs the proverb: 'When you have given your guest food and drink, escort him.' Hence, AND ABRAHAM WENT WITH THEM TO BRING THEM ON THE WAY.

[1] Or, two parts of a chain (Th.). [2] *Supra*, xx, 6.

CHAPTER XLIX (VAYERA)

1. AND THE LORD SAID: SHALL I HIDE FROM ABRAHAM (XVIII, 17)? R. Isaac commenced his discourse thus: *The memory of the righteous shall be for a blessing* (Prov. x, 7). Said R. Isaac: If one makes mention of a righteous man and does not bless him, he violates a positive command. What is the proof? '*The memory of the righteous shall be for a blessing.*' While he who mentions a wicked man and does not curse him also violates a positive command. What is the reason? *But the name of the wicked shall rot* (*ib.*). R. Samuel b. Naḥman said: The names of the wicked are like weaving implements, as long as you use them, they remain taut, if you lay them aside, they slacken Thus, have you ever heard a man call his son Pharaoh, Sisera, or Sennacherib? No: he calls him Abraham, Isaac, Jacob, Reuben, or Simeon, Levi or Judah.[1] Rab [whenever he mentioned Haman] would say, 'Cursed be Haman and his children.' R. Phinehas said: One must say, 'Harbonah, be he remembered for good.'[2]

R. Samuel b. Naḥman said: We find that when the Holy One, blessed be He, mentions Israel by name, He blesses them, as it says, *The Lord hath been mindful of us, He will bless . . . the house of Israel* (Ps. cxv, 12). R. Huna said in the name of R. Aḥa: I know this only of six hundred thousand.[3] How do we know that the Lord blesses every single Israelite when He mentions his name? Because it says: AND THE LORD SAID: SHALL I HIDE FROM ABRAHAM THAT WHICH I AM DOING; AND ABRAHAM

[1] Cur. edd. add. R. Berekiah, R. Ḥelbo in the name of R. Samuel b Naḥman and R. Jonathan, when they came to the verse, *Who had been carried away from Jerusalem with the captives . . . whom Nebuchadnezzar . . . had carried away* (Est. II, 6) would exclaim, 'Nebuchadnezzar, rot his bones!' Then why did they not say this (when they read his name) in the Book of Jeremiah? Because whenever Nebuchadnezzar occurs in Jeremiah he was yet alive; whereas here (in the book of Esther) he was already dead.

[2] V. Est. VII, 9. Text as emended according to Jer. Meg III *ad fin.*

[3] I e. God blesses Israel when He mentions the *whole* nation.

SHALL SURELY BECOME A GREAT AND MIGHTY NATION. Now Scripture need merely have said, *And the Lord said: Verily, the cry of Sodom and Gomorrah is great* (Gen. XVIII, 20), but the Holy One, blessed be He, said: 'Having made mention of this righteous man, shall I not bless him?' Hence, AND ABRAHAM SHALL SURELY BECOME A GREAT AND MIGHTY NATION.

2. It is written, *The secret* [E.V. '*counsel*'] *of the Lord is with them that fear Him and His covenant, to make them know it* (Ps. XXV, 14) [1]

Another interpretation: '*The secret of the Lord is with them that fear Him.*' At first the secret of the Lord was

[1] Cur. edd. add: Now what is the secret of the Lord? Circumcision, which He did not reveal until twenty generations after Noah, i.e. until Abraham arose and He gave it to him, as it says, *And I will give* [E.V '*establish*'] *My covenant between Me and thee* (Gen XVII, 7) [Radal *Between Me and thee* implies that it was in the nature of a secret which remains as it were between two] Now God said to him · 'If thou wilt circumcise thyself, thou wilt receive the secret (*sod*) of the Lord.' What is the secret (*sod*) of the Lord? *Samech* stands for sixty, *waw* for six, and *daleth* for four [that is the Hebrew spelling of *sod* (סוד)], making seventy in all [Thus God said] 'In the merit of circumcision I will cause seventy people to spring from thee, as it says, *Thy fathers went down into Egypt with threescore and ten persons* (Deut. X, 22). From them I will set up seventy elders, as it says, *Gather unto Me seventy men of the elders of Israel* (Num. XI, 16) From them I will raise up Moses, who will study the Torah in seventy languages,' as it says, *Moses took upon him to clarify* [E.V. '*expound*'] *this law* (Deut. I, 4). [By '*clarify*' the Rabbis understood that it was to be intelligible to all peoples, hence it must have been explained in all languages.] For the merit of what was all this? For the merit of circumcision, as it says, *The secret of the Lord is with them that fear Him, and His covenant* ['*Covenant*' was often understood to refer to circumcision.] The Holy One, blessed be He, said to Abraham: 'It is sufficient for a servant to be like his master.' [Mah. holds that this is out of place here. Some commentators attempt to fit it in, but not very plausibly.] Then Abraham said to Him. 'And who shall circumcise me?' 'Thyself,' He replied Abraham took a knife forthwith and held his foreskin and was about to cut it, yet he was afraid, being an old man. What did the Lord do? He put forth His hand and held it with him, whilst Abraham cut For it says, *Thou art the Lord God, who didst choose Abram* . . *and didst cut* [E V '*madest*'] *a covenant with him* (Neh. IX, 7 f.) Now it is not written, 'and didst cut a covenant *for* him,' but '*And didst cut a covenant* with *him*', which teaches that the Lord held [the foreskin] with him

with them that feared Him; later it was with the upright,[1] as it is written, *But His secret is with the upright* (Prov. III, 32); and finally with the prophets, as it says, *For the Lord God will do nothing, but He revealeth His secret unto His servants the prophets* (Amos III, 7). Now the Holy One, blessed be He, said: 'This Abraham is God-fearing,' as it says, *Now I know that thou art a God-fearing man* (Gen. XXII, 12); 'this Abraham is upright,' as it says, *The upright love thee* (S.S. I, 4)[2]; 'this Abraham is a prophet,' as it says, *Now therefore restore the man's wife, for he is a prophet* (Gen. XX, 7): 'shall I then not reveal it to him?'[3] Hence, AND THE LORD SAID: SHALL I HIDE FROM ABRAHAM, etc.

AND THE LORD SAID: SHALL I HIDE FROM ABRAHAM THAT WHICH I AM DOING, etc. R. Joshua b. Levi said: It is like a king who presented an estate to his friend and subsequently wished to cut down five non-fruit-bearing trees from it. Said the king: 'Had I wanted [to cut them] down even from his patrimony, he would certainly not refuse me: what then can I lose?[4] And so he consulted him about it. Similarly, the Holy One, blessed be He, said: 'I have already made a gift of this land to Abraham,' as it says, *Unto thy seed have I given this land* (*ib.* XV, 18). 'Now these five towns[5] were indeed in My territory; yet if I desired them even of his ancestral heritage he would not refuse Me: what then does it matter [if I ask him]? And so He consulted him. R. Judah b. R. Simon said: This may be compared to a king who had three friends without whose consent he did nothing. But on one occasion he desired to do something without their consent. Whereupon he evicted one from the palace,

[1] Heb. ישרים: from the context these appear to be of a higher spiritual level. [2] E.V. '*Sincerely do they love thee*' The verse is referred to Abraham; v. *supra*, XLVIII, 6; S.S. R. I, 4

[3] Sc. the impending destruction of Sodom and Gomorrah.

[4] Lit. 'what is in it'—if I ask him first

[5] Which I am to destroy, viz. Sodom and Gomorrah, Admah, Zeboiim, and Lasha, mentioned in X, 19. According to tradition all five were destroyed. They are likened to non-fruit-bearing trees, because they produced nothing good.

the second he put in prison, affixing his seal on it [the prison door]. But as for the third, whom he loved exceedingly, he said, 'I cannot do anything without his consent.' Similarly, Adam—*So He drove out the man* (Gen. III, 24); Noah—*And the Lord shut him in* (ib. VII, 16). But as He loved Abraham so much He said, 'I will do nothing without his consent.' R. Samuel b. Naḥman said: It may be compared to a king who had an adviser without whose consent He did nothing. On one occasion, however, he wished to do something without his consent, whereupon he observed: 'Surely I made him my adviser for no other reason than that I should do nothing without his consent.' R. Judan said: The Holy One, blessed be He, said thus: 'Did I designate him *The man of My counsel* (Isa. XLVI, 11) for any other reason than that I should do nothing without his consent? With them [the Sodomites] is Lot, his brother's son, yet I am not to reveal it to him [Abraham]!' The Rabbis said: I have already called him their father, as it says, *For the father of a multitude of nations have I made thee* (Gen XVII, 5): does one judge the son without the father's knowledge? Gehenna I have revealed to him: the giving of the Torah I have revealed to him; shall I not reveal to him Sodom's judgment![1]

R. Aḥa said in R. Alexandri's name, and R. Samuel b. Naḥman said in R. Nathan's name: Abraham knew even the laws of the *'erub* of courtyards.[2] R Phinehas, R. Ḥelkiah, and R. Simon in the name of R. Samuel said: Abraham even knew the new name which the Holy One, blessed be He, will one day give to Jerusalem, as it says, *At that time they shall call Jerusalem, The Throne of God* (Jer. III, 17). R. Berekiah, R. Ḥiyya, and the Rabbis of that country [Babylonia] in R. Judah's name said: Not a day passes in which the Holy One, blessed be He, does not teach a new law (*halachah*) in the heavenly Court. What is the proof? *Hear attentively the noise of His voice,*

[1] Cf. *supra*, XLIV, 21

[2] This and the following sentences are out of place, and belong to XXVI, 5: *Because that . . Abraham kept . . My laws*—hence the comments on Abraham's knowledge of God's laws.

and the meditation that goeth out of His mouth (Job XXXVII, 2). Now '*meditation*' refers to nought but Torah, as in the verse, *But thou shalt meditate therein day and night* (Josh. I, 8). Even those laws Abraham knew.

3. SEEING THAT ABRAHAM SHALL SURELY BECOME—HAYOH YIHYEH (XVIII, 18). R. Tanḥum said in the name of R. Ḥus Elai[1] in R. Berekiah's name: He informed him that the world must never contain less than thirty righteous men like Abraham.[2] R. Judan and R. Aha in R. Alexandri's name deduced it from this verse: SEEING THAT ABRAHAM SHALL SURELY BECOME—HAYOH YIHYEH: *yod* is ten, *heh* five, *yod* ten, and *heh* five.[3]

4. FOR I HAVE KNOWN HIM, TO THE END THAT HE MAY COMMAND HIS CHILDREN AND HIS HOUSEHOLD AFTER HIM THAT THEY MAY KEEP THE WAY OF THE LORD, TO DO RIGHTEOUSNESS AND JUSTICE—ZEDAKAH U-MISHPAT (XVIII, 19). R. Aḥa said in R. Alexandri's name: This (*ẓedakah*) refers to his hospitality [to wayfarers].[4]—The Rabbis said: It refers to visiting the sick. R. 'Azariah said in R. Judah's name: First *ẓedakah* and then *mishpat* (justice): how is this to be understood?[5] Abraham used to receive wayfarers. After they had eaten and drunk he would say to them, 'Now recite Grace.' 'What shall we say?' they asked. 'Blessed be the God of the Universe of whose bounty we have partaken,' he replied. If one consented to recite grace, he would [be allowed to] eat, drink, and depart. But if one refused, he would demand, 'Pay me what you owe me.' 'Why, what do I owe you?' he would reply. 'One *xestes*[6] of wine costs ten *follera*,[7] a pound of meat

[1] A name not occurring elsewhere; nevertheless it appears to be correct, being found in several MSS. [2] Cf. *supra*, XXXV, 2.
[3] These are the letters of יהיה. [4] Cur edd. to the (provision of) the mourner's meal—which had to be provided by neighbours.
[5] '*Zedakah*' and '*mishpat*' were often regarded as antithetical, '*mishpat*' being an insistence on the strict letter of the law, while '*zedakah*' connotes a kindly forbearance.
[6] A measure, nearly a pint. [7] Jast: A small debased coin.

costs ten *follera*; a round of bread costs ten *follera*. Who will give you wine in the wilderness; who will give you meat in the wilderness; who will give you bread in the wilderness?' Seeing himself thus driven into a corner, he who would say, 'Blessed be the God of the Universe of whose bounty we have eaten.' Hence ẒEDAKAH is written first and then MISHPAT.

TO THE END THAT THE LORD MAY BRING UPON ABRAHAM, etc. R. Simeon b. Yoḥai taught: He who leaves a son toiling in the Torah is as though he had not died. What is the proof?—The verse, TO THE END THAT THE LORD MAY BRING UPON ABRAHAM THAT WHICH HE HATH SPOKEN OF HIM. It does not say simply, THAT WHICH HE HATH SPOKEN, but THAT WHICH THE LORD HATH SPOKEN OF HIM.[1]

5. AND THE LORD SAID: VERILY, THE CRY OF SODOM AND GOMORRAH IS GREAT (XVIII, 20). R. Ḥanina interpreted: It waxed ever greater. R. Berekiah said in R. Johanan's name: We know that the generation of the Flood was punished by water, and the Sodomites by fire: whence do we know to apply what is stated here to the case above, and the reverse? Because 'great' is mentioned in both places, affording an analogy.[2]

6. I WILL GO DOWN NOW (XVIII, 21). R. Simeon b. Yoḥai taught: This is one of the ten descents mentioned in the Torah.[3] R. Abba b. Kahana said: This teaches that the Holy One, blessed be He, gave them the opportunity of repenting. For it says, I WILL GO DOWN NOW, AND SEE WHETHER THEY HAVE DONE ACCORDING TO THE CRY OF IT, THEN IT IS AN END[4]—they must be completely destroyed; AND IF NOT, I WILL KNOW, i.e. I will teach them that the Attribute of Justice exists in

[1] Implying that God's promises actually applied to Abraham himself. But of course Abraham died long before the land became his; hence he must still be regarded as alive, because his descendants are occupied in the study of the Torah. [2] V. *supra*, XXVII, 3.
[3] *Supra*, XXXVIII, 9 [4] E.V. . . '*have done altogether according*,' etc.

the world.[1] R. Levi said: [God said]: 'Even if I wished to keep silent, justice for a certain maiden (*ribah*) does not permit Me to keep silent.'[2] For it once happened that two damsels went down to draw water from a well. Said one to the other, 'Why are you so pale?' 'We have no more food left and are ready to die,' replied she. What did she do? She filled her pitcher with flour and they exchanged [their pitchers], each taking the other's. When they [the Sodomites] discovered this, they took and burnt her.[3] Said the Holy One, blessed be He: 'Even if I desired to be silent, justice for that maiden does not permit Me to keep silent.' Hence it does not say, WHETHER THEY HAVE DONE ACCORDING TO THEIR CRY; but ACCORDING TO *HER* CRY[4]—the cry of that maiden.

R. Jeremiah b. Eleazar said: The real prosperity of Sodom lasted fifty-two years only, and for twenty-five of these the Holy One, blessed be He, made the mountains to tremble and brought terrors upon them in order that they might reform, yet they did not. Hence it is written, *Who removeth the mountains, and they know it not, when He overturneth them in His anger* (Job IX, 5).

7. AND THE MEN TURNED (WAYYIFENU) FROM THENCE (XVIII, 22). This proves that angels have no back.[5] AND THEY WENT TOWARD SODOM; BUT ABRAHAM STOOD YET BEFORE THE LORD. R. Simon

[1] Rendering: AND IF NOT, they are not as evil now as the cry which has ascended to Me, I WILL KNOW how to punish them by suffering, thus vindicating the demands of justice for their past misdeeds, yet I will not utterly destroy them. Thus they were given an opportunity of repenting. This interpretation is adopted because otherwise it would appear that God, the omniscient, did not know whether they were evil or not, which is impossible (Mah.).

[2] By a play on words *rabbah*, great, is read *ribah*, a maiden, and the verse translated: The cry of Sodom and Gomorrah on account of the maiden.

[3] As they had strictly forbidden charity, cf. Sanh. 109 *a*, *b*.

[4] Lit. translation.

[5] M.K. and Y.T.: '*from thence*' is apparently superfluous, as it is obvious. Hence '*wayyifenu*' is connected with *panim*, face, and the verse translated: And the men went toward Sodom, yet their faces were still looking upon the place whence they came.

said: This is an emendation of the Soferim, for the *Shechinah* was actually waiting for Abraham.[1]

8. AND ABRAHAM DREW NEAR, AND SAID, etc. (XVIII, 23). R. Judah, R. Nehemiah, and the Rabbis each commented R. Judah said: He drew near for battle, as it says, *So Joab and the people that were with him drew nigh unto battle*, etc. (II Sam. X, 13). R. Nehemiah said: He drew near for conciliation, as in the verse, *Then the children of Judah drew nigh unto Joshua* (Josh. XIV, 6)—to effect a reconciliation. The Rabbis said: He drew nigh for prayer, as it says, *And it came to pass at the time of the offering of the evening offering, that Elijah the prophet came near, and said: O Lord, the God of Abraham, of Isaac, and of Israel, let it be known this day that Thou art God in Israel*, etc. (I Kings XVIII, 36).[2] R. Leazar said: Interpret it thus: I come, whether it be for battle, conciliation, or prayer. R. Phinehas, R. Levi, and R. Johanan, in the name of Menaḥem of Gallia,[3] said: When one passes before the Ark,[4] we do not say to him, 'Come and do,'[5] but 'Come and draw near', which means, Come and wage war for us, come and offer the public sacrifice [i.e. pray].[6] R. Tanḥuma said: Why did they institute that the fifteenth benediction should be 'who heareth prayer'?[7]—To correspond to the Divine Name which

[1] V. Ex. R. XLI, 4. The phrase, BUT ABRAHAM . . . LORD implies that he was still at the same place, which is incorrect, since he had accompanied the angels some distance. Hence it really means that the Lord was still standing before Abraham, since He is omnipresent, but as it would be derogatory to His honour to say that He was standing before Abraham, as an inferior before his superior, it is reversed Y.T. and Th.: this does not mean that the Soferim actually emended the Bible, but that it was originally written thus in such a way that it might loosely appear a Soferic emendation

[2] He drew near to do 'battle', i e argue with God, viz. *That be far from thee*, etc (v. 25); to conciliate: *Behold, now, I have taken upon me to speak unto the Lord*, etc. (v. 27); to pray: *Peradventure there are fifty righteous*, etc. (v. 24) —Mah v. *infra*, XCIII, 6

[3] Gallia or Galatia in Asia Minor [4] To officiate as Reader for the Congregation. [5] Which means, Come and do your duty.

[6] Because 'draw near' implies both.

[7] In the original *'Amidah* of eighteen Benedictions (before a nineteenth was added), the fifteenth ended with the formula, 'Who heareth prayer.'

occurs fifteen times in the Psalm, *Ascribe unto the Lord, O ye sons of might* . . . as far as *The Lord sat enthroned at the flood* (Ps. XXIX), which restrains punishment from visiting the world.[1]

WILT THOU INDEED SWEEP AWAY THE RIGHTEOUS WITH THE WICKED? R. Huna said in R. Aḥa's name: WILT THOU INDEED (HA-AF) SWEEP AWAY (TISPEH): Thou confinest anger, but anger cannot confine Thee.[2] R. Joshua b. Nehemiah interpreted it: The anger (*af*) which Thou bringest upon Thy world, wouldst Thou destroy therewith the righteous and the wicked![3] And not enough that Thou dost not suspend judgment of the wicked for the sake of the righteous, but Thou wouldst even destroy the righteous with the wicked!

Rabbi and R. Jonathan each commented. Rabbi said: [Abraham pleaded:] A human being is mastered by his anger, but the Holy One, blessed be He, masters anger, as it says, *The Lord avengeth and mastereth wrath* (Nahum I, 2).[4] R. Jonathan said: A human being is mastered by his jealousy, but the Holy One, blessed be He, masters His jealousy, as it says, *The Lord is God* [i.e. master] *over jealousy and vengeance* (*ib.* I).[5]

R. Simlai asked R. Jonathan: 'What is meant by the verse, *But there is that is swept away without judgment* (Prov. XIII, 23)?'[6] 'It means without judgment on his own town,'[7] he answered. Thus it once happened that a man was sent to collect [a fine] from the citizens of Tiberias and Sepphoris. Whilst he was thus collecting in Tiberias, he saw a citizen of Sepphoris, whereupon he arose and seized him.[8] 'I belong to Sepphoris,' he protested. 'I have warrants instructing me to collect in Sepphoris too,' he replied; but before he finished collecting in

[1] I.e Israel's prayers stay punishment. *The Lord sat enthroned at the flood* is understood as a reference to His oath not to repeat the flood.
[2] Translating *af*, 'anger,' and *tispeh* 'to take away', 'remove,' from *asaf*, whence 'to dominate'. Thou dost rule Thine anger.
[3] This gives *tispeh* its usual meaning of 'to destroy'.
[4] E.V. *'Is full of wrath.'* [5] E.V.: *'The Lord is a jealous and avenging God.'* [6] E.V. . . . *'by want of righteousness.'*
[7] As explained. [8] For payment

Tiberias, remission was granted to Sepphoris, and thus this man was 'gathered in' without the judgment of his own town. R. Levi and R. Simon commented. R. Levi said: [Abraham pleaded: 'Is Thine anger] like a she-bear ravaging among animals which, if it does not find another beast to destroy, destroys its own young!' R. Simon said: [Is Thine anger] like a scythe which cuts down thorns, but when it finds [no more] cuts down roses!

9. THAT BE FAR FROM THEE—ḤALILAH LAK (XVIII, 25). R. Judan interpreted: It is a profanation (*ḥalalah*) for Thee, it is alien to Thy nature. R. Aḥa said: ḤALILAH is written twice,[1] implying, Such action would profane (*hilal*) the Divine Name.[2] R. Abba said: Not 'to do this' is written here, but TO DO AFTER THIS MANNER: neither this or anything like it nor anything even of a lesser nature.

R. Levi said: Two men said the same thing, viz. Abraham and Job. Abraham: THAT BE FAR FROM THEE, TO DO AFTER THIS MANNER, TO SLAY THE RIGHTEOUS WITH THE WICKED. Job: *It is all one—therefore I say: He destroyeth the innocent and the wicked* (Job IX, 22). Yet Abraham was rewarded for it, while Job was punished for it! The reason is because Abraham said it in confirmation,[3] while Job said it in cavil: '*It is all one!*' R. Hiyya b. Abba said: We have here a merging of answers.[4] Thus Abraham said: THAT BE FAR FROM THEE, to which God replied: SO SHALL [THE WICKED] BE AS THE RIGHTEOUS! Thou desirest that judgment of the wicked should be suspended for the sake of the righteous; but are they righteous? Surely they are but counterfeit righteous! For R. Joḥanan said: Wherever *ẓaddiḳim* (righteous) occurs in connection with Sodom, it is spelled defectively.[5]

[1] In that verse, *q v.* [2] Thus the first '*halilah*' means 'foreign', and the second, it would profane Thee—by casting doubts upon Thy justice.
[3] I.e. surely God is not so unjust as to slay the righteous with the wicked!
[4] Abraham's question and God's answer are merged.
[5] I.e. צדקים instead of צדיקים, the second *yod* being missing. This intimates that the righteousness even of those who laid claim to it was defective, a hypocritical pretence.

That corresponds with R. Joḥanan's view, for R. Joḥanan said: *And our elders* (zeḳenenu) *and all the inhabitants of our country spoke to us* (Josh. IX, 11): it is spelled '*zekenenu*',[1] intimating that they were elders in wrong-doing, elders in wickedness.[2]

R. Joshua b. Levi said: [Abraham pleaded,] 'Combine their good deeds, and so they will amount to fifty.'[3] R. Judah b. R. Simon said: [Abraham pleaded:] 'Art Thou not the righteous One of the universe? Combine Thyself with them and they will amount to fifty.' R. Judah b. R. Simon said: [Abraham pleaded thus:] 'Even in the case of a human judge, an appeal can be made from the commander to the prefect and from the prefect to the governor; but Thou, because no appeal can be made from Thy judgment, wilt Thou not do justly?' R. Judah said further: When Thou desiredst to judge Thy world, Thou didst entrust it to two, Romulus and Remus,[4] so that if one wished to do something the other could veto him; while Thou, because there is none to veto Thee, wilt Thou not do justly?

R. Aḥa said: [Abraham pleaded:] 'Thou hast sworn not to bring a deluge upon the world. Wouldst Thou evade Thine oath! Not a deluge of water wilt Thou bring but a deluge of fire? Then Thou hast not acted according to Thine oath.' R. Levi commented: SHALL NOT THE JUDGE OF ALL THE EARTH DO JUSTLY? If Thou desirest the world to endure, there can be no absolutely strict judgment, while if Thou desirest absolutely strict judgment, the world cannot endure, yet Thou wouldst hold the cord by both ends, desiring both the world and absolute judgment! Unless Thou foregoest a little, the

[1] זקנינו instead of זקינינו.

[2] 'Elders' means chiefs: in wickedness and evil too they were elders.

[3] Many must have some little good in them, and if Thou combinest the good of all it will be equivalent to that of fifty righteous men.

[4] The legendary founders of Rome These are mentioned because Rome did appear as God's instrument for punishing the world. Or possibly (as Th.) this is a reference to the early Roman system of dyarchy, under which a duumvirate ruled, and appeal could be made from the decision of one to the other

world cannot endure. Said the Holy One, blessed be He, to Abraham: '*Thou hast loved righteousness* (Ps. XLV, 8): thou hast loved to justify My creatures; *and hated wickedness:* thou hast refused to condemn them. *Therefore God, thy God, hath anointed thee with the oil of gladness above thy fellows* (*ib.*). From Noah to thee were ten generations, and out of all of them I remembered but thee alone.'[1]

10. AND THE LORD SAID: IF I FIND IN SODOM (XVIII, 26). R. Judah b. R. Simon, in the name of R. Joshua b. Levi, quoted *For it is for God to have said: I have forgiven* (Job XXXIV, 31).[2] Thus, THEN WILL I FORGIVE ALL THE PLACE FOR THEIR SAKE. *Lo eḥbol* (*ib*) means, I will not take them in pledge, as in the verse,[3] *If thou at all take thy neighbour's garment to pledge*—taḥbol (Ex. XXII, 25). Yet they [men] abuse Me with words and say: 'He does not judge well.' *Apart from Myself, I will see* (Job XXXIV, 32)[4]: i.e. without Me, do thou go and scrutinise My judgment. And if I have erred, *Teach thou Me (ib.). And if I have wrought injustice* (*ib.*) to the earlier generations,[5] *I will do it no more* to the later generations.[6]

To him will I keep silence [and] *to his branches* (Job XLI, 4)[7]: [God said to Abraham:] 'To thee will I keep silence and to the branches that proceed from thee' [I will keep silence] to Abraham, who said: THAT BE FAR FROM THEE TO DO AFTER THIS MANNER; to Moses, who said: *Lord, why doth Thy wrath wax hot against Thy people* (Ex. XXXII, 11); to Joshua, who said: *Wherefore hast Thou at all brought this people over the Jordan* (Josh. VII, 7); and to David, who said: *Why standest Thou afar off,*

[1] V. *supra*, XXXIX, 6. [2] E V '*For hath any said unto God: I have borne chastisement, though I offend not?*' [3] I e. take them for their sins.
[4] I will see that you recognise the justice of My actions. E.V. '*That which I see not.*'
[5] The generations of the Flood and of the Separation of races
[6] The Sodomites. According to this interpretation God is the speaker in these verses, defending Himself before Abraham against the charge of injustice
[7] Reading לו (to him) instead of לא (not), and deriving בדיו from בד, a branch, i.e. to his descendants. E.V. '*Would I keep silence concerning his boastings.*'

O Lord, etc. (Ps. x, 1).[1] *Or his proud talk, or his fair* (ḥin) *array of words* (Job *loc. cit.*): his [sc. Abraham's] long speech was endowed with grace (*ḥen*) when he beseeched mercy for the Sodomites.

11. AND ABRAHAM ANSWERED AND SAID: BEHOLD NOW, I HAVE TAKEN UPON ME TO SPEAK UNTO THE LORD, WHO AM BUT DUST AND ASHES (XVIII, 27). He said: Had Nimrod slain me, would I not have been dust, and had he burnt me, would I not have been ashes?[2] Said the Holy One, blessed be He, to him: 'Thou didst say, I AM BUT DUST AND ASHES; by thy life, I will give thy children atonement therewith,' as it says, *And for the unclean they shall take of the ashes* ('afar) *of the burning of the purification from sin* (Num. XIX, 17)[3]; also, *And a man that is clean shall gather up the ashes of the heifer* (*ib.* 9).

We learnt[4]: What was the ritual of a fast?[5] The Ark was carried out into the public square of the town and burnt ashes were sprinkled on the Ark. R. Judan b. R. Manasseh and R. Samuel b. Naḥman disagreed. One maintained: [The ashes were to recall] the merit of Abraham, for it is written, I WHO AM BUT DUST AND ASHES.[6] But the other maintained that they were to recall the merit of Isaac[7]; he learnt 'ashes' only.[8] The following statement of R. Judah b. Pazzi disagrees, for he would publicly announce: If the congregational beadle cannot get to anyone [to pour ashes on his head], let him take ashes himself and pour them on his own head.[9] [That is not so, for] R. Judah b. Pazzi's announcement teaches that *'afar* (dust) and *efer* (ashes) are identical.[10]

[1] All these indirectly questioned God's justice.
[2] V. *supra*, XXXVIII, 13 *ad fin.*
[3] *'Afar* really means dust (of earth). [4] Ta'an 15*a*.
[5] Specially proclaimed in times of distress.
[6] Thus either dust or ashes might be sprinkled on the heads of the people.
[7] Who might have been reduced to ashes as a burnt-offering.
[8] Not dust. [9] But not dust. This disagrees with the first view.
[10] Either could be taken. The text and meaning are doubtful, and the rendering is conjectural

12. PERADVENTURE THERE SHALL LACK FIVE OF THE FIFTY RIGHTEOUS. R. Ḥiyya b. Abba said: Abraham wished to descend from fifty to five,[1] but the Holy One, blessed be He, said to him: 'Turn back.'[2] R. Levi said: This may be compared to a clepsydra[3] full of water; only as long as it contains water may the defending counsel plead; yet sometimes the judge desires him to continue his defence, and so he orders, 'Pour more water into it'[4]

13. AND HE SAID: OH, LET NOT THE LORD BE ANGRY . . . PERADVENTURE TEN SHALL BE FOUND THERE (XVIII, 32). And why ten? So that there might be sufficient for an assembly [of righteous men to pray] on behalf of all of them.[5] Another reason, why ten? Because at the generation of the Flood eight righteous people yet remained,[6] and the world was not given a respite for their sake. Another reason, why ten? Because he thought that there were ten there, viz. Lot, his wife, his four daughters and four sons-in-law.[7] R. Judah b. R. Simon and R. Ḥanin in R. Joḥanan's name said: Here ten were required, while in Jerusalem even one would have sufficed,[8] as it is written, *Run ye to and fro in the streets of Jerusalem . . . and seek . . . if ye can find a man, if there be any that doeth justly* (Jer. V, 1); and thus it says too, *Adding one thing to another, to find out the account* (Eccl. VII, 27). R. Isaac said: How far can an account be extended [for one city]? As far as one man.[9]

14. AND THE LORD WENT HIS WAY, AS SOON AS HE HAD LEFT OFF SPEAKING TO ABRAHAM (XVIII,

[1] Without the intermediate steps. He probably renders: Peradventure the fifty shall be lacking, and there be but five. [2] This is too great a jump. [3] Jast.: a water-clock used in courts of justice for measuring the time given for argument. [4] So too God desired Abraham to plead for the Sodomites, though He knew beforehand that it was useless (Mah.). [5] Ten is a quorum for public prayer. [6] Noah, his three sons, and their wives. [7] But he was mistaken in thinking them righteous (M.K.). [8] But not even one was to be found.
[9] Mah.. Translating, the righteousness of one man saving one town.

33). A judge waits as long as the advocate is pleading; when the advocate becomes silent, the judge rises [to go]. Similarly, AND THE LORD WENT HIS WAY, AS SOON AS HE HAD LEFT OFF SPEAKING TO ABRAHAM. Again, an advocate goes on pleading as long as the judge is willing to pay attention to him, but when the judge rises to go, the advocate becomes silent. Thus, AND THE LORD WENT HIS WAY, AS SOON AS HE HAD LEFT OFF SPEAKING TO ABRAHAM; AND ABRAHAM RETURNED UNTO HIS PLACE. Again, as long as the defender pleads and the judge shows himself willing to hear, the accuser waits; when the judge rises and the advocate is silent, the accuser sets forth on his mission. Similarly: AND THE LORD WENT HIS WAY, AS SOON AS HE HAD LEFT OFF SPEAKING TO ABRAHAM; AND ABRAHAM RETURNED UNTO HIS PLACE. This is followed by, *And the two angels came to Sodom at even* (Gen. XIX, 1).

Chapter L (VAYERA)

1. AND THE TWO ANGELS CAME TO SODOM AT EVEN etc. (XIX, 1). It is written, *And the living creature ran* (raẓo) *and returned as the appearance of a flash of lightning* (Ezek. I, 14). R. Aibu said: Not *raẓoth* (running) is written but '*raẓo*': they are eager (*raẓin*) to perform their mission.[1] '*As the appearance of a flash of lightning*' (bazaḳ): R. Judah b. R. Simon said in the name of R. Levi b. Parta: [Like the flames breaking forth] when one scatters (*bozek*) olive refuse in a stove. R. Ḥiyya b. Abba said: It was like wind driving sparks (*zika*). The Rabbis said: Like a lightning-flash to the eye.[2] Now [returning to our subject,] they take leave of Abraham at noon, and arrive in Sodom in the evening![3] The fact is, however, that they were angels of mercy, and they delayed, thinking that perhaps Abraham might find something in their favour; but when he found nothing in their favour, THE TWO ANGELS CAME TO SODOM AT EVEN.

2. THEN THE TWO ANGELS CAME, etc. *But He is at one with Himself, and who can turn Him? and what His soul desireth, even that He doeth* (Job XXIII, 13). It was taught[4]: One angel does not perform two missions, nor do two angels together perform one mission,[5] yet you read that two [angels came to Sodom]? The fact is, however, that Michael announced his tidings [to Abraham] and departed: Gabriel was sent to overturn Sodom, and Rafael to rescue Lot; hence, THEN THE TWO ANGELS CAME, etc.

It is written, *He sent forth upon them the fierceness of His anger, Wrath, Indignation, and Trouble, a sending of*

[1] Deriving *razo* from *raẓah*, to be willing, desire.
[2] As quickly as the eye perceives a flash of lightning. Cur. edd. (as rendered by Y.T. and Jast.) like a wind scattering clouds
[3] Surely angels that travel like a flash of lightning should have reached Sodom much earlier. [4] B.M 86*b*.
[5] Translating: And He (God) performs His purpose through one (angel).

messengers of evil (Ps. LXXVIII, 49)[1]; yet you say, TWO [ANGELS]! But the fact is that Michael announced his tidings and departed; Gabriel was sent to overturn Sodom, and Rafael to save Lot. Hence, THEN THE TWO ANGELS CAME.[2]

[AND THE TWO ANGELS CAME TO SODOM.] Here you call them angels, whereas earlier they were termed men? Earlier, when the *Shechinah* was above them, they were men; but as soon as the *Shechinah* departed from them they assumed the form of angels. R. Levi said: To Abraham, whose [religious] strength was great, they looked like men[3]; but to Lot they appeared as angels, because his strength was feeble.[4] R. Ḥunia said: Before they performed their mission they were called men; having performed their mission, they assumed the style of angels. R. Tanḥuma said: They may be likened to a man who received a governorship from the king. Before he reaches the seat of his authority, he goes like an ordinary citizen. Similarly, before they performed their mission, they are called men; having performed it, they assumed the style of angels.

3. SEDOMAH (TO SODOM). It was taught in R. Nehemiah's name: When a word requires a *lamed* as a prefix you add *heh* as a suffix [instead], e.g. SEDOMAH (TO SODOM), *se'irah* (to Seir), *mizraimah* (to Egypt), *ḥaranah* (to Haran).[5] An objection was raised: Yet it is written, *The wicked shall return* lisheolah—*to the netherworld* (Ps. IX, 18).[6] Said R. Abba b. Zabda: That means to the nethermost compartment of hell.[7]

BA'EREB (AT EVEN). The evening of Sodom had come,[8] its sun had set, and its doom was sealed. R. Levi said: The Holy One, blessed be He, judges the nations

[1] The Midrash regards *Wrath*, etc., as proper nouns, each being the name of a particular angel, each was sent *alone* on a separate mission.
[2] This passage is omitted in cur edd [3] Because he was as familiar with angels as with men [4] Hence he was overawed by them.
[5] Hebrew סדומה instead of לסדום, etc. [6] Heb. לשאולה, i.e. with both the prefix ל and the suffix ה. [7] Hence the double form is used.
[8] Reading BA'EREB as two words *ba 'ereb*, evening had come.

at night only, when they are asleep from their sins[1], while He judges Israel by day only, when they are engaged in good deeds. Hence it is written, *And He will judge* the world (*tebel*) in righteousness, *He will minister judgment to* the peoples with equity (*ib.* 9).[2]

AND LOT SAT IN THE GATE OF SODOM. Sat is written defectively,[3] intimating that only that day had he been appointed by them chief justice.[4] There were five principal judges in Sodom: False-Principles, Lying-Speech, Cad, Justice-Perverter, and Man-Flayer, while Lot was their chief judge. When he told them something which pleased them, they would say to him, '*Go further* (Gen. XIX, 9),[5] take a higher seat'; but if he said something which displeased them, they would say, '*This one fellow came in to sojourn, and he will needs play the judge!*' (*ib.*).

4. AND LOT SAW THEM, AND ROSE UP TO MEET THEM . . . AND HE SAID: BEHOLD NOW, MY LORDS, TURN ASIDE, I PRAY YOU (XIX, 1 f.). R. Judan interpreted: Even if I am not worthy, divert your course for my sake. R. Huna said: [He asked them:] 'Come to me by a circuitous route, so that you may not be seen coming to me.' AND TARRY ALL NIGHT, AND WASH YOUR FEET. Abraham asked them to wash first and then stay with him,[6] whereas Lot first invited them to stay with him and then to wash. The truth is that Abraham was particular about the pollution of idolatry, whereas Lot had no objection to it. Some say: This too Lot did with forethought, so that when they [the angels] went out, the dust

[1] So that His judgment can be more lenient

[2] *Tebel* (world) is regarded as a contrast to *peoples*, and hence refers to Israel, and the verse is understood thus: He judges Israel when they perform their righteousness, i.e. by day, but the peoples with grace, i.e. by night, when they are not engaged in wrongdoing.

[3] ישב instead of יושב. [4] IN THE GATE was the place where justice was dispensed. [5] E.V. '*stand back*'.

[6] The Heb. *linah* means to spend the night. Abraham of course did not invite them for the night, but the Midrash means that he asked them to wash their feet before accepting his hospitality; v. XVIII, 4 f.

would be seen on their feet,[1] and the Sodomites should not ask, 'Where have they spent the night?' AND THEY SAID: NAY, BUT WE WILL ABIDE IN THE BROAD PLACE ALL NIGHT [This teaches that] you may refuse an ordinary person, but not a great person.[2] AND HE URGED (WAYYIFẒAR) THEM GREATLY (XIX, 3): Through them he brought anger (*af*) and trouble (*zarah*) into his home[3] AND THEY TURNED ASIDE TO HIM. This supports R. Huna's contention that he asked them to take a circuitous path to him that they might not be seen entering his house.[4] AND HE MADE THEM A FEAST. He had been reared in the home of Abraham who showed hospitality to travellers. R Isaac said: A fierce quarrel[5] broke out over the salt, for he [Lot] said to her [his wife], 'Give these guests a little salt,' to which she replied, 'Do you want to introduce here that evil practice too?'

5. BUT BEFORE THEY LAY DOWN, they commenced questioning him, 'What is the nature of the people of this city?'[6] 'In every town there are people good and bad,' he replied, 'but here the overwhelming majority are bad.' THE MEN OF THE CITY, THE MEN OF SODOM, COMPASSED THE HOUSE ROUND, BOTH YOUNG AND OLD—not one of them objecting. AND THEY CALLED UNTO LOT, AND SAID UNTO HIM, etc (XIX, 5). R Joshua b Levi said in the name of R. Padiah: Lot prayed for mercy on their behalf the whole of that night, and they would have heeded him; but immediately they [the Sodomites] demanded, BRING THEM OUT UNTO US, THAT WE MAY KNOW THEM—for sexual

[1] If they left after spending the night without washing.
[2] Since they accepted Abraham's invitation without demur
[3] A play on '*wayyifzar*' The anger and trouble are those felt and caused by the Sodomites (Y.M).
[4] Otherwise there is no point in repeating that they turned aside
[5] This is a play on the text, AND DID BAKE UNLEAVENED BREAD, Heb *mazzoth*, which is read *mazẓuth*, a quarrel—he stirred up a quarrel.
[6] The verse is apparently divided: BUT BEFORE THEY LAY DOWN, they asked him about THE MEN OF THE CITY Then THE MEN OF SODOM CAME, etc.

purposes[1]—they said to him, '*Hast thou here* (poh) *any besides* (*ib.* XIX, 12)? Until now you had the right to plead in their defence, but from now you have no right to plead for them.'[2]

6. AND LOT WENT OUT UNTO THEM TO THE DOOR . . . AND HE SAID: I PRAY YOU, MY BRETHREN, DO NOT SO WICKEDLY. BEHOLD NOW, I HAVE TWO DAUGHTERS . . . ONLY UNTO THESE (HA-EL) MEN (XIX, 6 ff.): they are powerful men.[3] [Another interpretation]: they are men of godly strength.[4] FORASMUCH AS THEY ARE COME UNDER THE SHADOW OF MY ROOF: not in my merit, but in the merit of Abraham.[5] Another interpretation is that the verse FORASMUCH AS THEY ARE COME UNDER THE SHADOW OF MY ROOF teaches that she [Lot's wife] turned the house against them, saying to him, 'If you want to receive them, receive them in your portion.'[6]

7. AND THEY SAID: STAND BACK (XIX, 9)—out of the way! AND THEY SAID: THIS ONE FELLOW CAME IN TO SOJOURN, AND HE WILL NEEDS PLAY THE JUDGE—you wish to destroy the judgments of your predecessors![7] R. Menaḥema said in R. Bibi's name: The Sodomites made an agreement among themselves that whenever a stranger visited them they should force him to sodomy and rob him of his money; even him of whom it is written, *That they may keep the way of the Lord, to do righteousness and justice* (Gen. XVIII, 19),[8] we would use him bestially and rob him of his money.

[1] I.e. pederasty, '*know*' being understood as in Gen. IV, 1 *And the man knew Eve his wife, and she conceived.* [2] Reading *peh* (mouth) for *poh* (here): have you still a mouth to plead for them, after such iniquitous demands? [3] This is the interpretation of '*ha-el*'. [4] Translating: men of God. [5] M.K. '*shadow*' is understood in the sense of protector: they are come in the merit of the protector of my roof, sc. Abraham. [6] This stresses the word *ḳorathi*, lit. '*my* rafter'—she would only let them stay under a particular part of the house. Y.M. translates differently. [7] Who forbade hospitality. Possibly the verse is translated: and he would judge the judgments—condemning them and introducing new ones. [8] Sc. Abraham.

8. BUT THE MEN PUT FORTH THEIR HAND AND BROUGHT LOT INTO THE HOUSE TO THEM . . . AND THEY SMOTE THE MEN THAT WERE AT THE DOOR (PETHAḤ) OF THE HOUSE WITH BLINDNESS (XIX, 10). They were first to do the evil, and they were the first to be punished.[1] Similarly, *And He blotted out every living substance*, etc. (*ib.* VII, 23): he who was the first to do wrong was the first to be punished. Further, *And her belly shall swell, and her thigh shall fall away* (Num. V, 27): the limb that was first to sin was the first to be punished.[2]

SO THAT THEY WEARIED (WAYYILE'U) THEMSELVES TO FIND THE DOOR: they were maddened, as in the verse, *For My people is foolish*—ewil (Jer. IV, 22).[3]

9. AND THE MEN SAID TO LOT . . . FOR WE WILL DESTROY THIS PLACE (XIX, 13). R. Levi said in R Naḥman's name: Because the ministering angels revealed God's secret, they were banished from their precincts a hundred and thirty-eight years.[4] R. Tanḥuma expressed it in the word *kelaḥ*.[5] R. Ḥama b. Ḥanina said: [They were punished] because they expressed themselves boastfully, FOR *WE* WILL DESTROY THIS PLACE.

AND LOT WENT OUT, AND SPOKE UNTO HIS SONS-IN-LAW [AND] THOSE WHO WERE TAKING[6] HIS DAUGHTERS (XIX, 14). He had four daughters, two betrothed and two married, for it is not written, 'Who were married to his daughters,' but WHO WERE TAKING [i.e. MARRYING] HIS DAUGHTERS.[7] BUT HE SEEMED

[1] The house was encompassed by '*young and old*', 'young' first; hence they were smitten with blindness, 'BOTH YOUNG AND OLD'—young first. [2] Cur. edd add several other examples. [3] Cur edd add other interpretations [4] They were driven out of the sacred precincts within the Divine barrier, until they appeared at Jacob's dream (Mah.) The calculation is given in Th. [5] He used the word *ḳelah* (stalk or jet) to denote this period, its numerical value beng 138.

[6] E V '*who married*'; v. n. 7

[7] 'Betrothed' in this sense means married, but before the home-taking ceremony (*ḥuppah*), without which the marriage might not be consummated, v. Ḳid. 2*a* The Midrash understands SONS-IN-LAW to mean those who were already married, and THOSE WHO WERE TAKING HIS DAUGHTERS as different ones Hence it is assumed that there were two (as in v. 15) of each.

UNTO HIS SONS-IN-LAW AS ONE THAT JESTED. Said they to him: 'Organs and cymbals are in the land and the land is to be overthrown!'[1]

10. AND AS THE MORNING AROSE, THEN THE ANGELS HASTENED LOT, SAYING (XIX, 15). R. Ḥanina said: A man can walk four miles from dawn until it becomes light in the east; for it says, AND WHEN THE MORNING AROSE [i.e. at early dawn] . . . and then it is written, *The sun was risen upon the earth when Lot came unto Zoar* (*ib.* 23). Is it then four miles from Sodom to Zoar?[2] Said R. Ze'ira: The angel levelled the way for them.[3] And how do we know that one can walk four miles from the time it becomes light in the east until the sun begins to sparkle?—AND AS is written, intimating that one period is equal to the other.[4]

R. Jose b. Abin said: If a man tells you that the morning star is the morning dawn he is speaking falsely, for sometimes it is earlier and sometimes later; but two rays of light, as it were, issue from the east and light up the world.[5]

ARISE, TAKE THY WIFE AND THY TWO DAUGHTERS THAT ARE FOUND.[6] R. Tobiah b. R. Isaac said: Two 'finds' [would spring from them], Ruth the Moabitess and Naamah the Amonitess. R. Isaac commented: *I have found David My servant* (Ps. LXXXIX, 21): where did I find him? In Sodom.[7]

11. BUT HE LINGERED — WAYYITHMAHAMAH (XIX, 16). He kept on delaying, exclaiming, 'What a loss of gold and silver and precious stones!' Thus it is written,

[1] Absurd—the city is strong, everything is in order, and its inhabitants carefree! [2] Surely it is more? [3] And thus shortened it. Or perhaps it is meant metaphorically, by hurrying them.
[4] AND AS is regarded as an extension; hence two periods are envisaged, AND AS intimating that they are both alike.
[5] But the first light of dawn is not given by the morning star (the planet Venus). [6] Lit. translation. E.V. '*here*'.
[7] V. *supra*, XLI, 4. The point may be that something valuable may spring from the worst; cf. Sanh. 96*b* on the descendants of Nebuzaraddan, Sennacherib, and Haman.

Riches kept by the owner thereof to his hurt (Eccl. v, 12). R. Joshua b. Levi said: This applies to Lot. R. Samuel b. Naḥman said: It applies to Korah. R. Judah b. R. Simon referred it to Naboth; R. Levi, to Haman; R Isaac, to the tribes of Reuben and Gad[1]; the Rabbis applied it to the tribe of Levi, which became impoverished but subsequently regained their original state.[2]

AND THE MEN LAID HOLD UPON HIS HAND, AND UPON THE HAND OF HIS WIFE, AND UPON THE HAND OF HIS TWO DAUGHTERS, etc. Who was it? Rafael. A difficulty was raised: It is written, '*And it came to pass, when* they *had brought them forth*'? Read what follows, he replied; it is not written, 'And *they* said,' but AND *HE* SAID: ESCAPE FOR THY LIFE. If so, why does it say, AND *THEY* LAID HOLD, etc.? [Because it means], Abraham's merit together with Rafael.[3]

ESCAPE TO THE MOUNTAIN, i.e. for the sake of Abraham.[4] LEST THOU BE SWEPT AWAY—through the iniquity of the city.

AND LOT SAID UNTO THEM: OH, NOT SO, MY LORD; BEHOLD NOW, THY SERVANT HATH FOUND GRACE IN THY SIGHT . . . AND I CANNOT ESCAPE TO THE MOUNTAIN, LEST THE EVIL OVERTAKE ME, AND I DIE (XIX, 18 f.). R. Berekiah and R. Levi in the name of R. Huna b. Ḥanina said: Two people said the same thing, Lot and the woman of Zarephath. The woman of Zarephath said: Before you [Elijah] came to me, the Holy One, blessed be He, saw my [good] deeds and those of my fellow citizens, and mine exceeded theirs. Now, however, that you have come here, you have recalled my

[1] Who on account of their great flocks and herds chose their heritage on the east of the Jordan, and were subsequently the first to suffer exile.
[2] Translating there is wealth kept for its owner even when he falls on evil days.—Th.: Possibly this refers to the times of Ezra and Nehemiah, when the levitical dues were largely withheld (v. Neh XIII, 10 f.). Cur edd. read: The Rabbis applied it to Job, etc
[3] Thus there were two, as it were.
[4] Cur. edd.: who was called a mountain (in the verses) *Leaping upon the mountains* (S.S. II, 8) and *Hear, O ye mountains, the Lord's controversy* (Micah VI, 2).

sins and slain my son.[1] Lot said: Before I went to Abraham, the Lord saw my [good] deeds and the deeds of my fellow citizens, and mine exceeded theirs. Now that I am to go to Abraham, his good deeds are so much more than mine, and I cannot withstand his burning coals[2] Hence, I AM UNABLE [TO ESCAPE TO THE MOUNTAIN].[3]

R. Berekiah said in R. Levi's name: What is the source of what we learnt: Just as a bad dwelling puts one to the test, so does a good one?[4] This passage: AND I CANNOT ESCAPE TO THE MOUNTAIN; he dwells in a valley and they tell him to go to the mountain and he replies thus![5] This proves that even [in changing] from a bad dwelling to a good one [there may be danger], because [even] a good dwelling is a test.

BEHOLD NOW, THIS CITY IS NEAR TO FLEE UNTO . . . AND HE SAID UNTO HIM: SEE, I HAVE SHOWN THEE FAVOUR CONCERNING THIS THING ALSO (XIX, 20 f.). R. Taḥlifa of Ḳetireh[6] said: [God said to Israel:] 'If the angel showed favour to Lot because he [Lot] had shown him honour, will I not show thee favour for thine own sake and for the sake of thine ancestors!' [Hence it is written], *The Lord lift up His countenance upon thee, and give thee peace* (Num. VI, 26).

12. HASTEN THOU, ESCAPE THITHER; FOR I CANNOT DO ANYTHING TILL THOU BE COME THITHER, etc. (XIX, 22). R. Levi said: This may be compared to a great city which had two patrons, one from a large town and the other a provincial.[7] The king was angry with them [the citizens] and wished to punish them. Said the king: 'If I punish them in the presence of the townsman alone, they will say, "Had the provincial been here, he would have protected us"; while if I punish them in the presence of the provincial they will say, "Had the

[1] V. 1 Kings XVII, 9–18 [2] I e I cannot live in his vicinity. Cf. Ab. II, 10 [3] Which on the present interpretation refers to Abraham. [4] Keth. 110*b*. A change even from a bad dwelling to a good dwelling tests one's health, and if it is not good the change may affect it adversely. [5] Though mountain air is purer and healthier. [6] Probably an error for Cæsarea, as in cur. edd [7] From a small town.

townsman been here he would have protected us."' Similarly, because some of the Sodomites worshipped the sun and others the moon, God said: 'If I punish them by day they will say, "Had the moon been there it would have protected us"; while if I punish them at night they will say, "Had the sun been there it would have protected us."' Therefore [He destroyed them] on the sixteenth of Nisan, when both the sun and the moon are visible in the sky.[1] Hence it is written, THE SUN WAS RISEN UPON THE EARTH WHEN LOT CAME UNTO ZOAR (XIX, 23).[2]

[1] At the same time. [2] And at that time the moon was still visible.

Chapter LI (VAYERA)

1. THEN THE LORD CAUSED TO RAIN UPON SODOM AND UPON GOMORRAH BRIMSTONE AND FIRE FROM THE LORD OUT OF HEAVEN (XIX, 24). It is written, *Let them be like a snail which melteth and passeth away, like the untimely births of a woman, that have not seen the sun* (Ps. LVIII, 9). Like a snail, like a slug which dissolves in excrements; like a mole which sees not the light before it returns to the dust; like a married woman who has committed adultery,[1] and, being ashamed that her child should be discovered, casts it away at night before it sees the sun. Hence it is written, *The sun was risen upon the earth* . . . AND THE LORD [HAD] CAUSED TO RAIN UPON SODOM.[2]

2. THEN THE LORD CAUSED TO RAIN UPON SODOM, etc. This may be compared to two countries that revolted against the king, whereupon the king ordered one to be burnt down at its own cost and the other to be burnt down at the exchequer's cost. Similarly, elsewhere we find, *And the streams thereof* [sc. Edom] *shall be turned into pitch, and the dust thereof into brimstone* (Isa. XXXIV, 9)[3]; whereas here we read, THEN THE LORD CAUSED TO RAIN UPON SODOM AND UPON GOMORRAH, etc.[4] R. Abin said: It may be compared to a servant who was removing bread from the oven. Her child came and took out a loaf, whereupon she let him have it; but her mistress's child came and took out burning coals,[5] and she let him have them. Similarly, elsewhere it says, *Then the Lord said unto Moses: Behold, I will cause to rain* bread *from heaven for you* (Ex. XVI, 4); whereas here we read, THEN

[1] This is apparently the meaning of the original [2] By which time Sodom was already destroyed—the Sodomites did not see the daylight. [3] Thus it shall provide its own burning materials. [4] Providing the materials from His own treasury, as it were [5] To injure others with them.

THE LORD CAUSED TO RAIN UPON SODOM AND UPON GOMORRAH BRIMSTONE AND FIRE.[1]

Abba Hilfi, the son of Samkai, said in the name of R. Judah: THEN THE LORD CAUSED TO RAIN, etc. refers to Gabriel; FROM THE LORD (OUT OF HEAVEN, to the Holy One, blessed be He).[2] R. Leazar said: Wherever 'And *the Lord*' occurs, it means, He and His heavenly Court[3] R. Isaac said: Both in the Torah [Pentateuch], in the Prophets, and in the Writings we find a commoner[4] mentioning his name twice in one verse. In the Torah: *And Lamech said unto his wives: Adah and Zillah hear my voice;* this is not followed by, 'my wives,' but by *Ye wives of Lamech* (Gen. IV, 23). In the prophets: *And the king said unto them: Take with you the servants of your lord, and cause Solomon my son to ride upon mine own mule,* etc. (I Kings I, 33)—it does not say, 'Take my servants,' but '*Take . . . the servants of your lord*'.[5] In the Writings: *For the writing which is written in the king's name,* etc. (Est. VIII, 8).[6] Yet you wonder that the Holy One, blessed be He, mentions His name twice in one verse![7]

3. BRIMSTONE AND FIRE. Thus it is written, *Upon the wicked He will cause to rain* paḥim [E.V. '*coals*']—this means coals and snares[8]—*Fire and brimstone* (Ps. XI, 6). R. Judan said: Why does a man instinctively recoil when he smells brimstone? Because his soul knows that it will be punished therewith in the future. *The portion of their cup* (*ib.*). R. Ishmael b. Naḥman[9] said in R.

[1] Thus, Israel sought bread—for their own needs—and God granted it; the Sodomites sought fire to injure others—and God granted it likewise, but of course to their own destruction. [2] This is added from cur edd. [3] Here too the original means literally, 'And the Lord' (*wa-adonai*). [4] I.e a mortal. [5] Which is the equivalent of mentioning himself.—The rendering is that of an emended text (Y T) [6] He likewise did not say, 'written in my name,' Ahasuerus being the speaker [7] Thus he disagrees with the view which makes part of the present verse refer to God and part to Gabriel. [8] *Paḥ* (pl *paḥim*) generally means snares; also as a shortened form of *peham* (pl. *pehamim*) it means coals [9] Instead of R Samuel b. Naḥman, v. *Ag. Pal Am.* I, 484.

Jonathan's name: Like a double measure of poterion after a bath.[1]

R. Ḥanina b. Pazzi said: Nothing evil descends from above.[2] The scholars objected. Yet it is written, *Fire and hail, snow and vapour, stormy wind, fulfil His word* (Ps. CXLVIII, 8)? It is the stormy wind alone which fulfils His word, he answered them.[3] The following statement of R. Simeon b. Lakish disagrees with this. For R. Simeon b. Laḳish said: *The Lord will open unto thee His good treasure* (Deut. XXVIII, 12): hence it follows that He possesses treasures of a different kind too. FROM THE LORD OUT OF HEAVEN: like a blow from a powerful man.

4. AND HE OVERTHREW THOSE CITIES (XIX, 25). R. Levi said in the name of R. Samuel b Nahman: These five cities were built on one rock, so the angel stretched out his hand and overturned them, as it is written, *He putteth forth his hand upon the flinty rock, he overturneth the mountains by the roots* (Job XXVIII, 9). Two amoraim dispute this. One says, it means: With a fifth of his hand; while the other interprets: with a fifth of his finger.[4] AND WHICH GREW UPON THE GROUND intimates that even the spontaneous produce of the ground was smitten.[5] R. Joshua b. Levi said: To this very day, if a man collects rain from the atmosphere of Sodom and pours it over a furrow elsewhere, it does not promote growth.

[1] So does a spirit of trembling await the wicked in full measure. Poterion is the name of a shrub (Astragalus Poterium), a species of tragacanth, yielding a gum which was used for spicing wines (Jast.). This was generally taken after a bath. Both the text and the meaning are doubtful.

[2] Hence the present case, where we are told that *The Lord caused to rain . . . brimstone and fire . . . out of heaven* is an exception, showing that the extreme wickedness of the Sodomites caused a change. Or (as Rashi explains on the Pentateuch), He caused ordinary rain to descend, and it turned into brimstone and fire when it approached the earth.

[3] Cf. preceding note.

[4] The Heb. for 'flint' is חלמיש. By a play on words the ל is omitted and it is read חמש, a fifth.

[5] Rendering. Even things which normally grow without effort (Y.T.).

5. BUT HIS WIFE LOOKED BACK FROM BEHIND HIM, AND SHE BECAME A PILLAR OF SALT. R. Isaac said: Because she sinned through salt.[1]

6. AND IT CAME TO PASS, WHEN GOD DESTROYED THE CITIES OF THE PLAIN, THAT GOD REMEMBERED ABRAHAM, AND SENT LOT OUT OF THE MIDST OF THE OVERTHROW (XIX, 29). What recollection was brought up in his favour?[2] The silence which he maintained for Abraham when the latter passed off Sarah as his sister; he knew of this, yet was silent. AND SENT LOT OUT OF THE MIDST OF THE OVERTHROW, WHEN HE OVERTHREW THE CITIES IN WHICH LOT DWELT. (*ib.*). R. Samuel b. Naḥman said: This means that he actually dwelt in [all] of them.[3] The Rabbis said: It means that he lent money on interest there.[4]

7. AND LOT WENT UP OUT OF ZOAR, AND DWELT IN THE MOUNTAIN (XIX, 30). Thus it is written, *For the Leader; al-tashheth. [A Psalm] of David; Michtam; when he fled from Saul, in the cave* (Ps. LVII, 1). He [David] prayed to Him: 'Sovereign of the Universe! Before I entered this cave Thou didst show mercy to others for my sake[5]; now that I am in the cave, O grant that Thou destroyest not (*al tashheth*)!'

8. AND THE FIRSTBORN SAID UNTO THE YOUNGER: OUR FATHER IS OLD, AND THERE IS NOT A MAN IN THE EARTH, etc. (XIX, 31). They thought that the whole world was destroyed, as in the generation of the Flood. COME, LET US MAKE OUR FATHER DRINK

[1] Cur. edd. add On the night that the angels visited Lot, what did she do? She went about to all her neighbours and asked them, 'Give me salt, as we have guests,' her intention being that the townspeople should become aware of their presence Therefore, SHE BECAME A PILLAR OF SALT. Cf. also *supra*, L, 4 [2] The verse implies that he was saved for the sake of something he had done to Abraham.
[3] At various times. [4] And so he had a personal interest in all these cities. [5] Before I was born Thou didst spare Lot because I was to spring from him; cf *supra*, L, 10 *ad fin*.

WINE . . . THAT WE MAY PRESERVE SEED OF OUR FATHER (*ib.* 32) R. Tanhuma said in Samuel's name: It is not written, that we may preserve a child of our father, but, THAT WE MAY PRESERVE *SEED* OF OUR FATHER: viz. the seed that comes from a different source, which is the King Messiah.[1]

AND THEY MADE THEIR FATHER DRINK WINE . . . AND HE KNEW NOT WHEN SHE LAY DOWN, AND WHEN SHE AROSE—U-BEḲUMAH (*ib.* 33): this word [U-BEKUMAH] is dotted,[2] intimating that he did not indeed know of her lying down, but he did know of her arising.[3] AND IT CAME TO PASS ON THE MORROW, THAT THE FIRSTBORN SAID UNTO THE YOUNGER . . . LET US MAKE HIM DRINK WINE THIS NIGHT ALSO (*ib.* 34). Whence did they procure wine in the cave? Since they [the Sodomites] had an abundance of wine they stored it in caves. R. Judah b. Simon said: A specimen, as it were, of the Messianic Age was provided for them, as you read, *And it shall come to pass in that day, that the mountains shall drop down sweet wine* (Joel IV, 18).

9. THUS WERE BOTH THE DAUGHTERS OF LOT WITH CHILD BY THEIR FATHERS (XIX, 36). R. Leazar said: A woman never conceives by her first intimacy. The scholars raised an objection: Surely it is written, THUS WERE BOTH THE DAUGHTERS OF LOT WITH CHILD BY THEIR FATHERS? Said R. Tanḥuma: They put pressure on themselves and brought forth their virginity and thus conceived at the first act of intercourse. R. Naḥman b. Ḥanin observed: Whoever is aflame with adulterous desire is eventually fed with his own flesh.[4] R. Judan of Gallia and R. Samuel b. Nahman both said

[1] Y.M. and Rash.: SEED implies one of their posterity 'coming from a different source', viz. from a different mother and father. v. *supra*, XXIII, 5. [2] It is traditionally written ובקומה.

[3] Hence AND WHEN SHE AROSE is not the object of AND HE KNEW NOT, but belongs to the next sentence: *And after she arose, it came to pass on the morrow*, etc

[4] He commits incest; *supra*, XLI, 7; XLII, 3.

in the name of R. Elijah Enene[1]: We would not know whether Lot lusted after his daughters or they lusted after him, but that it says, *He that separateth himself seeketh desire* (Prov. XVIII, 1),[2] whence it follows that Lot desired his daughters. R. Tanḥum b. R. Ḥiyya said in the name of R. Hoshaya, his interpreter[3]: Not a Sabbath passes without this chapter on Lot being read.[4] What is the reason? Because it is written, *At every* [congregation of] *wisdom he is revealed*—or, *repelled* (*ib.*).[5] R. Aḥa commented: It is not written, 'They are repelled,' but '*He is repelled*': men were repelled [by this reading], but women were attracted.[6]

10. It is written: *I know his* [sc. Moab's] *conception, saith the Lord, that it was not so* (Jer. XLVIII, 30).[7] R. Ḥanina b. Papa and R. Simon disagree. R. Ḥanina b. Papa said: The original conception of Moab was brought about not in a spirit of immorality but with a noble motive[8]; but *His scions* [lit. 'branches'] *did not act thus* (*ib.*), but with immoral motives, as it says, *And Israel abode in Shittim, and the people began to commit harlotry with the daughters of Moab* (Num. XXV, 1). R. Simon said: The first conception of Moab was not with a noble motive but in a spirit of immorality; '*His scions did not act thus,*' but with a noble motive, as it says, *And she went down unto the threshing-floor, and did according to all that her*

[1] This name is not found elsewhere. Perhaps we should read simply R. Elijah.
[2] *He that separateth himself* is applied to Lot, to whom Abraham had said, *Separate thyself from me* (Gen. XIII, 9), while *desire* is understood to mean passion.
[3] The interpreter was a functionary who interpreted the Torah to the congregation at its public reading.
[4] M.K. and Y.T. assume that this was the ancient practice. Possibly it should be rendered. There is not a single assembly (of scholars) where this is not read—wherever scholars congregate this story is known and Lot's shame kept alive.
[5] E.V. '*And snarleth against all sound wisdom*'.
[6] This reading acted as a deterrent to men, but not to women.
[7] E.V. '*I know his arrogancy, saith the Lord, that it is ill-founded*', (*his boastings have wrought nothing well-founded*).
[8] As above in sec. 9, for the sake of the Messiah.

mother-in-law bade her (Ruth III, 6).[1] R. Levi said: If the first conception of Moab was in a spirit of immorality, then his subsequent actions too were in the same spirit, for '*Did not his scions act thus?*'[2] as it says, '*And Israel abode in Shittim,*' etc. While if his first conception was with a pure motive, his subsequent acts too were thus: '*Did not his scions act thus?*' [Surely], '*And she went down unto the threshing-floor,*' etc.

11. AND THE FIRSTBORN BORE A SON, AND CALLED HIS NAME MOAB (XIX, 37). R. Judan said in R. Aibu's name: Because the firstborn disgraced her father and called his name Moab, which means, 'by my father' (*me-'ab*), Scripture commanded, *Be not at enmity with Moab, neither contend with them in battle* (Deut. II, 9): thou mayest not wage war with them, yet thou mayest divert their rivers and burn their barns in fire. But because the younger spared her father's honour, for SHE CALLED HIS NAME BEN-AMMI, declaring, He is a son (*ben*) of one who was with me (*'immi*), Scripture ordered, *Harass them not, nor contend with them* (*ib.* 19)—in any way, whatsoever.

R. Judah and R. Ḥanan in R. Joḥanan's name said: Lot's daughters went to commit wrong, yet became pregnant! In whose merit was this? In the merit of Moab, i.e. of one who was a father (*mi 'ab*) [viz. Abraham, of whom it says], *For the father of a multitude of nations have I made thee* (Gen. XVII, 5).

[1] They both interpret the verse as meaning that the original conception (deriving '*ebratho* from '*ibbur*, conception) of Moab was not brought about in the same spirit in which a similar act was committed by his descendants. But R. Hanina contrasts it with the *impure* motive which animated the daughters of Moab when the Israelites were at Shittim, while R. Simon contrasts it with the *noble* motive which animated Ruth.

[2] He treats this as a rhetorical question

Chapter LII (VAYERA)

1. AND ABRAHAM JOURNEYED FROM THENCE, etc. (xx, 1). R. Abin commenced his discourse thus: *And surely the mountain falling crumbleth away*, etc. (Job xiv, 18). '*And surely the mountain falling*' alludes to Lot, who fell [morally] at a mountain[1]; *And the rock is removed out of its place* (*ib.*) alludes to Abraham. For in consequence of the destruction of the region of Sodom wayfarers ceased, and he said, Why should I permit hospitality to cease from my house? He therefore went and pitched his tent in Gerar. Hence it is written, AND ABRAHAM JOURNEYED FROM THENCE.

2. *A brother offended* (nifsha') *is harder to be won than a strong city* (Prov. xviii, 19). '*A brother*' alludes to Lot, the son of Abraham's brother. '*Nifsha'*': thou didst sin against Abraham, thou didst deny him, thou wast false to him.[2] And whom did he [as a result] stir up against himself?—*And judges*[3] *like the bars of a castle* (*ib.*): he brought judges against himself [who shut him out] like the bars of the Temple. As we read there, *That none that was unclean in any thing should enter in* (II Chron. xxiii, 19),[4] so here too, *An Ammonite or a Moabite shall not enter into the assembly of the Lord* (Deut. xxiii, 4).[5] Hence, AND ABRAHAM JOURNEYED FROM THENCE.[6]

3. *The wise in heart will take good deeds* (Prov. x, 8)[7]: this refers to Abraham; '*Will take good deeds*': the region of Sodom was now desolate and travellers had ceased,

[1] This disregards the exact translation. 'Rashi' his moral fall took place at the cave in the mountain, when he became drunk Y.T and Radal otherwise [2] The Midrash understands '*nifsha'*', the *nif'al* of *pasha'*, 'to sin', in the sense, he made himself offend—against Abraham.
[3] E.V. '*Their contentions are*'. [4] The bars of the Temple shut them out, as it were. [5] So judges keep out the Ammonites and Moabites from the Jewish fold. [6] He journeyed away from Lot, so that their descendants should not intermingle. [7] E.V. '*Will receive commandments*'.

with the result that his stores were now in no way diminished; therefore he said: 'Why should I allow hospitality to cease from my house?' And he went and pitched his tent in Gerar. *But the foolish of tongue* (*ib.*) alludes to Lot who was foolish with his tongue, for he should have said to his daughter, 'Shall we commit that sin for which the whole world was punished!'[1] What did it lead to?—*He shall fall* (*ib.*): he brought upon himself fall after fall[2]: as we read there, '*That none that was unclean in any thing should enter in*' (II Chron. XXIII, 19),[3] so here too, '*An Ammonite or a Moabite shall not enter into the assembly of the Lord.*' Hence, AND ABRAHAM JOURNEYED FROM THENCE.

4. AND ABRAHAM JOURNEYED FROM THENCE. He departed because of the ill-repute [of his family], as people would say, 'Lot, Abraham's nephew, has been intimate with his two daughters.' TOWARD THE LAND OF THE SOUTH (NEGEB). It has seven names: *Darom* (south), *Negeb* (the dry region), *Teman*, *Yamin* (the right), *Hadar*, *Yam*, and *Sinin*.[4] A difficulty was raised: But it is written, *Nor yet from the wilderness*, Harim (Ps. LXXV, 7)?[5] The answer was given: That too is *darom*.[6]

R. Ḥiyya b. Abba said: I was passing the Babylonian synagogue of Sepphoris, when I heard children sitting and reciting the verse, AND ABRAHAM JOURNEYED FROM THENCE. At that I remarked, How great are the words of the Sages, who said: Take heed of their glowing coals, that thou be not burnt, for their bite is the bite of a fox, etc.[7] For from the moment that our father

[1] Sc. incest and immorality, through which Sodom was destroyed; cf. *supra*, L, 5. Possibly the reference is to the Flood (M.K.); v. *supra*, XXXI, 6. [2] Or, trouble upon trouble.

[3] This is really irrelevant here, but is inserted because it was mentioned in the preceding section. [4] Th. gives the references.

[5] He understands *harim* to mean the south (lit. 'mountains'—i.e. the region of the hills and mountains). E.V. '*Cometh lifting up*'. There too it refers to the south.

[6] I.e. *Harim* too could have been included, just as *Darom* is.

[7] Ab. II, 10.

Abraham separated from Lot, the separation was for all time.[1]

AND HE SOJOURNED IN GERAR—in Geradike.[2]

AND ABRAHAM SAID OF SARAH HIS WIFE: SHE IS MY SISTER (XX, 2)—without her will or consent.[3]

5. BUT GOD CAME TO ABIMELECH IN A DREAM OF THE NIGHT (XX, 3).[4]

What is the difference between the prophets of Israel and those of other nations? R. Hama b. R. Ḥanina said: The Holy One, blessed be He, reveals Himself to heathen prophets with half-speech only,[5] as you read, *And God met* (wayyiḳḳor) *Balaam* (Num. XXIII, 4).[6] R. Issachar of Kefar Mandi[7] observed: The term '*wayyiḳḳor*' signifies uncleanness,[8] as in the verse, *If there be among you any man, that is not clean by reason of that which chanceth him* (mikreh) *by night* (Deut. XXIII, 11). But to the prophets of Israel He speaks with complete speech, in terms of love and sanctity, with language in which the ministering angels praise Him, as it says, *And one* [seraph] *called unto another, and said: Holy, holy, holy, is the Lord of hosts* (Isa. VI, 3). R. Jose said: *The Lord is far from the wicked* (Prov. XV, 29) refers to the prophets of other

[1] Y.T.. Lot's descendants might never be joined to Abraham's, since they were forbidden to enter the community. Thus Abraham's request, *Separate thyself, I pray thee, from me* (Gen XIII, 9), was like coals of fire, having such momentous consequences. Y.M explains differently.

[2] The place was better known under this Hellenised form, and so it is given here

[3] This can be explained as implied in the fact that it is not mentioned that Abraham asked her beforehand, as he did when approaching Egypt; also, that she was unwilling to permit it, since on the previous occasion it had led to her being taken to the house of Pharaoh ('Rashi,' M K., Y.T) It is better, however, to amend the whole passage as follows (it is so in Yalkuṭ): AND ABIMELECH KING OF GERAR SENT, AND TOOK SARAH (*ib*). Is it possible that she went by her own desire? No: it was without her will or consent.

[4] Cur. edd. insert here what in the present ed. comes at the end of the section

[5] I e. with incomplete prophecy.

[6] *Met* implies in a casual, incomplete manner.

[7] Kafr Menda, south of Sepphoris (Jast)

[8] As though God spoke to something unclean. Or perhaps, as though God dimmed the splendour of His glory by speaking to him

nations[1]; *But He heareth the prayer of the righteous* (*ib.*)—to the prophets of Israel.

R. Jose b. Bibah said: The Holy One, blessed be He, appears to the heathens only in the hour when people generally take leave of each other [sc. at night], as it says, *Now a word was secretly brought to me . . . at the time of leave-taking*,[2] *from the visions of the night, when deep sleep falleth on men* (Job IV, 12 f.). R. Leazar b. Menaḥem said: '*The Lord is far from the wicked*' refers to the prophets of other nations; '*But He heareth the prayer of the righteous*'—to the prophets of Israel. And God appears to the nations only like one who comes from afar, as you read, *They are come from a far country unto me* (Isa. XXXIX, 3).[3] But in connection with the prophets of Israel we read *And [the Lord] appeared* (Gen. XVIII, 1), *And the Lord called* (Lev. I, 1)—implying, from the immediate vicinity. What is the difference between the prophets of Israel and the prophets of other nations? R. Ḥanina said: It may be compared to a king who was with his friend in a chamber (but separated by a curtain; whenever he desired to speak to his friend), he folded up the curtain and spoke to him. (But He speaks to the prophets of other nations without folding the curtain back but from behind it.)[4] The Rabbis compared it to a king who has a wife and a concubine; to his wife he goes openly, but to his concubine he repairs with stealth. Similarly, the Holy One, blessed be He, appears to the heathens only at night, as it says, *And God came to Balaam at night* (Num. XXII, 20); *And God came to Laban the Aramean in a dream of the night* (Gen. XXXI, 24); AND GOD CAME TO ABIMELECH IN A DREAM AT NIGHT.

BEHOLD, THOU SHALT DIE, BECAUSE OF THE

[1] Even when He speaks to them He is still far from them (Y.T.)
[2] Lit. 'at the divisions'—when people separate from each other. This derives *se'ippim* from *se'if*, a branch—when people branch away. E.V. '*in thoughts*'.
[3] God's communication to the heathen prophets is introduced by the phrase 'and he came', denoting as from a distance.
[4] The bracketed passages are inserted from cur. edd.

WOMAN WHOM THOU HAST TAKEN; this teaches that no formal warning is necessary in the case of the Noachides.[1]

FOR SHE IS A MAN'S WIFE. R. Aḥa said: Her husband was crowned through her, but she was not crowned through her husband. The Rabbis said: She is her husband's ruler. Usually, the husband gives orders, whereas here we read, *In all that Sarah saith unto thee, hearken unto her voice* (*ib.* XXI, 12).[2]

6. NOW ABIMELECH HAD NOT COME NEAR UNTO HER; AND HE SAID: LORD, WILT THOU SLAY EVEN A RIGHTEOUS NATION (XX, 4)? If Thou didst sentence the generation of the Flood and the generation of the Separation in this fashion, he protested, then they were righteous.[3] R. Berekiah explained it: [Abimelech pleaded]: 'If Thou wouldst slay this nation [sc. Abimelech], then slay the righteous one [Abraham].'[4] SAID HE NOT HIMSELF UNTO ME: SHE IS MY SISTER? AND SHE, SHE TOO (GAM) HERSELF SAID HE IS MY BROTHER (XX, 5): she, her ass-drivers, and her camel-drivers, her domestics, and all her household.[5] IN THE INTEGRITY OF MY HEART AND THE INNOCENCY OF MY HANDS HAVE I DONE THIS: this proves that he mishandled her.[6]

7. AND GOD SAID UNTO HIM: YEA, I KNOW . . . AND I ALSO WITHHELD THEE FROM SINNING (MEḤATO) AGAINST ME (XX, 6). R. Isaac explained: Thine evil Demon (*maḥṭoneka*)[7] is in My power, THEREFORE

[1] Mah: This verse cannot be regarded as a warning, since the next verse states, *Now Abimelech had not come near her*, whence it follows that if he had, death would already have been the penalty, even before this was told him. Cf. *supra*, XXXIV, 14.

[2] For notes v. *supra*, XLVIII, 1. Here the passage is based on the phrase *be'ulath ba'al* (a man's wife), which being written defectively (בעלת instead of בעולת) can be read *ba'alath ba'al*, a ruler to her husband.

[3] This is deduced from the word NATION, which implies that he spoke of others in addition to himself.

[4] Seeing that he misled me by saying that she was his sister.

[5] '*Gam*' is an extension, hence all these are included

[6] Though he did not actually dishonour her. [7] A play on '*meḥaṭo*'—i.e. your impulse to sin. The rendering is conjectural.

SUFFERED I THEE NOT TO TOUCH HER (*ib.*). R. Aibun said: It is like the case of a warrior who was riding his horse at full speed, when seeing a child lying in the path, he reined in the horse, so that the child was not hurt. Whom do all praise, the horse or the rider? Surely the rider! [Similarly here God said]: THEREFORE SUFFERED I THEE NOT TO TOUCH HER, [and the credit is Mine, not thine].

8. NOW THEREFORE RESTORE THE MAN'S WIFE; FOR HE IS A PROPHET (xx, 7). 'Who will reassure him [Abraham] that I did not touch her?' asked he. '[It is unnecessary], FOR HE IS A PROPHET,' He replied. 'And who shall make it known to all?' he pursued. AND HE SHALL PRAY FOR THEE, AND THOU SHALT LIVE (*ib.*), was the answer.[1] AND IF THOU RESTORE HER NOT, KNOW THOU THAT THOU SHALT SURELY DIE (*ib.*): this proves that no formal warning is required in the case of the Noachides.[2]

9. AND ABIMELECH ROSE EARLY IN THE MORNING, etc. (xx, 8). R. Ḥanan said: Because they had seen the smoke of Sodom ascending like that of a fiery furnace, they said: Perhaps the angels that were sent to Sodom have come hither? On that account, AND THE MEN WERE SORE AFRAID (*ib.*).

10. THEN ABIMELECH CALLED ABRAHAM, etc. (xx, 9). What did he mean by, WHAT HAST THOU DONE UNTO US?—[This was said in reference to,] *Behold, thou shalt die, because of the woman whom thou hast taken;* AND WHEREIN HAVE I SINNED AGAINST THEE, in reference to, *And if thou restore her not, know that thou shalt surely die* (*ib.* 7); THAT THOU HAST BROUGHT ON ME AND ON MY KINGDOM A GREAT SIN, in reference to, *For the Lord had fast closed up all the wombs of the*

[1] That will be proof to all, for otherwise he would certainly not pray for you [2] V. *supra*, 5.

house of Abimelech (*ib.* 18). [As for his rebuke], DEEDS THAT ARE NOT DONE, R. Ḥelbo said: [Abimelech complained,] 'In all places prosperity went before thee, whereas here famine preceded thee.[1] Thus, THOU HAST DONE DEEDS UNTO ME THAT ARE NOT DONE [elsewhere].'

11. AND ABIMELECH SAID UNTO ABRAHAM: WHAT SAWEST THOU, THAT THOU HAST DONE THIS THING? AND ABRAHAM SAID: BECAUSE I THOUGHT: SURELY THE FEAR OF GOD IS NOT IN THIS PLACE . . . AND MOREOVER SHE IS INDEED MY SISTER, THE DAUGHTER OF MY FATHER (XX, 9–12): Said he [R. Meir] to them[2]: He answered them in accordance with their own views, for they permit [marriage with] the daughter of one's father, but interdict the daughter of one's mother[3]; therefore he answered them in accordance with their practice. AND IT CAME TO PASS, WHEN GOD CAUSED ME TO WANDER (HITHE'U) FROM MY FATHER'S HOUSE, etc. (XX, 13). R. Hanan said: Would that we may interpret this verse in three ways, and so discharge our duty![4] (i) When the nations of the world wished to fall upon me[5] while I was yet in my father's house, God came to my help. (ii) Again, when the nations of the world wished to mislead me [into idolatry], God revealed Himself to me and bade me, *Get thee . . . out of thy father's house* (Gen. XII, 1). And finally, (iii) when the nations of the world wished to stray from His ways,

[1] Each complaint of Abimelech referred to something said or done. Thus in WHAT HAST THOU DONE UNTO US? he upbraided Abraham for the threat, *Behold, thou shalt die*, maintaining that it was unjustified, seeing that the position had arisen because of what Abraham himself had done The others are to be explained in similar fashion

[2] For the reference v *supra*, XVIII, 5, of which this is a fragment.

[3] I e. a paternal sister is permitted but a maternal sister is forbidden.

[4] The verse contains two difficulties: (i) '*caused to wander*' is in the plural, whereas verbs referring to God should be in the singular, and (ii) the verb '*hithe'u*' literally means, 'caused to err.' R. Ḥanan gave three different renderings of the verse to obviate these difficulties.

[5] And destroy me, because I rejected idolatry.

He raised two great men out of my father's house [i.e. family], Shem and Eber, to warn them.[1]

12. AND ABIMELECH TOOK SHEEP AND OXEN . . . AND GAVE THEM UNTO ABRAHAM . . . AND UNTO SARAH HE SAID: BEHOLD, I HAVE GIVEN THY BROTHER A THOUSAND PIECES OF SILVER, etc. (XX, 14 ff.). R. Judah b. R. Ilai said: [Abimelech reproached Abraham:] 'You went to Egypt and made merchandise of her, and you came here and traded in her. If you desire money, here is money and cover up [your] eyes from her.'[2] That is the meaning of, BEHOLD, IT IS FOR THEE A COVERING OF THE EYES.

BEHOLD, IT IS FOR THEE A COVERING (KESUTH) OF THE EYES. R. Joḥanan explained it: [Abimelech said to Abraham:] 'Make thee a garment that all may look at *it*, not at her beauty,' A COVERING OF THE EYES meaning a garment which attracts the eyes. R Berekiah said: He [Abimelech] made her a noble lady, A GARMENT OF THE EYES meaning one in which she would be covered from the eyes.[3] R. Simeon b. Lakish said. He wished to make her discontented with her husband, that she might complain: All those years he had been with her and had not made her any finery, yet this man did all this for her because of a single night [4] [Another interpretation:] He [Abimelech] said to him: 'You covered my eyes[5]; therefore the son that you will beget will be of covered eyes.'[6]

[1] These are his three renderings: (i) AND IT CAME TO PASS WHEN (the nations) ERRED (by their idolatry and wished to slay me because I rejected it), GOD (saved) ME (in) MY father's HOUSE, (ii) AND IT CAME TO PASS, WHEN (the nations tried to) MISLEAD me, that GOD (bade me to get me gone) FROM MY FATHER'S HOUSE; (iii) AND IT CAME TO PASS, WHEN (THE NATIONS) ERRED, THAT GOD (RAISED MEN) OUT OF MY FATHER'S HOUSE (to teach them better) —Mah. [2] Do not look at her to trade in her. Or: cover other people's eyes from her, that they should not desire her.

[3] As ladies of high rank were generally covered.

[4] Perhaps Resh Laḳish understood his words to bear the subtle suggestion that now Sarah would cover her eyes from Abraham—not look at him but desire Abimelech. [5] Deceived me. [6] His eyesight will be dimmed; cf. XXVII, 1.

AND BEFORE ALL MEN THOU ART REPROVED.[1] He said to her: 'This man's [Abraham's] reproof is already with him.[2] For we learned[3]. If a woman revolts against her husband,[4] seven *denarii* are deducted from her settlement[5] weekly. And why *seven denarii?* Because of the seven labours which a woman owes to her husband: grinding corn, baking, laundering, cooking, suckling her child, preparing his bed, and working in wool: hence seven. Conversely, if a man revolts against his wife,[6] her settlement is increased by three *denarii* per week. Why three? Because he owes her food, raiment, and marital privileges: hence three. But consider: if she brought in [male and] female slaves [in her dowry], she owes him nothing at all.[7] Again, if he stipulated [at the time of marriage] to be free from the obligation of food, raiment, and marital rights, he owes her nothing?[8]—Said R. Johanan: A man's suffering exceeds a woman's,[9] as it says, *And it came to pass, when she pressed him daily with her words, and urged him* (Judg. XVI, 16). This means that she slipped away from him, [and the verse continues], *That* his *soul was vexed unto death*, but her soul was not vexed.[10] Why? Because[11] she took her pleasures elsewhere.

13. AND ABRAHAM PRAYED UNTO GOD (XX, 17). R. Ḥama b. R. Ḥanina said: From the beginning of the

[1] As A.V., not R V. or Jewish Version.
[2] The passage is very puzzling The Midrash apparently understands it to mean that she was now assured that *Abraham* stood reproved, in the sense that if he now refused her her rights, the law had already provided (as the Midrash proceeds to quote) that he should be fined.
[3] Keth. 63*a*
[4] Refusing him conjugal rights, v. Keth *loc. cit*
[5] To which she would be entitled on his death or if he divorced her.
[6] Refusing her her rights.
[7] She is not bound to do this work, since the slaves can do it.
[8] Hence revolt on the part of either should not always bring these penalties. Since, then, the Mishnah states the law in *general* terms, without making an exception for these cases, it follows that the *seven* and *three denarii* respectively do not correspond to their respective duties.
[9] When conjugal rights are denied.
[10] Which proves that his suffering was greater. And for this reason her fine is greater, seven and three respectively being a reasonable estimate of how much they should be fined.
[11] Jer. reads: But some say that she took, etc. This is preferable here.

Book [of Genesis] until here we do not find this expression.[1] But as soon as Abraham prayed, this knot was untied.[2]

FOR THE LORD HAD FAST CLOSED UP (XX, 18). This 'closing up' applied to the mouth, the throat, the eye, the ear, above and below.[3] And all admitted that it was BECAUSE OF SARAH ABRAHAM'S WIFE. R. Berekiah said: It was because he dared to approach the shoe of that lady. And the whole of that night Sarah lay prostrate on her face, crying, 'Sovereign of the Universe! Abraham went forth [from his land] on Thine assurance, and I went forth with faith; Abraham is without this prison while I am within!' Said the Holy One, blessed be He, to her: 'Whatever I do, I do for thy sake, and all will say, "It is BECAUSE OF SARAH ABRAHAM'S WIFE."' R. Levi said: The whole of that night an angel stood with a whip in his hand; when she ordered, 'Strike,' he struck, and when she bade him, 'Desist,' he ceased. And why such severity? Because she told him [Abimelech], 'I am a married woman,' yet he would not leave her. R. Eleazar said, and it was also taught in the name of R. Liezer b. Jacob: We know that Pharaoh was smitten with leprosy and Abimelech with the closing up [of the orifices] How do we know that what is said here is to be applied there, and vice versa? Because *'for the sake of'* occurs in both places, in order that an analogy should be drawn.[4]

[1] We do not find anyone praying to God for another's sake

[2] The 'knot' refers to the 'closing up' (v. 18), the knot was untied, and they were healed.

[3] This comment is based on the repetition of the verb in the Hebrew

[4] For the whole passage v *supra*, XLI, 2, and notes *ad loc*

Chapter LIII (VAYERA)

1. AND THE LORD REMEMBERED SARAH AS HE HAD SAID (XXI, 1). It is thus that Scripture writes, *And all the trees of the field shall know that I the Lord have brought down the high tree, have exalted the low tree, have dried up the green tree, and have made the dry tree to flourish; I the Lord have spoken and done it* (Ezek. XVII, 24). R. Judan said: Not like those who speak but do not perform. R. Berekiah said on the verse, '*I the Lord have spoken and done it*': Where did He speak it?—*At the set time I will return unto thee . . . and Sarah shall have a son* (Gen. XVIII, 14). '*And I have done it*'—AND THE LORD DID UNTO SARAH AS HE HAD SPOKEN. '*And all the trees of the field shall know*' refers to the people, as you read, *For the tree of the field is man* (Deut. XX, 19).[1] '*That I the Lord have brought down the high tree*' alludes to Abimelech; '*Have exalted the low tree*'—to Abraham; '*Have dried up the green tree*'—to Abimelech's wives, as it is written, *For the Lord had fast closed up all the wombs of the house of Abimelech* (Gen. XX, 18). '*And have made the dry tree to flourish*' alludes to Sarah. '*I the Lord have spoken*': Said R. Judan: Not like those who speak but do not perform. R. Berekiah commented: '*I the Lord have spoken*'[2]: Where did He speak it? '*At the set time I will return unto thee*,' etc. '*And I have done it*': thus it is written, AND THE LORD DID UNTO SARAH AS HE HAD SPOKEN.

2. *Shall a man be juster than God, shall a man be purer than his Maker* (Job IV, 17)? Is it possible for a mortal to be more righteous than his Creator; '*Shall a man be purer than his Maker*': is it possible for a mortal to be purer than his Creator? Now what did Elisha say to the Shunammite? '*At this season, when the time cometh round, thou shalt embrace a son.*' And she said to him: '*Nay,*

[1] E.V. '*For is the tree*' . . .?
[2] This passage is absent in cur. edd. and is apparently a mere repetition.

my lord, thou man of God, do not lie unto thy handmaid (II Kings IV, 16). For the angels who gave the good tidings to Sarah said thus to her: "*At the set time* I *will return unto thee,*" etc.'[1] 'Those angels, knowing that they live for ever, could say, "*At the set time* I *will return unto thee,*"' he replied. 'But I am mortal, here to-day and dead to-morrow; whether I am alive or dead [by then], "*At this season . . . thou shalt embrace a son.*"' Now what is written there further? *And the woman conceived, and bore a son* (*ib.* 17). Now if the words of a mere mortal were fulfilled, how much more those of the Holy One, blessed be He! Hence, AND THE LORD REMEMBERED SARAH AS HE HAD SAID, etc.

3. *For though the fig-tree doth not blossom,* etc. (Hab III, 17). This alludes to Abraham, as in the verse, *I saw your fathers as the first-ripe in the fig-tree at her first season* (Hos. IX, 10). *Neither is there fruit in the vines* (Hab. *loc. cit.*), alludes to Sarah, as you read, *Thy wife shall be as a fruitful vine* (Ps. CXXVIII, 3). *The labour of the olive faileth* (Hab. *loc. cit.*): the faces of those angels who gave the good tidings to Sarah shone like an olive: were they lying?[2] No, but *The fields* (shedemoth) *yielded no food,* which means, the withered breasts (*shadayim methin*) yielded no food.[3] *The flock is cut off from the fold* (Hab. *loc. cit.*) has the same connotation as in the verse, *And ye My flock, the flock of My pasture, are men* (Ezek. XXXIV, 31). *There is no herd in the stalls* (Hab. *loc. cit.*), has the meaning it has in the verse, *And Ephraim is a heifer well broken, that loveth to thresh* (Hos. X, 11).[4] Subsequently, however, Sarah exclaimed, 'What! am I to lose faith in my Creator! Heaven forfend! I will not lose faith in my

[1] Thus they promised to return—a guarantee that their promises would be fulfilled—whereas you do not promise this.
[2] Surely not! *Kiḥesh* (E.V. 'faileth') means primarily 'to lie', 'to fail' being a secondary meaning (not to be true to its function).
[3] Even if Sarah believed them, she still feared that she would be unable to suckle the child.
[4] Thus Sarah feared that 'flocks' would be cut off from her and there would be no *herd* in her stalls—she could not bring up children.

Creator, *For I will rejoice in the Lord, I will exalt in the God of my salvation'* (Hab. III, 18). Said the Holy One, blessed be He, to her: 'Since thou didst not lose thy faith, I too will not give thee cause to lose faith.' But rather, AND THE LORD REMEMBERED SARAH, etc.

The grass withereth, the flower fadeth (Isa. XL, 8): that means, the grass of Abimelech withereth and his flower fadeth.[1] *But the word of our God shall stand for ever* (*ib.*); hence, AND THE LORD REMEMBERED SARAH, AS HE HAD SAID.

4. *For ever, O Lord, Thy word standeth fast in heaven* (Ps. CXIX, 89)—but not on earth? But it means, what Thou didst say to Abraham in heaven[2]: *At the set time I will return unto thee*, etc. Hence, AND THE LORD REMEMBERED SARAH. R. Menaḥema and R. Naḥman of Joppa in the name of R. Jacob of Caesarea commenced with the text: *O God of hosts, return, we beseech Thee* (Ps. LXXX, 15). Return and do what Thou didst promise Abraham. *Look from heaven, and behold* (*ib.*)—as it says, *Look now toward heaven, and count the stars*, etc (Gen. XV, 5). *And be mindful of this vine* (Ps. *loc. cit.*): thus, AND THE LORD REMEMBERED SARAH.

R. Samuel b. Naḥman commenced thus: *God is not a man, that He should lie*, etc. (Num. XXIII, 18). Said R. Samuel b. Naḥman: In this verse the beginning does not correspond to the end, nor the end to the beginning. Thus it commences, '*God is not a man that He should lie,*' etc., while it concludes, *When He hath said, He will not do it, and when He hath spoken, He will not make it good.*[3] But the meaning is this: When the Holy One, blessed be He, decrees to bring good upon the world, then, '*God is not a man, that He should lie*'. But when He decrees to bring evil upon the world, then, '*When He hath*

[1] This probably refers to his wives; v. Gen. XX, 18
[2] I.e. His promise; *Look now toward heaven*, etc. (Gen XV, 5).—Mah., M K and Y T. explain differently.
[3] E.V. '*Will He not do it . . . will He not make it good'?* But the Midrash renders it as a positive statement

said, He will not do it'. When He said to Abraham: *For in Isaac shall seed be called to thee* (Gen. XXI, 12), then *'God is not a man, that he should lie', neither the son of man, that He should repent.* When He said to him, *Take now thy son, thine only one,* etc. (*ib.* XXII, 2), then, *'When He hath said, He will not do it, and when He hath spoken, He will not make it good.'* When God said to Moses, *I have surely remembered you* (Ex. III, 16), then, *'God is not a man, that He should lie, neither the son of man, that He should repent.'* But when He said to him, *Let Me alone, that I may destroy them* (Deut. IX, 14), then, *'When He hath said, He will not do it, and when He hath spoken, He will not make it good.'* When God said to Abraham, *And also that nation, whom they shall serve, will I judge,* etc. (Gen. XV, 14), then, *'God is not a man, that He should lie, neither the son of man, that He should repent.'* But when He said to him, *And they shall serve them, and they shall afflict them four hundred years* (*ib.* 13), then, *'When He hath said, He will not do it, and when He hath spoken, He will not make it good.'*[1] Finally, when God said to him, *I will certainly return unto thee,* etc. (Gen. XVIII, 10), then, *'God is not a man, that He should lie,'* etc., but, AND THE LORD REMEMBERED SARAH.

5. *Who hast kept with Thy servant David my father,* etc. (I Kings VIII, 24). *'Who hast kept with Thy servant'* alludes to Abraham.[2] *That which Thou didst promise him,* viz. *At the set time I will return unto thee,* etc. (Gen. XVIII, 14). *Yea, Thou spokest with Thy mouth, and hast fulfilled it with Thy hand, as it is this day* (I Kings *loc. cit.*), viz. AND THE LORD REMEMBERED SARAH.

Who maketh the barren woman to dwell in her house (Ps. CXIII, 9). This alludes to Sarah, as it is written, *And Sarai was barren* (Gen. XI, 30); *As a joyful mother of*

[1] The actual period of servitude was far less than four hundred years.
[2] Notwithstanding that David is explicitly mentioned, the Rabbis held that in addition to their plain meaning Biblical verses often have a hidden and subtle meaning; and in accordance with the latter this verse refers to Abraham too.

children, as it says, *Sarah has given children suck* (*ib.* XXI, 7).

AND THE LORD REMEMBERED SARAH AS HE HAD SAID. R. Judah said: AND THE LORD REMEMBERED SARAH AS HE HAD SAID refers to the promises which were prefaced with the term 'saying' (*amirah*); AND THE LORD DID UNTO SARAH AS HE HAD SPOKEN refers to the promises prefaced with the term 'speaking' (*dibbur*).[1] R Nehemiah said: AND THE LORD REMEMBERED SARAH AS HE HAD SAID refers to what He said to her through the angel, while AND THE LORD DID UNTO SARAH AS HE HAD SPOKEN refers to what He Himself said to her. R. Judah expounded: AND THE LORD REMEMBERED SARAH—to give her a son; AND THE LORD DID UNTO SARAH AS HE HAD SPOKEN—to bless her with milk. Said R. Nehemiah to him: Had she then already been informed about milk? This teaches, however, that God restored to her the days of her youth. R. Abbahu said: He inspired all people with fear of her, so that they should not call her 'barren woman'. R. Judan said: She lacked an ovary, whereupon the Lord fashioned an ovary for her.[2]

R Adda said: The Holy One, blessed be He, is a trustee[3]: Amalek deposited with Him bundles of thorns [wrong-doings]; therefore He returned to him bundles of thorns [punishment], as it says, *I remember that which Amalek did to Israel* (I Sam. XV, 2). Sarah laid up with Him a store of pious acts and good deeds; therefore the Lord returned her [the reward for] these, as it says, AND THE LORD REMEMBERED SARAH.

[1] *Amirah* refers to Gen. XVII, 19 *And God said* (wayyomer, same root as amirah): *Nay, but Sarah thy wife shall bear thee a son. Dibbur* refers to XV, 18: *Unto thy seed have I given this land*, this passage being introduced by the passage (XV, 1) *After these things the word* (debar, same root as dibbur) *of the Lord came unto Abram.*

[2] V. *supra*, XLVII, 2, for notes.

[3] He returns what is deposited with Him. He connects פקד in this verse (E.V. '*remembered*') with פקדון 'a deposit', and renders: And the Lord returned what Sarah had deposited, as explained.

6. R. Isaac said: It is written, *And if the woman be not defiled, but be clean; then shall she be cleared, and shall conceive seed* (Num. v, 28).[1] Then this woman [Sarah] who had entered the houses of Pharaoh and Abimelech and yet emerged undefiled—surely it was but right that she should be remembered.[2] R. Judah b. R. Simon said: Although R. Huna said that there is an angel appointed over desire, Sarah had no need for such, but He in His glory [made her conceive]; hence, AND THE LORD REMEMBERED SARAH.

AND SARAH CONCEIVED, AND BORE ABRAHAM A SON. (XXI, 2). This teaches that she did not steal seed from elsewhere. A SON IN HIS OLD AGE: this teaches that his [Isaac's] feature were like his own. AT THE SET TIME OF WHICH GOD HAD SPOKEN TO HIM. R. Judan said: He was born at nine months [of pregnancy], so that it might not be said that he was a scion of Abimelech's house. R. Ḥunia said: He was born at seven months, which were nine incomplete months.[3] R. Huna said in Hezekiah's name: He was born at midday. For 'set time' (*mo'ed*) is said here, while elsewhere it says, *At the season* (mo'ed) *that thou camest forth out of Egypt* (Deut. XVI, 6).[4]

7. AND ABRAHAM CALLED THE NAME OF HIS SON THAT WAS BORN UNTO HIM, WHOM SARAH BORE TO HIM, ISAAC—YIZḤAḲ (XXI, 3). [The name signifies] Law had gone forth (*yaẓa ḥoḳ*) to the world, a gift was made to the world. R. Isaac Ḥipusheh said: *Yod* is ten, corresponding to the ten commandments; *ẓaddi* is ninety: *And shall Sarah, that is ninety years old, bear* (Gen. XVII,

[1] The reference is to a woman suspected of adultery who successfully passed the water test. [2] I.e. conceive

[3] After she left Abimelech's house—it was seven months plus a day in the month before and a day in the month after. Each of these could count technically as months, so that they were nine incomplete months Y.T., however, reads more simply: he was born at seven incomplete months, i.e. after just over six months of pregnancy.

[4] V. Ex. XII, 51. *And it came to pass in the middle of that day* (E.V. .. *'the selfsame day'*) *that the Lord did bring the children of Israel out of the land of Egypt. Mo'ed* is assumed to have the same meaning in both places.

17); *kuf* is hundred. *Shall a child be born unto him that is a hundred years old* (*ib.*)? *heth* [is eight], in reference to circumcision, as it says, AND ABRAHAM CIRCUMCISED HIS SON ISAAC WHEN HE WAS EIGHT DAYS OLD (XXI, 4).

8. AND SARAH SAID: GOD HATH MADE JOY FOR ME; EVERY ONE THAT HEARETH WILL REJOICE WITH ME (XXI, 6). R. Berekiah, R. Judah b. R. Simon, and R. Ḥanan in the name of R. Samuel b. R. Isaac said: If Reuben has cause to rejoice, what does it matter to Simeon? Similarly, if Sarah was remembered, what did it matter to others? But when the matriarch Sarah was remembered [gave birth], many other barren women were remembered with her; many deaf gained their hearing; many blind had their eyes opened, many insane became sane. For 'making' [HATH MADE] is mentioned here, and also elsewhere, viz. *And he made a release to the provinces* (Est. II, 18). As the making mentioned there means that a gift was granted to the world,[1] so the making mentioned here means that a gift was granted to the world. R. Levi said: She increased the light of the luminaries: 'making' is mentioned here, viz. GOD HATH MADE FOR ME, while elsewhere it says, *And God made the two lights* (Gen. I, 16).[2]

9. AND SHE SAID: WHO WOULD HAVE SAID (MILLEL) UNTO ABRAHAM THAT SARAH SHOULD GIVE CHILDREN SUCK (XXI, 7)? R. Phinehas said in R. Ḥelkiah's name: Not *amar* or *dibber* but MILLEL is written[3]: thus she indirectly drew his attention to the fact that he had begotten child at the age of a hundred years.[4] R. Phinehas said in R. Ḥelkiah's name: [MILLEL signifies that] the standing crop of our father Abraham

[1] A remission of taxes

[2] Hence by analogy 'making' in the first verse bears a similar connotation.—This probably means poetically that Isaac's birth filled the house with light.—M.K.

[3] The usual word is *amar* (said) or *dibber* (spoke)

[4] This being the numerical value of '*millel*'; מ (40) and ל (30) twice = 100

had been dried up, but it now turned to ripe ears of corn (*meliloth*).[1] THAT SARAH SHOULD HAVE GIVEN CHILDREN SUCK: she suckled builders.[2] Our mother Sarah was extremely modest. Said Abraham to her: 'This is not a time for modesty, but uncover your breasts so that all may know that the Holy One, blessed be He, has begun to perform miracles.' She uncovered her breasts and the milk gushed forth as from two fountains, and noble ladies came and had their children suckled by her, saying, 'We do not merit that our children should be suckled with the milk of that righteous woman.' The Rabbis said: Whoever came for the sake of heaven[3] became God-fearing. R. Aḥa said: Even one who did not come for the sake of heaven[4] was given dominion [i.e. greatness] in this world. Yet they did not continue to enjoy it, for when they stood aloof at Sinai and would not accept the Torah, that dominion was taken from them. Thus it is written, *He looseth the bonds of kings, and bindeth their loins with a girdle* (Job XII, 18).

10. AND THE CHILD GREW, AND WAS WEANED (XXI, 8) R. Hoshaya the Elder said: He was weaned from temptation.[5] The Rabbis said: He was weaned from his mother's milk. AND ABRAHAM MADE A GREAT FEAST. R. Judah said: The great One of the Universe was there.[6] R. Judan said in the name of R. Jose b. R. Ḥanina: *Then the king made a great feast* (Est. II, 18) means that the great One of the world was there.[7] Thus it is written,

[1] A metaphor: he regained his youthful virility.

[2] By a play on words *banim* (children) is read *bana'im* (builders).—Those who were suckled by her (as explained in the text) became God-fearing and were granted dominion, and they built up the world, as it were. Cur edd.: It does not say 'She suckled a son', but '*She suckled sons (children)*'. [3] That her child might drink Sarah's milk and be imbued with a spirit of righteousness

[4] But merely to see whether the miracle was really true.

[5] He was thirteen years old, when the duties of manhood (in the religious sense) became incumbent upon him.—This is probably the source of the practice of celebrating the thirteenth birthday with a feast

[6] That is the meaning of GREAT. [7] God approved this feast in Esther's honour and was Himself there, as it were.

For the Lord will again rejoice over thee for good (Deut. XXX, 9)—in the days of Mordecai and Esther—*As He rejoiced over thy fathers* (*ib.*)—in the days of Abraham, Isaac, and Jacob.[1] R. Judah said: A GREAT FEAST means a feast for great people, for Og and all the great men were there. Said they to Og, 'Did you not say that Abraham is like a barren mule and cannot beget child?' 'Even now what is [the value of] his gift,' replied he; 'is he [Isaac] not puny? I can crush him by putting my finger on him' Said the Holy One, blessed be He, to him: 'What meanest thou by disparaging My gift! By thy life, thou wilt yet see countless thousands and myriads of his descendants, and thine own fate will be to fall into their hands,' as it says, *And the Lord said unto Moses: Fear him not; for I have delivered him into thy hand* (Num. XXI, 34).[2] (R. Levi said. The cradle was rocked for the first time in the house of our father Abraham.)[3] For R. Joshua b. Menahama said. The thirty-one kings slain by Joshua were all present at Abraham's banquet. Yet there were not thirty-one only, but as R. Berekiah and R. Ḥelbo and R. Parnak in R. Johanan's name said: *The king of Jericho, one* (Josh. XII, 9)[4]: why state '*one*'?[5] Because it means, he and his regent.[6]

11. AND SARAH SAW THE SON OF HAGAR THE EGYPTIAN, etc. (XXI, 9). R. Simeon b. Yoḥai said: R. Akiba used to interpret this to his [Ishmael's] shame.

[1] Yalkuṭ omits Isaac and Jacob, who are irrelevant here

[2] M.K. the past tense, *I have delivered*, implies long ere now—his fate had been sealed since the time of Abraham

[3] The meaning is doubtful Th. understands it as an allusion to the legend that originally children were born full grown (v. *supra*, XXXVI, 1); Isaac was the first to be born as a baby, and thus he was the first for whom a cradle was required. Or perhaps· the first step to the downfall of the heathen kings was taken then. This would explain the following statement Otherwise one must assume a lacuna in the text

[4] The passage there enumerates the thirty-one kings defeated by Joshua.

[5] Obviously each king was one.

[6] Thus we have a far larger number. Th. explains (on the basis of various passages) that the thirty-one kings were not really kings but regents of kings outside Eretz Israel; cf. *infra*, LXXXV, 14.

Thus R. Akiba lectured: AND SARAH SAW THE SON OF HAGAR THE EGYPTIAN, WHOM SHE HAD BORNE UNTO ABRAHAM, MAKING SPORT. Now MAKING SPORT refers to nought else but immorality, as in the verse, *The Hebrew servant, whom thou hast brought unto us, came in unto me to* make sport *of me* (Gen. XXXIX, 17). Thus this teaches that Sarah saw Ishmael ravish maidens,[1] seduce married women and dishonour them. R. Ishmael taught: This term SPORT refers to idolatry, as in the verse, *And rose up to* make sport (Ex. XXXII, 6).[2] This teaches that Sarah saw Ishmael build altars, catch locusts,[3] and sacrifice them. R. Eleazar said: The term sport refers to bloodshed, as in the verse, *Let the young men, I pray thee, arise and* sport *before us* (II Sam. II, 14).[4] R. 'Azariah said in R. Levi's name: Ishmael said to Isaac, 'Let us go and see our portions in the field'[5]; then Ishmael would take a bow and arrows and shoot them in Isaac's direction, whilst pretending to be playing. Thus it is written, *As a madman who casteth fire-brands, arrows, and death; so is the man that deceiveth his neighbour, and saith: Am not I in sport* (Prov. XXII, 18 f.)? But I say[6]: This term sport [mockery] refers to inheritance.[7] For when our father Isaac was born all rejoiced, whereupon Ishmael said to them, 'You are fools, for I am the firstborn and I receive a double portion.' You may infer this from Sarah's protest to Abraham: FOR THE SON OF THIS BONDWOMAN SHALL NOT BE HEIR WITH MY SON, WITH ISAAC (XXI, 10). WITH MY SON, even if he were not Isaac; or WITH ISAAC, even if he were not my son; how much the more, WITH MY SON, WITH ISAAC!

[1] The rendering is conjectural. Others: take forcible possession of gardens—where women were generally engaged.
[2] In connection with the Golden Calf.
[3] As children play.—He was yet too young to handle large animals.
[4] See v 16
[5] Let us see how the crops are faring
[6] R. Simeon b. Yohai now gives his own interpretation.
[7] Tosefta adds: Heaven forfend that a son who received training from Abraham should have engaged in idolatry, adultery, or bloodshed.

12. AND THE THING WAS VERY GRIEVOUS IN ABRAHAM'S SIGHT (XXI, 11). Thus it is written, *And shutteth his eyes from looking upon evil* (Isa. XXXIII, 15).[1]

AND GOD SAID UNTO ABRAHAM: LET IT NOT BE GRIEVOUS IN THY SIGHT . . . FOR IN ISAAC SHALL SEED BE CALLED TO THEE (XXI, 12): R. Judan b. Shilum said: Not 'Isaac', but IN ISAAC is written here.[2] R. 'Azariah said in the name of Bar Ḥuṭah: The *beth* (IN) denotes two, i.e. [thy seed shall be called] in him who recognises the existence of two worlds; he shall inherit two worlds. R. Judan b. R. Shalum said: It is written, *Remember His marvellous works that He hath done, His signs* [E.V. *'wonders'*], *and the judgments of His mouth* (Ps cv, 5): [God says]: 'I have given a sign [whereby the true descendants of Abraham can be known], viz. he who expressly recognises [God's judgments]: thus whoever believes in the two worlds shall be called "thy seed",[3] while he who rejects belief in two worlds shall not be called "thy seed".'

13. AND ABRAHAM AROSE UP EARLY IN THE MORNING, AND TOOK BREAD AND A BOTTLE OF WATER (XXI, 14). Abraham's household was liberal, yet it says, AND ABRAHAM AROSE UP EARLY IN THE MORNING . . . AND GAVE IT UNTO HAGAR? The reason is that such was the custom of slaves, to carry water in their pitchers.[4] PUTTING IT ON HER SHOULDER

[1] He shut his eyes from Ishmael's evil ways, and was reluctant to send him away.

[2] Without the IN, it would indicate that *all* Isaac's descendants will count as Abraham's descendants; the IN, however, limits it. only *some*, not all, Esau and his descendants being excluded.

[3] God's justice is not always apparent in this world, the righteous suffering and the wicked prospering. Hence belief therein demands as a corollary belief in another world, where the balance shall be redressed Hence the following verse continues· *O ye seed of Abraham His servant.*

[4] The passage is puzzling and commentators differ widely in their interpretations. The present translation is based on Radal, and possibly involves a slight emendation of the text, '*yet* it says' instead of '*as* it says'. Thus the Midrash asks: Surely Abraham, the head of a house

AND THE CHILD[1]: he was twenty-seven years old,[2] yet you say, PUTTING IT ON HER SHOULDER AND THE CHILD! This, however, teaches that Sarah cast an evil eye on him, whereupon he was seized with feverish pains.[3] The proof lies in the verse, AND THE WATER IN THE BOTTLE WAS SPENT (XXI, 15), a sick person drinking frequently. AND SHE CAST THE CHILD UNDER ONE OF THE SHRUBS—SIḤIM (*ib.*). R. Meir said: It was a juniper tree,[4] these usually growing in the desert. R. Ammi said: [UNDER ONE OF THE SIḤIM is an intimation] that there the ministering angels spoke (*hesiḥu*) to her.

AND SHE WENT AND SAT HER DOWN OVER AGAINST HIM (MI-NEGED) A GOOD WAY OFF (XXI, 16). Here you say, AND SAT DOWN OVER AGAINST HIM—MI-NEGED (whilst elsewhere it says, *Over against it* (mi-neged), *round about the tent of meeting* (Num II, 2). A GOOD WAY OFF: here you say, A GOOD WAY OFF (HARHEḲ), AS IT WERE A BOWSHOT),[5] whilst elsewhere you read, *Yet there shall be a space* (raḥoḳ) *between you and it, about two thousand cubits by measure* (Josh. III, 4). Thus we learn the meaning of *neged* from *neged* and *harḥek* from *raḥoḳ*.[6] R. Isaac observed: The phrase As

famed for its liberality, should not have sent her away with nothing more than this! The answer follows that it was the practice of slaves to carry pitchers of water, and Abraham was anxious that their servile rank should be known, so that Ishmael might not subsequently claim to be his free-born son and dispute Isaac's title to be heir. Possibly the Midrash means that he gave her much more, but that Scripture draws particular attention to the pitcher of water, for the reason stated. V. Ex. R. I, 1, for a different reason. [1] Disregarding the comma which in E.V. follows the word SHOULDER.

[2] Ishmael was fourteen years old at Isaac's birth (cf XVI, 16, with XXI, 5). This assumes that Isaac was now thirteen years old, cf. *supra*, 10, p. 468, n. 5 The Yalḳuṭ reads 'seventeen', on the assumption that Isaac was then three years old. [3] And became weak, so that he had to be carried [4] Text as emended; Radal.

[5] The bracketed passage is added from cur. add.

[6] I e by comparing these verses we learn that she sat at a distance of two thousand cubits. The exact point of the Midrash is doubtful, particularly if the passage added from cur. edd. is omitted, but the rendering gives the general idea.

THE SHOTS OF A BOW[1] [shows the distance, for] two bowshots cover a mile. R. Berekiah said: The phrase connotes, as a woman who impugned[2] God's justice, saying, 'Yesterday Thou didst promise me, *I will greatly multiply thy seed*, etc. (Gen. XVI, 10), and now he is dying of thirst!'

14. Thus it is written, *Thou hast counted* nudi (Ps. LVI, 9): which means, Thou hast counted my wanderings.[3] *Put Thou my tears into Thy bottle* (*ib.*). [Estimate them by] that woman of the bottle (*nod*).[4] *Are they not in Thy book* (*ib.*)? as it is written in the Book of Psalms, *Hear my prayer, O Lord, and give ear unto my cry; keep not silence at my tears* (XXXIX, 13): Thou didst not keep silence at Hagar's tears; wilt Thou keep silence at mine! And shouldst Thou reply, 'Because she was a stranger[5] she was more beloved,' then I too am thus, *For I am a stranger with Thee, a sojourner, as all my fathers were* (*ib.*).

AND THE ANGEL OF GOD CALLED TO HAGAR (XXI, 17)—for Abraham's sake; while [GOD HATH HEARD THE VOICE OF THE LAD] WHERE HE IS connotes for his own sake, for a sick person's prayers on his own behalf are more efficacious than those of anyone else.

WHERE HE IS. R. Simon said: The ministering angels hastened to indict him, exclaiming, 'Sovereign of the Universe! Wilt Thou bring up a well for one who will one day slay Thy children with thirst?'[6] 'What is he now?' He demanded. 'Righteous,' was the answer. 'I judge man only as he is at the moment,' said He. [Therefore Scripture continues], ARISE, LIFT UP THE LAD, etc.[7]

AND GOD OPENED HER EYES, etc. (XXI, 18 f.). R.

[1] Lit. translation, with the plural 'shots'.
[2] A play on words, *ki-metahawe* (as the shots) being connected with *ke-mateheth*, as one who criticises. [3] The Midrash renders *nudi* by a more familiar word, its rendering agreeing with E V.
[4] Sc Hagar. As Thou didst listen to her tears, so do Thou listen to mine.
[5] Not directly of Abraham's family but a convert.
[6] V Isa. XXI, 13 f., which is interpreted as an unheeded appeal by the Israelites to the Arabs, regarded as descendants of Ishmael.
[7] That is the meaning of WHERE HE IS, i.e in his present state.

Benjamin b. Levi and R. Jonathan b. Amram both said: All may be presumed to be blind, until the Holy One, blessed be He, enlightens their eyes. That follows from this verse: AND GOD OPENED HER EYES AND SHE SAW, etc.

AND SHE WENT AND FILLED THE BOTTLE WITH WATER. This proves that she was lacking in faith.[1]

15. AND GOD WAS WITH (ETH) THE LAD, AND HE GREW (XXI, 20). R. Ishmael asked R. Akiba: Since you have studied twenty-two years under Nahum of Gimzo [who interpreted every] *ak* (save that) and *rak* (except) as limitations, and *eth* and *gam* (also) as extensions, tell me what of the *eth* written here? If the text stated, 'And God was the lad,' it would be unintelligible, he replied[2]; hence, WITH (ETH) THE LAD must be written. Thereupon he cited to him, *For it is no empty thing from you* (Deut. XXXII, 47), and if it is empty, it is so on your account, because you are unable to interpret it rightly: ETH THE LAD, however, means with him, his ass-drivers, and his camel-drivers and his household.[3]

AND BECAME AN ARCHER—ROBEH ḲASHOTH (*ib.*). Even as he grew (*rabbah*), so did his cruelty (*kashiuth*) grow with him.[4] [Another version]: while a lad (*robeh*), he trained himself in the use of the bow. [Another interpretation]: Master (*rabbah*) of all archers.

AND HE DWELT IN THE WILDERNESS OF PARAN, etc. (*ib.*). R. Isaac said: Throw a stick into the air, and it will fall back to its place of origin [the ground]. Thus, because it is written, *And she had a handmaid, an Egyptian, whose name was Hagar* (*ib.* XVI, 1), therefore it is written, AND HIS MOTHER TOOK HIM A WIFE OUT OF EGYPT.

[1] 'Rashi' and M.K: because she *filled* the bottle, fearing that the well would disappear again.
[2] The *eth* is grammatically required. [3] Cf. *supra*, I, 14; XXII, 2.
[4] The rendering is conjectural and does not quite follow Th's. ed.

CHAPTER LIV (VAYERA)

1. AND IT CAME TO PASS AT THAT TIME, THAT ABIMELECH AND PHICOL THE CAPTAIN OF HIS HOST, etc. (XXI, 22). It is written, *When a man's ways please the Lord, He maketh even his enemies to be at peace with him* (Prov. XVI, 7). R. Johanan said: '*His enemies*' refers to his wife, as it says, *A man's enemies are the people of his own house* (Micah VII, 6). It once happened that a woman brought a charge against her husband to the governor, and he beheaded him. Some say, He executed her too. R. Samuel b. Nahman said: The verse refers to the serpent. The School of Halafta b Saul taught: A serpent is very fond of garlic. It once happened that a serpent went down into a house, where he found a dish of garlic, of which he ate, and he then spat [his poison] into it. Now there was a snake in the house, which could not fight against it; but as soon as the first departed, it went and filled the dish with earth.[1] R. Joshua b. Levi said: It refers to the Tempter.[2] Generally speaking, if one is brought up along with another for two or three years, he becomes closely attached to him; but this one [the Tempter] grows with man from his youth until old age, and yet if he can, he strikes him down even in his seventies or in his eighties. It was this that David said: *All my bones shall say: Lord, who is like unto Thee, who deliverest the poor from him that is too strong for him, yea, the poor and the needy from him that spoileth him* (Ps. XXXV, 10).[3] R. Aha observed: Is there a greater despoiler than he [the Tempter]? And of him Solomon said: *If thine enemy be hungry, give him bread to eat*, etc. (Prov. XXV, 21): [resist him] with the bread of the Torah, as you read, *Come, eat of my bread* (*ib.* IX, 5)[4]; *And if he be thirsty, give him water to drink* (*ib.* 25)—the water of the Torah, as

[1] So that they should not eat of it. Thus even the serpent, man's natural enemy (v. Gen. III, 15), became his friend.
[2] The evil desires personified. [3] Meaning the Tempter.
[4] The speaker is wisdom—the Torah—personified. Here too by the enemy the Tempter is understood.

in the verse, *Ho, everyone that thirsteth, come ye for water* (Isa. LV, 1). R. Berekiah said: 'Even (*gam*) *his enemies*,' instead of simply 'his enemies', includes the pests of his house,[1] such as insects, vermin, and flies.[2]

Another interpretation: '*When a man's ways please the Lord*,' etc. (refers to Abraham, who is called a man, as it is written, *Calling . . . the man of My counsel from a far country* (Isa. XLVI, 11)[3]; '*Even his enemies*' refers to Abimelech, as it is written),[4] AND IT CAME TO PASS AT THAT TIME, THAT ABIMELECH AND PHICOL THE CAPTAIN OF HIS HOST SPOKE, etc.

2. AND PHICOL. R. Judah and R. Nehemiah disagree. R. Judah said: Phicol was actually his name. R. Nehemiah said: [Phicol is an attributive, meaning] the mouth (*peh*) responsible for the provisioning of all (*kol*) his troops.

GOD IS WITH THEE IN ALL THAT THOU DOEST. Now the people of the world had said: If he were a righteous man, would he not have begotten children? Hence when he did beget a child, they said to him, GOD IS WITH THEE IN ALL THAT THOU DOEST. Again, if he were a righteous man, would he have heeded his wife?[5] But when, *In all that Sarah saith unto thee, hearken unto her voice* (Gen. XXI, 12), was said to him, they admitted, GOD IS WITH THEE IN ALL THAT THOU DOEST. Further, if he were a righteous man, would he have thrust away his firstborn son? But when they saw his behaviour, they said to him, GOD IS WITH THEE, etc.

Another interpretation: Because the region of Sodom was now desolate and travellers had ceased, with the result that his stores were now in no way diminished, [he said: Why should I allow hospitality to cease from my house? Therefore he went and pitched his tent in

[1] Cf *supra*, LIII, 15, on *gam*
[2] Even they cease to be harmful.—The idea may be that everything in nature has its place; cf. *supra*, X, 7.
[3] V *supra*, XV, 4.
[4] The bracketed passage is added from cur. edd.
[5] When she caused Hagar to flee the first time (Gen XVI, 6 *seq.*).

Gerar].[1] In consequence [all exclaimed], GOD IS WITH THEE IN ALL THAT THOU DOEST, etc.[2]

NOW THEREFORE SWEAR UNTO ME HERE BY GOD THAT THOU WILT NOT DEAL FALSELY WITH ME, NOR WITH MY SON, NOR WITH MY SON'S SON (XXI, 22 f.): thus far is a father's compassion for his son.[3] R. Abba b. Kahana said: Thus far for brothers in partnership.[4]

R. Jose b. Ḥanina said: It is written, *But mine enemies are strong in health* (Ps. XXXVIII, 20). What was given to Abraham for seven generations was given to Abimelech for three.[5] Why was it that *God led them not by the way of the land of the Philistines* (Ex. XIII, 17.)? Because his [Abimelech's] grandson was still alive then.[6]

BUT ACCORDING TO THE KINDNESS THAT I HAVE DONE UNTO THEE (*ib.*). What kindness then had he shown him? By saying to him, *Behold, my land is before thee: dwell where it pleaseth thee* (*ib.* XX, 15). Yet even so, Abraham had not accepted this offer.[7]

3. AND ABRAHAM REPROVED ABIMELECH, etc. (XXI, 25). R. Jose b. R. Ḥanina said: Reproof leads to love, as it says, *Reprove a wise man, and he will love thee* (Prov. IX, 8). Such indeed is R. Jose b. Hanina's view, for he said: Love unaccompanied by reproof is not love. Resh Laḳish said: Reproof leads to peace; hence, AND ABRAHAM REPROVED ABIMELECH.[8] Such is his view,

[1] The bracketed passage has been added from LII, 3, to complete the sense. [2] They were impressed by his hospitality.

[3] He is not interested in the generations after his grandson

[4] When brothers inherit an estate in partnership, it remains so until the third generation, the profits being shared. After that they can insist on a division

[5] 'Rashi' and M.K.: Seven generations of Abraham had passed by the time the Israelites entered the Promised Land, viz.: Abraham, Isaac, Jacob, Levi, Kohath, Amram, and Moses; whereas there were only four generations of Abimelech's seed, as it says, *And in the fourth generation they shall come back hither* (Gen XV, 16—'*fourth*' must refer to the Canaanites) [6] Hence Abraham's oath stood in the way.

[7] See v. 32, which shows that Abraham was not dwelling in their land at this period. [8] The outcome being an oath of peace, v. 32.

for he said: Peace unaccompanied by reproof is not peace.

BECAUSE OF THE WELL OF WATER, WHICH ABIMELECH'S SERVANTS HAD VIOLENTLY TAKEN AWAY—GAZLU (*ib.*). Who is called a robber (*gazlan*)? R. Leazar, the son of Kappara, said: One who robs openly, as in the verse, *And they robbed* (wayyigzelu) *all that came along that way by them* (Judg. IX, 25): as the way is public, so does a *gazlan* act openly. R. Simeon b. Yoḥai quoted this verse: *And ye have brought that which was taken by violence* (gazul), *and the lame* (Mal. I, 13): as the lame suffers from an open defect, so the *gazlan* acts openly. R. Jose in R. Abbahu's name, and R. Hezekiah reporting R. Abbahu in the name of Resh Lakish, said: [He who steals] in the presence of nine people is a thief (*ganab*); in the presence of ten, is a robber (*gazlan*). R. Tanḥuma said in R. Huna's name: One is not a robber (*gazlan*) unless he actually snatches the article from the victim's hand, as it says, *And plucked* (wayyigzol) *the spear out of the Egyptian's hand* (II Sam. XXIII, 21).[1]

AND ABIMELECH SAID: I KNOW NOT WHO HATH DONE THIS THING; NEITHER DIDST THOU TELL ME—by a message.[2]

4. AND ABRAHAM SET SEVEN EWE-LAMBS OF THE FLOCK, etc. (XXI, 28). The Holy One, blessed be He, said to him [Abraham]: 'Thou gavest him seven ewe-lambs; as thou livest, I will delay the joy of thy children for seven generations![3] Thou gavest him seven ewe-lambs; as thou livest, his descendants will slay seven righteous men of thy descendants, viz. Hofni, Phinehas, Samson, and Saul with his three sons.[4] Thou gavest him seven ewe-lambs; accordingly, thy descendants' seven sanctuaries shall be destroyed, viz. the Tent of Appointment, [the sanctuaries at] Gilgal, Nob, Gibeon, and Shiloah,

[1] There is a difference in law between a *ganab* (thief) and *gazlan* (robber), cf. Ex. XXII, 3, with Lev. V, 23 f., and v. B.K. 79*b*.
[2] Or perhaps; through an angel
[3] V. p. 477, n. 5.
[4] V. Judg. XVI, 30; I Sam. IV, 10 f.; *ib.* XXXI.

and the two Temples.[1] Thou gavest him seven ewe-lambs; My Ark will spend seven months in Philistine territory,' (as it says, *And He delivered His strength into captivity* (Ps. LXXVIII, 61), which refers to the Ark of the Covenant, as it is written, *And the ark of the Lord was in the country of the Philistines seven months* (I Sam. VI, 1). [Continuing the verse]· *And His glory into the adversary's hand* (Ps. *loc cit.*) refers to the priestly garments, as it says, *And thou shalt make holy garments for Aaron thy brother, for splendour and for glory* (Ex. XXVIII, 2)).[2]

R. Jeremiah said in the name of R Samuel b. R Isaac: (Why were the people of Beth-Shemesh smitten?[3] Because they made merry over the Ark.[4] The Holy One, blessed be He, said): 'If a fowl had been lost, would not its owner have gone in search of it through many houses to recover it? yet My Ark has been seven months in the country of the Philistines and ye care nought for it. I Myself will care for it,' hence, *His right hand, and His holy arm, hath wrought salvation for Him* (Ps XCVIII, 1). Thus it is written, *And the kine took the straight way*—wayyasharnah (I Sam. VI, 12): they went a straight path, turned their faces to the Ark and broke forth into song[5] What song did they sing? R. Meir said: The Song of the Sea, for here it is stated, *They went along . . . lowing* (ga'u) *as they went* (*ib.*), while there it says, *For He is highly exalted*—ga'oh ga'ah (Ex. XV, 1).[6] R. Johanan said: *O sing unto the Lord a new song* (Ps. XCVIII, 1). R. Leazar said: *O give thanks unto the Lord, call upon His name* (Ps. CV, 1). The Rabbis said: *The*

[1] These were not all destroyed, some simply ceasing to be used. Further, they were not all destroyed by the Philistines, and Th's ed reads simply: (people) will destroy, not 'his descendants will destroy' as in cur. edd.

[2] Abraham and Abimelech represent true belief and heathenism respectively, hence God predicted that a covenant between the two would prove of evil omen (Mah.)—The bracketed passage is added from cur. edd. [3] V. I Sam. VI, 19.

[4] V. Num. R v, 9. Here too the bracketed passage is from cur edd.

[5] *Wayyasharnah* is rendered as in E.V., they took a straight road; but also, by a play on words it is connected with *shirah*, song: they broke forth into song.

[6] Rather a daring play on words.

Lord reigneth, let the earth rejoice (Ps. XCVII, 1). R. Jeremiah said: They sang three [songs]: '*O sing unto the Lord a new song'; Sing unto the Lord, all the earth* (Ps, XCVI, 1), and, *The Lord reigneth, let the peoples tremble* (Ps. XCIX, 1). Elijah taught[1]: [They sang thus:] 'Rise, O rise, thou acacia,[2] soar, yea soar, in thine abundant glory, beautiful in thy gold embroidery, extolled in the innermost shrine of the Sanctuary, encased between the two Cherubim.' R. Samuel b. R. Isaac said: How much toil did the son of Amram expend before he taught the Song to the Levites,[3] while ye [cows] recite Song spontaneously! All strength to you![4]

5. AND HE SAID: VERILY, THESE SEVEN EWE-LAMBS SHALT THOU TAKE OF MY HAND (XXI, 30). The Rabbis said: Abraham's shepherds quarrelled with Abimelech's shepherds, each claiming, 'The well is ours.' Said Abraham's shepherds to them: 'It belongs to him for whose flocks the water will rise when it sees them.' When the water saw Abraham's flocks, it immediately ascended. Said the Holy One, blessed be He, to him: 'Thou art an augury, for thy children, that the well will rise for them'; thus it is written, *Spring up, O well—sing ye unto it* (Num. XXI, 17). R. Isaac b. Ḥaḳorah said: In this very passage there is no lack of proof.[5] It is not written, 'That it[6] was a witness unto me,' but, THAT IT WILL BE[7] A WITNESS [i.e. A SIGN] UNTO ME (*ib.*).

6. AND ABRAHAM PLANTED AN ESHEL (E.V. 'TAMARISK') TREE (XXI, 33). R. Judah said: ESHEL means an orchard, the word meaning ask (*she'al*) for whatever you wish, figs, grapes, or pomegranates. R.

[1] Cur. edd.: Tanna debe Eliyahu taught. The reference is to a Midrashic work said to have been taught by Elijah to R. Anan, Keth. 106*a*.
[2] The Ark was made of acacia wood
[3] Radal is inclined to emend.: Israel. [4] Lit. 'your strength be well', Heb *yeyasher*, another play on *wayyasharnah*
[5] It is unnecessary to quote a verse from elsewhere.
[6] Sc. the rising of the water
[7] Lit. translation, which is made to refer to the *distant* future.

Nehemiah said: ESHEL means an inn, the word connoting, ask whatever you desire, meat, wine, or eggs. R. 'Azariah said in the name of R. Judah: ESHEL means a court of law, as in the verse, *Now Saul was sitting in Gibeah, under the* eshel (E.V. '*tamarisk tree*') *in Ramah* (I Sam. XXII, 6).[1] According to R. Nehemiah's view that it was an inn, Abraham used to receive wayfarers, and after they had eaten and drunk he would say to them, 'Now say Grace.' When they asked what to say, he would reply, 'Blessed be the Everlasting God, of whose bounty we have eaten.' Hence it is written, AND CALLED THERE ON THE NAME OF THE LORD, THE EVERLASTING GOD (*ib.*)[2]

AND ABRAHAM SOJOURNED IN THE LAND OF THE PHILISTINES MANY DAYS (XXI, 34)—more than the time he spent in Hebron. In Hebron he stayed twenty-five years, while here he stayed twenty-six years.[3]

[1] It is assumed that he sat there for the purpose of giving judgment.
[2] Cf. *supra*, XLIX, 4.
[3] The calculation is given by Rashi in the Pentateuch, *ad loc.*

CHAPTER LV (VAYERA)

1. AND IT CAME TO PASS AFTER THESE THINGS, THAT GOD DID PROVE (NISSAH) ABRAHAM (XXI, 1). It is written, *Thou hast given a banner* (nes) *to them that fear Thee, that it may be displayed* (le-hithnoses) *because of the truth. Selah* (Ps. LX, 6): this means, trial upon trial, greatness after greatness, in order to try them in the world and exalt them in the world like a ship's ensign [flying aloft].[1] And what is its purpose? '*Because of the truth. Selah*': in order that the equity of God's justice may be verified in the world. Thus, if one says, 'Whom He wishes to enrich, He enriches; to impoverish, He impoverishes; whom He desires, He makes a king[2]; when He wished, He made Abraham wealthy, and when He wished He made him a king,' then you can answer him and say, 'Can you do what Abraham did?' *Abraham was a hundred years old, when his son Isaac was born unto him* (Gen. XXI, 5); yet after all this pain[3] it was said to him, TAKE NOW THY SON, THINE ONLY SON (XXII 2), yet he did not refuse. Hence, '*Thou hast given a banner to them that fear Thee, that it may be displayed*'; so it is written, THAT GOD DID PROVE ABRAHAM.

2. *The Lord trieth the righteous*, etc. (Ps. XI, 5). R. Jonathan said: A potter does not examine defective vessels, because he cannot give them a single blow without breaking them. What then does he examine? Only the sound vessels, for he will not break them even with many blows. Similarly, the Holy One, blessed be He, tests not the wicked but the righteous, as it says, '*The Lord trieth the righteous*.' R. Jose b. R. Ḥanina said: When a flax worker knows that his flax is of good quality, the more he beats it the more it improves and the more it glistens;

[1] *Nes* and *le-hithnoses* are connected with *nissah*, to prove or try, and with the idea of exaltation, from *nes*, an ensign flying aloft. The verse is then translated: God imposes a trial upon them that fear Him, so that He may then exalt them. [2] All arbitrarily and without cause or justification. [3] Of being childless so long.

but if it is of inferior quality, he cannot give it one knock without it splitting. Similarly, the Lord does not test the wicked but only the righteous, as it says, '*The Lord trieth the righteous.*' R. Eleazar said: When a man possesses two cows, one strong and the other feeble, upon which does he put the yoke? Surely upon the strong one Similarly, God tests none but the righteous, as it says, '*The Lord trieth the righteous.*'[1]

3. Another interpretation: '*The Lord trieth the righteous*' alludes to Abraham, as it says, THAT GOD DID PROVE ABRAHAM.

R. Abin commenced his discourse thus: *Forasmuch as the king's word hath power; and who may say unto him: What doest thou* (Eccl. VIII, 4)? Said R. Abin: This may be compared to a teacher who instructed his disciple, (*Thou shalt not wrest judgment* (Deut. XVI, 19), yet he himself wrested judgment; *Thou shalt not respect persons* (*ib.*), yet himself respected persons; *Neither shalt thou take a gift* (*ib.*), yet himself took gifts;)[2] do not lend money on interest, yet himself lent on interest. Said his disciple to him: 'Master, you tell me, "do not lend money on interest," yet you yourself lend on interest!' He replied: 'I tell you not to lend on interest to an Israelite, but you may lend on interest to other nations, for it is written, *Unto a foreigner thou mayest lend on interest; but unto thy brother thou shalt not lend upon interest* (*ib.* XXIII, 21).[3] Similarly, Israel said to the Holy One, blessed be He: 'Sovereign of the Universe! Thou didst write in Thy Torah, *Thou shalt not take vengeance, nor bear any grudge* (Lev XIX, 18), yet Thou doest so Thyself, as it says, *The Lord avengeth and is full of wrath, the Lord taketh vengeance on His adversaries, and He reserveth wrath for*

[1] *Supra*, XXXII, 3. [2] The bracketed passage is added from cur. edd. in accordance with Eccl. R. VIII, 4.
[3] V. Joseph M. *Judaism as Creed and Life*, p. 428, for the grounds of this distinction It is noteworthy that the other objections remain unanswered—perversion of justice, respecting persons, and taking bribes are not permitted under any conditions.

His enemies' (Nahum I, 2). Said God to them: 'I wrote in My Torah, "*Thou shalt not take vengeance, nor bear any grudge*" against *Israel;* but in respect of the nations —*Avenge the children of Israel,'* etc. (Num. XXXI, 2).[1] Similarly it is written, *Ye shall not try the Lord your God* (Deut. VI, 16), yet GOD DID PROVE ABRAHAM.[2]

4. AFTER THESE THINGS—misgivings were experienced on that occasion[3] Who then had misgivings? Abraham, saying to himself: 'I have rejoiced and made all others rejoice,[4] yet I did not set aside a single bullock or ram for the Holy One, blessed be He.' Said God to him: 'I know that even if thou wast commanded to offer thine only son to Me, thou wouldst not refuse.' According to R. Leazar who maintained that the employment of *wa-elohim*[5] where *Elohim* would suffice intimates, He and His Court, it was the ministering angels who spoke thus: 'This Abraham rejoiced and made all others rejoice, yet did not set aside for God a single bullock or ram.' Said the Holy One, blessed be He, to them: 'Even if we tell him to offer his own son, he will not refuse.'

Isaac and Ishmael were engaged in a controversy: the latter argued, 'I am more beloved than thou, because I was circumcised at the age of thirteen'; while the other retorted, 'I am more beloved than thou, because I was circumcised at eight days.' Said Ishmael to him: 'I am

[1] The Bible is full of predictions against Israel, unless they reformed The Rabbis, of course, were fully aware of this, and in the present passage they did not mean to teach that God is partial and favours Israel, but rather expressed their confidence that even when Israel sinned timely repentance would avert disaster, whereas the idolaters would never repent —Y.T. observes: In the illustration it may be assumed that the teacher did not in fact pervert judgment, etc , but that it merely appeared so to his disciple. In the same way, God never disobeys His own moral law, even when to man it appears so.

[2] The answer to the difficulty is not explicitly given but is left to be inferred from the general tenor of the preceding remarks. To try God is a sign of inadequate faith, whereas God tried Abraham in order to strengthen his faith in Him (Y.T)

[3] A play on '*ahar*' (after), which is now connected with *hirhur*, misgiving

[4] At the banquet in honour of Isaac's weaning.

[5] *And* God; in the present case E.V. '*that God*'.

more beloved, because I could have protested, yet did not.' At that moment Isaac exclaimed: 'O that God would appear to me and bid me cut off one of my limbs! then I would not refuse' Said God: 'Even if I bid thee sacrifice thyself, thou wilt not refuse.' (Another version: Said Ishmael to him: 'I am more beloved than thou, since I was circumcised at the age of thirteen, but thou wast circumcised as a baby and couldst not refuse.' Isaac retorted: 'All that thou didst lend to the Holy One, blessed be He, was three drops of blood. But lo, I am now thirty-seven years old,[1] yet if God desired of me that I be slaughtered, I would not refuse.' Said the Holy One, blessed be He, 'This is the moment!' Straightway, GOD DID PROVE ABRAHAM.)

5. *Wherewith shall I come before the Lord, and bow myself before God on high* (Micah VI, 6)? R. Joshua of Siknin said in R. Levi's name: Though this passage was [apparently] said about Mesha, king of Moab,[2] yet it refers to none but Isaac. For it says, '*Wherewith shall I come before the Lord, and bow myself before God on high*' . . . *Shall I give my firstborn for my transgression, the fruit of my body for the sin of my soul?* (Now in the case of Isaac the deed was not actually done, yet He accepted it as though it were completed, whereas in the case of Mesha it was not accepted.)[3]

6. THAT GOD DID PROVE (NISSAH) ABRAHAM. R. Jose the Galilean said: He exalted him like a ship's ensign

[1] Sarah was ninety years old at his birth and a hundred and twenty-seven years at her death, which, according to the Rabbis, was caused by shock when she was wrongly informed that Isaac had been sacrificed—*infra*, LVIII, 5. [2] Who sacrificed his son as a burnt-offering. The verse continues: *Shall I give my firstborn for my transgression*. For the incident v. II Kings III, 27.

[3] The bracketed passage is added from cur. edd. Y.T.: The following verse goes on to say that God requires man *To do justly, and to love mercy*, etc. Hence the whole may well refer to Isaac, whom God never intended to be sacrificed, His true worship consisting in acting with justice and love. But actual human sacrifice, such as Mesha's, is abhorrent to Him.

(*nes*). R Akiba said: He tested him unequivocally, that people might not say that He confused and perplexed him so that he did not know what to do.[1] AND SAID UNTO HIM: ABRAHAM; AND HE SAID. HERE AM I (*ib.*). R. Joshua said: On two occasions Moses compared himself to Abraham, and God answered him, *Glorify not thyself in the presence of the king, and stand not in the place of great men* (Prov. xxv, 6). Now Abraham said, HERE AM I—ready for priesthood, ready for kingship, and he attained priesthood and kingship. He attained priesthood, as it says, *The Lord hath sworn, and will not repent: Thou art a priest for ever after the manner of Melchizedek* (Ps. cx, 4); kingship: *Thou art a mighty prince among us* (Gen. xxiii, 5). Moses too said, *Here am I* (Ex. iii, 4)—ready for priesthood, ready for kingship—but God answered, *Draw not nigh hither*—halom (*ib* 5); now 'drawing nigh' refers to priesthood, as in the verse, *And the common man that draweth nigh shall be put to death* (Num. i, 51), while '*halom*' connotes kingship, as in the verse, *That Thou hast brought me thus far*—halom (ii Sam. vii, 18).[2]

7. AND HE SAID: TAKE, I PRAY THEE, THY SON, etc. (xxii, 2). Said He to him: 'TAKE, I PRAY THEE—I beg thee[3]—THY SON.' 'Which son?' he asked. 'THINE ONLY SON,' replied He. 'But each is the only one of his mother?'—'WHOM THOU LOVEST.'—'Is there a limit to the affections?' 'EVEN ISAAC,' said He. And why did He not reveal it to him without delay? In order to make him [Isaac] even more beloved in his eyes and reward him for every word spoken. This agrees with the dictum of R. Joḥanan, who said: *Get thee out of thy country* (Gen. xii, 1) means from thy province; *And*

[1] God did not order Isaac to be sacrificed immediately, but only after a three days' journey to Mount Moriah, during which Abraham had ample time for reflection. [2] This refers to David's royal rank.—For the full passage v Ex R. ii, 6, and Deut R. ii, 7.

[3] If you do not emerge successfully from this trial, it will be said that the previous trials by which I tested you were of no value (Sanh. 89*b*).

from thy kindred (*ib.*)—from the place where thou art settled; *And from thy father's house*—literally thy father's house. *Unto the land that I will show thee* (*ib.*). Why did He not reveal it to him there and then? In order to make it more beloved in his eyes and to reward him for every step.

R. Levi b. Ḥayyatha said: '*Get thee*' is written twice,[1] and we do not know which was more precious [in the eyes of God], the first or the second. But when it is written, AND GET THEE INTO THE LAND OF MORIAH (XXII, 2) it follows that the second occasion was more precious than the first.[2]

AND GET THEE INTO THE LAND OF MORIAH. R. Hiyya the Elder and R. Jannai discussed this. One said: To the place whence instruction (*hora'ah*) went forth to the world.[3] While the other explained it: To the place whence religious awe (*yirah*) went forth to the world.[4] (Similarly, the word *aron* (the Ark). R. Ḥiyya and R. Jannai—one said: The place whence *orah* (light) goes forth to the world; while the other explained it: The place whence *yirah* (religious reverence) goes forth to the world. Similarly, the word *debir*[5]; R. Ḥiyya and R. Jannai discussed this. One said: The place whence [God's] speech (*dibbur*) went forth to the world; while the other explained it: The place whence retribution (*deber*) goes forth to the world.) R. Joshua b. Levi said[6]: It means the place whence the Holy One, blessed be He, shoots (*moreh*)[7] at the other nations and hurls them into Gehenna. R. Simeon b Yoḥai said: To the place that

[1] Here, in connection with the sacrifice, and in ch. XII, 1, when Abraham was told to leave home.

[2] Mah : for the first was from without into Eretz Israel, while the second was in Eretz Israel itself, to a more sacred spot.

[3] It was the spot where in later times the Chamber of Hewn Stones in the Temple stood and the Great Sanhedrin sat and sent forth religious teaching to all Israel.

[4] The Temple radiated a spirit of awe and reverence.

[5] In I Kings VI, 19: E.V. '*sanctuary*'; A V. 'oracle'. It was the holy of holies, and the Rabbis now discuss the exact significance of the word.

[6] Reverting to the word MORIAH.

[7] M.K. Or perhaps: makes decrees (lit. 'instructs') about other nations.

corresponds (*ra'ui*) to the Heavenly Temple. R. Judan b. Palya said: To the place that He will show (*mareh*) thee.[1] R. Phinehas said: To the seat of the world's dominion (*marwetha*). The Rabbis said: To the place where incense would be offered, as you read, *I will get me to the mountain of myrrh*—Mor (S.S. IV, 6).[2]

AND OFFER HIM THERE FOR A BURNT-OFFERING (*ib.*). R Judah said: He [Abraham] said to Him: 'Sovereign of the Universe! Can there be a sacrifice without a priest?' 'I have already appointed thee to be a priest,' replied the Holy One, blessed be He: thus it is written, '*Thou art a priest for ever*' (Ps. CX, 4).

UPON ONE OF THE MOUNTAINS WHICH I WILL TELL THEE OF (*ib.*). For[3] R. Huna said on the authority of R. Eliezer: The Holy One, blessed be He, first places the righteous in doubt and suspense, and then reveals to them the real meaning of the matter. Thus, TO THE LAND THAT I WILL SHOW THEE (XII, 1); UPON ONE OF THE MOUNTAINS WHICH I WILL TELL THEE OF; *And make unto it the proclamation that I bid thee* (Jonah III, 2); similarly, *Arise, go forth into the plain, and I will there speak with thee* (Ezek. III, 22).

8. AND ABRAHAM ROSE EARLY IN THE MORNING, AND SADDLED HIS ASS (XXII, 3). R. Simeon b. Yohai said: Love upsets the natural order, and hate upsets the natural order.[4] Love upsets the natural order: AND ABRAHAM ROSE EARLY IN THE MORNING, etc.: surely he had plenty of slaves?[5] But the reason was that love[6] upset the natural order. Hate upsets the natural order: *And Baalam rose up in the morning, and saddled his ass* (Num. XXII, 21): surely he had plenty of slaves? Hate, however, upsets the natural order. Love upsets

[1] Probably by a special sign; v. *infra*, LVI, 1 [2] All these are plays on the word 'Moriah'. [3] This is really the middle of a passage (v. *supra*, XXXIX, 9), which explains the abrupt 'for'. Cur edd omit
[4] Through love or hate a man acts as he would not otherwise, disregarding his own dignity. [5] To saddle his ass, which was not a dignified proceeding for a man of his rank. [6] His love for God.

the natural order: *And Joseph made ready his chariot*, etc. (Gen. XLVI, 29): yet surely Joseph had plenty of slaves? But love upsets the natural order. Hate upsets the natural order: *And he made ready his chariot* (Ex. XIV, 6)[1]: yet surely he had plenty of slaves? Thus hate upsets the natural order.

R. Simeon b. Yoḥai said: Let saddling counteract saddling. Let the saddling done by our father Abraham in order to go and fulfil the will of Him at whose word the world came into existence counteract the saddling done by Baalam in order to go and curse Israel. Let preparing counteract preparing. Let Joseph's preparing [of his chariot] to meet his father counteract Pharaoh's preparing to go and pursue Israel. R. Ishmael taught: Let the sword of the hand counteract the sword of the hand. Let the sword taken in the hand of our father Abraham, as it says, *And Abraham stretched forth his hand, and took the knife to slay his son* (Gen. XXII, 10), come and counteract the sword grasped by Pharaoh's hand when he said, *I will draw my sword, my hand shall destroy them* (Ex. XV, 9).

AND TOOK TWO OF HIS YOUNG MEN WITH HIM, AND ISAAC HIS SON. R. Abbahu said: Two people behaved with propriety, Abraham and Saul: Abraham, as it says, AND TOOK TWO OF HIS YOUNG MEN WITH HIM; Saul, as it says, *And Saul . . . went, he and two men with him* (I Sam. XXVIII, 8).[2]

AND HE CLEAVED THE WOOD FOR THE BURNT-OFFERING. R. Ḥiyya b. R. Jose said in the name of R. Miasha, and it was also repeated in the name of R. Bannaiah: As a reward for the two cleavings wherewith our father Abraham cleaved the wood of the burnt-offering,[3] he earned that God should cleave [divide] the Sea before

[1] The Heb. is in the singular (not '*chariots*', as E.V.); hence it is assumed that Pharaoh did it himself.

[2] Both took companions because it would have been undignified for them to go alone, though the nature of their mission might have prompted them to go unaccompanied (Mah.)

[3] 'Wood' is in the plural, whence it is deduced that he cut up two logs

his descendants, as it says, *And the waters were divided* (Ex. XIV, 21). Said R. Levi: Enough of this![1] In truth Abraham acted according to his powers and the Holy One, blessed be He, according to His powers.

AND ROSE UP, AND WENT UNTO THE PLACE. He was rewarded for rising up and for going.[2]

[1] It is wrong to compare these two incidents as though they were on a par.

[2] For each separately Otherwise, why state AND ROSE UP, which is obvious? (M.K.).

CHAPTER LVI (VAYERA)

1. ON THE THIRD DAY, etc. (XXII, 4). It is written, *After two days He will revive us, on the third day He will raise us up, that we may live in His presence* (Hos. VI, 2). E g. on the third day of the tribal ancestors[1]: *And Joseph said unto them the third day: Ths do, and live* (Gen. XLII, 18); on the third day of Revelation: *And it came to pass on the third day, when it was morning* (Ex. XIX, 16); on the third day of the spies: *And hide yourselves there three days* (Josh. II, 16); on the third day of Jonah: *And Jonah was in the belly of the fish three days and three nights* (Jonah II, 1); on the third day of those returning from the Exile: *And we abode there three days* (Ezra VIII, 32); on the third day of resurrection: '*After two days He will revive us, on the third day He will raise us up*'; on the third day of Esther: *Now it came to pass on the third day, that Esther put on her royal apparel* (Est. V, 1)—i.e. she put on the royal apparel of her ancestor.[2] For whose sake?[3] The Rabbis say: For the sake of the third day, when Revelation took place. R Levi maintained: In the merit of what Abraham did on the third day, as it says, ON THE THIRD DAY, etc.

AND SAW THE PLACE AFAR OFF (*ib.*). What did he see?[4] He saw a cloud enveloping the mountain,[5] and said: 'It appears that that is the place where the Holy One, blessed be He, told me to sacrifice my son'

2. He then said to him [Isaac]: 'Isaac, my son, seest thou what I see?' 'Yes,' he replied. Said he to his two servants: 'See ye what I see?' 'No,' they answered. 'Since ye do not see it, ABIDE YE HERE WITH THE

[1] The children of Jacob.
[2] Viz. Saul (Y.T. and Radal). M.K. and Mah.: she was clothed in the holy spirit; or, her ancestors' merit stood her in good stead —The point of all these quotations is that relief from distress or the climax of events occurred on the third day.
[3] Did relief come to all these on the third day?
[4] Which told him that this was the place.
[5] And he recognised it as the cloud of God's glory.

ASS,' (XXII, 5), he bade them, for ye are like the ass,[1] whence it follows that slaves are like an ass.[2] The Rabbis proved [it from this verse spoken at] the Revelation: *Six days shalt thou labour, and do all thy work . . . thou, nor thy daughter, nor thy man-servant, nor thy maid-servant, nor thy cattle* (Ex. XX, 10).

R. Isaac said: This place shall one day be alienated from its Owner.[3] For ever? [No], for it is stated, *This is My resting-place for ever; here will I dwell for I have desired it;* (Ps. CXXXII, 14)—when he comes of whom it is written, *Lowly, and riding upon an ass* (Zech. I, 9).[4]

AND I AND THE LAD WILL GO YONDER—'AD KOH. Said R. Joshua b. Levi: We will go and see what is to be the eventual outcome of *koh.*[5]

AND WE WILL WORSHIP, AND *WE* WILL COME BACK TO YOU. He thus informed him[6] that he [Isaac] would return safely from Mount Moriah. R. Isaac said: Everything happened as a reward for worshipping.[7] Abraham returned in peace from Mount Moriah only as a reward for worshipping: AND WE WILL WORSHIP, AND WE WILL COME BACK TO YOU. Israel were redeemed only as a reward for worshipping: *And the people believed . . . then they bowed their heads and worshipped* (Ex. IV, 31). The Torah was given only as a

[1] Which has not seen it either

[2] In a legal sense, that they cannot acquire or transmit property Actually they had definite rights, and from the religious point of view were semi-Jews.

[3] The site of the sacrifice, which corresponded to Jerusalem, would one day be alienated from God; or (M.K.) from its owners, the Jews being exiled from it. This is hinted at in AND SAW THE PLACE AFAR OFF—far from its Owner

[4] Sc. the Messiah. This is based on a figurative interpretation of the present verse, *shebu lakem* (E.V 'abide ye'), which is now rendered· Return ye (the Hebrew can mean that) When? *With the ass*—when he (Messiah) comes travelling on an ass.

[5] God promised me, *Koh* (so) *shall thy seed be* (Gen XV, 5): we will see how that can be fulfilled, now that I am to lose my son.

[6] God informed Abraham, by making him unintentionally prophesy, AND *WE* WILL COME BACK Others (as in Tanḥuma)· His own mouth thus informed him, etc.

[7] The Hebrew word means 'prostration'.

reward for worshipping: *And worship ye afar off* (*ib.* XXIV, 1).[1] Hannah was remembered only as a reward for worshipping: *And they worshipped before the Lord* (I Sam. I, 19). The exiles will be reassembled only as a reward for worshipping: *And it shall come to pass in that day, that a great horn shall be blown; and they shall come that were lost . . . and that were dispersed . . . and they shall worship the Lord in the holy mountain at Jerusalem* (Isa. XXVII, 13). The Temple was built only as a reward for worshipping. *Exalt ye the Lord our God, and worship at His holy hill* (Ps. XCIX, 9).[2] The dead will come to life again only as a reward for worshipping: *O come, let us worship and bend the knee; let us kneel before the Lord our Maker* (Ps. XCV, 6).[3]

3. AND ABRAHAM TOOK THE WOOD OF THE BURNT-OFFERING (XXII, 6)—like one who carries his stake on his shoulder.[4] AND HE TOOK IN HIS HAND THE FIRE AND THE KNIFE (MA'AKELETH). R. Ḥanina said: Why is a knife called *ma'akeleth?* Because it makes food (*oklim*) fit to be eaten.[5] While the Rabbis said: All eating (*akiloth*) which Israel enjoy in this world, they enjoy only in the merit of that MA'AKELETH (KNIFE).

AND THEY WENT BOTH OF THEM TOGETHER (*ib.*): one to bind and the other to be bound, one to slaughter and the other to be slaughtered.[6]

4. AND ISAAC SPOKE UNTO ABRAHAM HIS FATHER, AND SAID: MY FATHER (XXII, 7). Samael[7]

[1] Though this comes after Revelation, the whole incident recorded in that passage is assumed to have taken place before Revelation

[2] God is exalted by the building of the Temple

[3] *Let us kneel*, etc., is not in the text, but has been added. Rash.: This is probably deduced from *Our Maker*, understood in the sense of our Maker in a new life Cf *supra*, XXXIX, 11: *And I will make thee:* after I have made thee newly created, etc

[4] The stake on which he is to be executed.

[5] An animal (food, *oklim*, from which *ma'akeleth* is now derived) is ritually slaughtered with a knife, and only then may it be eaten.

[6] Yet they went TOGETHER—in the same spirit.

[7] The name of a wicked angel; cf. Soṭ. 10*b*.

went to the Patriarch Abraham and upbraided him saying: What means this, old man! Hast thou lost thy wits? thou goest to slay a son granted to thee at the age of a hundred!' 'Even this I do,' replied he. 'And if He sets thee an even greater test, canst thou stand it?' said he, as it is written, *If a thing be put to thee as a trial,*[1] *wilt thou be wearied* (Job IV, 2)? 'Even more than this,' he replied. 'To-morrow He will say to thee, "Thou art a murderer, and art guilty,"' 'Still am I content,' he rejoined. Seeing that he could achieve nought with him, he approached Isaac and said: 'Son of an unhappy mother! He goes to slay thee.' 'I accept my fate,' he replied. 'If so,' said he, 'shall all those fine tunics which thy mother made be a legacy for Ishmael, the hated of her house?'[2] If a word is not wholly effective, it may yet avail in part'; hence it is written, AND ISAAC SPOKE UNTO ABRAHAM HIS FATHER, AND SAID: MY FATHER: why HIS FATHER . . . MY FATHER?[3] So that he should be filled with compassion for him.[4] AND HE SAID: BEHOLD, THE FIRE AND THE WOOD. 'May that man be drowned who has thus incited him,' exclaimed he. 'At all events, GOD WILL PROVIDE HIMSELF THE LAMB, O my son; and if not, THOU ART FOR A BURNT-OFFERING, MY SON.' SO THEY WENT BOTH OF THEM TOGETHER—one to slaughter and the other to be slaughtered.

5. AND THEY CAME TO THE PLACE WHICH GOD HAD TOLD HIM OF, AND ABRAHAM BUILT THE ALTAR THERE (XXII, 9). And where was Isaac? Said R. Levi: He had taken and hidden him, saying, 'Lest he who sought to seduce him[5] throw a stone at him and disqualify him from serving as a sacrifice.'[6] AND

[1] E.V. '*If one venture a word unto thee*'
[2] Or perhaps shall all the steps taken by thy mother against Ishmael have been for nought, and he, the hated of the house, be the heir?
[3] Why is the relationship stressed? [4] Thus, though Samael could not induce him to resist, he nevertheless induced him to plead indirectly.
[5] From obedience and willingness to allow himself to be sacrificed.
[6] By maiming him.

BOUND ISAAC HIS SON. R. Ḥanina b. Isaac said: Even as Abraham bound his son Isaac below, so the Holy One, blessed be He, bound the Princes of the heathens above.[1] Yet they did not remain [thus bound]. For when Israel alienated themselves [from God] in the days of Jeremiah, the Holy One, blessed be He, said to them: 'What think ye: that those fetters still exist?' as it says, *For shall they be like tangled thorns* (sirim) *for ever* (Nahum I, 10), which means: For are the Princes (*sarim*) to be entangled [i.e. bound] for ever? No; for *When they* [the Israelites] *are drunken according to their drink* (*ib.*),[2] their fetters are broken, for it is written, *They shall be devoured as stubble fully dry* (*ib.*).

When the Patriarch Abraham stretched forth his hand to take the knife to slay his son, the angels wept, as it says, *Behold, their valiant ones* [the angels] *cry without*—ḥuẓah (Isa. XXXIII, 7). What does '*huẓah*' mean? R. 'Azariah said: It is unnatural. It is unnatural that he should slay his son with his own hand. And what did they say? *The highways lie waste?* (*ib.* 8)—does not Abraham show hospitality to travellers? *The wayfaring man ceaseth*—shabath (*ib.*)—as in the verse, *It had ceased* (ḥadal) *to be with Sarah* (Gen. XVIII, 11).[3] *He hath broken the covenant* (Isa. *loc. cit.*), viz. *But My covenant will I establish with Isaac* (Gen. XVII, 21).[4] *He hath despised the cities* (Isa. *loc. cit.*), viz. *And* [Abraham] *dwelt between Kadesh and Shur* (Gen. XX, 1).[5] *He regardeth not man* (Isa. *loc. cit.*)—has Abraham no merit in his favour? And who says that this verse refers to the angels?[6]—Here it says, UPON (MI-MA'AL) THE WOOD, while in another passage it says, *Above* (mi-ma'al) *Him stood the seraphim* (Isa. VI, 2).

[1] Every nation was thought to possess a 'Prince'—a guardian angel and patron.—I.e. made them subservient to Israel.

[2] I.e. when they have forfeited their rights through sin.

[3] *Shabath* in the former verse is rendered by *hadal* in the latter, this being more familiar to the Rabbis (M K. Th.)

[4] That covenant will now be broken if he is sacrificed

[5] The angels urged in his favour that he 'despised' his former residence in order to practise hospitality; v. *supra*, LII, 1.

[6] How does this verse indicate a protest by the angels?

6. AND ABRAHAM STRETCHED FORTH HIS HAND, AND TOOK THE KNIFE. Rab asked R. Ḥiyya the Elder: Regarding Rabbi's teaching, in which he said: How do we know that ritual slaughtering must be with a movable object?[1] From this verse: AND ABRAHAM STRETCHED FORTH HIS HAND, AND TOOK THE KNIFE[2]—did he tell you this as *haggadah*, in which case he might retract[3]; or did he state it as a tradition, in which case he would not retract from it? For R. Levi taught: If they [e.g. sharp flints] were fast [to the ground or rocks] from the very beginning, they are unfit; but if they had been originally detached but subsequently fixed in the ground, they are fit. For we learned: If one slaughters with a hand-sickle,[4] a flint, or a reed, the slaughtering is fit.[5] R. Jose b. Abin said: Five things were said of a reed stalk: You may not slaughter, circumcise, cut meat, wipe your hands,[6] nor pick your teeth with it, because an evil spirit rests upon it.

7. AND THE ANGEL OF THE LORD CALLED UNTO HIM OUT OF HEAVEN, AND SAID: ABRAHAM, ABRAHAM (XXII, 11). R. Ḥiyya taught: This is an expression of love and encouragement. R. Liezer said: [The repetition indicates that He spake] to him and to future generations: There is no generation which does not contain

[1] But not something immovable that is part of the ground, e g a sharp ledge of rock which otherwise is fit, and against which the animal's throat can be drawn.
[2] Which implies that it was movable
[3] Deductions made in the spirit of *haggadah* are not binding laws.
[4] Jast: an implement combining knife and saw.
[5] Ḥul 15*b*, 16*a*. The point of Rab's question is this if the deduction from the verse was made as a true law, then an immovable object is absolutely unfit, even if it had been movable at one time; and, moreover, not only is it unfit at the outset, but even if one does slaughter with it the animal is not permitted for food. Obviously then Levi does not accept this view, and Rab's question is whether Rabbi stated this only as *haggadah*, in which case it may not represent his view as far as a practical ruling is concerned, and he can agree with Levi; or did he state it as an actual law, in which case he must disagree with Levi?
[6] Because sharp shreds or splinters detach themselves from it and these are dangerous.

men like Abraham, and there is no generation which does not contain men like Jacob, Moses, and Samuel.[1]

AND HE SAID: LAY NOT THY HAND UPON THE LAD, etc. (XXII, 12). Where was the knife? Tears had fallen from the angels upon it and dissolved it. 'Then I will strangle him,' said he [Abraham] to Him 'LAY NOT THY HAND UPON THE LAD,' was the reply. 'Let us bring forth a drop of blood from him,' he pleaded. 'NEITHER DO THOU ANY THING TO HIM,' He answered —'inflict no blemish upon him.[2] FOR NOW I KNOW— I have made it known to all—that thou lovest Me, AND THOU HAST NOT WITHHELD, etc. And do not say, "All ills that do not affect one's own person are not ills,"[3] for indeed I ascribe merit to thee as though I had bidden thee sacrifice thyself and thou hadst not refused.'[4]

8. (Another comment: R. Isaac said: When Abraham wished to sacrifice his son Isaac, he said to him: 'Father, I am a young man and am afraid that my body may tremble through fear of the knife and I will grieve thee, whereby the slaughter may be rendered unfit and this will not count as a real sacrifice; therefore bind me very firmly. Forthwith, HE BOUND ISAAC: can one bind a man thirty-seven years old? (another version: twenty-six years old)[5] without his consent? Presently, AND

[1] We find the names of these men repeated as in the present passage, and this intimates that He spoke to future generations, too, each of which would contain such men —They represent respectively the spirit of philanthropy, service of God, study of the Torah, and civil justice, which may be regarded as the fundamentals of civilisation.—Y.T

[2] A play on words, *me'umah* (anything) being read *mumah*, a blemish.

[3] Great though the sacrifice was, it nevertheless did not demand his own life.

[4] This is based on the Heb YEHIDEKA (E.V. 'THINE ONLY SON'), which the Midrash renders, thy soul (life), as in the verse, *Deliver my life from the sword, my soul* (*yehidathi*, same root; this is the Midrashic rendering, approximating to E.V '*mine only one*') *from the power of the dog* (Ps. XXII, 21)

[5] Sarah was ninety years old at his birth and 127 at her death, which according to some was occasioned by the false report that Isaac had actually been sacrificed. The second view rejects this, and is based on the statement *supra*, LIV, 6, that Abraham spent 26 years in Hebron, the beginning of which coincided with Isaac's birth and the end with his sacrifice.

ABRAHAM STRETCHED FORTH HIS HAND—he stretched forth his hand to take the knife while the tears streamed from his eyes, and these tears, prompted by a father's compassion, dropped into Isaac's eyes Yet even so, his heart rejoiced to obey the will of his Creator. The angels assembled in groups above. What did they cry? *The highways lie waste, the wayfaring man ceaseth, He hath broken the covenant, He hath despised the cities* (Isa. XXXIII, 8) —has He no pleasure in Jerusalem and the Temple, which He had intended giving as a possession to the descendants of Isaac? *He regardeth not man* (*ib.*) : if no merit has stood in Abraham's favour, then no creature has any value before him.)[1]

R. Aḥa said: [Abraham wondered]: Surely Thou too indulgest in prevarication! Yesterday Thou saidest, *For in Isaac shall seed be called to thee* (Gen. XXI, 12); Thou didst then retract and say, *Take now thy son* (*ib.* XXII, 2); while now Thou biddest me, LAY NOT THY HAND UPON THE LAD! Said the Holy One, blessed be He, to him: 'O Abraham, *My covenant will I not profane* (Ps. LXXXIX, 35), *And I* will *establish My covenant with Isaac* (Gen. XVII, 21). When I bade thee, "*Take now thy son,*" etc., *I will not alter that which is gone out of My lips* (Ps. *loc. cit.*). Did I tell thee, Slaughter him? No! but, "*Take him up.*"[2] Thou hast taken him up. Now take him down.'[3]

9. AND ABRAHAM LIFTED UP HIS EYES, AND LOOKED, AND BEHOLD BEHIND HIM (AḤAR) A RAM (XXII, 13). What does AḤAR mean? Said R. Judan: After all that happened,[4] Israel still fall into the clutches of sin and [in consequence] become the victims of persecution; yet they will be ultimately redeemed by the ram's horn, as it says, *And the Lord God will blow the horn,* etc. (Zech. IX, 14). R. Judah b. R. Simon interpreted: At the end of [after] all generations Israel will fall into the clutches of sin and be the victims of persecution; yet eventually

[1] The bracketed passage is added from cur. edd. [2] Lit. translation. [3] In cur. edd. a parable illustrating this follows. [4] 'E J.: After all that God has done for Israel, redeeming them from Egypt, etc.

they will be redeemed by the ram's horn, as it says, '*And the Lord God will blow the horn,*' etc.[1] R. Ḥanina b. R. Isaac said: Throughout the year Israel are in sin's clutches and led astray by their troubles, but on New Year they take the *shofar* and blow on it, and eventually they will be redeemed by the ram's horn, as it says, '*And the Lord God will blow the horn.*' R. Abba b R Pappi and R. Joshua of Siknin in R. Levi's name said: Because the Patriarch Abraham saw the ram extricate himself from one thicket and go and become entangled in another, the Holy One, blessed be He, said to him: 'So will thy children be entangled in countries, changing from Babylon to Media, from Media to Greece, and from Greece to Edom; yet they will eventually be redeemed by the ram's horn,' as it is written, *And the Lord God will blow the horn . . . the Lord of hosts will defend them* (*ib.* 14 f.).

AND ABRAHAM WENT AND TOOK THE RAM, AND OFFERED HIM UP FOR A BURNT-OFFERING IN THE STEAD OF HIS SON (*ib.*). R. Judan said in R. Banai's name: He prayed to him: 'Sovereign of the Universe! Look upon the blood of this ram as though it were the blood of my son Isaac; its *emurim* as though they were my son's *emurim*,' even as we learned[2]: When a man declares: This animal be instead of this one, in exchange for that, or a substitute for this, it is a valid exchange [3] R. Phinehas said in R. Banai's name · He prayed: 'Sovereign of the Universe! Regard it as though I had sacrificed my son Isaac first and then this ram instead of him,' [IN THE STEAD being understood] as in the verse, *And Jotham his son reigned in his stead* (II Kings XV, 7).[4]

It is even as we learned[5]: [When one declares · I vow a sacrifice] like the lamb or like the animals of the Temple stalls,[6] R. Joḥanan said: He meant, like the lamb of the

[1] They understand *aḥar* (lit. 'after') and 'ram' to hint at the Messianic future. [2] Tem. 26*b*.

[3] 'It is a valid exchange' is a technical expression denoting that *both* are holy; v. Lev. XXVII, 23.

[4] Not, of course, as a substitute but as his successor, and so Abraham too prayed that the ram might be regarded as *additional* to Isaac.

[5] Ned. 10*b* [6] I e. the animals kept for sacrifice.

daily burnt-offering[1]: Resh Lakish said: He meant, like Isaac's ram.[2] There [in Babylon] they say: Like the offspring of a sin-offering. Bar Kappara taught: He meant, like the lamb which has never given suck.[3]

10. AND ABRAHAM CALLED THE NAME OF THE PLACE ADONAI JIREH—THE LORD SEETH (XXII, 14). R. Bibi Rabbah said in R. Johanan's name: He said to Him: 'Sovereign of the Universe! When Thou didst order me, "*Take now thy son, thine only son*" (*ib.* 2), I could have answered, "Yesterday Thou didst promise me, *For in Isaac shall seed be called to thee* (*ib.* XXI, 12), and now Thou sayest, '*Take now thy son,*' etc." Yet Heaven forfend! I did not do this, but suppressed my feelings of compassion in order to do Thy will. Even so it may be Thy will, O Lord our God,[4] that when Isaac's children are in trouble, Thou wilt remember that binding in their favour and be filled with compassion for them.'

Abraham called it 'Jireh': AND ABRAHAM CALLED THE NAME OF THAT PLACE ADONAI—JIREH Shem called it Salem [Shalem]: *And Melchizedek king of Salem* (Gen. XIV, 18).[5] Said the Holy One, blessed be He: 'If I call it Jireh as did Abraham, then Shem, a righteous man, will resent it; while if I call it Salem as did Shem, Abraham, the righteous man, will resent it. Hence I will call it Jerusalem, including both names, Jireh Salem.'[6] R. Berekiah said in R Helbo's name: While it was yet Salem the Holy One, blessed be He, made Himself a tabernacle and prayed in it, as it says, *In Salem also is set His tabernacle, and His dwelling-place in Zion* (Ps. LXXVI, 3). And what did He say: 'O that I may see[7] the building of the Temple!'

Another interpretation: This verse teaches that the Holy One, blessed be He, showed him the Temple built,

[1] And this must be brought. [2] Hence he must bring a ram.
[3] The relevance of this whole paragraph is obscure. Th. conjectures that something has fallen out of the text.
[4] This phrase is now liturgical, with the addition, 'and the God of our fathers.' [5] The Midrash on Psalm LXXVI shows that this was Shem.
[6] 'He will see peace.' [7] So cur edd

destroyed and rebuilt. For it says, AND ABRAHAM CALLED THE NAME OF THAT PLACE ADONAI—JIREH (THE LORD SEETH): this alludes to the Temple built, as in the verse, *Three times in a year shall all thy males be seen . . in the place where He shall choose* (Deut. XVI, 16)[1]; AS IT IS SAID TO THIS DAY: IN THE MOUNT refers to it destroyed, as in the verse, *For the mountain of Zion, which is desolate* (Lam. V, 18); WHERE THE LORD IS SEEN refers to it rebuilt and firmly established in the Messianic era, as in the verse, *When the Lord hath built up Zion, when He hath been seen in His glory* (Ps. CII, 17).

11. AND THE ANGEL OF THE LORD CALLED UNTO ABRAHAM A SECOND TIME OUT OF HEAVEN, AND SAID: BY MYSELF HAVE I SWORN (XXII, 15 f.). What was the need of this oath? He had begged Him: 'Swear to me not to try me again henceforth, nor my son Isaac.' R. Levi in the name of R. Ḥama b. R. Ḥanina gave another reason for this oath: He had begged: 'Swear to me not to test me again henceforth.'[2] This may be likened to a king who was married to a noble lady. She gave birth to her first son by him, and he divorced her; a second, and he divorced her; a third, and he divorced her.[3] When she had given birth to a tenth son by him, they all assembled and demanded of him: 'Swear to us not to divorce our mother again.' Similarly, when Abraham had been tried for the tenth time,[4] he said to Him: 'Swear to me not to test me again.' R. Ḥanan commented: BECAUSE THOU HAST DONE THIS THING (*ib.*)—it was the tenth trial, yet you say, BECAUSE THOU HAST DONE *THIS THING*! The fact, however, is that this was the last trial, which was as weighty as all the rest together, and had he not submitted to it, all would have been lost.

[1] Sc. the Temple; thus 'seeing' is connected with the Temple while it was standing. [2] But he did not plead for Isaac too.
[3] Remarrying her after each divorce.
[4] The ten trials have been variously computed

THAT IN BLESSING I WILL BLESS THEE, etc (XXII, 17): a blessing for the father and a blessing for the son; AND IN MULTIPLYING WILL I MULTIPLY: an increase for the father and an increase for the son.[1] AND THY SEED SHALL POSSESS THE GATE OF HIS ENEMIES (*ib.*). Rabbi said. This alludes to Tadmor.[2] Happy is he who will see the downfall of Tadmor which took part in both destructions[3] R. Judan and R. Hanina—one of them said. At the destruction of the first Temple she supplied eighty thousand archers, and at the destruction of the second, eight thousand archers.

SO ABRAHAM RETURNED UNTO HIS YOUNG MEN (XXII, 19). And where was Isaac? R. Berekiah said in the name of the Rabbis of the other place[4]: He sent him to Shem to study Torah.[5] This may be compared to a woman who became wealthy through her distaff.[6] Said she: 'Since I have become wealthy through this distaff, it will never leave my hand.' (Thus said Abraham: 'All that has come to me is only because I engaged in Torah and good deeds; therefore I am unwilling that it should ever depart from my seed')[7] R. Jose b. R. Ḥanina said: He sent him [home] at night, for fear of the [evil] eye.[8] For from the moment that Hananiah, Mishael, and Azariah ascended unscathed from the fiery furnace they are no more mentioned. Whither then had they gone? R. Leazar said: They died through the spittle[9]; R. Jose b. R Ḥanina said: They died through an [evil] eye. R. Joshua b. Levi said: They changed their locality and went to Joshua, the son of Jehozadak, to study Torah; that is meant by the verse, *Hear now, O Joshua the high priest, thou, and thy*

[1] In both cases the verb is repeated in the original, and that is the basis of the present comment. [2] Palmyra. [3] Sc. of the two Temples.
[4] Sc. Babylon. [5] Cf. *supra*, XLIII, 6. [6] I.e her spinning.
[7] Bracketed passage added from cur. edd.
[8] The admiration that would be shown on account of his narrow escape might adversely affect him.
[9] The nations spat at them in scorn that a people with such a God should yet breed apostates, so much spittle collected that the heroes were drowned in it! Y.T.: This is metaphorical: they died through the anguish of knowing that by their faith they had brought scorn upon Israel. V. also Sanh. (Sonc. ed.), p. 623, n. 3.

fellows that sit before thee, for they are men that are a sign (Zech. III, 8) R. Tanḥuma b. Abina commented in R. Hanina's name: For this very purpose did Hananiah, Mishael, and Azariah descend into the fiery furnace, that a sign should be wrought through them.[1]

[1] Either of God's greatness, or of loyalty to God even at the cost of one's life.

CHAPTER LVII (VAYERA)

1. AND IT CAME TO PASS AFTER THESE THINGS, THAT IT WAS TOLD ABRAHAM, SAYING: BEHOLD, MILCAH, SHE ALSO HATH BORNE CHILDREN, etc (XXII, 20). It is written, *A tranquil heart is the life of the flesh* (Prov. XIV, 30): thus, while he was yet on Mount Moriah he was informed that his son's mate [Rebekah] had been born, as it says, BEHOLD, MILCAH, SHE ALSO HATH BORNE, etc.[1] *It shall be health to thy navel, and marrow to thy bones* (*ib.* III, 8). R. Berekiah said in R. Isaac's name: If thou healest, it will be for thyself What is the proof? '*If thou healest, it will be for thine own flesh*',[2] for while he was yet on Mount Moriah he was informed that his son's mate had been born, as it says, BEHOLD, MILCAH, SHE ALSO HATH BORNE CHILDREN

2. *As cold waters to a faint soul, so is good news from a far country* (*ib.* XXV, 25). We learned elsewhere[3]: As for good tidings one recites the blessing: 'Blessed be He who is good and doeth good,' so for cold water [i.e. rain] one recites the blessing, 'Blessed is He who is good and doeth good' And '*As cold water to a faint soul, so is good news from a far country*'; while he [Abraham] was still on Mount Moriah, he was informed that his son's mate had been born, in accordance with the verse, BEHOLD, MILCAH, SHE ALSO HATH BORNE, etc.[4]

3. AND IT CAME TO PASS AFTER THESE THINGS: misgivings were entertained on that occasion.[5] By whom?

[1] And so Abraham might have *a tranquil heart* Th.: the Midrash renders, A tranquil heart is the life of kinsmen—through being informed that a new kinswoman had been born, who would eventually be Isaac's wife, Abraham had a tranquil heart.
[2] This is his rendering of the verse, reading *le-shareka* (to thy navel) as *li-she'ereka*, for thy flesh.—Abraham, being healed and tranquillised after his fears for Isaac, now found that a wife was ready for 'his own flesh'—Isaac —The translation and explanation are conjectural
[3] Ber. 54*a*. [4] *Supra*, XIII, 15. The longer passage there is included here in cur. edd. [5] V. *supra*, XLIV, 5.

By Abraham. He reflected: Had he died on Mount Moriah, he [Isaac] would surely have died without children! Therefore now I may indeed give him in marriage to one of the daughters of Aner, Eshcol, or Mamre, who are righteous women; for what does their birth[1] matter to me?[2] Said the Holy One, blessed be He, to Him. 'You do not need this, for Isaac's mate has already been born'; hence, BEHOLD, MILCAH, SHE ALSO HATH BORNE.

Why state SHE *ALSO*?[3] To teach that just as in her case there were eight children from the mistress [i.e. the legal wife] and four from the concubines,[4] so in this case there were eight children from the mistress and four from the concubines.[5]

4. Another interpretation: [Abraham entertained misgivings,] being afraid of suffering.[6] Said the Holy One, blessed be He, to him. 'Thou needst have no fear, for already he has been born who is to receive them, viz. UZ HIS FIRSTBORN, AND BUZ HIS BROTHER (XXII, 21).[7]

When did Job flourish? R. Simeon b. Lakish said in Bar Kappara's name: In the days of Abraham, for here it says, UZ HIS FIRSTBORN, while it is written, *There was a man in the land of Uz* (Job I, I). R. Abba b. Kahana said: In the days of Jacob, for R. Abba b. Kahana said: Dinah was Job's wife (for in the case of Job's wife it is written, *Thou speakest as one of the foolish women* (nebaloth) *speaketh* (*ib.* II, 10), while with respect to Dinah, it says, *Because he had wrought a vile deed* (nebalah) *in Israel* (Gen. XXXIV, 7)) [8] R. Levi said: He flourished in the days

[1] I e their Amoritish descent (Mah.). [2] Following cur. edd

[3] '*Also*' (Heb. *gam*) denotes addition or extension. [4] V. vv 21-4

[5] The meaning is not quite clear Mah.: Jacob, Sarah's descendant, had eight sons from his two chief wives, Rachel and Leah, and four from Zilpah and Bilhah, who were of inferior status.

[6] Viz of being involved in further trials; cf. *supra*, LVI, 11.

[7] The reference is to Job, this agreeing with the view that Job was identical with Uz or a contemporary of his.

[8] Bracketed passage added from cur. edd.

of the tribal ancestors,[1] as it is written, *Which wise men have told, and have not hid it from their fathers* (Job XV, 18).[2] And what reward did they receive for this? That *unto them alone the land was given* (*ib.* 19).[3] R Jose b. Halafta said: He was born when they went down into Egypt, and died when they went up out of Egypt. You will find that in essence his life's span was two hundred and ten years,[4] while Israel spent two hundred and ten years in Egypt.[5] Now when Satan came to denounce [Israel],[6] He [God] incited him against Job [instead].[7] R. Ḥanina, the son of Aḥa, and R. Ḥama, the son of R Ḥanina, discussed this. R. Ḥanina, the son of Aḥa, said · It may be compared to a shepherd who stood watching his flocks, when a wolf came to attack him, whereupon he ordered: 'Throw him a he-goat on which to vent his rage.' R. Ḥama b. R. Ḥanina said: It may be compared to a king sitting at his meal when a dog came and attacked him, whereupon he ordered, 'Give him a bone to worry.' Thus it is written, *God delivereth me to the ungodly, and casteth me into the hands of the wicked* (*ib.* XVI, 11): and would that the people

[1] I.e Jacob's twelve sons

[2] Lit. translation, cur. edd. which alludes to Reuben and Judah who confessed their sins to Jacob, cf Soṭ 7*b*. The preceding verse states: *That which* I have seen *I will declare*, hence he was their contemporary.

[3] Rashi in Soṭ. *loc. cit.*: Royalty descended from Judah, while Reuben was the first tribe to receive his territory

[4] In Job XLII, 12, it says, *So the Lord blessed the latter end of Job more than his beginning*. The Rabbis take this to mean that he was now given twice as much of *everything* which he had enjoyed before his sufferings, including his years of life. Since it states further in v. 16, *And after this Job lived a hundred and forty years*, it follows then that he had lived seventy before, making two hundred and ten in all.—The words 'in essence' (Heb. עיקר) are difficult, implying as they do that he lived more, but that the other years are disregarded. Th suggests that the original reading may have been, Job's lifetime in essence was *seventy* years: i.e. this was his originally allotted span, but that God gave him an additional hundred and forty years.

[5] V. B B. 15*a*.

[6] That they were not worthy of being redeemed, for they too were guilty of immorality and idolatry. 'E.J. Satan denounced Israel *immediately* after Joseph's death, when they took the first step toward degeneration by ceasing to practise circumcision.

[7] Th.: this does not refer to his sufferings as recounted in the Book of Job, but assumes additional sufferings at the end of his life, to distract Satan's attention, as it were. Mah and 'E.J. explain differently.

were righteous, but they are indeed wicked![1] R. Jose b. R. Judah said: He flourished in the days when the judges judged. Hence it is written, *Behold, all ye yourselves have seen it; why then are ye become altogether vain?* (*ib.* XXVII, 12)[2]: ye have seen my deeds, ye have seen the deeds of my contemporaries: ye have seen my deeds—piety and noble acts; ye have seen the deeds of my contemporaries, who seek to pay harlots out of the granaries, but righteous men do not pay harlots out of the granaries; thus it is written, *Thou hast loved a harlot's hire out of every corn-floor* (Hos. IX, 1). R. Samuel b. Naḥman said: He lived in the days of the Chaldeans, for it says, *The Chaldeans set themselves in three bands* (Job I, 17).[3] R. Nathan said: In the days of the Queen of Sheba, as it says, *And the Sabeans made a raid, and took them away* (*ib.* 15). R. Joshua said: In the days of Ahasuerus, in connection with whom is written, *Let there be sought for the king young virgins fair to look on* (Est. II, 2), while it is written, *And . . . were no women found so fair as the daughters of Job* (Job XLII, 15). R Simeon b. Lakish said: Job never existed at all. This view of Resh Laḳish is self-contradictory, for elsewhere he said in the name of Bar Ḳappara: He flourished in the days of Abraham,[4] while here he maintains thus? He means, however, that he was never exposed to the sufferings ascribed to him.[5] Why then were they ascribed to him? Because had they come upon him, he would have been able to withstand them R. Joḥanan said: He was one of those who returned from the [Babylonian] Exile, an Israelite. Therefore he [R. Joḥanan] learned from him the laws of mourners,[6] as it is written, *Then Job arose, and rent his mantle* (*ib.* I, 20), whence we derive that a man must rend his garments standing. R. Ḥanina said:

[1] This apparently means: If the people had been righteous, God need not have incited Satan against me.
[2] In B.B. 15*b* this is held to be a description of the period of the Judges.
[3] Mah.: in the days of Nebuchadnezzar.
[4] V. beginning of this section.
[5] Y.T. for it is inconceivable that God would have permitted Satan to inflict so much suffering on an innocent person.
[6] Since he was an Israelite his practice throws light on Jewish law.

He was a heathen. R. Hiyya taught: [God said:] 'One righteous man arose among the nations of the world, and I gave him his reward and let him go'; and who was that? Job.

UZ HIS FIRSTBORN, AND BUZ HIS BROTHER, AND KEMUEL THE FATHER OF ARAM (XXII, 21). R. Judan and R. Judah b. R. Simon in R. Joshua's name said. Kemuel was Laban; and why was he called Kemuel? Because he arose (*kam*) against the people of God (*El*).[1]

AND HIS CONCUBINE, WHOSE NAME WAS REUMAH, SHE ALSO BORE TEBAH, AND GAHAM, AND TAHASH, AND MAACAH (XXII, 24). R. Isaac said: All these names signify chastisement: TEBAH means they slaughter (*ṭabḥin*): GAHAM, they burn (*gamḥin*): TAHASH, they silence (*taḥshin*), MAACAH, they crush (*ma'akin*).[2]

[1] By showing enmity toward Jacob and in pursuing after him. Radal, however, emends: Kemuel was Balaam.
[2] Other peoples. Cur. edd.: slaughter *them*, etc.

CPSIA information can be obtained at www.ICGtesting.com
Printed in the USA
LVOW03s1613300714

396753LV00012B/479/P

9 781293 822685